NE AND

STEPPE

CULTURES

KUBAN AND TEREK CULTURES
(CAUCASUS)

C A S P I A N   S E A)

E A)

ash

ITE
PIRE

(Lake
Van)

(Lake
Urmiah)

emish   Haran
Barsip PADAN-
        ARAM   Nineveh   Tepe Gawra
Khalab LAND OF THE   Asshur ASSYRIA
Aleppo AMORITES   Arrapkha
                                              Tepe Giyan   Ter
Hamath Tirqa   Euphrates   E
Jatna   Tadmar   Tigris River   L
        Mari   River   Eshnunna   A
              Tuttul   River   Der   M
Damascus   BABYLONIA
              Babylon   Kish   Susa
                        Nippur   Shushan
or
                        Erech
hem   Larsa
alem   Ur
re   AR   Eridu
heba
on

Record of the Fulfillment: The New Testament

OTHER BOOKS IN THE SERIES

Record of Revelation: The Bible
Record of the Promise: The Old Testament

Record of the Fulfillment

THE NEW TESTAMENT

WILFRID J. HARRINGTON, O.P.

THE PRIORY PRESS • CHICAGO, ILLINOIS

NIHIL OBSTAT: *Rev. Bernard O'Riley, O.P.;*
Rev. Augustine Rock, O.P.,
Censores Deputati

IMPRIMATUR: ✠*Most Rev. John P. Cody, D.D.*
Archbishop of Chicago
May 25, 1966

The Nihil Obstat and Imprimatur are official declarations
that a book or pamphlet is free of doctrinal or moral
error. No implication is contained therein that those
who have granted the Nihil Obstat and Imprimatur agree
with the contents, opinions, or statements expressed.

The Bible text in this publication is from the
Revised Standard Version of the Holy Bible,
copyrighted 1946 and 1952 by the Division of
Christian Education, National Council of Churches,
and used by permission.

Library of Congress Catalogue Number 66-24107
© *Copyright 1965 by* THE PRIORY PRESS
1165 East 54 Place, Chicago, Illinois 60615
Manufactured in the United States of America

Preface

In my Prefaces to the preceding volumes of this series,*
I have set out the purpose and scope of the whole work: to provide
an introduction to the Bible which takes account of modern biblical
studies and which might serve the needs both of seminarians and of
interested layfolk. Now encouraged by the tenor of many reviews,
I make bold to suggest that it may also be of help to pastoral clergy
and to Sisters engaged in religious education.

My treatment of the New Testament follows the general pattern
set by the approach to the Old Testament. However, I have been
able to devote much more space to the individual writings. Even so,
I should have liked to develop theological themes more fully, apart
from the fact that other themes which I would have wished to include had to be omitted altogether. I could not forget that this book
is, after all, an introduction to Scripture, and literary criticism had
to retain its rightful place. Eventually I would wish to provide an
outline of the doctrine of both Testaments.

Some may feel that the allotment of space is rather unbalanced. The
chapters on the Synoptic Gospels, for instance, are proportionately
not long; but it must be pointed out that the introductory chapter on
the formation of the Gospels is to be taken along with each of them.
It would appear that a work like the Apocalypse, so confusing to most

---

*Record of Revelation: The Bible; Record of the Promise: The Old Testament
(Chicago: The Priory Press, 1965).

v

people, demands as full an explanation as one can manage. A summary of a remarkably thorough literary analysis does seem to make the article on Hebrews unduly long, in relation to the Pauline Epistles, but its inclusion, as an example of literary criticism, is not out of place in a book of this sort. In short, although I am sure that others would arrange the matter differently, I would suggest that my arrangement is not haphazard.

For a third time, and with a keener sense of gratitude, I acknowledge the co-operation of my colleagues, Fathers Liam G. Walsh and Thomas P. McInerney, who, as before, have carefully read through my typescript. I have received valuable help from my confrere, Father Jerome Murphy-O'Connor; my one regret is that his contribution has not been more considerable. The painstaking editor of the series, Father Bernard O'Riley, O.P., is also responsible for layout and design; I thank him for his splendidly competent work and for his unfailing patience.

I am grateful also to Father Kevin A. Lynch, C.S.P., who has kindly granted me permission to make free use of material taken from *Explaining the Gospels,* published by the Paulist Press and copyrighted by the Missionary Society of St. Paul the Apostle.

W.J.H.

Table of Contents

THE BOOKS OF THE BIBLE

Gn.: Genesis	Wis.: Wisdom	Mk.: Mark
Ex.: Exodus	Sir.: Sirach	Lk.: Luke
Lv.: Leviticus	(Ecclesiasticus)	Jn.: John
Nm.: Numbers	Is.: Isaiah	Acts: Acts
Dt.: Deuteronomy	Jer.: Jeremiah	Rm.: Romans
Jos.: Joshua	Lam.: Lamentations	1,2 Cor.: 1,2
Jgs.: Judges	Bar.: Baruch	Corinthians
Ru.: Ruth	Ezek.: Ezekiel	Gal.: Galatians
1,2 Sm.: 1,2 Samuel	Dn.: Daniel	Eph.: Ephesians
1,2 Kgs.: 1,2 Kings	Hos.: Hosea	Phil.: Philippians
1,2 Chr.: 1,2	Jl.: Joel	Col.: Colossians
Chronicles	Am.: Amos	1,2 Thes.: 1,2
Ez.: Ezra	Obad.: Obadiah	Thessalonians
Neh.: Nehemiah	Jon.: Jonah	1,2 Tm.: 1,2
Tb.: Tobit	Mi.: Micah	Timothy
Jdt.: Judith	Na.: Nahum	Ti.: Titus
Est.: Esther	Hb.: Habakkuk	Phm.: Philemon
Jb.: Job	Zeph.: Zephaniah	Heb.: Hebrews
Ps.: Psalms	Hag.: Haggai	Jas.: James
Prv.: Proverbs	Zech.: Zechariah	1,2 Pt.: 1,2 Peter
Qoh.: Qoheleth	Mal.: Malachi	1,2,3 Jn.: 1,2,3 John
(Ecclesiastes)	1,2 Mc.: 1,2	Jude: Jude
Ct.: Canticle of	Maccabees	Ap.: Apocalypse
Canticles	Mt.: Matthew	(Revelation)

WORKS OF REFERENCE

Atlante Biblico: Atlante Storico della Bibbia

BJ: *Bible de Jérusalem*

(BJ): A separate fascicle of the *Bible de Jérusalem*

BW: *Bibeltheologisches Wörterbuch*

CBQ: *Catholic Biblical Quarterly*

DBS: *Dictionnaire de la Bible* (Supplement)

IB: *Introduction à la Bible*

PBC, *Instr.: Instruction on the Historical Truth of the Gospels*

PCB: *Peake's Commentary on the Bible*

VTB: *Vocabulaire de Théologie Biblique*

Record of the Fulfillment: The New Testament

A History of New Testament Times

This chapter is meant to sketch, in outline form, the historical, religious, and cultural background of the New Testament. Christianity did not, any more than the religion of Israel, come into being in a vacuum. Although essentially something new, Christianity is also a phenomenon of the first century A.D. and can be fully understood only in the setting of that century.

1. THE GRAECO-ROMAN WORLD
1) The Roman Empire

Roman history is usually divided into three parts: the period of the Kings; the period of the Republic; and the period of the Empire. Traditionally, Rome was founded in 753 B.C.; the first period reached from that year until 510 B.C. when Tarquinius Superbus, last of the kings, was deposed. The period of the Republic (509-27 B.C.) is the age in which Rome won her position in Italy, and then in the Mediterranean, and in which she gained political and administrative experience and learned from the civilization of other peoples—particularly from the Greeks. The years 133 B.C. onwards was a time of commercial expansion but political disorder. The third period, that of Imperial Rome, dates from the accession of Augustus in 27 B.C. It is true that Augustus himself wished to be known as *Princeps* or "first citizen," carefully avoiding the title of Emperor; but, in reality, the Roman Empire did begin with him. Here we are interested only in the last years of the Republic and the first years of the Empire.[1]

In 66 B.C. Pompey, armed with the greatest powers a Roman general had ever enjoyed, marched to the East. He conquered Asia Minor and led his troops to the foot of the Caucusus and to the shores of the Caspian Sea. In the spring of 63 B.C. he was in Damascus and late that same year he beseiged and took Jerusalem, thus bringing to an end the last period of Jewish independence. Pompey celebrated his triumph in Rome in 61 B.C. Rivalry between him and Julius Caesar (who had meanwhile conquered Gaul) flamed into civil war in 49 B.C. Caesar won control of Italy and Spain and followed Pompey into Greece; the decisive battle of Pharsalus in 48 B.C. resulted in complete victory for Caesar. Then, on the Ides of March, 44 B.C., Julius Caesar was assassinated. Again there was civil war: Mark Antony and the young Octavian (Caesar's adopted son), supported by Lepidus, faced the conspirators, Brutus and Cassius; the latter were disastrously defeated at Philippi in 42 B.C. The Triumvirs, Antony, Octavian, and Lepidus, divided the Roman dominions among them—but Octavian soon took over the army and territory of Lepidus. The West declared for Octavian, while Antony, in Egypt, dallied with Cleopatra. Soon there was open conflict and Antony's fleet was destroyed at the battle of Actium in 31 B.C. Antony and Cleopatra committed suicide, leaving Octavian as sole ruler of the Roman world. In 27 B.C. he received from the Senate the new name Augustus and until his death in 14 A.D. was unchallenged ruler of the most powerful Empire the world had known. He restored peace, order, and justice throughout the Empire. His beneficial rule seemed all the greater blessing in contrast to the long years of civil strife.

Augustus was succeeded by his stepson Tiberius (14-37 A.D.). He was an able and experienced ruler but his suspicious temperament found vent, in his last year, in a reign of terror. His successor, the young Caligula (37-41 A.D.) was depraved and ruled as a capricious despot. On his assassination, the unwilling Claudius became emperor (45-54 A.D.) and proved a not incompetent ruler. He was succeeded by Nero (54-68 A.D.), the first great persecutor of Christians.

---

[1]See A. A. M. van der Heyden and H. H. Scullard, editors, *Atlas of the Classical World* (London: Nelson, 1960), pp. 122-34.

His assassination was followed by a period of civil strife and the appearance of the ephemeral emperors: Galba, Otho, and Vitellius. At this point it became clear that real power now lay with the army. The legions of the Danube and the East chose as emperor the general Vespasian, then engaged in Palestine. Vespasian (69-79 A.D.) proved a happy choice. His son and successor, Titus, reigned for two years only (79-81 A.D.), the days of Nero returning under the rule of the latter's son, Domitian (81-96 A.D.)—the second great persecutor of Christians. An elderly lawyer, Nerva (96-98 A.D.), was appointed by the Senate after the murder of Domitian. He adopted as his son the able general Trajan—who soon, in fact, succeeded him. The reign of Trajan (98-117 A.D.) marked a new era for Rome.

At the death of Augustus, the Roman Empire, stretching from Italy, took in Spain, Gaul, much of Germany, the Balkans, Asia Minor, Syria and Palestine, Egypt and North Africa. The Mediterranean had become a Roman lake and the authority of Rome extended to all its shores. During the first century A.D. the Roman legions pushed ever farther afield. Throughout the Empire the different ethnic groups were juxtaposed rather than amalgamated; national characteristics and traditions were preserved. Yet, many contacts in the economic, cultural, and religious spheres tended to offset the differences. In the cities the most common spoken language was the *Koine* (common or current) Greek, but in rural areas the native languages were still in possession. The Empire was divided into provinces. The older provinces were called senatorial and were governed by a proconsul appointed by the Senate; the other provinces were called imperial and were governed by a legate appointed by the emperor. Palestine was ruled by a procurator who was subject to the legate of Syria. A vast network of roads linked the wideflung provinces of the Empire. Along these roads, in a world governed by a single power, the preachers of a new faith were soon journeying. And the followers of this faith before long would clash with that power.

A feature of Roman society was the enormous number of slaves: there were almost as many slaves as free citizens. A slave could be set at liberty by his master or by the state and so become a freedman, but he did not thereby become a citizen. Roman citizens alone enjoyed the fullest civil rights. Among other privileges, they were immune from corporal punishment and could not be executed by crucifixion if condemned to death; and they had the right to appeal to Caesar's tribunal. Roman citizenship could be given as a reward for services rendered, or it could be bought (cf. Acts 22:25-28) and was hereditary.

2) *Philosophical Trends*[2]

In the Graeco-Roman world the metaphysics of Plato and Aristotle had lost their appeal. Now the emphasis was on the problems of human life, notably the conduct and happiness of the individual. The philosophers of the first Christian century were in fact eclectics (i.e., they chose elements from a variety of philosophical systems), but Stoicism and Epicureanism contributed most to their generalized philosophy.

EPICUREANISM   Epicureanism has suffered from a misunderstanding of its ethical idea. The founder of the system was Epicurus of Samos (342-270 B.C.), who did indeed make pleasure the end of life; but we must understand what he meant by *pleasure*.

> Two facts are to be noted: first that Epicurus meant, not the pleasures of the moment, individual sensations, but the pleasure which endures throughout a lifetime; and secondly, that pleasure for Epicurus consisted rather in the absence of pain than in positive satisfaction. This pleasure is to be found pre-eminently in serenity of soul.[3]

Since the only durable pleasure is health of body and tranquility of soul, moderation and self-control are necessary on the one hand, and the avoidance of embroilment in political and public affairs on the other. Epicurus admitted the existence of the gods, but the gods stood apart from the world and were indifferent to human affairs. Although the appeal of Epicureanism was always limited, even in the first century B.C., its views were adopted by such thinkers as Lucretius and Cicero and by poets like Vergil and Horace, and its influence continued into the next century at least.

---

[2]See R. H. Pfeiffer, *History of New Testament Times,* With an Introduction to the Apocrypha (London: A. & C. Black, 1963[2]), pp. 116-27; R. McL. Wilson, *Peake's Commentary on the Bible,* M. Black and H. H. Rowley, editors (London: Nelson, 1962), n. 624 a-d (henceforth references to this work will be abbreviated PCB); H. C. Kee and F. W. Young, *The Living World of the New Testament* (Englewood Cliffs, N. J.: Prentice-Hall, 1965[2]), pp. 15-19; F. Copleston, *A History of Philosophy* (New York: Doubleday Image Books, 1962[2]), I, Pt. II, Greece and Rome, pp. 145-71.

[3]Copleston, *op. cit.,* p. 151.

STOICISM   The founder of the Stoic school was Zeno (336-264 B.C.). The influence of Stoicism continued after his death and was the dominant philosophy in the Graeco-Roman period. Since the sincere Stoic was a man of outstanding moral integrity, he, and the challenge of self-discipline and asceticism demanded by the Stoic way of life, appealed to many in an age of prevailing low moral standards in public and private life.

The Stoic divinity is material; he existed from eternity in the form of primeval fire, and yet he is the mind or soul of the universe that has emerged from him. God, the Logos, is the active principle which contains within itself the forms (the "seeds") of all things that are to be. The soul of man is part of the divine Fire which descended into men at their creation; personal immortality is not possible because all souls return to the primeval Fire at the conflagration when the universe is consumed to be born anew—the cycle goes on eternally. Since the human soul is essentially one with the divine element, to live in accordance with the highest dictates of one's own being is to live in harmony with the divine purpose and so to attain to virtue.

The Stoic ethic is largely a struggle against the passions and affections, an attempt to reach a state of moral freedom and independence of externals. Since man is necessarily a social being, to live in society is a dictate of reason. Division of mankind into warring states is wrong and all men have a claim to our good will. "The ethical ideal is attained when we love all men as we love ourselves or when our self-love embraces all that is connected with the self, including humanity at large, with an equal intensity."[4]

Stoicism was the principal element of what might be termed the "popular" philosophy of the first century A.D. This philosophy was propagated by Stoic preachers—highly regarded by the people— who had a special teaching method: doctrinal or moral expositions in dialogue form, with questions and answers, apostrophes and exclamations—the *diatribe* (cf. Rm. 3:1-9). These later teachers no longer shared the pantheistic views of the earlier Stoics; rather, they preached a universal God, the soul and reason of the world, father

_____

[4]*Ibid.*, p. 144.

of gods and men. They proclaimed the equality and brotherhood of all men; they taught that superiority lay only in the practice of virtue, and that virtue alone, entailing asceticism and self-control, can bring happiness. In short, a philosophic system had taken on something of the character of a religion.

> It is quite true that the Stoic philosophy remained theoretically materialist and more or less determinist; but from the practical viewpoint, the insistence on man's kinship with God, on purification of the soul by self-control and moral education, on submission to the "Divine Will," together with the broadening influence of its cosmopolitanism, served as a preparation in some minds for the acceptance of the universal religion which, while transcending the materialism of the Stoics, insisted on the brotherhood of men as children of God and introduced a dynamic influence which was wanting in the Stoic system. Moreover, insofar as an ethical Stoicism was an answer to the contemporary need for moral guidance and direction as to the right course to be pursued by the individual, swamped in the great cosmopolitan Empire, this need was far better met by the Christian doctrine, which could appeal to the uneducated and simple in a way Stoicism could hardly do and which held out the prospect of complete happiness in the future life as the term of moral endeavor in a way that Stoicism, by its very system, was debarred from doing.[5]

3) Religious Trends[6]

THE MYSTERY RELIGIONS   Even before the Hellenistic era the traditional worship of the Olympian gods had declined among the Greeks. After Alexander, its influence, at least on the minds of cultivated men, grew less and eventually disappeared altogether. The Roman attitude toward the national religion was more conservative; but in the first century A.D. it too, at least in the cosmopolitan capital, had to yield to other influences. In fact, men were seeking something that the traditional religions could not offer: personal religious feeling and the prospect of immortality. This longing was promised fulfillment in the mystery cults. By mystery cults are meant sacred rites by which one was initiated into religious and divine secrets; knowledge of these secrets guaranteed the protection of the

---

[5]*Ibid.*, pp. 248 f.

[6]See Pfeiffer, *op. cit.*, pp. 127-65; Kee and Young, *op. cit.*, pp. 21-24; R. McL. Wilson, PCB, nn. 620-626; A. Tricot, *Introduction à la Bible*, A. Robert and A. Feuillet, editors (Tournai: Desclée, 1957; second edition, 1959), II, pp. 23-29 (henceforth references to this work will be abbreviated IB).

god or goddess of the mystery religion in question, and assured the eternal bliss of the initiate.

The Eleusinian mysteries had developed around the myth of Demeter. Persephone, the daughter of Demeter, goddess of the earth, had been carried to the underworld by Hades. Through the intervention of other gods, Persephone was restored to her mother, but must return to the underworld for four months of every year. The mysteries celebrated at Eleusis re-enacted the mourning of Demeter and the joyous return of Persephone—symbolizing the revival of nature in spring. Originally, the cult of Demeter would seem to have had the purpose of guaranteeing good crops; but later, the cycle of the life and death of nature was seen as a symbol of man's life and death, and participation in the Eleusinian mysteries would assure new life in a world beyond death.

The oldest and most popular of Hellenistic mystery cults was that of Dionysus, and in the beginning of the Christian Era the Dionysian mysteries were celebrated throughout the Graeco-Roman world. Dionysus was god of wine. His devotees, mostly women, after preparatory fasting and purification, were, by means of night-long ceremonies and the drinking of wine, overcome by a "divine" frenzy. In the rapture of their ecstasy, they achieved mystical union with the deity for a moment, a foretaste of eternal bliss.

In Rome, the Egyptian mysteries of Osiris had won a footing. The myth tells of Isis wandering over the earth searching for the dismembered body of her consort Osiris, who had become the god of the underworld. In the mysteries, the initiate, by re-enacting the sufferings and journey to death of Osiris, became united with the god of the dead. As a consequence, he had no further fear of death and was assured of life beyond the grave.

The secret of full initiation into the mysteries has been well kept and no more than a general outline of these religions is known to us. However, it is clear that the emphasis was on external rites which had to be carried out scrupulously. Salvation was guaranteed merely by a ceremony of initiation. Hence, the mystery cults had no really beneficial influence on moral conduct; they offered no challenge to a change of life. Indeed, in this sphere, the contribution of Stoicism was much more effective. But, on the other hand, the mysteries did foster belief in a life beyond the grave and did promote recourse to "savior" gods, and did give rise to a sense of personal unity with the divinity. All this emphasized the yearning of men for something more satisfying than the traditional religions could offer, and goes far to explain the appeal of Christianity to those who were also prepared to live up to its demanding standard.

THE IMPERIAL CULT   The notion of the divinity of kings was an ancient and common one in the East. Alexander the Great found that his Eastern (and Egyptian) subjects regarded him as a god, and his successors, Seleucids and Ptolemies both, complacently assumed divine titles—for instance, Antiochus IV was "Epiphanes" ([god] manifest). The practice was slower to find a foothold in Rome, but was eventually seized upon as a valuable political factor. In the Hellenistic age, Rome itself had attained the status of a deity and the cult of the *Dea Roma* (the goddess Rome) had grown up. In the East it was soon accompanied by the cult of the emperor.

After his death in 44 B.C., Julius Caesar, by decree of the Senate, was declared one of the divine protectors of the state. Augustus did not claim divine honors in Rome, but he was worshiped as a divinity in the East where temples were raised to him (like the temple of Augustus built by Herod the Great in Sebaste, the restored Samaria). Later emperors openly claimed divine honors during their lifetime. The imperial cult had secured a firm grip and was nowhere more enthusiastically propagated than in Asia Minor.

The common emperor cult served as a unifying principle, a point of contact for the varied peoples of the Empire—and Rome, somewhat cynically, fully realized and exploited its political value. But there was one religious group which could not and would not give even token recognition to the divinity of the emperor. The Roman emperor was "Savior" and "Lord"—divine titles. In the eyes of Christians the claim was blasphemous: Jesus Christ was the only Savior and Lord. In Asia Minor more than elsewhere their singular attitude was manifest. The Roman authorities could not ignore their refusal to participate in the imperial cult, and Christians could not honor the emperor as god. A clash was inevitable. The Apocalypse bears witness to the bitter trials of those who "held fast the Name"—who would grant the title of "Lord" to Jesus Christ alone.

2. THE JEWISH WORLD

1) Palestine under the Romans[7]

THE HERODIAN   1. *Herod the Great (37-4 B.C.).* Although Herod
DYNASTY[8]   never gained the affection, or even the respect of
his Jewish subjects (who regarded him as a "half-Jew" because of
his Idumaean origin), he was an able and energetic ruler—at least
in Roman eyes. In relation to Rome his status was that of *rex socius,*
or allied king, enjoying autonomy and freedom from tribute, but
subject to Rome in matters of foreign policy and obliged to furnish
troops to the imperial army in time of war.

Herod, in the spring of 37 B.C. had married the Hasmonaean prin-
cess Mariamne, and was persuaded (against his will) by his mother-
in-law, Alexandra, to appoint her son Aristobulus as high priest.
That was early in 35 B.C. Late that same year Aristobulus was
drowned in Jericho at the instigation of Herod. From Egypt, Cleopatra cast envious eyes on Herod's territory and won from Antony
(who had been in Egypt since 40 B.C.) the coastal plain and the
region of Jericho. Herod was already guarantor for the Nabataean[9]
payment of tribute to Cleopatra: the queen had astutely set the
two most important rulers at her Asiatic frontier at loggerheads. As
it happened, the situation turned to the advantage of Herod. When
civil war between Antony and Octavian broke out in 32 B.C., Herod
was prepared to bring aid to Antony, but Cleopatra insisted that
he move against the Nabataeans. Thus, he was saved from taking
the field against Octavian—a move that might have prejudiced his
career beyond recovery. Herod's campaign was successful, but the
defeat of Antony at Actium (31 B.C.) seemed fatal to his position.
However, he appeared before Octavian in Rhodes in the spring of
30 B.C. and was confirmed as king of the Jews. Later in the year
he helped Octavian in the latter's march from Ptolemais to Egypt.
The coastal strip and Jericho were restored to him and Samaria was

---

[7]See P. Lemaire and D. Baldi, *Atlante Storico della Bibbia* (Rome: Marietti,
1955), pp. 197-208. Henceforth references to this work will be abbreviated *Atlante
Biblico (Biblical Atlas)*; Pfeiffer, *op. cit.,* pp. 24-45; A. Tricot, IB, pp. 85-97.

[8]For Herod's rise to power see Wilfrid J. Harrington, *Record of the Promise:
The Old Testament* (Chicago: The Priory Press, 1965), pp. 96-98.

[9]The Nabataeans were a powerful Arab nation with a territory stretching from
north of Damascus, along the edge of the desert, to the border of Egypt. Their
capital was the rock-hewn Petra, that "rose-red city, half as old as time."

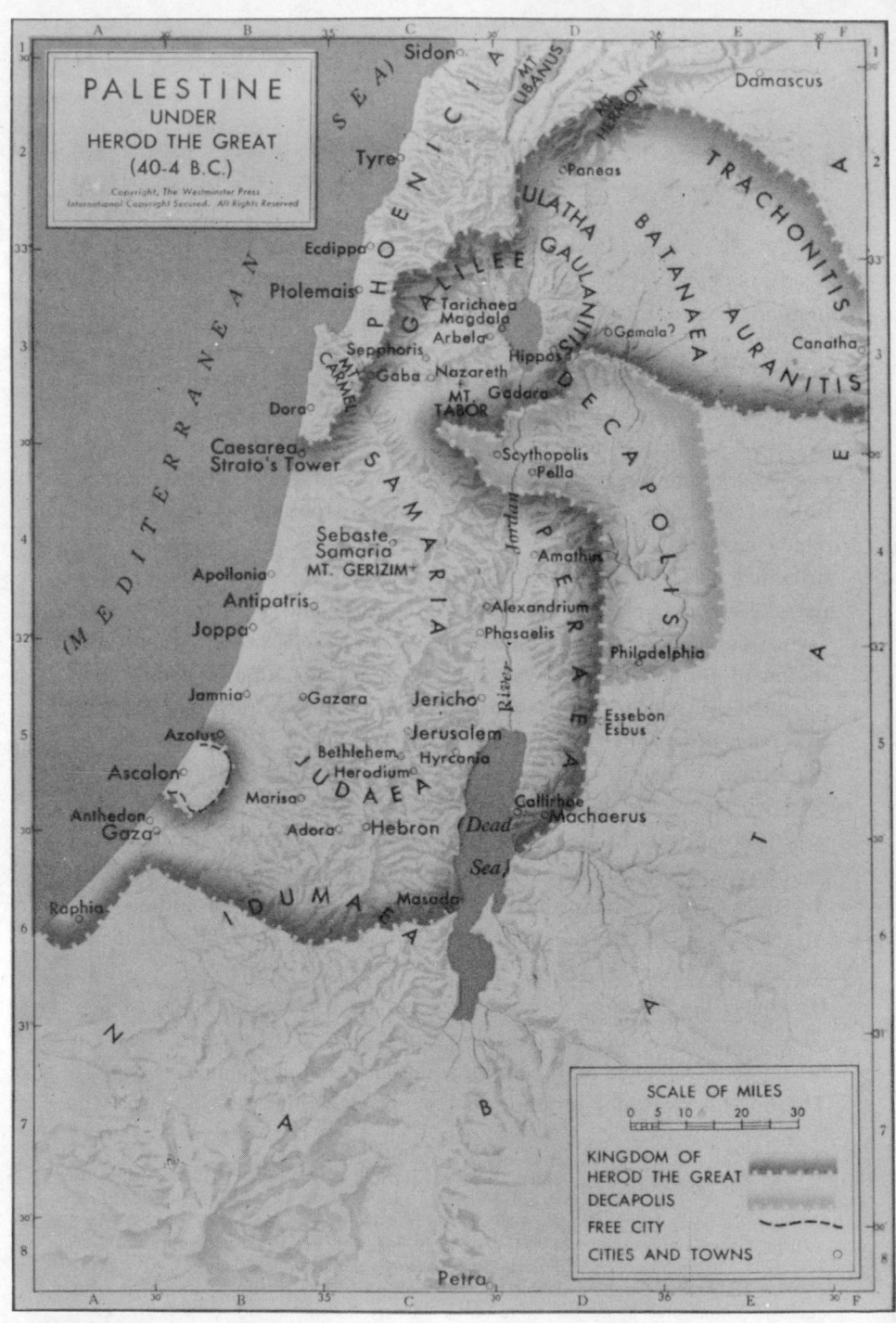

PALESTINE
UNDER
HEROD THE GREAT
(40-4 B.C.)

Copyright, The Westminster Press
International Copyright Secured. All Rights Reserved.

Damascus

Sidon

TRACHONITIS

Tyre

MT. LIBANUS

MT. HERMON

Paneas

ULATHA

PHOENICIA

Ecdippa

BATANAEA

Canatha

AURANITIS

Ptolemais

GALILEE

GAULANITIS

Tarichaea
Magdala
Arbela

Gamala?

Sepphoris

MT. CARMEL

Gaba

Nazareth

Hippos

Dora

MT. TABOR

Gadara

DECAPOLIS

Caesarea
Strato's Tower

Scythopolis
Pella

SAMARIA

Sebaste
Samaria
MT. GERIZIM

Amathus

Apollonia

Antipatris

Alexandrium

Phasaelis

Philadelphia

Joppa

Jericho

Essebon
Esbus

Jamnia

Gazara

Jerusalem

Azotus

Bethlehem

Hyrcania

Herodium

Ascalon

JUDAEA

Anthedon
Gaza

Marisa

Callirhoe

Machaerus

Adora

Hebron

(Dead

Sea)

Raphia

IDUMAEA

Masada

(MEDITERRANEAN SEA)

Jordan River

PERAEA

Petra

SCALE OF MILES

0   5   10   20   30

KINGDOM OF
HEROD THE GREAT

DECAPOLIS

FREE CITY

CITIES AND TOWNS   ○

added to his kingdom. Before Herod died, his territory had come to include Idumaea, Judaea, Samaria, the coastal plain (to Caesarea), Galilee, Peraea (in Transjordan), and Gaulinitis-Ituraea-Batanaea-Trachonitis-Auranitis (districts north and east of the Sea of Galilee).

The reign of Herod was marked by great constructions which permitted him to give expression to his admiration for things Greek and enabled him to express his devotion to Augustus. He built temples to Augustus in Hellenistic cities; he restored Samaria and renamed it Sebaste (Greek *Sebastos* = Augustus); he rebuilt Strato's Tower and renamed it Caesarea. In Jerusalem he built the palace of Herod on the west side of the city and the tower of Antonia north of the Temple enclosure. He provided an amphitheater, and constructed gymnasia, theaters, and stadia throughout the land. In 20 B.C. he began his most ambitious project, the rebuilding of the Temple. Work was still in progress forty-six years later (cf. Jn. 2:20) and the restoration was not finished until 63 A.D., a few years before its total destruction (70 A.D.).

In the domestic sphere, Herod's reign was very troubled. He was of a suspicious nature (in 29 B.C. he had his favorite wife, Mariamne the Hasmonaean, executed for alleged adultery). He was jealous of his power and reacted violently against any attempt on it. In 28 B.C. his mother-in-law Alexandra was put to death on the charge of plotting against him. In 7 B.C. Alexander and Aristobulus, his sons by Mariamne, were strangled at Sebaste. A few days before his death, the king had his son Antipater executed. Herod died at Jericho in March/April, 4 B.C., and was buried on the Herodium near Bethlehem.

2. *The Sons of Herod.* In his will Herod had divided his kingdom among his sons Archelaus (whom he named king), Antipas, and Philip (both named tetrarchs). The will was subject to the approval of Augustus, but already Archelaus had to face disorders in Jerusalem and crushed an incipient rebellion at the cost of many lives. He went to Rome to plead his cause and a delegation of Jews set out to oppose his claim (cf. Lk. 19:14). Sabinus, the procurator sent by Augustus to take charge of the territory of Herod until the succession had been settled, overstepped his authority and stirred up a revolt which was promptly and savagely put down by Varus, legate of Syria. Eventually Augustus did approve Herod's will; but Arche-

laus was named ethnarch, not king, and all three sons were vassals of Rome and subject to the legate of Syria.

1. Archelaus (4 B.C.-6 A.D.), Ethnarch of Judaea, Idumaea, and Samaria. In 6 A.D. Archelaus was summoned to Rome to answer charges of misgovernment. He was deposed and exiled to Vienne in Gaul, and his former territory was placed under a Roman procurator.

2. Philip (4 B.C.-34 A.D.), Tetrarch of Gaulanitis, Ituraea, Batanaea, Trachonitis, and Auranitis. His reign was peaceful. He restored Panias, renaming it Caesarea Philippi, and rebuilt Bethsaida-Julia. He married his niece Salome, daughter of Herodias, and left no descendants; at his death his territory was annexed to the province of Syria. (In 37 A.D. Caligula granted it to Agrippa I.)

3. Antipas (4 B.C.-39 A.D.), Tetrarch of Galilee and Peraea. He restored Sepphoris in Galilee, and by the southeast corner of the Lake of Gennesareth built the new town of Tiberias. He had married the daughter of Aretas IV, king of the Nabataeans, but repudiated her in order to marry Herodias (formerly the wife of his brother Herod Philip)—a union condemned by John the Baptist (Mt. 14:3 f. parr.). In 36 A.D. Antipas suffered a severe defeat at the hands of Aretas who was bent on avenging the insult to his daughter. Antipas (urged by Herodias who was jealous of the favor shown by Caligula to her brother Agrippa) went to Rome in 39 A.D. to request the royal title, and found himself exiled to Gaul. (His territory was given to Agrippa.)

3. *Agrippa I, King (41-44 A.D.).* In 37 A.D., when Caligula had become emperor, he granted to Agrippa, grandson of Herod the Great, the former territory of Philip, plus Abilene (between Damascus and Anti-Lebanon). In 39 A.D. Agrippa received, in addition, the former territory of Antipas. Agrippa was in Rome in 41 A.D. when Caligula was assassinated and he helped in the appointment of his friend Claudius. The new emperor granted him the title of king and added to his realm the territory formerly ruled by the Roman procurator. In other words, Agrippa I was now (41 A.D.) master of the whole kingdom of Herod the Great. His brother, Herod, was made king of Chalcis, a small state between Lebanon and Anti-Lebanon (41-48 A.D.).

The reign of Agrippa I was peaceful and prosperous. Although himself a sceptic, he was careful to respect the religious scruples of the Jews and supported the Pharisees. In order "to please the Jews," he judged it politic to take action against the Christians and executed James the brother of John (Acts 12:1-3). He planned to fortify Jerusalem, but his "third wall" was not completed by the time of his sudden death at Caesarea in 44 A.D. (Acts 12).

4. *Agrippa II.* The son of Agrippa I (also named Agrippa) did not inherit his father's kingdom, but in 50 A.D. he was given Chalcis, the territory of his late uncle Herod; and was, at the same time, appointed supervisor of the Temple with the right of appointing the high priest. In 53 A.D. he exchanged Chalcis for the former territory of Philip, plus Abilene. When in 60 A.D., accompanied by his sister Berenice, he visited Caesarea, he was invited by the procurator Festus to hear Paul (Acts 25:13—26:32). He was a faithful subject of Rome, and although he had sought to prevent rebellion, he supported the Romans in the Jewish revolt (66-70 A.D.) once it had broken out. He died in 92/93 A.D., the last of the Herodian kings.

DESCENDANTS OF HEROD THE GREAT
Herod the Great

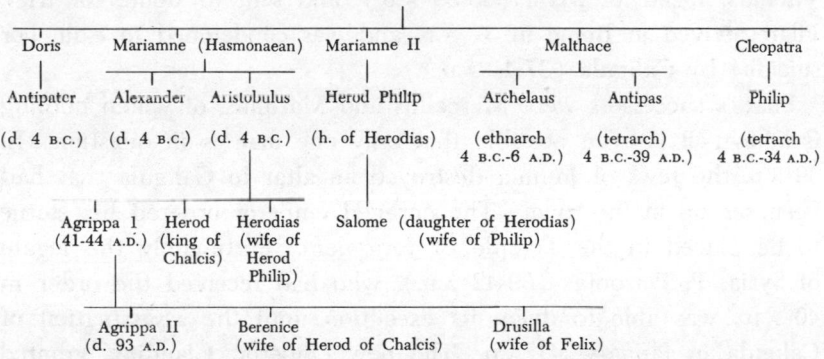

Doris	Mariamne (Hasmonaean)		Mariamne II	Malthace		Cleopatra
Antipater	Alexander	Aristobulus	Herod Philip	Archelaus	Antipas	Philip
(d. 4 B.C.)	(d. 4 B.C.)	(d. 4 B.C.)	(h. of Herodias)	(ethnarch 4 B.C.-6 A.D.)	(tetrarch) 4 B.C.-39 A.D.)	(tetrarch 4 B.C.-34 A.D.)

	Agrippa I (41-44 A.D.)	Herod (king of Chalcis)	Herodias (wife of Herod Philip)	Salome (daughter of Herodias) (wife of Philip)

	Agrippa II (d. 93 A.D.)	Berenice (wife of Herod of Chalcis)	Drusilla (wife of Felix)

THE ROMAN PROCURATORS[10] After the deposition of Archelaus in 6 A.D., his territory (Idumaea, Judaea, and Samaria) was annexed to the province of Syria and was governed by a Roman procurator subject to the legate of Syria. The procurator had troops at his disposal and his powers included the appointment and removal

---

[10]See *Atlante Biblico*, pp. 208-12.

of the high priest. His official residence was in Caesarea, but he moved to Jerusalem for the great feasts—to be on the spot in case of trouble. Procuratorial government was interrupted from 41 A.D. to 44 A.D. during the reign of Agrippa I and ended with the outbreak of the Jewish revolt in 66 A.D.

We know scarcely anything of the first three procurators: Coponius (6-9 A.D.), Marcus Ambivius (9-12 A.D.), and Annius Rufus (12-15 A.D.). Tiberius appointed Valerius Gratus (15-26 A.D.), who deposed the high priest Ananus (Annas of Lk. 3:2; Jn. 18:13), and eventually appointed Caiaphas (18-36 A.D.). Valerius was succeeded by Pontius Pilate (26-36 A.D.), who continually irritated and provoked the Jews. He tried to bring the imperial standards (carrying the image of the emperor) into Jerusalem and later placed shields with the emperor's name on the walls of Herod's palace; these were removed by order of Tiberius. He requisitioned funds from the Temple treasury to construct an aqueduct to the city. All this, and his general attitude, were sore points with the Jews, but the policy of Tiberius was to leave his representatives in office as long as possible. Eventually Pilate overreached himself by a senseless massacre of Samaritans; in 36 A.D. he was suspended from office by Vitellius, legate of Syria (35-39 A.D.), and sent to Rome for trial. Pilate arrived in Rome in 37 A.D. and was condemned to exile (or suicide) by Caligula (37-41 A.D.).

Pilate's successors were Marcellus and Marullus, of whom nothing is known—it is even possible that only one man is in question. In 39 A.D. the Jews of Jamnia destroyed an altar to Caligula that had been set up in the town. The enraged emperor ordered his statue to be placed in the Temple of Jerusalem. Fortunately the legate of Syria, P. Petronius (39-42 A.D.), who had received the order in 40 A.D., was able to delay its execution until the assassination of Caligula in January, 41 A.D. The new emperor, Claudius, granted the procuratorial territory to Agrippa I.

On the death of Agrippa (44 A.D.), Claudius again placed Palestine under a Roman procurator, but added the regions of Gaulanitis, Ituraea, Batanaea, Trachonitis, and Auranitis. (This, the former tetrarchy of Philip, was assigned to Agrippa II in 53 A.D.) The political situation in Palestine, which had eased somewhat under

Agrippa I, now became still more troubled. National sentiment grew stronger under foreign domination, and the extreme party of the Zealots[11] became active.

Cuspius Fadus (44-46 A.D.) was sent to Claudius to take possession of the territory of Agrippa I. He came into open conflict with the Zealots. Tiberius Alexander (46-48 A.D.) was an apostate Jew, a nephew of the philosopher Philo.[12] He took action against the Zealots and crucified James and Simon, the sons of Judas the Galilean, one of the original leaders of the group. During his term of office there was a severe famine (Acts 11:27-30). Vemtidius Cumanus (48-52 A.D.) supported the Samaritans in a clash with the Jews and had many Jews executed. The legate of Syria, Quadratus (50-60 A.D.), removed Cumanus from office and sent him to Rome. Antonius Felix (52-60 A.D.) was a freedman, yet he married Drusilla, sister of Agrippa II. Felix was extremely venal (cf. Acts 24:26—he hoped to receive a bribe from Paul) and unscrupulous. There was mounting tension in the land, fanned by false messianic hopes and claims; the procurator's reaction was ruthless and he was recalled by Nero. Porcius Festus (60-62 A.D.) was an honest and prudent magistrate who, unfortunately, died in office. He was the one who sent Paul to Rome after the latter had invoked his privilege as a Roman citizen and had appealed to the imperial tribunal. The death of Festus left the way open for the persecution of Christians by the high priest Ananus II (Ananias), and James the "brother of the Lord" was stoned in 62 A.D.

Meanwhile, the situation in Palestine was getting more and more out of hand and the new procurator, Albinus (62-64 A.D.), did nothing to improve matters. A venal man, he became a tool in the hands of the high priest Ananias whom St. Paul had called a "whitewashed wall" (Acts 23:2 f.). The Zealots were now much more active. The last procurator, Gessius Florus (64-66 A.D.), was possibly the worst of the lot. When in 66 A.D. he realized that his unscrupulous and ruthless conduct would not go unpunished in Rome, he incited the Jews to rebellion. In June of 66 A.D. organized revolt against Rome did break out.

---

[11]See p. 29.
[12]See p. 32.

THE JEWISH WAR   Agrippa II tried to dissuade the Jews from
AND AFTERMATH[13]   the final irrevocable step, but in vain. In
Jerusalem the extremist party, led by Eleazar, gained the upper
hand and openly rebelled against Rome. The Roman troops in the
city surrendered, and were massacred. In October, 66 A.D., Cestius
Gallus, the legate of Syria, attacked Jerusalem. Deciding that he
lacked sufficient forces for an effective siege he retired; he was
ambushed and disastrously defeated at the pass of Beth-horon.
This victory stirred up all Jews against Rome, but, unhappily, hatred
of a common foe was not enough to overcome the divisions that
soon began to prove suicidal.

The defense of Jerusalem was entrusted to the ex-high priest
Ananias and to Joseph ben Gorion. The Zealots, let by Eleazar, were
dispatched to Idumaea, apparently with the hope of keeping them
out of the way. Flavius Josephus, the future historian, became
governor of Galilee and found himself opposed by John of Giscala
and his band of Zealots. Nero sent his most experienced general,
Vespasian, to quell the rebellion in Palestine. In 67 A.D. Vespasian
was in Ptolemais at the head of three legions, together with auxiliary
troops—a total of 60,000 men. Galilee was conquered in the course
of the year, but John of Giscala and his Zealots escaped to Jerusalem.
These and other refugees from Galilee increased the extremist element. In the ensuing conflict the aristocratic leaders were executed
or assassinated and John of Giscala became master of the city.

Vespasian was content to let the Jews destroy one another, and
turned to Peraea (68 A.D.). He was about to invade Judaea when
he got word of Nero's death (June 9, 68 A.D.) and suspended opera-
tions. This unexpected respite proved disastrous for the Jews. In
the spring of 69 A.D. Simon bar-Giora, leader of a band of Zealots,
entered Jerusalem and immediately came into conflict with John of
Giscala. In July of 69 A.D. the legions of the East acclaimed Vespasian as emperor; he, leaving his son Titus in command in Palestine,
went to Alexandria and, early the following year, to Rome. Meanwhile, a third party, led by Eleazar, son of Simon, had taken a
hand in the civil strife that raged in the capital; he was overcome
by John of Giscala.

---

[13]See *Atlante Biblico*, pp. 213-17; Pfeiffer, *op. cit.*, pp. 41-45.

In March, 70 A.D., Titus, at the head of four legions, moved from Caesarea against Jerusalem. Famine, in addition to civil strife, had by now become another ally of his within the walls. On May 25, 70 A.D., the Romans broke through the "third wall" (the unfinished fortifications of Agrippa I had been hastily completed), but the city still held out and Titus waited for famine to do its work. In a fresh assault the fortress of Antonia fell on July the twenty-fourth, and finally, on August the ninth, the Temple was taken and destroyed by fire. Still the Jews resisted, but by the end of September the whole city was in Roman hands and both John of Giscala and Simon bar-Giora were prisoners. The war was not quite over: the fortresses of the Herodium and Machaerus had to be taken and the strongest position of all, Masada by the Dead Sea, fell only in April of 73 A.D. This was the end of the disastrous Jewish War.

Palestine, under the name of Judaea, became an independent imperial province governed by a legate, and the Tenth Legion was stationed in Jerusalem. Gradually the Jewish survivors began to regroup around their spiritual leaders, the scribes and Pharisees. A rabbinical school was established at Jamnia where the oral traditions that had grown around the written Torah were collected and shaped, eventually to take their place in the Mishna.[14] Jerusalem lay in ruins and the Temple was gone, but Judaism survived. Not only that, but the Jews, in little more than half a century, were again rising in a final desperate revolt.

In 130 A.D. the Emperor Hadrian (117-138 A.D.) ordered the rebuilding of Jerusalem as Aelia Capitolina; a temple to Jupiter Capitolinus was to be erected on the site of the Temple. This decision, joined to an imperial decree forbidding circumcision, fomented another rebellion (132-135 A.D.). Its leader was Simon bar Kochba ("son of the star"; cf. Nb. 24:17) whose real name was Ben Koseba. He was supported by Rabbi Akiba who hailed him as the messiah. The ruins of Jerusalem were, for a time at least, occupied by the rebels; we also know that insurgents lived in the caves of Wadi Murabba'at and elsewhere in the desert of Judah. In 1950 two letters of Bar Kochba were found at Wadi Murabba'at; in 1960 a further fifteen letters of the Jewish leader were found in a cave farther south,

---

[14]See p. 24.

near the Dead Sea.[15] The details of the struggle are not clear, but the fact that it dragged on for over three years—even though the Romans had dispatched four legions with auxiliaries under the command of Julius Severus, recalled from Britain for the purpose— indicates the seriousness of the rebellion.

The losses on both sides were very heavy; the surviving Jews were sold into slavery. Jerusalem, now named *Colonia Aelia Capitolina,* became a Roman colony, which no Jew might enter, and the temple of Jupiter was built on the site of Yahweh's Temple—just as Hadrian had ordered in the first place. The words of Lk. 21:24, which in their present form may be colored by the events of 70 A.D., find their most literal fulfillment after the Second Revolt: "They will fall by the edge of the sword, and be led captive among all nations; and Jerusalem will be trodden down by the Gentiles, until the times of the Gentiles are fulfilled." But the final note of hope should not be overlooked (cf. Rm. 11:25 f.).

2) *Jewish Religious Sects*[16]

PHARISEES AND SADDUCEES[17]   1. *The Pharisees.* The Hasidim movement of the Maccabaean period survived, in later times, in two branches: Pharisees and Essenes.[18] The Pharisees (whose name means the "separated ones") emerged during the reign of John Hyrcanus (135-104 B.C.). During his reign and that of his successor, Alexander Jannaeus (104-76 B.C.), they cut themselves adrift from, and stood in opposition to, the Hasmonaean dynasty. Later they refused to take an oath of allegiance to Herod the Great; they practiced passive resistance but avoided embroilment in political affairs; and they maintained a similar attitude toward the Roman authorities. However, they also "separated" themselves from the 'am ha-ares, the "people of the land"—the mass of the people "who knew not the law" (Jn. 7:49). Like the Hasidim before them,

---

[15]See Y. Yadin, *The Biblical Archaeologist,* 24 (1961), 34-50, 86-95.

[16]See A. Tricot, IB, pp. 67-74; M. Black, PCB, nn. 604 e-605 d; Kee and Young, *op. cit.,* pp. 39-45; Pfeiffer, *op. cit.,* pp. 54-59; F. V. Filson, *A New Testament History* (Philadelphia: Westminster Press, 1964), pp. 48-56.

[17]Under this heading we may conveniently treat of the scribes, although they did not, of course, constitute a sect; and we may consider the Sanhedrin.

[18]See Wilfrid J. Harrington, *Record of Revelation: The Bible* (Chicago: The Priory Press, 1965), pp. 78 f.

they were champions of the Torah and, since they had withdrawn from political activity, their religious character became more and more marked.

On the whole, the Pharisees came from the middle classes. According to Josephus, the members of the party numbered 6,000 in the time of Herod, and those in sympathy with their views must have been more numerous. What set them apart was an exact and detailed knowledge of the Mosaic Law and of the "traditions of the Elders," the oral interpretation of the Torah. Insistence on the oral tradition was at once the strength and the weakness of pharisaism. On the one hand it offered a means of adapting the prescriptions of the Torah to changing circumstances. It also meant that the Pharisees were more open to the acceptance of new ideas; thus, they readily gave assent to doctrines such as personal immortality, judgment after death, the resurrection, and the existence of angels. While stressing the action of divine Providence they also insisted on human freedom. They looked forward eagerly to the establishment of the kingdom of God on earth and they had a lively messianic expectation. As moral theologians they were much more open and progressive than the Sadducees.

On the other hand, preoccupation with the oral prescriptions— which they set on a par with the written Law—could and did lead to legalism and even to puerile casuistry. The severe indictment of the Pharisees in Mt. 23 lists some of the extremes of their legalistic interpretation. They had turned the observance of the Torah into an insupportable burden and since, in their view, faithfulness to God was expressed through faithfulness to the whole Torah (written and oral) they had effectively "shut the kingdom of heaven against men" (Mt. 23:13). Besides, pride in their knowledge and observance of the Law led to self-righteousness, an attitude strikingly illustrated in the parable of The Pharisee and the Publican (Lk. 18:9-14). The Pharisee believed that he was the author of his own salvation, that he was justified by his observance of the Law. St. Paul—the former Pharisee—came to realize that perfect observance of the whole law was not possible (Rm. 7); he bluntly stated that the Pharisees did not, in fact, observe the Law (Rm. 2:17-24).

Even though the Pharisees despised "the common breed without the Law," their influence over the people was immense. They were zealous for the Law, their religious ideals were high, and their moral conduct was often exemplary. Paul himself bears witness to the sincerity of his former life: ". . . as to the law a Pharisee . . . as to righteousness under the law blameless" (Phil. 3:5 f.). Besides, their independent attitude toward the Roman authorities appealed to the people. Not that the Pharisees were extremists; indeed, they cautioned against open revolt.

The trust of the people (in one sense at least) was not misplaced, for it was the Pharisees who saved Judaism from extinction. Their stand had always been on the Torah (understood in the wider sense), even though they did not despise the Temple cult. When the Temple was destroyed in 70 A.D., they were able to rebuild on the basis of the Torah alone. Their belief had always been that the destiny of the Jews was religious rather than political. Thus, political disaster did not spell the end of everything. Although their faults were glaring and although their opposition to and rejection of the Messiah was a national tragedy, we cannot but admire the faith and the courage that survived the shattering experiences of the two Jewish wars and we cannot but marvel at the spirit, bequeathed by them, that has enabled Judaism to survive (against all reasonable expectation) to the present day.

2. *The Sadducees.* The Sadducees (their name probably means "Zadokites," descendants or partisans of Zadok, Solomon's priest— 1 Kgs. 2:35) first appear as an organized party in the time of John Hyrcanus. It was due partly to the conflict of Sadducees and Pharisees that the Jews eventually lost their political independence: the appeal of both parties to Rome led to Pompey's intervention in 63 B.C. The conflict was not surprising; the two parties differed widely in social structure as well as in outlook and practice.

> In general the Pharisees belonged to the middle classes, the Sadducees to the wealthy priestly aristocracy. The Pharisees claimed the authority of piety and learning, the Sadducees that of blood and position; the Pharisees were progressive, the Sadducees conservative; the Pharisees strove to raise the religious standards of the masses, the Sadducees were chiefly concerned with Temple administration and ritual, and kept themselves aloof from the masses.[19]

The Sadducees stressed the importance of the Law of Moses, espe-

---

[19]Pfeiffer, *op. cit.*, p. 56.

cially the regulations governing the priesthood and sacrifice. However, they are not simply to be identified with the priesthood; they also included members of the lay aristocracy. In fact, they took their stand on the Torah alone (in the strict sense) and rejected the oral tradition. Hence, they denied the resurrection of the dead, personal immortality, and recompense beyond the grave, as well as the existence of angels and devils (cf. Acts 23:8). Since they interpreted the Law very literally, in moral matters they held extremely rigid views. Politically, they easily accepted Roman rule because the preservation of the status quo was to their advantage. It is readily understood that they did not have the sympathy of the people and had little or no influence in the religious and moral sphere. When the Temple and its cult came to an end, they had no further *raison d'être* and they, too, disappeared from history.

3. *The Scribes.* Scribes first appear in the reign of Solomon as educated civil servants; they are the originators and the authors of the wisdom literature in Israel.[20] In postexilic times, the scribe was one versed in the Law, like Ezra (Ez. 7:6, 11 f.; Neh. 8:1). In the first century A.D., the scribes, who were lawyers, moralists, and theologians, were the guides and teachers of the Jewish community: "The scribes sit on Moses' seat; so practice and observe whatever they tell you" (Mt. 23:2). They were named "lawyer," "teacher," "doctor of the Law," and were given the title of *rabbi* ("my master"). Some of them were celebrated founders of schools like Hillel and Shammai in the early part of the first century A.D.; others had great authority, like Gamaliel, St. Paul's master (cf. Acts 5:34-39; 22:3).

Although in the Gospels the scribes are most often associated with the Pharisees, the term "scribe" and "Pharisee" are not identical. For one thing, the scribes, even in the narrower sense of doctors of the Law, were in existence long before the Pharisee party emerged. Then, too, there were scribes with Sadducee leanings who held and taught the tenets of that party. However, it remains true that the great majority of scribes inclined to Pharisaism and their position as teachers of the people greatly increased the influence of the Pharisees.

---

[20]See Harrington, *Record of the Promise: The Old Testament, op. cit.,* pp. 243 f.

This seems a convenient point to insert a word of explanation about the Talmud, for its compilation was the work of later scribes. The earliest written codification of oral law is called the *Mishna* ("repetition"). The *Mishna* is essentially a collection of *halakoth* —rules of conduct deduced from the Law—that are earlier than the year 200 A.D. The *Tosephta* ("complement") is a body of material similar to the *Mishna* in form and content. Finally, the *Gemara* ("completion") contains traditions not incorporated in the *Mishna,* the solutions of later rabbis as well as moral exhortations and legends. *Mishna* and *Gemara* together make up the Talmud—the compilation of rabbinical oral traditions. There are two Talmuds, differing widely in content and extent: the Jerusalem Talmud (fifth century) and the Babylonian Talmud (seventh century).

4. *The Sanhedrin.* The beginnings and original composition of the Sanhedrin are not clear, but, under the Roman procurators, it had assumed a precise form and character. It was a senate of priests and laymen with seventy members—not counting the high priest who was *ex officio* president of the assembly. The sanhedrites were divided into three groups: the heads of the priestly families, the elders (representing the lay aristocracy), and the scribes. The third group was Pharisaic in spirit, the others were Sadducees. Paul skillfully played on this division when he was brought before the Sanhedrin (Acts 23:1-9).

Under the procurators, the Sanhedrin had considerable power. It could handle all cases involving infringement of the Torah: this included the civil as well as the religious sphere since Judaism knew one Law only. The council had its own police force and could arrest malefactors and punish them when convicted. It might pass sentence of death; but the sentence had to be ratified by the Roman procurator (cf. Jn. 18:31).

Outside of Jerusalem, in the communities of Palestine and throughout the Diaspora, local tribunals were also called "sanhedrin." They settled local affairs in the light of precedents established by the great Sanhedrin of Jerusalem, whose decisions were communicated to the various Jewish groups.[21]

---

[21]See A. Tricot, IB, pp. 63-65.

THE ESSENES   Josephus (the Jewish historian of the late first century A.D.), who presents the Jewish sects as "philosophies," describes the Essenes as a "third philosophy"—after the Pharisees and Sadducees. He gives the impression that they emerged during the reign of Jonathan (160-142 B.C.), and it seems that we may regard the sect as an offshoot of the Hasidim. Philo[22] asserts that the Essenes dwelt in large numbers in many towns and villages of Judaea, and he interprets their name as meaning the "pious ones." Essenianism, as presented by Josephus and Philo,[23] is seen as a monastic movement of priestly ascetics. All things were held in common, the members of the sect being charitably received in any of their settlements. Although Josephus knew a group of Essenes who permitted marriage, the sect as a whole observed perfect continence.

A candidate for admission to the order first had to undergo a postulancy of one year, after which he was admitted to the purification rites. Only after a further novitiate of two years was he admitted to the common religious meal and so received into the community. He also had to swear "dread oaths" to revere God, to act justly toward men, and to do harm to no man; he had to hate the wicked and take the part of the just; he had to be obedient to his superiors, avoid lies and theft, and keep the community teachings secret. Each community had a superior and was arranged in hierarchical order. The sectarians had very great respect for the Torah and were notably meticulous in observance of the sabbath. They sent offerings to the Temple, but did not themselves participate in the Temple cult; it would appear that they regarded the assumption of the high priesthood by Jonathan (and his successors) as a usurpation, and even as a profanation; this may have been the reason for their withdrawal from normal Jewish life.

Another ancient writer, Pliny the Elder, a Roman, tells of an Essene settlement on the western shore of the Dead Sea, between Ain Gedi and Jericho: "A lonely people, the most extraordinary in the world, who live without women, without love, without money,

---

[22]See p. 32.

[23]The relevant texts, together with the testimony of Pliny the Elder, all in English translation, are conveniently assembled by E. F. Sutcliffe, *The Monks of Qumran* (Westminster, Md.: Newman Press, 1960), pp. 224-38.

with the palm trees for their only companions." Pliny is undoubtedly referring to Qumran (which is the only important ruin in the area indicated by him). He named his "lonely people" Essenes. The majority of scholars agree that the Qumran sectarians, if they are not identical with the Essenes, are closely related; we shall regard them as identical. (An historical outline of the Qumran settlement, together with an evaluation of the abundant scroll material discovered in the neighborhood of the settlement can be found in *Record of Revelation: The Bible*.[24]) At this point we shall indicate the importance of Qumran (that is to say, of the Essene movement) for an understanding of the New Testament.[25]

The age immediately before the coming of Jesus, the last century B.C., is a relatively obscure period of Jewish history. The recently discovered Essenian texts have raised the veil to some extent, so that we now know something of a corner of that Jewish world into which Jesus was born. We are aware of an unexpected aspect of Jewish theology: a theology based on a dualism, a doctrine of two spirits, the spirit of God and the spirit of Belial (the devil). Light and darkness stand in opposition: they fight in the world, and the same conflict takes place within every man. But this dualism is monotheistic, for God is the creator of both spirits. It is dualism of a moral order: the influence of the spirit of truth is seen in the practice of virtue, while vice shows the hand of the spirit of iniquity. The combat is not unending, but will close with the utter destruction of evil and the victory of the "children of light."

Certain elements of the Qumran organization and certain tenets of the sect show an analogy with those of the primitive Christian community: there may be an Essenian influence on nascent Christianity. It is just possible that John the Baptist may have been an Essene. According to Lk. 1:80, John "was in the wilderness [i.e., in the desert of Judah] until the day of his manifestation to Israel." The only necessary conclusion from this statement, however, is that John must have known the Qumran settlement. Besides, if he had ever been an Essene, he had broken with the sect: his baptism, public

---

[24]See Harrington, *Record of Revelation: The Bible, op. cit.,* pp. 73-79.
[25]We follow the judicious assessment of J. Jeremias, "Qumran et la théologie," *Nouvelle Revue Théologique,* 85 (1963), 675-90.

and not repeated, differed radically from the daily ritual baths of the Essenes; and his universal call to repentance contrasted sharply with their marked exclusiveness.

At first sight there is a striking resemblance in external organization between the Essenes and the primitive Jerusalem community. According to Acts 2:44 f.; 4:32, 34-37; 5:1-11, the first Christians held all things in common. Each day (Acts 2:46) they partook of a common meal. The three stages to be observed in fraternal disciplinary correction (man to man; before one or two witnesses; before the assembled community [Mt. 18:15-17; cf. Ti. 2:10]) are paralleled in Qumran procedure. In doctrinal matters, the Pauline Epistles and the Fourth Gospel show some contacts with Essenian doctrine.

It is with John that the greatest number of points of contact, both literary and doctrinal, have been discovered. In John a form of dualism is expressed in contrasts: light-darkness, truth-falsehood, life-death; on the evidence of the Qumran texts, such dualism is authentically Jewish and is not due to gnostic influences (as had formerly been suggested by certain scholars). The evangelist treats light, truth, and life as kindred, and often as identical, images; the same holds true for darkness, falsehood, and death. The meaning of these expressions is very close to that of similar ones in the Qumran texts, where they occur a number of times in practically the same sense.

In these texts, too, stress is laid on a spirit of unity and fraternal love. Such ideas are frequent in John, but with notable differences. Thus, the fraternal love so insisted upon in Qumran is limited to members of the sect; all others must be hated as enemies of God. This is not Christian charity. It is the word "Christian" indeed that underlines the essential difference between the Scrolls and the Gospel. The occurrence of the various themes in the Fourth Gospel and in the Essene writings points to a common Jewish background, but in John these same ideas have been quite transformed by the impact of Christian revelation and of Christian faith. There is also a wider relationship between Qumran and the primitive Christian community: a religious awakening marked by a spirit of exultation before the gift of salvation, and marked, too, by intensity and by generosity.

But the differences that separate the Essene movement and Christianity run far deeper than any mutual contacts. A most notable difference is the extreme exclusiveness of the sectarians. They are the Remnant, the true people of God, the Israel of the end-time. By the practice of the moral virtues, by their common life, by prayer and meditation, and also by the meticulous observance of the Law and the strict discipline of their order, they strove to be an authentically priestly community. In order to become the immaculate people of God, they cut themselves off, not only from any contact with sinners—from all, that is, who did not belong to the sect—but also they would accept no one with a bodily deformity into their community; only priests without blemish might officiate in the liturgy of the New Covenant.

> No man afflicted in such a way as to be unable to take a place in the congregation, and no one with a bodily affliction, crippled in feet or hands, lame or blind, or deaf or dumb, or afflicted with a bodily disfigurement visible to the eye, or tottering with age so as to be unable to support himself among the congregation—these may not enter to take a place in the congregation of the Name; because holy Angels are in the congregation.[26]

How very different the outlook and practice of Jesus. He came to seek out and save the lost (Lk. 19:10). He associated with sinners and welcomed and healed the sick and the lame and the blind. And he never tired of teaching that the self-righteousness of men, reliance on their own efforts, cut them off from God. Salvation is not a distant goal which a man must reach by his own striving, it is the gift of a loving God. But it presupposes repentence, the tears of the prodigal son. And the gift is offered to all who will accept it.

In short:

> [The Qumran texts] set in unexpected relief the contrast between Jesus and the religion of his time. There below, in that Dead Sea monastery, the small army of ascetics, the saints of God, the militia of the Most High, live a life of the most severe penance. Striving after perfect purity, engaged in the strictest legal observance, they hate, without quarter, the enemies of God, holding themselves apart from the reprobate, excluding even the sick and the blind. Here, Jesus

---

[26]IQSa, 2:3-9; see Sutcliffe, *op. cit.*, p. 151.

proclaims to the poor, the miserable, the destitute of Yahweh, the incomprehensible, the infinite love of God, the dawn of that joyous time when the blind see, the crippled walk, and the poor have the Good News preached to them. Two worlds are there, face to face. On the one hand, the universe of the Law and of observance; Qumran had pushed to the extreme both its admirable sincerity and the limitation of its love. On the other hand the world of the Good News—the preaching of the limitless love of God and the joy of children forgiven by their Father. Better than ever before we see the splendor and the originality of the message of Jesus: that is the service, the great service, that the new texts have rendered us.[27]

OTHER GROUPS

1. *The Zealots.* When in the year 6 or 7 A.D. the legate Quirinius[28] set in operation a general census in Palestine, the exasperated Jews rebelled; the leaders of the revolt were a Pharisee called Sadduk and a Galilean named Judas of Gamala. These men gathered a group of insurgents around them and carried on a campaign against the Romans, first in Galilee and later in Judaea. This was the origin of the Zealots: ardent patriots who regarded themselves as the agents of God's wrath and the instruments of the deliverance of his people. Although the initial revolt was crushed, the party survived—men who owed allegiance to God alone, the sole Master.

The Zealots cut themselves adrift from the Pharisees who, in their eyes, were too conciliatory and too passive. They made use of any means, not excluding assassination, to free themselves from the foreign oppressor and to punish Jews suspected of collaboration. Since, in getting rid of their enemies, they usually used a short dagger called a *sica*, they were known as *sicarii* by the Romans. The Zealots were largely responsible for goading their countrymen into the fatal rebellion of 66 A.D. And the supporters of Bar Koseba in the final desperate rising of 132-35 A.D. were animated by the Zealot spirit: they were men who preferred death to pagan domination.

2. *The Herodians.* The Herodians are named three times in the New Testament (Mk. 3:6; 12:13; Mt. 22:16) and are also mentioned by Josephus. They were not a religious sect nor an extremist party like the Zealots, but the friends and supporters of the Herod family. They were found principally in Galilee, the dominion of Herod An-

---

[27]Jeremias, *art cit.*, 690.
[28]See p. 39.

tipas, although some Jerusalem families had remained attached to the Herods. It appears that, under the procurators, the Herodians allied themselves with the Pharisees. Although they were soon to disappear from the Palestinian scene, the Gospels would suggest that, at the time of Jesus, they were an important factor in the existing situation.

3. *The Samaritans.* The Samaritans were not a Jewish sect or group, but it is convenient to consider them here. The Samaritans of New Testament times were descendants of the heterogeneous people planted in Samaria after 721 B.C. The seeds of the enmity between them and the Jews were sown in the early days of the return from the Exile;[29] the final break came in the time of Alexander the Great when (according to Josephus) the schismatic temple was built on Mt. Gerizim. When their temple was destroyed by John Hyrcanus in 128 B.C., they continued to maintain their cultic autonomy and to celebrate their Pasch on the sacred mountain—a rite that they have faithfully followed to the present day. Their sacred Scripture was the Pentateuch alone.

In the time of Jesus they formed a small group localized in Samaria. With regard to doctrine they were monotheists, and they venerated Moses as the prophet *par excellence* who had given them the Torah. They believed that, from the days of the high priest Heli, God had been angry with his sinful people. However, they looked for the coming of a messianic figure—the *Taheb*—another Moses (cf. Dt. 18:15). Jn. 4:25 makes allusion to this messianic expectation. Several Gospel texts reflect the bitter feeling between Jews and Samaritans (e.g., Jn. 4:9; 8:48; Lk. 9:52-54). With supreme courtesy Jesus held up a Samaritan as the model of Christian charity; and Acts 8 relates how Samaria welcomed the Good News.

3) *The Jewish Diaspora*[30]

The term *Diaspora* ("dispersion"; cf. 2 Mc. 1:27) is frequent in the Judaism of the Hellenistic period as a technical term for the settlement of Jews abroad. The movement began in the sixth century B.C. when many of those exiled in Babylon elected to remain there, but

---

[29]See Harrington, *Record of the Promise: The Old Testament, op. cit.,* pp. 72 f.
[30]See A. Tricot, IB, pp. 98-105; Pfeiffer, *op. cit.,* pp. 166-96; W. D. Davies, PCB, nn. 598-603; *Atlante Biblico,* pp. 205-7; Harrington, *ibid.,* pp. 85 f.

it really got under way from the time of Alexander the Great. In the first century A.D., the total number of Jews settled throughout all the countries of the Mediterranean world may have been in the neighborhood of four million; Acts 2:9-11 gives an idea of their geographical distribution. Characteristic features of the Diaspora were, first of all, the strict community life of Jews living in the different centers; and then the close contact maintained between the various cells, with Jerusalem as the focal point of the whole vast network.

The constitution of the individual communities varied according to place and according to the juridical position of each in a particular city or state. Each community was governed by a *gerousia* ("council") formed of "Elders." Everywhere synagogues sprang up and the offices of *archisynagogos* ("president over the cult") and of *archontes* ("chief magistrates") were constant elements in the communities. Roman law not only recognized and protected this special organization, but also granted special privileges to Jews. Their right to collect the Temple tax and to dispatch it to Jerusalem was scrupulously safeguarded. They were dispensed from participation in pagan ceremonies and from swearing on the name of the emperor—they were expected to pray for the emperor—and the sabbath observance was respected.

One of the most important Jewish communities was that of Alexandria. There, beginning in the third century B.C., the Hebrew Bible was translated into Greek. This version, the Septuagint, became the Bible of the Greek-speaking Diaspora. In Roman times, the Jews of Alexandria enjoyed a considerable degree of autonomy (the Jews had welcomed Octavian's conquest of Egypt and had shown themselves openly in favor of Rome), although they did not possess full Alexandrian citizenship. They were disliked by their Gentile neighbors for their exclusiveness and for their pro-Roman tendencies. Serious disturbances occurred during the reign of Caligula (37-41 A.D.), but order was restored by Claudius (41-54 A.D.). The Jewish war in Palestine (66-70 A.D.) had repercussions in Alexandria, and many thousands of Jews lost their lives.

Jews in the cosmopolitan and intellectual atmosphere of Alexandria were conscious of the influence of the Hellenistic milieu in which they lived and their reaction was not only defensive. True, they did defend the Jews and Judaism from the attacks of pagans, but they also sought to prove the superiority of the Jews and Judaism over the nations and their religions. The most outstanding figure in this work of propaganda was the philosopher Philo.[31] Born about the year 20 B.C. of a prominent family, Philo was leader of a Jewish embassy to the emperor Caligula in 39 A.D.; he died some time after 40 A.D. His great achievement was his attempt to present Judaism in terms of contemporary Hellenistic philosophy. This involved a thoroughgoing allegorical exegesis of the Torah (by seeking a deeper meaning beneath the plain surface of the narrative): he strove to show that the biblical writers were saying the same thing as the philosophers of his own day. The influence of Philo is visible in at least one New Testament writing, the Epistle to the Hebrews, for the unknown author of the Epistle was almost certainly an Alexandrian Jewish convert.

For Philo, God is absolute Being who, by reason of his transcendence, is outside the scope of human knowledge. This supreme Being has used intermediaries in his work of creation and continues to make use of them in his conservation of the world; the intermediaries are ideas (*logoi*). The highest of them and the nearest to God is the *Logos*, the original Idea which contains all the others. The Logos, shadow and image of God, the exemplar of all created things, stands between the absolute Being and sensible creation: it is through the Logos that the human soul can attain to God in mystical contemplation. Philo had no intention of changing Judaism: he wished to make it relevant in a milieu imbued with intellectual speculation. The God of Philo is still the Yahweh of the Old Testament, yet there is a great distance between the Alexandrian philosopher and the views of the Palestinian rabbis.

Jews had, naturally, settled in Rome, but the colony in the capital was not as large or as compact as that of Alexandria and did not enjoy the same civil autonomy. In recognition of Jewish support in Judaea and in Egypt, Julius Caesar had looked with favor on the Roman colony; Augustus also regarded the Roman Jews favorably. Such an occurrence as the expulsion order of Claudius (Acts 18:22) would have been unusual, and that particular decree does

---

[31]See IB, pp. 103 f., 128 f.

not appear to have been very effective; at least, Jews were soon able to return.

A notable characteristic of Judaism in this period was proselytism (cf. Mt. 23:15). In Alexandria especially a deliberate attempt was made to propagate Jewish beliefs by means of such works as 1 (3) Esdras, the Letter of Aristeas, and the Jewish Sibylline Oracles.[32] Philo, we have noted, presented Judaism in terms of Greek philosophy. But a similar approach would have had a limited appeal and the real attractive power of Judaism lay in its superiority over the other religions of the Graeco-Roman world and in the high moral standards and conduct of Jews.

Many Gentiles who had wearied of the pagan religions and who were prepared to admit the principle of monotheism, were drawn to Judaism. They were freely admitted to the synagogue worship. They came to know and to appreciate the main tenets of the religion, and began to observe certain Jewish practices. If they were prepared to accept circumcision, a ritual baptism, and Jewish citizenship, they became true proselytes (incorporated into the Israel of God) and were subject to all the prescriptions of the Law. It seems, however, that the number of proselytes was not great—and the bulk of them would have been women. A much larger class was formed of "God-fearers" (cf. Acts 13:43, 50; 17:4; Rm. 2:19 f.). They accepted monotheism and certain Jewish practices, but objected to circumcision and to Jewish citizenship, and hence would not take the final step of full incorporation into the Jewish religion. For, despite praiseworthy efforts to remove barriers, Judaism remained a nationalistic religion. The Christian message of true universalism offered something that Judaism could never really give, and Christian missionaries made many converts among the God-fearers of the synagogues. In two ways at least, by producing the Septuagint, which became the Christian Bible, and by the good seed sown among the Gentiles, the Jewish Dispersion had prepared the way for the Christian Church.

This sketch of Jewish influence may give a wrong impression unless seen against a somber background. If some Gentiles came to appreciate the qualities of Judaism, many more were suspicious of

---

[32]See p. 38.

and hostile to the exclusive communities in their midst. The Jews were known to have a supreme contempt for any cult other than that of the God of Israel and they held themselves aloof from the religious and social life of the cities in which they dwelt (almost always in closely-knit colonies). Misunderstanding and misrepresentation were only too easy: their religion had no place for temple, statue, or sacrifice (Were they atheists?); they practiced the "mutilation" of circumcision; and the sabbath observance was taken as a proof of indolence on their part. The privileges they enjoyed gave more cause for resentment. Reaction not infrequently took a violent turn. In the first century A.D., the phenomenon that we term antisemitism reared its ugly head in many parts of the Mediterranean world. In Alexandria in 34 A.D. and in Caesarea and Antioch in 66 A.D. many thousands of Jews were massacred. These crimes might be put down to the exasperated reaction of paganism to a religion and a code of morals whose very presence was a constant irritant.

4) Jewish Apocryphal Literature[33]

Both in Palestine and in the Diaspora, during the last century B.C. and the first century A.D., living Jewish tradition gave birth to a varied literature. In these writings—many of them, by accepted convention, pseudonymous, that is, attributed to notable personages of the past—we perceive the spirituality, the prayer, and the hopes of Judaism, and we become aware of the atmosphere in which Christianity took root. Brief descriptions of the most important of the apocryphal books follow.[34]

THE ENOCH   1. *The Book of Enoch* (Ethiopic Enoch or 1 Enoch)
LITERATURE   is a compilation, in five parts, of exhortations, prophecies, and writings attributed to Enoch. The whole work is now extant only in an Ethiopic version. Fundamentally, it is an exposé of the religious and moral, messianic and eschatological beliefs of Judaism shortly before the Christian Era. The main divisions of the book are:

---

[33]See IB, pp. 109-28; A. Tricot, *Initiation Biblique* (Paris: Desclée, 1954³), pp. 79-83; English edition, A. Robert and A. Tricot, editors, *Guide to the Bible*, trans. E. P. Arbez and M. R. P. McGuire (New York: Desclée, 1960²), I, pp. 107-23; Pfeiffer, *op. cit.*, pp. 60-90, 187-230.
[34]See Harrington, *Record of Revelation: The Bible, op. cit.*, pp. 64 f.

1) Introduction	1-5
2) Angels and Universe	6-36

PARABLES OR SIMILITUDES (37-71)

THE BOOK OF DREAMS—APOCALYPTIC (72-82)

APOCALYPSE OF WEEKS AND FINAL JUDGMENT (91-104)

APPENDICES (105-108)

The sections are of different dates and the whole may fall between 170-60 B.C. The most interesting part is that of the parables or similitudes (vv. 37-71); it is largely concerned with the coming of the Messiah, the "Son of Man" (cf. Dn. 7). As it stands, this would appear to be a Jewish interpretation of "Son of Man" in a messianic sense, and hence a preparation of the use that Jesus was to make of the title. However, scholars (for example, Lagrange) have seen here Christian interpolations; this view seems to be supported by evidence from Qumran. The *Book of Enoch* is represented by ten manuscripts (fragmentary) from cave IV; the language is Aramaic. Four of the five parts found in the Ethiopic version are represented; the absence of fragments from the second part, the "similitudes," is significant: it can scarcely be the work of chance. The "similitudes" are probably to be considered the work of a Jew, or Jewish Christian, of the first or second century A.D.[35] At any rate, the parables are the latest part of the book and their author is, very likely, the compiler of the whole. The *Book of Enoch* had considerable influence in the early Church and, in its extant form, we must certainly admit the presence of Christian interpolations.

2. *The Book of the Secrets of Enoch* (Slav Enoch) is a typically apocalyptic writing. Enoch relates the revelations granted him in a journey through the seven heavens. He describes the creation of the world and discloses the secrets of the future. It was written by a Palestinian Jew (or possibly by a Judaeo-Christian) who

---

[35]See J. T. Milik, *Ten Years of Discovery in the Wilderness of Judaea* (Naperville, Ill.: Allenson, 1959), pp. 33 f.

wrote in Greek in the first century A.D. It is extant in a Slav version.

3. *3 Enoch* (Hebrew Enoch) is a rabbinical compilation of the third or fourth century A.D. It is of some importance for a study of Jewish mysticism.

THE BOOK   *Jubilees* tells again the story of salvation from the
OF JUBILEES   creation until the theophany of Sinai. The account
of the origins of the Chosen People is given in periods of 49 years and the number of periods itself is 49, so that the whole forms a jubilee of jubilees. The work is presented as a vision granted to Moses on Sinai; hence it is apocalyptic in form. But, since the author's aim is to find, especially in the story of the patriarchs, justification for the laws and customs of his time, he has made wide use of the haggadic technique.[36] Fragments of some ten Hebrew manuscripts of the work have been found in Qumran; the text corresponds closely to the archetype presupposed by the extant (complete) Ethiopic and (incomplete) Latin versions. The insistence on a special form of calendar and on fixed dates for the main festivals—both important characteristics of the Qumran sect—suggest that the work was itself written by a member of the sect. Historical allusions make it probable that its composition was well before 100 B.C.

THE TESTAMENTS   This work is close to Jubilees in spirit and
OF THE   outlook. The twelve sons of Jacob appear
TWELVE PATRIACHS   one after another with words of advice and
warning for their descendants; the whole is a moral treatise and is a striking testimony to the lofty standards of Jewish morality. The complete writing is extant only in a Greek version. Fragments of the *Testament of Levi,* in Aramaic, and a fragment of the *Testament of Naphtali,* in Hebrew, have turned up at Qumran. Some scholars (for example, Charles and Lagrange) had suggested the presence of Christian interpolations in the *Testaments of the Twelve Patriarchs;* now, others (for example, Milik) suggest that the whole is a Christian compilation, based on Jewish sources, such as the Qumran manuscripts. At any rate, the Jewish work (or sources) dates from the first or second century B.C.

---

[36]See Harrington, *Record of the Promise: The Old Testament, op. cit.,* pp. 325 f.

THE PSALMS   These are eighteen psalms, very similar to those
OF SOLOMON   of the psalter, composed in Hebrew but extant only
in a Greek translation and in a Syriac version made from the Greek
text. Pss. 2 and 17 refer to the taking of Jerusalem by Pompey in
63 B.C.; it is likely that the other psalms also date from about the
middle of the first century B.C. Teaching on the resurrection, free
will, and the messianic hope (particularly in Ps. 17) indicates the
Pharisaic origin of these psalms. The *Psalms of Solomon* should be
carefully distinguished from the *Odes of Solomon* which are second
century A.D. Christian canticles of Syrian origin.

APOCALYPSES   1. *The Assumption of Moses,* partly extant in an
Old Latin version, was apparently written in Hebrew shortly after
the death of Herod the Great, and seems to have been of Essene
rather than of Pharisaic origin. The author is very insistent on observance of the Law, hostile to the Sadducees and violently nationalistic.

2. *2 (4) Esdras* (Apocalypse of Esdras) is the Jewish apocryphal
work most widely known and used by Christians and (with 1 (3)
Esdras and the Prayer of Manesseh) is printed as a supplement in
editions of the Vulgate. Extant in Latin (and in Oriental versions),
it was written in Aramaic or Hebrew shortly after the destruction of
Jerusalem in 70 A.D. It consists of seven visions: dialogues with God
on the woes of Israel. It is an affirmation of Jewish faith and hope
in the face of overwhelming trials.

3. *The Apocalypse of Baruch* (Syriac Baruch) was written about
the same time as 2 (4) Esdras and seems to have been influenced
by the work; like Esdras it is divided into seven parts. It was originally written in Aramaic or Hebrew, but is extant only in a Syriac
translation of a Greek version.[37]

GREEK   1. *1 (3) Esdras* is a mosaic of passages taken from 2
APOCRYPHA   Chronicles, Ezra, and Nehemiah and is concerned
with the return from the Exile. The only original part is 3:1–5:6,
haggadic in form, a story about Zerubbabel which, in a charming
manner, turns on the theme that Truth (that is, wisdom) is victor
over all things. The book, a work of Jewish propaganda, was written

---

[37]For Qumran sectarian literature see Harrington, *Record of Revelation: The
Bible, op. cit.,* pp. 77 f.

in Greek in the first century B.C., most likely in Alexandria. The Vulgate carries a Latin version of it as an appendix.

2. *3 Maccabees* is an edifying story. It tells of a persecution of the Jews of Alexandria during the reign of Ptolemy IV (221-205 B.C.) and of their miraculous deliverance from a planned massacre. The work was written by an Alexandrian Jew before 70 A.D., and may have had in view the encouragement of Alexandrian Jews during a persecution under Caligula.

3. *4 Maccabees* was written to demonstrate the supremacy of reason over the passions. It is really a philosophical treatise in the form of a diatribe. The thesis is supported by the heroic example of Eleazar and the seven brothers of 2 Maccabees. The author was almost certainly an Alexandrian Jew who wrote in the first century A.D.

4. *The Prayer of Manasseh* was suggested by 2 Chr. 33:11-13 —a penitential psalm is put in the mouth of the repentant king. Written by a Hellenized Jew about the beginning of the Christian Era, it is a magnificent example of what is best in Jewish spirituality. A Latin version is appended to the Vulgate.

5. *The Letter of Aristeas*, purporting to be a letter written by Aristeas, an official of Ptolemy Philadelphos (285-247 B.C.), gives a legendary account of the translation of the Pentateuch into Greek by seventy-two elders brought from Jerusalem for the purpose. This story of the origin of the Septuagint is a pretext for extolling Jewish wisdom and the Mosaic Law and for showing their superiority over pagan philosophy and morality. A work of Alexandrian Jewish propaganda, it dates about 100 B.C.

6. *The Sibylline Oracles.* From the fifth century B.C. onward, oracles, attributed to the Sibyl (a Greek prophetess), circulated in Greece and Asia. The Alexandrian Jews saw here an effective method of propaganda. Thus, from the second century B.C. they composed and circulated "Sibylline oracles" inculcating Jewish beliefs. Christians continued the practice so that, in fact, the extant collection of twelve books is mainly Christian in tone. Books III (a collection of separate fragments from the second century B.C.), IV (about 80 B.C.), and V (about 125 A.D.) are the only Jewish oracles in the collection; and even these have been retouched to some extent.

3. CHRONOLOGY OF THE LIFE OF JESUS

The evangelists, who had no intention of writing a biography of Jesus in the modern sense, were not worried about precise chronology. We can date few of the events of our Lord's life, and even then we have to be content with approximations. No date can be established with absolute certainty, because the evidence at our disposal is meager and open to conflicting interpretations. We shall be content to indicate a chronology based on a reasonable evaluation of the available data.

1) The Birth of Jesus

Jesus was born during the reign of Herod the Great. This is attested to by Mt. 2:1 and Lk. 1:5. Hence, the birth occurred not later than 4 B.C., the date of Herod's death.[38]

According to Lk. 2:1 f., Jesus was born at a time of a census ordered by Augustus and carried out by Quirinius, governor of Syria.[39] Augustus was emperor (27 B.C.-14 A.D.). The general census of the Roman Empire ("all the world" = the *orbis Romanus*) was in view of tax assessment; Luke sees it as the providential means of ensuring that Jesus would be born in Bethlehem. There is evidence for a census in Gaul in 12 B.C., and there was provision for the taking of a census in Egypt every fourteen years; the series seems to have begun in 10/9 B.C. According to Tacitus,[40] a *Breviarium Imperii*, in Augustus' own hand, found at his death, gave not only the numbers of regular and auxiliary troops and the strength of the navy, but provided statistics on the provisions of dependent kingdoms, direct and indirect taxation, and recurrent expenditures. This information must have resulted from a general census which, of course, need not have been carried out simultaneously in all parts of the Empire. The possibility of a Roman census in the domain of

---

[38]According to Josephus (*Antiquities*, XVII, 8:1; 9:3; *Jewish War*, I, 33:8; II, 1:3), Herod died in Jericho a few days before the Pasch of 750 A.U.C. (= March/April, 4 B.C.). The monk Denis the Small, in the sixth century, erroneously fixed 754 A.U.C. as the beginning of the Christian Era.

[39]See M.-J. Lagrange, *Évangile selon Saint Luc* (Paris: Gabalda, 1921), pp. 65 f.; G. Ricciotti, *Vita di Gesù Cristo* (Rome: Società Editrice Internazionale, 1951[14]), pp. 195-202; Tricot, *Initiation Biblique*, *op. cit.*, pp. 635-37; English edition, pp. 124-27; *Atlante Biblico*, pp. 219 f.; J. Schmid, *Das Evangelium nach Lukas* (Regensburg: Verlag F. Pustet, 1960[4]), pp. 66-70; G. Ogg, PCB, n. 635.

[40]*Annals*, 1, 11.

Herod the Great has been questioned. But Augustus knew that Herod, a puppet king, must bow to his wishes, and besides there was a distinct coolness in their relations following Herod's unauthorized campaign against the Nabataeans (9/8 B.C.). In view of the evidence it is reasonable to suppose that Luke is standing on sound historical ground when he refers to the edict of Augustus.

The celebrated chronological difficulties raised in Lk. 2:2 are still unsolved. It is widely accepted, on the sole authority of Josephus,[41] that a census was held in 6/7 A.D., when Publius Sulpicius Quirinius was legate of Syria and was resisted by the Zealots under John the Galilean.[42] If this dating is accepted, we must look for an earlier census carried out by Quirinius. On the evidence of inscriptions from Tivoli and Antioch of Pisidia, it has been argued that he was legate of Syria between 4 and 1 B.C. and also that he had a special commission to carry out a census in Palestine during 10-8 B.C. Tertullian[43] attributed the nativity census to Sentius Saturninus, legate of Syria (8-6 B.C.); he could well have completed a census begun by Quirinius. On the evidence, the best we can say is that Jesus was born between 8 B.C. (the census of Quirinius) and 4 B.C. (the death of Herod). The years 7 or 6 B.C. are commonly proposed as the most probable.

2) *The Public Ministry*[44]

In Luke 3:1 f., the evangelist is at great pains to date exactly the ministry of the Baptist; his real purpose is thereby to date the beginning of our Lord's ministry. His elaborate synchronization serves to set the Gospel event in the framework of world history and to describe the political situation in Palestine. Unfortunately, however, only one element is of any use to us: the fifteenth year of Tiberius Ceasar. The reign of Tiberius began on August 19, 14 A.D.; the fifteenth year would be—in the Roman system—from August 19, 28 A.D. to August 18, 29 A.D. It is more likely that Luke follows the Syrian calendar with its year beginning on October 1. In this case the short period August 19-September 30 would be reckoned as the

---

[41]*Antiquities*, XVII, 13:5; XVIII, 1:1; *Jewish War*, VII, 8:1.
[42]See p. 29.
[43]See *Adversus Marcionem*, 4:19.
[44]See Tricot, *op. cit.*, pp. 638-43; G. Ogg, PCB, n. 636 a-b; *Atlante Biblico*, p. 220.

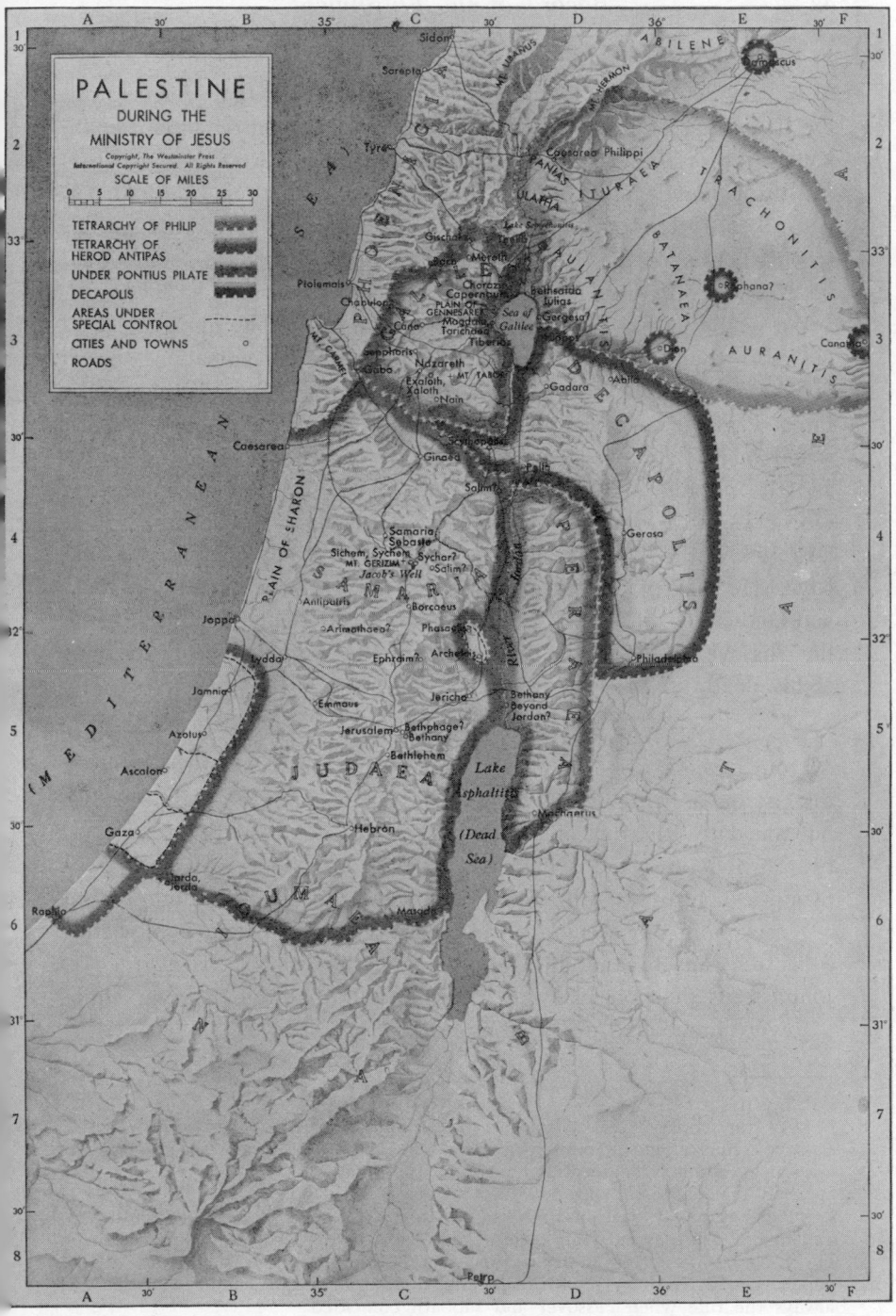

PALESTINE
DURING THE
MINISTRY OF JESUS

Copyright, The Westminster Press
International Copyright Secured. All Rights Reserved.

SCALE OF MILES

0   5   10   15   20   25   30

TETRARCHY OF PHILIP
TETRARCHY OF
HEROD ANTIPAS
UNDER PONTIUS PILATE
DECAPOLIS
AREAS UNDER
SPECIAL CONTROL
CITIES AND TOWNS
ROADS

first year of Tiberius; the fifteenth year of his reign would be October 1, 27 A.D.-September 30, 28 A.D. Thus, it seems that we can put the beginning of the ministry of Jesus, coming shortly after the inauguration of the Baptist's mission, in the year 28 A.D.

An incidental indication of importance is that of Jn. 2:20: "It has taken forty-six years to build this temple." Herod began his reconstruction of the Temple in 20 B.C.; forty-six years later would be 27 or 28 A.D., thus agreeing with the indication of Lk. 3:1.

We would gather from the Synoptics that the public ministry lasted not more than one year, although there are some indications that it may have been longer.[45] The Fourth Gospel, by clearly distinguishing three Passovers, leaves us in no doubt that the ministry really lasted more than two years.[46] After his encounter with the Baptist and the miracle of Cana, Jesus went to Jerusalem for the Passover (Jn. 2:13, 23). Back in Galilee, he multiplied the loaves by the lake "when the Passover was at hand" (Jn. 6:4), obviously a year later. He was in Jerusalem for the feasts of Tabernacles (Jn. 7:2) and Dedication (Jn. 10:22); thus, his visit to Bethany, "six days before the Passover" (Jn. 12:1), took place in the following year, the year of his death.

3) The Death of Jesus[47]

All four Gospels agree that Jesus died on the *parasceve* of the sabbath, that is, on a Friday (Mk. 15:42; Mt. 27:62; Lk. 23:54; Jn. 19:31), but the date (the day of the month) of his death is disagreed upon by the Synoptics and John.

Synoptics: Jesus ate the Passover on 15 Nisan (according to our reckoning the evening of 14—the Jewish day began immediately after sunset) and died on the afternoon of 15 Nisan.

John: Jesus died on 14 Nisan (at the hour that the Passover lambs were immolated in the Temple).[48]

45See p. 74.

46An unidentified feast (Jn. 5:1) has sometimes been regarded as another Passover, thus giving a ministry of over three years. It is more likely that the feast in question is Pentecost, or possibly Tabernacles.

47See Tricot, *op. cit.*, pp. 643-46; G. Ogg, PCB, n. 636 c.

48Passover always fell on 15 Nisan, whatever day of the month it should happen to be. The paschal lambs were slaughtered in the Temple on the afternoon of 14 Nisan, i.e., after 2:00 P.M., and were eaten that same day after sunset—which was 15 Nisan by Jewish reckoning. From the second century B.C. this was always the rule when Passover and sabbath coincided.

In detail, we observe that, according to the synoptists, the last supper eaten by Jesus with his disciples was a Passover meal. He had the preparations made for the Passover on the "first day of Unleavened Bread," that is, on 14 Nisan (Mk. 14:12 parr.; cf. 14:14 parr.). On taking his place at table, he remarked: "I have earnestly desired to eat this passover with you before I suffer" (Lk. 22:15).

But, John begins his account of the passion in this way: "Before the feast of the Passover" (Jn. 13:1); and at the trial scene before Pilate he remarks that the Jews refused to enter the praetorium "so that they might not be defiled, but might eat the passover" (Jn. 18:28). Jesus was condemned to death on the "day of the Preparation for the Passover" (Jn. 19:14) and was crucified on the same day (Jn. 19:42). John's dating is confirmed by 1 Cor. 5:7: Jesus *died* on the day the paschal lamb was immolated, that is, 14 Nisan.[49]

When we look again at the Synoptics we find that the day of the death of Jesus was not a day of sabbath rest. The guards who took part in the arrest carried arms (Mk. 14:47). Simon of Cyrene came from the fields where, apparently, he had been working (Mk. 15:46 parr.). The shops were open: Joseph of Arimathea could buy a winding-sheet (Mk. 15:46 parr.) and the women could buy spices (Lk. 23:56). All such activity could not have taken place on the solemn day of the Pasch, 15 Nisan. It may be that the Paschal character of the Last Supper, stressed in the Synoptic tradition, has upset the chronological perspective, and that the perspective has been restored in the Fourth Gospel. We recognize with John that Jesus died on 14 Nisan and with the synoptists that the Last Supper was a paschal meal—although it anticipated by twenty-four hours the Passover of the Jews. Various explanations of this last factor have been proposed,[50] but it seems best to acknowledge that Jesus freely

---

[49]In fairness we should observe that a strong case can be made for the synoptic dating. In an important *excursus* (*Das Evangelium nach Markus* [Regensburg: Verlag F. Pustet, 1954³], pp. 268-73), J. Schmid argues that John had changed the date of the death of Jesus for theological reasons.

[50]A. Jaubert (*La Date de la Cène*, Calendrier biblique et liturgie chrétienne [Études Bibliques; Paris: Gabalda, 1957]) proposes the theory that, although 14 Nisan of the crucifixion year was a Friday, Jesus followed an older calendar (which was still in use at Qumran) in which 14 Nisan was Tuesday of Passion Week. For an excellent critique of Miss Jaubert's book, see P. Benoit, "La Date de la Cène," in *Exégèse et Théologie* (Paris: Cerf, 1961), I, pp. 255-61.

anticipated the paschal meal. "Since he would be unable to celebrate the Passover on the morrow, except in his own person on the Cross (Jn. 19:36; 1 Cor. 5:7), Jesus instituted his own new rite in the course of a meal which had all the characteristics of the Jewish Passover."[51]

The crucifixion must have taken place between 26 and 36 A.D.—the term of Pilate's procuratorship. Since we have accepted the view which dates the death of Jesus to Friday, 14 Nisan, we can limit our scope to the years in which these factors were verified: 27, 30, and 33 A.D. When we consider that the public ministry opened in 28 A.D. and lasted more than two years, but less than three years, we see the years 27 and 33 are eliminated. Hence, we may assert, with some confidence, that Jesus died on Friday, 14 Nisan, 30 A.D., that is to say, on April 7, 30 A.D.

In conclusion, we may set in tabular form our relatively exact chronology of the life of Jesus:

7/6 B.C.	Birth of Jesus
28 A.D. (before Passover)	Beginning of the public ministry
April 7, 30 A.D.	Crucifixion
April 9, 30 A.D.	Resurrection (and Ascension)

4. THE APOSTOLIC AGE[52]

In this and the next section we shall be content to follow the main lines of the Acts of the Apostles. The whole of the chapter offers no more than the broad background and general historical outline of New Testament times.

1) The Jerusalem Community

The first Christian community was founded in Jerusalem where the group of Galileans, Apostles and disciples of Jesus, were gathered. They had been commanded to await the promise of the Father (Acts 1:4, 8); and the outpouring of the Spirit on Pentecost 30 A.D. marked the birth of the Church.

THE TWELVE The Twelve, naturally, took the first place in the community. As companions of Jesus, hearers of his words, witnesses

---

[51]*La Sainte Bible,* traduite en français sous la direction de l'École Biblique de Jérusalem (Paris: Cerf, 1957), p. 1325. See also the second revised edition in fascicle form. Henceforth references to this Bible will be abbreviated BJ; references to the fascicles will be abbreviatd (BJ).

[52]See Tricot, *op. cit.,* pp. 811-38; *Atlante Biblico,* pp. 241-47.

of his works and of his resurrection, their position was unique. From the beginning it was recognized, spontaneously—though it may not have been fully grasped until later—that the Twelve were the foundation of the Church: "The wall of the city had twelve foundations, and on them the twelve names of the twelve apostles of the Lamb" (Ap. 21:14). It is not surprising, then, to find them functioning as a group in the early days of the Church. Their first act was to fill the vacancy left by Judas and to restore the sacred symbol of the twelve tribes of the New Israel. If it was Peter who spoke on Pentecost, he was not alone, but stood "with the Eleven" (Acts 2:14); and at the close of his discourse those who heard turned to "Peter and the rest of the Apostles" (Acts 2:37). It was the Twelve who selected and laid hands on the new ministers (Acts 6:2 f.). When the Good News had reached Samaria and had been welcomed there, "the apostles at Jerusalem . . . sent to them Peter and John" (Acts 8:14). All the while the Twelve had been busy at "the ministry of the word" (Acts 8:14) in Jerusalem. But they were Galileans; besides, their mission was to be witnesses of Christ to the "ends of the earth" (Acts 1:8); it was the task of others to rule the church of Jerusalem.

THE ELDERS   A council of Elders was set up under the direction of James the "brother of the Lord"; its responsibility was to watch over the spiritual and material interests of the Jerusalem community. This arrangement was modeled on the council of Elders of the Jewish synagogues in Palestine and throughout the Diaspora. Acts bears ample witness to the influence of the Elders (Acts 11:30; 15; 16:4; 21:18).

PETER   Peter, first of the Twelve, was undoubtedly head of the Christian community; Acts 1-12 leaves no room for doubt on that score. He made decisions, presided over, and governed the infant Church. We see him act in the election of Matthias (Acts 1:15-26); he was the first preacher (Acts 2:14-36; 3:12-26) and the spokesman before the Sanhedrin (Acts 4:8-12); he took the initiative in the case of Ananias and Sapphira (Acts 5:3-11); he went on an official visit to the Samaritan converts (Acts 8:14-24) and undertook an apostolic journey to the coastal region (Acts 9:32-43); he baptized Cornelius (chap. 10). The role of Peter is confirmed by the testimony of Paul. Peter was the first disciple to see the Risen Christ

(1 Cor. 15:5). When Paul visited Jerusalem three years after his conversion, it was with the sole purpose of meeting Peter (Gal. 1:18). Eleven years later, at the "council" of Jerusalem, it was Peter who upheld Paul's case—and appealed to his own experience with Cornelius.

Although the evidence leads to the conclusion that Peter was leader of the Twelve and head of the primitive community, yet, "to see him as someone apart from the apostolic group is to sever the head from the body. Peter's role in 'confirming his brethren' (Lk. 22:32) should not lead us to overlook the fact that those to be confirmed are his 'brethren'—and so much his 'brethren' that one of them, Paul, did not hesitate to rebuke Peter at Antioch (Gal. 2:11-14)."[53]

JAMES, THE "BROTHER OF THE LORD" A James is named "brother of the Lord" in Mk. 6:3 and Mt. 13:55; and we learn that the Risen Lord appeared to him (1 Cor. 15:7). He is certainly not to be identified with the Apostle James, son of Zebedee, who was martyred in 44 A.D. (Acts 12:2). His identification with the Apostle James, son of Alphaeus, is possible, but is generally rejected by modern scholars. It is clear that his authority in the church of Jerusalem was second only to that of the Twelve.

Acts 1:14 informs us that the "brethren" of Jesus were with the Apostles in the "upper room" on the day of Pentecost; hence, James was, from the first, a member of the Church. Obviously, his position as head of the family of the Lord marked him out as natural leader of the Hebrew Christians. When Paul visited Jerusalem three years after his conversion—he had come to see Peter—he also made a point of meeting James (Gal. 1:19), whom, with Peter and John, he names one of the "pillars" of the Church (Gal. 2:9). In his account of the council of Jerusalem (Acts 15), Luke brings out the eminent position of James. In 44 A.D., when Peter had fled Jerusalem as a result of the persecution of Herod Agrippa I, he clearly designated James as head of the Jerusalem community (Acts 12:17). James was able to remain on in the city because his zeal for the Law was well known and because he was respected by the Jews

---

[53]B. M. Ahern, "The Witness of Sacred Scripture to the Collegiality of Apostles and Bishops," *The Bible Today* (October, 1964), 860.

as head of the Hebrew group. Finally, when Paul returned to Jerusalem in 58 A.D., after his third missionary journey, he found only James (Acts 21:18).

For information on the death of James we depend on Josephus.[54] He relates that the high priest Ananias had James stoned in 62 A.D., in the interval between the death of the procurator Festus and the appointment of his successor, Albinus. The tradition of Hegesippus that James was cast from the pinnacle of the Temple is secondary. It is said that James was succeeded by his brother Simeon, who, before the disaster of 70 A.D., led the Hebrew community to Pella in Transjordan.

THE TWO GROUPS Acts 6:1 speaks of two groups in the primitive Jerusalem community: "Hebrews" and "Hellenists." The Hebrews were Palestinian Jews who spoke Aramaic and who read the Bible in Hebrew in their synagogues. James, we have noted, was leader of the converts from among the Hebrews. They were distinguished by their zeal for the observance of the Law and were treated tolerantly by orthodox Jews. These Hebrew converts were not, as such, "Judaizers," that is, converts from Judaism who held that full observance of the Mosaic Law was necessary for salvation. It is understandable, however, that there were some among them with Judaizing leanings and that some of them may indeed have been Judaizers (cf. Acts 15:1, 5; Gal. 2:4). They did tend to look askance at the freedom from observance of the Law enjoyed by Gentile converts (cf. Acts 11:1-3, 22; 21:21). It is not surprising that missionary activity sprang not from this group but from the other.

The Hellenists (cf. Acts 6:1; 9:29) were Jews of the Diaspora who lived outside Palestine and who had synagogues of their own in Jerusalem where the Bible was read in Greek. They normally spoke Greek rather than Aramaic. Faithful to the Law and its observance, proud of their Jewish blood, they, at the same time, had a broader outlook than their Palestinian brethren and did not share their aversion for pagans. Acts 2:8-11 testifies to the presence of many Hellenistic Jews in Jerusalem on the fateful Pentecost. We gather that the converts from their ranks were not fewer than from

[54] *Antiquities*, XX, 9:1.

among the natives of Jerusalem. The Hellenists did not at once break with the Law or with the Temple; all the brethren—Hebrews and Hellenists—assembled daily in the Temple (Acts 2:46). However, friction soon arose between the two groups; the Hellenists complained that their widows were being neglected in the daily distribution (Acts 6:1). Accordingly, the Twelve asked them to designate seven of their own group who were then appointed to the service of alms. (The title "deacon" does not occur in the text, but the verb *diakonein*, "to serve," is used in Acts 6:2.) The seven bear Greek names, and one of them, Nicolaus, was a proselyte from Antioch.

2) The Spread of the Church

The plan for the expansion of his Church was traced by Christ himself in a charge to the Twelve before his definitive ascension: "You shall be my witnesses in Jerusalem and in all Judaea and Samaria and to the end of the earth" (Acts 1:8).

JERUSALEM   The coming of the Holy Spirit transformed the Twelve and those with them. Peter began to preach the Good News boldly and confidently. Those who heard, and repented, were initiated into Christianity by baptism in the name of Jesus, for the remission of sins and by the gift of the Spirit (Act 2:38). On the first day there were over 3,000 converts. At the close of a summary statement Luke can declare: "And the Lord added to their number day by day those who were being saved" (Acts 2:47); and afterwards repeatedly refers to the numerical increase of the Church. The first Christians were assiduous in following the teaching of the Apostles. They were of one heart and one soul; they frequented the Temple daily and were united in the breaking of bread and in prayer. All things were in common among them and they were highly thought of by the people (Acts 2:42-47; 4:32-35; 5:12-16). Barnabus, a Levite of Cyprus, was specially commended for generosity (Acts 4:36).

The Jewish authorities could not fail to react to the growing strength of the Church. The Apostles were arrested (Acts 5:17 f.); miraculously delivered from prison (Acts 5:19-21), they were summoned before the Sanhedrin where the prudent counsel of Gamaliel prevailed (Acts 5:27-42). Friction within the community itself was allayed by the appointment of seven "deacons" (Acts 6:1-6). One of these, Stephen—probably of Alexandrian origin—at once became prominent and was bitterly opposed by some of the Hellenistic Jews; he was brought before the Sanhedrin (Acts 6:8-15). In an impassioned speech he showed how the Old Testament prophecies had been fulfilled in the person of Jesus of Nazareth. He ended by attacking the emptiness of the Temple cult, the formalism of the scribes, and the blindness of the religious authorities of Jerusalem (Acts 7). The enraged hearers dragged him outside the city and summarily stoned him (Acts 7:57-60); and Saul approved of the murder (Acts 8:1).

The martyrdom of Stephen seems to have been the first episode in a violent persecution (Acts 8:1). It appears to have been aimed at the Hellenists; the Twelve were undisturbed. The execution of Stephen and the persecution—highhanded and quite illegal action on the part of the Jewish authorities—would not have been possible under Pilate. He was recalled to Rome in the autumn of 36 A.D.; the legate of Syria, Vitellius, a man favorable to the Jews, was in immediate charge until the appointment of a new procurator. We may with some justification put the death of Stephen and the outbreak of persecution in the winter of 36 A.D. The Hellenists were dispersed and went from place to place, preaching the Good News (Acts 8:4): Christian missionary activity had begun—born of persecution.

JUDAEA AND SAMARIA   Another of the seven, Philip, preached the Gospel in Samaria with great success (Acts 8:5-13); this was the first missionary activity outside of Jerusalem. When the Twelve had heard of Philip's success, they sent Peter and John, who not only approved but themselves carried on the work of evangelization (Acts 8:14-25). Philip baptized the eunuch minister of Candace, queen of the Ethiopians (i.e., of Nubia, the modern Sudan); the man was obviously a "God-fearer" (Acts 8:26-39). Philip continued to evangelize the coast area (Acts 8:40) and, indeed, seems to have settled in Caesarea (Acts 21:8 f.). Other Hellenist Christians were busy elsewhere: there were many converts. Meanwhile, the greatest of them all had been converted by the Risen Lord in person (Acts 9:1-19).

The conversion of Paul seems to have been followed by a period of tranquillity for the churches: "So the church throughout all Judaea and Galilee and Samaria had peace and was built up" (Acts 9:31). The inclusion of Galilee is significant: the Church had spread there. Peter availed of the calm to visit the brethren of Judaea and the coastal plain. He remained for a time at Joppa (Jaffa) in the house of Simon a tanner. Providentially, his steps had been guided toward an event, simple in itself, but of capital significance: the reception, by the leader of the Christian community, of the first Gentile convert. The conversion of the Roman officer Cornelius, a "God-fearer"—but still a Gentile—was, in the accompanying circumstances, not an individual case but an event of universal import; it was to be a deciding factor at the assembly of Jerusalem (Acts 15:7-11, 14). Peter (Acts 10) had learned a twofold lesson: God had shown him that pagans must be received into the Church without being constrained to the observance of the Law; God also had made clear to him that he ought to accept the hospitality of the uncircumcised. One senses the problem of relations between Christians of Jewish and of pagan origin. True enough, Peter was called upon, by Hebrew Christians, to justify his action (Acts 11: 1-18).

Some time after this event, when Agrippa I was king of Judaea and Samaria (41-44 A.D.), he "laid violent hands upon some who belonged to the church" and had James, son of Zebedee, beheaded (Acts 12:1). In order to please the Jews still further, Agrippa had Peter arrested, but the latter was miraculously delivered and departed for "another place" (Acts 12:3-17). All this happened during the Passover season (Acts 12:3). The death of the king, reported in Acts 12:20-23, seems to have followed soon after his return to Caesarea from Jerusalem (where he had attended the Pasch). This would date his repressive measures to the year 44 A.D. Peter returned to Jerusalem, for he was back there at the assembly of 49 A.D.

Shortly after Paul and Barnabas had returned to Antioch from their journey in Asia Minor (45-49 A.D.), certain brethren came from Jerusalem and taught that circumcision was necessary for salvation (Acts 15:1; Gal 2:4). The church at Antioch decided to send Paul and Barnabas, with some of their own number, to Jerusalem (Acts 15:2; Gal. 2:1). In Jerusalem they were received by the community and by the Apostles and Elders (Acts 15:4); but some converts from pharisaism immediately demanded that Gentile converts should be subjected to circumcision (Acts 15:5). The Apostles and Elders examined the question (Acts 15:6). Peter brought forward the case of Cornelius: it would be "tempting God" to impose any burdens on the converts since he had manifested his will so clearly. It was by the grace of the Lord Jesus alone that Jews and Gentiles were saved (Acts 15:7-11). James, arguing from the Old Testament for the call of the Gentiles, agreed fully with Peter on the question of circumcision. However, he added the "James-clause": the Gentile Christians were to abstain from meat sacrificed to idols, from marriage within the forbidden degrees of kindred (*porneia*), from strangled animals, and from blood (Acts 15:13-21); this would be a gesture to the Hebrew Christians. A letter was drawn up, addressed to "the brethren who are of the Gentiles in Antioch and Syria and Cilicia." It was sent with Paul and Barnabas, who were accompanied by two distinguished members of the Jerusalem church, Judas and Silas (Acts 15:22-29). Thus was the authority of the mother-church invoked to settle a problem that had troubled the great missionary church of Antioch and had imperiled the future of Christianity. Jerusalem had approved the "gospel" of Paul; and Paul himself was officially recognized as Apostle of the Gentiles (Gal. 2:7-9).

It is not our intention to linger over the difficulties raised in Acts 15—especially in its confrontation with Gal. 2—but it would be well to indicate them. In general, we should recognize that the Epistle and Acts represent, from different points of view, the relations of Paul with the Jerusalem Apostles. Paul wrote an *apologia*, defending his apostolate; Luke had no such concern. Paul took his stand on personal recollection, and his statements have an importance all their own; Luke was obliged to compile details from different sources. There is no question of setting Paul and Luke in opposition or in contradiction.[55] It is likely that the journey of Barnabas and Saul to Jerusalem, with help for the famine-stricken brethren (Acts 11:27-30), is identical with that of Acts 15:2 (cf. Gal. 1:18; 2:1 f.). The famine is the one mentioned by Josephus as having occurred during the procuratorship of Tiberius Alexander (46-48 A.D.); it

---

[55]See L. Cerfaux, IB, p. 352.

was aggravated by the sabbatical year of 47/48 A.D. In that case, Barnabas and Saul carried the alms from Antioch on their journey to the assembly in Jerusalem in 49 A.D.[56]

With regard to Acts 15, it seems probable that Luke has fused two accounts. One concerned a dispute about circumcision and the attitude of Gentile converts to the Mosaic Law. Paul and Barnabas went up to Jerusalem and the matter was settled on the authority of Peter. This is described by Paul in Gal. 2:1-10 and by Luke in Acts 15 and Acts 11:27-30. The later controversy, in which James (in the absence of Peter) played the decisive role, concerned the problem of social contacts between converts from Judaism and from paganism (Acts 15:13-21; cf. Gal. 2:11-14). A letter, embodying the decision on this question, was sent to the churches in Syria and Cilicia.

Luke's rearrangement of the material may be explained by his intention of bringing out more effectively the approval by the Jerusalem church of the Gentile mission.

> He probably wishes to show (a) that James and the "apostles and elders" disapproved of the Judaizing party, who claimed to speak in their name; (b) that they recognized the divine approval of Paul's Gentile mission, both in the signs and wonders done in Asia Minor and also in the prophetic scriptures rightly interpreted; (c) that Paul was scrupulously loyal to the authorities at Jerusalem in carrying out his Gentile mission.[57]

The pre-eminence of the Jerusalem church was short-lived. In 62 A.D. James was stoned, and a few years later all Palestine was in a ferment as the Zealots rose against Rome. Before the catastrophe of 70 A.D., Simeon led his flock to Pella in Transjordan. Later, some few returned to live in and near the ruins of the city. The last survivors disappeared under Trajan (98-117 A.D.). Thus, in fact, Judaeo-Christianity ended with the City and the Temple.

THE END OF   Some of those who had been dispersed after the
THE EARTH   death of Stephen went farther afield, to Phoenicia and Cyprus and Antioch (Acts 11:19). In the latter city they preached to Gentiles as well as to Jews (Acts 11:20), thus giving a decisive turn to the work of spreading the Good News. Antioch,

---

[56]See BJ, p. 1454.
[57]G. W. H. Lampe, PCB, nn. 791 f.; cf. BJ, pp. 1458 f.

at the mouth of the Orontes, was capital of Syria and the third city of the Empire. It was a busy commercial city with a cosmopolitan population. Converts were won from the first. When news of the new trend had reached Jerusalem, Barnabas was sent to investigate. He wholly approved of the work that had been done, and his influence gave a fresh impetus to the spread of the Gospel (Acts 11:21-24). Barnabas went to Tarsus to fetch Saul (who had retired to his own city after his apostolic efforts at Damascus and Jerusalem had been blocked by the Jews), and the two spent a year together preaching in Antioch where "the disciples were for the first time called Christians" (Acts 11:25 f.).

Antioch became the headquarters of Paul, the source of missionary expansion. From chapter 13 of Acts onward we are concerned almost exclusively with the mighty figure of the Apostle. Paul is Luke's hero, but he is also much more: the incarnation of the dynamism of the Church. Luke had taken the plan of his book from Christ's own words (Acts 1:8) and, tracing the expansion of the Church from Jerusalem, he leads the Apostle of the Gentiles to the capital of the Roman Empire, the heart of the world. There, with high dramatic effect, he leaves Paul—technically a prisoner—"preaching the kingdom of God and teaching about the Lord Jesus Christ quite openly and unhindered" (Acts 28:31). The book is not principally a study of personalities; it is the story of the Church.

> Acts is the history not of Paul nor of the Apostles, but of the Holy Spirit and the Church. In these lines Paul is not Paul alone, he is the Church, the Church which although hemmed in by a hostile world goes on with its task of preaching openly and fearlessly to all who come to it. So the Acts ends as it began, with Christ and the Kingdom.[58]

3) New Testament Apocrypha[59]

Although the New Testament apocryphal literature is not of the same standard of many of the Old Testament apocrypha, it has exercised an enormous influence on popular piety, on the liturgy, and on religious art. These varied writings reflect the preoccupa-

---

[58]C. H. Rieu, *The Acts of the Apostles*, A New Translation with Introduction and Notes (Baltimore, Md.: Penguin Books, 1957), p. 176.
[59]See Tricot, *Initiation Biblique, op. cit.*, pp. 85 f.; English edition, pp. 123-26; J. Bonsirven and C. Bigaré, IB, pp. 745-62.

tions and the curiosity of the common man among the early Christians; and also—since many are patently heretical—the deviations that were possible almost from the beginning. They also bear witness to the early origin of Marian devotion. Many of the New Testament apocrypha are no longer extant, and a number of those that have survived are of no value and of little interest. We shall indicate only the most noteworthy.

AGRAPHA   The Gospels do not purport to give us all the sayings of Jesus. Indeed, St. John has warned us plainly that only a small proportion of his words has been written down (Jn. 21:25). Yet, the early Christians were convinced that the Gospels had given us the essential message of the Lord; and sayings of his, outside the canonical Gospels, are rare. Such a saying is named an *agraphon*: ". . . any isolated saying traditionally attributed to Jesus and absent from our canonical Gospels."[60]

A few *agrapha* occur in other New Testament writings; these, obviously, stand in a class apart. In fact they number only five; and two of them are paralleled in the Gospels: Acts 1:4-8 in Lk. 24:45-49; and 1 Cor. 11:24 f. in the three Synoptics. Of the others (Acts 20:35; 1 Thes. 4:15; Ap. 12:15), the first alone offers something entirely new—the maxim: "It is more blessed to give than to receive." However, we also find certain variant readings in some manuscripts. We may note two of these: the Freer Logion[61] added in W to Mk. 16:14; and in *Codex Bezae* (D), in place of Lk. 6:5, the saying: "On the same day, seeing one working on the sabbath, he said unto him: 'Man, if indeed you know what you are doing, blessed are you; but if you know not, you are accursed and a transgressor of the Law.' "

Many *agrapha* are found in the patristic writings, but most of them seem to have been inspired by Gospel sayings. Some of them, indeed, may be authentic sayings of Jesus or may be based on genuine sayings of his not recorded in the Gospels. Nevertheless, it is extremely difficult to decide whether a particular saying is genuine or not. A careful study will eliminate certain of them;

---

[60]L. Vaganay, "Agrapha," *Dictionnaire de la Bible* (Supplement) (Paris: Letouzey et Ané, 1928), I, col. 162. Henceforth references to this work will be abbreviated DBS.

[61]See p. 129.

but we can never be sure that the rest—and they are few—are indeed sayings of Jesus. The tendency is to reduce the number of alleged genuine *agrapha*.

GOSPELS   1. *The Gospel according to the Hebrews* was the most important of the apocryphal gospels, although it is known to us only by citations in patristic writers. It was written in Aramaic about the end of the first century, and seems to have been a rather free translation of canonical Matthew for the use of Judaeo-Christians.

2. A *parchment fragment* discovered in Akhmin, Upper Egypt, in 1886 is almost certainly part of the *Gospel of Peter* mentioned by Origen and Eusebius. The work seems to have been written, in Syriac, in the first half of the second century. The extant fragment describes the last scenes of the passion, with the resurrection of Christ and his first apparitions, and is based on the canonical Gospels.

3. *The Protoevangelium of James* consists of two edifying but legendary narratives concerning the birth and infancy of Mary and the circumstances of the birth of Jesus. It was composed in Greek by an Alexandrian about the middle of the second century. It has greatly influenced Christian art.

4. *The Gospel of Pseudo-Matthew,* written in Latin in the fifth or sixth century, was inspired by the Protoevangelium of James. The first part of the writing treats of the nativity of Mary and the infancy of Jesus; the second part deals with the miracles of the infant Jesus.

5. *The Transitus Beatae Mariae Virginis,* written originally in Greek, in the fourth or fifth century, is closely related to the two previous writings and forms a complement to them. It bears witness to an early popular belief in the Assumption.

6. *The Gospel of Pseudo-Thomas,* extant in Greek, Latin, Syriac, Georgian, and Slav, appears to be no earlier than the fifth century, although, doubtlessly, it contains earlier material. It treats of the infancy of Jesus. The later Armenian and Arabic gospels of the infancy are based on it and on the Protoevangelium of James. The many stories contained in them vary from the charming to the puerile; and not a few are in bad taste.

7. *The Acts of Pilate* or *Gospel of Nicodemus* is extant in Greek, Syriac, Coptic, Armenian, and Latin. It appears to date from the fourth century. It is composed of two quite distinct parts. The first

part, based on the canonical Gospels, is a justification of Pilate who is seen as a witness to the innocence and divinity of Jesus. The second part, in the Latin version entitled *Descensus Christi ad Inferos,* describes that mysterious descent of Christ to the abode of the dead.

8. *The Gospel of Thomas*[62] belongs to a collection of thirteen volumes of papyri (containing forty-four secret writings) found at Nag Hammadi, close to ancient Chenoboskion, Egypt, about 1945. It is made up of 118 sayings of Jesus. The work may possibly have started off as an orthodox collection of the sayings of Jesus but, in its present form, it has an undeniable gnostic slant and it seems reasonable to regard it as being a gnostic work from the beginning. Many of the sayings are patently the interweaving of texts taken from the canonical Gospels. Frequently these are combined in order to achieve a gnostic interpretation. There is a marked tendency to rearrange the sequence of Gospel sayings. It is also noteworthy that, when the sayings are very close to the canonical forms, certain slight variations give the impression that the writer is striving to cover up his borrowing. The work shows how Gnostics understood, or rather misunderstood, Jesus and his Gospel. The Coptic manuscript is from the second half of the fourth century; the original, possibly in Greek, may have been second century.

ACTS   The earlier aprocryphal Acts (second-fourth centuries) have much in common. They have a similar literary form and the same doctrinal outlook. Although substantially orthodox, they show certain gnostic or encratistic tendencies and have suffered gnostic interpolations.

1. *The Acts of John* is a legendary life of the Apostle John, beginning with his appearance in Rome, from Ephesus, during the reign of Domitian. Extant in Greek, it was written about 160 A.D.

2. *The Acts of Paul,* an edifying narrative of the missionary journeys of Paul, is, together with the Martyrdom of Paul and 3 Corinthians, part of a larger work called the *Acts of Paul and Thecla,* written by a priest of the province of Asia, about 180 A.D.

3. *The Acts of Peter,* extant in a Greek fragment, in a Coptic fragment, and in a free Latin version is a second- or third-century

---

[62]See J. Doresse, *The Secret Books of the Egyptian Gnostics,* trans. Philip Mairet (New York: Viking Press, 1959); R. M. Grant and D. N. Freedman, *The Secret Sayings of Jesus* (Garden City, N.Y.: Doubleday, 1960).

popular narrative. It is the source of the episode of the "Quo Vadis" and of the tradition that Peter was crucified head downward.

4. *The Acts of Thomas*, extant in Greek and Syriac, seems to have originated in Syria in the third century. It gives an account of the missionary activities of Thomas in India. Although it has been described as a gnostic work, it is perhaps more true to say that certain gnostic tendencies have been emphasized by later interpolations.

5. *The Acts of Andrew* is known through Greek and Latin developments of it. The original, in Greek, is dated about 200 A.D. The liturgy of the feast of the Apostle (November 30) has been colored by the writing.

EPISTLES AND 1. *The Third Epistle to the Corinthians* is the final
APOCALYPSES part of the Acts of Paul and Thecla. It is a short exposition, in the name of Paul, of the orthodox doctrines of the Incarnation and the resurrection of the body.

2. *The Epistle to the Laodicians* is a brief mosaic of texts from the canonical Epistles. It is of Western origin, written at the end of the second century.

3. *The Letter of the Apostles* is extant in Coptic and Ethiopic versions of a Greek original composed in Asia or Alexandria about 180 A.D. In form it is a letter addressed by the Eleven in Jerusalem to all the churches. It is perfectly orthodox and of importance from the viewpoint of doctrine and liturgy.

4. *The Apocalypse of Peter* is extant in a Greek fragment found with the Gospel of Peter, and in a free Ethiopic version. It seems to have been of Alexandrian origin and dates from the middle of the second century. In the form of a revelation made by Christ to Peter—and transmitted by the latter to his disciple Clement—it describes the general judgment, with great emphasis on the torments of the damned. It had a notable influence on Christian literature and art.

5. *The Apocalypse of Paul*, of Palestinian origin, and written in Greek in the third century, is closely related to the Apocalypse of Peter. It describes paradise and the life of the elect—without neglecting a treatment of hell. Extant in Greek and in many versions, it was also popular in the middle ages.

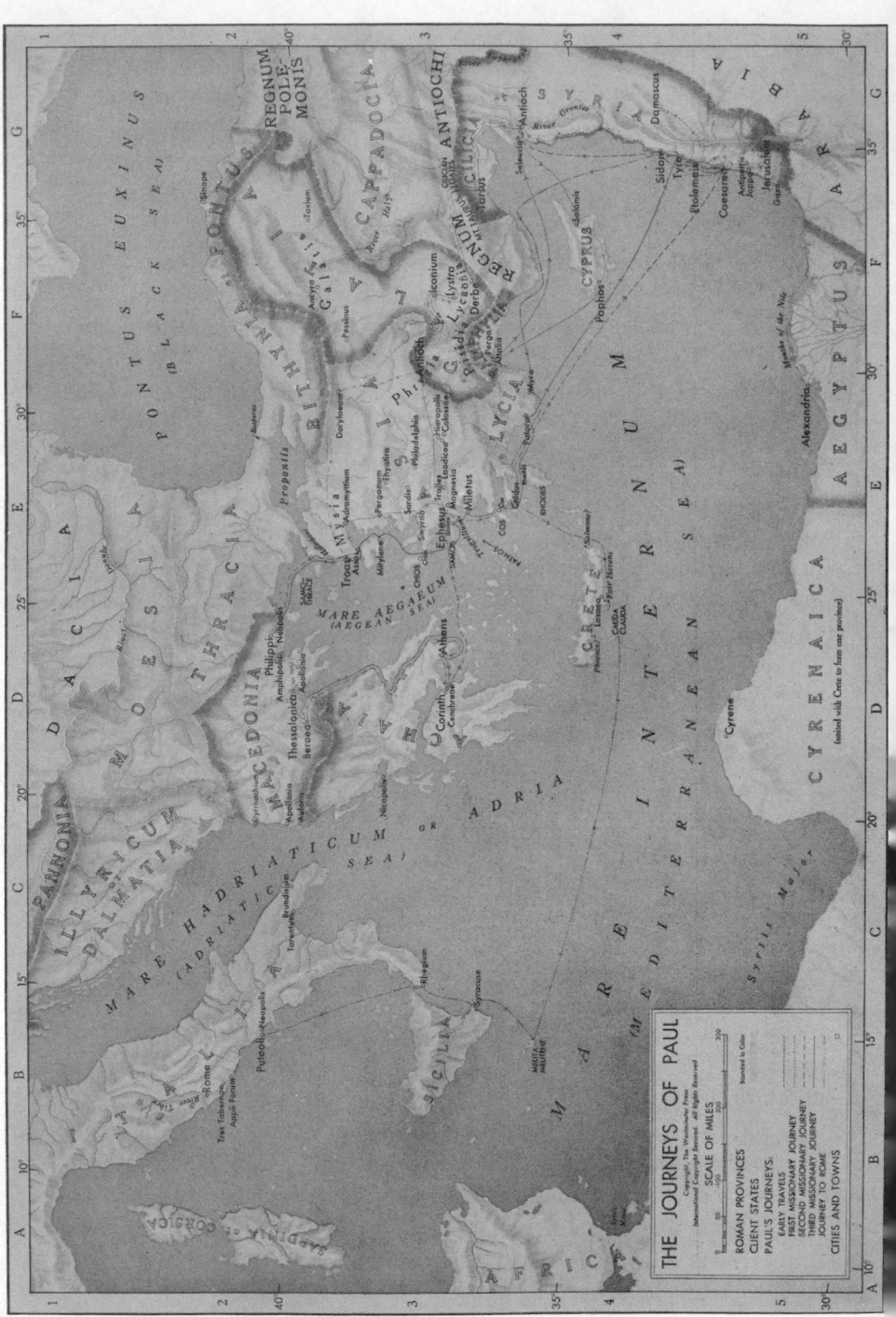

THE JOURNEYS OF PAUL

ROMAN PROVINCES
CLIENT STATES
PAUL'S JOURNEYS:
EARLY TRAVELS
FIRST MISSIONARY JOURNEY
SECOND MISSIONARY JOURNEY
THIRD MISSIONARY JOURNEY
JOURNEY TO ROME
CITIES AND TOWNS

5. ST. PAUL: CHRONOLOGY AND MISSIONARY JOURNEYS[63]

The literary work of Paul will be treated in some detail in later chapters. It is convenient, at this point, to sketch the framework of his life and to outline his missionary activities.

1) Chronology

CHRONOLOGICAL INDICATIONS FROM PROFANE HISTORY

1. *Proconsulate of Gallio in Achaia.* An inscription found in Delphi in 1905 gives a rescript of Claudius in which Lucius Junius Gallio (brother of Seneca) is named as proconsul of Achaia. The rescript was written after Claudius had been acclaimed—a special honor decreed for the emperor after a victory—for the twenty-sixth time, that is, very probably between January 25 and August 1, 52 A.D. Achaia was a senatorial province; the proconsul was in office only one year, from spring to spring. It is likely that Gallio was proconsul in Achaia from the spring of 52 A.D. to the spring of 53 A.D. Paul's appearance before him (Acts 18:12-17) was, plausibly, early in the proconsul's term of office—the Jews were attempting to take advantage of his inexperience—and toward the close of the Apostle's one and one-half year stay in Corinth; in other words, the summer of 52 A.D. Thus, we may, with some confidence, date Paul's stay in Corinth during his second missionary journey: winter 50 A.D.-summer 52 A.D.

2. *Recall of Felix and Appointment of Festus.* Antonius Felix took office as procurator of Judaea in 52 A.D. He was recalled by Nero, according to many scholars, in 60 A.D. His successor was Porcius Festus (60-62 A.D.). According to Acts 24:27, Paul was arrested at Pentecost two years before Felix was recalled. His case was reopened by Festus soon after he had taken office; Paul's appeal to Rome forestalled a protracted trial. We may date Paul's departure for Rome to the autumn of 60 A.D.; and his imprisonment in Caesarea to the years 58-60 A.D.

---

[63]See *Atlante Biblico,* pp. 247-54; L. Cerfaux, IB, pp. 377-84; B. Rigaux, *Saint Paul et ses Lettres* (Paris: Declée de Brouwer, 1962), pp. 99-138.

CHRONOLOGICAL INDICATIONS
IN THE NEW TESTAMENT
1. *Conversion of Paul.* The martyrdom of Stephen seems to have been the first episode of a persecution on the part of the Jews (Acts 8:1, 3). This would not have been possible under Pilate, who would have welcomed such a disturbance in order to pay off the Jews. He was recalled in the autumn of 36 A.D., and the legate Vitellius, favorable to the Jews, would have turned a blind eye to their activities. We may reasonably date the martyrdom of Stephen in the autumn of 36 A.D. The conversion of Paul followed soon after: during the winter of 36 A.D.

2. *Episodes Dating from the Conversion.* According to Gal. 1:8, Paul visited Jerusalem three years after his conversion. In Gal. 2:1 he tells us that he again visited the city fourteen years after his conversion. According to the manner of computation then in vogue, both first and last years of a period were reckoned, and, even when incomplete, were counted as full years. Hence, "three years" could be anything from one and a half to three years, and "fourteen years" could be from twelve and a half to fourteen. If we put the conversation at 36 A.D., three years after would be 38-39 A.D.; fourteen years after would be 49-50 A.D.

3. *Birth of Paul.* Here we have only the vaguest indications. In Philemon 9 (written about 62 A.D.) Paul is called *presbutēs,* an "old man"; and in Acts 7:58 (just before his conversion in 36 A.D.), he is called *neanias,* "young man." This would put his birth about 10 A.D.

2) *The Missionary Journeys*

FIRST MISSIONARY JOURNEY:
SPRING 45 A.D.-SPRING 49 A.D.
(ACTS 13-14)
Success in Antioch had fired the apostolic ambition of the Christians there. In the course of a liturgical reunion, Barnabas and Saul were "set apart" for a new venture farther afield. The first goal was Cyprus, homeland of Barnabas. Taking with them John Mark (cousin of Barnabas), they sailed from Seleucia, port of Antioch, and landed at Salamis, on the east coast of Cyprus and the chief port of the island. There they began to preach in the synagogues, thus setting a pattern that they were to maintain throughout; Paul would continue to preach the Good News to the Jews before turning to the Gentiles. At Paphos,

on the west, the administrative capital of the island, they were
favorably received by the proconsul, Sergius Paulus. At this point
in Acts, the Jewish name Saul is dropped, and Paul is named
before Barnabas.

The apostles crossed to Asia Minor and came to Perga, capital
of the province of Pamphylia. At this point, Mark left them and
returned to Jerusalem—a step that Paul regarded as desertion (Acts
15:36-39). Paul and Barnabas moved on to Pisidian Antioch, a
Roman colony by then incorporated in the province of Galatia. An
important stage on the main route from Syria to Ephesus, it had
a cosmopolitan character and a considerable Jewish population. The
Good News was rejected by the Jews but gladly accepted by the
Gentiles; the missionaries may have spent the best part of a year
here. Eventually, the Jews succeeded in having them driven from
the district. Paul and Barnabas went to Iconium, some eighty miles
southeast of Antioch. Here they met with notable success among
both Jews and Gentiles, but the inevitable opposition forced them
to move on to the Roman colony of Lystra, twenty-three miles south-
west of Iconium. There was no Jewish synagogue in Lystra, but
it was the home of Timothy (Acts 16:1-3). Roused by the cure
of a cripple, the people of Lystra hailed Barnabas and Paul as
Zeus and Hermes. Later, at the instigation of Jews who had come
from Antioch, they stoned Paul.

After this the missionaries went to Derbe, a frontier town of the
province of Galatia, about thirty miles southeast of Lystra. The
mission here was highly successful. After they had preached for
some time, the apostles decided to retrace their steps. They organized the local administration of each of the churches they had
founded. However, they did not revisit Cyprus, but from Attalia,
port of Perga, sailed directly to Syrian Antioch. News of the remarkable success of the venture, especially among the Gentiles,
disturbed some elements in Jerusalem; at a solemn assembly in
Jerusalem, Gentile freedom from the Mosaic Law and the special
apostolate of Paul were recognized (Acts 15; Gal. 2). It was a
momentous decision: Christianity was now, in fact, established as
a universal religion.

SECOND MISSIONARY JOURNEY:
AUTUMN 49-AUTUMN 52
(ACTS 15:36–18:22)

Heartened by the happy solution of the problem that had threatened to wreck his work, Paul soon began to look toward Asia Minor again. On this new journey his companion was Silas. They traveled overland from Antioch, through the Cilician Gates, and so reached Derbe and Lystra. At Lystra he met Timothy (converted on the first visit: Acts 16:1-3) and took him as a companion; Timothy would remain a valued friend of Paul until the end.

When Paul had visited the churches already established, he wished to go directly westward to the province of Asia, but, receiving a prohibition from the Spirit, he went north toward Bithynia instead. Here again he received a divine prohibition and turned due west, on a route that must lead to Troas, a port and Roman colony on the coast of Mysia (near the site of ancient Troy). At last the mysterious directions were made clear: Paul had a vision and heard the urgent cry of Macedonia.

At Troas the party was joined by Luke (the first "we-passage"[64] begins at Acts 16:10) and all set sail for Europe. They landed at Neapolis (modern Cavalla), the port of Philippi, and hurried on to that important Roman colony. Apparently there was no synagogue in Philippi, the few Jews who lived there meeting for prayer outside the town. A God-fearer named Lydia, a native of Thyatira, was converted, together with her household. Paul's cure of a possessed girl was the occasion of the arrest of himself and Silas and their imprisonment as disturbers of the peace. The incident had as a sequel the conversion of their jailer and the apology of the magistrates who had flogged and imprisoned Roman citizens without trial.

The missionaries then took the Egnatian Way through Amphipolis and Apollonia to Thessalonica, the capital of Macedonia. Paul and Silas preached in the synagogue and converted many of the Gentile adherents of the synagogue and some influential women. The Jews quickly stirred up a rabble against the missionaries; the brethren prevailed on Paul and Silas to slip away by night to Beroea, a small town west of Thessalonica. Here many Jews were converted, but the arrival of troublemakers from Thessalonica forced the brethren

---

64See p. 170.

to send Paul (obviously the chief target) on to the coast and by sea to Athens, while Silas and Timothy remained behind.

In Athens, Paul spoke to Jews and God-fearers in the synagogues, and daily in the market place held disputations with passers-by and also entered into controversy with Epicurean and Stoic philosophers. He was called upon to justify his teaching before the Council of the Areopagus, the Athenian Senate. He won a few converts, notably a member of the Council of the Areopagus named Dionysius.

Soon afterwards Paul left for Corinth, capital of the province of Achaia, residence of the proconsul, and a major commercial center. Here he met the couple Aquila and Priscilla, converts from Judaism, and lodged with them. He preached in the synagogue sabbath after sabbath; and was soon joined by Silas and Timothy. Repulsed by the Jews, he turned to the Gentiles with considerable success. He spent a year and one-half in Corinth (winter 50 A.D.-summer 52 A.D.) and wrote 1 and 2 Thessalonians during his stay.

The Jews took advantage of the arrival of the new proconsul, Lucius Junius Gallio, to bring a trumped-up charge against Paul. The proconsul dismissed the charge without hesitation. However, soon afterwards Paul sailed for Ephesus, taking with him Priscilla and Aquila whom he left in that city. He himself preached briefly in the synagogue, promised to return, and sailed to Caesarea. He went to pay his respects to the church of Jerusalem and then returned to Antioch (autumn of 52 A.D.).

THIRD MISSIONARY JOURNEY: SPRING 53-SPRING 58 (ACTS 18:23–21:16)   After a short stay in Antioch Paul decided to visit Asia Minor. Yet again: "He went from place to place through the region of Galatia and Phrygia, strengthening all the disciples" (Acts 18:23). But this time his jail was Ephesus, capital of the province of Asia, a city of wealth and magnificence, one of the great cities of the age. It was famed for its Artemesion—the temple of Artemis (Diana)—one of the seven wonders of the world. In Ephesus, Paul was received by Aquila and Priscilla. He instructed and baptized a small group of the disciples of John the Baptist. As usual, he preached first in the synagogue—for three months—but, inevitably, he was eventually rejected by the Jews. For more than two years after this (his whole stay in Ephesus was nearly three years: Acts 19:8-10; 20:31) he carried on his mission among the Gentiles, using for this purpose the lecture hall of a certain Tyrannus. Meanwhile, his disciples worked throughout Asia (cf. Col. 1:7 f.; 4:12 f.). A striking testimony to the success of Paul's preaching is provided by the reaction of the silversmiths whose main business was the manufacture of silver statuettes of Artemis for devotees of the goddess. They recognized in Paul a serious threat to this lucrative business, and organized a riot in an attempt to get rid of him; soon afterwards (before Pentecost, 57 A.D.), Paul did leave the city. During his stay in Ephesus, the Apostle wrote 1 Corinthians (and, perhaps, Philippians). It seems likely that 1 Cor. had been followed by a brief visit to Corinth (cf. 2 Cor. 1:23–2:1; 12:14; 13), and that after his return to Ephesus he wrote the "letter written in tears" (2 Cor. 2:3 f., 9; 7:8 ff.). Galatians was also written in Ephesus; whether before or after 1 Cor. is not clear.

From Ephesus, Paul went to Macedonia where he wrote 2 Corinthians; and then went on to Corinth where he spent three months (winter, 57/58 A.D.). While there he wrote the Epistle to the Romans. He had planned to sail directly from Corinth to Antioch, but he was warned of a plot against him and he decided to travel overland by way of Macedonia instead. At Philippi he met Luke and they sailed for Troas just after Easter of 58 A.D. Paul was anxious to be in Jerusalem for Pentecost; in order to avoid inevitable delay, he bypassed Ephesus and had the elders of the church come to meet him at Miletus, where he took a touching leave of them. Eventually the party landed at Tyre and spent a week with the brethren there. Then they continued the voyage to Caesarea, stopping off at Ptolemais on the way. In Caesarea they stayed with Philip, one of the seven deacons; there the prophet Agabus foretold the imminent imprisonment of Paul. On arrival at Jerusalem they were warmly welcomed by the brethren. The next day Paul was received by James and the Elders. As a conciliatory gesture to the Judaeo-Christians, it was suggested that Paul should defray the expenses of four men under a Nazirite vow; he agreed with alacrity. However, Jews from Asia who had seen Paul in the company of the Ephesian Trophimus—a non-Jew—accused him of bringing a Gentile into the Temple; prompt action by the tribune Claudius

Lysias saved Paul from being lynched. Paul's address to the mob only inflamed them the more, and the tribune, not understanding Aramaic and believing that his prisoner was provoking the crowd, was on the point of flogging him when Paul appealed to his rights as a Roman citizen. Next day the tribune had Paul brought before the Sanhedrin where he deftly set Pharisees and Sadducees at loggerheads. The Apostle's nephew warned him of a plot against him; the tribune, without delay, sent Paul under heavy escort to Caesarea where he was handed over to the procurator Antonius Felix. After a preliminary trial, the venal Felix, hoping for a bribe, held Paul a prisoner in Caesarea during the remaining two years of his term of office (58-60 A.D.).

JOURNEY TO ROME (AUTUMN 60-SPRING 61) AND LAST YEARS   In 60 A.D. Porcius Festus succeeded Felix. The new procurator, briefed by the Jewish leaders, wanted Paul to stand trial in Jerusalem. But Paul, realizing the murderous intention of the Jews, appealed to the imperial tribunal. That settled the matter: the procurator was now bound to send his prisoner to Rome for trial. Before leaving Caesarea, Paul had an opportunity of stating his case before Agrippa II and his sister Berenice who had come on a state visit to Festus.

In the autumn of 60 A.D., Paul was handed over to the custody of a centurion of the Augustan Cohort (imperial couriers) named Julius. The party boarded a ship bound for Asia Minor. When they had reached Myra in Lycia, the centurion transferred his prisoners to a ship bound for Italy. The voyage, described in dramatic detail in Acts 27-28, ended in shipwreck in Malta. The party spent the winter on the island and arrived in Rome in the spring of 61 A.D. There Paul was under house arrest for two years. He was able to carry on a fruitful apostolate; and he wrote his "capitivity epistles": Colossians, Ephesians, Philemon, and, probably, Philippians. His enemies knew that it was useless to proffer their charges against Paul in the imperial tribunal. Hence, after the statutory two years, Paul was set at liberty.

We know little about the last phase of Paul's life (63-67 A.D.). He may have fulfilled his intention of visiting Spain (cf. Rm. 15:24 f.). The Pastoral Epistles indicate that he visited Ephesus

(1 Tm. 1:3) and Crete (Ti. 1:5); while 1 Timothy and Titus appear to have been written in Macedonia about 65 A.D. From 2 Timothy we learn of a second Roman captivity, much more severe than the first (2 Tm. 1:8, 12; 2:9). Paul realizes that death is in store for him this time (2 Tm. 4:6-8). He was likely a victim of the persecution of Nero. The traditional date of his martyrdom is 67 A.D.

3) Chronological Table

c. 10 A.D.	Birth of Paul in Tarsus
after 30 A.D.	Jerusalem—disciple of Gamaliel
c. 36 A.D.	Conversion
36-39 A.D.	Damascus and Arabia
39 A.D.	Visit to Jerusalem
39-43 A.D.	Tarsus
43-44 A.D.	In Antioch with Barnabas
45-49 A.D.	First missionary journey
49 A.D.	Assembly in Jerusalem
50-52 A.D.	Second missionary journey
	Corinth: winter, 50 A.D.-summer, 52 A.D.
	1, 2 Thessalonians
53-58 A.D.	Third missionary journey
	Ephesus: autumn, 54 A.D.-spring, 57 A.D.
	[Philippians] Galatians
	1 Corinthians
	Visit to Corinth: 57 A.D.
	Macedonia: summer, 57 A.D.
	2 Corinthians
	Corinth, winter, 57/58 A.D.
	Romans
58 A.D. (Pentecost)	Arrest in Jerusalem
58-60 A.D.	Prisoner in Caesarea
60-61 A.D.	Journey to Rome
61-63 A.D.	Prisoner in Rome
	Colossians, Ephesians, Philemon
	[Philippians]
63 A.D.	End of first captivity
	Perhaps journey to Spain

c. 65 A.D.	Ephesus, Crete, Macedonia
	1 Timothy, Titus
c. 67 A.D.	Second Roman captivity
	2 Timothy
c. 67 A.D.	Death

TWO

The Formation of the Synoptic Gospels

THE WORDS AND WORKS OF JESUS

THE APOSTOLIC TRADITION

THE EVANGELISTS

In order to determine correctly the trustworthiness of what is transmitted in the Gospels, the interpreter must take careful note of the three stages of tradition by which the teaching and the life of Jesus have come down to us.[1]

The Greek word for gospel is *euangelion,* whence the Latin *evangelium.* (Our "gospel" is from the early English "god spel" = "good news.") In the early Church, *euangelion* signified, not a book dealing with the words and works of Christ, but the Good News of messianic salvation, the message of salvation. The word was already found in the LXX (the Greek translation of the Old Testament).[2] For example, we read in Isaiah: "How beautiful upon the mountains are the feet of him who brings *good tidings* of good" (52:7). The word is the same, but in the Old Testament the good news is of future salvation, whereas the gospel is the good news of a salvation that has been achieved.

The gospel may be the Good News that Jesus himself preached (for example, Mk. 1:15; Mt. 11:5; Lk. 4:18); or it may be the apostolic preaching about Christ and the salvation that is found in

---

[1]*Instruction on the Historical Truth of the Gospels,* issued by the Pontifical Biblical Commission, April 21, 1964. Excerpts are from the authentic English translation of the *Instruction.* Henceforth references to this work will be abbreviated PBC., *Instr.*

[2]See Wilfrid J. Harrington, *Record of Revelation: The Bible* (Chicago: The Priory Press, 1965), p. 67.

him (for example, Acts 5:42; Rm. 1:1 f.). Both come to the same thing because the question is always one of Christ and of his teaching. We should note that it is a matter of *preaching*, not of the written word, and that Christian missionaries are called "evangelists" (Acts 21:8; Eph. 4:11; 2 Tm. 4:5). We must realize that, in the New Testament itself, the word "gospel" means the preaching of Christ and the "evangelist" is a preacher.

But words often change; frequently, a word that has quite a broad meaning acquires a precise, technical sense. So it was that, in the second century A.D., *euangelion* came to designate the written account of the life and teaching of our Lord. At this same time, the authors of the Gospels were named evangelists. Hence, we should keep in mind that our very special meaning for "gospel" and "evangelist" is not quite that of the New Testament itself.

The Gospels tell us of Christ and of his teaching, but they were not written by him. Jesus did not describe such and such a miracle; he worked it. Jesus suffered and died and rose from the dead; he did not give an account of these happenings. The same is true of his teaching. His words were spoken by him, but they were written down by others. They have come down to us, not as he spoke them, but as others remembered them. They may have been remembered and recorded exactly as he spoke them, and they may not; an examination of the Gospels convinces us that we must consider the second alternative. Hence, we must turn to the evangelists.

The Gospels were written by the four evangelists, but the evangelists wrote many years after the resurrection, after the events they relate. They did not write the Gospels out of their heads, relying only on what they had seen and heard and remembered. We have only to recall that St. Mark was not an Apostle and that St. Luke was not even a disciple of Jesus in order to realize that they, at least, must have been dependent on others. Quite apart from this, however, it is now clear that the evangelists set about their task in a perfectly natural way by making use of such accounts or documents as served their purpose.

We must go beyond the evangelists because, although they have given us a fourfold account of the Good News, they themselves are not the authors of the Good News; they have put the story of our Lord in writing, but that story existed long before they wrote. Between Christ and the evangelists come the Apostles and the first preachers. Thus we get back, ultimately, to the early Church; for it was the Church, represented by the Apostles, that formed the basic Gospel which was afterwards passed on to us, according to the viewpoint of each, by the four evangelists.

Therefore, we have three stages: Jesus Christ, the apostolic Church, and the evangelists. Only when we have taken all three into account can we really hope to understand the Gospels. In the light of this realization, many apparent problems are seen to be no problems at all. We must have noticed, for instance, that the evangelists rarely agree verbatim, even when repeating sayings of our Lord; and, indeed, there are some notable differences. That they do differ is really what we should expect. They are genuine authors, writing with a definite purpose in mind; and, too, they often owe their information to sources that are not always identical. It is to be hoped that this and the following chapters will help the reader to realize these facts; otherwise, he will never have a really intelligent grasp of the Gospels.

1. THE WORDS AND WORKS OF JESUS

1) *The Sayings*

Our Lord, when expounding his teaching by word of mouth, observed the methods of reasoning and of exposition which were in common use at the time; in this way he accommodated himself to the mentality of his hearers, and ensured that his teachings would be deeply impressed on their minds and would be easily retained in memory by his disciples (PBC, *Instr.*).

We shall see that the Gospels are not biographies of Jesus. They do purport, however, to present his teaching, and they do put before us certain stages and events of his earthly career. But, if we are to attain to the words and deeds of Jesus, we can do so only by working backward from the third and second stages of the tradition. For the moment we simply presuppose the work of the evangelists and of the Apostles and indicate how we may reach the very kernel of the Gospel.

When we turn to the sayings of our Lord, we find that, on the whole, the same sayings are recorded by the three evangelists— although Mark has notably less of them than Matthew and Luke.

But rarely do we find that any saying occurs in identical form in any two Gospels. Generally, the differences are insignificant, but frequently enough they are more far-reaching. We must see the problem in proper perspective. It would be unreasonable to have the words of Jesus always recorded in just the same way. Indeed, it is impossible to have any of his sayings *exactly* as they came from his lips, for the good reason that he spoke Aramaic while our Gospels are written in Greek. However, an Aramaic substratum is sometimes discernible and can be a valuable pointer to sayings of his that still retain the form and cast he gave them (for example, expressions like *Abba,* Mk. 14:36; *talitha cumi,* Mk. 5:41; *Ephphatha,* Mk. 7:34 that still stand in Aramaic), while features of the oral style—such as rhythm, parallelism, and the *inclusion*—surely illustrate his care to instruct his disciples.

FEATURES OF THE   In the Old Testament writings, rhythm is large-
ORAL STYLE   ly present in the psalms and prophetical books.
The parallel with the prophetical books is particularly instructive because these were precisely the parts of the Old Testament which were first preached in public before being written down. We should expect to find traces of rhythm in the sayings of our Lord (for example, Mt. 6:9-13; 7:17; Mk. 7:8). A striking example is Mt. 16:17-19; here we give it in an English translation of a Greek text that is itself based on an Aramaic original. Even at third hand the balance and rhythm are obvious; surely we are close to the accents of Jesus.

The passage consists of three verses, each verse contains three lines and each line is divided into two balanced parts:

Blessed are you/ Simon Bar-Jona!
for flesh and blood/ has not revealed to you,
but my Father/ in the heavens.

And I say to you/ that you are Rock (Peter)
and on this rock/ I will build my Church
and the gates of hell/ shall not prevail against it.

I shall give you the keys/ of' the kingdom of heaven,
and whatever you bind on earth/ shall be bound in heaven,
and whatever you loose on earth/ shall be loosed in heaven.

In parallelism we again have a feature that is prominent in the psalms and prophetical literature; it is distinctive of Hebrew poetry.[3] The different types of parallelism are represented in the sayings of Jesus.

1. *Synonymous parallelism.* Two members of a couplet express the same idea; the second renders the sense of the first in different words. For example:

He who receives a prophet because he is a prophet shall receive a prophet's reward.
and he who receives a righteous man because he is a righteous
man
shall receive a righteous man's reward (Mt. 10:41).

Everyone to whom much is given, of him will much be required;
and of him to whom men commit much they will demand the
more (Lk. 12:48).

2. *Antithetical parallelism.* The terms of the second member contrast with those of the first. For example:

The sabbath was made for man,
not man for the sabbath (Mk. 2:27; cf. Mt. 7:17; Lk. 12:47 f.).

3. *Progressive parallelism.* The sense of the first member is developed in the second. For example:

He who receives you receives me,
and he who receives me receives him who sent me (Mt. 10:40;
cf. Mk. 9:37; Lk. 12:4 f.).

---

[3]See Wilfrid J. Harrington, *Record of the Promise: The Old Testament* (Chicago: The Priory Press, 1965), pp. 282 f.

All three types are found in the passage Mt. 10:39-41. These examples show that our Lord deliberately cast his sayings into forms that are redolent of the Old Testament. More important still, the sayings thereby became more easily remembered; we are close to the very words of Jesus.

The *inclusion*, found in Hebrew and Aramaic, is a sort of refrain arranged in such a way that a discourse, which may be quite short, begins and ends with the same word or words, or with the same idea. The passage in question is thus clearly marked off as a unit (for example, Mt. 5:3b,10b; 7:16a,20; 16:6,12; 19:30, 20:16). Jesus certainly employed this technique; nevertheless, it is difficult to determine whether an existing inclusion is his or was shaped in the tradition.

A fascinating field of study is provided by the parables. It would seem that, in the parables we indeed have hope not only of discerning the authentic teaching of our Lord but of hearing that teaching in his own words. In fact, however, the parables have been worked over by the Church and the evangelists. The circumstances of the early Church were not those of the ministry of Jesus; hence, if his parables were to suit later needs, they had to be adapted to some extent. Although the parables have two settings—their original setting in the ministry of Jesus and their later setting in the life of the primitive Church—we can, in many cases, recover the original form with some measure of success.[4]

2) The Narratives

[His disciples] grasped correctly the idea that the miracles and other events of the life of Jesus were things purposely performed or arranged by him in such a way that a man would thereby be led to believe in Christ and to accept by faith the doctrine of salvation (PBC, *Instr.*).

We learn from the early chapters of Acts that, after Pentecost, Peter was the principal witness of Christ. In his preaching he traced the main lines of the public life of Jesus, always after a definite pattern (cf. Acts 1:21 f.; 2:22-24; 10:37-41). This order is basic to the first three Gospels:

---

[4]See Wilfrid J. Harrington, *A Key to the Parables* (New York: Paulist Press, 1964).

1. Preparation and baptism in Judaea, that is, the preaching of John the Baptist and the inauguration of the public ministry.
2. Ministry in Galilee.
3. Journey from Galilee to Jerusalem.
4. In Jerusalem: passion, death, resurrection.

The last part, the Passion-narrative, was the first to take shape; this is attested by the close parallelism of all four Gospels. The other details from the life of our Lord and many of his sayings were added. Indeed, the Gospels have been described, not unjustly, as "Passion-narratives with an introduction." It is manifest that, in the eyes of the primitive Church, the most remarkable events in the life of Christ were his passion, death, and resurrrection.

It is important to realize from the beginning that, in the process of preaching the Good News according to this four-fold division and within this framework, the life and ministry of Jesus have been considerably simplified. If we had only the first three Gospels we might think that the ministry of Christ lasted less than a year. Only one Pasch is mentioned, that of the passion; apparently, then, he would have begun his work some time after the same feast of the previous year. It would appear also that, during his ministry, he visited Jerusalem only once, on the journey to his death. As a matter of fact, however, certain texts of Luke (9:51-53; 13:22; 17:11) suggest differently. But, we have a Fourth Gospel; in it St. John makes it clear that the ministry of our Lord lasted more than two years: he mentions three Paschs. He also tells us that Jesus visited Jerusalem frequently and preached there at length.

Obviously, both of these presentations cannot be historically accurate; we may accept John's view of the longer ministry. The other Gospels are much more closely attached to the original preaching and follow more nearly the plan drawn up by the Apostles. This original plan was devised with missionary interests in view. There had to be agreement on the selection of the events of our Lord's life and of points from his teaching; an inevitable result was simplification, schematization.

Let us consider just the events of our Savior's life. We have noted that the death and resurrection are central and that this saving event was considered first. In a broader view, however, it was seen that Jesus was preceded by one who had come to prepare the

way for him. Therefore, something had to be said about John the
Baptist; he was the first herald of the Good News, but when
Christ appeared his task was finished. The baptism of Jesus, in
fact and conveniently, brought him and John together and thus
dramatically introduced the public ministry. It is indeed the beginning of the Gospel.[5] After this, our Lord carried out his mission
in Galilee. Accounts of his journeys and of his miracles were
grouped with records of typical preaching of his, and even isolated
sayings. The journey of Christ to his death is all the more dramatic
when it is presented as his only entry into Jerusalem.

The framework is conventional, but there is no falsification of
historical facts because, in this respect, the intention is not primarily historical. We are not presented with a biography of Jesus
and there is no real interest in chronology. Yet, the plan does correspond to an historical and theological reality. At first Jesus was
favorably received by the people, but his humble and spiritual
messianism disappointed their hopes—enthusiasm waned. Already,
too, the bitter opposition of the ruling classes was evident. Then
he withdrew from Galilee to devote himself to the formation of a
little group of faithful disciples. He won their unconditional support after Peter's confession of faith at Caesarea Philippi. This
was a decisive turning point: the road now led to Jerusalem. In the
face of mounting opposition, the drama of the passion was played
out and seeming failure was turned to triumph by the resurrection.

This is the reality, at once theological and historical, which lies
behind the plan of the apostolic preaching. It is not concerned
with giving a detailed biography of Jesus—this is a modern preoccupation—but it has given the essentials; there is no falsification.
From the first three Gospels, it would appear that the public ministry
lasted less than a year; that is no more than an impression, however, for it is nowhere asserted that such was the case. One might
come to this conclusion if he does not understand the methods and
intentions of those who formed the tradition. The object was to
show the ministry of the Messiah from its favorable beginning in

---

[5]Matthew and Luke go back to the birth of our Lord, but the Primitive
preaching began with the Baptist and the baptism of Jesus. It was later that
interest in the human origin of the Son of God gave rise to the Infancy-
narratives.

Galilee to the tragedy and ultimate triumph in Jerusalem: the Gospels do bring home to us that historical process.

For us moderns, the time element, a detailed chronology, would be an obvious part of any such presentation. But does the duration of the ministry of Jesus really affect the purpose and the achievement of that ministry? Is not the question of chronology very secondary indeed? The converts came to believe that the Son of God had lived and preached among men, had suffered, died, and risen from the dead. This is all they needed to know in order to acknowledge their Savior. We have no intention of studying the historicity of the Gospels at length, but we may assert with confidence that an historical figure, Jesus of Nazareth, stands behind the Gospel tradition. We may accept the broad lines of his public career and we can be sure that the substance of his teaching has been preserved for us. For the Apostles and evangelists, however, the vital factor was not biographical interest; rather, it was their firm belief that "Jesus is the Christ, the Son of God" (Jn. 20:31), that "Jesus is Lord" (Rm. 10:9).

2. THE APOSTOLIC TRADITION

1) The Source

THE WITNESSES

> Christ our Lord attached to himself certain chosen disciples who had followed him from the beginning, who had seen his works and had heard his words, and thus were qualified to become witnesses of his life and teaching (PBC, *Instr.*).

From among his disciples Jesus chose a special group as his collaborators. He had a double purpose in view in choosing his Apostles, as we gather from Mk. 3:14. First he wanted them "to be with him" in order to form them and fill them with his spirit. But his principal purpose was to make them associates in the founding of the kingdom of God on earth. In order to prepare them for this task, he sent them to preach, to drive out devils, and to heal the sick (Mt. 10:1). He sent them out just as the Father had sent him (Mt. 10:5-40). In the eyes of men they were representatives of Jesus and, as it were, extensions of his person: whoever received them received him; whoever despised them despised him (Mt. 10:40).

After the resurrection, Christ commissioned them to preach the Gospel throughout the world (Mt. 24:14). This is why they had been witnesses of Jesus (Acts 1:8). They must proclaim before men the events from the baptism of John to the ascension of Jesus, and especially the crowning event of the resurrection (Acts 1:22; 2:32). On the road to Damascus, Paul also was made a witness of the Risen Christ (Acts 22:15; 26:16); he henceforth proclaimed the resurrection of Jesus (1 Cor. 15:15), and his preaching met with faith (2 Thes. 1:10; 1 Cor. 1:6). The Gospel narrative of John rests on the authority of an eyewitness (Jn. 19:35; 21:24).

The Apostles, then, are witnesses of Christ, men, especially, who have seen the Risen Christ. But they must attest, too, that this Risen Christ is the same Jesus with whom they had lived (Acts 1:8,21). This sets the Twelve apart even from the great Apostle of the Gentiles and gives their apostolate an unique character (Lk. 24:48). They are witnesses filled with the Spirit (Lk. 24:49; Acts 1:8)—inspired witnesses. They form a group, a college, the foundation stones of the new Jerusalem (Ap. 21:14). The Church was organized around these "pillars" (Gal. 2:9), the chosen, Spirit-enlightened witnesses and hearers of the Incarnate Word. These are the molders of the Gospel tradition.

The Acts of the Apostles describes the stages of the proclamation of the Good News, a program that would reach to the "ends of the earth" (Acts 1:8). It is still the good tidings of the kingdom (Acts 8:12; 14:21 f.), but now, more emphatically, the good tidings of Jesus (Acts 8:35, 17:18) and the resurrection of Christ take the central place. The preaching is accompanied by "signs" (Mk. 16:17; Acts 4:30; 5:12,16; 8:6 ff.) and everywhere finds hearts open to the word of God (Acts 13:7,12), men who "hear" (Acts 2:22,37; 3:22 f.), "receive" (Acts 8:14; 11:1; 17:11), and "obey" (Acts 6:7).

Founded on the solid "institution" of witnesses, and animated by the breath of the Spirit, the Church continues to develop and to nourish itself on a living gospel tradition. . . . The soul of the infant Church is the Twelve witnesses and behind them stands Jesus himself, the living Lord who guides his Church by means of the Holy Spirit. So, it is with entire confidence that we can turn to the work of the witnesses, whether in their gospel preaching or in the progressive formation of the Gospels.[6]

THE ORAL TRADITION

The Apostles, bearing testimony of Jesus, proclaimed first and foremost the death and resurrection of the Lord, faithfully recounting his life and words and, as regards the manner of their preaching, taking into account the circumstances of their hearers (PBC, *Instr.*).

Before the Gospels were written, they were preached. If the evangelists (and this is chiefly true of the first three evangelists) do differ in some respects, they agree in giving more or less the same teaching of our Lord and in telling much the same things about him. There would be nothing strange in this if they had told us *all* that he had said and *all* that he had done. Obviously, this is not so, and St. John was well aware of it (Jn. 21:25). But, if it is patent that they tell us only a few of the things he did and that they give us only a part of his preaching, then it is clear that they could not all have chosen the same events and sayings quite independently of common or similar sources.

The first problem that confronted the Apostles when they set about their task of preaching Christ was how to present that message. If each of them and each of the disciples was to preach what had struck him about the Lord and the words of the Lord that he had remembered, those to whom they preached would have been utterly confused. There had to be organization from the start. For practical missionary purposes, a selection had to be made from the deeds and sayings of Christ. This task fell to the Twelve, but under the leadership of Peter.

An oral tradition lies behind our Gospels. This does not merely mean that the Gospel message was first preached, or merely that it was cast in a definite mold from the beginning. It also means that we may still discern traces of that oral tradition in our Gospels. The first preachers and teachers were at pains to ensure the retention of the Gospel message; hence, the episodes and sayings were, as far as possible, presented in a way that could be easily remembered. We can still identify some of these forms. As we analyze

---

[6]X. Léon-Dufour, *Les évangiles et l'histoire de Jésus* (Paris: Éditions du Seuil, 1963), pp. 255 f.

them, we can see the Gospel taking shape before our eyes. We may certainly say, for instance, that the following elements of the "oral style" are the work of the Church.

1. *Schematization,* that is, narrative episodes are often built on the same model, after a very simple plan. Miracle stories especially are stripped down to the essentials and appear in a stereotyped form. For example, in Mark the casting out of an evil spirit and the stilling of a tempest are related in almost identical terms (Mk. 1:25-27; 4:39-41; cf. 7:32-37 and 8:22-26; 11:1-6 and 14:13-16).[7]

2. *Mnemonic aids,* that is, sayings are joined together by a system of catchwords (for example, Lk. 16:9-13; Mt. 18:1-35; Mk. 9:33-50; Lk. 9:46-50). The *inclusion* is a type of mnemonic aid.

As we study these forms of the oral tradition, we get back to the origin of the Gospels and, in the case of sayings, we approach as closely as it is possible for us to do to our Lord himself. But, if we are to understand the apostolic tradition from its entirely oral stage to the stage of pregospel literary units, we must examine the method of Form Criticism.

2) Form Criticism of the Synoptic Gospels

In appropriate cases the interpreter is free to seek out what sound elements there are in "the method of Form-history," and these he can duly make use of to gain a fuller understanding of the Gospels (PBC, *Instr.*).

Immediately after World War I, in the years between 1919 and 1922, a new approach to the Synoptic Gospels developed in Germany. The explanation of the relations between the Gospels in terms of common literary sources had led to the Two-Source theory: Mark is the earliest of our Gospels and the other two are dependent on Mark and on a collection of sayings of the Lord, designated by Q (for German *Quelle* = "source").[8] But these two sources were relatively late and represented a developed stage of the tradition. Attempts to break them down into earlier written sources met with no real success. The course of the Gospel tradition between its beginnings and its well-nigh final form in Mark and Q remained shrouded in darkness. Literary criticism alone seemed powerless

---

[7]See p. 130.
[8]See p. 108.

to pierce the gloom. The only hope lay in going back behind the written sources and studying the oral tradition. The name given to the new approach, *Formgeschichtliche Methode,* indicates a method which concentrates on the form or structure of the primitive Gospel tradition; in English it has become known as Form Criticism.

The method was not entirely new: it had already been applied to parts of the Old Testament, notably Genesis and Psalms, by H. Gunkel; but it is within the field of synoptic criticism that it has grown and developed. Here we shall study Form Criticism as it has been presented by its two most influential exponents: Martin Dibelius[9] and Rudolf Bultmann.[10]

THE METHOD OF   1. *Principles.* a) The Synoptic Gospels are not
FORM CRITICISM   literary units but mosaics of varied fragments.
Consequently, the evangelists are not true authors but compilers who have grouped isolated and disparate elements within a framework of their own devising. The Passion-narrative alone has a certain literary coherence. Apart from it, the Synoptic Gospels are not literature in a true sense; rather, they belong to the category of popular literature (or they may be described as "infraliterary").

b) The Gospels are not biographies; none of them gives an historical and consistent picture of the life of Jesus. We look in vain for a description of Jesus; we find no study of his personality, no manifestation of his interior life; the development of his thought is not traced. The other personages in the Gospels are treated no differently. Similarly, chronological and topographical indications are rare. The Gospels in fact are not concerned with the Jesus of history; rather, they are testimonials to the faith of the Christian community in the Savior of the world.

c) The constituent elements of the Gospel tradition are the product of the first-generation Christian communities. The faith

---

[9]*Die Formgeschichte des Evangeliums* (Tübingen: Mohr, 1919; second edition, 1933); "Zur Formgeschichte der Evangelien," *Theologische Rundschau* (1929), 185-216; "Zur Formgeschichte des Neuen Testaments," *Theologische Rundschau* (1931), 207-42; *Die Botschaft von Jesus Christus* (Tübingen: Mohr, 1935).

[10]*Die Geschichte der synoptischen Tradition* (Göttingen: Vandenhoeck & Ruprecht, 1921; second edition, 1931); *Die Erforschung der synoptischen Evangelien* (Giessen, 1930[2]); "The New Approach to the Synoptic Problem," *Journal of Religion* (1926), 335-62.

of these first-century Christians was colored and shaped by the *Christus-Mythus*, the "myth of Christ," which is the work of Paul; for Paul had transformed Jesus into the Incarnate Son of God who died for the salvation of men and rose from the dead. In the light of this faith, the community created the Gospel; the Gospel message was "lived" by the believers before it took shape. The demands of preaching, apologetics, and cult gave birth in the primitive communities to popular narratives developed around sayings or actions (real or invented) of Jesus. This combination of creative faith and practical demands leaves room for little or nothing of real historical value in the Gospels.

2. *Analysis and Classification of the Gospel Material.* Since Dibelius and Bultmann viewed the Gospels as compilations of varied fragments, they set about analyzing the Gospels and classifying their component parts. It is a basic assumption of Form Criticism that originally the tradition circulated in separate oral units which may be classified according to their forms. Many of the forms identified are really independent units, but dissection has been carried to extremes and the over-all effect of the classification is artificial.

The Gospel material as a whole falls into the two main groups: Logia (sayings of Jesus) and narrative material (stories about Jesus). Although the two critics accept this general division, they do not quite agree in subsequent classification.

a) Classification of the Logia. Bultmann distinguishes six groups:

i.   Wisdom sayings and proverbs (for example, Mt. 6:19-34; 12:34; 24:28).

ii. Prophetic and apocalyptic sayings (for example, Mt. 5:3-9; 11:5 f.; 13:16 f.).

iii. Law words and community rules (for example, Mt. 6:2-18; 18:15-22; 5:21 f., 27 f., 33 f.).

iv. "I-words" (*Ich-Worte*). Jesus speaks in the first person of his coming or of his person (for example, Mt. 10:34-36; 11:18 f.; 25-30; 16:18 f.).

v.   Similitudes and parables (for example, Mt. 13).

vi. Apophthegms: polemical (for example, Mk. 2:1-12, 23-28; 12:13-17); didactical (for example, Mk. 10:17-22); biographical (for example, Mk. 6:1-6; 10:13-16; Lk. 9:57-62).

Dibelius classifies the Logia under the general denomination of parenesis ("persuasion," "exhortation")—for, in his view, they were collected for instructive or hortatory purposes—and does not treat them in detail.

b) Classification of the narratives. The analysis of the narrative material has proved more difficult and here the two critics differ widely. Bultmann is satisfied with three headings:

i. Miracle-stories.
ii. Anecdotes and legends (edifying and unhistorical passages).
iii. The Passion-narrative.

Dibelius has five groups:

i. Paradigms ("models"), which are used as illustrations in sermons (for example, Mk. 2:1-12, 23-28; 10:17-27).
ii. *Novellen* ("tales," "stories"), that is, miracle stories.
iii. Legends (in the etymological sense), that is, espisodes in the life of Jesus (for example, Lk. 2:41-50; 19:1-10) or of the disciples (for example, Lk. 5:1-11; Mt. 14:28-31; 17:24-27).
iv. Myths, that is, passages influenced by the *Christus-Mythus* of Paul (cf. Phil. 2:5-11) (for example, Mk. 1:9-11; 4:1-11; 9:28 parr.).
v. The Passion-narrative.

The most striking divergence in classification is this: whereas the apophthegms of Bultmann correspond to the paradigms of Dibelius, the former are placed among the logia and the latter among the narratives. To these apophthegms = paradigms the British scholar Vincent Taylor has given a name that is simple and descriptive; he calls them Pronouncement Stories.[11] The point is that the narrative leads up to and is concerned solely with a saying or pronouncement of Jesus (for example, Mk. 12:13-17). Hence, there is the possibility of classifying them as narratives or logia according to whether one chooses to concentrate on the story or on the saying.

It is important to observe that, after this painstaking analysis, the critics admit that the forms rarely occur in a pure state and that for the most part we have to deal with *Mischformen,* with "mixed types."

---

[11]See V. Taylor, *The Formation of the Gospel Tradition* (New York: St. Martin's Press, 1933), p. 30.

3. *The Sitz im Leben of the Literary Forms.* The classification of the traditional material is only a first step. It is far more important to trace the origin and development of these different literary forms. For that purpose, they must be seen against the background of the primitive community, and the needs that gave rise to them, and the tendencies they represent established. In a word, their *Sitz im Leben,* the life-situation out of which they have sprung, must be determined. To discover the *Sitz im Leben* of the various Gospel elements, two approaches are possible:

    a) Deduction *a priori*—to deduce the literary forms from a study of the community organization;

    b) Induction *a posteriori*—to identify the interests of the community from a study of the literary forms.

Dibelius has chosen the deductive method. He starts with the offices or functions of the primitive community, especially with the fundamental office of preaching. *Am Anfang war die Predigt* ("In the beginning was the sermon") is his foundation thesis. He can assert: "The connections of an essential part of the tradition about Jesus with preaching appears to me an assured assumption of all further discussions."[12] This preaching naturally demanded examples, illustrations; thus, the paradigms were born. As time went on, details were added and the *Novellen* appeared: the miraculous powers of Jesus were related with complacency. These stories are the work, not of preachers, but of storytellers. Clearly, then, the *Novellen* are later than the paradigms. The latter have come from the first preachers, eyewitnesses; the *Novellen* are due to later anonymous storytellers—there is more scope for the imagination and less guarantee of historical accuracy. Dibelius is vague about the legends and myths and does not attribute them to a communitary office; they are later than the other forms and are quite unhistorical.

Bultmann follows the inductive method. He starts with the Gospel text and, by a close analysis of it, eliminates additions and retouchings. The additions and modifications are due to motifs and points of view that may be identified as we study the tradition which evolves as it passes from one Gospel to another (for example, Mk. 9:17 tells of a father who brought Jesus to his son "for he has a

---

[12]Cf. *ibid.*, p. 27.

dumb spirit." More details appear in Mt. 17:15–"for he is an epileptic and suffers terribly: often he falls into the fire and often into the water." Luke [9:38 f.] gives further symptoms and adds that he was an only child. Or, in Mk. 14:47, one of the followers of Jesus "drew his sword and struck the slave of the high priest and cut off his ear"; Luke [22:50] specifies the right ear, and John [18:10] adds the names: Peter and Malchus); and especially as it passes from the canonical Gospels to the apocryphal gospels. When we have determined the laws of this evolution, in their light we can fix the initial phase of the tradition and rediscover its primitive form; or, at least, we can discover the "motif" that has given rise to the tradition. The *Sitz im Leben* of the elements is to be sought in "debates" within the communities; in these "debates," the tradition was shaped under the influence of apologetic, polemical, and dogmatic needs. Bultmann believes that, for the most part, the process took place in the Palestinian communities, but that the miracle-stories and legends took shape in Hellenistic circles. Some of the discourse-tradition, for instance the "I-words," is also traced to the Hellenistic world.

Dibelius and Bultmann agree in attributing to the community a role of paramount importance in the formation of the tradition.[13] But Bultmann is the more radical of the two: everything, or almost everything, in the Gospels is attributed by him to the creative genius of the *Gemeinde,* the primitive community. Jesus did not lay down rules governing fasting or the sabbath observance, but the Christians of Jerusalem, in their controversies with the Jews, invented them and, for greater authority, put them in the mouth of the Master. Jesus did not cure a leper or raise the young man of Nain; the Christians of Antioch, to match the miracles of pagan gods, had attributed these wondrous deeds to him. The narrative portions of the apophthegms are sheer fiction. Thus, for instance, the description of the call of Peter and Andrew (Mk. 1:16-20) has no other basis than the saying: "I will make you fishers of men." Things of this kind are seen throughout the Gospel material. And, although it

---

[13]See P. Benoit, "Réflexions sur la *Formgeschichtliche* Methode," in *Exégèse et Théologie* (Paris: Cerf, 1961), I, pp. 25-61. I have been helped greatly by this article.

remains possible that Jesus really may have uttered certain sayings or may have done certain deeds, we can never be sure because the community stands between him and us. We can only know what it tells us about Jesus; we cannot know what Jesus has said or done.

Dibelius does not share Bultmann's extreme scepticism. He is prepared to admit, for instance, that the paradigms, the earliest form of the tradition, go back to eyewitnesses; but, on the other hand, he also attributes an important creative role to the community. Even the first preachers, eyewitnesses though they were, have interpreted as they preached. Jesus had said: "Behold my mother and my brothers." The preacher, for the edification of his hearers, added: "Whoever does the will of God is my brother, and sister, and mother" (Mk. 3:34 f.). Jesus had said: "Those who are well have no need of a physician, but those who are sick." In order to emphasize the theological application of this saying, the preacher added: "I came, not to call the righteous, but sinners" (Mk. 2:17). The preacher can go so far as to correct a word of the Lord. Jesus had said: "The friends of the bridegroom cannot fast," thereby forbidding his disciples to follow the Jewish practice of fasting. But the early Christians did in fact fast! There had to be an explanation of this custom which was contrary to the word of the Master. The preacher solved the difficulty by making Jesus add: "The days will come when the bridegroom is taken away from them, and then they will fast in that day" (Mk. 2:19 f.).

In the face of such liberties, it is not surprising to learn that the *Novellen* are borrowings from Jewish and Hellenistic milieux. The cure of a possessed man at Gerasa was originally an account of a Jewish exorcism. The miracle of Cana is of pagan origin, for it is obvious that its hero is a god of wine, like Dionysus. It follows that the biographical details of the legends are of no historical value. As for the legends of Jesus—the theophany at the baptism, the Transfiguration, the prophecies of the passion, the resurrection—all these have been manifestly invented to introduce into the Gospel tradition the *Christus-Mythus* of Paul, that is, that Jesus was the Incarnate Son of God, who died for men and rose from the dead.

What then of historical value remains when one has eliminated from the tradition all these creations of the community? Very little indeed, a harmless residue: Jesus of Galilee, who believed himself to be a prophet, who may have spoken and acted in that belief, nobody can truly say why or how, and who finally died an ignominious death. All the rest—his divine origin and his mission of salvation, together with the supporting words and miracles, even the Resurrection which set the seal on his work—is sheer fiction, a child of faith and cult cast in the shape of legendary tradition and formed by the preaching and controversies of the primitive community.[14]

CRITIQUE OF
THE METHOD

The method [of Form Criticism] is often found alloyed with principles of a philosophical or theological nature which are quite inadmissable, and which not infrequently vitiate both the method itself and the conclusions arrived at regarding literary questions. For certain exponents of this method, led astray by rationalistic prejudices, refuse to admit that there exists a supernatural order, or that a personal God intervenes in the world by revelation properly so called, or that miracles or prophecies are possible and have actually occurred. There are others who have as their starting point a wrong notion of faith, taking it that faith is indifferent to historical truth, and is indeed incompatible with it. Others practically deny *a priori* the historical value and character of the documents of revelation. Others finally there are who on the one hand underestimate the authority which the Apostles had as witnesses of Christ, and the office and influence which they wielded in the primitive community, whilst on the other hand they overestimate the creative capacity of the community itself. All these aberrations are not only opposed to Catholic doctrine, but are also devoid of any scientific foundation, and are foreign to the genuine principles of the historical method (PBC, *Instr.*).

1. *It is true that the Gospels are not biographies of Jesus.* They are, essentially, collections of his words and works. It is a fact that the Gospel elements are not arranged in strict chronological order. The various units of the tradition may be separated from the redactional setting in which they now find themselves, to be considered apart. What follows is that the framework alone is artificial: the individual sayings of Jesus and the individual stories are traditional. It is not true to say that the evangelists are mere compilers. In a healthy reaction against the assertion that they are, it is almost universally acknowledged today that the evangelists are authors, and that the Gospels are personal works, each having its own plan and individual characteristics. They are far from being mosaics of disparate fragments.

---

[14]*Ibid.*, p. 46.

2. *The classification of the material is, to a large extent, artificial.* The logia present the least difficulty, and Bultmann's classification may, in the main, stand. His terms do little more than describe stylistic features; they do not denote popular forms into which an individual or a community unconsciously throws sayings. The same cannot be said of his, or of Dibelius', classification of narratives. Miracle-story is, perhaps, a legitimate designation, but the titles "legends" and "myths" are not only arbitrary but false. The critics also have to admit that the forms they have identified or postulated are rarely found in a pure state in our Gospels.

A more serious error is their unwarranted leap from literary criticism to historical criticism. Dibelius not only attributes his paradigms to "preachers" and his *Novellen* to "storytellers," but asserts that the *Novellen* are a later form and hence less historical. It is not easy to see why the minister of the word could not use both pronouncement-story and miracle-story, and it is reasonable to feel that both forms go back to the earliest tradition. With regard to the preacher's alleged invention of sayings, as exemplified in the sayings about fasting (Mk. 2:19 f.),[15] the argument of Vincent Taylor is apposite.

> This (Mk. 2:19b-20), say the Form-Critics, is not the word of Jesus; it is a "community-product." The later Christian community has departed from an earlier attitude of freedom, and it justifies its practice by putting back upon the lips of Jesus a prophecy which adapts his words to the existing situation. Now this explanation may be true; but it transcends any principles belonging to form, and is really a study in historical probability. I should prefer to describe it as a study in historical improbability. It overstresses the undoubted freedom of Jesus and his disciples in respect of Jewish ritual practices; for the words: "When ye fast, be not, as the hypocrites, of a sad countenance" (Mt. 6:16), show that Jesus made no decisive breach with Jewish customs, while the alleged change on the part of the first Christians from a liberal to a conservative attitude reverses the actual process visible in such matters as circumcision and the question of eating with Gentiles. Moreover, the explanation passes too lightly over the question how the words of Jesus could be so neatly transformed into a composite utterance which combines a historical report with something which Jesus never said.[16]

---

[15]See p. 85.
[16]*Op. cit.*, pp. 34 f.

When Dibelius takes up his legend and myth, he no longer refers to an "office" of the primitive community (for example, those of "preacher" and "storyteller"), but appeals to "motifs"; this is an unwarranted change of formal principle. Similarly, it is because (as he asserts) the paradigms are concerned with the Jesus of the Palestinian tradition while the *Novellen* look to the miracle worker of the Hellenistic communities that he can assert the later date of the *Novellen*. Considerations of historical criticism are constantly encroaching on what purports to be a purely literary investigation; this is a grave methodological fault.

Bultmann, too, is guilty of the same error. The "motifs" he invokes are doctrinal and are concerned with the substance rather than with the form. Hence, he affirms that a word of Jesus justifies a practice of the primitive Church (for example, Mk. 2:20 and the question of fasting); that a discussion of Jesus with the Pharisees throws light on a living issue between Christians and Jews (for example, Mk. 2:27 and the sabbath observance); that an action of Christ establishes a matter of faith or cult (for example, Mk. 2:10 and the power to forgive sins; Mk. 14:22-25 and the Eucharist). We shall see that these observations are indeed enlightening, but Bultmann takes a fatal step: the words of Christ have not been recalled in view of such circumstances, they have been invented. It is a step that takes him well beyond the limits of literary criticism.

3. *A cardinal postulate of Form Criticism is the creative power of the community.* A notable part of the synoptic material is either a free creation of the community or was formed under the influence of motifs borrowed from Jewish and Hellenistic milieux. In truth, a community as such does not create; it is always an individual who produces something new. This is evident in the field of history; in the field of literature the position is even clearer. Many have argued that Bacon is the real author of the plays of Shakespeare, but no one has ever suggested that the plays are the work of the audience of the Globe theater. Nor can we believe that the Gospel parables are the creation of a community. Finally, and most damaging of all, the postulate leaves no room for eyewitnesses.

It is on this question of eyewitnesses that Form Criticism presents a very vulnerable front. If the Form Critics are right, the disciples must have been translated to heaven immediately after the resurrection. As Bultmann sees it, the primitive community exists *in vacuo*, cut off from its founders by the walls of an inexplicable ignorance. Like Robinson Crusoe it must do the best it can. Unable to turn to anyone for information, it must invent situations for the words of Jesus, and put into his lips sayings which personal memory cannot check. All this is absurd; but there is reason for this unwillingness to take into account the existence of leaders and eyewitnesses. . . . By the very nature of his study, the Form Critic is not predisposed in favor of eyewitnesses; he deals with oral forms shaped by nameless individuals, and the recognition of persons who would enrich the tradition by their actual recollections comes as a disturbing element to the smooth working of the theory. He is faced by an unknown quantity just where he wants to operate with precise "laws of the tradition." . . .

However disturbing to the smooth working of theories, the influence of eyewitnesses on the formation of the tradition cannot possibly be ignored. The one hundred and twenty at Pentecost did not go into permanent retreat. . . . The presence of personal testimony is an element in the formative process which it is folly to ignore. By its neglect of this factor Form Criticism gains in internal coherence, but it loses its power to accomplish its main task which is to describe the *Sitz im Leben* of the tradition.[17]

4. *The amazing tour de force of the Form Critics in consistently disposing of eyewitnesses is indeed forced upon them by a philosophical presupposition that underlies their whole approach.*[18] This is the denial of the supernatural. Rationalistic biblical criticism, influenced by the system of Hegel, had substituted for a personal and transcendent God an impersonal and immanent Idea expressing itself in human development. The earlier religions, including Christianity, with their marvels and their myths, were stages in this evolution; this is why the origin and transmission of the religious legends of the Gospel must be rationally explained. The creative role of the community is a concept founded on the same philosophy: the Idea immanent in humanity finds expression in collective activity. Hence, we have the primacy accorded to the community, to the detriment of individual witnesses. In this philosophy, "historical" and "supernatural" are incompatible terms; the Form Critics have accepted this principle also. But, for them, there is no question

[17]*Ibid.*, pp. 41-43.
[18]See Benoit, *art. cit.*, 54-60.

of distinguishing the Jesus of history from the Christ of faith: since the transformation of Jesus (under the influence of Paul's *Christus-Mythus* contribution) began as far back as our traditions go, Jesus is forever lost to sight behind the primitive community.

THE POSITIVE CONTRIBUTION   The picture we have drawn of Form
OF FORM CRITICISM   Criticism does not seem a promising one. Yet, we must observe that the *Instruction* of the Biblical Commission prefaces its litany of the shortcomings of the method with the statement: "In appropriate cases the interpreter is free to seek out what sound elements there are in 'the Method of Form-history,' and these he may duly make use of to gain a fuller understanding of the Gospels." In the context of the document, it is clear that the positive contribution of Form Criticism is acknowledged to be important; for when the *Instruction* goes on to list and study the "three stages of tradition by which the teaching and the life of Jesus have come down to us," it is stressing an appreciation of the development of the Gospel material that we owe, in large measure, to the Form Critics. Here we shall briefly indicate what the method has taught us.

1. *We are well aware now of literary units within the Synoptic Gospels and of the frequent loose linking of these units.* We no longer seek to trace a strictly logical sequence of thought throughout a Gospel or throughout a long passage of it; rather, we recognize that, at times—quite frequently in fact—we have to study a pericope sentence by sentence, for isolated sayings may be joined by a system of catchwords, or simply juxtaposed. It is no longer open to question that many smaller literary compositions stand behind our written Gospels.

The work of the evangelists appears more complex. Often they were dealing with pre-existing units and found their scope restricted whenever and to the extent that they desired to respect those units. On the other hand, in direct contrast to the view of the earlier Form Critics, the role of the evangelist in choosing, arranging, and interpreting the material is being more and more stressed. The three Gospels are personal works, each with its own definite stamp and character. They are far from being mosaics of disparate fragments. Neither the evangelists nor the early Christians were interested in producing a biography of Jesus according to our modern standards, but this does not render their work unhistorical. "The early Christians had not, perhaps, our regard for 'history,' but they had regard for the 'historical.' The preachers of the new faith did not intend to relate *everything* about Jesus, but were careful to relate only what was solidly founded."[19]

2. *We cannot accept the "storyteller" of Dibelius and we recognize that the "preacher," as conceived by him, is an artificial figure, but we do admit that the first Christian preachers did help to shape the tradition.* We also realize that there was a development of the tradition, a process that, partially at least, is still visible in the Gospels. It is not only legitimate but illuminating to seek the *Sitz im Leben* of the units of the tradition. We understand the parables better when we realize that many of them have a twofold setting: in the ministry of Jesus and in the life of the primitive Church. The "motifs" of the critics are arbitrary, but there are other, genuine factors which did govern the selection and presentation of the words and deeds of the Lord.

3. *The community did not create the Gospels but, at the same time, we must admit that the needs of the early Church did influence the selection of the sayings of our Lord and the stories about him.* Thus, for instance, the sayings about fasting (Mk. 2:20), about sabbath observance (Mk. 2:27), and about tribute to Caesar (Mk. 12:17) were remembered and treasured precisely because they met practical problems or pointed the way to a particular line of conduct; but this is a far cry from inventing the sayings.

The Church did not create the Gospel in the sense that it invented it, yet it obviously is responsible for much of the Gospel. It composed the narrative parts, and the needs and interests of the Church did influence the selection of the sayings of our Lord. This creative activity is mainly concerned with the literary forms into which the traditional data were cast, but it is not limited to these. There was also a certain amount of interpretation and adaptation. It would be false to the words of Christ, when he promised to send the Holy Spirit on his disciples, if their role were limited to a mechanical passing on of his teaching: "The Counselor, the Holy

---

[19]*Ibid.*, pp. 47 f.

Spirit, whom the Father will send in my name, he will teach you all things, and bring to your remembrance all that I have said to you" (Jn. 14:26; cf. 16:13). It is evident from the Gospels and the early chapters of Acts that the Apostles needed more than a recollection of the words of Jesus. Only after the resurrection did they fully understand Christ, and the account of Pentecost dramatically shows how the coming of the Spirit enlightened them. Not until then were their eyes fully opened. Not until then could the Gospel have taken shape.

When it has been relieved of the impossible load it had been asked to carry, the method of Form Criticism does show us the real influence of the early Church on the formation of the Gospel tradition. It did not create that tradition, as Bultmann would have it, but it did mold the forms of it and it did interpret the tradition in the light of experience—for the Church has ever been a living entity. We owe to Form Criticism the awareness of these facts and, to some extent, the explanation of them, and we owe to it the identification of many of the literary units of the tradition.

3) Pre-Synoptic Literary Units

The varied ways of speaking which the heralds of Christ made use of in proclaiming him must be distinguished one from the other and carefully appraised: catecheses, narratives, testimonies, hymns, doxologies, prayers, and any other such literary forms as were customarily employed in Sacred Scripture and by the people of that time (PBC, *Instr.*).

THE LITERARY We shall indicate some of the literary units that
UNITS have predated the written Gospels; these will crop up again in our study of the individual Gospels. We shall also briefly examine the milieux of the primitive community in which the units took shape, and the interests that formed them.

Thus far we have seen that the apostolic Church gave the Gospel story its shape. The passion, death, and resurrection form the central part, and the other events were chosen to trace the development from the beginning of the public ministry to Calvary. But the discourses and sayings of Jesus were also selected. Very often, sayings were preserved because they solved some pressing problems or showed the way to a line of conduct. We have seen units which stand behind the Gospels and which took shape within the Church.

Some of the forms go back to our Lord himself; the parables are an obvious example. But we have to recognize that, more often than not, the parables have been adapted or reinterpreted in the tradition. Other forms are due to the Church. Jesus worked miracles, but it was the Apostles who first told of them; from this we get miracle-stories. The Church also is the one who composed pronouncement-stories, in which a narrative leads up to and concentrates on a saying or pronouncement of Jesus; for example:

> And they sent to him some of the Pharisees and some of the Herodians, to entrap him in his talk. And they came and said to him, "Teacher, we know that you are true, and care for no man; for you do not regard the position of men, but truly teach the way of God. Is it lawful to pay taxes to Caesar, or not? Should we pay them, or should we not?" But knowing their hypocrisy, he said to them, "Why put me to the test? Bring me a coin, and let me look at it." And they brought one. And he said to them, "Whose likeness and inscription is this?" They said to him, "Caesar's." Jesus said to them, "Render to Caesar the things that are Caesar's, and to God the things that are God's." And they were amazed at him (Mk. 12:13-17).

It is evident that the narrative builds up to a climax; the saying is what matters, the details serving only to set it in relief. The relations of Church and State, the clash of civil and religious rights, is nothing new. The early Christians had to face this problem and that is why the saying of our Lord was remembered and treasured. Other literary units will be studied below.[20]

THE INTERESTS OF THE PRIMITIVE COMMUNITY[21] We may distinguish three "milieux" in which the Gospel tradition was formed: the cult, the mission, and the catechesis. Acts is our capital source for identifying these milieux. Three summaries (Acts 2:42-47; 4:32-35; 5:12-16) sketch the activities of the first community. We read that the Christians "devoted themselves to the apostles' teaching and fellowship, to the breaking of bread and the prayers" (Acts 2:42); while "with great power the apostles gave their testimony to the resurrection of the Lord Jesus" (Acts 4:33), and "many signs

---

[20]See pp. 126 f.
[21]See Léon-Dufour, *op. cit.*, pp. 266-79.

and wonders were done among the people by the hands of the apostles" (Acts 5:12). From this it appears that the essential activity of the Apostles was formed by cult, catechesis, and preaching supported by miracles.

1. *The Liturgy.* Acts 2:42 already gives us an indication of this milieu, for the "breaking of bread" is a technical term for the celebration of the Eucharist (cf. 1 Cor. 10:16; 11:23-25). It is widely recognized that the differences between the Matthew/Mark and Luke/Paul[22] formulas of institution are to be traced to the liturgy: Matthew and Mark have followed the formula in use in Jerusalem, while Paul and Luke have echoed the liturgical text with which they were familiar, doubtless the one in vogue at Antioch and then in the Pauline churches. The Passion-narrative very likely was shaped in the liturgical assemblies. The account of the multiplication of loaves may have been influenced by liturgical concern; this is suggested by Jn. 6. The "hymns, doxologies, and prayers" mentioned in the Pontifical Biblical Commission's *Instruction* are more readily discernible in other New Testament writings (for example, 1 Thes. 5:16-22; Phil. 2:6-11; 1 Pt. 1:3-5; 3:18-22; 2:22-25; 5:5-9; Ap. 4:8,11; 5:9 f., 12; 7:15-17; 11:17 f.; 15:3 f.).

2. *The Mission Preaching.* The missionary preaching to Jews and pagans is called *kērygma*: the proclamation of the Lord, crucified, risen, and to come. The earliest résumé of the kerygma is found in 1 Cor. 15:3-5: "I delivered to you as of first importance what I also received, that Christ died for our sins in accordance with the scriptures, that he was buried, that he was raised on the third day in accordance with the scriptures, and that he appeared to Cephas, then to the twelve." To preach Jesus, to proclaim that he has reconciled us with God, that he is our peace—that is the kerygma.[23] In the mission preaching, the miracles of Jesus had an important part. They are a sign of his messianic role (cf. Lk. 7:18-23). In the approach to the Jews, the scriptural argument was stressed. Hence, the preservation of sayings that speak of the fulfillment of Scripture (for example, Mt. 5:17 f.), of Jesus' presentation of himself as the Suffering Servant (for example, Mk. 8:31), and of episodes that were

---

[22]See Mt. 26:26-29; Mk. 14:22-25; Lk. 22:19-20; 1 Cor. 11:23-25.
[23]See J. Jeremias, *Paroles de Jésus* (Paris: Cerf, 1963), pp. 31 f.

seen as particular fulfillments (for example, Mk. 4:14-16; 8:17; 12:17-21). To this apologetic preaching was added the memory of conflicts with the scribes and Pharisees (for example, Mk. 2:1—3:6). The missionary activity of the infant Church was addressed to both Jews and Gentiles, and kerygmatic interest has left its mark on the Gospel tradition.

3. *The Didachē.* The catechetical preaching to those already within the fold, to the Christian community is called *didachē*. It includes the content of the kerygma, but goes on to the further instruction of the community: moral teaching (for example, Mt. 18:7-20), the doctrine of the sacraments (for example, Jn. 6), and additional episodes in the life of Jesus (for example, Mt. 1-2; Lk. 1-2). The Sermon on the Mount (Mt. 5-7; Lk. 6:20-49) is a classic example of didache: a collection of the sayings of Jesus which form an instruction addressed to Christians, one aimed at their Christian formation.

These are some of the interests of the early Church, the milieux in which elements of the tradition were shaped: cult mission, catechetics—the activities of a living community. There were, of course, other preoccupations; but all of them sprang from the impact of the new faith on men who had accepted Jesus as Lord. We can be grateful to Form Criticism for making us conscious of these factors, for now we are more keenly aware that our Gospels have taken rise within the Church of Christ: they are the inspired and written form of the apostolic tradition.

4) Fact and Interpretation in the Tradition

> The Apostles, when handing on to their hearers the things which in actual fact the Lord had said and done, did so in the light of that fuller understanding which they enjoyed as a result of being schooled by the glorious things accomplished in Christ, and of being illuminated by the Spirit of Truth. Thus it came about that, just as Jesus himself after his resurrection had "interpreted to them" both the words of the Old Testament and the words which he himself had spoken, so now they in their turn interpreted his words and deeds according to the needs of their hearers (PBC, *Instr.*).

THE EASTER   The delightful narrative at the close of Luke's Gospel
FAITH   (the disciples on the road to Emmaus, Lk. 24:13-35)
brings home to us an important truth that should be kept in mind

when studying the Gospels. As the two disciples discussed the shattering experience of the preceding days, Christ appeared, evidently as though he had just overtaken them. In reply to this "stranger's" question, they acknowledged their belief that Jesus was a mighty prophet; as such, his violent death was not exceptional. But they had seen in him something more, the Messiah, although their expectation was thoroughly Jewish. Like the Jews in general, they had not accepted *all* that the prophets had spoken: they had closed their eyes to the suffering of the Messiah (cf. Lk. 18:31; Acts 26:23). This is the reason the death of Jesus had been a fatal stumbling block. Nevertheless, they should have known that, by the path of suffering and death, Christ would enter into his glory; hence, starting with the Pentateuch, he explained the messianic prophecies.

The fact remains, however, that the disciples had not expected the resurrection; and we must realize that, during the lifetime of Jesus, they were not conscious of the full implication of his claims; the Gospels do not hide from us that even the Twelve did not understand him. Certain texts of John are apposite here. After the clearing of the Temple, and again after the entry into Jerusalem on Palm Sunday, the evangelist remarks that the disciples did not grasp the full meaning of these events until after the resurrection (Jn. 2:22; 12:16; cf. 13:7; Lk. 9:45; 18:34). Similarly, our Lord had foretold his resurrection not once but many times; yet, when Peter and the beloved disciple came to the empty tomb, we are faced with the blunt statement: "For as yet they did not know the scripture, that he must rise from the dead" (Jn. 20:9). They had not yet received the Holy Spirit, and it was he alone who could help them to understand the teaching of Christ (Jn. 14:26; 16:13). The Easter experience was the basis of their faith. When they did receive the Paraclete, however, the faith that was theirs after the resurrection, and especially after Pentecost, was centered on the life and words of their Master. It is by men filled with this faith, and certain of the great truth that Jesus the Messiah was, in the strictest sense, the Son of God, that the Gospel tradition was formed. But this fuller perception was not found during the ministry of Jesus.

It is not surprising that one of the earliest Christian credos lays special stress on the resurrection: ". . . that he was raised on the third day in accordance with the scriptures, and that he appeared to Cephas, then to the Twelve. Then he appeared to James, then to all the apostles. Last of all, as to one untimely born, he appeared also to me" (1 Cor. 15:4-8). Jesus had reserved the postresurrection manifestations of himself to witnesses whom he had chosen (Acts 2:32; 10:41; 13:21; 1 Cor. 15:8). From Pentecost onward, the resurrection became the center of apostolic preaching because it revealed the fundamental object of Christian faith (Acts 2:22-35). This Gospel of Easter is first and foremost testimony to a fact: Jesus was crucified and had risen. This is the message of Peter to the Jews (Acts 3:14 f.) and his confession before the Sanhedrin (Acts 4:10); it is the teaching of Philip (Acts 8:35); it is the argument of Paul (Acts 13:33; 17:3) and his profession of faith (Acts 23:6). Always it is the same Easter experience; and it is consistently presented as a fulfillment of Scripture (for example, 1 Cor. 15:3 f.; Acts 2:34; 4:30; 7:56).

The apostolic preaching developed a theological interpretation of the fact of the resurrection.[24] It is the Father's glorification of the Son (Acts 2:22 ff.; Rm. 8:11), and thus sets the seal of God's approval on the redemptive act. By it, Jesus is constituted "Son of God in power" (Rm. 1:4), "Christ and Lord" (Acts 2:36), "chief and savior" (Acts 5:31), "judge and Lord of living and dead" (Acts 10:42; Rm. 14:9; 2 Tm. 4:1). Returned to his Father, he can now send the Spirit (Jn. 20:17, 22). Now at last the full meaning of his earthly life appears: he was the manifestation of God here below, of God's love and of his grace (2 Tm. 1:10; Ti. 2:11; 3:4).

> The resurrection is God's public witness to his designation of Jesus as Son of God. As such, it is not merely another sign that the new age had dawned with the coming of Jesus; it is the decisive act of God, demonstrating to all that the rejected Jesus of Nazareth has been declared Lord and Christ, triumphing over sin and death. The new age, anticipated in the mighty works that Jesus performed, has now begun.[25]

---

[24]See X. Léon-Dufour, *et al.*, *Vocabulaire de Théologie Biblique* (Paris: Cerf, 1961), pp. 916 f.

[25]H. C. Kee and F. W. Young, *The Living World of the New Testament* (Englewood Cliffs, N.J.: Prentice-Hall, 1965²), p. 61.

It is inevitable that the words and works of Christ, seen now in the full light of Easter faith, should present a new dimension to those who had formerly heard and seen without fully understanding.

SPIRIT-GUIDED   After the resurrection, it was just not possible
INTERPRETATION   for the Apostles to view Jesus only as they had known him before the great Easter-event. Meeting him now as Risen Lord, they recognized that the Master whom they had heard and served was indeed the Son of God, even though they had not been aware of it. But, apart from this psychological factor, the words and deeds of Christ held a wealth of meaning that had to be diawn out and made available. The promised gift of the Spirit would enable the Apostles to understand the true significance of what Jesus had said and done (Jn. 14:26; 16:13).

> The religious purpose with which the Gospels were written required that they should contain not the bare facts and teachings of Jesus exclusively as such, but the facts together with their interpretation; the facts, and together with them, inhering in them as they are presented, authentic intimations of their supernatural significance in the history of God's dealings with his people. This deep significance of his own words and deeds Christ himself was of course deeply conscious of, for it was integral to the revelation of God which he came to communicate. He himself was the first to draw attention to it, deliberately planning his words and his deeds in such a way that they would make their impact on the minds of those about him, and elicit from them the response of faith in himself and in his mission. "The miracles and other events of his life were purposely performed or arranged by him in such a way that men were thereby led to believe in him, and to accept by faith the doctrine of salvation" (PBC, *Instr.*).[26]

The process of interpretation reaches its climax in the Fourth Gospel,[27] but the tendency was present from the beginning. A particularly interesting field of study is provided by the parables.[28] We shall content ourselves with one example of the process. It is generally recognized that The Talents (Mt. 25:14-30) and The Pounds (Lk. 19:12-27) are fundamentally the same, two versions of one parable. Details have been changed, of course: the three servants

---

[26]C. Kearns, "The Instruction on the Historical Truth of the Gospels: Some First Impressions," *Angelicum*, 41 (1964), 218-34.

[27]See pp. 406 f.

[28]See J. Jeremias, *Die Gleichnisse Jesu* (Göttingen: Vandenhoeck & Ruprecht, 1956[4]); Harrington, *A Key to the Parables, op. cit.*

of Matthew become ten in Luke; but, on the other hand, the sum entrusted to them is much smaller. We may reconstruct the common story along these lines: A man summoned his servants, gave them sums of money in trust and went away. When he returned he called them to account. All, except one, had notably increased the capital and were commended. The other admitted that he had been unwilling to risk losing the money and had carefully hidden it. He produced it and, no doubt, expects to be commended in his turn for his prudence. Instead, he is soundly berated for his inexcusable lack of enterprise: he might at least have earned interest on the money. As it is, the sum he had received is taken from him and given to another.

The parable was addressed by Jesus to the Jewish religious leaders, to the scribes especially (cf. Lk. 11:52): to them the word of God had been entrusted and they, like the unprofitable servant, had failed in their trust. But, with the founding of the Church, this role of the scribes was over; the early Christians were no longer very interested in the scribes as such, but they were passionately interested in what the words of the Master might mean for themselves. Hence, they gave to the parable of The Talents its widest application by adding to it the maxim: "For to every one who has will more be given, and he will have abundance; but from him who has not, even what he has will be taken away" (cf. Mt. 25:29; Mk. 4:25; Lk. 19:26). The parable now has to do with the absolute freedom of God in regard to his gifts. The grading of the amounts of money entrusted to the three servants (in Matthew's version) is a further modification to illustrate the variety of human endowments.

Soon a new preoccupation was to bring about a fresh interpretation of the parable, one that was to mark it profoundly. It had become apparent to the Christians that the *parousia*, the second coming of Christ, would be delayed; they began to read The Talents in the light of his frequent warnings to keep awake and be prepared, for he would come "like a thief in the night." In Matthew, the master is seen as the Son of Man himself, and his reckoning with his servants has become the Last Judgment. Luke, in his introduction (Lk. 19:11), makes explicit the application to the second coming; his version, by added details from another parable (vv.

12,14,17,19,27), describes Christ as ascending to heaven in order to return as king.

The differences in the sources used by the evangelists make clear that the changing interests of the early Church brought about changes in interpretation. In the process, not only has the original parable been modified in its details, but the setting has been altered completely, and the new interpretations have been worked out by the familiar methods of secondary conclusion and allegorization. The surprising result of all this is that, although the audience has changed and although the interest is different, the teaching remains very much that of the original parable; indeed, this teaching has been underlined more urgently. Christians, too, are entrusted with a great treasure: they are expected to bear fruit (Jn. 15:2) and their Master will hold a reckoning.[29]

3. THE EVANGELISTS

The sacred authors, for the benefit of the churches, took this earliest body of instruction, which had been handed on orally at first and then in writing—for many soon set their hands to "drawing up a narrative" of matters concerning the Lord Jesus—and set it down in the four Gospels. In doing this, each of them followed a method suitable to the special purpose which he had in view. They selected certain things out of the many which had been handed on; some they synthesized, some they explained with an eye to the situation of the churches, painstakingly using every means of bringing home to their readers the solid truth of the things in which they had been instructed. For, out of the material which they had received, the sacred authors selected especially those items which were adapted to the varied circumstances of the faithful as well as to the end which they themselves wished to attain; these they recounted in a manner consonant with those circumstances and with that end. And since the meaning of a statement depends, among other things, on the place which it has in a given sequence, the evangelists, in handing on the words or the deeds of our Savior, explained them for the advantage of their readers by respectively setting them, one evangelist in one context, another in another. For this reason, the exegete must ask himself what the evangelist intended by recounting a saying or a fact in a certain way, or by placing it in a certain context. For the truth of the narrative is not affected in the slightest by the fact that the evangelists report the sayings or the doings of our Lord in a different order, and that they use different words to express what he said, not keeping to the very letter, but nevertheless preserving the sense (PBC, *Instr.*).

---

[29]See Harrington, *ibid.*, pp. 41-46.

1) Redaction-history

We have seen that, from the first, there was a certain amount of adaptation and interpretation. The Church lived by the teaching of Christ; its role was not limited to the passing on of his words. Form Criticism has helped to make us aware of the importance of the pregospel traditions; *Redaktionsgeschichte* ("redaction-history") —in part a reaction against the excesses of earlier Form Critics— has drawn our attention to the contribution of the evangelists. They were not entirely free, because they were working with traditional material and they often wished to respect pre-existing literary units. But we are aware at last that they worked with more freedom than we had been wont to believe. The task of an evangelist was not a private undertaking; he was, in fact, the last link of a chain. The Gospel, founded on the works and words of Jesus, was first lived in the Church. The evangelist, although himself directly inspired by God, was also the spokesman of a Church guided by the Spirit of God. But the evangelists are authors, and the Gospels are personal works, each having its own definite stamp and character. Therefore, the evangelist, too, further interpreted and adapted the teaching of the living Lord.

We shall have occasion to note many of the redactional touches of the evangelists. A notable feature, singled out in the Pontifical Biblical Commission's *Instruction,* is a significant variation in the order and context of events and teachings from one evangelist to another. We may turn again to the fruitful field of the parables and study an illuminating example of editorial work on the part of an evangelist.[30] According to Luke, the parable of The Lost Sheep (Lk. 15:4-7) was occasioned by the Pharisees' complaint: "This man receives sinners and eats with them" (Lk. 15:2). In reply, Jesus tells of the shepherd who went in search of the sheep that was lost and of his joy when he had found the stray. There can be no missing the moral of the story: "Even so, I tell you, there will be more joy in heaven over one sinner who repents than over ninety-nine righteous persons who need no repentance" (Lk. 15:7). Quietly, but unmistakably, the critics are told that they are being utterly

---

[30]See *ibid.,* pp. 39-41.

unreasonable, that, in fact, they are presuming to question the mercy of God.

The same parable occurs in Matthew (18:12-14). Here it is no longer addressed to the critics of the Good News, but to the disciples; the discourse of which it forms a part begins: "So it is not the will of my Father who is in heaven that one of these little ones should perish" (Mt. 18:14). Even if the application were not already clear, the context quite clinches the issue, for the warning not to despise one of the least (v. 10) and the admonition regarding fraternal correction (vv. 15-17) leave no doubt about the interpretation of verse 14. It is evident that Luke has preserved the original setting of the parable and Matthew has placed it in the setting of his artificially constructed ecclesiastical discourse (chap. 18). Our next consideration will also help to illustrate the editorial methods of the evangelists.

2) *The Synoptic Problem*

THE FACT   The first three Gospels are closely related; St. John goes his own way. The narratives and discourses of Matthew, Mark, and Luke have common or corresponding passages which may be arranged in parallel columns. Thus, the reader gets a double or triple form of the same Gospel event or saying and he may see at a glance, and in detail, the resemblances and differences. The text so arranged is called by the Greek term *synopsis* ("seeing together"). This is the reason the name "synoptics" has been applied, since the end of the eighteenth century, to the first three Gospels.

The Synoptic Gospels have much material in common, although they are of unequal length:

1) Mark contains 661 verses (excluding 16:9-20); over 600 of these are found in Matthew and Luke. Hence, Mark has about 30 verses proper.

2) Matthew contains 1068 verses. This includes the substance of over 600 verses of Mark. Thus, Matthew has about 230 verses proper to it, and about 235 verses in common with Luke.

3) Luke contains 1149 verses. This includes more than half of Mark. Thus, Luke has 548 verses proper to it, and about 235 verses in common with Matthew.

However, more is involved than a mere quantitative comparison. The following texts will illustrate what we mean by the term "synoptic" and will give an indication of the complexity of the problem involved in the relationship of these Gospels.

1. A Question about Fasting.

MT. 9:14-15	MK. 2:18-20	LK. 5:33-35
Then the disciples of John approached him saying:	Now the disciples of John and the Pharisees were fasting, and people came and said to him:	And they said to him: The disciples of John fast often and offer prayers and so do those of the Parisees,
Why do we and the Pharisees fast?	Why do the disciples of John and the disciples of the Pharisees fast?	
but your disciples do not fast?	but your disciples do not fast?	but yours eat and drink.
And Jesus said to them:	And Jesus said to them:	But Jesus said to them:
Can the children of the wedding-f e a s t mourn as long as the bridegroom is with them?	Can the children of the wedding-feast fast while the bridegroom is with them? As long as they have the bridegroom with them they cannot fast.	Can you make the children of the wedding-feast fast while the bridegroom is with them?
The days will come when the bridegroom will be taken away from them and then they will fast.	The days will come when the bridegroom will be taken away from them and then they will fast in that day.	The days will come— and when the bridegroom will be taken away from them—then they will fast in those days.

2. In the Synagogue at Capharnaum.

MK. 1:23-28	LK. 4:33-37
And then there was in their synagogue a man with an unclean spirit and he cried out, saying:	And there was in the synagogue a man who had the spirit of an impure devil and he cried out in a loud voice:
What is your business with us Jesus the Nazarene? Have you come to destroy us? we know who you are, the Holy One of God.	Ha! what is your business with us Jesus the Nazarene? Have you come to destroy us? we know who you are, the Holy One of God.
Jesus rounded on him, "Hold your tongue," he said, "and come out of the man." And the unclean spirit convulsed the man, gave a	Jesus rounded on him, "Hold your tongue," he said "and come out of the man." And the demon flung him into their midst and

loud cry and came out of him. And all were amazed as they questioned one another, saying: what is this? a new doctrine with authority He even commands unclean spirits and they obey him. From that moment his fame spread everywhere through all the countryside of Galilee.

without having done him any harm came out of him. And amazement fell on all and they discussed among themselves, saying: what is this thing?, for he commands unclean spirits with authority and power and they come out! And his renown spread into every part of the countryside.

The relationship between the Synoptics is a strange combination of agreement and disagreement (often described as a *concordia discors*). It pervades the Gospels in such a way that there are variations in important matters and perfect accord in mere details. This fact, and the problem it raises, is not just academic. No attempted solution has been generally accepted, but the discussion of the problem, and the indication of the lines along which the solution must lie, are of real help in understanding the Gospels. We shall first consider, briefly, the agreements between the Gospels and their differences.

1. *Agreements.* The main lines of the Gospel story are the same in all three narratives:

	MARK	MATTHEW	LUKE
Preparation	1:1-13	3:1—4:11	3:1—3:13
Ministry in Galilee	1:14—9:50	4:12—18:35	4:14—9:50
Journey to Jerusalem	10:1-56	19:1—20:34	9:51—18:43
Passion and Resurrection	11—16	21—28	19—24

The following should be noted:

a) The similarity between the three narratives is particularly striking in the case of certain important facts in the life of Christ: the baptism; controversies with the opponents; the multiplication of loaves; the confession of Peter; the foretelling of the passion; the last days in Jerusalem; the arrest; judgment and death of the Savior.

b) In general, the elements of the Gospel story are arranged in the same order in the three Synoptics. In many instances the episodes of the history follow on one another and are linked in an identical manner in the three narratives (for example, the paralytic of Capharnaum, the call of Levi, the question of fasting [Mt. 9:1-17; Mk. 2:1-22; Lk. 5:17-39]; the calming of the storm, the demoniac of Gerasa, the daughter of Jairus [Mt. 8:18—9:34; Mk. 4:35—5:43; Lk. 8:22-56]; the confession of Peter, first prediction of the passion, the Transfiguration, the cure of an epileptic, the second prediction of the passion [Mt. 16:13—17:23; Mk. 8:27—9:32; Lk. 9:18-45]). It is obvious that such an accord cannot be fortuitous.

c) The literary form. Even a quick examination of the parallel texts shows that frequently the expression is almost identical and that the differences in style and vocabulary are insignificant (for example, the ears of corn on the sabbath [Mt. 12:1-4; Mk. 2:23-26; Lk. 6:1-4]; the grain of mustard seed [Mt. 13:31-32; Mk. 4:30-32; Lk. 13:18-19]; the rich young man [Mt. 19:16-26; Mk. 10:17-27; Lk. 18:18-27]).

d) Old Testament citations. Sometimes there is perfect agreement in the form of an Old Testament citation found in the Synoptics, even when the form is that of a version somewhat different from the Hebrew and the accepted Greek translation.

Such agreement cannot be the result of chance; the contacts are too numerous and the agreements are too marked and continuous. On the other hand, we must be careful not to overplay the extent of agreement.[31] We may find partial agreements within passages that differ on a wider showing (for example, Mk. 1:21-45 and Mt. 7:28—8:16; Mk. 2:1-22 and Mt. 9:1-17; Mk. 2:23—3:6 and Mt. 12:1-14). We may just as easily encounter disagreement in a generally similar grouping (for example, the order of Mk. 1:21-39; 1:40-45 and that of Mk. 4:13-24; 13:25 is inversed in the corresponding passages of Matthew). Luke follows the order of Mark closely; yet, we find the call of the first disciples after the preaching at Capharnaum (Lk. 5:1-11; cf. Mk. 1:16-20—

---

[31]See X. Léon-Dufour, IB, pp. 259-95; *Les évangiles et l'histoire de Jésus, op. cit.*, pp. 225-41.

the call comes before the preaching); the visit to Nazareth is set in a different context (compare Lk. 4:16-30 with Mk. 6:1-6). Differences are multiplied in the Passion-narrative. This fact of numerous transpositions within a common framework should be kept in mind.

2. *Differences.* The agreement between parallel texts is manifest. On the other hand there are differences that are no less marked and no less characteristic.

a) Sayings of Christ. Here one would expect a high degree of conformity. In fact, the disagreements are sometimes disconcerting. Classic examples are: The Lord's Prayer (Mt. 6:9-13; Lk. 11:2-4); institution of the Eucharist (Mt. 26:26-28; Mk. 14:22-24; Lk. 22:19-20).

b) The elements of the Gospel story. Matthew and Luke alone give an account of the Birth and Infancy, but independently. Mark alone has the parable of the Seed Growing Secretly. Matthew alone contains the parables of the Cockle, Hidden Treasure, Precious Pearl, Leaven, Net, and Unjust Steward.

Only Luke writes the parables of The Prodigal Son, Good Samaritan, Pharisee and Publican, Rich Man and Lazarus.

c) The order of events and discourses:

Matthew: Sermon on the Mount (chaps. 5-7).

Mark: omits the Sermon on the Mount.

Luke: has most of the material found in Mt. 5-7 distributed throughout chapters 6, 11, 13, 14, 16.

Luke is independent of Matthew-Mark in 9:51—18:14.

Luke is in perfect accord with Mark in 4:31—6:19; 8:4—9:50; 18:15—21:38.

d) The Passion-narrative is essentially the same in the three Snoptics, yet there are notable differences:

Mt. 27:46; Mk. 15:34—one word of Christ from the Cross.

Lk. 23:34,43,46—gives three others and omits that of Mt.-Mk.

Mt. 28:16-20; Mk. 16:6-7—the Risen Christ appears in Galilee.

Lk. 24:13-53—the Risen Christ appears in Jerusalem only.

Mt. 27:62-66; 28:11-20—Matthew alone mentions guards at the Tomb.

Lk. 24:13-35—Luke alone mentions the disciples at Emmaus.

Here again we have to advert to the fact that the combination of disagreements and agreements can be very complicated.[32] We may find that, while the structure of a narrative remains identical in different Gospels, the details will have changed. In the parables of The Talents (Mt. 25:14-30) and The Pounds (Lk. 19:11-27), and again in the two versions of The Great Feast (Mt. 22:1-10; Lk. 14:16-24) the basic plan is the same but the words are quite different. The exact opposite may happen: in the same episode words can remain identical but they have changed place or even sense. Crying out "with a loud voice," the unclean spirit came out of the possessed man (Mk. 1:26); in Lk. 4:33 the spirit cried "with a loud voice" in addressing Jesus. The crowd present at the exorcism was amazed at the authoritative teaching of Jesus (Mk. 1:27)—or at the authority displayed in the exorcism itself (Lk. 4:36). Jesus *raised up* Peter's mother-in-law (Mk. 1:31); in Mt. 8:15 she *rose*. In Mk. 1:45 *logos* means "news," while in the same episode in Lk. 5:15, it means "renown." The same Greek word *basanizō* signifies in Mt. 14:24 that the boat "was *beaten* by the waves" and in Mk. 6:48 that the disciples "were *distressed* in rowing." In the discussion on divorce, reference to Moses' authorization of a certificate of divorce appears at an early stage in the discussion as an answer to a question of Jesus (Mk. 10:4)—and, at a later stage, as an objection put to Jesus (Mt. 19:7). This sort of thing pervades the Gospels.

THE PROBLEM   The existence of such a welter of agreements and differences constitutes the synoptic fact; the explanation of the strange relationship between the three Gospels is the synoptic problem. It is clear, even from our rather hurried presentation of the data, that there can be no simple solution to the problem. It is here that all we have written above about the oral tradition and the respective roles of community and evangelists is drawn together. Key elements of the solution lie in the prehistory of the Gospels;

---

[32]See *Les évangiles et l'histoire de Jésus, ibid.*, pp. 232 f.; cf. IB, pp. 266-71.

it will not do to study the evangelists alone. On the other hand, the oral tradition by itself will not account for the intricate relationship that exists between the three Gospels: there are literary contacts between them. An immense amount has been written on the question since it came into prominence in the nineteenth century. The discussion of this problem has greatly contributed to a better understanding of the three Gospels.

TOWARD A   As a basis for the study of the problem we may ac-
SOLUTION   cept: (1) that Mark is independent of Matthew and
Luke; (2) that Matthew and Luke are mutually independent. On these points there is virtual unanimity among scholars. For the rest there is wide divergence of opinion. Here we shall content ourselves with two hypotheses.

1. *The Two-Document Hypothesis.* This theory is held, in one form or another, by a great number of scholars. In general it asserts the following: Mark is the earliest of our Gospels; Mark is followed by Matthew and Luke, independently of each other. Then, in order to explain the further agreement of Matthew/Luke against Mark, a special document is posited, one that contained sayings and discourses only. This hypothetical document, which must have been written in Greek, is named Q, from the German *Quelle* ("source"). Many attempts have been made to reconstruct Q; all are subjective, and no two authors agree on the extent or arrangement of the document. The Two-Document Hypothesis, in its simplest form, may be set out in a plan:

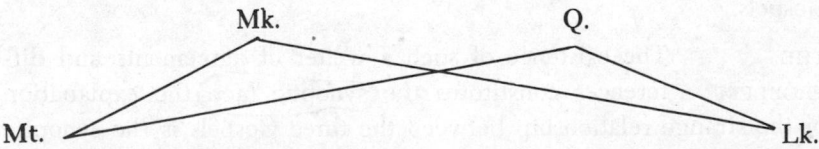

A somewhat more complicated form of the Two-Document Hypothesis has appealed to Catholic scholars:[33] Matthew and Luke depend on Mark; Matthew and Luke have no direct literary inter-

[33]See A. Tricot, *Initiation Biblique*, A. Robert and A. Tricot, editors (Paris: Desclée, 1954[3]), pp. 371 f.; A. Wikenhauser, *Einleitung in das Neue Testament* (Frieburg: Herder, 1956[2]), pp. 180-82.

dependence. The common source of Matthew/Luke (beside Mark) is made up especially, but not exclusively, of logia. This source is the logia-writing of Matthew mentioned by Papias.[34]

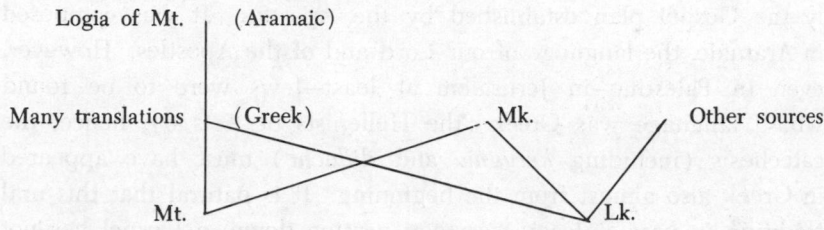

Logia of Mt. (Aramaic)

Many translations (Greek) Mk. Other sources

Mt. Lk.

We have seen above that the Two-Document (or Two-Source) Theory has appeared to many to be incapable of accounting for the real complexity of the synoptic fact.[35]

2. *A More Satisfactory Theory.*[36] We know that an oral tradition lies behind the Gospels, but its influence must be carefully gauged. Attempts have been made to explain the complicated relations between the Synoptics by recourse to the stereotyped form of the Gospel preaching, but these attempts have not proved wholly satisfactory. There was simplification and schematization, that is true, but not to the extent and in such detail to account for the highly complicated situation that exists. Our Gospels were composed at a relatively long distance in time from the primitive apostolic preaching in Palestine. Oral tradition plays its part, but literary criticism of the Synoptics shows that they must have had common written sources. On the other hand, we should keep in mind that the oral tradition is not just a first stage that was supplanted by literary sources: it accompanied the formation of the Gospels. It began to shape the tradition and continued to modify it right up to its final written form. We have noted something of the importance of the community in the forming of the tradition; it may be

---

[34]See p. 140.

[35]See pp. 79 f.

[36]The theory outlined here is basically that proposed by L. Vaganay in *Le Problème Synoptique* (Paris: Desclée, 1954), but modified in the light of the observations of X. Léon-Dufour in IB, pp. 259-95, and in *Les évangiles et l'histoire de Jésus, op. cit.*, pp. 225-41. The present sketch may be filled out by reference to the subsequent literary analysis of the individual Gospels.

that certain differences can be explained, not on the grounds of diversified sources, but as modifications of the tradition wrought within a community.

At any rate, we must start with the oral tradition, which is basically the Gospel plan established by the Apostles. It was composed in Aramaic, the language of our Lord and of the Apostles. However, even in Palestine—in Jerusalem at least—Jews were to be found whose language was Greek (the Hellenists of Acts 6); hence, the catechesis (including *kērygma* and *didache*) must have appeared in Greek also almost from the beginning. It is natural that this oral tradition in part at least, was soon written down; a Gospel has not yet arisen, but some of the writings may have been rather long. St. Luke tells us that "many have undertaken to compile a narrative of the things which have been accomplished among us" (Lk. 1:1). Just like the oral tradition, these accounts must have appeared both in Aramaic and in Greek. But the oral tradition still continued; the teaching of the Master was adapted and interpreted to meet new needs, and the different units were being shaped by the interests of the community.

A Gospel, written in Aramaic, is traditionally attributed to St. Matthew. It is not unreasonable to suppose that this writing was a schematized form of the Palestinian catechesis, the apostolic Gospel preaching. It too was soon translated into Greek and, on the authority of Papias (bishop of Hierapolis in Asia Minor c. 130 A.D.), we know that there were many Greek versions.[37] On the reasonable hypothesis that the Aramaic Gospel is in some manner incorporated in our Greek Matthew, it is not too rash to expect that literary criticism of Matthew may, within broad limits, trace the extent of this writing.[38] It seems that Greek versions of Aramaic Matthew were known to all three evangelists. We have to bear in mind, however, not only that these versions may have differed rather widely among themselves, but also that they may have been modified, within the communities, by the living tradition.

---

[37]See p. 140.
[38]See p. 144.

A study of Matthew and Luke makes it clear that they must have had a special source in common for much of their material.[39] Yet, it is impossible to give coherent form to this source; it may be described as a common source only with qualifications. For the most part, it appears to have contained sayings and parables of Jesus and, originally written in Aramaic, would soon have appeared in Greek translation. It may be more reasonable to believe that an oral Aramaic collection of sayings and parables assumed written form in Greek-speaking communities. It is not difficult to imagine that the rather formless collection would have been freely modified and expanded in different communities. The "common" source of Matthew and Luke may well have been two widely diversified forms of original traditions that had stood close together.

Now we come to the first of the Gospels as we know them. This is not Matthew, as might have been expected, but Mark: the Gospel of Mark is the earliest of the Gospels as they have come down to us. St. Mark was not an Apostle, an eyewitness; hence, he followed closely a Greek version of the Aramaic Gospel of Matthew. The Gospel of Mark is noted for the vivid details and lifelike touches that abound in it.[40] Tradition informs us that Mark was a disciple of St. Peter. This association readily explains the many details that could have come only from an eyewitness.

Since Matthew and Luke are independent, it is not possible to say which preceded the other; in the circumstances it is a matter of little moment. Matthew, we would naturally suppose, is based primarily on a Greek version of the Aramaic Gospel attributed to the Apostle Matthew. Here we have a source common to Mark and Matthew; however, the relationship between these Gospels would seem to suggest as well some dependence of Matthew on Mark. Matthew also follows a source (described above) common to himself and Luke; besides, he gathers material (for example, the Infancy-narrative) from other, distinct, sources.

It is almost universally recognized that Luke used Mark as a source, indeed that Mark is his chief source, and he has manifestly followed the order of Mark. Yet, there are many differences

---

[39]See p. 178.
[40]See pp. 121 f.

between Mark and Luke which may be explained, in large part, by the editorial freedom of St. Luke. Perhaps Luke made use of a Greek version of the Aramaic Gospel of Matthew, so that some of the changes of Luke with regard to Mark may be due to the order and content of the earlier source. Like Matthew, Luke follows a form of the common source and he too is greatly indebted to other sources. Indeed, the material proper to Luke gives us an idea of the breadth and richness of the tradition.

It may be helpful to present these data in the form of a plan.

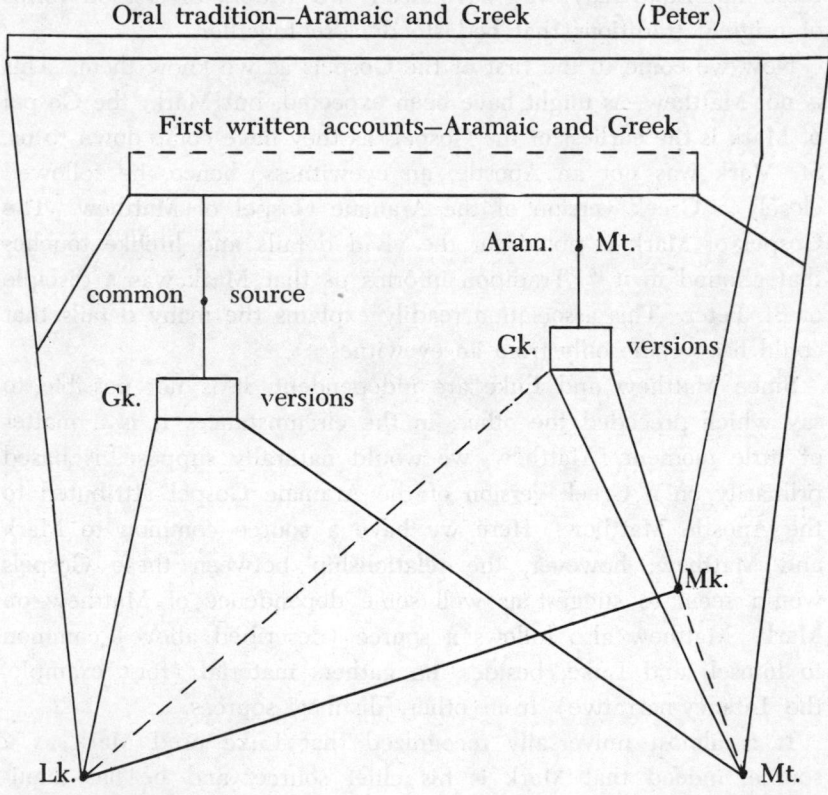

Oral tradition—Aramaic and Greek   (Peter)

First written accounts—Aramaic and Greek

Aram. ● Mt.

common ● source

Gk. ● versions

Gk. ● versions

● Mk.

Lk. ●   ● Mt.

Mark is dependent on: a Greek version of Aramaic Mt. and on oral tradition (via Peter).

Matthew is dependent on: a Greek version of Aramaic Mt.; a Greek version of the common source; other oral and written traditions; probably Mark.

Luke is dependent on: Mark; a Greek version of the common source; other oral and written sources; possibly a Greek version of Aramaic Mt.

The Synoptic Problem is a complicated one; hence, a simple and ready solution cannot be found. The theory sketched above does face up to the difficulties and does give a reasonable explanation both of agreements and differences between the Gospels, and it does make use both of a close literary study of the Gospels and of the traditional data regarding the relationship of the Gospels. The sources of the three Gospels, and more particularly of Matthew and Luke, are, in the main, the same, but they may have differed widely in detail. Beyond this, however, there is the important factor that the evangelists are authors who wrote with a purpose in view and adapted the material to suit that purpose.

This last point will be considered more closely as we study each Gospel. For instance, we find that St. Luke, who writes better Greek than the others, is at pains to improve the style of his source: many of the lesser differences between his Gospel and Mark's may be ascribed to this fact. Taking a longer look at the facts, we find that St. Matthew, who has written primarily for Jews, presumes that matters of Jewish interest will be readily understood. St. Luke, writing for Gentiles, consistently omits passages and references that are too specifically Jewish. We can see immediately that, in this sphere, differences between Matthew and Luke may be explained without difficulty.

It is hoped that the influence of one Gospel on another will be more clearly understood when the individual Gospels have been studied. Nevertheless, even at this stage it is important to have some notion of the relationship between them. We can see, dimly at least, how differences and apparent contradictions can be reasonably explained. Not everything will be clear, but it should be obvious that it is only by facing up honestly to undoubted difficulties that we may hope to understand the Gospels.

| THREE | *The Gospel of St. Mark* |

1. THE AUTHORSHIP OF THE GOSPEL

1) *The Testimony of Tradition*

The tradition of the early Church is unanimous in attributing a gospel to St. Mark. The earliest and most important witness is that of Papias, who was bishop of Hierapolis in Phrygia (Asia Minor) before 120 A.D., and the author of a five-volume work entitled *Explanation of the Lord's Sayings*. This work is not extant, although a few passages have been preserved by Eusebius, the Church historian. Papias obtained his information from "John the Elder" (and *not* John the Apostle, as some have thought), a man of the first Christian generation who had known the Apostles. Thus, Papias' testimony regarding the origin of Mark carries great weight. Here is what he says:

> And the Elder said this also: "Mark, having become the interpreter of Peter, wrote down accurately all that he remembered of the things said and done by the Lord, but not however in order." For neither did he hear the Lord, nor did he follow him, but afterwards, as I said, [followed] Peter who adapted his teaching to the needs [of the hearers], but not as though he were drawing up a connected account of the Lord's sayings. So then Mark made no mistake in thus recording some things just as he remembered them, for he took care to omit nothing that he had heard and to make no false statement.

The Elder's statement ends with the first sentence; the rest is the opinion of Papias himself. The second part is really a commentary

114

on the statement of the Elder.[1] The statement and comment both contain three parts:

1. The Elder remarks that Mark is the interpreter of Peter.

2. He then notes the essential quality of his work: Mark has written accurately all his recollections of the words of Peter.

3. He concludes by saying that St. Mark did not put in order the sayings of Christ.

These three points are taken up by Papias, but in a different order:

1. He explains the dependence of Mark: he is not a disciple of the Lord, but at a later date became a disciple of Peter.

2. Then he takes the third point of the Elder: the order of Mark. He remarks on the homely method of Peter, who did not try to make an ordered grouping of the sayings, and of Mark, his faithful disciple, who proceeded in the same fashion.

3. Papias defends the accuracy of Mark's account. He had only one purpose: to omit nothing of what he had heard and to add nothing that was inaccurate.

Thus, Papias not only unhesitatingly attributes the Gospel to St. Mark, but even goes out of his way to defend the evangelist's method. He appears to be replying to unfavorable criticism of the ordering of material in Mark as compared with that of Matthew.

Other witnesses are:

1. *The Anti-Marcionite Prologue* (*c. 160-180* A.D.).[2] ". . . Mark declared, who is called 'stump-fingered,' because he had rather small fingers in comparison with the stature of the rest of his body. He was the interpreter of Peter. After the death of Peter he wrote down this same Gospel in the region of Italy."

2. *Irenaeus* (*end of second century* A.D.). "And after the death of these (Peter and Paul) Mark, the disciple and interpreter of Peter, also transmitted to us in writing the things preached by Peter."

3. *Origen* (d. 254). "And second, that according to Mark, who did as Peter instructed him, whom also he acknowledged as a son in the

---

[1]See L. Vaganay, *Le Problème Synoptique* (Tournai: Desclée, 1954), pp. 52 f., 154-56.

[2]The "Anti-Marcionite Prologues" were prefaces attached to the Gospels (and many of the Epistles) to defend their authenticity against the attacks of the heretic Marcion, who accepted as canonical only Luke and ten epistles of St. Paul. The beginning of the Prologue to Mk. has not been preserved.

Catholic Epistle in these words: 'She that is Babylon, who is likewise chosen, sends you greetings, as does Mark my son' " (1 Pt. 5:13).

The verdict of modern scholarship on the traditional evidence may be summarized in the words of an eminent scholar:

> There can be no doubt that the author of the Gospel was Mark, the attendant of Peter. This is the unbroken testimony of the earliest Christian opinion from Papias onwards. In an age when the tendency of Christian tradition was to assign the authority of the Gospels to Apostles, Mark is not likely to have been named as the author unless there was very good reason to make that claim.[3]

2) The New Testament Witness

Tradition names St. Mark, interpreter and disciple of Peter, as the author of the Second Gospel. This is the same Mark who is frequently mentioned in the New Testament.[4]

1. Acts speaks six times of a person variously called "John surnamed Mark" (Acts 12:12, 25; 15:37) or "John" (Acts 13:5, 13) or "Mark" (Acts 15:39). It is the same person in each case. The companion "John surnamed Mark," whom Barnabas and Paul took with them from Jerusalem to Antioch (Acts 12:25), is no other than the helper called "John" who later accompanied them on the first missionary journey (Acts 13:5) and who left them shortly afterward (Acts 13:13). On the other hand, the "John surnamed Mark," who was the occasion of the separation of Barnabas and Paul (Acts 15:37), is evidently the "Mark" with whom Barnabas returned to Cyprus (Acts 15:39).

2. In the Epistles of St. Paul the name is mentioned three times, always in the form "Mark": Col. 4:10 (where he is described as the cousin of Barnabas); Phm. 24; 2 Tm. 4:11. When these texts are compared it is certain that the same person is meant in each case.

3. In 1 Pt. 5:13, Peter sends his readers the greetings of "Mark my son." In Acts 12:12-17, Peter, delivered from prison, went straight to the house of Mary, the mother of "John surnamed Mark." It is natural to suppose that Peter had baptized the family and that Mark was thus his spiritual son.

From this New Testament evidence the following picture emerges:

---

[3]V. Taylor, *The Gospel according to St. Mark* (New York: St. Martin's Press, 1953), p. 26.

[4]See Vaganay, *op. cit.*, pp. 152-54.

The Mark whom Peter calls his "son" (1 Pt. 5:13), and who was with him in Rome when the Epistle was written, is the same man whose family the Apostle knew quite well (Acts 12:12). It is the same Mark who accompanied Paul and Barnabas on their first missionary journey (Acts 12:25; 13:5, 13), and who later was the occasion of a quarrel between them (Acts 15:37, 39). But we find him again with Paul during the latter's first captivity (Phm. 24; Col. 4:10); and later, Paul sent for him during his second captivity (2 Tm. 4:11). His Jewish name was John; the form John Mark is explained by the assumption of a Greek surname, which was a frequent practice of Jews throughout the Roman Empire.

The fact that Mark, who had been the cause of a misunderstanding between Paul and Barnabas, should later be the trusted companion of Paul, raises no difficulty. It is readily understandable too that Mark, who was first in contact with Peter, should be the disciple of Paul in the years 44-46 A.D. and later in 60-63 A.D. to be again the disciple of Peter about 63-64 A.D. The New Testament texts which refer to St. Mark are all the more striking since there is no suggestion of harmonization. It follows that the evangelist was in the very best position to know the preaching of Peter, both in Jerusalem and in Rome, and he was also aware of the preaching of Paul.

3) Destination and Date

The Gospel of St. Mark was written for non-Jewish Christians. This is evident from the explanation of Aramaic expressions (for example, "Boanerges, that is, sons of thunder" [Mk. 3:17]; "'Talitha cum,' which means, 'Little girl, (I say to you), arise'" [Mk. 5:41; cf. 7:11, 34; 14:36; 15:22, 34], as well as of Jewish customs [Mk. 7:3 f.; 14:12; 15:42]).

According to early tradition, the Gospel was written in Rome. In general, the many Latinisms found in Mark may be written off as current military and technical terms. Nevertheless, on two striking occasions a Greek expression is explained by its Latin equivalent: ". . . two *lepta* [Greek coins], that is, a *quadrans* [Roman coin]" (Mk. 12:42); the "interior of the palace, that is, the *praetorium*" (Mk. 15:16). These suggest that the Gospel was written in Rome.

St. John Chrysostom says that Mark was written in Egypt. This claim cannot be reconciled with the words of Clement of Alexandria and of Origen, however, and is probably due to the misunderstanding of an ambiguous statement of the Church historian Eusebius. Antioch is also mentioned. But the weight of evidence, supported by internal criticism (that is to say, the study of the Gospel itself), is overwhelmingly in favor of the Roman origin of Mark.

There is almost unanimous agreement that the Gospel was written before the year 70 A.D. (the date of the destruction of Jerusalem by the Romans). We have the testimony of Irenaeus and of the Anti-Marcionite Prologue that St. Mark wrote after the death of Peter (c. 64 A.D.); we cannot be far wrong if we take 65 A.D. as the date of the Gospel.

2. LITERARY CONSTRUCTION OF THE GOSPEL

1) The Plan[5]

PART ONE	
INTRODUCTION (1:1-13)	
THE GALILEAN MINISTRY (1:14–3:6)	
1) Opening summary statement	1:14 f.
2) Call of the first disciples	1:16-20
3) *The ministry at Capharnaum*	1:21-39
4) The cure of a leper	1:40-45
5) *Conflicts with the scribes*	2:1–3:6
THE HEIGHT OF THE GALILEAN MINISTRY (3:7–6:13)	
1) Summary statement: crowds by the lake	3:7-12
2) Appointment of the Twelve	3:13-19a
3) *Charges brought against Jesus*	3:19b-35
4) *Parabolic teaching*	4:1-34
5) *A group of Miracle-stories*	4:35–5:43
6) Rejection at Nazareth	6:1-6a
THE CLOSE OF THE GALILEAN MINISTRY (6:6b–7:23)	
1) The mission charge to the Twelve	6:6b-13
2) Herod's fears and the death of the Baptist	6:14-29
3) *Feeding of the five thousand and sequel*	6:30-56
4) *The question of defilement*	7:1-23

[5]This plan is based on that given by Taylor, *op. cit.*, pp. 107-111.

JOURNEYS BEYOND GALILEE (7:24—8:26)	
1) *Withdrawal to the region of Tyre*	7:24-37
2) Feeding of the four thousand	8:1-10
3) Demand for a sign from heaven	8:11-13
4) The mystery of the loaves	8:14-21
5) The cure of the blind man	8:22-26
PART TWO	
CAESAREA PHILIPPI: JOURNEY TO JERUSALEM (8:27—10:52)	
1) *Messiahship and suffering*	8:27—9:29
2) The journey through Galilee	9:30-50
3) The journey through Peraea and Judaea	10:1-31
4) Final stage of the journey to Jerusalem	10:32-52
THE MINISTRY IN JERUSALEM (11—13)	
1) The events preceding the ministry	11:1-25
2) *Teaching in Jerusalem*	11:27—12:44
3) The eschatological discourse	13
THE PASSION AND RESURRECTION NARRATIVE (14—16)	
1) The events culminating in the arrest	14:1-52
2) Trial scenes, crucifixion, and burial	14:53—15:47
3) The resurrection	16:1-8
	(+16:9-20)

In this plan the longer sections of continuous narrative (Mk. 1:21-39; 4:35—5:43; 6:30-56; 7:24-37; 8:27—9:29) stand out, so much so that it seems special information was available to the evangelist. At the same time it would also appear that the passages Mk. 2:1—3:6; 3:19b-35; 4:1-34; 7:1-23; 11:27—12:44 are units which Mark found already formed and which he preserved intact; for it is apparent that these interrupt or halt the course of events. Thus, for example, Mk. 3:19b-35 comes as an anti-climax (although this does not affect its intrinsic worth) after Mk. 2:1—3:6; and this latter section, in turn (cf. Mk. 3:6), occurs too early in the Gospel.

Nevertheless, these stylistic shortcomings really add to the historical value of Mark. A more gifted writer would have arranged things differently, and the Gospel would have been improved from the literary point of view. But in the process it would have lost something of inestimable value, its close link with the earlier tradition. As it stands, its arrangement can best be understood if it is seen that Mark has preserved, more or less intact, traditional groupings that were already familiar to his first readers.

Although, on the whole, the plan of Mark is not very systematic, it does follow the main lines of the primitive kerygma.[6] The prelude (Mk. 1:1-13) deals with the preaching of John the Baptist, the baptism of our Lord, and the Temptations. Then follows a period of ministry in Galilee (Mk. 1:14–7:23), followed by journeys to Tyre, Sidon, and Decapolis, with a return to Galilee. The confession of Peter at Caesarea Philippi is a cardinal point, even in the sense that the Gospel is divided in two here. Hitherto Jesus had appeared as the Messiah, but now the passion is in view; henceforth, he is a suffering Messiah who goes to his death. Although there is a return to Galilee (Mk. 9:30-50), in reality the final journey to Jerusalem begins after the descent from the mount of Transfiguration (Mk. 9:2-8), a journey that ends in the passion and resurrection.

Corresponding to the division of the Gospel, there is a development in the self-manifestation of Jesus. At first—during the Galilean ministry—he taught the people. He spoke openly, in a manner that was congenial to his hearers, by means of parables. Yet, this teaching gave only an outline of his message, and he took care to explain it more fully to those whose task it would be to preach it to all men after his resurrection.[7] The reaction of his hearers is also a fact that must be considered. At first he was favorably received by the crowds, but his humble and spiritual messianism disappointed their hopes; enthusiasm waned. Hence, in the second period he turned to his disciples, devoting himself almost exclusively to their formation. Therefore, we can say that, despite a few inconsistencies—due to the fact that the evangelist was using pre-existing material—the plan of Mark corresponds closely to the historical course of events.

2) The Sources of the Gospel

THE
SOURCES
We have already indicated that Mark is based on literary sources; nevertheless, the Gospel as we know it is clearly the work of a single author, for the method of construction and the style are consistent throughout. The Greek is quite unpretentious, even poor; the Gospel is full of Aramaisms and not a few Latinisms. A striking feature is the curious blend of dry, stereo-

---

[6]See pp. 123 f.

[7]See M.-J. Lagrange, *Èvangile selon saint Marc* (Paris: Gabalda, 1929), p. lxiv.

typed phrases and vivid details. St. Mark was not an imaginative writer, nor was he even a skillful writer; yet, his work has an undeniable individuality. Even so, the problem of the sources of Mark is not an easy one.

In the previous chapter we suggest that Mark is dependent on two main sources (which are closely related):

1. *A Greek Translation of Aramaic Matthew.* This is a schematized condensation of the apostolic preaching or, in other words, it is essentially the Palestinian kerygma of Peter.

2. *The Roman Kerygma of Peter.* This is basically the same as the other, but it includes the vivid touches found throughout Mark that can be due only to an eyewitness. The reasonableness of this view becomes apparent when we examine the Markan passages that find parallels in Matthew and Luke. Three different types of these may be distinguished:[8]

a) Passages which contain picturesque touches not found, or rarely found in Matthew and Luke. These give a special coloring to the Markan narrative (for example, Mk. 2:1-12; 4:35-41).

b) Passages which differ very little from those of Matthew and Luke. Here there is rarely any personal note in Mark. This type is most frequent in the discourses (for example, Mk. 4:1-34).

c) Markan passages which are manifestly abbreviations, by comparison with Matthew and Luke (for example, Mk. 1:4-13).

The problem raised is how to explain the blend of such sections which have clearly differing characteristics.

The difficulty can be solved by taking into account the influence of the two main sources: the Palestinian kerygma and the Roman preaching of Peter. The stylized passages—very like those of Matthew in parallel passages—come from a Greek translation of Aramic Matthew, which is, in fact, a condensed form of the apostolic preaching in Jerusalem. In the passages with more vivid touches, the influence is that of the Roman kerygma of Peter. In this the schematic framework is still that of the original Aramaic Gospel. Understandably, however, Peter would not have been satisfied with the bare bones of the simplified Gospel, and would have added his own reminiscences. In fact, the lifelike touches that abound in the Gospel can be due

---

[8]See Vaganay, *op. cit.*, pp. 156-74.

only to Mark's familiarity with the living preaching of Peter. With regard to the abbreviated passages, some of them have had that form in the Aramaic Gospel, while others were undoubtedly condensed by Mark himself. Thus, the problem of the sources of Mark can be satisfactorily solved by recourse to the traditional data: the existence of an original Aramaic Gospel, and the fact that Mark was a disciple of Peter.

It will be helpful to consider more closely the influence of Peter. A study of the Gospel does show that this influence—that of an eye-witness—is very marked.[9] When he preached the Gospel, Peter heard again the familiar voice of Jesus and saw him move again before his eyes—all of this comes through in Mark. Peter saw not only Jesus but also those who were associated with Jesus. For this reason, in Mark's Gospel particularly, the Lord and the other personages are people of flesh and blood, insignificant touches and details of every-day life bringing them vividly to life.

At the call of Jesus, the sons of Zebedee rose up and followed him, leaving their father in the boat "with the hired servants" (Mk. 1:20). On the evening of the first sabbath spent at Capharnaum, "the whole city was gathered together about the door" (Mk. 1:33) of the house where Jesus was staying. At other times there was such a concourse of people that he and his disciples had no time to eat (Mk. 6:31). The sick man who was brought on his bed to Jesus was "carried by four men" (Mk. 2:3). The accounts of the cure of the deaf-mute and of the blind man at Bethsaida abound in details that were seen and remembered: Jesus putting his fingers in the ears of the deaf man and touching his tongue with spittle and exclaiming: "Ephphata" (Mk. 7:33-34); and the spontaneous remark of the blind man when he began to regain his sight: "I see men; but they look like trees, walking" (Mk. 8:24). On the way to Jerusalem for the passion, Christ walked in front of his disciples (Mk. 10:32). When he sent two of his disciples to procure a donkey, they found the colt tied up at a door in the open street (Mk. 11:4). There is also the unforgettable picture of Jesus lying asleep on a cushion at the stern of the boat, during the storm on the

---

[9]See J. Huby and X. Léon-Dufour, *L'Évangile et les Évangiles* (Paris: Beauchesne, 1954), pp. 156-58.

lake (Mk. 4:38). These are only a few of the details that make the Markan narratives so delightful. In every case, we can discern behind the prose of Mark the accents of the Prince of the Apostles.

MARK AS KERYGMA[10]   Mark's dependence on the preaching of Peter no doubt explains his fidelity to the Jerusalem kerygma—the earliest form of missionary preaching of the Good News. It is precisely in the sermons of Peter (Acts 2:14-36, 38 f.; 3:12-26; 4:8-12; 10:36-43; cf. 13:17-41—Paul) that we discover the outline of the kerygma. Its content may be summarized as follows:[11]

1. The age of fulfillment—the messianic age—has dawned: the prophecies are fulfilled.

2. This has come about through the ministry, death, and resurrection of Jesus of Nazareth, son of David.

3. By virtue of his resurrection he has exalted to the right hand of God, as Lord and Christ, the messianic head of the new Israel.

4. The Holy Spirit in the Church is the sign of Christ's present power and glory.

5. The messianic age will reach its consummation in the return of Christ.

6. The kerygma always closes with an appeal for repentance and a call to be baptized for the forgiveness of sin.

When we turn to the Gospel of Mark, we find that it "may be regarded as an expanded form of what we may call the historical section of the kerygma."[12] The evangelist's intention to give an account of the Good News is clear from the title of his work: "The beginning of the gospel of Jesus Christ, the Son of God" (Mk. 1:1). An analysis of the book supports the traditional evidence that Mark's Gospel is in fact a rendering of the apostolic preaching.

The Gospel begins: "As it is written in Isaiah the prophet" (Mk. 1:2); the theme of fulfillment is at once in view. The prophecies cited (Mal. 3:1; Is. 40:3) refer to the immediate prelude to the Day of the Lord, which is fulfilled in the appearance of the Baptist. John's reference to baptism in the Spirit (Mk. 1:8) points to a sign of the New Age. The descent of the Spirit on Jesus at his baptism

---

[10]See C. H. Dodd, *The Apostolic Preaching and Its Development* (London: Hodder & Stoughton, 1963³), pp. 46-52.

[11]See *ibid.*, pp. 21-24. See also below, pp. 213-17.

[12]*Ibid.*, pp. 46 f.

(Mk. 1:10) evokes the interpretation of that event as the messianic "anointing" of Jesus (Acts 10:38), and the divine voice points to the Lordship of Jesus. The summary statement (Mk. 1:14 f.), which gives the theme of the preaching of Jesus, provides the framework within which the Jerusalem kerygma had been set.

After the introduction and the summary of the preaching of Jesus (Mk. 1:1-15), the first part of the Gospel (Mk. 1:16—8:26), which is composed of more or less detached elements in no ordered sequence, follows. Yet, there is a conscious development as the Galilean ministry is described and the narrative moves on to journeys beyond Galilee. Jesus has revealed himself as Messiah, but in a manner consonant with the mysterious manner of his messiahship: the works of Jesus are works of divine power. The climax comes with Peter's profession of faith, which marks a turning point in the Gospel.

The second part (from Mk. 8:27 onward, that is, more than half the Gospel) is dominated by the thought of the approaching passion. Mark is pre-eminently the Gospel of the Passion. The works and words of the first part lead to the momentous question: "Who do you say that I am?" (Mk. 8:29.) Peter's answer—that Jesus is the Messiah—brings out the purpose of all that has gone before. The ministry of the son of David has been described, the messianic age has dawned; now the way is open for the proclamation of the suffering and death of Christ and of his resurrection: "The Son of man must suffer many things . . . and be killed, and after three days rise again" (Mk. 8:31).

Yet, from the start, the story of the passion is set within a frame of glory, and the balance of the original kerygma is maintained. The first announcement of suffering is followed immediately by the glory of Christ at the Transfiguration. The eschatological discourse (chap. 13) is a reminder of the triumph that lies beyond the story of suffering and death. The Passion-narrative ends on a similar note, drawing attention to the rending of the Temple veil and to the confession of the centurion.

> It is the veil that lay between men and the presence of God. Christ has now consecrated a new and living way through the veil: God is revealed in his kingdom, power, and glory. Not even Paul himself could have set forth more startlingly the divine paradox of the glory of the Cross. "And when the centurion saw that he so died, he said, 'Truly this man was the Son of God.'" As Peter's confession prepared

the way for the story of the Passion, so the confession of the pagan soldier provides the final comment upon it.[13]

Although Mark's Gospel breaks off short, it does record how Christ rose again on the third day, according to the Scripture, and the present ending is true to his perspective and true to the kerygma. The disciples are commanded to preach the Good News; whoever repents, believes in the Gospel, and is baptized will be saved (Mk. 16:15 f.). And with regard to the Messiah himself: "The Lord Jesus . . . was taken up into heaven, and sat down at the right hand of God" (Mk. 16:19).

3) The Markan Material

CLASSIFICATION   The material contained in Mark is varied. A classification of it according to the principles and categories of Form Criticism has been attempted by many scholars. The following is an outline of the painstaking analysis of Vincent Taylor,[14] who distinguishes six groupings:

1. *Pronouncement-stories.*[15] These are short narratives which set in relief sayings of Jesus of special interest and importance to the primitive communities. Some twenty Markan narratives belong to this type (for example, Mk. 2:5-10a, On Forgiveness; 2:18-20, On Fasting; 11:27-33, On Authority).

2. *Miracle-stories.* The main interest of such stories is the account of the miracle itself. They normally have a threefold structure in which the circumstances, the wonder itself, and the effect produced on the witnesses and hearers are successively described. Seventeen of these narratives may be listed (for example, Mk. 1:40-45, The Cure of a Leper; 6:35-44, The Feeding of the Five Thousand).

3. *Stories about Jesus.* In form these are not unlike the Miracle-stories, but differ from them in subject matter. Many, if not all of them, appear to have come to Mark as existing units of tradition, although we have to allow for certain editorial modifications. Some twenty-nine narratives of this kind are listed (for example, Mk. 1:9-11, The Baptism of Jesus; 6:1-6a, Rejection at Nazareth; 15:21-24, The Crucifixion).

---

[13]*Ibid.*, p. 51.
[14]*Op. cit.*, pp. 78-89.
[15]See pp. 82, 93.

4. *Markan Constructions.* Other stories about Jesus lack the vivid characteristics of the stories listed above—as if Mark lacked fuller information—and appear to have been constructed by the evangelist himself from traditonal material. "At the time when Mark wrote they did not exist as self-contained narratives, traceable directly or indirectly to informants. The tradition they contain is *given,* but the narratives are constructed"[16] (for example, Mk. 3:13-19a, The Appointment of the Twelve; 9:9-13, The Descent from the Mount; 14:17-21, the Prophecy of the Betrayal).

5. *Summary Statements.* The Gospel contains a number of summaries which describe the activity of Jesus over a period, and which sketch the course of events. The two most striking of these are Mk. 1:14 f., which indicates the opening of the public ministry and gives the theme of the preaching of Jesus, and Mk. 3:7-12, which describes the external features of the ministry (cf. also Mk. 1:12 f., 39; 2:13; 6:7, 12 f., 30).

6. *Sayings and Parables.* The heading adequately indicates the basis of classification for this group.

The above classifications are enough to suggest the great variety of the Markan material. Most of it is not far removed from the original eyewitnesses and, as we have seen, is close to the cast of the apostolic preaching. To a lesser extent, some of it has been shaped and adapted for catechetical purposes. But, one way or another, almost all of it pre-existed the Gospel.

PRE-EXISTING LITERARY UNITS   Scholars are agreed that much of St. Mark's material was found already grouped in units, and that the evangelist merely reproduced many of these complexes. This view is in full accord with the picture that emerged from our consideration of the formation of the Gospels. In the second stage of the formation, the first written accounts appeared; that is to say, certain groupings of sayings and narratives were set down in writing. We find proof of these literary units in Mark; but the evangelist, in his turn, found them already grouped in his principal source: the apostolic kerygma. It will be helpful to look more closely at some of these.

---

[16]Taylor, *op. cit.,* p. 82.

Mk. 2:1-36 presents a series of five conflicts of Christ with the Pharisees in Galilee: concerning forgiveness of sins (Mk. 2:1-12); concerning eating with publicans and sinners (Mk. 2:13-17); concerning fasting (Mk. 2:18-22); concerning the plucking of ears of grain on the sabbath (Mk. 2:23-28); concerning healing on the sabbath (Mk. 3:1-6). These are arranged in progressive order.[17] At the cure of the paralytic, the opposition is latent: the scribes "questioned in their hearts" (Mk. 2:6-7). During the meal in the house of Levi, they addressed the disciples, although they were really attacking the Master (Mk. 2:16). With regard to fasting, they questioned Jesus about an omisson of his disciples (Mk. 2:18); but in the case of the ears of grain on the sabbath, the charge is a direct violation of the law (Mk. 2:24). In the last episode, the adversaries spy on Jesus (Mk. 3:2) and then meet in council to plot his destruction (Mk. 3:6). This last point makes it clear that we are dealing with a pre-existing arrangement, one which emphasized the growing opposition to Jesus, for such official action against him did not take place so early in the ministry, and the plot is not mentioned again until much later (Mk. 11:18; 12:12). It is obvious that Mark has reproduced the unit just as he found it, deciding to insert it at this point in his Gospel.

Further on, the author presents another series of five conflicts which seems to correspond to the other. These center around: the mission of Jesus and the baptism of John (Mk. 11:27-33)—the parable of The Wicked Husbandmen (Mk. 12:1-12) is inserted at this point; the tribute to Caesar (Mk. 12:13-17); the resurrection (Mk. 12:18-27); the greatest commandment (Mk. 12:28-34); the origin of the Messiah (Mk. 12:35-37). Again the question is one of narratives already grouped before they took their place in the Gospel. It is noteworthy that the "Herodians" are mentioned by the evangelist twice only, and then in the context of these conflicts: Mk. 3:6; 12:13.

Having thus illustrated what is meant by pre-existing units, they can now be classified.[18] The importance of this step is that the recognition of different kinds of traditional material, and the evangelist's use of it, will enable us to explain a certain lack of logical order in Mark, and, what is more important, it will take us back beyond the Gospel to an earlier stage of the tradition.

---

[17]See Vaganay, *op. cit.,* pp. 44 f.
[18]See Taylor, *op. cit.,* pp. 78-104; X. Léon-Dufour, IB, pp. 207 f.

1. Groups of narratives based on personal testimony, most probably that of Peter: Mk. 1:21-39; 4:35-5, 43; 6:30-56; 7:24-37; 8:27–9:29. These are groups of vivid narratives that are linked together by statements which fix them at a given time or place. Mark fitted them into his general plan as simply as he could.

2. Groups containing sayings and pronouncement-stories: Mk. 2:1–3:6; 3:20-35; 4:1-34; 7:1-23; 11:27–12:37; 13:1-37. In all these, the center of interest is a saying of Jesus; the groups were compiled in order to make his mind known on matters of vital importance to the Christian community.

3. Less well-defined groups: Mk. 1:1-13; 3:13-19; 6:6-13; 9:30–11:25. These also seem to indicate previous groupings of material in the oral period or, perhaps more accurately, in the period of the first written accounts.

Some idea of how Mark worked arises from all this. He was content to take the pre-existing material and fit it in, as best he could, into his own plan. This plan itself was essentially that of the apostolic kerygma, and went back, like the Aramaic Gospel which was his main written source, through the intermediary stages to the oral tradition. In Mark we see most clearly the true role of an evangelist. The Gospel is not a private undertaking, and the evangelist is only the last link in a chain. Behind him stand the preachers and the Apostles, the whole teaching activity of a living Church. The Gospel, founded on the words and works of Jesus, was lived in the Church, and the evangelist, although himself directly inspired by God, is also the spokesman of a Church guided by the Spirit of God.

THE MARKAN ENDING   In very many Greek manuscripts of the
(MK. 16:9-20)   Gospel, and in important manuscripts of
early versions, the passage Mk. 16:9-20 is omitted. Eusebius and St. Jerome attest that it was wanting in almost all Greek manuscripts known to them. Some manuscripts have another ending, known as the "Shorter Ending," which is inserted after Mk. 16:8 instead of (or sometimes combined with) Mk. 16:9-20. The Shorter Ending is: "And all that had been commanded them they made known briefly to those about Peter. And afterwards Jesus himself appeared to them, and from the East as far as the West sent forth through them the sacred and incorruptible proclamation of eternal salvation." The

so-called Freer Ending is really a gloss in Codex W added to Mk. 16:14.

The vocabulary and style of Mk. 16:9-20 indicate that the passage was not written by Mark; it is based on a knowledge of the traditions found in the other Gospels, especially in Luke. For example: in verse 9, the description of Mary Magdalen as she "from whom he had cast out seven devils" equals Lk. 8:2; verse 12, the apparition to two disciples, equals Lk. 24:13-35. The title, "the Lord Jesus" (v. 19) is frequent in Acts, but is found nowhere else in the Gospels.

It is not probable that Mark originally ended at 16:8; nevertheless, how the original ending disappeared is obscure. The mutilation of the original papyrus manuscript and deliberate suppression have been conjectured. It is also suggested that Mark may have died before he was able to complete the Gospel. At any rate, Mk. 16:9-20 was added at a very early date. Catholics need have no doubt regarding the inspiration of this passage, for it has been accepted by the Church as forming an integral part of Sacred Scripture.

4) The Author

THE LANGUAGE AND STYLE OF MARK   Mark is written in a relatively simple and popular form of Greek that has striking affinities with the spoken language of everyday life. The evangelist is by no means a skillful writer. He uses only the simplest constructions; a glance at the Gospel will show that sentences are most often strung together by the simple conjunction "and." Aramaisms[19] abound in his pages, to such an extent that some few have suggested that his Gospel was originally written in Aramaic. The great majority of scholars reject this view; one of them has put the position rather neatly: "The strong Semitic coloring of the Gospel indicates, not that it is the translation of an Aramaic original, but that its author is Palestinian born and that his mother-tongue is Aramaic."[20]

There are many Latin terms in Mark, but most of them are of a technical nature (for example, denarius, legion, centurion). The fact that these occur more frequently than in the other Gospels.

---

[19] Aramaisms are turns of speech which, although found in the Greek text of the Gospel, are really Aramaic idiom.

[20] A. Wikenhauser, *Einleitung in das Neue Testament* (Freiburg: Herder, 1956²), p. 121.

and that on two occasions a Greek expression is explained by its Latin equivalent (Mk. 12:42; 15:16) would suggest that the evangelist wrote in a Roman environment. Thus, in fact, considerations of language and style support the traditional view of the origin of Mark. The remark of Vincent Taylor is apposite: "The sympathies of Mark are Gentile in their range, but his tradition is Jewish Christian to the core."[21]

A point to be borne in mind when examining the style of Mark is the limitation imposed on the evangelist by the earlier groupings of gospel material. He wished to retain many of these unbroken; therefore, he was not in a position to write freely. He had to fit them into his general plan as best he could, and very often the artificiality of the result is manifest. "The apparently poor literary style of St. Mark is often only a manifestation of his fidelity to his sources. This must certainly be taken into account when judging the merits of his work."[22]

In this context we may consider a notable tendency in Mark, that of schematization, or the casting of narratives, miracle-stories especially, in the one mold. For example, the following are two distinct and quite different miracles described according to the same pattern and in almost identical terms.[23]

The Tempest Stilled (Mk. 4:39-41)	*An Exorcism* (Mk. 1:25-27)
And he awoke and *rebuked* the wind and *said* to the sea *'Be Silent,* be still'	*And* Jesus *rebuked* him *saying* "*Be silent,* and go out of him."
[Effect of the command: the sea stilled]	[Effect of the command: cure of the possessed person]
And they were filled with awe and *said* to one another, *Who* then is this?	And they were all amazed, so that they questioned one another, *saying, What* is this?

In the same way we can compare the cure of the blind man at Bethsaida (Mk. 8:22-26) and that of the deaf-mute (Mk. 7:32-36); the preaching of Jesus in his own country (Mk. 6:1-2) and in Cap-

---

[21]*Op. cit.,* p. 65.
[22]Taylor, *op. cit.,* p. 105.
[23]See X. Léon-Dufour, IB, p. 202.

harnaum (Mk. 1:26-27); the preparation of the Supper (Mk. 14:13-16) and the entry into Jerusalem (Mk. 11:1-6).

It is clear that frequently the same, or a similar, framework has been used for different narratives. This stereotyped construction may possibly be the work of the evangelist, but it can be most reasonably explained by seeking its origin in the oral teaching. Admittedly, the preaching of Christ was very personal, and the teaching of the Apostles must have been modeled on that of the Master. But, as time passed, it was necessary to make a résumé of the words and works of Jesus for the use of missionaries; it was then that the schematized narratives appeared.

St. Mark's Gospel was long regarded as no more than an abridged version of Matthew. For this reason it was rather neglected, not coming into its own until recent times. Today it is recognized clearly that Mark is in no way an abridgement of Matthew; if anything, the opposite may be true in some few cases. Mark stands on its own merits, and indeed, as the earliest of our Gospels, it is of special significance: it is nearer the source.

Still, Mark is quite obviously much shorter than the other Synoptics. We note at once just how few of the sayings of our Lord are found in it. There are only three discourses, all of which are very brief: the discourse in parables (Mk. 4:1-34); the ecclesiastical discourse (Mk. 9:33-50); and the eschatological discourse (Mk. 13:1-37). It seems that St. Mark has consciously omitted the Sermon on the Mount.

On the other hand, in narratives common to the three Synoptics, Mark is usually richer in detail and more picturesque. We have a striking example of this in the account of the raising of the daughter of Jairus; it is certainly quite plain that here Mark is not abbreviating, as is obvious from a comparison of the texts of the three synoptists (Mt. 9:18-26; Lk. 8:40-56; Mk. 5:21-43).[24]

This passage is no isolated case, for there are many other examples, especially in the first part of the Gospel: for instance, the cure of the paralytic (Mk. 2:1-12; Mt. 9:1-8; Lk. 5:17-26); the stilling of the tempest (Mk. 4:35-41; Mt. 8:23-27; Lk. 8:22-25); the first multiplication of loaves (Mk. 6:30-44; Mt. 14:13-21; Lk. 9:10-17). Mark is no abridgement. Although it is shorter than Matthew and Luke, this

---

[24]See Huby and Léon-Dufour, *op. cit.*, pp. 145-51.

is due to the evangelist's own choice and method, just as it was his choice to record the vivid details he had learned from Peter.

We must not be deceived by the brevity or the simple style of this Gospel. Those—even those saints—who neglected Mark because they believed that all of it was to be found in Matthew, were the poorer for their neglect. Today, Mark has come into his own as we learn from this noble tribute to the evangelist and his Gospel.

> In Mark we have an authority of first rank for our knowledge of the Story of Jesus. Separated at the time of writing by little more than a generation from the death of Jesus, its contents carry us back further into the oral period before Mark wrote, to the tradition first of the Palestinian community and subsequently that of the Gentile Church at Rome. The historical value of Mark depends on the evangelist's fidelity to that tradition, including his special advantage as a hearer of Peter's preaching. . . . We may say of the Gospel what St. Paul says of the first missionaries; we have this treasure in earthen vessels that the exceeding greatness of the power may be of God (2 Cor. 4:7). Without this Gospel, it is impossible to account for the history of primitive Christianity, or to imagine the perils from which it was preserved; for it sets at the center the personality of Jesus himself and his redemptive work for men.[25]

INTERESTS VISIBLE IN THE GOSPEL[26]   Form Criticism has made us conscious that the selection and shaping of gospel material was governed, to some extent, by the special interests of the communities in which the tradition was formed, and of the evangelists. With regard to Mark, we may say that a liturgical interest can, perhaps, be discerned in the allusions to fasting (Mk. 2:20), anointing (Mk. 6:13), and prayer (Mk. 9:29; 11:24 f.). A cultic interest is more marked in the attention given to the institution of the Eucharist (Mk. 14:22-25) and its association with the Pasch (Mk. 14:16-20). The narrative of the Last Supper, because of its starkness and of its emphasis on the words of Jesus, gives the impression of having been forged in early liturgical usage. Liturgical interest seems to be reflected in the two stories of miraculous feeding (Mk. 6:35-44; 8:1-10).

Although the Gospel is faithful to the main lines of the primitive kerygma, it is also touched by catechetical motives. Some of the

---

25Taylor, *op. cit.*, pp. 148 f.
26See *ibid.*, pp. 131-35; X. Léon-Dufour, IB, pp. 218-21.

longer pre-existing units (for example, Mk. 2:1–3:6; 4:1-34; 7:1-23) and the compilations along topical lines or by mnemonic techniques (for example, 4:21-25; 8:34–9:1; 9:37-50; 10:1-31) point to the life and teaching of a settled Christian community. A doctrinal motive is evident in the confession ascribed to demons and to the centurion at the foot of the Cross of the divine Sonship of Jesus. The emphasis on the messianic secret and on the eschatological aspect of the message of Jesus (by omitting sayings that speak of the here and now of the kingdom) may be put down to theological motives. A special tendency also appears in the Apocalypse (chap. 13), that is, the underlining of watchfulness; but this is still in the realm of early Christian thought: Mark has shared the common expectancy of the nearness of the end of the world.

Our study of the formation of the Gospels has led us to expect the influence of such interests and has assured us that they do not affect the historical value of the Gospels. They are the vital manifestations of a living Church in which tradition and Gospel took shape.

3. DOCTRINE

1) Son of Man

The title, "Son of Man," is—because of its use in the Gospels—such a familiar one that perhaps we do not advert to it or to its meaning. What *does* Son of Man mean? The title is a literal translation of the Aramaic expression *bar enash*, which simply means "man." But, in its emphatic form (*nasha*), the second noun is capable of conveying the notion "*the* man," and hence of being used in a special, messianic sense. As found in the Gospels, the origin of the title goes back to Daniel.[27] In a judgment scene, Daniel saw one "like a son of man," that is, a human figure, in contrast to four beasts (representing world empires); and, again in contrast to the beasts' origin from the depths of the sea, he saw him appear "on the clouds of heaven." This Son of Man was presented to the Ancient of Days (God) and received universal and everlasting dominion. As presented in Dn. 7:13 f., the figure certainly appears as an individual. Yet, in the interpretation of the vision (Dn. 7:26 f.), "Son of man" stands for the

---

[27]See Wilfrid J. Harrington, *Record of the Promise: The Old Testament* (Chicago: The Priory Press, 1965), p. 370.

"saints of the Most High"—the messianic people, the purified Remnant of Israel. It appears that the "saints of the Most High" and the "Son of man" must stand for the same reality, at once collective and individual: the messianic people and the Messiah who represents and contains them.

It must be admitted that this mysterious figure, coming on the clouds of heaven and receiving universal dominion and an everlasting kingdom, evokes a conception "which is very different from that of the traditional Messiah—an earthly king, descended from David, who conquers his enemies in war. This leader has become a transcendent personage, of heavenly origin, who receives his dominion by a sovereign and direct intervention of God."[28] Although it is probable that in certain restricted circles a Messiah was awaited who was "Son of Man,"[29] it is understandable that, among the Jews, "Son of Man" never became a current messianic title. Despite this, or rather, as we shall see, precisely because of this, "Son of Man" does designate the Messiah who had come.

Before turning to the use of "Son of Man" in Mark, we have to consider another Old Testament concept that is essentially linked to this title in the Gospels. In Second Isaiah, four poems or canticles may be regarded as distinct, in some way, from the rest of the book: Is. 42:1-9; 49:1-6; 50:4-9; 52:13–53:12.[30] These have to do with a mysterious figure called the "Servant of Yahweh." While the identification of the Servant is a widely-discussed problem, almost all scholars would agree that he is a messianic figure. But, like the Son of Man, it is hard to deny that the Servant has both corporate and personal characteristics; he is at one and the same time the messianic people and the Messiah. What is undoubted is that Jesus made his own, and accomplished, the mission of the Servant. For our present purpose, the most important of these poems is the fourth. It is concerned with the sufferings of the Servant; the noteworthy feature is that the suffering is vicarious, that is to say, he suffers and dies for, and in the place of, others:

---

[28]P. Benoit, *Exégèse et Théologie* (Paris: Cerf, 1961), I, p. 136.

[29]See *ibid.*, pp. 137 f. For the occurrence of the title in the Book of Enoch see above, p. 35.

[30]See Harrington, *op. cit.*, pp. 234-36.

He was despised and rejected by men;
   a man of sorrows, and acquainted with grief . . .
Surely he has borne our griefs
   and carried our sorrows . . .
He was wounded for our transgressions,
   he was bruised for our iniquities;
   upon him was the chastisement that made us whole,
   and with his stripes we are healed.
All we like sheep have gone astray;
We have turned every one to his own way;
   and the Lord has laid on him
   the iniquity of us all (Is. 53:3-6).

Although the Suffering Servant is undoubtedly a messianic figure, we do not find that Is. 53, any more than Dn. 7, was, in the time of Christ, interpreted in a messianic sense. Although in some circles the concept of a suffering Messiah may have arisen, nevertheless, official Judaism in New Testament times did not regard the Servant of Yahweh in a messianic light. This is understandable perhaps if we realize that, for the Jews in general, the idea of a Messiah who had to suffer was unthinkable. The Gospels, on the other hand, make it clear that Jesus (although he did not designate himself by the title "Servant of Yahweh") applied to himself the idea of vicarious suffering and death. The Suffering Servant, no less than the heavenly figure of Daniel, stands behind the title "Son of Man."

This title, found exclusively in the Gospels (with the exception of Acts 7:56, which refers to the reply of Jesus before the Sanhedrin, cf. Mt. 26:64, and Ap. 1:13; 14:14, which are explicit references to Dn. 7:13), is always a self-designation of Jesus. The title occurs fourteen times in Mark and, apart from Mk. 2:10, 28, is found only in the second part of the Gospel, subsequent to the confession of Peter at Caesarea Philippi (Mk. 8:29). The list is: Mk. 2:10, 28; 8:31, 38; 9:9, 12, 31; 10:33, 45; 13:26; 14:21 (twice), 41, 62. In three cases (Mk. 8:38; 13:26; 14:62), it is the glory of the Son of Man that is envisaged. For instance, during that trial, when the high priest asked our Lord if he were the Messiah, he replied that he was, and added: "You will see the Son of man sitting at the right hand of Power, and coming with the clouds of heaven" (Mk. 14:62). This is almost a citation of Dn. 7:13. Elsewhere (always excepting Mk. 2:10, 28), the sufferings of the Son of Man are in question.

Thus, after Peter's confession we read: "And he began to teach them that the Son of man must suffer many things, and be rejected by the elders and the chief priests and the scribes, and be killed and after three days rise again" (Mk. 8:31).

This and related texts look to the Suffering Servant of Is. 53, the Man of Sorrows who bore the iniquity of us all and who went like a lamb to slaughter.

In short, the title Son of Man occurs in two contexts. It designates: (1) the glorious Christ who will come at the end of the world to judge mankind; (2) Christ, the Suffering Servant, the Man of Sorrows. Jesus, by using this title, linked together the two notions of the great Judge of the world and of the Servant of Yahweh—notions that would seem mutually exclusive—and showed that both were united in his person.

We have yet to consider Mk. 2:10, 28. Elsewhere, the title "Son of Man" occurs after the confession of Peter, and always in an eschatological setting, but Mk. 2:10, 28 refer to a time in the beginning of the ministry. However, we have already noted that the passage Mk. 2:1—3:6—a series of five conflicts—is a unit which Mark inserted, just as he had found it, at an early stage of his Gospel. The anticipated use of the title shows Mark's fidelity to his source, while his own care to reserve the title for the second part of his Gospel is linked with his presentation of the messianic secret.

When we turn to the texts themselves we find that, in each case, a divine prerogative is in question: remission of sins (Mk. 2:10); Lord of the sabbath (Mk. 2:28). For the Jews, these prerogatives were exclusively divine. But, as Son of Man, Jesus laid claim to them. In these passages, Jesus presents himself as a heavenly being; he claims that he has brought down on earth the very source of pardon which hitherto had existed only in heaven: "That you may know that the Son of man has authority *on earth* to forgive sins" (Mk. 2:10). He claims the right to dispense the disciples from the divine law of the sabbath observance; in practice, this amounts to the declaration that he is introducing a new order in which the sabbath observance will no longer have place.[31] Here, no less than elsewhere, the title "Son of Man" is most certainly messianic.

---

[31]See A. Feuillet, IB, p. 792.

Jesus the Messiah is Son of God, Son of Man. Either title enshrouds the mystery of his person, but it was the second that he chose to use, and, in the circumstances, he could not have introduced himself in any clearer terms. While it is probable that in certain circles of Judaism a Messiah was awaited who was "Son of Man," it is certain that this conception of the Messiah was not widespread, and the crowds were manifestly puzzled by the title (cf. Jn. 12:34; Mk. 8:27-30). But the Jewish leaders realized that Jesus claimed to be more than the traditional Messiah; this is the reason why he was accused of blasphemy. "In likening himself to the 'Son of Man' of Daniel he gave to the title 'Son of God' itself a meaning that was not metaphorical, but proper and transcendent, one that was unacceptable to their strict monotheism (cf. Lk. 22:70; Jn. 19:7; Mt. 27:40). That is why they decided on his death."[32]

The disciples must have understood, better than the crowds who listened to Jesus, what "Son of Man" meant. Yet, the Gospels make it clear that, before his death, they did not really grasp the mystery of his person.

> The humanity of Jesus was a veil difficult to pierce. The mystery that surrounded him could not be really lifted while he was still with them as one of themselves. It needed the passion to make them understand that he was in very truth the Suffering Servant who makes atonement for the sins of the world; it needed the resurrection and the outpouring of the Spirit to convince them that he truly belonged to the divine world.[33]

2) *The Messianic Secret*

Son of Man, then, expresses the complexity and the fullness of the messianic idea, but it remains a mysterious title. Why should our Lord have used a mysterious title? In order to answer this queston, another feature must be taken into account, one that is found in other Gospels too, but which is most obvious in Mark.

Throughout this Gospel, Jesus is at pains to hide his Messiahship. The devils know him and cry out: "You are the Son of God"—and he commands them to be silent (Mk. 1:25, 34; 3:11 f.). Silence is enjoined after notable miracles. For instance, after he had raised the daughter of Jairus, he turned to those who were present "and he

---

[32]Benoit, *op. cit.*, p. 141.
[33]*Loc. cit.*

strictly charged them that no one should know this" (Mk. 5:43; cf. 1:44; 7:36; 8:26). Again, when at Caesarea Philippi Peter had recognized his Messiahship, and later when he was transfigured before Peter and James and John, he admonished them to tell nobody until he had risen from the dead (Mk. 8:30; 9:9). From time to time he withdrew from the crowd on secret journeys (Mk. 7:27; 9:30). He gave his disciples private instructions (for example, Mk. 4:10-11, 33:34).

We might say that the Messianic Secret lies behind almost every narrative in Mark. Nevertheless, it must be admitted that the warnings to preserve silence, as found in the Gospel, are artificial and stereotyped to some extent. Sometimes silence is imposed when its observance is impossible, for example, at the raising of the daughter of Jairus (Mk. 5:21-43), and at the healing of the deaf-mute (Mk. 7:36 f.) and of the blind man (Mk. 8:26). Yet, the theme is not Mark's invention—it occurs in the other Gospels also, notably in Mt. 9:27-31 which has no parallel in Mark.

A partial explanation of the reticence of Jesus may be found in the conflict between his own messianic consciousness and the prevalent false notions about the Messiah. Jesus was indeed the Messiah, but he did not present himself as Son of David; instead, he called himself Son of Man because, although not a current messianic title, it could—as in fact it did—designate the Messiah. He imposed silence because the idea of Messiahship, as he conceived it—the spiritual Messiahship of a suffering Messiah—would be unacceptable to his contemporaries.

This explanation does not go deep enough, however; we must seek a more profound reason for his conduct.[34] In the first place, he could not really explain who he was until his death and resurrection had shed their light on his person—not that any title could convey the whole mystery of his person. Then, too, the strangeness of the title he had chosen and the veiling of his messianic dignity expressed a condition of revelation itself: the appeal to human liberty. Jesus continually invited the question: "Who do you say that I am?"

It is fitting to conclude with the verdict of Vincent Taylor, to whom this chapter has owed much:

---

[34]See X. Léon-Dufour, IB, pp. 216-18; *Les évangiles et l'histoire de Jésus* (Paris: Éditions de Seuil, 1963), pp. 383-85.

Jesus imposed silence because of the nature of Messiahship as he conceived it to be. To him it was not primarily a matter of status but of action. In his own estimation Jesus is Messiah in his works of healing, his exorcisms, his victory over Satanic powers, his suffering, dying, rising, and coming with the clouds of heaven. Messiahship is a destiny; it is that which he does, that which the Father is pleased to accomplish in him and which he fulfills in filial love. It is for this reason that he silences the demoniacs and commands his disciples to tell no man his secret till after the resurrection. The Messiah already, he would not be the Messiah until his destiny was fulfilled. We may agree that it is necessary to read the Story in terms of doctrine; but the doctrine is that of Jesus himself. This view of the Messianic Secret is in line with the Markan Christology and soteriology. The agreement is too astonishing to be a work of art; it is the reflection of historical reality.[35]

---

[35]*Op. cit.*, pp. 123 f. For the theme of the Suffering Messiah see Wilfrid J. Harrington, *Explaining the Gospels* (New York: Paulist Press, 1963), pp. 86-88.

| FOUR | *The Gospel of St. Matthew* |

THE AUTHORSHIP OF THE GOSPEL

LITERARY CONSTRUCTION OF THE GOSPEL

DOCTRINE

1. THE AUTHORSHIP OF THE GOSPEL

1) *The Testimony of Tradition*

The unanimous tradition of the early Church is that St. Matthew was the first of the four evangelists to write a gospel, and that he wrote it in Aramaic. The tradition is quite definite. Nevertheless, the Gospel of Matthew, as it has come down to us in the New Testament, was written in Greek. The relationship between the original Aramaic and the later Greek gospel raises a question that must be considered. First, however, the tradition must be established and examined.

Papias[1] is again the earliest witness. In substance, he says: Matthew, in Aramaic, grouped the sayings in order, and each translated (*hērmēneuse*) them according to his ability. Protestant scholars have long argued that, by "sayings" (*logia*) is meant a *collection* of sayings of Jesus, a work that was quite distinct from the Gospel of Matthew. Many Catholic scholars, on the other hand, have held that *logia* here is equivalent to "gospel." In fact, both views seem incorrect.[2] *Logia* cannot mean "gospel," but neither does the term refer to a mere collection of sayings. When this statement of Papias is compared with his statement regarding Mark,

---

[1]See p. 114.

[2]See L. Vaganay, *Le Problème Synoptique* (Paris: Desclée, 1954), pp. 51-54.

the real meaning of the former is seen to be: "Matthew, in Aramaic, grouped in order [in his Gospel] the sayings [of the Lord] . . ." The point at issue is that, in Matthew, the sayings of Jesus, in reality, are grouped in five long discourses, while in Mark there is no such order. Other witnesses are:

1. *Irenaeus* (end of second century A.D.): "Matthew, in the language of the Hebrews, published a gospel when Peter and Paul were preaching in Rome and founding the Church there."

2. *Eusebius* (third century A.D.): "Matthew wrote a gospel in Hebrew [that is, Aramaic]."[3]

3. *Origen* (d. 254): "The First Gospel was written in Aramaic for converted Jews by Matthew, who was a tax-collector and an Apostle of Jesus Christ."

The verdict of early ecclesiastical tradition comes to this: Matthew the Apostle wrote a gospel in Aramaic for Jewish converts in Palestine.

2) *The Greek Gospel*

The tradition that Matthew was the author of an Aramaic gospel seems to be unassailable. It is not legitimate to limit the *logia,* mentioned by Papias, to a mere compilation of sayings independent of the Gospel. The Aramaic writing appears to have been a somewhat condensed form of the Palestinian kerygma, the original Gospel plan drawn up by the Apostles. Papias tells us that it was soon translated into Greek ("each translated it according to his ability"); it is one of these translations that is the basis of our Greek Matthew —the Gospel that we know.

Our Gospel and the Aramaic Gospel are substantially identical, in the sense that the Greek Gospel incorporates the material of the Aramaic source; it does not follow that the Greek Gospel is a direct translation of the other. For one thing, the language of Matthew does not give the impression that it is a translation; for instance, it has a better Greek style than Mark, and certainly the latter was written in that language. However, this personal Greek

---

[3]Although "Hebrew" or the "language of the Hebrews" are the expressions used in these testimonies, there is no doubt that Aramaic is meant. Hebrew was no longer generally spoken, and the current Aramaic was, by non-Jewish Christians, loosely termed "Hebrew."

style is not inconsistent with the tradition of the Aramaic origin of the Gospel, for the source of Matthew is probably not the Aramaic Gospel itself, but a Greek translation of it. The original Gospel was meant for Jewish Christians; many of these, however, even in Palestine, were Greek-speaking, and they must have wanted versions in that language.

Besides, we have seen[4] that Matthew is dependent on other sources, notably on a special source common to Matthew and Luke, and probably on Mark as well. Thus, in general, Matthew is based on three accounts or documents: (1) a translation of Aramaic Matthew; (2) the source common to Matthew and Luke; and (3) Mark. All of these are Greek sources. Matthew is not, in any way, a direct translation of Aramaic writings.

Traditionally, it is quite certain that St. Matthew wrote the original Aramaic Gospel, but it is unlikely that he is the author of the Greek Gospel as we know it. The fact that we cannot be sure who wrote this Gospel is not as disturbing as might appear at first sight. We are sure, on the authority of the Church which has accepted this Gospel as Scripture, that the author of it was inspired. The fact that we are unable to name him is of secondary importance. Of course, we shall continue to refer to the writing as the Gospel according to St. Matthew. That is a convenient designation; furthermore, St. Matthew had a large part in its composition, even though it was not he who gave it its final form.

3) Destination and Date

Obviously, Aramaic Matthew was meant for Aramaic-speaking Jews and converts. It was essentially the Palestinian kerygma; and, if we allow time for the development of the oral teaching, we may date its composition at about 40-50 A.D. Its Greek versions would date from about the same time.

Matthew was addressed to Palestinian readers too, that is, to Greek-speaking Jews and Jewish Christians. It is natural, then, that the Palestinian character of Matthew should be more marked than that of the other Synoptics. And, indeed, we do find local color (Herod the *tetrarch*, his correct title, Mt. 14:1; the parasceve, Mt.

---

[4]P. 111.

27:62), the use of traditional expressions (*raca, gehenna,* Mt. 5:22; Beelzebul, Mt. 10:25), allusions to Jewish customs (washing of hands before eating, Mt. 15:2; the wearing of phylacteries, Mt. 23:5) —and the author rarely feels it necessary to give an explanation. The Gospel was written primarily for Jews, a fact to be kept in mind when reading it.

Since Matthew seems to be dependent on Mark to some extent, it cannot have been written before 65 A.D., which is the most likely date for Mark. Catholic writers have generally placed the composition of Matthew before 70 A.D., the date of the destruction of Jerusalem by the Romans. This event is foretold in Mt. 24:15-20, and the text gives no hint (by filling out the details) that the prophecy had been fulfilled at the time of writing. But, perhaps Matthew is merely faithfully reproducing his sources here, so that the passage may not necessarily be an argument for an early date. We find eminent Catholic scholars[5] who believe that our Greek Matthew was written shortly after 70 A.D. There is, then, some uncertainty, but it is recognized clearly today that the question of date is quite a secondary one, since the Gospels go back ultimately to the apostolic Church.

2. LITERARY CONSTRUCTION OF THE GOSPEL

1) The Plan[6]

BIRTH AND INFANCY OF JESUS (1–2)	
I. THE PROMULGATION OF THE KINGDOM OF HEAVEN (3–7)	
1) Narrative section	3–4
2) Evangelical discourse (Sermon on the Mount)	5–7
II. THE PREACHING OF THE KINGDOM OF HEAVEN (8–10)	
1) Narrative section (ten miracles)	8–9
2) Apostolic discourse	10

[5]Cf. A. Wikenhauser, *Einleitung in das Neue Testament* (Freiburg: Herder, 1956[2]), p. 144.; J. Schmid, *Das Evangelium nach Matthäus* (Regensburg: Pustet, 1956[3]), p. 31.

[6]The plan followed here is that given in the *Bible de Jérusalem*.

III. THE MYSTERY OF THE KINGDOM OF HEAVEN (11:1—13:52)	
1) Narrative section	11—12
2) Discourse: seven parables	13:1-52

IV. THE CHURCH, FIRSTFRUITS OF THE KINGDOM OF HEAVEN (13:53—18:35)	
1) Narrative section	13:53—17:27
2) Ecclesiastical discourse	18

V. THE NEAR ADVENT OF THE KINGDOM OF HEAVEN (19—25)	
1) Narrative section	19—22
	(+Discourse, 23)
2) Eschatological discourse	24—25
3) Passion and resurrection	26—28

If we leave aside the Infancy-narrative and the Passion-narrative, the central portion of Matthew's Gospel falls naturally into five parts, each containing a narrative and a discourse section. Each of the discourses has a brief introduction: Mt. 5:1-2; 10:1-5; 13:1-3; 18:1-2; 24:1-3; and each is closed by a stereotyped formula: "And it came to pass, when Jesus had finished these sayings . . ." (Mt. 7:28; 11:1; 13:53; 19:1; 26:1). Chapter 23, our Lord's severe censure of the scribes and Pharisees, does not quite fit into this plan, since chapters 24-25 form the discourse which corresponds to the narrative section chapters 19-22. It seems that chapter 23 has been inserted into the original plan by the evangelist himself, and the fifth part is really built on the same model as the others. It has been suggested that the fivefold division is consciously modeled on the Pentateuch. This is no more than a possibility. Furthermore, Matthew has added the Infancy-narrative and the Passion-narrative so that the alleged pentateuchal construction is obscured.

The five central parts of Matthew are not so many disconnected units; there is a close link between them. The narratives indicate the progressive movement of events, while the discourses illustrate a parallel progress in the messianic concept of the kingdom of heaven. The following is a summary of their content[7] (the Roman numbers refer to the sections indicated in the plan).

After his baptism in Judaea, which marked the inauguration of his public ministry as Messiah, our Lord began, in Galilee, to preach the coming of the kingdom of heaven. In the Sermon on the Mount, he laid down the conditions for participation in the kingdom (I). He chose his disciples, who became his constant companions, and he commissioned them to preach the kingdom. To that end he instructed them, pointing out particularly that they must be ready to face all dangers, even death (II). Christ himself encountered difficulties: the violent opposition of the Jewish authorities and the apathy of the crowd. Many of his parables were addressed to his opponents, who did not heed the clear warnings of these parables or listen to his appeals, but hardened their hearts against his message. The secret of the kingdom—that it is present in his words and works—was revealed only to the few chosen and faithful ones (III).

At this stage, Christ gave himself to the formation of his disciples: he knew that the time was short and the crisis near. He still had compassion on the multitude, but he did not preach to them any more; he likewise avoided discussion with the Jewish leaders. He organized the earthly phase of the kingdom by instituting the Church with Peter as the foundation. He instructed the Apostles in their duties to the community (IV). At last he left Galilee altogether. His going to Jerusalem was a journey to death. He censured the Jewish leaders in the presence of a crowd that was once again enthusiastic. His last discourse, the eschatological prophecies, was for the Apostles alone (V).

The Infancy- and Passion-narratives are not extraneous to this plan; rather, they fit in to form one broader, unified plan. Indeed, the whole Gospel has been characterized as "a drama in seven acts on the coming of the kingdom of heaven."[8]

1. The preparation: the Infant Messiah (Mt. 1–2).

2. The promulgation of the program of the kingdom in the Sermon on the Mount (Mt. 3–7).

---

[7]See Vaganay, *op. cit.*, pp. 200 f.
[8]P. Benoit, BJ, p. 1287.

3. The preaching of the kingdom by specially-instructed missionaries whose words were authenticated by the miracles of Christ (Mt. 8–10).

4. The opposition to the kingdom, illustrated by the parables (Mt. 11:1–13:52).

5. The beginnings in a group of disciples headed by Peter; these are the firstfruits of the Church whose way of life is sketched in the community discourse (Mt. 13:53–18:35).

6. The crisis which must precede the final appearance of the kingdom: the eschatological discourse (Mt. 19–25).

7. The advent of the kingdom in suffering and triumph through the passion and resurrection (Mt. 26–28).

It is only fair to observe that the fivefold division, which seems so obvious, may, in fact, veil the dramatic development of the Gospel, which can be regarded as falling into two parts.[9] After the prologue (chaps. 1-2), Jesus presents himself: he proclaims the admission of Gentiles into the kingdom and demands of his people an absolute commitment to himself. The Jews refuse (chaps. 3-13). Jesus then follows the path which leads to his passion and then to Glory, and lays the foundation of his Church (chaps. 14-28). Thus, the following plan emerges:

PROLOGUE (1–2)	
THE JEWISH PEOPLE REFUSE TO BELIEVE IN JESUS (3–13)	
1) Introduction	3:1–4:11
2) Jesus all-powerful in works and words	4:12–9:34
3) The disciples sent out by their Master	9:35–10:42
4) The decision: for or against Jesus	11–13:58
PASSION AND GLORY (14-28)	
1) To Jerusalem	14–20
2) In Jerusalem	21–28

The Jewish people's acceptance of Jesus would have meant their

---

[9]See X. Léon-Dufour, IB, pp. 172-78; *Les évangiles et l'histoire de Jésus* (Paris: Éditions du Seuil, 1963), pp. 153 f.

fulfillment as people of God. Instead, the Church is now the new Israel, the true people of God.

2) The Discourses

The discourses of Matthew, clearly marked by the repeated formula: "And when Jesus had finished these sayings . . ." (Mt. 7:28; 11:1; 13:53; 19:1; 26:1), set down in ordered fashion the teaching of the Master. Within each discourse the material is thematically distributed.[10] For instance, it seems that the nucleus of the apostolic discourse (chap. 10) is to be found in Mt. 10:5-16; to this has been added the long development Mt. 10:17-42; then the whole was provided with an introduction (Mt. 10:1-4). Although Mt. 13:34 reads like a conclusion to the parabolic discourse, further parables are added, and a second conclusion appears in Mt. 13:53. A question about the greatest in the kingdom of heaven (Mt. 18:1-4) leads to a series of lessons on Christian community life (18:1-35). The parables of chapter 25 illustrate the properly eschatological discourse of chapter 24. In short, when the discourses are examined, we find that each of them has been formed by grouping together related sayings of Jesus; it is the evangelist who has shaped this varied teaching into unified "sermons."'

THE SERMON ON THE MOUNT   The Sermon on the Mount offers a splendid example of this method;[11] for this reason we shall consider it in detail. Jesus formulated the special character, the new spirit of the kingdom of God, in a discourse which Mark has omitted and which Matthew and Luke (Lk. 6:20-49) have preserved in widely-different versions. The discourse of Matthew is much longer than that of Luke. On the other hand, however, many of the passages found in Mt. 5–7 are found elsewhere in Luke, in chapters 11,13,14, and 16. It can be shown that Luke has omitted, as being of little interest to his Gentile readers, all that concerned Jewish law and customs (Mt. 5:17–6:18). In general, we may say that Matthew has added to the original Sermon and that Luke has omitted some of it.

---

[10]See X. Léon-Dufour, IB, pp. 168 f.

[11]See J. Dupont, *Les Béatitudes* (Bruges: Abbaye de Saint-André, 1958[2]), pp. 43-204. I am entirely indebted to this brilliant study for the following analysis of the Sermon.

It is not enough to assert that Matthew has made additions; we must be sure that he has done so. The fact can be established without much difficulty; a study of the Lord's Prayer, for example, bears it out. Luke informs us that it was the sight of Jesus in prayer, alone, in an unspecified place, that moved the disciples to ask him to teach them to pray (Lk. 11:1). Here Luke has undoubtedly given the circumstances in which the Savior spoke the prayer. Matthew has presented the Our Father in the context of the Sermon on the Mount; it is not difficult to understand why he has done so.

In Mt. 6:1-18 we find first (in v. 1) a general statement on the performance of good works. This is followed by a consideration of the three great Jewish works of piety: almsgiving, prayer, and fasting. It may be seen that verses 2-4, 5-6, and 16-18 treat each of these in exactly the same manner: a warning not to imitate the hypocrites is followed by an indication of the proper attitude of disciples. The very close parallel of these passages is remarkable:

MT. 6:2-4	MT. 6:5-6	MT. 6:16-18
When, therefore you give alms, sound no trumpet before you as the hypocrites do	And when you pray, you must not be like the hypocrites for they love to stand and pray	When you fast, do not look dismal as the hypocrites do for they disfigure their faces
in the synagogues and in the streets That they may be honored by men.	in the synagogues and at the street corners that they may be seen by men.	that they may be seen by men to fast.
Amen, I say to you, they have already received their reward. As for you, when you give alms, do not let your left hand know what your right hand is doing, so that your alms	Amen, I say to you, they have already received their reward. As for you, when you pray, retire to your room and shut the door, and pray to your Father,	Amen, I say to you, they have already received their reward. As for you, when you fast, anoint your head and wash your face, so that your fasting may not be seen by men, but by your Father,
may be in secret; and your Father, who sees in secret, will reward you.	who is there, in secret; and your Father, who sees in secret, will reward you.	who is there, in secret; and your Father, who sees in secret, will reward you.

This uniform plan is disturbed by Mt. 6:7-15. What has happened is that Matthew has taken advantage of the reference to prayer, in order, first, to add a warning against praying like the Gentiles (vv. 7 f.) and then to give an example of the perfect prayer (vv. 9-15). He even carries the process a step further, in verses 14-15 developing the idea expressed in the Our Father (v. 12), on forgiving others. Thus, we are given a summary of Jesus' teaching on prayer.

If the additions that Matthew has made to his source can be recognized and isolated, the original plan of the Sermon may be found. The analysis that follows is not arbitrary; rather, it is based on a close and detailed study of the text of Matthew. Nevertheless, within the scope of this work, we must be satisfied with the result of that investigation.

The basic discourse. In Matthew 5, verse 17 is to be attached to verse 20 (vv. 18 f. break the sequence). These two verses introduce the theme which is developed in verses 21-48 in the form of five concrete examples showing how Jesus perfected the Law and enlarged its demands. Each of these examples opens with a precept of the Law. Chapter 6 gives three parallel developments of the three great works of piety of Judaism: almsgiving, prayer, and fasting. The point of view expressed in Mt. 6:1 is a little different from

INTRODUCTION: THE BEATITUDES (5:3-12)	
PART I: PERFECT JUSTICE	
1) General statement: perfect justice	5:17, 20
2) Five concrete examples	5:21-24, 27 f., 33-37, 38-42, 43-48
PART II: GOOD WORKS	
1) General statement	6:1
2) Three concrete examples	6:2-4, 5 f., 16-18
PART III: THREE WARNINGS	
1) Do not judge	7:1 f.
Example: Parable of the Mote and the Beam	7:3-5
2) Beware of false prophets	7:15
Example: Parable of the Tree and its Fruit	7:16-20
3) Practice justice	7:21
Example: Parable of the Two Houses	7:24-27

that put forward in chapter 5: Jesus no longer seeks to extend and to deepen religious demands; rather, he is concerned with the purity of intention required in doing good works. Chapter 7 has the same triadic structure as chapter 6: it is composed of three warnings, each illustrated by a short parable. Thus, the plan as found on the preceding page emerges.

The procedure of the discourse is uniform throughout: a general recommendation is illustrated by concrete examples. The first recommendation (Mt. 5:20) is the most general and has five applications. The second (Mt. 6:1) is more concrete; it has three applications. The three sayings of chapter 7 refer directly to conduct; one example is enough to illustrate each of them. The discourse is by no means a mere collection of sayings; it has a real unity and is highly original.

The many additions of Matthew have not changed the plan of the discourse: the structure of the original is preserved. Into this framework, however, he has inserted material taken from another source, one used by Luke also (because almost all these sayings are found in Luke too, although not as part of the Sermon). The passages in question are numerous: Mt. 5:13-16, 18 f., 25 f., 29-32, 36; 6:7-15, 19-34; 7:6-14, 22 f.—about one-half of the discourse as Matthew presents it. These additions respond to a desire for completeness. Matthew is manifestly anxious to give a view as wide as possible of the teaching of his Master and to hold out the ideal of the perfect life to which he had called his disciples. In this same spirit he has composed the other four discourses.

But Matthew does not expand the text lightly; sometimes he abridges his sources (cf. Mt. 5:29 f., 46 f.; 7:1, parr.). When he does make an addition, he can skillfully work the new element into its new context. The third antithesis (Mt. 5:31 f.) offers a striking example. The evangelist had taken advantage of the antithesis on adultery to insert a saying on divorce. In order that it may fit, he gives it, too, an antithetical structure by contrasting it with the precept of Dt. 24:1. Similarly, he is careful to emphasize the parallelism of the sayings on salt (Mt. 5:13) and on the lamp (Mt. 5:15) by the introduction formulas: "You are the salt of the earth"; "You are the light of the world'" (Mt. 5:13 f.).

Matthew is preoccupied with the conduct of Christians; he tries to indicate all that the Master requires of them. Therefore, he speaks of the duty of concord among brethren (Mt. 5:25 f.), and of forgiveness (Mt. 5:14 f.). He insists on detachment (Mt. 6:19-34) and on the necessity of good works (Mt. 17:22 f.). Obscure sayings like Mt. 5:13a, 14a, 16 are given a concrete application. In short, he is concerned with immediate results and he sees the Sermon on the Mount as, primarily, a program of life; this is the reason he fits in so many sayings of Jesus that have a bearing on conduct. Thus, the final plan of Mt. 5-7 can be given:

INTRODUCTION: THE BEATITUDES (5:1-12)

SAYINGS: SALT OF THE EARTH; LIGHT OF THE WORLD (5:13-16)

PART I: PERFECT JUSTICE

The fulfillment of the Law	5:17-20
Concrete examples: six antitheses	5:21-26
	5:27-30
	5:31 f.
	5:33-37
	5:38-42
	5:43-48

PART II: GOOD WORKS

General statement	6:1
Concrete examples: Almsgiving in secret	6:2-4
Prayer in secret	6:5 f.
True prayer: the Pater	6:7-15
Fasting in secret	6:16-18
The true treasure	6:19-21
Light of the body	6:22 f.
God and mammon	6:24
Trust in Providence	6:25-34

This whole question is not just a matter of literary criticism; it also has a practical bearing, for, if it can be shown that isolated sayings of our Lord have been grouped together, this fact must be kept in mind in interpreting these sayings. The context in which they are found, their relation to one another, are, in some degree at least, artificial. It would be misleading, for instance, to take the Sermon in Mt. 5-7 as one closely-knit unit, and study it as one would a theological essay. There is a certain unity, and there is a plan, but to a large extent these chapters are made up of pre-existing and distinct parts. The realization of this factor can save us from being disturbed by a lack of strict logical order, and can prevent us from doing violence to the text by reading into it a too rigid sequence of ideas.

St. Luke's approach to the Sermon is different from that of St. Matthew, and it does not concern us here. But, it should be noted that Dom Dupont concludes his study of the method of both evangelists in terms that give further force to a point we were at pains to emphasize in our study of the formation of the Gospels.

> These retouches indicate the concept which the evangelists had of their task and the preoccupations which guided them in their work. Their role, as they saw it, was not that of simple annalists. As evangelists they were very conscious of the concrete aspect of the teaching which they handed on and which was destined to nourish the Christian life of those for whom they wrote. They seem to have been more interested in the application of principles to conduct than in the principles as such. It was not enough for them to tell their readers what the Master had taught, they wanted to bring that teaching to bear on their lives.

The spirit which animated their work was the spirit of the primitive Church. The Gospel tradition is not to be conceived as a mechanically exact repetition of the words of Jesus; it is a question of witness, of testimony. The words of Jesus are living, life-giving words; the early Church passed them on clothed also with its own life.[12]

THE NATURE OF THE SERMON — We have observed that the fivefold division of the central part of Matthew is, possibly, modeled on the Pentateuch. In a similar strain, it is argued that certain Exodus parallels have been stressed and that Matthew has wished to present Jesus as a new Moses. Although sometimes the evidence has been pressed too far, it does seem true that "Matthew was well aware of that interpretation of Christ which found its prototype in Moses, and that, at certain points, he may have allowed this to color his Gospel. But the restraint with which the New Exodus and New Moses motifs are used is noticeable."[13] We may take it, then, that the evangelist did see the Jesus of the Sermon as a new Moses—but also as more than a Mosaic figure. The Sermon is not another version of the Law, it is a definitive formulation. Suggestive of the Law of a new Moses, it is also the authoritative word of the Lord, the Messiah: it is the messianic Torah.[14]

The new Law of Christ does not stand in sharp antithesis[15] to that given on Sinai: it is a fulfillment of the Law of Moses (Mt. 5:17). A similar outlook may be discerned in the messianic expectations of the Old Testament and of the Qumran sectarians. In Jer. 31:31-34, it seems possible to understand the "new covenant" not as something utterly divorced from the old Torah: Jeremiah's hope for the latter days, the law written on the hearts of men, is the old ideal renewed and brought to perfection. In the Qumran writings[16] it is expected that the laws of the community will be changed in the messianic age; these changes may be radical and current interpretations will be obsolete, but it does not appear that the Law

---

[12]*Ibid.*, p. 204.

[13]W. D. Davies, *The Setting of the Sermon on the Mount* (New York: Cambridge University Press, 1964), pp. 92 f. What I have to say here is based largely on this remarkable historical study of the Sermon.

[14]See *ibid.*, p. 93.

[15]The designation "antitheses" applied to Mt. 5:21-48 should not be overstressed.

[16]CD and 1QS; see Wilfrid J. Harrington, *Record of Revelation: The Bible* (Chicago: The Priory Press, 1965), pp. 74-78.

will cease or will be changed entirely. We may justly say that, against the overall eschatological expectation of Judaism, the evidence for a *new* messianic Torah is not impressive.[17] Yet, Judaism did anticipate that the messianic age would bring a new teaching, with authority; and Matthew does certainly present Jesus as teaching with authority (Mt. 7:28 f.).

When the Sermon is compared with the rest of the New Testament, it becomes clear that these words of Jesus—his moral teaching —were preserved primarily because they were part of the essential structure of the Gospel. Jesus did make demands, he did lay down the law of the Messiah. There is no conflict between Gospel and Law—the Law of Christ. The Gospel is not only kerygma, not only kerygma and didache, it is also a moral code, and this was so from the beginning. We may put it another way and say that the kerygma involves the acceptance of Christ and of his demands, and that the didache includes precepts and rules of conduct for Christian living. "For some in the primitive Church, if not for all, the penetrating demands of Jesus, no less than the great kerygmatic affirmations about him, were part of 'the bright light of the Gospel,' that is, they were revelatory."[18] Jesus revealed himself not only in his works and words but also by the exigency of his demands.

The Sermon on the Mount is didache, a preaching to the Christian community—to those already within the fold. But didache presupposes and contains kerygma: it sets out the basis of the faith, the saving events, and then goes on to teach; instruction in morals has a large part in it. The teaching will differ according to audience and circumstances (for example, the instruction on prayer in Mt. 6:5-15 and Lk. 11:1-13). Matthew has four sayings which are concerned largely with how *not* to pray; in this context, the Lord's Prayer stands as a model of a short prayer in contrast to longwinded effusions. In Luke, the Our Father is given in answer to the disciples' request to be taught to pray; the passage, then, goes on to urge perseverance in prayer and closes with the image of the father who will not turn a deaf ear to his son. Clearly, the Matthaean passage is addressed to men who have come from a milieu where

---

17See Davies, *op. cit.*, p. 188.
18*Ibid.*, p. 437.

prayer is not unknown, but where it has been open to misconceptions and abuses: it is a Judaeo-Christian didache. Luke is concerned with people who have to learn to pray and who need to be encouraged: it is a didache for converts from paganism.[19]

The Sermon on the Mount, then, is a classic example of didache. It is a collection of sayings of Jesus, compiled for the purpose of Christian formation; it probably served for the instruction of catechumens or for the further direction of the newly baptized. It follows that something is presupposed: the proclamation of the Lord, crucified, risen and to come—the declaration that Jesus has reconciled us with God and that he is our life. What is presupposed is the conquering attraction of the Good News, a sincere conversion; what has already taken place is the witness which Jesus has given, in words and works, to what he is; what is presupposed is faith in the Risen Lord.[20]

This is the reason Jesus is so demanding, why he goes so far beyond the Law (cf. Mt. 5:21-48). His teaching is addressed to men who have been rescued by the Good News from the power of Satan, men who already stand in the kingdom of God. He addresses men who have been pardoned, prodigal sons who have been received back into the house of their Father. Men who have received that gift and who have experienced the love and mercy of God are urged, by inner compulsion, to do the will of that heavenly Father. The Commandments of Christ are not further reminders of sin (cf. Rm. 7:7-13), but carry with them the divine help that enables men to obey and gives men the possibility of living as children of God.

The Sermon on the Mount shows us the spirit and the demands of the Gospel of Jesus—demands far more exacting than those of the Law, and a spirit of freedom unknown to the most sincere observer of the Law. Above all, he who listens to the demands of Christ and earnestly seeks to carry them out is given the means to achieve that task, the liberal gift of grace. Here we put our finger on the difference between Law and Gospel: the Law makes demands, but does not give the means of carrying them out—it leaves

[19]See J. Jeremias, *Paroles de Jésus* (Paris: Cerf, 1963), p. 33.
[20]See *ibid.*, pp. 15-48.

man to himself; the Gospel sets man before the gift of God (salvation through Jesus Christ) and demands of him that he should make that ineffable gift the sole foundation of his life. Yet, in the new life there is still room for precepts, there is still need for law, the Law of Christ (Gal. 6:2).

3) *The Narratives*

Distinct from the discourses, in literary style, are the narrative sections, which deal with the activity of Jesus, his journeys and miracles. Matthew, as we have seen, is later than Mark and has used that Gospel, but it is also largely independent of Mark. This can be observed in the style of Matthew which is more polished than that of the other Gospel. There are many Aramaisms, but these are not as frequent as in Mark. Yet, in the narratives, there is a large field of agreement between the two Gospels. In general, it is true that Mark has many vivid details not found in Matthew, but the latter may have deliberately developed a more austere style. If we take, for example, the account of the cure of Peter's mother-in-law (Mt. 8:14 f.; Mk. 1:29-31; Lk. 4:38 f.), we find that the suppression of all accessory details in Matthew gives a certain solemnity to the narrative. At the same time Matthew also tends to be clearer than the other synoptists.

After the Infancy-gospel (Mt. 1-2), the first narrative is composed of a triptych which shows John the Baptist preaching (Mt. 3:1-12), the baptism of Jesus (Mt. 3:13-17), and the Temptations (Mt. 4:1-11), and is followed by the beginning of the Galilean ministry (Mt. 4:12-25). The grouping of material, so evident in the discourses, is also present in the second narrative section: ten miracles are grouped (Mt. 8:1–9:34). The disbelief and hostility of the Jews is brought out in the various episodes of the third narrative (Mt. 11-12). After the account of the rejection of Jesus at Nazareth (Mt. 13:53-58), chapters 14-17 show him constantly journeying. Three times he withdraws: to the eastern side of the lake (Mt. 14:13); to pagan territory (Mt. 15:21); from the Pharisees and Sadducees (Mt. 16:1-5), in order to found his Church (Mt. 16:13-20): he has turned from Israel to the new people of God. Chapters 19-20 treat of the journey of Jesus through Peraea and Jericho to Jerusalem for the

Pasch, the journey to his death. The entry of the Son of David who takes possession of the Temple and the symbolic action of the withered fig tree are described in Mt. 21:1-22; in Mt. 21:23—23:39 he is face to face with his enemies. Like the others, this Gospel concludes with the narrative of the passion, death, and resurrection of Jesus (chaps. 26-28).

The narrative sections are an integral part of the Gospel; yet, the great discourses are the parts that have won for it a unique position in the Church. Taken as a whole, discourse and narrative, it forms the basis of Christian teaching on the life and doctrine of Christ. This is the reason Father Lagrange can write:

> It is the First Gospel that has always been dearest to pious souls and to preachers. St. Dominic included it and the Epistles of St. Paul among the few belongings he carried with him on his missionary journeys. The Christ of St. Matthew is less homely than the Christ of St. Mark who is so indulgent towards disciples slow to understand. He is less the Savior of the world than in Luke, and he is never called the Word as in John. He is the revealer of a doctrine that is essentially interior, and he is the founder of the Christian institution built on Peter. Meek and humble of heart, he does not quench the smouldering wick, but he challenges the hypocrites and unmasks them. He is the Messiah, a Lawgiver, not like Moses in the name of another, but as God: the only Son of God whom Israel has rejected but whom the Church has received. If St. Matthew, in his narrative, has not the striking realism of St. Mark, or the gentle charm of St. Luke; if his gaze is not fixed on divine things like that of St. John, he has many more sayings of Christ, sayings simple and straightforward, sayings that are so penetrating that one seems to hear them, with the accent and intonation almost, that they had on his lips. Indeed, the oldest witness of the Church's tradition, Papias, has seen in Matthew, above all else, *the divine Words*. It is these words, too, that we must study.[21]

3. DOCTRINE

1) The Messiah

The First Gospel is dominated by this idea: Jesus is the Messiah who was foretold and promised in the Old Testament and whose arrival was awaited by the Jews; but when he came his own people rejected him. That Jesus is indeed the promised Messiah is proved first of all by reference to the prophets; no other evangelist uses

---

[21]*Évangile selon St. Matthieu* (Paris: Gabalda, 1923), p. i.

and cites the Old Testament so freely. In this respect, the so-called "reflection-citations" (because they are personal "reflections" of the evangelist) are noteworthy. In them Matthew shows that Christ has fulfilled the Old Testament prophecies. There are eleven such distinctive quotations: five in the Infancy-narrative (Mt. 1:22 f., 2:5 f., 15, 17 f., 23); five in the central part of the Gospel (Mt. 4:14-16; 8:17; 12:17-21; 13:35; 21:4 f.); one in the Passion-narrative (Mt. 27:9 f.). We may remark with regard to all of these:

1. *They are proper to Matthew.* Neither the citations nor their introductory formulas are found elsewhere in the Synoptics, or in the New Testament for that matter.

2. *All eleven are personal reflections of the evangelist.* All other quotations are attributed to Jesus or to some other character in the Gospels.

3. *The introductory formula is essentially the same in all eleven citations*: "In order that the oracle of (the Lord . . . Jeremiah . . . the prophet) might be fulfilled"; or, "Then was fulfilled the oracle of (the Lord . . . Jeremiah . . . the prophet)."

4. There is a certain artificiality in the application of these texts to events in the life of Jesus. Thus, for example, when the evangelist has told us that the holy Family, on their return from Egypt, settled in Nazareth, he adds that this was in order that "what was spoken by the prophets might be fulfilled, 'He shall be called a Nazarene'" (Mt. 2:23). Significantly, reference is to "the prophets," for the precise text is nowhere to be found. Matthew was evidently thinking of a *nazir*, one dedicated to God as in Jgs. 13:5,7, and he read this into the word "Nazareth"; the Old Testament is full of similar word-play and popular etymology; this should be evaluated as such where it occurs.

Note further that all the quotations are easily detached from their context; this is because they have been added by the evangelist. It would seem to follow that Matthew has been referring to a special collection of Old Testament "proof-texts," that is to say, to a list of texts which were used by Christians as arguments to show that Christ had fulfilled the prophecies. "In these quotations Matthew applies rules for interpretation similar to those used at Qumran and arrives at a substantiation of the claim that the Church is right in hailing Jesus of Nazareth as the Christ, and his believers as the true heirs to the prophecies and their promises."[22]

Yet, in these citations, Matthew is only echoing the reflection of a living Church, seeking and finding justification in the Scriptures for the events of Jesus' life and for his conduct. Scripture enlightens the stages of the Infancy: born of a virgin (Mt. 1:22 f.), at Bethlehem (Mt. 2:5 f.), he sought refuge in Egypt (Mt. 2:15); he was the occasion of a massacre of Bethlehem infants (Mt. 2:17 f.) and went to live in Nazareth (Mt. 2:23). During his ministry he dwelt in Capharnaum, in the Galilee of the Gentiles (Mt. 4:14-16)— and not in Jerusalem. Like the Servant of Yahweh (and not as the Judge preached by the Baptist), he has taken our infirmities and healed our sicknesses (Mt. 8:17) and did not cry out in the streets (Mt. 12:17-21); he preached in parables (Mt. 21:4 f.); and he was sold for thirty pieces of silver (Mt. 27:9 f.). Jesus is therefore the Christ whom the Scriptures have foretold; but his contemporaries had failed to accept his message and had been in error regarding the true nature of the expected Messiah. "The story of Jesus, thus illuminated by faith in the Scriptures, is not simply an event merged in the past; it remains today, for every reader of Matthew, the summit of the history of God's saving plan."[23]

While we may admit that the "reflection-citations" have something forced and artificial about them, we should recognize that the evangelists' (and the New Testament writers' in general) use of the Old Testament is particularly enlightened.[24] They do not regard the prophets as fortunetellers of a sort, and they do not seek to show an exact correspondence between prophecy and fulfillment. Nor do they try to demonstrate, as was attempted in later ages, that everything in the Old Law has direct reference to Christ. Closer study of their method has established that they concentrated on certain passages—mainly from Isaiah, Jeremiah, some of the minor prophets, and Psalms—and the sections in question were considered as units and taken in their totality.

---

[22]K. Stendahl, PCB, n. 673 g.
[23]X. Léon-Dufour, IB, pp. 182 f.
[24]See C. H. Dodd, *According to the Scriptures: The Substructure of New Testament Theology* (London: Nisbet, 1952).

As a rule, only a particular verse of one of these passages is quoted, but the whole context should be kept in mind if the true meaning of the citation is to be established. For example, Matthew and Mark place the first verse of Ps. 22 (21) ("My God, my God, why hast thou forsaken me?") on the lips of Jesus on the Cross. John (19:24) quotes verse 11 of the same psalm: "They parted my garments among them, and for my clothing they cast lots." In each case, it is not the isolated verse but the whole Psalm that should be considered. And the Psalm, opening on a note of dereliction, ends as a hymn of thanksgiving for deliverance (vv. 19-21), and thus admirably fits the double aspect of the Passion of our Lord. The two passages that have most influenced the Gospels are Is. 53 (the Servant of Yahweh) and Dn. 7 (the Son of Man).[25] Always, of course, the appeal to Scripture is an integral part of the kerygma. In the typical passage, 1 Cor. 15:3-5, it is said that Christ died and rose the third day "according to the Scriptures." In the summary outlines of the kerygma found in Acts, it is a constant theme that, in the coming of Christ and in his death and resurrection, the prophecies are fulfilled.[26]

The prophecies of the Old Testament are interpreted according to the evangelists' understanding of history, and the history of the people of God followed a plan designed by God. But the pattern into which the events of the Old Testament fall is not clearly seen until it is illuminated by the revealing light of the Gospel. The Old is only a prelude to the New, but it is the same God who has brought to pass both the one and the other. Hence, the evangelists looked to the Old Testament to find the threads that ran through it, reaching to Christ.

But, to return to Matthew. Jesus the Messiah, as the evangelist saw him, was, in a special way, the "son of David." The Gospel opens with a genealogy which demonstrates that he was descended from David (Mt. 1:1). In fulfillment of the prophecy of Micah (5:1), he was born in David's city of Bethlehem (Mt. 2:5). As son of

---

[25]See Wilfrid J. Harrington, *Record of the Promise: The Old Testament* (Chicago: The Priory Press, 1965), pp. 234-39.

[26]See C. H. Dodd, *The Apostolic Preaching and Its Developments* (London: Hodder & Stoughton, 1963³). See above p. 123 and below p. 214.

David, he was "king of the Jews," and it was as such that his life was sought by Herod (Mt. 2:13-23). The Baptist's query (Mt. 11:2 f.) does, despite appearances, receive a direct answer (Mt. 11:4-6), for the works there listed are the works of the Messiah (cf. Is. 26:19; 29:18 f.; 35:5 f.; 61:1), and John must have concluded that he who did these things was indeed the Messiah. The healing of a man who had a blind and dumb spirit moved the people to ask if this were the son of David (Mt. 12:23). The two blind men (Mt. 9:27) and the pagan woman (Mt. 15:23) addressed him as "son of David." On his entry into Jerusalem, this son of David was acclaimed by the people (Mt. 21:10) and received the homage of the children (Mt. 21:15). Soon, however, his people were to call for his crucifixion (Mt. 27:22 f., 25), and thus, paradoxically, ensured the success of his mission. Yet, this rejection of the Messiah was the great tragedy that was so deeply to affect Paul, the passionate lover of his people (Rm. 11).

2) Son of God

In Matthew, as in the other Gospels, Jesus is frequently called "Son of God." This designation is not quite as obvious as it appears; hence, it must be examined more closely. The biblical title, "Son of God," does not necessarily imply natural divine sonship. It can, and very often does, indicate adoptive sonship, which follows on the divine choice and establishes particularly intimate relationships between God and his creatures.

In the Old Testament, the term is applied to angels (Jb. 1:6; 36:7; Ps. 29 (28):1), to the Chosen People (Ex. 4:22; Wis. 18:13), to the Israelites (Dt. 14:1; Hos. 2:1), to their leaders (Ps. 83 (82):6), to the king (2 Sm. 7:14; Ps. 89 (88):27). In later Judaism, with the advent of individualistic religion (that is, of a more personal relationship between the individual and God), the pious man became a "son of God" (Sir. 4:10; 23:1; Wis. 2:16). In Jewish literature, the Messiah was not called Son of God—which is understandable in view of the very wide meaning of the title. Thus, it seems that, at the time of Jesus, "Son of God" had no necessary messianic connotation.

In the Synoptic Gospels, the title "Son of God" is often colored by the evangelists' faith in the true divine Sonship of Christ. We can see this influence in Mt. 16:16—where Peter acknowledges the Messiahship of Jesus—when we compare this text with Mt. 8:29. In Mt. 16:16, the declaration of Peter reads: "You are the Christ, the Son of the living God." But Mark (8:29) has: "You are the Christ"; and Luke (9:20): "The Christ of God." Some have understood the words of Peter (in Matthew) as referring to the divine Sonship of Christ. However, in view of Mark ("Christ" is the Greek translation of "Messiah") and of the general lack of understanding on the part of the disciples, it is better to take them as referring to his messianic dignity. Besides, Peter's rebuke to Jesus, immediately after the confession (Mt. 16:22), is scarcely compatible with an acknowledgement of his divinity. We have seen[27] how very difficult it was for the disciples of Jesus to grasp his notion of a spiritual Messiahship, and Peter would certainly have required a divine revelation if he were to accept it (Mt. 16:17). The full title employed by Matthew does not, *of itself,* go beyond the messianic significance, but it is certain that the evangelist, *when he wrote the Gospel*—and therefore in the light of his postresurrection faith—had in mind the divine Sonship in the strict sense.

The Easter faith is clear too in Mt. 14:33 (cf. Mk. 6:51 f.). Nor must we suppose that the title had originally the full meaning in the mouth of Satan (Mt. 4:3,6) or of the demoniacs (Mt. 8:29). The declaration of the centurion at the foot of the Cross is a striking case in point. According to Mark, he says: "Truly this man was a son of God!" (Mk. 15:39), whereas Luke has: "Certainly this man was innocent!" (Lk. 23:47.) This title even at the Baptism (Mt. 3:17) and at the Transfiguration (Mt. 17:5) did not, for its hearers, imply more than the special divine favor bestowed on the Messiah. However, it would seem that the solemn question of the high priest (Mt. 26:63) did extend to the superhuman rank which Jesus claimed.

The title "Son of God" is, of course, open to the meaning of true divine Sonship. In fact, Jesus did suggest this by designating himself as "Son" (Mt. 17:26 f.; 21:37). In Mt. 7:21, he calls

---

[27]See p. 138.

God "my Father." So, too, he never speaks of "our Father" (except in the prayer which is meant for his disciples), but always of "my Father" or "your Father." The most explicit text of all, which is quite in the style of John, but undoubtedly belongs to the synoptic tradition, clearly asserts his divine Sonship: "All things have been delivered to me by my Father; and no one knows the Son except the Father, and no one knows the Father except the Son and any one to whom the Son chooses to reveal him" (Mt. 11:27). These statements, confirmed by the resurrection, give to the title "Son of God" the properly divine meaning which it has, for example, in the Pauline Epistles.

3) The Kingdom of God[28]

In his presentation of the preaching of Jesus, Matthew insists on the theme of the kingdom of heaven. The reader of the Gospels will have noted that Mark and Luke speak, not of the "kingdom of heaven,'" but of the "kingdom of God," and it may seem that there is a corresponding difference in meaning. But this is not so. In Matthew, "heaven" is used in place of "God," because the Jews of the time avoided, whenever possible, the use of the divine name. Hence, "kingdom of heaven" is exactly the same as "kingdom of God." Indeed, it is very likely that Jesus, addressing Jews, employed the current expression and spoke of the "kingdom of heaven."

The basic idea of the "kingdom of God" is that of the "rule" or "reign" of God. This corresponds to the meaning of the Aramaic *malkutha* (the term used by Jesus): "kingship," "kingly rule," "sovereignty." But, while the reign of God is the primary idea, that of domain or kingdom is also necessarily implied; there can be no reign, in any real sense, without a kingdom.

Jesus, in speaking of the kingdom of God, obviously took it for granted that his hearers would know what he meant. He spoke of something already familiar to them, and he did not have to begin by explaining the term. In the Old Testament, however, the ex-

---

[28]See R. Schnackenburg, *God's Rule and Kingdom* (London: Herder/Nelson, 1963); J. B. Bauer, editor, *Bibeltheologisches Wörterbuch* (Graz-Wien-Köln: Verlag Styria, 1962²), I, pp. 966-88 (henceforth references to this work will be abbreviated BW).

pression occurs only rarely and then in the later books (for example, Tb. 13:1; Ps. 146 (145):11 f.; Dn. 2:37; Wis. 10:10). In nonbiblical Jewish literature, however, there was frequent reference to the kingdom of God. This was largely due to the tendency, already noted, to avoid mention of the name of God or to speak of him in abstract terms. For instance, in Is. 24:23, instead of "Yahweh shall reign," the Aramaic version reads: ". . . the kingdom of God will be manifest." Yet, although the name is not prevalent, the reality of the kingdom of God is very much in evidence in the Old Testament[29] and the synoptic use of the term has Old Testament roots (for example, Nm. 23:21; 1 Sm. 12:13; Is. 52:7; 1 Chr. 29:11).

In the teaching of Jesus, the kingdom is, first and foremost, an intervention of God in history. This is also true of the Old Testament concept; but in the New Testament view, the divine intervention is made manifest in the coming of the Son of God. God intervenes in history; in other words, it is he who establishes the kingdom, it is his work. He is like the sower, like the owner of the vineyard, like the king who gave a feast. And he, too, grants vitality to the kingdom so that it grows, from within, like a seed, so that it spreads out, irresistibly, as leaven permeates the mass of dough. Although it is the work of God, nevertheless, in the concrete, the kingdom is identified with the work and with the very person of Jesus Christ.

This insistence on the supernatural origin of the kingdom and on its spiritual nature does not mean that the idea of a domain can be ignored. God, in establishing his reign among men, sets up a kingdom in which he will be acknowledged as King and over which he will reign. This is the reason there is question of entering into the kingdom (Mt. 5:20; 7:21; 18:3). This is the reason it is like a feast in which those who belong to the kingdom have a place (Mt. 8:11). In the interpretation of the parable of The Cockle, we read that the Son of Man will send his angels who will "gather out of his kingdom all causes of sin and all evildoers" (Mt. 13:41). In these and similar passages, it is clear that a kingdom is meant and not a reign only.

---

[29]See Harrington, *Record of the Promise: The Old Testament, op. cit.*, pp. 218 f.

The question may be asked whether, in the teaching of Jesus, the kingdom is already present, or whether he sees it as something lying wholly in the future. The truth of the matter is that he considered it under both aspects, for it has this twofold aspect. In many passages of the Gospels, it appears as a future reality (cf. Mt. 10:7; 24:14), and many of the parables refer to a kingdom that awaits its completion and perfection: The Mustard Seed, The Wheat and the Cockle (Mt. 13:24-32, 47-50). But these same parables just as obviously presuppose that the kingdom is already present and what they teach is that, despite every obstacle, it will come to fulfillment—the mustard seed grows and the sown wheat ripens to harvest.

> The character of God's rule as actually "present" may be briefly described as follows. Jesus proclaims the eschatological kingship of God as something that is close and insistent, operative and tangible, bound up with his own person and activity and summoning his hearers to an inescapable decision. In this sense it is present in him, in his words and works.[30]

We might say that the final age has a beginning and an end. With Jesus, the reign of God is present, but as an initial salvation which awaits fulfillment. The intervening period is the era of the Church and its activity in the service of the perfect reign that is to come. Because in Jesus and in his works God's reign with its saving power is actually in operation, its final phase is certain; there exists an indissoluble connection between the dawn of God's reign and its coming full manifestation in glory. But the fulfillment remains an object of hope and the present era of salvation looks to its consummation.

It may be asked how and when the perfect kingdom of God will come. No definite answer can be given to either question, but its coming is assured.

> It will one day come, and unexpectedly, but in a form visible to all men, according to God's sovereign will and only through his all-powerful action. This will occur when the "Son of Man" accompanied by the hosts of heaven, comes "with power." This "Son of Man" is no other than Jesus himself. For the present, in the form of humiliation

---

[30]Schnackenburg, *op. cit.*, p. 159.

and to a certain degree in concealment, he is fulfilling his messianic tasks on earth. But then he will manifest himself to all the world as possessed of kingly dignity and divine power to establish in God's name, God's perfect, universal, cosmic reign.[31]

For the intervening period between the first appearance of the kingdom in the person of Jesus and its fulfillment at the end of this age, Jesus had established his earthly community, the pilgrim people of God, the Church, which is distinct from the perfect eschatological society: *ekklesia* and *basileia* should not be identified. We may propose the relationship between the Ecclesia and the Reign of God as follows:

1. *God's reign and the earthly community of Jesus are not identical but they are related.* "Because God's eschatological reign was already present in the person and action of Jesus and will manifest itself in power and glory at the Parousia, the community established by and attached to him has a share in the saving graces of the present and the promises for the future."[32]

2. *The Ecclesia is orientated toward the future kingdom.* It will, one day, after the test of Judgment, become God's community of the perfect *basileia*.

3. *In the community, the powers of God's kingdom are already operative.* Jesus' disciples are commissioned and empowered to lead men into the future kingdom of glory (Mt. 18:18; Jn. 20:21 f.).

4. *Jesus assures his community that the "gates of hell" will not prevail against it.* It will not only endure to the advent of the perfect reign of God, but must fight against the forces of evil.

5. *Membership of the Ecclesia is not in itself a guarantee of entrance into the future kingdom.* The earthly community includes many who will be cast out at the final judgment.

6. "The basic thought, uniting present and future, must be that of the eschatological people of God. This people is considered as assembled—but also, from another point of view, as God's flock scattered in the world—yet genuinely God's flock over which God exercises his sovereignty. The Ecclesia is the assembly ground of the

---

[31]*Ibid.*, p. 177.
[32]*Ibid.*, pp. 230-32.

elect (*eklektoi*) who still have to endure their earthly combats. Again, it is the flock of Jesus, the messianic shepherd who not only gathers them around himself at God's instance (Mk. 6:34; 14:28) but gives his life for their salvation (Lk. 22:20; Mk. 14:24; Jn. 10:11)."[33]

Jesus' community of salvation came to effective life after Easter and the descent of the Holy Spirit. Jesus was now the glorified Lord, seated at God's right hand (Acts 2:30-35), who directed his Church through his Spirit. God's kingship is now, throughout the duration of the "times of the Church" exercised through the rule of Christ, the universal Lord (Phil. 2:11); for the Father has established his Son "King of kings and Lord of lords" (Ap. 19:16). Christ's rule over the world is exercised through his Church: inwardly through its own growth in grace and outwardly through its mission. In the present era of salvation, God's kingship is realized in Christ's rule here and now over Church and world.

At the end of time, Christ, conqueror of all his enemies, will deliver the kingdom to God the Father (1 Cor. 15:24). Then this kingship will have indeed become "the kingdom of our Lord and of his Christ" (Ap. 11:15; 12:10) and the faithful will receive their inheritance in "the kingdom of Christ and of God" (Eph. 5:5). Then at last, finally and perfectly, "the Lord our God the Almighty will reign" (Ap. 19:6).[34]

---

[33]*Ibid.*, pp. 231 f.
[34]See VTB, p. 956. For a treatment of the Church in Mt., see Wilfrid J. Harrington, *Explaining the Gospels* (New York: Paulist Press, 1963), pp. 58-63.

FIVE	*The Gospel of St. Luke*

1. THE AUTHORSHIP OF THE GOSPEL

1) *The Testimony of Tradition*

The testimony of tradition regarding the authorship of the Third Gospel is unhesitating: It is the work of St. Luke. The chief witnesses are:

1. *Irenaeus* (end of second century A.D.): "Luke, the companion of Paul, wrote the latter's Gospel in a book."

2. *Anti-Marcionite Prologue* (c. 160-180 A.D.):

> Luke, a Syrian of Antioch, doctor by profession, was the disciple of the Apostles. At a later date he was the disciple of Paul until the death of the latter. After having served the Lord without fault and never having married, he died, full of the Holy Spirit, at Boeotia, aged 84. As Gospels had already been written by Matthew in Judaea and by Mark in Italy, Luke, under the impulse of the Holy Spirit, wrote his Gospel in the region of Achaia. In the prologue he shows that other Gospels had been written before his, but that it was necessary to present to the faithful converted from paganism an exact account of the economy of salvation, lest they should be impeded by Jewish fables or caused to stray from the truth by the deceits of heretics.

3. *The Muratorian Canon* (end of second century A.D.)[1] "Luke, a doctor and companion of Paul, wrote the Third Gospel. He himself had not seen the Lord."

4. *St. Jerome gives a summary of the traditional data*:

> Thirdly, Luke the physician, by nation a Syrian of Antioch, whose praise is in the Gospel [cf. 2 Cor. 8:18], and who himself was a disciple of the Apostle Paul, wrote in the region of Achaia and Boeotia, seeking material from the ancients, and, as he admits in his preface, writing rather from hearsay than from eyewitness.

The main points of the impressive traditional witness come to this: The author of the Third Gospel is Luke, a companion of St. Paul and a doctor. Present-day scholarship, in general, is agreeable to accept the tradition. It follows that Luke is also the author of Acts, for Luke and Acts are demonstrably two volumes of the one work.

2) *The New Testament Witness*

Just as in the case of Mark, the New Testament also has much to tell us about Luke; once again, that information is found in the Epistles of St. Paul and in the Acts of the Apostles.

THE PAULINE EPISTLES   Luke is named three times: "Luke the beloved physician and Demas greet you" (Col. 4:14); "Epaphras, my fellow prisoner in Christ Jesus, sends greetings to you, as do Mark, Aristarchus, Demas and Luke, my fellow workers" (Phm. 23 f.); "Luke alone is with me" (2 Tm. 4:11).

Thus, according to Colossians and Philemon, Luke was with Paul in Rome during the latter's first captivity (61-63 A.D.); and according to 2 Timothy, he was with him during the second Roman captivity (67 A.D.). In Col. 4:10-14, the collaborators of Paul are divided into two groups: (1) Aristarchus, Mark, and Justus, "the only circumcised" (that is, Jews); (2) Epaphras, Luke, and Demas, who, by implication, are of pagan origin.

The designation "beloved physician" (Col. 4:14) reveals that Luke belonged to an educated class, and also that his services were appreciated by Paul, especially during the second captivity.

---

[1]The Muratorian Canon is a list of the inspired books which were accepted in Rome about the end of the second century. The list, which is fragmentary, takes its name from the fact that it was discovered in the Ambrosian Library, Milan, by the Italian scholar Muratori, and was published by him in 1740.

THE ACTS OF   The "we-passages" (Acts 16:10-17; 20:5-15; 21:
THE APOSTLES   1-18; 27:1–28:16). In these sections, the author
of Acts (who, beyond all reasonable doubt, is Luke) writes in the
first person—hence, the designation "we-passages"—obviously as an
eyewitness. We gather that Luke met Paul at Troas during the
latter's second missionary journey (50-52 A.D.). He went to Macedonia
with him, to Philippi, where Paul founded a church (Acts 16:10-17).
Luke appears to have remained at Philippi because the next "we-
passage" occurs in the context of the third missionary journey (53-58
A.D.). Luke joined Paul at Philippi about 57 A.D. (Acts 20:5-15),
and went with him to Jerusalem. On this occasion, Paul was arrested
and spent two years as a prisoner at Caesarea, on the Palestinian
coast (58-60 A.D.). This afforded Luke ample time to search out
sources, oral and written, both for his Gospel and for Acts. He
accompanied Paul on the journey to Rome in 60-61 A.D. (Acts 27:1–
28:16). There Luke could have met the people mentioned in Col.
4:10-14 and Phm. 24—especially Mark. Here again the data of the
Pauline Epistles and of Acts are in perfect accord, and it is clear
how a disciple of Paul came to know the Palestinian tradition.

3) Destination and Date

St. Luke dedicated his Gospel (and Acts) to a certain Theophilus.
The title given to him, kratiste ("Excellency"), indicates a man of
high social standing. According to ancient custom, the man to whom
a book was dedicated was expected to promote its circulation.[2]

Luke certainly wrote for Gentile Christians; this is quite evident
from a study of his Gospel. Thus, he consistently avoids many
matters which might appear too specifically Jewish. He omits whole
passages: the traditions of the ancients (Mk. 7:1-23); the return of
Elijah (Mk. 9:11-13); the antitheses (Mt. 5:21-22, 27 f., 33-37).
Sometimes, instead of suppressing a passage, he rearranges it or
omits details. For instance, compare Mt. 5:38-48 with Lk. 6:27-36;
and Mt. 7:24-27 with Lk. 6:47-49. He is also careful to omit or
play down anything that might shock his Gentile Christian readers:
sayings liable to be misunderstood—"Of that day or hour no one

---

[2]See A. Wikenhauser, *Einleitung in das Neue Testament* (Freiburg: Herder,
1956²), p. 161.

knows . . . nor the Son" (Mk. 13:32); and the cry from the Cross: "My God, My God, why hast thou forsaken me?" (Mk. 15:34); sentiments of Jesus like anger, indignation, sorrow (in this regard, compare: "And he looked around at them with anger, grieved at their hardness of heart" [Mk. 3:5], with "And he looked around on them all" [Lk. 6:10]; Lk. 19:45 f. and Mk. 11:15-17; Lk. 22:39-46 and Mk. 14:32-42); anything which might cast doubt on the omnipotence of Christ (in this regard, compare: "And he could do no mighty work there (in his own country) . . . and he marvelled because of their unbelief" [Mk. 6:5 f.], with Lk. 4:25-30; Lk. 4:40 and Mk. 1:34; Lk. 5:15 f. and Mk. 1:45).

Luke also omits or changes details that do not redound to the credit of the Apostles: he has omitted Mk. 4:13; 8:22 f.; 9:10, 28 f., 33 f. Elsewhere, he has modified the text of Mark (see Lk. 8:24 f. and Mk. 4:38, 40; Lk. 18:25 f. and Mk. 10:24-26; Lk. 22:31-34 and Mk. 14:27-31). This conduct of St. Luke is explained by Father Lagrange: "Luke, because he was addressing Gentiles, especially Greeks prone to discussions and criticism, did not wish to raise difficulties for them. . . . He felt that the transition from the Semitic to the Greek world of ideas would be rendered easier by saying nothing about matters difficult to understand."[3]

Some scholars date Luke 60-62 A.D. One of their arguments is that this date is demanded by the date of Acts. Since, in the latter writing (they say), Luke gives no indication of the outcome of Paul's appeal to Caesar, it follows that Acts must have been written before 63 A.D., the end of Paul's first captivity. The Gospel is certainly earlier; hence, it must have been written about 60-62 A.D.

This argument, however, cannot be taken as proving its point. To do so it would have to show that Luke intended to give the result of Paul's appeal to Caesar. In fact, the plan of Acts shows that this lay beyond Luke's purpose, and that the ending of the book is indeed just as it should be. Luke indicates the plan of Acts by quoting Christ's own words before his ascension: "You shall receive power when the Holy Spirit has come upon you; and shall be my witnesses in Jerusalem and in all Judaea and Samaria and to the

---

[3] *Evangile selon Saint Luc* (Paris: Gabalda, 1921), p. cxl.

ends of the earth" (Acts 1:8). Luke followed this plan; and at the close—having traced the expansion of the Church from Jerusalem—he has led the great Apostle of the Gentiles to the capital of the Roman Empire, the center of the world, and there, although technically a prisoner, Paul was "preaching the kingdom of God and teaching about the Lord Jesus Christ quite openly and unhindered" (Acts 28:31). This is a masterly ending to a book that has shown the triumphal advance of Christianity and is one more proof of the literary artistry of St. Luke. This, then, is obviously the ending intended by Luke. To say that he does not go on to give the outcome of Paul's appeal to Caesar, is not a proof, therefore, that Acts, and consequently Luke, was written before 63 A.D.

The early dating of the Gospel is more compellingly excluded by the date of Mark (not earlier than 64 A.D.) and by the fact that Luke has used Mark. On the whole, Catholic scholars tend to date Luke between 65 A.D. (the probable date of Mark) and 70 A.D. Most Protestant, and not a few Catholic,[4] scholars would put the composition of Luke in the decade 70-80 A.D. Their main reason for doing so is based on the detailed form of the prediction of the destruction of Jerusalem (Lk. 19:43 f.; 21:20, 24; 23:28-30). Where Mt. 24:15 and Mk. 13:14 have "abomination of desolation" (cf. Dn. 9:27; 11:31; 12:11), Lk. 21:20 reads: "When you see Jerusalem surrounded by armies, then know that its desolation has come near." Verse 24 adds that the inhabitants of the city "will fall by the edge of the sword, and be led captive among all nations; and Jerusalem will be trodden down by the Gentiles until the time of the Gentiles are fulfilled." These would seem to be an *ex eventu* clarification of the veiled prophecy of the destruction of Jerusalem in 70 A.D. The argument is not conclusive, however, because the expressions, general in themselves, may well have been suggested by the Old Testament (cf. Dt. 28:54; Hos. 9:7; Zech. 12:3). Luke may have written shortly before 70 A.D. In the long run, however, the exact date of the Gospel, apart from being uncertain, is hardly a vital question; it has no bearing, direct or indirect, on matters of faith or morals.

---

[4]See Wikenhauser, *op. cit.*, pp. 161 f.; J. Schmid, *Das Evangelium nach Lukas* (Regensburg: Pustet, 1960⁴), pp. 26 f.; X. Léon-Dufour, IB, pp. 255-57.

2. THE LITERARY CONSTRUCTION OF THE GOSPEL

1) *The Plan*

PROLOGUE (1:1-4)

FROM THE TEMPLE TO THE CLOSE OF THE GALILEAN MINISTRY (1:5—9:50)

BIRTH AND HIDDEN LIFE OF JOHN THE BAPTIST AND JESUS (1:5—2:52)

1) Annunciation of the birth of John	1:5-25
2) Annunciation of the birth of Jesus	1:26-38
3) The Visitation	1:39-56
4) Birth of John and Circumcision	1:57-80
5) Birth of Jesus and Circumcision	2:1-21
6) Manifestation of Jesus	2:22-40
7) The Finding in the Temple	2:41-52

PREPARATION OF THE MINISTRY OF JESUS (3:1—4:13)

1) Preaching of John the Baptist	3:1-20
2) Baptism of Jesus	3:21-38
3) Temptation in the Wilderness	4:1-13

THE GALILEAN MINISTRY (4:14—9:50)

1) The beginning	4:14—5:16
2) Conflict with the scribes and Pharisees	5:17—6:11
3) Preaching of Jesus	6:12-49
4) Reception of the works of Jesus	7:1—8:3
5) Teaching in parables	8:4-21
6) A Group of miracles	8:22-56
7) Mission charge to the Twelve	9:1-6
8) Herod's fears	9:7-9
9) Feeding of the five thousand	9:10-17
10) Confession of Peter; first prediction of the passion	9:18-22
11) The following of Jesus	9:23-27
12) The Transfiguration	9:28-36
13) An exorcism	9:37-43a
14) Second prediction of the passion	9:43b-45
15) Ecclesiastical discourse	9:46-50

JOURNEY FROM GALILEE TO JERUSALEM

THE JOURNEY TO JERUSALEM (9:51—19:27)

1)	In Samaria	9:51-56
2)	The apostolic vocation; mission of the Seventy-two	9:57—10:24
3)	The true piety	10:25—11:13
4)	Conflicts with opponents	11:14-54
5)	Warnings to the disciples	12:1-53
6)	Call to repentance	12:54—13:25
7)	A meal in the house of a Pharisee	14:1-24
8)	Renunciation	14:25-35
9)	The three mercy parables	15
10)	Further parables	16
11)	Varied teaching	17:1-19
12)	The Day of the Son of Man	17:20-37
13)	Parables on prayer	18:1-14
14)	Jesus and children: danger of riches	18:15-30
15)	Third prediction of the passion	18:31-34
16)	At Jericho	18:35—19:27

LAST DAYS OF THE SUFFERING AND RISEN CHRIST IN JERUSALEM

MINISTRY IN JERUSALEM (19:28—21:38)

1)	Messianic entry	19:28-46
2)	Teaching in the Temple	19:47—21:4
3)	Discourse on the destruction of Jerusalem	21:5-36
4)	The last days of Jesus: summary	21:37 f.

THE PASSION (22—23)

1)	The events culminating in the arrest	22:1-53
2)	Trial scenes, crucifixion, and burial	22:54—23:56

AFTER THE RESURRECTION (24)

1)	Apparitions	24:1-49
2)	The ascension	24:50 f.
3)	The Apostles in the Temple	24:52 f.

Luke, like Matthew and Mark, has followed the original fourfold gospel plan; but he has made two important changes in this order, and thus has given quite a different bias to his Gospel. By placing at the beginning the long Infancy-narrative (chaps. 1-2), which balances the Passion- and Resurrection-narratives, he has presented the story of Jesus in perfect equilibrium. By his insertion of the long section (Lk. 9:51–18:14), he has fitted cleverly into the Gospel narrative a very important collection of episodes and sayings which are entirely absent from Mark and only partially represented in Matthew. This Lucan section is dominated by the perspective of the passion: the journey to Jerusalem is seen as a journey to death (cf. Lk. 9:51; 13:22; 17:11). In Luke the story of Jesus falls into three parts:

1. From the Temple to the close of the Galilean ministry (Lk. 1:5–9:50).

2. The Journey from Galilee to Jerusalem (Lk. 9:51–19-27).

3. The last days of the Suffering and Risen Christ in Jerusalem (Lk. 19:28–24:53).

Thus, despite the general agreement with Matthew and Luke, the Third Gospel has a distinctive character. The main division is very clear, but it is not so easy to give a satisfactory arrangement of the details, and this is the reason the plan given above is rather complicated. It respects a complexity that really exists and does not seek to falsify the picture by oversimplification.

2) *The Sources*

It is universally recognized that Luke has used Mark as a source—indeed, that Mark is his chief source—and he has manifestly followed the order of Mark. We may put the relationship between them in schematic form.[5]

	Luke	Mark
Prologue	1-2	
A. In Galilee 3:1–9:50	3:1 — 6:19	→ 1:1–3:19 3:20-35
	6:20— 8:3	
	8:4 — 9:50	→ 4:1–6:44 + 8:27–9:40 6:45–8:26
B. To Jerusalem 9:51–19:27	9:51–18:14	
	18:15–19:27	→10:13-52
C. In Jerusalem	19:28–24:53	→11:1–16:8 (20)

[5]See X. Léon-Dufour, IB, p. 233.

The chief differences that meet the eye (apart from the omission of Mk. 6:45—8:26) are the additions made by Luke (6:20—8:3, and especially 9:51—18:14). It is instructive to see how this last section has, in fact, been inserted into the order of Mark. In Lk. 9:18—9:50 and Mk. 9:50—9:40, the sequence of events is: profession of faith by Peter; the Transfiguration; the epileptic; the second prediction of the passion; who is the greatest?; use of the name of Jesus. At this point Luke makes the insertion that comprises some nine chapters. At the end of it (Lk. 18:15) he takes up the plan of Mark again, almost where he had left off, so that in Lk. 18:15-43 and Mk. 10:13-52 the sequence is: Jesus and children; the rich young man; the danger of riches; detachment rewarded; the third prediction of the passion; the blind man at Jericho.

While it is undoubtedly, and indeed obviously, true that Luke follows Mark, he does not, by any means, merely reproduce his source. We may classify the changes he makes under the general headings of *Omissions, Additions and Retouches,* and *Transpositions.*[6] Many of these changes are due to the theological plan of Luke.

OMISSIONS   Lk. has omitted Markan passages which might not be understood by his readers, such as specifically Jewish matters (Mk. 7:1-23; 9:9-13; 10:1-12); or matters which might raise difficulties for them (Mk. 3:20 f.; 7:24-30; 11:12-14, 20-25; 6:45-52). Luke avoids Markan passages that occur in another context in his Gospel: Mk. 1:16-20 (Lk. 5:1-11); Mk. 3:22-30 (Lk. 11:14-23); Mk. 4:30-32 (Lk. 13:18-21); Lk. 6:1-6a (Lk. 4:16-30); Mk. 8:11-13 (Lk. 11:29-32); Mk. 9:42-48 (Lk. 17:1 f.); Mk. 9:49 (Lk. 14:34 f.); Mk. 10:35-45 (Lk. 22:24-27); Mk. 12:28-34 (Lk. 10:25-28). He also avoids the repetition of closely-related narratives; thus, he omits: the Parable of the Seed Growing Secretly (Mk. 4:26-29); Jesus walking on the waters (Mk. 6:45-52); the second multiplication of loaves (Mk. 8:1-10); the anointing at Bethany (Mk. 14:3-9); the first appearance before the Sanhedrin (Mk. 14:55-64); the episode of the wine mingled with myrrh (Mk. 15:23). Further omissions are motivated by reverence toward Jesus: passages in which his human sensibility appears to be too boldly expressed (Mk. 1:43; 3:5; 9:36;

---

[6]See E. Osty, *L'Évangile selon Saint Luc,* (BJ), pp. 10-18.

10:16, 21, 14; 14:33 f.); or where his knowledge seems to be limited (Mk. 13:32; 15:34); and, of course, Mk. 3:21. Similarly, the Apostles are spared by leaving aside the passages Mk. 4:13, 38; 5:31; 9:10, 28 f., 33 f.; 10:35-45; 14:50. In general, Luke omits the picturesque, but unessential, details of Mark's narrative. Finally, certain topographical data are omitted in view of the theological plan of the Gospel.

ADDITIONS AND   These are variously motivated by Luke's desire
RETOUCHES   for clarity and by his literary and religious sensibility. They include: Lk. 4:31; 5:1; 8:24; 19:37; 23:51 (geographical data); 6:15 (explanation of an Aramaic expression); 4:1, 40, 43; 8:18, 30 f., 53, 55; 9:9; 22:51, 69 (varied). Especially notable are Lk. 21:20, 24; see also 22:45, 47 f., 41. The favorite themes of Luke frequently make their appearance: Lk. 5:25; 18:43; 19:37; 23:47 (praise); 3:6–cf. Mk. 1:3–(universalism); Lk. 3:21; 6:12; 9:28; 23:34 (prayer); 5:11, 28; 14:26; 18:22, 29 (detachment); 4:14; 10:21; 11:13 (the Holy Spirit).

TRANSPOSITIONS   Again the motives are varied. The arrest of the Baptist (Lk. 3:19 f.; cf. Mk. 1:14; 6:17-20) emphasizes the fact that the Baptist now fades into the background. The expulsion from Nazareth (Lk. 4:16-30; cf. Mk. 6:1-6a), placed by Lk. at the beginning of the ministry, symbolizes Israel's rejection of Jesus. The call of the first disciples (Lk. 5:1-11), placed after the first miracles at Capharnaum—and not before as in Mk. 1:16-20—makes their immediate response more understandable. The introduction of the Sermon (Lk. 6:17-19) follows after the choice of the Twelve (cf. Mk. 3:7-19); hence, the discourse itself (Lk. 6:20-49) can follow immediately and naturally. In the Passion- and Resurrection-narrative (Lk. 22:1–24:53), the transpositions seem to assure a more correct literary presentation. The institution of the Eucharist is placed before the announcement of the betrayal and after the Jewish pasch (Lk. 22:14-23), in a logical order (cf. Mk. 14:17-25). The announcement of Peter's betrayal is placed at the Supper, after another admonition to the Apostles (Lk. 22:31-34), and not on the way to Gethsemane (Mk. 14:26-31). For the same reason, the question on precedence (cf. Mk. 10:42-44) and the recompense promised to the Apostles (cf. Mt. 19:28) have been added here (Lk. 22:24-30). The narrative of the arrest of Jesus (Lk. 22:47-53; cf. Mk. 14:43-50) has been rearranged in a better literary style.

These examples give, at this stage, an idea of Luke's freedom in regard to his sources. It should be noted, however, that, although Luke does follow Mark, there is room for qualification. Since both have made use of a Greek version of the Aramaic Gospel of Matthew,[7] it may be that some of the changes of Luke with respect to Mark are due to the order of the earlier source.

Another, and very important, source of Lk. comes to light when we analyze the long section Lk. 9:51—18:14, which has been inserted into the plan of Mark. In this part of his Gospel, Luke has grouped "under the sign of Jerusalem and the Passion," and in no strict chronological order, a great bulk of material which did not come to him via Mark or the Aramaic Gospel, whereas—and this is the significant point—many of these elements are found in Matthew also. The only reasonable explanation is that, besides Aramaic Matthew, another common (or partly common) source was known to Matthew and Luke. An analysis of Lk. 9:51—18:14 permits us to distinguish, apart from a large body of material peculiar to Luke: (1) elements common to Matthew and Luke and absent from Mark; (2) elements common to Matthew, Mark, and Luke.[8] With regard to (1): there are thirty-three of these elements, for the most part of only a few verses each and, in general, they are simple sayings (for example, Lk. 13:24 = Mt. 22:1-10; Lk. 10:13-15 = Mt. 11:21-23). It is noteworthy that the resemblances between Matthew and Luke in these passages are relatively more numerous than in passages common to all three synoptists. It is clear that, in these cases, Matthew and Luke follow a common source. The material under (2) is of greater significance, for here we have the question of doublets. By doublets we mean the passages—in most cases they consist of sayings—which are met with more than once in the same Gospel but in a different context. Some of these may be due to repetition, but many of them point to the use of different sources. An examination of these doublets leads to the conclusion that, as a rule, in the case of each doublet, the first form of the text appears in parallel passages of the tradition Mt.-Mk.-Lk., while the second form, never occurring in Mark, frequent in Matthew, and almost always present in Lk. 9:51—18:14, points to

---

[7]See pp. 111 f.
[8]See L. Vaganay, *Le Problème Synoptique* (Paris: Desclée, 1954), pp. 112-26.

a tradition common to Matthew and Luke. Some examples will clarify this statement. The saying, "If any man would come after me, let him deny himself and take up his cross and follow me," occurs in Mk. 8:34b; Mt. 16:24b; Lk. 9:23 after the first prediction of the Passion, and in Mt. 10:38; Lk. 14:27, in another context. The saying, "To him who has will more be given . . ." occurs in Mk. 4:25; Mt. 13:12; Lk. 8:18, after the Parable of The Measure, and in Mt. 25:29; Lk. 8:18, after the Parable of The Talents (Pounds, Lk.). The conclusion would seem to be inevitable: Mark has no doublet because it follows one source only; the agreement of Matthew and Luke, independently of Mark, postulates another and common source. The passages common to the two evangelists make up, primarily, a collection of sayings and parables; these Matthew has distributed throughout his Gospel, while Luke has grouped most of them in the long section under review. The three principal sources, then, of Luke are: Mark; a Greek translation of Aramaic Matthew; and the special source common (more accurately, in part common) to himself and Matthew.

But Luke is not confined to these. We know that he had ample time (the two years 58-60 A.D.) for personal research in Palestine; and not only his own prologue ("having followed all things closely for some time past"), but a study of his Gospel, afford proof that he did not waste his time. First of all there is the Infancy-narrative (chap. 1-2), which is proper to Luke and independent of Matthew's first two chapters. The coloring of Lk. 1-2 is highly Semitic; it has been suggested that this section is based on a Greek translation of an Aramaic source, while some contend that these chapters were first written in Hebrew. Perhaps the most satisfactory explanation is this: Luke may have had Aramaic sources, but he has written chapters 1-2 of his Gospel in a Greek that is modeled on the style of the LXX (Septuagint). These chapters, as they stand, are the work of Luke but, manifestly, he has followed a source of some sort. It is conceivable that Our Lady may have been his informant; the two references to her meditation on the things that concerned her Son (Lk. 2:19, 51) would seem to indicate as much. At any rate, most of the information must have come from her ultimately.

Not only in the Infancy-narrative but throughout his Gospel, Luke presents to us the fruits of his research. It is surprising to discover that much of what we had learned to take for granted is owed to Luke alone. For instance, the following lovely parables: The Prodigal Son; The Good Samaritan; The Pharisee and the Publican; and The Rich Man and Lazarus are found only in Luke. In the Passion- and Resurrection-narrative, the Third Gospel has many additions. It is a good idea to consider some of these in order to appreciate the extent of our debt. In Lk. 22:8, it is specified that "John and Peter" were the disciples sent to prepare for the Last Supper; and Lk. 22:15 f. tell us of our Lord's desire to celebrate that last Pasch with his disciples. In Lk. 22:35-38, he tells them of the hour of the decisive combat. Luke alone informs us of the sweat of blood at Gethsemane (Lk. 22:43 f.), and that Jesus healed the wound inflicted by Peter (Lk. 22:51). He alone tells of our Lord's appearance before Herod (Lk. 23:6-16), and of the daughters of Jerusalem who wept over Christ (Lk. 23:27-31). He alone speaks of the pardon of the "good thief" (Lk. 23:40-43). While the cry of dereliction on the Cross is not given in this Gospel, we find instead three other sayings of our Lord (Lk. 23:34, 43, 46). And after the resurrection, it is in Luke that we read the delightful episode of the disciples on the way to Emmaus (Lk. 24:13-35).

Luke shows certain affinities with John, notably, in the Passion- and Resurrection-narrative. He cannot have known John, and it is unlikely that John used Luke; yet, the contacts are there, numerous and varied. It seems that Lk. would have known the Johannine tradition before it had taken final shape in the Fourth Gospel.

Luke shows a curious complexity in his approach to his sources. He can, and does, follow the order of Mark very closely, while at the same time he fits it into a new plan. He can depart from that order when it suits him and make deliberate changes in it. Most important of all, he has had recourse to new sources and, indeed, the elements proper to Luke make up almost half of the work. These additions include especially the Infancy-narrative and the special source-section, but they also extend to many elements of the Passion- and Resurrection-narrative. The Infancy-narrative enables the evangelist to begin the history of Jesus with the annunciation of the birth of the Precursor. The central source-section is the treasury of Luke; there he has grouped the loveliest parables in the Gospels. And in the Passion- and Resurrection-narrative, as we have seen, the additions of the evangelist are of real importance. We have good reason to be grateful to St. Luke.

3) Language and Style

Luke has the best Greek style among the evangelists. Greek is certainly his mother tongue. St. Jerome testifies: *"Lucas . . . inter omnes evangelistas graeci sermonis eruditissimus fuit."*[9] He often avoids the literary faults he finds in his sources; he chooses more exact Greek words and he usually suppresses foreign words and expressions. It is true, however, that he does not carry out these improvements consistently; not infrequently, he reproduces his sources just as he finds them. This causes an unevenness in the style of the Gospel that is something of a mystery.[10] For instance, although he regularly corrects Mk., we find that the *metemorphōthē* of Mk. 9:2 becomes, in Lk. 9:29, *kai egeneto . . . to eidos tou prosōpou heteron.* More curious still, in Lk 9:42, *daimonion* replaces the Hebraistic *pneuma* of Mk. 9:20, but the verse then goes on to speak of *pneuma akatharton.* The problem which emerges is not so much Luke's paucity of Aramaisms and his frequency of Greek expressions in relation to Mark, as it is the inconstancy of his stylistic changes.

Although Luke has preserved traces of the Aramaic originals of his sources, as a rule he avoids Aramaisms and translates Aramaic words. For example, instead of "Rabbi" (Mk. 9:5; 10:51), he has "Master" (Lk. 9:33) and "Lord" (Lk. 18:41); and instead of "Abba" (Mk. 14:36), he has "Father" (Lk. 22:42). On the whole, although Aramaisms are less frequent than in Mark and Matthew, they are nonetheless more in evidence than is commonly suggested, and witness to the Semitic substratum of the Gospel.

On the other hand, true Hebraisms are found almost exclusively in Luke; for example, *egeneto . . . kai* (Lk. 5:12, 17; 8:1; 9:51; etc.); *eleusontai hēmerai* (Lk. 5:35; 17:22; 21:6; etc.); *kai idou* (Lk. 2:25; 5:12; 8:41; etc.); *enōpion* (Lk. 1:15, 19, 76; 12:6, 9; 15:6; etc.); *Hierousalēm* instead of the Grecized form *Hierosolyma.* The presence of these Hebraisms is almost certainly due to the influence of the LXX; it seems that Luke has consciously imitated the style of the

---

[9]Epist. 19, 4, *Ad Damasum; PL* 22:378.
[10]See X. Léon-Dufour, IB, pp. 231-33.

Greek Bible. This viewpoint is not infrequently contested, however, especially with regard to the Infancy-narrative.

An interesting feature of Luke's style is his habit of rounding off
one subject before passing on to another; it is a characteristic that
might easily lead to misinterpretation. When he says: "Mary remained with her about three months and returned to her home"
(Lk. 1:56), and goes on to tell of the birth of John, he does not
mean to imply that Mary had departed before this event; he merely
wanted to complete the episode of the Visitation before taking up
another matter. In chapter 3, he ends his account of the preaching
of the Baptist by stating that Herod had John cast into prison (Lk.
3:19 f.), and then immediately tells of the baptism of Jesus (Lk.
3:21 f.); in other words, he finishes what he has to say about the
ministry of John before going on to that of Jesus.

In the same way, he indicates well in advance matters that will
be dealt with later, thus ensuring the unity and flow of the narrative. In Lk. 1:80, he mentions the sojourn of the Baptist in the
desert, and later that it was in the desert that the divine call came
to him (Lk. 3:2). At the close of the temptations, the devil departed from Jesus "to return at the appointed time" (Lk. 4:13),[11]
that is to say, the hour of his arrest: ". . . this is your hour and the
power of darkness" (Lk. 22:53; cf. 22:3). In Lk. 8:2 f., we are told of
the women who accompanied our Lord on his journeys; these reappear, quite naturally, and with no need of any explanation of their
presence, as those who prepare the spices and ointments for the
body of Jesus (Lk. 23:55 f.). We may also consider Lk. 3:20 and
9:9; 5:33 and 11:1; 9:1-6 and 10:1; 9:9 and 28:8; 18:31 and 24:25 f.;
20:19 and 22:2; 20:25 and 23:2; 21:27 and 22:39.

It is certainly true that the author of the Third Gospel is the
most versatile of the New Testament writers. Left to himself, his
Greek is excellent, but it is less good when he wishes to be faithful
to his sources; and, lastly, he can imitate perfectly the style of the
LXX. The language and style of the Gospel reveal a Christian
who is familiar with the Old Testament and an author familiar with
the Greek literary style of his time. If the style of the Third Gospel is

---

[11]See E. Osty, (BJ), p. 49.

complex, it is, in great measure, because Luke is undoubtedly a poet. According to a late tradition, he was an artist: he is credited with the first painting of Our Lady. It is easy to see how the legend could have grown out of the word-picture he has drawn of her in his Infancy-narrative. And surely it is because of its poetic depth that the same story has inspired, dominated indeed, Christian art. Speaking still more broadly, we can scarcely realize how different our picture of Christmas would be without these chapters. At the other end of the Gospel, we find the delightful story of the two disciples and the unknown Traveler on the road to Emmaus, while in-between there is so much beauty. We should be thankful to St. Luke not only for the treasures he has searched out for us and so carefully preserved, but also for the artistry that went into the setting of these many pearls of great price.

4) The Method of Luke

Our quick glance at the language and style of Luke is hardly enough to give us an adequate idea of his literary skill; we must look more closely at the Gospel and examine certain passages in some detail. This is the most practical way—and the one that is likely to be the most profitable—of studying the method of Luke.

THE LITERARY   Luke's Infancy-narrative is composed in the
STRUCTURE OF LK. 1-2   form of a diptych; it has two phases: (1) before the births of John and of Jesus (Lk. 1:5-38); and (2) the accounts of the birth of both (Lk. 1:56—2:40). Each of these phases has a complementary episode: the Visitation (Lk. 1:39-56) in the first case, and the Finding (Lk. 2:41-52) in the other.[12] There are seven episodes in all.

1. *Diptych of Annunciations* (*Lk. 1:5-56*)

I. Annunciation of the Birth of John (Lk. 1:5-25)	II. Annunciation of the Birth of Jesus (Lk. 1:26-38)
Introduction of the parents	Introduction of the parents
Apparition of the angel	Entry of the angel
Zechariah troubled	Mary troubled
Fear not . . .	Fear not . . .
Annunciation of the birth	Annunciation of the birth

---

[12]See R. Laurentin, *Structure et Théologie de Luc 1-2* (Paris: Gabalda, 1957), pp. 32 f.

Q. How shall I know?
A. *Reprimand* by the angel
Constrained silence of Zecha-
riah
Departure of Zechariah

Q. How shall this be done?
A. *Revelation* by the angel
Spontaneous reply of Mary
Departure of the angel

III. Complementary episode 1:39-
56
Visitation
Conclusion: Return of Mary.

2. *Diptych of Births* (*Lk.* 1:57-2:52)

IV. Birth of John 1:57-58
Joy at the birth
with canticle element

V. Birth of Jesus 2:1-20
Joy at the birth
Canticle of angels and
shepherds.

Circumcision and Manifestation of John 1:59-79
Manifestation of the "Prophet"

VI. Circumcision and Manifestation of Jesus 2:21-35
Manifestation of the "Sav-
iour"

Canticle: *Benedictus*

Canticle: *Nunc Dimittis*
Supplementary episode:
Anna 36-38

Conclusion:
Refrain of growth 1:80

Conclusion
Refrain of growth 2:40

VII. Complementary episode 2:
41-52
The Finding in the Temple
Refrain of growth 2:52

A glance at this plan of the Infancy-narrative points up Luke's intention. John the Baptist and Jesus are compared and contrasted,
but the greatness of Jesus is emphasized even by the more-developed
account of his earthly origins. Within the parallel narratives, the same
point is made. Mary is clearly shown to be far superior to Zechariah
and, more explicitly, the Son of Mary is set on a pedestal and towers
above the son of Zechariah. The parent cell of these two chapters
is the infancy of Jesus and, more precisely, the Annunciation, while
the infancy of the Baptist is no more than a prelude, composed by
Luke, in order that the Messiah may be introduced by his Precursor
as in the primitive Gospel. It is obvious that these two chapters have
been constructed with great care; indeed, they offer a striking proof
of Luke's literary skill. Despite the artificial framework, there is
an air of spontaneity about them. The composition, although in fact
carefully studied, appears to be effortless; it is this quality that
separates art from anything less than art. These chapters are domi-

nated by the idea of messianic fulfillment. The different scenes build up to the climax of the entry into the Temple, for Luke saw in that event the formal manifestation of Jesus the Messiah. He has achieved his effect, in large measure, by his use of Dn. 9-10 in the annunciations to Zechariah and to Mary, and by his use of Mal. 3 in the annunciation to Zechariah, the Benedictus, and the Presentation. Taken together with the pregnant *eplēsthēsan* ("accomplished" [Lk. 1:23, 57; 2:6, 21 f.]), this use of messianic texts underlines the arrival of the messianic age. These chapters are a religious history written in the biblical manner. Reflecting on the facts, Luke has rethought them and has recounted them in terms of scriptural precedents; hence, there is a constant echoing of Scripture. This gives rise to what we may term an "allusive theology" that lies beneath the surface throughout, a wealth of meaning which has been overlooked by an exegesis that is philological and historical only.

When the chapters are read on this deeper level, the fact emerges that Luke has wished to present Jesus as a transcendent, divine Messiah. The titles given to him (Great, Holy, King, Light, Glory, Son of God, Savior, Christ the Lord, Lord), when taken together, point in that direction. In short, we may say that the assimilation of Jesus to Yahweh is "the final word of the Christology of Lk. 1-2."[13] We should note, too, that the transcendent dignity of Jesus sheds a reflected glow on Mary. As mother of the Messiah, she is the true daughter of Sion, where God has come to dwell among his people—a truth brought out by the use of Zeph. 3 and Mi. 4-5.

THE SERMON ON THE MOUNT[14]   Jesus formulated the special character of the kingdom of God in a discourse which Matthew (chaps. 5-7) and Luke (6:20-49) have preserved in widely-different versions. The original plan of the Sermon on the Mount can be found on page 149 above. In his Gospel, Matthew made considerable additions to the original Sermon, while Luke did quite the opposite and has omitted much of it. Luke sets aside the section regarding our Lord's attitude to the Law (Mt. 5:17-48) and the passage concerning

---

[13]*Ibid.*, p. 130.

[14]See J. Dupont, *Les Béatitudes* (Bruges: Abbaye de Saint-André, 1958²), pp. 43-204. See above, p. 147.

the Jewish works of piety. This is in perfect accordance with his method of adapting the Gospel for his Gentile readers.

In Luke, the discourse is introduced by the beatitudes and woes (Lk. 6:20b-26). Only a small part of the matter dealt with in the antitheses (of the Sermon) is included: the recommendations of the fifth and sixth antitheses of Matthew; but this is sufficient to prove that Luke had known the series of antitheses and had deliberately omitted all the rest. He has combined two sayings by introducing into the middle of the positive part of the sixth antithesis the corresponding part of the fifth:

Mt. 5:43-48	= Lk. 6:27-28	Lk. 6:32-36.
Mt. 5:39-42	=	Lk. 6:29-30

Lk. 6:27-36, then, becomes an instruction on the love of enemies. The whole section, beginning with the commandment, "Love your enemies" (v. 27a)—repeated in the conclusion (v. 35a)—is a unit that is rounded off by verse 36.

Lk. 6:37-42 also forms a unit. The warning not to pass judgment on others, the Parable of the Mote and the Beam, and the other elements, are all linked together. Here the question is no longer one of love of enemies (as in the foregoing passage), but of love of the brethren. The last part of the discourse (Lk. 6:43-49) regards the necessity of proving good dispositions in action, and the necessity of putting into effect the teaching one receives.

As a result of these changes, the plan of the discourse in Luke takes the following form:

INTRODUCTION: BEATITUDES AND WOES (6:20b-26)
PART I: LOVE OF ENEMIES (6:27-36)
PART II: FRATERNAL CHARITY (6:37-42)
CONCLUSION: NECESSITY OF GOOD WORKS (6:43-49)

Mainly because of the omissions, the discourse of Luke has a different character from that of Matthew. But it is also true that the omissions were motivated by Luke's outlook and, consequently, by his editorial emphasis. In this way, the Parable of the Two Trees (Lk. 6:43-44), instead of illustrating a warning against false prophets (Mt. 7:15), has become a recommendation addressed to the disciples. Similarly, in Lk. 6:32-34, the reference to "publicans and pagans" is omitted (cf. Mt. 5:46 f.), and the conduct of Christians is opposed to that of "sinners" in general. In brief, Luke opens up a wider perspective and detaches the teaching of Jesus from its Jewish background.

This lack of emphasis on opposition to traditional Judaism characterizes Luke's version of the Sermon. It shows how Luke's purpose is different from Matthew's when both report the original discourse. We can see that the original Sermon defined Christianity in terms of perfect righteousness and in terms of a religion that is more interior and purer than that of official Judaism. The additions which Matthew makes from other discourses of our Lord serve to underline the practical consequences of this teaching. Luke is concerned, rather, to emphasize the essential trait of that message: charity. It is around this theme of charity that the elements of the central section of Luke's discourse are grouped: the duty of loving one's enemies (Lk. 6:27-36); the obligations of fraternal charity (Lk. 6:37-42). It seems that Luke is far less interested in defining the spirit of Christianity than in pointing out the conduct which can give concrete expression to that spirit.

THE JOURNEY TO JERUSALEM, 9:51—19:46 We have seen that the long section (Lk. 9:51—18:14) has been inserted by Luke into the plan of Mark, which he follows so closely. The sayings and narratives of this section are grouped together and the whole is fitted into the framework of a journey to Jerusalem, a journey which ends at Lk. 19:46. On examination, it can be perceived that this arrangement is artificial.

It is a striking fact, for instance, that, although these chapters are supposed to describe a journey from Galilee, all topographical references to any other place except Jerusalem are suppressed.[15] The journey is explicitly indicated in Lk. 9:51: "When the days drew near for him to be received up [that is, out of this world] he set his face to go to Jerusalem." The Samaritans would not receive

---

[15]See X. Léon-Dufour, IB, pp. 238-40.

him "because his face was set toward Jerusalem" (Lk. 9:53), and so he went on to "another village" (Lk. 9:56). In Lk. 10:1, there is reference to "every town and place" where he was to go; and in Lk. 10:38, while on his way, he entered "a village." In Lk. 11:1, he prayed "in a certain place." In short, we may say with Father Lagrange: "In vain do we try to discover where he is; we know only that he is still in the land of Israel, because there is no indication that he has left it. Apart from references to Jerusalem, there is no indication of place; the scene is always just 'somewhere.'"[16]

In Lk. 13:22, we are again reminded of the goal: "He went on his way through towns and villages, teaching and journeying toward Jerusalem." When he was warned to get away "from here" (Lk. 13:31), he replied: "I must go on my way today and tomorrow and the day following; for it cannot be that a prophet should perish away from Jerusalem" (Lk. 13:33)—and he apostrophied the city (Lk. 13:34 f.). In Lk. 14:25, we read that "great multitudes" accompanied him; it is like a solemn procession.

A reference in Lk. 17:11 shows beyond doubt that the framework is artificial. Although he had begun his journey from Galilee in Lk. 9:51, and had been on his way ever since, we are now told: "On the way to Jerusalem he was passing between Samaria and Galilee." He is still at the starting place! In Lk. 18:31-33, he tells his Apostles plainly that this journey to Jerusalem is a journey to his death; from then on, the tempo speeds up remarkably; and other placenames appear to mark the final stages of the journey.

He drew near to Jericho (Lk. 18:35) and entered the town (Lk. 19:1). This was near the holy city (Lk. 19:11), and he went on ahead of the others, "going up to Jerusalem" (Lk. 19:28). He drew near to Bethphage and Bethany (Lk. 19:28) and came to the Mount of Olives (Lk. 19:37). He wept over the city that now at last lay before him (Lk. 19:41). Finally, he entered the Temple, his Father's house (Lk. 19:45 f.).

The intention of the evangelist is manifest: to present dramatically the last journey of Jesus to Jerusalem. The overall effect is striking, especially the mounting tension of the final chapters. Obviously, however, he used this same journey to frame, and to give a certain

---

[16]*Op. cit.*, p. xxxviii.

unity to, an important collection of sayings and parables. It is significant that we have to be reminded (Lk. 13:22 and 17:11) that there is a journey at all. This framework sets these sayings of our Lord in relief and gives them an added solemnity. And all the while the literary skill of Luke is in evidence.

5) The Author

THE MINISTER
OF THE WORD
1. *The historian.*[17] Luke's careful wording of his prologue and his dedication of the work to the "excellent Theophilus" introduce a work that does not purport merely to tell us about the Good News; his object is to establish the soundness of the catechetical teaching; for this reason, his express intention is to weigh his sources. In view of this, he shows care in presenting historical data. By the detailed synchronisms prefixed to his narrative of the birth of Jesus (Lk. 2:1-3) and of the ministry of John (Lk. 3:1 f.), he sets these events in the framework of general history. On occasion, he can correct the chronology of his sources. Thus, while in Mark we are told that the Transfiguration took place six days after Peter's profession of faith at Caesarea Philippi (Mk. 9:2), Luke quietly modifies the statement and says: ". . . about eight days after" (Lk. 9:28); and he regularly qualifies round numbers by adding "about" (Lk. 1:56; 3:23; etc.). He speaks of Herod as "tetrarch," his correct title (Lk. 9:7), and not, as he was popularly described, as "king" (Mk. 6:14). Similarly, he speaks of the "lake of Gennesareth" (Lk. 5:1) rather than of the "sea of Galilee" (Mk. 1:16). He mentions contemporary facts: the massacre of Galileans by Pilate (Lk. 13:1-3), and the fall of the tower of Siloam (Lk. 13:4 f.). In this same spirit, he has had recourse to new sources.

We may not, however, judge the work of Luke as we would that of a modern historian; his Gospel is not scientific history, nor is it, any more than Matthew and Mark, a biography of Jesus. Even though he has retouched his sources in this respect, he has scarcely anything of the modern passion for precise chronology and detailed topography. He is interested in historical facts, but he does not have our regard for "history." If he does promise to write an "orderly account," that order is primarily theological, for his concern is with

---

[17]See Vaganay, *op. cit.*, pp. 263-67.

the things delivered by those who were not merely eyewitnesses of events but "ministers of the word" (Lk. 1:2).

2. *The evangelist.* Luke himself is first and foremost a "minister of the word," an evangelist;[18] and his work is, in the strict sense, a "gospel." This is why he has remained faithful to the general plan of Mark, the consecrated plan of the apostolic kerygma. For, in the New Testament itself, the word "gospel" means the *preaching* of Christ, and the evangelist is a *preacher* (Acts 21:8; Eph. 4:11; 2 Tm. 4:5). When, in the second century, *euaggelion* came to designate the written account of the life and teaching of our Lord, these writings were still regarded as filling a missionary need and served the same purpose as the spoken word: to waken and to strengthen faith (cf. Jn. 20:31). Similarly, the evangelist is also a preacher; behind him stands the whole teaching activity of a living Church; of that Church he is a spokesman. His work is kerygmatic, in the proper sense of that overworked term: to herald Jesus Christ, his works and words. And because this is so, an evangelist has, necessarily, a care for the historical and a certain biographical interest: the Good News that he preaches is all concerned with a Person who lived and moved among men and taught them, a Man who died at a given time and place, and rose from the dead. The person of Jesus, seen and interpreted in the light of the resurrection, is the very center of *Heilsgeschichte;* and the presentation of his words and deeds is necessarily theological. While Luke, no doubt because of his Greek background, is somewhat more meticulous than the other synoptists about historical data, his intention remains, fundamentally, kerygmatic and theological.

THE PURPOSE To appreciate the overall purpose of Luke one must
OF LUKE take his second work into consideration. Then, one can see that his object is to present the definitive phase of God's saving intervention, from the birth of the Baptist to the proclaiming of the Gospel in the capital of the Gentile world. His theme is the progress of the Good News from Jerusalem to Rome; it is above all a message of salvation to the Gentiles. Simeon had seen in Christ "a light for revelation to the Gentiles" (Lk. 2:32); Paul's last words

---

[18]See X. Léon-Dufour, IB, p. 240.

ta the Roman Jews are: "Let it be known to you then that the salvation of God has been sent to the Gentiles: they will listen" (Acts 28:28).

All of this follows, in the plan of God, on Christ's rejection by Israel, for that rejection led to his death and exaltation and to universal salvation (Lk. 24:46 f.). "Thus it is written, that the Christ should suffer and on the third day rise from the dead, and that repentance and forgiveness of sins should be preached in his name to all nations, beginning from Jerusalem" (Lk. 24:46 f.). It is indeed a constant (theological) preoccupation of the evangelist to center his whole Gospel around Jerusalem, because, for him, Jerusalem is the holy city of God and the theater of the great redemptive event, the passion and triumph of Christ. In Jerusalem, the Gospel begins (Lk. 1:5), and in Jerusalem it closes (Lk. 24:52 f.). The Infancy-narrative has two significant entries into the holy city (Lk. 2:22-38, 41-50). It is this same interest that explains why, unlike the natural climax of Matthew (Mt. 4:3-10), the culminating temptation of our Lord in Luke is at the pinnacle of the Temple (Lk. 4:9-12). The long central section (Lk. 9:51—18:14) is presented as a journey to Jerusalem and, to heighten the effect, all other place names are omitted. The journey outside of Galilee (Mk. 6:45—8:26) is not given, and Caesarea Philippi is not named as the place of Peter's profession of faith (Lk. 9:18-22). It is this concern too that explains why Luke has no mention of an apparition of Christ in Galilee. Jesus had come to Jerusalem and there had suffered and died and risen from the dead, and it was from Jerusalem that he was to ascend, finally, into heaven; a departure from the holy city would, in Luke's plan, be an anticlimax. And, consistently, when he came to write his second book, he took care to show the Christian message radiating from that same center: "You shall be my witnesses in Jerusalem and in all Judaea and Samaria and to the ends of the earth" (Acts 1:8).

Luke, we have seen, is an evangelist rather than an historian; here we may go further and describe him as a theologian of salvation-history. For him, that *Heilsgeschichte* falls into three periods: (1) the period of Israel; (2) the period of Christ; (3) the period of the Church. The Old Testament is the time of preparation for the culminating event of Christ's coming: "The law and the prophets were until John; since then the good news of the kingdom of God is preached" (Lk. 16:16). Yet, even though this is true, the period of Christ is pre-eminently that of his ministry; and the time since the Ascension is that of the Church, looking back to the period of Christ and forward to the Parousia. In this perspective, the Ascension, followed by the sending of the Spirit, is more the beginning of Acts than the close of Luke.[19]

All this is more understandable, and the outlook of Luke is clearer, if we see it in a wider perspective. In the Old Testament view, the midpoint of time is marked by the future coming of the Messiah. For Christians, this is no longer so: the midpoint of time is now in the past, in the historical life and work of Jesus Christ. There is another difference. For Christians, the midpoint of time does not coincide with the Parousia (as it did in the Old Testament perspective); there is a space of time between Christ and the Parousia. These factors account for a certain tension that we find throughout the New Testament writings. There is still an expectation, a looking to the future, as there was in the Old Testament, but that future event (the Parousia) is no longer the center of salvation-history; that center is found in an historical event. The New Testament outlook is based on "the thoroughly *positive* conviction that the mighty Christ-event has given a new center to time, and so it roots in the faith that the fulfillment has already taken place, that it is no longer the Parousia but rather the Cross and the resurrection of Christ that constitute the middle point and meaning of all that occurs."[20] Luke, in his Gospel, is concerned with that midpoint of salvation-history, the Christ-event, which he sees as the climax of the preceding period of Israel. In Acts, he deals with the opening moments of the time between the great saving event and the Parousia, the period of the Church.

3. DOCTRINE

1) *Universalism*

Luke wrote his Gospel for the Gentile Church; hence, he stressed the universal import of the Good News. This intention is already

---

[19]See H. Conzelmann, *The Theology of Saint Luke*, trans. Geoffrey Buswell (New York: Harper & Row, 1960), pp. 13-17, 202-6.

[20]See O. Cullmann, *Christ and Time* (Philadelphia: Westminster Press, 1964), pp. 81-86.

present in the Infancy-narrative, despite its marked Semitic character. It is expressed in the canticle of the angels ("peace among men with whom he is pleased" [Lk. 2:14]), and Simeon saw that the Child would be a light to the Gentiles. In his genealogy of Jesus, Luke does not stop at Abraham (as Matthew does), but goes back to Adam, the father of all men. The Baptist, in his preaching, cites the prophecy of Isaiah: "All flesh shall see the salvation of God" (Lk. 3:6; cf. Is. 40:5); Lk. 2:30-32 refers to another universalist text of Second Isaiah (Is. 52:10). Jesus' charge to the Twelve not to go among the Gentiles or Samaritans (Mt. 10:5 f.) is not recorded by Luke; indeed, Jesus sought hospitality in a Samaritan village (Lk. 9:52). A Samaritan is found among the ten lepers healed by Jesus—the only one who returns to give thanks (Lk. 17:11-19). One of the most striking parables is The Good Samaritan, with its lesson that all barriers fall before the demands of love (Lk. 10:30-37). The Jews are warned that they will be supplanted at the Messianic Feast by men from every land. And the last commission of the Risen Lord is that the Gospel should be preached to all nations (Lk. 24:47; cf. Mt. 28:19 f.).

Apart from these clear pointers, the universalist bearing of the Gospel is also indicated by several deft touches which open up a wider perspective than the original Palestinian one. The Pharisees tithe not only mint and rue but "every herb" (Lk. 11:42; cf. Mt. 23:23); not only the fig tree (Mk. 13:28) but "all the trees" (Lk. 21:29) herald summer. In the parable of The Two Builders (Lk. 6.47-48; Mt. 7:24-27), Luke has wholly changed the details so that the story might be readily intelligible to his non-Palestinian readers. The omissions and explanations we have noted have the same effect: the Gospel for all men is presented in a way that all men can understand.

2) *The Influence of St. Paul*

We are assured that Luke was a disciple of St. Paul, and the influence of Paul can indeed be traced in the Third Gospel. This is not so much a matter of vocabulary (although there are resemblances) or of traditions (although in the account of the institution of the Eucharist [Lk. 22:19 f.; 1 Cor. 11:23-25] both follow a similar tradition) as a common atmosphere of thought and sentiment. Both, for example, insist on the theme of the universality of salvation (Lk. 2:30 f.; 3:23, 38; 13:28 f.; 14:23; 24:46 f.; Rm. 1:16; 1 Tm. 2:4;

Ti. 2:11). This is not to say that the other Synoptics do not make it clear that salvation is offered to all men (and not to the Jews only), but rather that it is more emphatically the view of Luke as it is of Paul.

The atmosphere of joy that we have noted in Luke is like that of the Pauline Epistles. In both we find frequent invitations to serve the Lord in thanksgiving and joy (Lk. 5:25 f.; 10:17; 18:43; 19:37; 24:52 f.; Phil. 4:4; 1 Thes. 5:16; Rm. 12:12; etc.). In both we find the same pressing exhortation, by word and example, to have recourse to prayer (Lk. 3:21; 5:16; 6:12; 9:18, 28 f.; 11:1-13; 18:1-5, 9-14; 22:32; 33:34, 46; 1 Thes. 5:17; Col. 4:2; Eph. 6:18; Phil. 1:3-6; etc.), and the same manner of indicating the action of the Holy Spirit on the conduct of life (Lk. 3:16, 22; 4:1, 14, 18; 10:21; 11:13; 12:10, 12; 24:49; Gal. 3:2-5, 13 f.; 5:22; 1 Cor. 6:11; 12:13; 2 Thes. 2:13; Rm. 8:2, 9; 14:17, etc.).

Luke, alone among the synoptists, gives Christ the title *Kyrios* (Lk. 7:13, 19; 10:1, 39, 41; 11:39; 12:42; 13:15; 16:8; 17:5 f.; 18:6; 19:8; 22:61; 24:3, 34). In the LXX, "Yahweh" was rendered *kyrios*, and the early Christians, from the first, gave this same divine title to Christ. For us, "Lord" has lost its specific meaning, but the definite signification it had in the primitive Church is brought out by such texts as these: "If you confess with your lips that Jesus is Lord . . . you will be saved" (Rm. 10:9); and "every tongue should confess that Jesus Christ is Lord" (Phil. 2:11); in both cases the divinity of Christ is professed. When Luke uses the title, he is writing as a Christian firm in his faith, and hence applies this Christian title to the Savior; for Jesus was not addressed as "Lord," in this full sense, during his lifetime.

It is not necessarily the influence of Paul only that has moved the evangelist to use the title "Lord" so frequently; for many of the concepts in the Epistles go back beyond Paul to the primitive tradition. Such are the divine Sonship of Jesus, the universality of salvation, and the importance of faith as a condition of entry into the kingdom of God. It is precisely these, and similar, ideas that we find in Luke, and not as part of the preaching of the Apostle, but as they figured in his own written sources. Doubtless, in reproducing these concepts, he was influenced by the teaching and expressions of his master. But, despite his origin and his education, despite his close contact with Paul, despite the Gentile-Christian readers to whom his Gospel is addressed, Luke reproduced, substantially, the primitive catechesis, the tradition of the apostolic Church.[21]

[21]For a fuller treatment of the doctrine of Lk. see Wilfrid J. Harrington, *Explaining the Gospels* (New York: Paulist Press, 1963), pp. 117-23.

| *The Acts of the Apostles*

1. THE BOOK

1) The Author

In his preface, the author of Acts presents his writing as the continuation of a single work addressed to Theophilus (Acts 1:1; cf. Lk. 1:3). A consideration of the theme of both volumes and of the close similarity of style and vocabulary bears out the obvious meaning of the preface. The title of the work, "Acts of the Apostles," or "Acts of Apostles," adequately describes a book that forms a sequel to the "Acts and Words of Jesus" (cf. Acts 1:1)—the Gospel. The designation "Acts" was common enough as a description of the deeds of prominent men. It is not quite clear how "Apostles" is to be understood. On the one hand, some of those who figure here, such as Barnabas, Stephen, Philip, and Apollos, are not Apostles, and Paul himself is not one of the Twelve. On the other hand, although the Twelve figure as a group in the opening chapters, most of the Twelve are not named. The writing, in fact, records the acts of two outstanding Apostles, Peter and Paul, and even here the events are incomplete. But then, as we shall see, Acts is not meant to be a biography of Peter and Paul.

Ancient tradition is unanimous in attributing Acts to Luke, the author of the Third Gospel. Irenaeus, for instance, assigns the Book to him and emphasizes its trustworthiness. The Muratorian Canon makes the same attribution and adds that Luke was present at the events he relates (an obvious reference to the "we-passages"). The Anti-Marcionite Prologue of the Third Gospel also asserts that Luke wrote Acts after the Gospel. In short, then, from the time of Irenaeus onward the Book has been regularly attributed to Luke; internal evidence supports the attribution. Having accepted the "we-passages" at their face value, we have already seen[1] what they, and some passages from the Pauline Epistles, can tell us about the person of Luke.

2) Date

We have dealt above[2] with the view that sets the writing of Acts before the end of Paul's first Roman imprisonment. This view is based on the apparently abrupt ending of the Book; it finds some support in Eusebius. However, the Anti-Marcionite Prologue and the Muratorian Canon put the composition of the work after Paul's death. The oldest view throughout the Church holds that Luke wrote Acts, in Achaia, some time after Paul's death (c. 67 A.D.). Furthermore, the arguments for the dating of the Third Gospel are relevant here since Acts, as its sequel, must have come afterward. If the Gospel were written before 70 A.D. then Acts would also, quite reasonably, come before that date. But since it is possible that the Gospel was written in the decade 70-80 A.D., the possible composition of Acts in the same decade must be allowed for. However, the writing of Acts cannot be placed too late, since it shows no acquaintance with the Pauline Epistles. The author of the whole work, who so explicitly expresses his intention of doing careful research (Lk. 1:1-4), could not have passed over these important sources for the second part of Acts.

3) Purpose and Scope

Since Acts is the second volume of one work, it cannot be understood except as a continuation of Luke's Gospel; it is more correctly seen as a sequel to the Gospel than as a history of the primitive Church. After his account of the infancy of John and of Jesus, Luke turns to the preaching of the kingdom of God in Palestine, first by the Precursor and then by the Messiah; and at the end of his work

---

[1] See p. 170.
[2] See pp. 171 f.

he has Paul proclaiming the same kingdom at the center of the Roman world. The Gospel tells of the mission of Jesus and of the saving event of his death and resurrection; it ends with his glorification in the ascension. Jesus had come as the Messiah of his people and had found himself rejected by them. But his mission had not failed: he had brought salvation to a new Israel—repentance and forgiveness of sins must be preached in his name to all nations, beginning from Jerusalem (Lk. 24:47).

> The Gospel is not only the proclamation that the messianic promises of God are fulfilled in Jesus, but also the declaration that through his saving work Israel has been reconstituted; though the leaders of the covenant people rejected first Jesus and then his apostles, Israel has been given a new structure by the operation of the Spirit through the apostolic mission. . . . This re-creation of Israel is made possible because God has vindicated and exalted his Messiah. . . . The glorification of Jesus in the Ascension is thus the decisive turning-point of Luke's work, but it is by no means the end of his story; it demonstrates that Jesus is Lord and Messiah, but it remains for Luke to tell how the people of the Messiah was brought into being out of the faithful among the Jews and out of Samaritans and Gentiles.[3]

Given the close relationship between Gospel and Acts, we are not surprised to find that the composition of both runs along parallel lines.[4] The narrative of the ministry of Jesus is formed of two more or less equal parts: the first, covering the preaching in Galilee, centers in the Twelve and ends with the mission confided to the Twelve; it is very like the accounts of Matthew and Mark. The other part, the journey to Jerusalem, begins with the mission charge to the Seventy and has material not found in Matthew and Mark. Similarly, Acts has two parts: one in which Peter has the leading role, and which looks to Jerusalem; the second, centered in Paul, breaks out of this geographical framework and turns toward Rome. In following this plan, Luke had to strike a compromise between a systematic procedure and one which arose from the organization of the sources he followed. This causes—and explains—an unevenness in the composition.

In Acts, Luke is concerned with showing the triumphal progress of the Gospel throughout the whole known world. The plan of his

---

[3]G. W. H. Lampe, PCB, n. 772 b.
[4]See L. Cerfaux, IB, p. 340.

work is dictated by the commission of the Risen Christ to his disciples: "You shall be my witnesses in Jerusalem and in all Judaea and Samaria and to the end of the earth" (Acts 1:8). He is especially interested in the passing of the preaching from the Jews to the Gentiles and in the progress of the Gentile mission. Behind the continuous progress of the Good News through the provinces of the Roman Empire, he sees the power of the Holy Spirit. Indeed, the theme of his book may be expressed in this manner: "Acts depicts the universal spread of the Christian religion as it was begun and maintained by the power of the Holy Spirit."[5]

It is necessary, then, that the origin of the Gentile mission and its spread should be marked by the divine guidance. In view of this, it is not surprising to learn that the missionary activity was born of persecution: after the martyrdom of Stephen, the Hellenists fled to Samaria and elsewhere, but continued to preach the Gospel. It was a divine revelation that led Peter to baptize the Gentile household of Cornelius, an event of great significance for the future of the Church. Saul was dramatically confronted by the Risen Lord in person, and this former persecutor of Christians was transformed into the great Apostle of the Gentiles. Under his leadership, the mission penetrated Asia Minor and, at a later date, Europe; and he who had been set apart by the Spirit (Acts 13:2) continued to be divinely guided (Acts 16:6-10). The sufferings of Paul, his trial and imprisonment, were providential (Acts 20:22 f.); and storm and shipwreck offered no hindrance to the design of God (Acts 27:23 f.). In Rome, following his constant practice, Paul preached first to the Jews; when they rejected the Gospel, he turned to the Gentiles, confident that they would accept it (Acts 28:23-28). Thus, the book ends, its purpose achieved. The word had gone forth from Jerusalem to the end of the earth for, in the capital of the world, Paul was "preaching the kingdom of God and teaching about the Lord Jesus Christ quite openly and unhindered" (Acts 28:31).

Luke was aware that the Gentile mission had been set on foot before Paul began to play his part, and he knew that Paul was not the only architect of the Gentile Church. But, since his purpose was to portray the progress of the Church, he could not have chosen

_____
[5]A. Wikenhauser, *Die Apostelgeschichte* (Regensburg: Pustet, 1956³), p. 7.

a more effective and dramatic way of doing so, and it is typical of the genius of Luke that he should have gone about it in this way. For it is true that Paul the missioner and Paul the theologian has set his stamp on Christianity for all time. The alleged antithesis between the religion of Jesus and the religion of Paul is based on a complete misunderstanding of the teaching of both; but the fact that Paul could be put forward, with some plausability, as the real founder of Christianity (or as the great perverter of the Gospel of Jesus) is an indication of his stature. That stature Luke has perceived. When he had written the acts of Jesus, culminating in the great saving event, he turned to the emergence of a new Israel; then, after his "Infancy-narrative" of the Church, he went on to trace its progress in the "Acts of Paul." Just as Christianity is grateful to him for his strikingly beautiful portrait of Jesus, it is also grateful for his portrait of Paul.

Luke appears to have had a certain apologetical purpose, at least when he turns his attention to the work of Paul. Important Roman officials (Sergius Paulus, Gallio) attest that the Apostle's preaching is not a danger to the State. Felix and Festus (as well as Agrippa II) do not find Paul guilty of a capital charge, or of any charge. The centurion Julius, to whom he had been committed as a prisoner, treated Paul with great consideration. The latter's appeal to Caesar's tribunal had saved him from assassination at the hands of the Jews; and in Rome, until the statutory two years had elapsed, he was held under a remarkably lenient form of house arrest (Acts 28:30 f.). The whole presentation has the effect of underlining the political harmlessness of the Christian religion: a matter of moment for the preaching of the Gospel in Rome and throughout the Empire. This was all the more necessary in view of Jewish attempts to present the new religion as a political danger. Nevertheless, the apologetical interest is never more than a secondary theme.

4) The Text

Acts has come to us in two different text forms. The text that figures in critical editions of the New Testament is of the Alexandrian or Neutral type, represented by B S A C, P[45]; while another form is represented by D, Old Latin, Syriac and Latin Fathers—

the "Western" type. Although it has been argued that both recensions stem from Luke himself—the Western text is a first draft, which later was given the more polished form of the Alexandrian text—this undoubtedly oversteps the evidence. Yet, the view does indicate that the differences are notable. In general, the Western text tends to be more verbose. Although, in the past, its readings have been discounted, it is generally agreed today that a critical edition of Acts must take account of the Western additions and weigh them carefully on their merits. Some of the more interesting readings of the Western text, which could well be authentic, are the following: before the baptism of the Ethiopian: "And Philip said, 'If you believe with all your heart, you may.' And he replied, 'I believe that Jesus Christ is the Son of God'" (Acts 8:37); concerning Peter and the angel: ". . . they descended the seven steps" (Acts 12:10); Paul occupied the hall of Tyrannus "from the fifth hour to the tenth" (Acts 19:9); Gaius "of Doberus"—and not of Derbe (Acts 20:4); a halt between Samos and Miletus, "after remaining at Trogyllium" (Acts 20:15); on arriving in Rome, "the centurion handed over the prisoners to the camp commander" (Acts 28-16).

2. THE LITERARY CONSTRUCTION OF ACTS

1) The Plan

INTRODUCTION (1:1-11)		
A.	I.	THE JERUSALEM CHURCH (1:12—5:42)
	II.	THE FIRST MISSIONS (6—12)
	III.	BARNABAS AND PAUL (13:1—15:35)
B.	IV.	THE MISSION OF PAUL (15:36—19:20)
	V.	THE PRISONER OF CHRIST (19:21—28:29)
EPILOGUE (28:30 f.)		

2) Analysis

Acts, as we have seen, falls into two main parts. At the beginning of his second missionary journey (Acts 15:36), we find Paul, officially recognized as Apostle of the Gentiles, embarking on work that is truly his own. From this point on, the Book may be regarded as the narrative of a journey which leads from Antioch to Rome (compare the analogous journey to Jerusalem in Lk. 9:51–19:46). The first part of Acts does not have the same marked coherency; rather, it is more like a mosaic of varied episodes, all serving to illustrate the progress of Christianity.

A brief prologue (Acts 1:1 f.) indicates that Acts forms one work with the Gospel and recalls the dedication of the whole to Theophilus. In Acts 1:3-11, the ending of the Gospel (Lk. 24:13-53) is resumed, thus linking the volumes. (For Old Testament parallels, compare Jos. 24:28-31 and Jg. 2:6-9; 2 Chr. 36:22 f. and Ez. 1:1-3a.)

I. Acts 1:12–2:41: after the ascension, the Eleven, together with other disciples and "Mary the mother of Jesus," assembled regularly in the supper room; Matthias was chosen to replace Judas. The coming of the Holy Spirit at Pentecost transformed the Twelve and marked the emergence of the Church into the light of day. Peter's discourse stressed Jesus' fulfillment of Scripture—a distinctive feature of kerygma.[6] The first converts were baptized.

Acts 2:42–5:42: a summary statement sketches the life of the primitive community. This is followed by an account of the miracles and teaching of the Apostles; the people react favorably, but the Sanhedrin seeks to quell the movement. Two further summary statements describe the life of the first Christians.

II. Acts 6:1–8:3: with the appointment of the deacons, especially with the preaching of Stephen, the Hellenists come to the fore. Stephen is the first victim of a persecution; in his discourse before the Sanhedrin, he asserts that Christians are not tied to Jewish observances. The scattered Hellenist converts become the first Christian missionaries.

Acts 8:4-40: the story of Philip: evangelization of Samaria and conversion of the Ethiopian eunuch.

---

[6]See p. 214.

Acts 9:1-30: conversion and vocation of Saul.

Acts 9:31—11:18: Peter's tour of inspection of the communities along the Palestinian coast led to his reception of the centurion Cornelius, together with his household.

Acts 11:19-30: the founding of a community at Antioch; Barnabas and Saul are active there.

Acts 12: persecution of the Jerusalem community by Herod Agrippa I: James, brother of John, is beheaded; Peter is imprisoned but miraculously released; Agrippa dies at Caesarea.

III. Acts 13-14: Barnabas and Paul are sent out as missionaries by the Antiochian community and evangelize Cyprus and southern Galatia.[7]

Acts 15:1-35: the apostolic assembly at Jerusalem decided that Gentile converts were not to be subjected to the Mosaic Law. Paul henceforth was free to devote himself to—and spend himself in— the mighty task for which the Risen Christ had chosen him. A new era begins and the second part of Acts opens.

IV. Acts 15:36—18:22: departing from Antioch, Paul and Silas journeyed through Asia Minor (they were joined at Lystra by Timothy) to Troas and thence to Macedonia. Paul eventually reached Corinth, the most important stage on the journey, and later returned from there to Antioch.

Acts 18:23—19:20: very soon, Paul set out through Asia Minor again. This time he reached Ephesus, capital of the province of Asia, where he spent some two years.

V. Acts 19:21 f.: during his stay at Ephesus, Paul had worked out his plans for the future; the laconic statement given here may be filled out from the Epistles: Gal. 2:10; 1 Cor. 16:1-4; 2 Cor. 8:1-5; Rm. 15:25-28; cf. Acts 24:17. His idea was to bring to Jerusalem the proceeds of a great collection made in all the churches; this would serve to forge a bond between Gentile Christians and the Jerusalem community. After that, he could, with a light heart, embark on more ambitious projects: to preach the Gospel in Rome itself, and, beyond Rome, in Spain, the western limit of the world.

---

[7]For an account of the journeys of St. Paul see pp. 60-67.

Acts 19:23–21:26: shortly after the riot of the silversmiths, Paul left Ephesus; he visited Macedonia and moved on to Corinth. After a stay of three months he set out for Jerusalem—overland to Philippi (where he was joined by Luke) and thence by sea to Caesarea. At Jerusalem he was received by James.

Acts 21:27–28:29: the implacable hatred of the Hellenistic Jews finally caught up with Paul. His rescue by the tribune Claudius Lysias led to two years of imprisonment in Caesarea; then to a further two years in Rome, after he had appealed to the imperial tribunal.

Acts 28:30 f.: the plan of God is not thwarted by human factors. Paul had got to Rome, as he had wished (not only as he had wished but as God had designed: Acts 23:11; 27:24); and there, quite openly and unhindered, he bore witness to Christ.

3) The Sources

In the prologue to the first volume of his work (Lk. 1:1-4), Luke has candidly admitted his reliance on sources. A study of his Gospel has enabled us to discern some of them.[8] It is a priori certain that, in Acts, he has also made constant use of sources, but here there are no parallel writings (like the other Synoptic Gospels) to aid in the search. The problem of the sources of Acts is an involved one; for our purpose, we will rely largely on a recent and admirable survey of the question.[9] In our source-study we shall find it convenient (indeed necessary) to take the two parts of Acts separately.

ACTS 1:12–15:35   The Semitic coloring of the first part of the book (in particular chaps. 1-12) is undoubted. Thus, it seems possible to posit an original Aramaic source, perhaps reaching all the way to Acts 15:35. According to this view, these chapters are the Greek translation, clumsy in places, of an Aramaic writing; but the theory does not take account of Semitisms that come from a Hebrew rather than an Aramaic background and which show the influence of the LXX on Luke's style. On the other hand, it does point to the Aramaic origin of much of the material in the early

---

[8]See pp. 175-81.
[9]See J. Dupont, *The Sources of Acts,* trans. Kathleen Pond (London: Darton, Longman, & Todd, 1964).

chapters. Many attempts have been made to explain considerable portions of chapters 1-12 as the combination or juxtaposition of two parallel sources, but no delineation of the sources has stood up to penetrating criticism.

Some have seen in Acts 2:41—5:40 a basic source, a single descriptive document, emanating from the community in Jerusalem. Other traditions have been linked with Caesarea (Acts 1:15—2:40; 8:1b-13, 26-40; 9:1-30; 9:31—10:48), and Acts 1:1-14 has been regarded as a Galilean tradition. Nowadays, because of the contribution of Form Criticism, scholars are loath to posit the existence of clearly-defined written documents; it is found preferable to speak of traditions, or of a varied documentation on which Luke has built his narrative. It must always be kept in mind, too, that Luke has put his personal stamp on the material and that his whole work shows signs of considerable editorial activity.

Yet, although the sources must be envisaged in a more elastic manner, and although Luke's freedom of composition must be respected, it still seems possible to discern the presence of written sources.[10] Also to be observed is the fact that Luke has proceeded by stages: he wrote passages which he has later on fitted into his general plan by way of insertion or by means of link-passages. When, however, such a fragment is singled out, it must be seen as a passage already edited by Luke; we cannot put our finger on the basic document as such.

The account of the first missionary journey seems a good example of a passage that has been artificially inserted into a redactional framework, for it can be shown that Acts 12:25 and Acts 15:1 f. are link-verses, anchoring the passage in its present context. It is not difficult to see that Acts 11:27-30 plus Acts 15:3-33 was originally a coherent narrative of the journey of Barnabas and Saul to Jerusalem, with an account of the discussion that followed their arrival, and their subsequent return to Antioch. This narrative is now interrupted by Acts 12:1-23 which stands apart as a special Palestinian source, and by the Pauline tradition (Acts 13-14). Since this last describes a journey which began and ended in Antioch,

---

[10]See P. Benoit, "La deuxième visite de St. Paul à Jérusalem," *Biblica*, 40 (1959), 778-92.

the editor, in combining the sources, had to have Paul and Barnabas back in Antioch for the beginning of the missionary journey and had to give a reason for their going up to Jerusalem again; this he managed by the addition of Acts 12:25 and Acts 15:1 f. Strict chronology has yielded to reasons of literary composition.[11]

It follows that Acts 11:27-30 does not describe a journey distinct from that of chapter 15, for the passages, now separated, were originally one narrative. This fact is important for ironing out an apparent discrepancy between Acts 15 and Gal. 2:1-10. In the actual form of Acts, the journey of chapter 15 appears to be Paul's third visit to Jerusalem, after his conversion; therefore, it cannot be the second visit of Gal. 2. But, if Acts 11:27-30 does not really refer to another journey (distinct from that of chapter 15), then Acts 15 and Gal. 2 do treat of the same second visit. Acts 15:1 f. is redactional; in Jerusalem, the whole question of circumcision came to a head (Acts 15:5; Gal. 2:4). Paul and Barnabas had come to the city, after their return from the missionary journey, to carry alms to the famine-stricken poor (Acts 11:29 f.; cf. Gal. 2:10) and to announce the success of their mission (Gal. 2:2; Acts 15:3 f.). The question of circumcision was raised by some of the converted Pharisees (Acts 15:5 = "false brethren," Gal. 2:4), and the matter was taken up by the Apostles and elders, among them Peter, James, and John (Gal. 2:9). Paul's special apostolate was approved and it was decided not to impose the yoke of the Law on Gentile converts (Gal. 2:6-9; Acts 15:7-19).

Comparison of Gal. 2 with Acts 15 has been further complicated by the fact that the narrative of Acts 15:3-29 is composite. Luke has combined the accounts of two distinct discussions: one which concerned the obligation of the Mosaic Law, especially with regard to circumcision, on Gentile converts; the other (later), which laid down the dietary observances indispensable for achieving community of meals and good relations between Jewish and Gentile converts.[12] The first matter, of capital and universal import, was settled, not by the local Jerusalem community, but by the apostolic college assembled there—James' "brother of the Lord," being associated with

---

[11]See *ibid.*, pp. 785-88.
[12]See P. Benoit, *Exégèse et Théologie* (Paris: Cerf, 1961), II, pp. 254 f.

them. The second discussion, of lesser import and of more local interest (since it applied only where Jewish Christians were numerous), was taken up later, perhaps after the Antioch incident (Gal. 2:11-14), this time under the presidency of James and in the absence of Peter and Paul. The latter, in fact, makes no mention of this further decree when treating of the Council of Jerusalem (Gal. 2:6) and on other obvious occasions (1 Cor. 8-10; Rm. 15); indeed, Paul learns of it from James himself only at the end of the third missionary journey (Acts 21:25). Luke, seeing that both problems were in fact connected, combined them in a striking literary unit. He was motivated not only by literary concern but also by his desire to achieve a synthesis of the facts, an end which did not exceed his right as an historian.

It seems possible to discover three main sources in the first part of Acts: (1) Palestinian traditions (Acts 9:32—11:18; 12:1-23); (2) Pauline traditions (Acts 9:1-30; 13:3—14:28); (3) Antiochian traditions (Acts 11:19-30; 15:3-33). It should be kept in mind, however, that these passages, as they occur in Acts, had already been rewritten by Luke before he set about dovetailing them into his work. In other words, although the presence of different traditions may be noted, it is not wholly possible to distinguish between the basic sources and their editorial treatment. How far Luke's editing can go has been seen from a study of Acts 11:27-30 and Acts 15:3-33. But when cognizance of his method is taken, certain features of his work will seem less surprising. As a writer, Luke manifests a notable freedom in relation to his sources; as an historian, he is more concerned with the development of history than with the material details of events.[13]

Throughout Acts, Luke takes care to note the steady growth of the Christian community: Acts 2:47; 5:14; 6:7; 9:31; 12:24; 16:5; 19:20; the narratives too have many passing references to the same fact. Of special interest are three more developed summaries: Acts 2:42-47; 4:32-35; 5:12-16; these are tableaux recapitulating the life of the primitive community. From the viewpoint of literary criticism, the most noteworthy feature of these summaries is that they

---

[13]See Benoit, *art. cit.*, 790-92.

are composite. Thus, for example, the verses 2:44 f. anticipate the second summary, and in the latter the verse 4:33 is an intruder. A study of the passages indicates that Acts 2:42, 46 f.; 4:32, 34 f.; and 5:12a, 15 may be regarded as original, with Acts 2:43-45; 4:33; and 5:12b-14 as secondary. The purpose of the additions is to broaden the scope of each summary by reference to the themes developed in the others. Thus, in the first summary, the theme of the pious and edifying life of the community has been bolstered by reference to miracle working and common sharing of goods, which are the themes of the third and second respectively. In its turn, the second summary recalls, in a very condensed form (v. 33), the themes of the others. Similarly, in the third summary, the recalling of the common prayer-life and of the regard in which the community was held by the people fills out the theme of miraculous cures. In each case the final result has been achieved by an insertion into a pre-existing summary. The result is rather awkward and is not typical of Luke who would have preferred to rewrite the sources. It may be that the summaries already had their present form when they came to his notice; furthermore, it is not outside the bounds of probability that the insertions were made by a disciple of Luke who had edited his work.[14]

ACTS 15:36—28:28   Although much has been written about the sources used in the second half of Acts,[15] the situation is far less complicated; there is no real problem if Luke's authorship of the work is accepted. Granted that he is the author, it does seem hypercritical to deny that in the "we-passages" (Acts 16:10-17; 20:5—21:18; 27:1—28:16) he writes as an eyewitness. It is reasonable to believe that here Luke had recourse to written notes—a kind of diary; some such source seems required by the vividness and graphic detail of these passages. For the rest of the material—all concerned with Paul—it is not unreasonable to suppose that Luke had questioned the Apostle and other companions of his. An obvious explanation is not to be despised just because it happens to be straightforward and simple. The further question, whether Luke's

---

[14]See Benoit, *Exégèse et Théologie, op. cit.,* pp. 181-92.
[15]See Dupont, *op. cit.,* pp. 75-165.

sources for his narrative of Paul's journeys were scattered notes, an itinerary or a travel diary, is of secondary importance once we realize that, whatever form it may have taken, the source material was Luke's own.

In the conclusion of his summary, Dom Dupont notes that the result of it has been both negative and positive. On the negative side, it is a fact that no definition of the sources used by the author of Acts has met with widespread agreement among scholars. On the positive side, however, the conviction emerges that Luke did not write his work at one sitting, and it seems possible to describe his literary technique:

> He is not satisfied with transcribing his sources, he rewrites the text by putting the imprint of his vocabulary and his style everywhere. Perhaps it would be necessary to go even further, taking account of the fact that, as a whole, the materials used in Acts reveal, at the same time as the author's main interests, his very individual turn of mind. The information is not only reported in his own style, in its very substance it generally reflects his personality. Everything is done as if Luke were at the origin not only of the edited version, but even of the sources on which this version is based.[16]

THE
DISCOURSES   Although the general study of the sources of Acts has been concluded, it is well, before passing on, to turn briefly to the discourses.[17] These are an integral part of the book and play an important role in bringing out the significance of the events described in the narratives. Each stage in the historical development of the Church is marked by an accompanying discourse which indicates the corresponding development of Christian thought.

At the very beginning, the Risen Christ specifies the role of his Apostles and maps out their activity; Peter's words in the supper room underline the importance of the Twelve. His discourse on Pentecost points to the meaning of the ecstatic phenomenon and the intervention of the Holy Spirit; it is also the first message addressed to the Jews by the group of Apostles. This message is further developed in Peter's subsequent addresses (Acts 3:12-26; 4:8-12; 5:29-32; 10:34-43). His reception of Cornelius marks a turn-

[16]*Ibid.*, pp. 166 f.
[17]See L. Cerfaux, IB, pp. 355-58.

ing point, for now the admission of Gentiles must be justified (Acts 11:5-17; 15:7-11). Stephen's speech provides a valuable insight into the frame of mind of the Hellenists.[18] It also shows an incipient impatience with the demands of the Mosaic Law and with the Temple ceremonies that eventually will lead to a rupture with Judaism and bring Christians to a full consciousness of their own separate identity. Philip (Acts 8:30-33) explicitly identifies the Suffering Servant of Is. 53 with Christ.

Discourses effectively bring out the meaning of Paul's mission. After reading Acts 13:16-41, there is no doubt that the Apostle of the Gentiles anxiously longs for the conversion of the Jews of the Diaspora—he echoes the theme of Peter. His speeches at Lystra (Acts 14:15-17) and before the council of the Areopagus (Acts 17:22-51) show how he could accommodate himself to the style of Hellenistic religious propaganda which owed much to Stoicism. His farewell address to the elders of Ephesus at Miletus (Acts 20:18-35) is the Apostle's testament. His later discourses, at Jerusalem (Acts 22:1-21; 23:1-6), at Caesarea (Acts 24:10-21; 26:2-23), and at Rome (Acts 28:17-20, 25-28) are personal apologiae; yet, we may gather from them something of the situation of Christians in face of Judaism and of the Roman authorities.

The theological importance of the discourses is undoubted; we may ask if they are authentic. Luke's freedom in regard to his sources in the narrative part of his work has been noted. It must be admitted that many of the discourses—by their language and style—also show the editorial hand of Luke. There is also the consideration that Luke is capable of divining the distinctive character of men like Peter, Stephen, Paul, and James and of composing for

---

18"The Greek-speaking Jews had always irritated the homelanders by their disdain for the physical elements of Israel's worship. Living in the Diaspora, they had found God away from the Temple and had worshiped him with a spiritual devotedness which spurned the smell of blood and burning flesh. In coming to know Jesus these Hellenists found the way of spiritual worship wide open to them in the 'Temple not made by hands.' When Stephen the Hellenist, therefore, spoke of Jesus, his hearers had ears only for that irritating sentence which echoed the old anti-Temple polemic: 'Solomon built him a house; yet not in houses made by hands does the Most High dwell' (Acts 7:47 f.)" (B. M. Ahern, *New Horizons,* Studies in Biblical Theology [Notre Dame, Ind.: Fides, 1963], p. 183).

them discourses in character. At the same time, it is reasonable to believe that the tradition—of which Luke was so conscious—had preserved the main themes of these outstanding witnesses. And, in the discourses, the use of Scripture, the theology, the apologetic arguments, and the presentation of the Christian message are theirs even if the actual form of each discourse is the work of Luke. "Whatever may have been the penetrating power of his own developed theology, Luke often presents the thoughts of Peter and Stephen just as they thought them in that first burst of Pentecostal light."[19] Whereas it would be naïve to imagine that the discourses are, or are meant to be, verbatim reports, it is not less injudicious to claim that they are free compositions of the author of Acts. Luke does manifest editorial freedom, but this concerns the arrangement and presentation of his material; he exercises considerable restraint in regard to his sources and shows little tendency to invent.

4) Historicity

Some may say that Luke's object was to trace the history of Christian beginnings. This is true, up to a point, for it is obvious that he had no intention of writing, in detail, the story of the primitive Church; we must not think that Acts is, or was meant to be, an ecclesiastical history. If he does trace the expansion of the Church, he is aware that its growth was due to the action of the Holy Spirit (Acts 2:47; 9:31); and the Book shows us how the Holy Spirit has completed the work begun by Jesus, for it is he who guided the Apostles in their missionary task. Luke's whole work (Gospel and Acts) is a theology of redemptive history. Between the limits of this history, Creation and Parousia, he envisages three phases:[20]

1) The period of Israel, of the Law and the Prophets.

2) The period of Jesus, which gives a foretaste of future salvation.

3) The time since the ascension: the period of the Church and of the Spirit.

In his Gospel, Luke was concerned with the second period, which had brought the first to an end; in Acts he is concerned with the

---

[19]*Ibid.*, p. 180.
[20]See H. Conzelmann, *The Theology of St. Luke*, trans. Geoffrey Buswell (New York: Harper & Row, 1960), p. 150.

beginning of the last phase. No more than the Gospel is Acts profane history, or ecclesiastical history; it is a page of *Heilsgeschichte*.

But, since Christianity is an historical religion, it is necessary that Luke should deal with historical facts, although it does not follow that he should seek meticulous exactitude of detail. Much of Acts may be checked with information provided in the Pauline Epistles. From this the fact emerges that, although Luke has not used the Epistles, he gives a picture of the missionary activity of the Apostle which tallies with theirs. The celebrated discrepancy between Acts 15 and Gal. 2 is, as has been seen, capable of being explained on literary grounds. We have no similar term of comparison for the early chapters, but the intrinsic credibility of the events themselves and Luke's proven fidelity to his sources are all in favor of their historicity.

The trustworthiness of the historical data of Acts may also be measured by extrabiblical evidence; it has stood up to such verification. In most cases, what we know about contemporary profane history squares remarkably well with Acts. Luke is perfectly well acquainted with the religious, political, and social conditions of Paul's world.

> The officials with whom Paul and his companions were brought into contact are those who would be there. Every person is found just where he ought to be: proconsuls in senatorial provinces, Asiarchs in Ephesus, *strategoi* in Philippi, politarchs in Thessalonica. . . . The magistrates take action against them in a strictly managed Roman colony like Pisidian Antioch or Philippi, where legality and order reigned: riotous crowds try to take the law into their own hands in the less strictly governed Hellenistic cities like Iconium and Ephesus and Thessalonica.[21]

An important factor, in this context, is Luke's taste for geographical details, at least when they fit in with the course of his narrative.[22] He carefully locates places and towns he mentions; for example: ". . . the mount called Olivet, which is near Jerusalem, a sabbath day's journey away" (Acts 1:12); "Perga in Pamphylia" (Acts 13:13); "Lystra and Derbe, cities of Lycaonia" (Acts 14:6);

---

[21]W. Ramsay, *The Bearing of Recent Discoveries on the Trustworthiness of the New Testament* (London, 1915), p. 96.
[22]See Dupont, *op. cit.*, pp. 159-62.

"Myra in Lycia" (Acts 27:5); ". . . a place called Fair Havens, near which is the city of Lasea" (Acts 27:8). Similarly, Luke notes the addresses of people in his narrative: the place where they live, the house where they lodge. For example, in Damascus, Paul lodged in the house of Judas, situated in the street called Straight (Acts 9:11); in Joppa, Peter lodged with Simon, a tanner whose home was by the sea (Acts 10:6). At Philippi, Paul lodged with Lydia (Acts 16:14 f.), in Thessalonica with Jason (Acts 17:5-7), in Corinth with Aquila and Priscilla (Acts 18:3) and with Titius Justus whose house was next door to the synagogue (Acts 18:7); in Caesarea, he stayed with Philip the evangelist (Acts 21:8); and on a stage to Jerusalem in the house of Mnason of Cyprus (Acts 21:16). It is not credible that a writer with such an eye for detail would have been careless about historical facts.

Acts remains our most important source for the history of the primitive Church. At the same time, however, true to its real character, it shows us the beginning of Christian theology more effectively than any other document, and enables us (especially by means of the discourses of Peter) to grasp the primitive Christian message. Here history and theology go hand-in-hand, for Luke has desired to trace, in broad lines, a crucial phase of salvation history.

3. DOCTRINE

1) The Kerygma[23]

The Semitic character of the first part of Acts is readily discernible. Sometimes this is due to Luke's conscious imitation of the style of the LXX which is so marked by Hebraisms. In other passages—in Peter's speeches for instance—it comes from an Aramaic substratum. This factor, taken in conjunction with Luke's quest of and respect for sources, makes it certain that the speeches attributed to Peter are based on material which proceeded from the Aramaic-speaking church at Jerusalem; in other words, they represent the primitive kerygma of that church.[24]

---

[23]See C. H. Dodd, *The Apostolic Preaching and its Developments* (London: Hodder & Stoughton, 1963³), pp. 17-29.

[24]See p. 123.

The first four speeches of Peter (Acts 2:14-36, 38 f.; 3:12-26; 4:8-12; 5:17-40) cover substantially the same ground; they are complementary and give a comprehensive view of the content of the early kerygma:

1) The age of fulfillment has dawned. "This is what was spoken by the prophet" (Acts 2:16); "What God foretold by the mouth of all the prophets . . . he thus fulfilled" (Acts 3:18); "All the prophets who have spoken, from Samuel to those who came afterwards, also proclaimed these days" (Acts 3:24). Rabbinical exegesis of the Old Testament referred the predictions of the prophets to the "days of the Messiah"; hence, Peter declares that the messianic age has dawned.

2) Fulfillment has been achieved, in accordance with God's will and determinate plan, through the ministry, death, and resurrection of Jesus, the son of David; this is expressed quite emphatically, with proof from the Scriptures. The Davidic descent of Jesus is attested by David himself: "[David] being therefore a prophet, and knowing that God had sworn with an oath. to him that he would set one of his descendants upon his throne, he foresaw [Christ]" (Acts 2:30 f.). The ministry is described: "Jesus of Nazareth, a man attested to you by God with mighty works and wonders and signs which God did through him in your midst" (Acts 2:22); "Moses said, 'The Lord God will raise up for you a prophet from your brethren as he raised me up'" (Acts 3:22). His death is proclaimed: "This Jesus, delivered up according to the definite plan and foreknowledge of God, you crucified and killed by the hands of lawless men" (Acts 2:23); "Him you delivered up and denied in the presence of Pilate, when he had decided to release him. But you denied the Holy and Righteous One, and asked for a murderer to be granted to you, and killed the Author of life" (Acts 3:13-15). His resurrection is boldly asserted: "God raised him up, having loosed the pangs of death, because it was not possible for him to be held by it" (Acts 2:24); "God raised him from the dead; to this we are witnesses" (Acts 3:15); "Jesus Christ of Nazareth, whom you crucified, whom God raised from the dead" (Acts 4:10).

3) By virtue of the resurrection, Jesus has been exalted at the right hand of God, as messianic head of the new Israel. "Being therefore exalted at the right hand of God . . . God has made him both

Lord and Christ" (Acts 2:33, 36); "The Lord of our fathers glorified his servant Jesus" (Acts 3:13); "God exalted him at his right hand as Leader and Savior" (Acts 5:31).

4) The Holy Spirit in the Church is the sign of Christ's present power and glory. "Being therefore exalted at the right hand of God, and having received from the Father the promise of the Holy Spirit, he has poured out this which you hear and see" (Acts 2:33); "We are witnesses to these things, and so is the Holy Spirit whom God has given to those who obey him" (Acts 5:32).

5) The Messianic Age will reach its consummation in the return of Christ. "That he may send the Christ appointed for you, Jesus, whom heaven must receive until the time for establishing all that God spoke by the mouth of his holy prophets from of old" (Acts 3:20 f.). Compare this with Acts 10:42: "He commanded us . . . to testify that he is the one ordained by God to be judge of the living and the dead."

6) The kerygma always closes with an appeal for repentance, the offer of forgiveness and of the Holy Spirit, and the promise of salvation. "Repent, and be baptized every one of you in the name of Jesus Christ for the forgiveness of your sins; and you shall receive the gift of the Holy Spirit. For the promise is to you and to your children and to all that are far off, every one whom the Lord our God calls to him" (Acts 2:38 f.); "Repent, therefore, and turn again, that your sins may be blotted out . . . and that he may send the Christ appointed for you, Jesus" (Acts 3:19 f.); "There is salvation in no one else, for there is no other name given among men by which we must be saved" (Acts 4:12).

Such is the Jerusalem kerygma. It is significant that its main points are indicated in a Gospel summary of the preaching of Jesus: "Jesus came into Galilee, preaching the gospel of God, and saying, 'The time is fulfilled, and the kingdom of God is at hand; repent, and believe in the gospel' " (Mk. 1:14 f.). The kerygma follows the lines of this summary.

> The first clause, "The time is fulfilled," is expanded in the reference to prophecy and its fulfillment. The second clause, "The kingdom of God has drawn near," is expanded in the account of the ministry and death of Jesus, his resurrection and exaltation, all conceived as an eschatological process. The third clause, "Repent and believe in the

Gospel," reappears in the appeal for repentance and the offer of forgiveness with which the apostolic *kerygma* closes. Whether we say that the apostolic preaching was modeled on that of Jesus, or that the evangelist formulated his summary of the preaching of Jesus on the model of that of the primitive Church, at any rate the two are identical in purport. The kingdom of God is conceived as coming in the events of the life, death, and resurrection of Jesus, and to proclaim these facts, in their proper setting, is to preach the gospel of the kingdom of God.[25]

The discourse of Peter in Acts 10:34-47 differs from the others, not because it does not contain the principal elements of the kerygma, but because it concentrates on the historical facts concerning Jesus. We learn that, after the baptism of John, Jesus began to preach the Good News in Galilee and to proclaim it throughout Judaea. He went about doing good, healing the sick, casting out devils. He was crucified and was raised by God on the third day; he manifested himself to chosen witnesses and commanded them to preach to the people. The speech is addressed to a Gentile audience—Cornelius with his relatives and friends (Acts 10:24)—to people, unlike the Palestinian Jews, unacquainted with the main facts. "We may perhaps take it that the speech before Cornelius represents the form of *kerygma* used by the primitive Church in its earliest approaches to a wider public."[26]

Although Luke undoubtedly leaned on traditions that reached far back, it is Paul who provides our earliest extant written records. His writings, although not of the nature of kerygma, are a valuable basis of investigation, and in them we find a term of comparison with Acts.[27] In 1 Cor. 15:3-7, Paul gives a brief summary of the kerygma, explicitly declaring that it is something he had received from his instructors in the faith. Passages in Galatians and Romans, as well as a speech in Acts (13:17-41), provide all the elements of the kerygma. Furthermore, it is clear that Paul regarded it as the outline of an apostolic Gospel which he believed to be common to himself and other Christian missionaries.

25Dodd, *op. cit.*, p. 24.
26*Ibid.*, p. 28.
27See *ibid.*, pp. 9-17.

Yet, there are three points in the Pauline kerygma which appear to be absent from the Jerusalem kerygma of Acts.[28] In the first place, Jesus is not called "Son of God" in the speeches of Peter (cf. Acts 9:20: "And in the synagogues immediately [Paul] proclaimed Jesus, saying, 'He is the Son of God'"). We may remark that Peter's discourses are colored by the prophecies: he speaks of Jesus as the "Servant of God" of Second Isaiah. Then, too, it seems that the phrase "Lord and Christ" (Acts 2:36) means quite the same thing as "Son of God in power" (Rm. 1:4). It is not irrelevant to observe that the Synoptic Gospels regard Christ as Son of God and not through Pauline influence. Secondly, the Jerusalem kerygma does not assert that Christ died for our sins (cf. 1 Cor. 15:3). Again, it may be said that the fact is implicit in the presentation of Jesus as Servant of God; the importance of Is. 53 in the early preaching is strikingly manifest in Acts 8:32-35. Finally, the Jerusalem kerygma does not state that the Risen Christ intercedes for us (cf. Rm. 8:34). But, surely, the fact is implicit in the declaration that the remission of sins and salvation are offered only "in his name" (Acts 2:38; 4:12; 10:43).

It seems clear, then, that even on these points there is no real difference between the contents of the Jerusalem kerygma as presented in the early chapters of Acts and the contents of the kerygma known to Paul; in all other respects agreement is manifest. In Acts, we can trace the essential elements of the apostolic preaching at a very early date. As should be expected, the center of the preaching was Jesus Christ, his life, death, and resurrection; and it was marked by an awareness that the age of fulfillment had dawned, that Christ was Lord, and that the Holy Spirit has been poured out on the Church.

2) *The Holy Spirit*[29]

Following on the Third Gospel, which, more than the other Synoptics, underlines the action of the Holy Spirit in the ministry of Jesus (cf. Lk. 4:1, 14, 18; 10:21), Acts gives the impression that the primi-

---

[28]See *ibid.*, pp. 25 f.
[29]See Wikenhauser, *op. cit.*, pp. 99-103; A. Feuillet, IB, pp. 828-31; J. Guillet, VTB, pp. 320 f.

tive Christian community lived entirely under the motion of the Spirit; Acts is like a "gospel of the Spirit." Before his ascension, the Risen Christ had assured his disciples that he would send upon them the promised gift of the messianic age, the Holy Spirit, who would empower them to carry out their task of witnesses to Jesus (Lk. 24:47-49; Acts 1:5, 8). The fulfillment of the promise was the "baptism in the Spirit" (Acts 1:5) of Pentecost. This marked the beginning of the time of the Church, just as the baptism in the Jordan inaugurated the public ministry of the Savior; in both cases, Luke insists on the sensible manifestation of the Spirit (Lk. 3:22; Acts 2:3).

In his discourse, Peter explained that the ecstatic speaking in tongues was a sign that the Risen Christ had indeed poured out his Spirit upon them (Acts 2:33), thus fulfilling the prophecy of Joel (Acts 2:16-21). Since, however, Joel had spoken of "all flesh," the gift of the Holy Spirit is not for the circle of disciples alone but for all who will believe in Christ. Peter, then, can assure his hearers that they too will receive the Spirit if they will believe and be baptized (Acts 2:38 f.)—not only they but "all that are far off, every one whom the Lord our God calls to him" (Acts 2:39). Possession of the Spirit is part of the equipment of every Christian.

The activity of the Spirit is manifold. The charisms, especially speaking in tongues and prophecy, are an obvious expression of his activity. Not only at Pentecost, but also at other times, the Spirit gives the faculty of "speaking in tongues," that is, of praising God in the language of ecstasy, like Cornelius (Acts 10:46) and the disciples of John at Ephesus (Acts 19:6). The Holy Spirit moves the prophets, like Agabus (Acts 11:28; 21:11 f.), who were to be found in many of the churches: in Antioch (Acts 13:1), in Jerusalem (Acts 15:32), and at Caesarea (Acts 21:9).

If the charisms offer a striking manifestation of the Spirit's action, his role as guide and strengthener of the Christian preachers is of far greater importance. In the strength of the Spirit just received, Peter bore witness before the crowd of Jews and proselytes (Acts 2:5 f.) to Jesus as the Messiah sent by God (Acts 2:22-36). The witness of the Apostles is explicitly designated as the work of the Spirit (Acts 5:32). Stephen is filled with "wisdom and the Spirit," and his enemies cannot withstand him (Acts 6:10). The Spirit guides the Apostles and the leaders of the community and dictates their line of conduct (cf. Acts 8:29: "The Spirit said to Philip"; 10:19: "the Spirit said to Peter"). Peter was enlightened by the Spirit in the crucial matter of the acceptance of the pagan Cornelius into the Christian community (Acts 10:19; 11:12); and when the whole question of Gentile converts was in the balance, the Spirit guided the apostolic council (Acts 15:28). The Spirit called Barnabas and Saul to the first Gentile mission and directed the Church at Antioch to set them apart for that task (Acts 13:2-4). At the beginning of the second missionary journey, Paul was hindered by the Spirit from carrying out his original plan of preaching in the province of Asia (Acts 16:6 f.). In critical situations, the preachers, and the communities themselves, could look to the Spirit for support. Thus, Peter (Acts 4:8, 13, 21; 5:40) and Stephen (Acts 6:15; 7:55) spoke out boldly before the Sanhedrin, and the disciples were encouraged (Acts 13:52).

Acts has little to say about the manner of the outpouring and reception of the Spirit, and what it does say is sometimes difficult to understand. The visible descent of the Holy Spirit on the disciples at Pentecost and on the household of Cornelius was exceptional. As a rule, only those who have been baptized in the name of the Lord Jesus receive the Spirit; the question is whether the Spirit is received through baptism, or in connection with baptism, or by a separate imposition of hands. The Samaritans baptized by Philip received the Spirit through the laying on of hands by Peter and John (Acts 8:15 f.) and, similarly, the Spirit came upon the disciples of John at Ephesus after Paul's imposition of hands. Is the reception of the Spirit, then, bound to the Apostles' imposition of hands? The examples cited seem to point in that direction. But, in Acts 9:17, Ananias said to Saul: "The Lord Jesus has sent me to you that you may regain your sight and be filled with the Holy Spirit"—and the filling with the Spirit was achieved by baptism (Acts 9:19). And we are surely not meant to think that all those baptized by others lacked the Holy Spirit until an Apostle came along and imposed hands on them. The baptized person did, then and there, receive the Spirit. The gift that followed on the imposition of hands by

Apostles was the special "charismatic spirit"; they alone were able to transmit this further activity of the Spirit. With regard to the disciples themselves, they received the Spirit on Easter day (Jn. 20:22); the charismatic outpouring of Pentecost fitted them for their task as witnesses. Indeed, Pentecost is an unique event of world-wide dimensions destined to introduce into humanity the era of the outpouring of the Spirit.

3) The Person of Christ[30]

Although Acts does not have much to say about the earthly life of Jesus, it does reveal that, in the primitive preaching, the reality of Christ's humanity was taken for granted. He was a descendant of David (Acts 2:30; 13:23) from Nazareth (Acts 2:22; 3:6; 4:10; 6:14; 10:37; 22:8; 26:9). His mother Mary and his "brothers" are named (Acts 1:14), and mention is made of his works and teaching (Acts 1:22; 10:37 f.; 13:34); his passion, death, and resurrection figure prominently (Acts 2:23; 3:15; 4:28; 5:30; 7:52; 13:27, 29). The Apostles were privileged witnesses of Christ not only because they saw his post-Easter apparitions, but also because they had shared his earthly existence and had gone up with him from Galilee to Jerusalem (Acts 13:31; cf. 1:21 f.).

Yet, the resurrection of Jesus from the dead did not appear by way of afterthought in the early preaching. He who had been taken from the cross and laid in the grave (Acts 13:39), God had raised (Acts 2:24, 32; 3:15; 4:10; 5:30; 10:40; 13:30, 33 f., 37; 17:31; 26:6-9), and definitively: ". . . no more to return to corruption" (Acts 13:34). The Risen Christ appeared to his disciples and ate and drank with them (Acts 10:40 f.; 13:31). On the ground of these appearances of the Risen One, their faith, shaken by the crucifixion (Lk. 24:21), was firmly established, and they bore witness to the resurrection of Jesus (Acts 2:32; 3:15; 10:40 f.; 13:31). Hence, from the beginning, Christian faith maintained and underlined the perfect identity of Jesus, the historical person who lived in Galilee and died in Jerusalem, and the Risen Christ of the Easter apparitions. In grasping the mystery of the Incarnation, the first Christians did not start, as

---

[30]See Wikenhauser, *op. cit.*, pp. 126-32; A. Fueillet, IB, pp. 819-26; V. Taylor, *The Person of Christ in New Testament Teaching* (New York: St. Martin's Press, 1958).

we do, with the idea of God assuming a human nature; their starting point was the experimental knowledge of the man Jesus, an historical person. The discovery that this man was in reality infinitely more than an ordinary man, that he was a properly divine being, and especially the precise expression of this truth, could only be acquired little by little. But the first step was the realization that Jesus of Nazareth and the Risen Lord were one and the same.

From the beginning, too, the resurrection was seen as the peremptory proof that Jesus was the Christ, the Messiah promised by the prophets. In the eyes of the primitive community, composed of converted Jews, this was a matter of supreme importance. Following on an ignominious death which seemed to contradict the messianic claims, the miracle of Easter was an irrefutable divine response. For, by raising him from the dead, God had set the supreme seal on the testimony which he had already rendered by giving him power to work wonders (Acts 2:22; 3:15; 4:10; 10:38, 40). On Easter morning, Jesus not only rose from the dead but was exalted to the right hand of the Father (Acts 2:23; 3:13, 21; 5:31; 7:56).

By his resurrection and his elevation to the right hand of God, Jesus has taken a share in the divine power, in virtue of which he sent the Holy Spirit on his disciples at Pentecost, and will continue to send him; and will appear as Judge of the world. The declaration of Peter (Acts 2:36) that God had "made him both Lord and Christ" means that it was through his elevation that the messianic Lordship of Jesus was made manifest, while hitherto his messiahship had been humble and hidden. To preach the name of Jesus is to proclaim that he had received the dignity of Lord (Acts 9:27-29). The resurrection was, for Jesus, his enthronization, or his establishment in royal power or Lordship. Since the Jewish title of Messiah was not very meaningful for pagans, to them it was announced that Jesus is Lord—not simply a title of honor, but an expression of the messianic royalty to which Jesus had attained by his resurrection, and an acknowledgment of his divine prerogatives.

Among the many passages where the title Lord occurs, some, almost always citations of the Old Testament, refer directly to God (Acts 2:39; 3:22; 4:26; 5:19; etc.), while others refer to Jesus (Acts 7:59 f.; 9:10 ff.; 11:17; etc.). In a third class of texts, it is difficult to decide whether the title refers to God or to Jesus; the am-

biguity is significant (cf. Acts 9:28, 30; 11:23; 13:43; 1:23). At any
rate, the primitive community did not hesitate to set Jesus side-by-
side with God, at the very center of the plan of salvation. The theology of the Name, characteristic of Acts, points in the same direction.
Just as the people of God of the Old Testament was marked by the invocation of the name of Yahweh (Jer. 14:9; Ps. 99 [98]:6; 116 [115]:4;
Sir. 36:11; etc.), so also the Christian people is distinguished by the
invocation of the name of Jesus. The text of Joel (3:5), "Whoever
calls on the name of the Lord will be saved," is applied by Peter to
Jesus (Acts 2:21). In the name of Jesus alone can men find salvation (Acts 4:12). It is this name that the Apostles preach, in virtue
of it they act, and for it they suffer (Acts 3:6, 16; 4:10, 17 f.; 5:28,
40 f.; 8:12, 16; 9:15 f.; 27:28). The invocation of the name of Jesus
is a practical acknowledgment of his divinity.

> When St. Peter declares that God has made the Crucified One
> "Both Lord and Christ" (Acts 2:36) he puts a meaning upon these
> names which hitherto they had not borne. A deeper meaning is present
> also in the phrase "the name of Jesus Christ," since the Apostle goes
> on to speak of repentance and of baptism leading to the remission
> of sins and the gift of the Holy Spirit (Acts 2:38). In the context in
> which the phrase appears it has a divine content, although this is not
> brought out. The same also may be true of the command of St. Peter
> to the lame man at Jerusalem, "In the name of Jesus of Nazareth,
> walk" (Acts 3:6). Indeed, we may say that the names used in the
> early preaching hide rather than reveal a meaning they are forced
> to bear. Conviction precedes expression. This is exactly what might
> be expected in the history of the proclamation of a new message.
> Values appear first, adequate names later.[31]

---

[31]Taylor, op. cit., pp. 196 f.

| *The Pauline Epistles*

THE NEW TESTAMENT EPISTLES

1, 2 THESSALONIANS

THE MAJOR EPISTLES

THE CAPTIVITY EPISTLES

THE PASTORAL EPISTLES

HEBREWS

The title of this chapter implies nothing more than the existence of a traditional Pauline corpus; it does not follow that all the epistles treated here are Pauline in a strict sense. Thus, not only the Pastorals and Ephesians, whose authenticity is doubtful, but Hebrews too—certainly not written by the Apostle—find a place. Furthermore, not only are the grouping and the general designation convenient, but also they find justification in the Pauline character, direct or indirect, of the whole.

1. THE NEW TESTAMENT EPISTLES[1]

1) Letter and Epistle

Many epistolary writings of antiquity have been preserved and are known to us. They fall into two classes: 1) *Letters* strictly so called; these were written on a particular occasion to a particular person or group of persons and are meant only for these readers. 2) *Epistles;* these are treatises cast in letter form and addressed to a wide circle or, simply, to any reader. The Pauline writings are true letters because there is always a special occasion and a definite group of receivers; but, with the exception of Phm., they are official, not

---

[1] See A. Wikenhauser, *Einleitung in das Neue Testament* (Freiburg: Herder, 1956²), pp. 245-48; English translation by J. Cunningham (London: Herder/Nelson, 1958), pp. 346-50; J. Cambier, "Paul (Vie et Doctrine de Saint)," DBS, VII, cols. 329-41.

private letters. Most of them are addressed to a single community, or to a small group of churches (Gal.; Eph.); three are addressed to the holder of an ecclesiastical office and through him to the church in his charge (1, 2 Tm.; Ti.). These letters deal with various aspects of the missionary activity: the instructing, confirming, and admonishing of the faithful; the settling of misunderstandings in the churches; and the refutation of false teachers. They are the writings of an apostle, instruments of his apostolic ministry; in them, he speaks with authority.

The other New Testament epistles are closer to the form of a theological treatise (Heb.), or are homiletical (1, 2 Pt.; 1 Jn.) or exhortatory (James). Yet, although we have pointed to, and are conscious of, the difference between epistle and letter, we shall continue to designate the relevant New Testament writings by the traditional term "epistle."

2) *The Epistolary Formulas*

Most Greek and Latin letters have the following epistolary formulas: 1) The *praescripto* or address, which contained the name of the sender (nominative), the name of the receiver (dative), and a greeting, all in one sentence; for example, "Claudius Lysias to his Excellency the governor Felix, greeting" (Acts 23:26). Acts 15:23 is the only other New Testament example of the classic address. 2) The final greeting: *errōso, vale,* or the like. This was of more than conventional importance since, in effect, it served to authenticate a letter; it was, or could be, the equivalent of our signature. When a letter was dictated, the sender added the closing greeting in his own hand (see 2 Thes. 3:17; Gal. 6:11).

The New Testament writings do not adhere closely to the Greek practice. The address of the Pauline Epistles and of 1, 2 Pt., 2 Jn., and Jude is made up of two sentences: the first names the sender and receiver, but usually also carries certain titles and attributes and sometimes instructions (Rm.; Gal.; Ti.). The second is a blessing expressed as a wish. This two-sentence address, however, is found in Jewish letters. Paul, too, in eight epistles (1, 2 Thes.; Gal.; 1, 2 Cor.; Phil.; Col.; Phm.) names one or more fellow senders; this rarely occurs in profane letters. Nor does he always observe the strict rule of Greek letters that the address must be in the third person (e.g., Gal. 1:1; cf. 1, 2 Jn.). Paul usually begins the text of his letter with thanksgiving to God (e.g., 1 Thes., Col.)—Jewish discourses opened in this way and the Apostle doubtless followed the practice in his preaching—and with the assurance of his prayers (e.g., Rm.; Phil.). The text generally ends with personal remarks (e.g., Rm. 15:25 ff.; 1 Cor. 16:5) and greetings. The closing formula is never *errōso* or the like, but a blessing: "The grace of the Lord Jesus Christ be with you" (or something similar). The Apostle, while he owes much to his background, nonetheless is notably original in his use of epistolary formulas.

3) *The Language and Style of Paul*

The language of Paul betrays his background and training. A Jew of the Diaspora, born in Tarsus (a celebrated center of learning), he is marked by the influence of Greek culture. This is to be noted, for instance, in his use of the diatribe[2] (cf. Rm. 3:1-19, 27-31; 2 Cor. 6:4-10), in ideas borrowed from Stoicism (for example, the departure of the separated soul for the divine world [2 Cor. 5:6-8], the cosmic "pleroma" of Col. and Eph.), and in certain formulas (1 Cor. 8:6; Rm. 11:36; Eph. 4:6). At the same time, since he was a Pharisee, Aramaic-speaking from his infancy, a disciple of Gamaliel, the Jewish heritage is manifest and preponderant. Although he handles Greek with ease, as a second mother tongue, it sometimes seems that he thinks in Aramaic, and he is certainly indebted to the language of the LXX.

The Apostle's style is distinctive. "Never perhaps has the celebrated dictum *le style est l'homme même* been more truly verified than in the case of Paul whose style and eloquence are marked by the love of Christ and by a passion for the preaching of the gospel."[3] These influences not only account for the striking quality of so much of his work, but also explain its defects. Carried along by the pressure of his love and the urgency of his message, words can literally fail him (cf. 1 Cor. 9:15). More than once we get the impression that a passage was written or dictated at white heat

---

[2]See p. 7.
[3]Cambier, *art. cit.*, col. 341.

(see Gal. and 2 Cor.). The complex character of Paul is mirrored in the many moods and shades of his writing.

4) The Epistles in Chronological Order

Like the other New Testament writings, the Pauline Epistles can be dated only approximately. In this case the date assigned to each is determined by one's view of the chronology of the Apostle's life.[4]

A.D.	PLACE OF WRITING	EPISTLES
51	Corinth	1, 2 Thessalonians
56	Ephesus	Philippians
57	Ephesus Macedonia	Galatians 1 Corinthians 2 Corinthians
57/58	Corinth	Romans
61-63	Rome	[Philippians] Colossians Ephesians Philemon
65	Macedonia	1 Timothy Titus
67	Rome	2 Timothy
67	Rome	Hebrews

2. 1, 2 THESSALONIANS

1) 1 Thessalonians

THE THESSALONIAN CHURCH   The city of Thessalonica was the capital of the Roman province of Macedonia; by special privilege of Augustus, it was a free city. As a seaport and a stage

---

[4]See pp. 58-60.

on the great Egnatian Way which led from Dyrrachium to Byzantium, the city was a flourishing commercial center, cosmopolitan in population. It had a democratic constitution and its chief magistrates bore the title of "politarchs" (Acts 17:8).

Paul visited Thessalonica for the first time in the course of his second missionary journey, probably in the year 50 A.D. He was accompanied by Silas. Both missionaries turned first to the Jews, preaching in the synagogue on three consecutive sabbaths. Their preaching won over many of the "God-fearers" (Gentile adherents of the synagogue) and some influential women. The exasperated Jews, cleverly adapting their tactics to the political situation, played on the feelings of the people and stirred up a mob against the preachers. The brethren prevailed on Paul and Silas to slip away by night to Beroea, a small town some miles to the west. It is manifest that the Thessalonian church was predominantly Gentile in composition.

It is not easy to determine the length of Paul's stay in Thessalonica. The account of Acts would suggest that it cannot have been long. The best we can say is that it may have been two or three months—scarcely more than that.

PURPOSE AND SUMMARY   Paul did not remain long in Beroea, but
OF THE EPISTLE   soon proceeded to Athens; Silas and Timothy, whom he had left behind, were expected to join him there before long. The Apostle was worried about the Thessalonian church which had so soon been left to itself; when the two arrived he sent Timothy back to Thessalonica (1 Thes. 3:1 f.). Timothy returned with a comforting report for the Apostle who now was in Corinth (51 A.D.). The latter straightway gave expression to his relief in a letter, but, pastor that he was, he seized the occasion to draw attention to certain shortcomings and to issue instructions.

The customary address (1 Thes. 1:1 f.) is followed by a long thanksgiving (1 Thes. 1:3-10) for the manifest fruits of a conversion wrought by the Spirit. Then, the integrity and disinterestedness of the Apostle's preaching and way of life are stressed (1 Thes. 2:1-12). On their part, the converts received his message as the word of God (1 Thes. 2:13-16). The passage 1 Thes. 2:17–3:13 outlines

Paul's sentiments after he had left Thessalonica and the steps he had taken to keep in touch: his desire to see them again (1 Thes. 2:17-20); the sending of Timothy (1 Thes. 3:1-5); the Apostle's joy at his envoy's encouraging report (1 Thes. 3:6-10); his heartfelt prayer for their future progress (1 Thes. 3:11-13).

The second part of the writing, following the usual practice of Paul, takes up matters of personal import and exhorts the faithful to the practice of Christian morality. He urges the observance of chastity and brotherly love and advocates quiet attention to one's own affairs and work (1 Thes. 4:1-12). Evidently in reply to a problem of the community, he has comforting words on the fate of brethren who had passed away: they are with the Lord and will be witnesses of his Coming (1 Thes. 4:13-18). But, since the Lord will come unexpectedly, the living must be vigilant (1 Thes. 5:1-11). Finally, he has advice to offer on different aspects of community life (1 Thes. 5:12-22) and a concluding prayer (1 Thes. 5:23 f.). The letter ends in typical Pauline fashion (1 Thes. 5:25-28).

THE PLAN

THE ADDRESS (1:1 f.)	
INITIAL THANKSGIVING (1:3-10)	
THE APOSTLE AND THE THESSALONIANS (2–3)	
1) Paul's preaching and conduct	2:1-12
2) The reaction of the faithful	2:13-16
3) His subsequent solicitude	2:17–3:10
4) His prayer for them	3:11-13
INSTRUCTION AND EXHORTATION (4:1–5:24)	
1) Chastity and charity	4:1-12
2) Living and dead at the Parousia	4:13-18
3) Vigilance in view of the Day of the Lord	5:1-11
4) Various recommendations	5:12-22
5) Final prayer	5:23 f.
CONCLUSION (5:25-28)	

2) 2 Thessalonians

PURPOSE AND
SUMMARY

It cannot be doubted that Paul's principal reason for writing a second letter to the Thessalonians was to set right certain erroneous views on the Parousia which had arisen in that church. Although it has been urged that these views may have sprung from a misinterpretation of 1 Thes. (especially 4:13-18), it is not easy to see how his words could have been so misconstrued. Reference to a "letter purporting to come from us" (2 Thes. 2:2)—frequently regarded as pointing to 1 Thes.—is, in its context, more readily understood of an hypothetical letter. There was also another reason for the Epistle, one apparently not unconnected with the other. Some of the Thessalonians no longer worked (2 Thes. 6:11 f.), probably because, believing in an imminent Parousia, they saw no point in work. The Apostle deals with both problems in forthright fashion.

2 Thes. opens with an address (2 Thes. 1:1 f.) followed by a thanksgiving for the faith and fidelity of the Thessalonians (2 Thes. 1:3 f.). Next comes a statement on God's final retribution (2 Thes. 1:5-10) and a prayer for the faithful (2 Thes. 1:11 f.). The letter then takes up the question of the Parousia and its preceding signs (2 Thes. 2:1-12): the Day of the Lord has not yet come because, beforehand, there will be a great apostasy and the "man of lawlessness" (Antichrist) must appear. But, the Lord Jesus will overcome all his enemies. The Apostle again thanks God for the Christian vocation of the Thessalonians and urges them to persevere in their calling (2 Thes. 2:13-15), and he prays for that end (2 Thes. 2:16 f.). He asks for the prayers of the faithful and expresses his confidence in their regard (2 Thes. 3:1-5). This sounds like a conclusion but, abruptly, Paul turns to another matter, probably just come to his notice (see 2 Thes. 3:11). The brethren must not live in idleness; they should work, following the example of the Apostle (2 Thes. 3:6-15). The writing ends with the customary salutation (2 Thes. 3:16) and a greeting and blessing added in Paul's hand (2 Thes. 3:17 f.)—his authentication of the letter.

PLAN

ADDRESS (1:1 f.)	
INITIAL THANKSGIVING (1:3 f.)	
1) The retribution of God	1:5-10
2) Prayer for the faithful	1:11 f.
3) The Parousia and its Signs	2:1-12
4) Exhortation to perseverance	2:13–3:5
5) Warning against idleness	3:6-15
CONCLUSION (3:16-18)	

AUTHENTICITY[5]   Since the authenticity of 1 Thes. has scarcely ever been questioned, it was not necessary to consider it. However, the authenticity of 2 Thes. has been challenged. In the first place, there is the evidently more impersonal tone of the second letter. Of greater significance is the relationship between the letters; throughout, the second seems to depend on the first to a notable extent (cf. 2 Thes. 1:3–1 Thes. 1:2 f.; 2 Thes. 1:5–1 Thes. 2:12; 2 Thes. 1:7–1 Thes. 3:13; 2 Thes. 2:16 f.–1 Thes. 3:11 f.; 2 Thes. 3:8–1 Thes. 2:9; 2 Thes. 3:16–1 Thes. 5:23; 2 Thes. 3:18–1 Thes. 5:28; the list is by no means exhaustive). Because the rise of new problems which necessitated the writing of 2 Thes. would seem to set a space of at least two or three months between the two letters, it is not likely that Paul could have recalled, so faithfully, the phraseology of 1 Thes. And if he had happened to use that letter, it is strange that he makes no reference to it (we have seen that 2 Thes. 2:2 is probably not to be interpreted in this sense). On the other hand, all are agreed that the language of 2 Thes. is Pauline. Thus, despite the difficulties indicated, the Pauline authenticity of the writing is accepted by the great majority of scholars. Is not the role of a secretary (cf. 2 Thes. 3:17) an important factor in solving the difficulties?[6]

It seems, then, that the date of the writing of both Epistles may be placed within a few months of each other, in 51 A.D. at Corinth.

---

[5]See Wikenhauser, *op. cit.,* pp. 262-65; Eng. trans., pp. 368-72.
[6]See p. 289.

3) *The Eschatology of 1, 2 Thessalonians*[7]

Although eschatology is not the only concern of 1, 2 Thes., it does have a prominent place in the Epistles and merits further treatment on that score. There is also the fact that the relevant texts present undoubted difficulties; the student can, in fairness, expect some clarification. Because of the scope of this work and the need to keep it within certain limits, theological notes in this chapter will be confined to the leading or distinctive themes of the Epistles. It will not be possible to give more than a suggestion of the great doctrinal riches of these writings.

The eschatology of 1, 2 Thes. is to be understood according to the normal acceptation of the term: the hope of a divine intervention which brings about a radical change in the conditions of human life and in the relations between God and men. Here, however, two central themes are stressed: the Parousia, regarded as the beginning of an era in which believers are reunited to the Lord, and the Parousia as envisaged in its preparatory signs and in its unfolding.

Already in the opening part of 1 Thes., before the subject had been explicitly introduced, there are five references to the Parousia (1 Thes. 1:10; 2:12, 16, 19; 3:13); the theme is taken up explicitly in 1 Thes. 4:13–5:11. The Thessalonians believe that the Coming is near at hand, and yet Christians have died and hence cannot be present. Are these less privileged than others? Paul's reply is that the dead (in Christ) will not be deprived of their share in the Parousia; they will rise from the dead, so that those who may be alive at the time will have no advantage over those who had died (1 Thes. 4:16-18). It should be noted that the scenario of the Parousia is, in general, the common property of early Christianity and has been colored by the Old Testament prophets and apocalyptic. Terms and images which give expression to Christian eschatology, here and throughout the New Testament, are largely borrowed from the Old Testament descriptions of the Day of Yahweh.[8]

In view of his own vivid expectation of the Second Coming of his Lord, the Apostle has ranged himself among those who will be alive

---

[7] I follow B. Rigaux, *Saint Paul: Les Épîtres aux Thessaloniciens* (Paris: Gabalda, 1956), pp. 195-280.
[8] See pp. 462 f.

at that coming. Did he believe and does he teach that the Parousia is really near at hand? In the very next passage, he admits that he does not know the date of the Parousia (1 Thes. 5:1-3). But, he urges the faithful to be vigilant and to live the Christian life to the full (1 Thes. 5:6-11), just as later he castigates those who, thinking that the last hour was imminent, saw no further purpose in work (2 Thes. 3:6-13). Hopeful expectation of the Lord's Coming is one thing—and this expectation Paul shared with the early Christians— but, a declaration that the Parousia was near at hand is another matter. This Paul never uttered.

The main object of the second letter is to make clear to the Thessalonians, or to some among them, that the Day of the Lord had not yet come, and the perspective of the Parousia is present from the start. In the first Epistle, Paul passed from the fate of the dead to the Coming of the Lord; here, persecutions suggest the consideration of judgment and retribution. The Parousia coincides with the just judgment of God on unbelievers and, for the righteous, with their entering into the kingdom (2 Thes. 1:5). The Lord Jesus will be revealed, coming from heaven with his mighty angels, in flaming fire, inflicting vengeance on those who do not obey the Gospel (2 Thes. 1:8). They will experience eternal loss, far from God and his glory (2 Thes. 1:9), while the saints will share in the glory of that day (2 Thes. 1:10-12).

Before the revelation of the Lord Jesus, however, two events must occur: the apostasy, and the appearance of the "man of lawlessness," both the product of Satan (2 Thes. 2:1-12). The lawless one already acts, but in secret, because someone, or something, restrains him and keeps his activity hidden. But always, the Christian remains one called to salvation (2 Thes. 2:13), to the possession of the glory of our Lord Jesus Christ (2 Thes. 2:14).

In setting an "apostasy" as a sign of the Parousia, Paul is following a Jewish tradition which saw a religious apostasy as a sign of the end.[9] But the apostasy of 2 Thes. has no more than a general and vague form; it is a feature of the end-time, without further specification. In the Apostle's mind, there seems to be a close asso-

---

[9] Cf. *Jubilees* 23:14-23; 4 *Esdras* 5:1 f.; 1QpHab, II, 1-6; VIII, 10.

ciation of the apostasy with the man of lawlessness, because once he has mentioned the latter he no longer refers to the former. And at the end of the passage he pictures the lost as those whom the Antichrist had seduced by his deceptive signs and miracles. These are the apostates who had turned away from the call of love and truth that would have saved them.

In 2 Thes. 2:1-12, Paul speaks of the "man of lawlessness," the obstacle that "restrains" him, and the "mystery of lawlessness." It would be well to have in mind that the passage is apocalyptic and that, especially in his development of the theme of the lawless one (2 Thes. 2:3 f.), he is inspired by Old Testament parallels (Dn. 11:36; Is. 14:13 f.; Ezek. 28:2; Is. 11:4). Each of the three factors will be taken up in turn.

The Pauline description of the lawless one (Antichrist) leads one naturally to think of an individual of the end-time. The appearance of this individual is a sign. Paul, in fact, argues that the non-appearance of the Antichrist is a proof that the Day of the Lord has not come; the Parousia of the Antichrist and the Parousia of Christ are closely associated in 2 Thes. 2:8 f. The Apostle does not specify who the individual is, however, and he is content to speak in general terms. He sees clearly that the world, the human race, is the stake in the struggle of Satan and the Lord; hence, he gives Satan his representative, standing opposed to Christ the envoy of God. He has added his own contribution to the picture of the final events, which he had inherited from Jewish and Christian tradition.

Paul declares that the "mystery of lawlessness" is already at work (2 Thes. 2:7); in other words, iniquity is mysteriously or secretly at work. The mystery of lawlessness, although associated with Antichrist, is not identical with him; the distinction is evident in 2 Thes. 2:7 f. In view of the implied continued activity of the mystery of lawlessness and of the reference to the activity of Satan in 2 Thes. 2:9, it seems best to understand the former to mean "Satan's malign plan to frustrate as far as possible the redemptive work of Christ."[10]

Nevertheless, the satanic activity is being restrained, and with it the revelation of Satan's representative. Who or what constitutes

---

[10]P. H. Furfey, "The Mystery of Lawlessness," *Catholic Biblical Quarterly,* 8 (1946), 189.

the restraining obstacle? It is obviously a force already present, and a beneficent force at that. It does not seem possible to be more specific. The view of certain Fathers—followed by many exegetes —that the restraining force is the Roman Empire or the emperor, is an exegetical conjecture and not a traditional datum.

On the whole, it does seem that Paul has in mind two signs: the apostasy and the man of lawlessness. These will precede the Parousia. Meanwhile, Satan is already at work, but his action is being hindered; some person or influence obliges him to work in secret. This is why his representative—the lawless one, Antichrist—cannot manifest himself for the moment; his day will not come while the obstacle remains. Paul is concerned with assuring the Thessalonians that the Day of the Lord has not come; the absence of the apostasy and of the lawless one is the sign that it has not come. He does not specify or explain further. We simply have to admit that, like many apocalyptic texts, this passage is obscure. It is surely better to make a candid avowal of the fact than to embark on conjectural interpretations.

Our conclusion is that the Epistles to the Thessalonians distinctly affirm the return of Jesus, his manifestations at the end of this age. However, the circumstances and the description of his Coming are so presented that it is difficult to distinguish between image and reality. The close of the age—the period immediately preceding the Parousia—will be marked by Satan's redoubled activity, issuing in the apostasy and the emergence of Antichrist. Paul has spoken in vague terms of the apostasy and he has presented the Antichrist as an unspecified individual, but, vague or not, he regards the signs as real. At the same time, the eschatology of the Apostle is not concerned with the Parousia only; he makes an important statement on the resurrection of the dead: Jesus, Christ and Lord, has risen, and all who die in Christ will rise to live eternally with him.

3. THE MAJOR EPISTLES
1) Galatians

THE GALATIAN CHURCH   The Galatians (*Galatai* = *Keltai*) were a Celtic people which in the fourth century B.C. had emigrated from Gaul to Asia Minor, eventually settling in the territory round about Ancyra (Ankara). The last Galatian king, Amyntas

(d. 25 B.C.), willed his kingdom to the Romans; at his death, it became a Roman province with its capital at Ancyra. By Paul's time the province had embraced a much wider area, incorporating Pisidia, Phrygia, Lycaonia, Paphlagonia, Isauria, Pontus Galaticus, Pontus Polemonianus, and Armenia. Although a few Roman writers did refer to the whole province as "Galatia," it does seem that, in practice, the current language of the first century A.D. reserved the name for the *region*, that is, the original Galatian kingdom.

Because of the ambiguity of the name, some have argued that the "Galatians" of the Epistle are the inhabitants of Pisidia and Lycaonia whom Paul had evangelized on his first missionary journey. This is known as the "South Galatia theory." In favor of this view, it is urged that the second visit of Paul to Jerusalem (Gal. 2:1-10) must be the second visit mentioned in Acts 11:30; 12:25, and not the third visit (Acts 15:2-30); this explains why Gal. seems to be unaware of the apostolic decree of Acts 15: the Epistle was, in fact, written before the Council of Jerusalem. Supporting arguments are that Paul, in speaking of Macedonia, Achaia, and Asia, means the Roman provinces, that he supposes Barnabas (his companion of the first missionary journey) known to the Galatians, and the silence of ancient tradition on the existence of a church in North Galatia.

However, not one of the points raised is conclusive. We have already seen[11] that the second visit of Paul to Jerusalem (Gal. 2:1-10) is most likely to be identified with the journey of Acts 15; and furthermore, that the decree of Acts 15:19 f., 23-29 may well be later than 49 A.D., so that the lack of reference to it in Gal. is not surprising. Paul is not consistent in his reference to Roman provinces: in Gal. 1:21, "Syria" clearly means the region of Antioch, for Judaea was in the province of Syria. If he does name Barnabas, he also speaks of Peter, James, and John who were scarcely known personally to the Galatians. The silence of tradition indicates nothing more than the church of Galatia never achieved celebrity.

In support of the "North Galatia theory"—the common opinion until the nineteenth century—we may point to the *O Galatai* of Gal. 3:1; Paul, a native of Cilicia, and aware of the ethnic differences

---

[11]P. 206.

and national susceptibilities of the peoples within the provinces of Asia Minor, would not have thus addressed inhabitants of Lycaonia and Pisidia (cf. Acts 14:11). Furthermore, the evangelization of Galatia was almost incidental, due to an illness of the Apostle (Gal. 4:13); this does not fit in with the planned campaign of the first missionary journey. Also to be noted is the fact that Paul addresses former pagans (Gal. 4:8; 5:2 f.; 6:12 f.), but in the South Galatia church there would have been many Judeo-Christians, as is clear from the account of the first missionary journey.[12]

Therefore, we may reasonably regard the Galatians as not the inhabitants of Pisidia and Lycaonia, but—North Galatia theory— inhabitants of the Galatian region visited by Paul on his second and third missionary journeys. The Epistle was probably written during the Apostle's stay at Ephesus (54-57 A.D.). Because of its close affinity with Romans, it cannot have been written long before that Epistle. On the other hand, we cannot be sure if it was written before or later than 1 Cor. The most likely date would seem to be 57 A.D. Its authenticity has never been seriously contested.

PLAN

ADDRESS (1:1-5)
REPROOF (1:6-10)
PERSONAL APOLOGIA (1:11—2:21)
THE GOSPEL OF PAUL (3:1—4:11)
EXHORTATION (4:12—6:10)
EPILOGUE (6:11-18)

OCCASION AND SUMMARY   The purpose of Gal. is clearly defined: to refute the errors of Judaizers who had come to disturb the faith of the Galatians by teaching the necessity of the observance of the Mosaic Law, and especially of circumcision; and, posi-

---

[12]See Wikenhauser, *op. cit.*, pp. 266-68; Eng. trans., pp. 374-76, and L. Cerfaux, IB, pp. 404-6 for lists of exponents of the rival theories.

tively, to justify Paul's gospel. The Apostle argues that the Law is a provisional institution and that with the coming of Christ its role has ended; since Christ is now the only Mediator, the Mosaic observances are obsolete. These Judaizers had appealed to the authority of the Apostles and leaders of the Church, like Peter and James, who themselves observed the Law. They attacked the apostolic authority of Paul: since he had been converted after the resurrection, he was not a true Apostle. Besides, his doctrine differed from that of the true Apostles: before the Galatians he denied the necessity of the Law merely to win them more easily; elsewhere he accommodated himself to the customs of the Jews. As the result of the campaign, the Galatians were shaken in their allegiance to Paul and had begun to observe the rites of the Law. They had not yet gone so far as to accept circumcision, but there was danger that they might. When Paul learned of this, overflowing with rightful anger and fatherly solicitude, he wrote this letter. Writing authoritatively and with severity, he showed that the observance of the Mosaic Law was not only not necessary any more, but was worthless for salvation.

The address (Gal. 1:1-5) is unusually solemn. It stresses two points: the divine origin of Paul's apostolate and the saving power of Christ's sacrifice. The indignation of the Apostle accounts for the fact that this is the only one of his Epistles that does not contain an initial thanksgiving; instead, he starts off abruptly with an expression of pained surprise at the fickleness of the Galatians and with a sharp reproof. His adversaries cannot accuse him this time of trying to win favor with men (Gal. 1:6-10). Then he proceeds to assert and to justify his apostolic authority (Gal. 1:11–2:21). When Paul states (Gal. 1:11 f.) that his "gospel" has come to him by direct revelation, he has in mind not all of his knowledge of the faith, but the particular doctrine of justification without the works of the Law. His gospel could not have come to him from the primitive community because he who, before his conversion, was a fanatical upholder of the Law (Gal. 1:17 f.), first came in contact with the leaders of the Christian community only three years after his conversion (Gal. 1:15-20), and after that brief visit to Jerusalem he preached, far from the city, in Syria and Cilicia (Gal. 1:21-24). On the other hand, his gospel had been formally approved by the Jerusalem church (Gal. 2:1-10); furthermore, he had openly defended that gospel of freedom in a confrontation at Antioch with Peter himself (Gal. 2:11-21). In Gal. 2:15-21, we find a clear exposition of his doctrine of justification by faith alone.

The following section (Gal. 3:1—4:11) develops the doctrine. The Galatians should know from their own experience that the Spirit came to them by faith in Jesus, and not by the works of the Law (Gal. 3:1-5); the history of Abraham supports this doctrine (3:6-14), for he had received the promise that cannot be annulled by the later Law (Gal. 3:15-18). Since it was nothing more than the pedagogue or tutor of the people of God who were still in a state of childhood, the role of the Law was transitory (Gal. 3:19-24); but now, by their faith in Christ, Christians are the true descendants of Abraham, heirs of the promise, sons of God (Gal. 3:25—4:7). How, then, can the Galatians dream of going back to the old way of life? (Gal. 4:8-11.)

In Gal. 4:12—6:10, Paul turns to his children with words of affection, with remonstrance, and with practical advice. An illness of the Apostle was the occasion of the conversion of the Galatians—a striking example of God's way of doing things (Gal. 4:12-20). This passage gives a precious insight into Paul's character; the stern words of Gal. 1:6-10; 3:1-5 must be understood in the light of these verses. In order to inherit the promise, it is not enough to be a son of Abraham: one must be a son not like Ishmael but like Isaac, a son of the free woman and not of the slave (Gal. 4:21-31). But, by accepting circumcision, the Galatians would again become slaves and turn their backs on Christ (Gal. 5:1-12). On the other hand, Christian freedom is not license, and the fruits of the Spirit are opposed to the works of the flesh (Gal. 5:13-26). The Christian outlook is not vague; rather, it demands practical charity (Gal. 6:1-6) and the sowing of good seed in view of a harvest (Gal. 6:7-10). Paul, who had dictated the letter, now takes the pen himself and concludes with a warning against the Judaizers and an avowal that, for him, Christ is the center of all things (Gal. 6:11-18).

DOCTRINE[13]   We have noted that the specific purpose of Gal. is to defend the doctrine of justification by faith in Christ, without the works of the Law—Paul's gospel. Yet, it is not an entirely new teaching, although Paul's insistence on it is something new. The Jerusalem leaders were able to approve his stand because they too believed that salvation was from Christ alone. Nor did Paul object to the fact that the Judaeo-Christians of Palestine remained faithful to the Mosaic observances. Yet, he saw the inherent danger and realized that the true Christian doctrine involved freedom from the Law in theory and in fact.

The same basic teaching, in different terms—redemption by the death and resurrection of Christ—runs through the Epistle (cf. 1 Cor. 13:3 f.). Crucified with Christ, the Christian is dead to the Mosaic Law in order to participate in the life of the Risen Christ (Gal. 2:19). For the Christian is animated by the very life of Christ, even while still in the flesh he is spiritualized through faith (Gal. 2:21 f.). But Christians are united to Christ not only through faith but also by baptism; for, by baptism, they are brought into contact with the death and resurrection of Christ and live now the life of him who rose from the dead. We are Christians not only because we belong to Christ but also because we live by him. Assimilated to Christ, clothed in him, forming one with him, we are the true posterity of Abraham, heirs of God (Gal. 3:26-29).

Although the Jew was the heir of the promises, yet, being under the Law—still a minor—he is no better than a slave; and the Christian who wished to take on the practices of the Law would find himself in the same state (Gal. 4:1–5:9). In the fullness of time, when the Son of God came forth, born of a woman (Gal. 4:4), those under the Law came of age and were acknowledged as sons; but only—the whole Epistle makes clear—if they recognized and accepted the Son. When they have done that, the Spirit of God, sent into their hearts, will make them conscious of their new filial relationship (Gal. 4:6 f.).

In reply to the attacks of his adversaries, Paul has made an impassioned defense of his special mission as Apostle to the Gentiles;

---

[13]See L. Cerfaux, IB, pp. 411-16; A. Viard, "Paul: Galates (Épître aux)," DBS, VII, cols. 221-24.

he could even urge his vocation as another argument in favor of his central teaching. For he, before his conversion a committed Jew (Gal. 1:13 f.), had learned from his own experience that the Law is incapable of achieving that justification which is to be found in Christ alone (Gal. 2:16). Conscious though he was of his own special calling (Gal. 1:1, 15) and of his independence of others (Gal. 1:11 f.), he was still careful to show his basic accord with the other Apostles. Thus, his visit to Jerusalem after three years of solitude was specifically to see Peter (Gal. 1:18); in that fortnight spent together, Paul's knowledge of Christ and his assurance of his mission must have become abundantly clear to Peter. He had also met James—the acknowledged head of the Hebrew Christians—whose authority the later Judaizers had invoked against Paul. He, too, had firsthand knowledge of Paul's gospel; and he approved of it as later events were to show. When, fourteen years after his conversion, Paul was again in Jerusalem, this time to make a public stand for his gospel, James and Cephas and John—the "Pillars"—approved of his teaching and acknowledged his special mission (Gal. 2:1-10; Acts 15). The Antioch incident (Gal. 2:11-21) is no indication of fundamental conflict between the Apostle to the uncircumcised and the Apostle to the circumcised (Gal. 2:7). The fact simply was that the wavering conduct of Peter, although he may not have realized it, could undermine the doctrine of freedom and would certainly confuse the faithful. A principle was at stake, and Paul challenged Peter precisely *because* he recognized the latter's authority; a man in Peter's position could not afford to act as he had acted.

The autobiographical passages in Gal. do make us aware that Paul's conviction of his divine vocation, and the power and authority it gave him, guided his missionary career. He was an Apostle no less than the others. But, since his work and theirs was the building up of the Christian Church, he would work in his wide field, not aloof, but in harmony and contact with the others. He proclaimed at once his independence and his solidarity with the apostolic group. Above all, however, it was Christ who mattered; he was the ultimate motive power of his activity, of his life. When Paul wrote to the Galatians, he had, for many years now, preached Christ and suffered for him; he bore on his body the marks of Jesus (Gal. 6:17).

This is why, at the beginning, he can introduce himself as a slave of Christ (Gal. 1:10).

2) 1 Corinthians

THE CORINTHIAN   The celebrated city of Corinth had been de-
CHURCH   stroyed by the Roman consul L. Mummius in
146 B.C.; a century later it was rebuilt by Julius Caesar as a Roman colony (*Colonia laus Julia Corinthus*). Soon it had become the capital of the Roman province of Achaia and the seat of the proconsul. Lying on the narrow isthmus between the ports of Cenchreae in the East and Lechaeum in the West, it was a vital stage in traffic between West and East. Because of its position and commercial status, it had an extremely varied population. Famous for its temple of Aphrodite on the summit of Acrocorinth—the steep hill above the city—it was, by the same token, a byword for sexual immorality; and that even in the world of Paul's day (cf. Rm. 1:26-32).

Paul visited Corinth for the first time on his second missionary journey; there he founded a church and remained for eighteen months, from the winter of 50 A.D. to the summer of 52 A.D. As usual, he began his preaching in the synagogue—on the sabbath. When Silas and Timothy arrived from Macedonia, he was able to devote himself entirely to preaching; but soon the Jews rejected him. Then he went to the house of a Gentile "God-fearer" called Justus. Many Corinthians were subsequently converted and baptized. The Corinthian church was mainly Gentile in composition (although there were some Jews [cf. Acts 18:8]) and was recruited mainly among the poorer classes (although not exclusively [cf. 1 Cor. 1:26-28; 11:22-32]). Shortly after Paul's departure from Corinth, a gifted Alexandrian Jewish convert named Apollos came from Ephesus and preached with notable success (Acts 18:24-28; 1 Cor. 3:5-9).

PLAN OF THE EPISTLE

ADDRESS (1:1-3)

THANKSGIVING (1:4-9)

PARTY STRIFE AND SCANDALS AT CORINTH (1:10—6:20)

1) The rival parties		1:10—4:21
2) A case of incest		5:1-13
3) Christians before pagan courts		6:1-11
4) On fornication		6:12-20

SOLUTION OF PROBLEMS SUBMITTED (7:1—11-1)

1) Marriage and virginity		7:1-40
2) Meats offered to idols		8:1—11:1

ON LITURGICAL ASSEMBLIES AND CHARISMS (11:2—14:40)

THE RESURRECTION OF THE DEAD (15:1-58)

CONCLUSION (16:1-18)

GREETING (16:19-24)

OCCASION AND SUMMARY   While Paul was at Ephesus during his third missionary journey (54-57 A.D.), he wrote what may be termed a "pre-canonical" letter—not extant—to Corinth, warning the converts "not to associate with immoral men" (1 Cor. 9:1; cf. 5:9-13). Some time later he was informed by "Chloe's people" of rival parties in the Corinthian church (1 Cor. 1:12-17). He learned, too, perhaps from the same source, of some who challenged his apostolic authority (1 Cor. 9:1-3). It had also come to his notice that the brethren submitted their differences to the judgment of pagan courts instead of regulating their own affairs (1 Cor. 6:1-8), and he was told of scandals in the church (1 Cor. 5:1; 6:12-20). Besides, the Corinthians, in a letter to the Apostle, had submitted a number of problems (1 Cor. 7:1); this letter was probably carried by a delegation comprised of Stephanas, Fortunatus, and Achaicus (1 Cor. 16:17). The questions involved regarded the relative merits of marriage and virginity (chap. 7), the use of meats offered to idols (chaps. 8-10), and the matter of charisms (1 Cor. 7:1—11:1). Paul had also heard of disorders in the cultic assemblies, notably in the celebration of the Eucharist (chap. 11), and of doubts concerning the resurrection of the dead (chap. 15). The Epistle faces up to the various problems.

In the address (1 Cor. 1:1-3), Paul insists on his own standing as apostle and on the vocation of the Corinthians; the thanksgiving (1 Cor. 1:4-9) regards the riches that the converts have received from God in Christ.

The first part of the letter (1 Cor. 1:10—6:20) is concerned with party spirit among the Corinthians. Rival parties in a Christian community are a contradiction, because Christ is not divided (1 Cor. 1:10-16). Who were those followers of Paul, of Apollos, of Cephas, and of Christ? If the fourth group was made up of those who claimed that, as followers of Christ, they were independent of any human intermediary, it seems clear that three of the parties challenged the authority of Paul while the other group, in reaction, would have gone too far in their attachment to him. The wisdom of God— the folly of the Cross—proclaimed by Paul stands in contrast to the human wisdom that had motivated the dissensions (1 Cor. 1:17—2:5). True Christian wisdom is revealed by the Spirit (1 Cor. 2:6-16). Party strife is further denounced and the proper role of preachers emerges (1 Cor. 3:1-17). The converts must turn from human wisdom which had led to strife and realize that they are all one in Christ (1 Cor. 3:18-23). Paul does not stand trial before the Corinthians—some of whom believe that they have become kings!—he looks only to the scrutiny of the Lord (1 Cor. 4:1-13). With a sudden change characteristic of him, he switches from irony to a paternal appeal (1 Cor. 4:14-21).

Paul then turns to the question of abuses in the community (1 Cor. 5:1—6:20). The Corinthian church had tolerated a case of incest, a man living with his stepmother; he orders the excommunication of the culprit, in the hope of bringing him to his senses (1 Cor. 5:1-5). A warning that a little leaven can ferment a whole lump of dough introduces the theme of the new pasch (1 Cor. 5:6-8). In a previous letter, he had warned them of associating with immoral men (1 Cor. 5:9-13). It is unseemly that Christians should appear before pagan courts; besides, it is shameful to have lawsuits at all. Unrighteousness excludes from the kingdom and should be unheard of in those who had been washed and sanctified in the name of Christ (1 Cor. 6:1-11). In urging freedom from the Mosaic Law, Paul had taught his converts that "all things are lawful"; this does not mean, as some of them had thought, that Christian liberty is license. It does not imply that fornication is licit, for this is a profanation of the body, that temple of the Holy Spirit (1 Cor. 6:12-20).

In the second part of the letter (1 Cor. 7:1–11:1), the Apostle answers the queries raised in the letter of the Corinthian community; in the first place, the merits of marriage and of celibacy. He favors the celibate state, but he acknowledges that marriage is good and he insists on the mutual conferring of conjugal rights (1 Cor. 7:1-9). Concerning divorce, Paul reiterates the Lord's teaching (1 Cor. 7:10 f.), but he gives his own view on mixed marriages (1 Cor. 7:10-16). Then, by association of ideas, he turns to exhort Christians to remain in the way of life which the Lord has assigned to each (1 Cor. 7:17-24) and follows this general admonition with further advice on virginity (1 Cor. 7:25-38) and for widows (1 Cor. 7:39 f.). The essential teaching of the whole section is: In principle, one should remain in the state of life in which one found oneself on accepting the faith; virginity is a more perfect state than marriage and is spiritually more advantageous; marriage is recommended to those who cannot otherwise resist concupiscence—it is a safeguard. One should turn to Eph. 5:22-33 to get the Apostle's positive teaching on marriage.[14]

A particular problem exercising the community was the use of meats offered to idols. In the pagan society of the time, the frequent feasts and ceremonies always involved sacrifices. Portions of the victims were offered to the gods, the priests, and the donors, while the rest of the meat was eaten at a sacred meal or was sold in the market. All this raised a series of problems for Christians: Might one take part in a sacred meal? Might one buy the meat of a victim that had been offered to idols? Might one eat such meat at a meal to which one had been invited? It appears that the majority at Corinth, taking their stand on monotheism and arguing that an idol had no real existence, maintained that the meats in question were clean. Paul approved of this reasoning and attitude (at least in

---

[14]See E. Osty, *Les Épîtres de Saint Paul aux Corinthiens*, (BJ), p. 38.

principle, cf. 1 Cor. 10:14-22), but he warns that, in practice, knowledge is not enough (1 Cor. 8:1—11:1). His general principle is that, while the enlightened Christian will see his way clearly (1 Cor. 8:1-6; 10:15, 25, 29 f.), he must, at the same time, carefully avoid scandalizing those of his brethren whose outlook is still colored by their pagan background (1 Cor. 8:7-13; 10:23 f., 28 f.).

The third part of the letter (1 Cor. 11:2—14:40) is taken up with instructions concerning the liturgical assemblies of the community and the relative importance of spiritual gifts. In 1 Cor. 11:2-16, Paul urges that the subordinate place of women in Christian assemblies is founded on the order of creation. His tastes have been offended by the fact that Christian women of Corinth were praying and prophesying in public worship with heads uncovered. "His repugnance to the growing custom was due to the convention of the ancient world according to which ladies appeared in public with a veil over their hair, ears, and forehead, or else they were no ladies."[15] The arguments that Paul adduces are weak; he recognizes this himself in verse 16 and falls back on an appeal to the custom of the churches.

Even in the celebration of the Lord's Supper dissension among the Corinthians was manifest. They had turned the liturgical celebration into a social occasion. Before the celebration of the Eucharist, there was an ordinary meal; but, the tendency was for the wealthy to meet without waiting for their poorer brethren to join them. Worse still, these convivial gatherings were in danger of becoming occasions of gluttony and drunkenness. If they wanted no more than that it would be better for them to eat their meals at home (1 Cor. 11:17-34).

In chapters 12-14, Paul treats of the final question raised in the letter of the Corinthians, one concerning the "charisms" or spiritual gifts granted to certain members of the community. Their purpose was to manifest the presence of the Spirit and, in the absence of any fully-established hierarchy, to ensure the good order of the churches. However, their number, and the rather disturbing character of some of them, tended to cause confusion. Hence, Paul intervened and clarified the situation: All these gifts come from the same Spirit; they are granted in view of the good of the community;

---

[15]C. S. C. Williams, PCB, n. 838 a.

their relative importance is based on the importance of the services they render; charity stands far above the gift of speaking in tongues (*glossolalia*), a gift of which the Corinthians were inordinately proud; in fact, charity surpasses all the charisms.[16] The long reply contains an important statement on the Body of Christ (1 Cor. 12:12-30) and the famous hymn to *agapē*—fraternal charity, a love which is self-giving, which seeks the good of others. Its source is God, who has first loved us (1 Jn. 4:19) and who has given his Son in order to reconcile sinners with himself. The love of Christians is to be modeled on this love of God and of his Son.[17]

Chapter 15, no longer a reply to a specific question in the Corinthian letter, is an instruction on the resurrection of the dead. Paul had heard of a tendency at Corinth, one influenced by the Greek outlook, to think of the afterlife in terms of the immortality of the soul apart from the body. He argues that the fundamental fact is the resurrection of Jesus (1 Cor. 15:1-11). Christ's resurrection is the guarantee of the resurrection of those "in Christ"; for, if Christ has not risen, his work has failed—he cannot help those who believe in him. And the Christian life, which involves so much self-denial, is foolishness if it ends with death (1 Cor. 15:12-19). At his Second Coming, those who belong to Christ will rise; then he, to whom all things have been made subject, will hand over the kingdom of the Father (1 Cor. 15:20-28). Arguments *ad hominem* support the reasoning (1 Cor. 19:29-34). Verse 29 refers to a practice at Corinth, perhaps vicarious baptism undertaken by Christians on behalf of dead friends and relatives. Paul does not commend the practice, but uses it as an argument.

Next, the manner of the resurrection and the nature of the risen body are considered (1 Cor. 15:35-58). On the analogy of the seed that dies and springs to new life, the resurrection will bring about a profound transformation of the body (1 Cor. 15:35-44). What is sown a physical body, sharing the natural and corruptible principle of life common to all creatures, like that of the first Adam, will be raised a spiritual body, like that of the last Adam, freed from the laws of earthly matter, incorruptible, immortal (1 Cor. 15:45-49).

16See Osty, *op. cit.*, pp. 52 f.
17See pp. 449-51.

In 1 Cor. 15:50-53, Paul refers to the common belief that the Parousia would come soon and that many would be alive at the Lord's Coming (cf. 1 Thes. 4:13-17). The chapter closes with a hymn of thanksgiving for Christ's victory over death (1 Cor. 15:54-58).

The final chapter comes almost by way of an appendix. Paul gives instructions about the collection for the faithful of Jerusalem (1 Cor. 16:1-4); outlines his projected travel plans (1 Cor. 16:5-9); recommends Timothy to the Corinthians (1 Cor. 16:10 f.); and announces that Apollos will not return to the city (1 Cor. 16:12). After a call to faith, courage, and love (1 Cor. 16:13), he recommends the three envoys (1 Cor. 16:15-18) and sends greetings (1 Cor. 16:19 f.). The concluding words are written by the Apostle himself (1 Cor. 16:21-24).

No other epistle gives so clear an idea of the life of a primitive community and of the problems that faced the converts. At the same time, it gives us a precious glimpse of Paul, for it is the letter of a man of action who goes right to the heart of things, of a leader who rigorously combats error and gives precise directions, of a father who loves his children despite their faults, and of an apostle whose only care is to win men to Christ.

DOCTRINE   1. *The Eucharist.*[18] Twice in 1 Cor. Paul speaks of the Eucharist: apropos of pagan sacred meals in which no Christian may participate (1 Cor. 10:14-21); and to censure the abuses which had come to be associated with the celebration of the Lord's Supper (1 Cor. 11:23-32). In the latter passage, he recalled the essential ceremony which gives its meaning to the sacred meal of the Christian community. The words of institution (1 Cor. 11:23-25) doubtless echo the liturgical text with which the Apostle was familiar, that in vogue at Antioch and in the churches founded by him (cf. Lk. 22:15-20). In full accord with the synoptists, Paul teaches the faithful of Corinth that, the night on which he was delivered up, Christ took bread and pronounced over it the words: "This is my body." Then, he took a cup of wine and pronounced the words which we may paraphrase: "This (the wine contained in this cup) is my

---

[18]See M.-E. Boismard, "L'Eucharistie selon saint Paul," *Lumière et Vie*, 31 (1957), 93-106.

blood which ratifies the New Covenant." Each time he added: "Do this in remembrance of me."

Of itself, the phrase "This is my body" need mean no more than "This bread represents my body." The context, however, shows that Paul understood the words of Jesus in a very realistic sense. Thus, he adds that those who receive unworthily "will be guilty of profaning the body and blood of the Lord" (1 Cor. 11:27); and, before eating, a man must examine himself and eat of the bread and drink of the cup in such a manner that he can "discern the body" (1 Cor. 11:28 f.). In other words, for Paul, the body and blood of Christ are *really* present. He had already made the point in chapter 10: "The cup of blessing which we bless, is it not a participation in the blood of Christ? The bread which we break, is it not a participation in the body of Christ?" (1 Cor. 10:16.) He goes on to affirm that, if the Christian community can form the "body of Christ" in the wider sense, it is precisely because it partakes of the physical body of Christ: "*Because* there is one loaf, we who are many are one body, *for* all partake of the same loaf" (1 Cor. 10:17). In short, for Paul, after the words of consecration, the bread and wine have become really, physically, the body and blood of Christ; he does not say how the transformation is wrought.

Jesus had said: "This is my body, which is [given] for you"; and Paul had added: "As often as you eat this bread and drink this cup, you proclaim the Lord's death until he comes" (1 Cor. 11:24, 26). The celebration of the Supper is thus a proclamation of the death of Christ, it is a redemptive sacrifice ("for you"). Jesus had also said: "This is the new covenant in my blood" (1 Cor. 11:25): his approaching death is presented as a sacrifice, like that of the victim whose blood sealed the Sinai Covenant (Ex. 24:5-8); his sacrifice is about to inaugurate the New Covenant which Jeremiah had foretold (Jer. 31:31-34). Furthermore, he had added: "Do this in remembrance of me" (1 Cor. 11:24 f.). The disciples must repeat what he had done and said, his actions and his words. It is not a mere commemoration, but the renewal of a rite by means of which the sacrifice of the living Christ is made actual in bread and wine; their action will be as real and efficacious as that of Jesus. The gestures, the words, will be repeated, but the reality will persist unchanged: the sacrificial offering of the body and blood of Christ made once for all. Thus, Christ, literally, physically, will be with his own to the end of time—"until he comes." The last phrase makes clear that Paul sees that the Supper which Christians now actually celebrate is immediately ordered to the Parousia; for the body of Christ, present on the Eucharistic table, is the body of the Risen Christ—that body, transformed by the Spirit, in which he will return.

2. *The Body of Christ.* We have noted above that the verses 1 Cor. 10:16 f. witness to the realism of Paul's view of the Eucharist; the context will not permit us to see in the one body formed by Christians only a metaphor expressing their common union in Christ.

> It is very clear indeed that this body is first and foremost the individual body of the Lord, dead and risen, in which they participate by receiving the Eucharistic bread. The word *soma* [body] must have the same meaning in verses 16 and 17. There is a remarkable inference from the relation of one verse to the other: by receiving in their body, through the sacramental rite, the body of Christ, they "are," all together, one body, that is to say, this body, at first individual but now drawing into itself all the bodies of those whom it unites to itself.[19]

By the Eucharistic experience, we become aware that we are members of the body of Christ, and our union with Christ should therefore be understood in a very realistic sense (cf. 1 Cor. 6:15). Hence, when Paul states that we form one body (1 Cor. 12:12), he is not speaking metaphorically and is not referring primarily to a Greek fable of the body and its members (1 Cor. 12:14-26). It is the personal body of Christ which draws together the many members of the body which believers have become through baptism (1 Cor. 12:13, 27) and by Eucharistic communion (1 Cor. 10:17). Around the individual body of Jesus, the unity of men, called to join themselves to this body, is achieved.[20]

The highest point reached by 1 Cor. on the theme of the body of Christ is found in 1 Cor. 12:12 f., 27: "For just as the body is one and has many members, and all the members of the body, though many, are one body, so it is with Christ. For by one Spirit we are all baptized into one body. . . . Now you are the body of Christ and

---

[19]P. Benoit, *Exégèse et Théologie* (Paris: Cerf, 1961), II, p. 117.
[20]See F. Amiot, VTB, p. 166.

individually members of it." At this period in his thought, *sōma* meant the physical body of Christ; it is the real body of Christ present in the Eucharist. (Indeed, the expression "Mystical Body of Christ," now applied to the Church, originally designated the Eucharistic body of the Lord.) Union with the body of Christ means union with his Eucharistic body, or the union which comes about through baptism into the death of Christ. Although Paul was influenced by the Hellenistic figure of the body and its members as representative of the social order, there is not yet a concept of the Body of Christ in the sense of the Church as it will appear in the Captivity Epistles.

> All Christians as a group, insofar as they are a spiritual organism, are mystically united with the body of Christ. We must never go beyond the bounds of this statement. We may go beyond it unduly either when we identify the organism with the *person* of Christ, or when we speak of the *mystical body* of Christ as a collective person which forms the Church.[21]

3) 2 Corinthians

OCCASION AND DATE   Shortly after he had written 1 Cor., a sudden crisis demanded a brief and painful visit of Paul to Corinth (2 Cor. 1:23–2:1; 12:14; 13:1 f.). He returned to Ephesus, promising to go back for a longer stay (2 Cor. 1:15 f.); but soon a fresh incident, in which it seems that the authority of Paul was flouted in the person of his representative (2 Cor. 2:5-10; 7:12), called forth a "severe letter" (2 Cor. 2:3 f., 9), which had a salutary effect (2 Cor. 7:8-13). It was in Macedonia, not long after his arrival from Ephesus (1 Cor. 15:22; 2 Cor. 1:8-10; Acts 19:23-40), that Paul received this comforting assurance from Titus (2 Cor. 2:12 f.; 7:5-16); and there, toward the close of 57 A.D., he wrote 2 Cor. It was the fourth time—or at least the fourth time—that he had written to Corinth; the other letters being the "precanonical letter" (1 Cor. 5:9), 1 Cor., and the "severe letter."

There is no reference in 2 Cor. to the problems raised in 1 Cor.; hence, this letter seems to have been effective. When he wrote 2 Cor.,

---

[21]L. Cerfaux, *The Church in the Theology of St. Paul*, trans. G. Webb and A. Walker (London: Herder/Nelson, 1959), pp. 282 f.

Paul was planning to visit Corinth "for the third time" (2 Cor. 12:14; 13:1). He did in fact arrive in the city in 57 A.D. and spent the winter there (Acts 20:3). The intermediary visit (2 Cor. 13:2) was short, and painful—both for the Corinthians and Paul. This visit had not brought order to Corinth. The severe letter, written "with many tears," makes mention of a situation involving "one who did wrong" and "one who suffered a wrong" (2 Cor. 7:12). It is not the case of the incestuous man (1 Cor. 5:1-13), for the circumstances are notably different. As we have suggested, it seems to concern one who had challenged the authority of the Apostle's representative. Judaizing missionaries had arrived (cf. 2 Cor. 11:22)—the "arch-apostles" (2 Cor. 11:5) or "false apostles" (2 Cor. 11:13) who strove to undermine Paul's prestige and authority. The culprit of 2 Cor. 7:12 was, very likely, one of these "superlative apostles." Paul's severe letter had a salutary effect; and his relief found vent in 2 Cor., although it does seem that chapters 10-13 were occasioned by reports of further unrest in the community.

UNITY   It is not necessary to dwell on the authenticity of 2 Cor.: it is freely admitted by almost all scholars (although we may have to allow for a short interpolation). The unity of the letter is another matter. Do we have a single letter, written as such by the Apostle, or a combination of two or more letters? Tradition, supported by the textual evidence, unhesitatingly regards the Epistle as a unit. But many modern scholars feel that the internal evidence points in the direction of the second alternative. Three passages especially call for attention: 2 Cor. 6:14—7-1; chapters 8-9; chapters 10-13.

1. *2 Cor. 6:14—7:1.* This passage gives the impression of having been interpolated into its present context. It brusquely introduces a new idea and breaks the flow of the argument; 2 Cor. 7:2 follows naturally on 2 Cor. 6:13. It has been suggested that there is a fragment of the "precanonical letter" (cf. 1 Cor. 5:9-13), but the suggestion must remain gratuitous. More to the point is the observation that the passage shows a remarkable affinity with the Qumran literature. The struggle between Light and Darkness is an idea that is characteristic of Qumran dualism; here we find that the writer sharply contrasts righteousness and iniquity, light and dark-

ness, Christ and Belial. The name "Belial," frequently occurring in the sectarian literature, is found nowhere else in the New Testament. It is hard to deny some influence of Qumran ideas, and the impression of an interpolation is a strong one. Perhaps the passage may be the work of an Essene disciple of Paul.[22] At any rate, we must admit that the authenticity of the passage is in some doubt.

2. *Chapters 8-9.* Each of these chapters is concerned with the collection for the Jerusalem church and both cover the same ground; it appears that they represent two distinct letters. In 2 Cor. 9:1, Paul declares that it is "superfluous for me to write to you about the offering for the saints"; coming just after a whole chapter devoted to the collection, this rings strangely. Then, in 2 Cor. 8:1-5, he seeks to stir the Corinthians to emulation by recalling the eagerness and liberality of the churches of Macedonia, while in 2 Cor. 9:1-6 he tells the Corinthians how, in Macedonia, he had boasted of their zeal and generosity. Also, the motives for a ready response are presented twice and differently (2 Cor. 8:7-15; 9:6-14). On the evidence, it seems that we may reasonably regard chapter 9 as a letter, or part of a letter, originally written to churches of Achaia other than Corinth. Its insertion after chapter 8 must have occurred very early, because all extant manuscripts contain it as part of the Epistle. (The same is true of 2 Cor. 6:14—7:1.)[23]

3. *Chapters 10-13.* To one who has read through the Epistles, the sharp tone of these final chapters comes as a surprise. Nor is it only a matter of tone. Certain expressions of the last four chapters are not easily reconcilable with passages in the earlier parts (cf. 2 Cor. 1:24 and 13:5; 2 Cor. 7:4; 14:16; 8:7 and 10:2; 11:3 f., 20 f.; 13:2-10). While it is not difficult to imagine that Paul could have written to the Corinthians in terms of chapters 10-13, it is not so easy to comprehend why he should have started off, and continued for so long, on a different line. The reverse order would have been readily understandable; the present order cries out for an explanation.

It has been suggested that chapters 10-13 form part of the "severe letter," and hence were indeed written before chapters 1-9. But, from the references to that letter "written with many tears," we

22See p. 304.
23See Osty, *op. cit.*, pp. 78 f.

would expect to meet with sad reproaches and hurt tenderness, not with the anger and indignation of chapters 10-13. Besides, there is no mention here of the "offender" and the "injured one," in other words, of the incident that was the motive and theme of the severe letter. An alternative solution is that news of further trouble reached Paul before he had completed his letter (cf. 2 Thes. 3:6-15); or, perhaps, when he had ended it, for, with the addition of a brief final greeting, chapters 1-9 could very well stand as a complete letter. At any rate (the theory goes), disturbed and indignant at the latest report, he added chapters 10-13; thus, the unexpected order of the letter is explained by the circumstances of its composition.[24]

Perhaps, however, we have been demanding of Paul a cold logic and an academic methodology that do not fit his Semitic mentality and volatile temperament—and in a letter as personal as 2 Cor. at that. Since we can offer no certain answers to the factors that point to unity or to lack of it, we shall, in practice, take the letter as it stands.

PLAN

ADDRESS (1:1 f.)	
THANKSGIVING (1:3-11)	
PAUL'S APOLOGIA (1:12—7:16)	
1) The Journey to Corinth	1:12—2:17
2) The apostolic ministry	3:1—6:10
3) Appeal and consolation	6:11—7:16
THE COLLECTION FOR THE JERUSALEM CHURCH (8—9)	
POLEMICAL APOLOGIA (10:1—13:10)	
1) Reply to accusations	10
2) Paul's apostolate	11:1—12:18
3) The third visit	12:19—13:10
CONCLUSION (13:11-13)	

[24]See *ibid.*, pp. 80 f.

SUMMARY   The address (2 Cor. 1:1 f.) is followed by Paul's thanksgiving to God for support in the trials of the ministry and for deliverance from grave danger (2 Cor. 1:3-11). His explanation of his former conduct toward the Corinthians forms the first part of the letter (2 Cor. 1:12–7:16). He explains why he had changed his travel plans. Refuting a charge of duplicity, he declares himself to be not a man who answers "yes" and "no" in the same breath. It was to spare their feelings that he had not come to Corinth: one painful visit was more than enough. Instead, from Macedonia he had written a severe letter, "with many tears." Now that the culprit had been duly punished by the community, it was time to pardon him. But Paul was still anxious for his Corinthians and he had left Troas for Macedonia in order to meet Titus who would bring him news of them. He joyfully thanks God for the good tidings received (2 Cor. 1:12–2:17).

Next he turns to the grandeur and the demands of the apostolic ministry (2 Cor. 3:1–6:10). Paul needed no recommendation to or from the converts, such as his adversaries doubtlessly required; the community at Corinth was his recommendation, an open letter for all to read. He is a minister of the New Covenant, one of the Spirit and not of the letter; the administration of the New Covenant is more glorious than Moses' administration of the old. Basing himself on a free exegesis of Ex. 34:33-35, he argues that the Jews fail to see that the Old Testament has reached fulfillment. Yet, they have only to turn to Christ for the veil to be removed. The role of an apostle is to preach Jesus Christ as Lord, to bring to men the knowledge of God revealed in Christ (2 Cor. 3:1–4:6).

Apostles, it is true, are earthen vessels, to show that divine, not human, power is at work in them. Paul may be worn down by the tribulations of the ministry, but the life of Jesus flows from him to other men, and he is confident that he will share in the resurrection of Jesus. All the while, his spiritual life is being renewed and his sufferings are a prelude to his reunion with Christ (2 Cor. 4:7–5:10). The climax of the apologia is reached in 2 Cor. 5:11–6:10. He does not commend himself to the Corinthians, but he would wish them to be proud of him—this is why he has explained his conduct so fully. It is the love of Christ that stirs him and he, in his turn, proclaims Christ dead and risen again. For, in Christ, God has reconciled the world to himself. It was for our sake that God made him "to be sin" (2 Cor. 5:21); that is, God had sent his Son "in the likeness of sinful flesh" (Rm. 8:3), in order to become a sacrifice for sin. By dying in his flesh, the sensible sign of the sinful world, and by rising in a body made new, Christ himself and in him, virtually, all humanity passed from the carnal to the spiritual life.[25] Paul commends himself by the sufferings he has undergone in the service of Christ; he entreats his faithful not to receive the grace of God in vain.

A tender appeal (2 Cor. 6:11–7:4) is unexpectedly interrupted by an exhortation not to associate with unbelievers and a warning to have no part with Belial (2 Cor. 6:14–7:1). The Apostle declares that his mind is now fully at rest. Titus has brought good news; he realizes that the severe letter had produced a salutary effect and he is confident that he can depend on his Corinthians (2 Cor. 7:5-16).

The letter passes to the question of a collection for the church of Jerusalem (chaps. 8-9). This matter of a collection in favor of the "saints" of Jerusalem was of great importance in Paul's eyes (cf. Gal. 2:10; 1 Cor. 16:1-3; 2 Cor. 8-9; Rm. 15:25-27). Since, for him, the Christian is a member of the Body, and life in Christ is the life of the people of God, the unity of the Church is essential. He developed his theology of unity especially in the face of differences between Judaeo-Christian and Gentile converts and under the impetus of internal strife in the Corinthian community. In view of this, and of his great regard for Jerusalem as the holy city of the new people of God, the collection was much more than a work of charity.

> The carrying into effect of this project of the collection was perhaps the happiest stroke of genius in the whole of his life as an apostle. By it Jerusalem won a religious empire and the Gentile Christians saved not only their unity, but also their living connection with the center of monotheism and purity of life.[26]

Paul holds up for imitation the churches of Macedonia which, in spite of their difficulties and extreme poverty, had contributed volun-

---

[25]See L. Sabourin, *Rédemption Sacrificielle* (Bruges: Desclée de Brouwer, 1961), p. 445.

[26]L. Cerfaux, *The Church in the Theology of St. Paul, op. cit.,* p. 261.

tarily and liberally to the needs of the brethren of Jerusalem. Titus
had been urged to complete the work already begun in Corinth.
The Corinthian church, outstanding in every way, also must be
foremost in this. Paul's ultimate argument is not friendly emulation,
but the self-abasement of the Incarnation, the great charity of Jesus
Christ, for the only driving motive that he knew, the only motive
that really matters to a Christian, is the example of Christ and the
imitation of him. The Corinthians are not expected to impoverish
themselves, but they should give generously whatever they can spare.
Paul is sending two delegates besides Titus (one is very likely Luke
[2 Cor. 8:15 f.]); they should be warmly welcomed at Corinth (chap.
8).

Chapter 9 covers the same ground as chapter 8; we have suggested
that it was originally addressed to churches other than Corinth. Paul
has pointed to the churches of Achaia in order to stir the generosity
of the Macedonians (in 2 Cor. 8:1-6, it was the other way about).
Generosity is urged: almsgiving is a sowing of seed, and there exists
between the seed and the harvest a strict law of proportion. But it
is a question of one's attitude rather than of the amount one gives;
the important thing is that the gift, whether big or little, should be
given freely, gladly: "God loves a cheerful giver" (2 Cor. 9:7). God
will see to it that the generous giver will not suffer on account of
his generosity. He will receive spiritual blessings, but he will be
blessed in temporal matters too—so that he may be able to give more
liberally still! This work does not end with the relief of those in
need; the benefactor will benefit from the prayers of those he has
helped, and glory is given to God (chap. 9).

In the final part of the letter (chapters 10-13), Paul turns again
to a personal apologia, but this time with a marked polemical tone.
It seems that Titus, sent by Paul to organize the collection (2 Cor.
8:6, 17 f.), had found that the Apostle's adversaries had renewed
their attacks on him. When Paul had received word of the latest
development, he quickly wrote chapters 10-13. His adversaries had
accused him of weakness: Paul can speak boldly when he is at a safe
distance, but is timid and wavering when confronted. He assures
them that he is quite prepared to take strong action whenever it is

necessary. He will not class himself with those who so love to blow their own trumpet. He is not trespassing when he exercises his authority at Corinth, a church founded by himself. The Lord has called him to the apostolic ministry—this is approbation and praise enough; self-praise would sound foolishly beside it (chap. 10).

Although much of chapter 11 is bitingly sarcastic, Paul begins by excusing himself for his self-defense. He had been called a "fool"; then, they must be prepared to put up with his "folly." He had been driven to this self-defense by the fickleness of the Corinthians who were ready to accept a different gospel. He is not a whit inferior to the "super-apostles," those self-styled representatives of the mother-church to whom the Corinthians have turned; his unyielding insistence on financial independence marks him off from those others. Now he is obliged to boast in order to prove his apostleship genuine (2 Cor. 11:1-21a). While he cannot compete with the arrogance of his adversaries, he can match their claims of race (Hebrews), religion (Israelites), and inheritance (descendants of Abraham). And if they claim to be servants of Christ, his litany of sufferings *proves* him to be a true minister of Christ (2 Cor. 11:21b-33). Although boasting about visions is out of place, Paul is compelled to recall an extraordinary experience he had fourteen years previously: he had found himself caught up to the divine presence. However, a keen reminder of his human weakness kept him from being carried away by the experience. We do not know the nature of the "thorn in the flesh"; most likely it was a recurring illness; there are no grounds for regarding it as the urge of concupiscence (2 Cor. 12:1-10). Again he is forced to justify himself (2 Cor. 12:11-18). He fears that he will have to take strong action when he visits them anew, and he is quite ready to do so. But he hopes that the sinners will repent, because he has no desire to lord it over them. The Corinthians are strong when their conduct is fully Christian, and in this case Paul is weak since he does not have to invoke his apostolic authority against them (2 Cor. 12:19—13:10). The conclusion (2 Cor. 13:11-14) makes a final appeal for a Christian life in the joy of union. The closing wish, trinitarian in form, is possibly a liturgical formula.

4) Romans

THE ROMAN   The origin of the Roman church is shrouded in
CHURCH   darkness, but it is unquestioned that Christians had
gained a footing in Rome in the early days of the Church. Most
probably, the foundation of a church there was not due to a planned
mission, but was the result of the migration of Christians to the
capital of the empire. Some of the early converts were to be found
among the Jews and proselytes who had heard the preaching of
Peter at Pentecost (Acts 2). It is not likely that Peter himself was
the founder of the Roman church, for he seems to have come to
Rome for the first time in the decade 50-60 A.D.

Some have contended that the Roman community was predominantly Judaeo-Christian in composition. Paul addresses self-satisfied
Jews (Rm. 2:17–3:8); he contrasts faith and the Law (Rm. 3:21-31);
he speaks of "Abraham, our forefather according to the flesh" (Rm.
4:1); he answers objections against his doctrine of freedom from
the Law (Rm. 6:1–7:6); he dwells at length on the fate of Israel
(chaps. 9-11); finally, the "weak" of Rm. 14:1–15:13 are said to be
Judaeo-Christians. To all this evidence must be added the weighty
fact that the main doctrine of Rm. is this: Not circumcision and
the Law, but faith without the works of the Law brings salvation.

Yet, strong as these indications seem, they are outweighed by
arguments in favor of a Gentile-Christian majority. In his prologue
and at the close, Paul expresses his desire of visiting Rome and insists on his vocation of Apostle to the Gentiles. He addresses the
Romans as Gentile-Christians: he had received from Christ the mission of the apostolate among the nations, "including yourselves" (the
Romans) (Rm. 1:5 f.). Hitherto he had been prevented from visiting Rome, where he would wish to bear fruit "as among the rest
of the Gentiles" (Rm. 15:16). He addresses them quite deliberately
as Gentiles: "Now I am speaking to you Gentiles—inasmuch as I am
an apostle to the Gentiles" (Rm. 11:13). These texts are conclusive. The Roman church was composed, for the greater part, of
Gentile-Christians; the evidence to the contrary indicates no more
than a minority of Judaeo-Christians.[27]

---

[27]See Wikenhauser, *op. cit.*, 288-90; Eng. trans., pp. 403-5.

OCCASION AND
DATE

Paul had long desired to visit Rome. He had proclaimed the name of Christ in the East, and in Europe as far as Illyricum; now he wanted to preach in the West, especially in Spain. On the journey to Spain he planned to pass through Rome. As Apostle to the Gentiles he was more anxious than ever to establish contact with the Roman church for, in view of that apostolate, its position as church of the empire's capital was of paramount importance. He who did not wish to build on foundations laid by others, nevertheless saw clearly that the roads which led from Rome to all parts of the *orbis Romanus* could become so many roads of missionary expansion. Romans, then, was written to prepare the way for the visit of Paul: he wished that the Romans should know beforehand the main lines of "his" gospel.

For Paul is concerned to expound his gospel, his manner of presenting the Good News of Christ. From the moment of his conversion, he had perceived with clarity the unique role of Christ in the salvation of men. His work among the Gentiles had colored his attitude to Jewish law and practice; the enmity of Jews and the opposition of Judaeo-Christians further sharpened his appreciation of the central truth of salvation through faith in Christ. The writing of Gal. had given an opportunity of stating his thesis, but in a polemical atmosphere; now he can take it up again in a calmer fashion and more leisurely. It is not, however, a synthesis of his theology—there are too many omissions for that. But Paul does take occasion to expound a theme which he had pondered at length: The salvation of God, presented by the preaching of the Gospel first to Jews and then to Gentiles; salvation, a divine force, necessary for all and offered to all (Rm. 1:1 f., 16 f.).[28]

Paul had not lost sight of the controversial and the apologetic, and the problem which he faced was, for him, a practical one. That problem, as presented, may have no more than an historical interest for us, but behind the temporary form of the question lie permanent interests.

> The discussion of the relation of Christianity to the religion out of which it sprang can never be obsolete while the Old Testament retains any place in Christian worship or instruction—that is, while

---

[28]See J. Cambier, IB, pp. 456 f.

Christianity remains an historical religion. Moreover, although the Jewish Law is a matter of indifference to us, yet the legalist conception of religion is by no means obsolete. In our times, as in Paul's, it besets the minds of many Christian people, and often gives a distorted view of the Christian religion to the general public.[29]

Yet, the Epistle remains essentially a doctrinal exposition in which the Apostle develops his conception of salvation and of the Christian life. He teaches the Romans that the Gospel understood in the sense of integral Christianity is the sole efficacious saving force: "It is the power of God for salvation to every one who has faith, to the Jew first and also the Greek" (Rm. 1:16).

Rm. was written at Corinth toward the close of the third missionary journey, during the winter 57/58 A.D. That Corinth was the place of origin is indicated by Paul's recommendation of Phoebe, deaconess of Cenchreae, the eastern port of Corinth (Rm. 16:1), and by the fact that he is the guest of Gaius who is, very likely, the same man named in 1 Cor. 1:14 (Rm. 16:23). We may add that, according to Acts 20:2 f., Paul left from Corinth on his last journey to Jerusalem (cf. Rm. 15:25).

UNITY OF THE EPISTLE The authenticity of Rm. is universally accepted; "Attempts to question it may be reckoned among the eccentricities of criticism."[30] On the other hand, there is a question of the integrity of the letter; specifically, whether chapters 15-16 or, at least, the doxology (Rm. 16:25-27) originally belonged to it.

There is evidence that, in the second and third centuries, three recensions of Rm. were current. Thus, for instance, the position of the doxology (which of its nature should end the Epistle) varies. It is found after Rm. 16:23 in many of the earliest manuscripts, after Rm. 14:23 in many mainly later manuscripts, and after Rm. 15:33 in the important P[46]. Besides, a system of Latin chapter headings (*capitula*)—certainly earlier than the fourth century A.D.—leave no place for chapters 15-16, but pass directly from Rm. 14:15-23 (chap. 50) to the doxology (chap. 51); hence, the Latin version for which the *capitula* were compiled lacked Rm. 15-16.

---

[29]C. H. Dodd, *The Epistle of Paul to the Romans* (London: Collins; Fontana Books, 1959[2]), p. 26.

[30]T. W. Manson, PCB, n. 815 a.

The shortest form, ending at Rm. 14:23 (and breaking off in the middle of an argument that really continues on to Rm. 15:13), is, according to Origen, the work of the heretic Marcion (c. 150 A.D.) who deliberately cut the letter at that point. Although the *capitula* point to a corresponding short Latin version, it is not represented by a single extant Latin manuscript. The authority of P⁴⁶ (our earliest manuscript of the Epistle—third century A.D.) is weighty, but its setting of the doxology at the end of chapter 15 may mean nothing more than that the scribe regarded chapter 16 as not very suitable for liturgical reading in church. We may reasonably take it that chapter 15 forms an integral part of the Epistle.

A difficulty is raised by the long list of names in chapter 16, for it does seem surprising that Paul should have had so many friends in a church he had never visited. Then, there is the unexpected warning against false teachers (Rm. 16:17-20). In face of these facts, it has been suggested that Rm. 16 is a short letter to some other church, probably Ephesus, where Paul was well known. This must remain a gratuitous hypothesis and, perhaps, not a very likely one: "A letter consisting almost entirely of greetings may be intelligible in the age of the picture postcard; for any earlier period it is a monstrosity."[31] Or, the chapter may have served to introduce Phoebe to the Ephesians, and Paul seized the occasion to send them a copy of the letter he had just written to the Romans; this is another doubtful hypothesis. The presence of many of Paul's friends in Rome may not be so surprising. We know that travel to the capital from all parts of the empire was common in the first century A.D. It is also possible that many of those listed would have been temporarily exiled from Rome in 49 A.D. by the edict of Claudius;[32] Paul could have met them in the eastern provinces. It appears that we cannot say with certainty that chapter 16 was originally part of Rm., but evidence to the contrary is far from being conclusive.

From the viewpoint of textual criticism, doubt about the authenticity of the doxology springs solely from the hesitation of the manuscript tradition on the place to be assigned to it; only Marcion,

---

[31]H. Lietzmann, quoted by Dodd, *op. cit.*, p. 13.
[32]See p. 32.

Ephrem, and a few manuscripts omit it altogether. Hence, on internal evidence—it is certainly not un-Pauline in style—and on the testimony of the practical totality of manuscripts, it is to be judged authentic and an integral part of Rm. ·

PLAN

THE ADDRESS (1:1-7)	
THE THANKSGIVING (1:8-15)	
PART I. SALVATION BY FAITH (1:16—11:36)	
A. JUSTIFICATION	
THE THEME (1:16 f.)	

1) The universal sway of sin and retribution	1:18—3:20
2) The justice of God and faith	3:21—4:25
a. The doctrine of justification	3:21-32
b. The example of Abraham	4:1-25

B. SALVATION	
THE THEME (5:1-11)	

1) Liberation from sin, death, and the Law	5:12—7:25
a. Adam and Christ	5:12-21
b. Union with Christ in death and resurrection	6:1-14
c. Freedom from sin	6:15-23
d. Freedom from the Law	7:1-6
e. The role of the Law	7:7-25
2) Life in the Spirit	8:1-39
3) The situation of Israel	9—11
a. The privileges of Israel	9:1-5
b. Divine sovereignty	9:6-29
c. Israel's responsibility	9:30—10:21
d. God has not rejected his people	11:1-32
e. Hymn to the divine mercy	11:33-36

PART II. THE JUSTICE OF GOD IN CHRISTIAN LIVING
(12:1—15:13)

1) Sacrifice of self	12:1 f.
2) Proper use of charisms	12:3-8
3) Charity	12:9-21
4) Christians and the state	13:1-7
5) Love fulfills the Law	13:8-10
6) The Christian is a child of light	13:11-14
7) The "Strong" and the "Weak"	14:1—15:13

EPILOGUE (15:14—16:27)

1) Personal explanations	15:14-33
2) Recommendation of Phoebe	16:1 f.
3) Greetings to friends in Rome	16:3-16
4) A final word of warning	16:17-20
5) Greetings of Paul's companions	16:21-23

DOXOLOGY (16:24-27)

SUMMARY   The address (Rm. 1:1-7) is unusually solemn: Paul presents his credentials to a church where he is unknown and over which he has no authority. He is a servant of Jesus Christ, called to be an apostle. He preached to the Gentiles that gospel foretold by the prophets and realized in Christ, a descendant of David, but now by his resurrection established Son of God in the glory of his power according to his spirit of holiness—our Lord. Christ is presented in his salvific role: the Risen Lord has become "a lifegiving spirit" (1 Cor. 15:45). The thanksgiving (Rm. 1:8-15) acknowledges the good name of the Roman church and expresses the Apostle's eager desire to preach among them. In Rm. 1:16 f., we find the theme of the Epistle: The Gospel (the revelation of God's justice), the very power of God, working for the salvation of all who receive it by faith. It is preached first to the Jews whose historical role as Chosen People entitles them to hear it first; after that there is no distinction between Jew and Gentile.

In contrast to the revelation of God's justice, is the manifestation of his anger against Gentile and Jew (Rm. 1:18—3:20). In a passage inspired by Wis. 13:1-9, Paul declares that contemplation of the wonderful works of God should have led the Gentiles to an acknowledgment of the Creator; instead, men have perversely worshiped creatures. Idolatry is punished by depraved morals (cf. Wis. 14:22-31). The Apostle is passing judgment on the pagan world as such, not on individuals (Rm. 1:18-32). Then he turns to the Jews (Rm. 2:1–3:20). The Jew who sets himself up as a judge of other men will not be spared if he acts like them. Neither the Law, nor circumcision, nor the Scripture will dispense him from interior righteousness. All men, Jews and Gentiles, must face the judgment of God and will receive reward or punishment according to their deeds. The Gentiles who have not the advantage of a Law positively revealed can still follow the law written on the heart of every man. Paul does admit that the Jew has the honor of belonging to the Chosen People, but this alone is not sufficient to save him. Many Jews have, in fact, proved unfaithful, but then the failure of men cannot hinder the fulfillment of God's promises. The Law, an external norm of conduct, has not, in God's plan, the role of remitting sin; rather, it brings the sinner to an awareness of sin.

After the preliminary stage of his argument—apart from the Gospel all that is to be found in the world is sin and its retribution—Paul can turn to the thesis announced in Rm. 1:17: "The righteousness of God is revealed through faith for faith" (Rm. 3:21–4:25). The plan of God is presented in Rm. 3:21-26. Paul combines three metaphors: from the law-court (justification), from the institution of slavery (emancipation), and from sacrificial ritual (expiation by blood): "They are justified by his grace . . . through the redemption which is in Christ Jesus . . . and expiation by his blood" (Rm. 3:24 f.). He describes an act of God for men, the metaphors serving to emphasize the change of status involved.

> But what he is here concerned to make clear is that by no possible effort of his own could man alter his status before God, any more than a guilty prisoner could acquit himself, or a slave free himself, or an "unclean" person become "clean" without supernatural means; but that God, by a sheer act of grace, has made this change possible.[33]

---

[33]Dodd, *op. cit.,* p. 80.

For man is justified by faith alone and not by the works of the Law. Paul contrasts two regimes: one consists in believing, that is, in submitting oneself to the justifying activity of God; the other is a vain striving to find grace through works (Rm. 3:27-31).

Paul now brings Abraham forward in support of his doctrine of justification by faith (Rm. 4:1-25). In Jewish tradition, Abraham, by his constancy in trial, had become the model of justification by works. The Apostle argues that the faith of Abraham was his justification, and that even in Abraham the faith and justice of the Christian Era were prefigured; he is the first of believers. According to Genesis (15:6), Abraham was declared justified before he had been circumcised. It was only afterward that circumcision was imposed as a seal on the justification he had received through faith. Spiritual descent from Abraham is not based on circumcision, and the rite so valued by Jews and converts from Judaism is of no advantage to them. The promise made to Abraham did not reach him through the Law but through the "righteousness of faith," that is, through a justification which consists in believing or, quite simply, through a living faith. Paul argues that Abraham is the father of Gentiles too, and specifically of Christians. As their father he is the model of Christians, of all who are justified by faith in Christ. Abraham believed in God and trusted in the power of God who could vivify, miraculously, his body and the body of Sarah; hence, he reached, by anticipation and in type, the object of the Christian faith. For justification is a first participation in the life of the Risen Christ.

We come to the central section of the letter. We have learned that men are justified, freely, by God (chaps. 1-4); henceforth (chaps. 5-11), we shall see that the Christian, justified through faith, finds in the love of God and the gift of the Spirit the guarantee of salvation. Christ has won for us the entry into the friendship of God; the love of God for us bears the hallmark of divine love: it is while we were sinners that Christ died for us (Rm. 5:1-11). Paul is desirous to show that Christ has repaired, in superabundant fashion, the sin of the first man and its consequences. He describes with complacency the great contrast between the ravages of sin, however fearful, and the grace of God conferred on men through Jesus

Christ. The Law was not able to remove sin; instead, it made men more conscious of sin (Rm. 5:12-21).

Paul takes up the objection that, if the work of salvation is entirely God's, and we can do nothing of ourselves, then why not remain on in sin so that there may be all the more room for grace (Rm. 6:1). First, he shows how baptism, the sacramental initiation into the Christian life, brings about a death and a renewal. Baptism by immersion symbolizes the effect of the sacrament: the baptized person is "buried" in the water and is dead to sin, but then coming out of the water, he "rises" to share the new life in Christ. The Christian, dead and risen with Christ, now lives in the Spirit. Although baptism destroys sin in men, still, until his body has "put on immortality" (1 Cor. 15:54), sin can again gain possession of this "mortal" body (Rm. 6:1-14). Next, he represents liberation from sin as freedom from slavery. No man can serve two masters; justification means the service of God and the free gift of eternal life in Christ (Rm. 6:23-25). The Christian, however, is free not only from sin but also from the Law; the argument is in terms of the laws of marriage. By their link with the death of Christ in baptism, Christians have died to the Law; a new life in the Spirit follows the old regime of the letter (Rm. 7:1-6).

Having introduced the Law, the Apostle, in Rm. 7:7-25, goes on to discuss its role. The Law is itself good and holy, but it has not justified men. It is a light which enlightens men's consciences, but does not give interior strength; it is powerless to prevent sin. In a certain sense, it is an occasion of sin, since it makes sin more obvious and more culpable. The argument is scriptural: it is inspired by the biblical description of the sin of Adam, the type of all sin (Rm. 5:12-21).

> Translated into terms of individual experience the story runs: *I lived at one time without law myself, but when the command came home to me, sin sprang to life and I died; the command that meant life proved death to me. The command gave an impulse of sin, sin beguiled me and used the command to kill me.* It fits like a glove; and there are enough verbal echoes of the Greek translation of Gn. 3 to make it likely that Paul actually had the passage in mind.[34]

---

[34]*Ibid.*, p. 124.

Of course, Paul is not thinking merely of the person of Adam, but takes him as a type of humanity. What he has said can be applied, with the necessary nuances, to every man; yet, it is not drawn from personal experience or from abstract speculation, but from the story of Adam.[35] Left to himself, then, man is in a hopeless state: "Who will rescue me from this body of death?" But, Paul knows that deliverance has been won and thanks God for it (Rm. 7:24-25a). Verse 25b is clearly an afterthought, and would be more in place before verse 24.

Having traced the unhappy state of a man in the bondage of sin and death, Paul now turns to the Christian already justified and filled with the Spirit. For, the new regime of the Spirit—the law of the Spirit of life in Christ Jesus—has replaced the regime of sin and death (chap. 8). The Mosaic Law, an external norm, was not a principle of salvation. Christ, by coming into the world "in the likeness of sinful flesh," and by offering himself as a sacrifice for sin, broke the power of sin and the stranglehold of the flesh. Henceforth, united to Christ, man is spiritualized. Because of sin the body is destined for physical death and is the instrument of spiritual death, but the spirit has life in Christ. The body, however, will rise again, and already the Spirit of God dwells in it (Rm. 8:1-13; cf. 1 Cor. 15:35-55). By the indwelling of the Spirit, Christians are made sons of God, sharing the divine life; this is the reason they can address their Father with the intimate title used by Jesus himself (Rm. 8:14-17; cf. Mk. 14:36). The material world, created for man, shares in his destiny. Cursed by reason of man's sin (Gn. 3:17), it will share in man's redemption. Whereas Greek philosophy would liberate spirit from matter, regarded as something evil, Christianity sets matter itself free.[36]

Like nature, Christians wait for the final redemption; salvation remains an object of hope. The image of God in man was tarnished by sin; Christ, the Image of God, enables men to acquire again, more fully, the divine likeness: he and Christians form the one family of

---

[35]See S. Lyonnet in Huby-Lyonnet, *Saint Paul, Épître aux Romains* (Paris: Beauchesne, 1957²), p. 604; cf. M.-J. Lagrange, *Saint Paul: Épître aux Romains* (Paris: Gabalda, 1922), p. 168.

[36]See BJ, p. 1502.

the Father. God has destined his elect for glory and has ordered everything to that end (Rm. 8:18-30). Paul ends with a hymn of Christian hope: the certainty of salvation. The fact of the redemption and justification wrought by God gives the faithful the assurance of triumphing in the midst of the tribulations of the present life: nothing can part them from God's love in Christ Jesus their Lord (Rm. 8:31-39). "There is no arguing with such a certainty. Either you simply don't believe it or you recognize it as the word of God."[37]

Paul has sketched the universal saving plan of God, but, in that plan, what has become of Israel, the people of the promises? As it is, the Jewish resistance to the Gospel seems to be a flat contradiction of all he has said. Hence, in diatribe style, he discusses the historical role of Israel (chaps. 9-11). First, he points to the privileges which the people of Israel, as chosen race, enjoys: adoption as sons of God; the glory of God's dwelling in their midst; the covenants with the patriarchs and with Moses; the cult of the true God; the Law that is the expression of his will; the messianic promises; and the fact that Christ was born of their race (Rm. 9:1-5).

After this short introduction, Paul deals with the problem in three stages:

1) God is absolutely sovereign and is completely free to choose the recipients of his favor and the instruments of his purpose. The freedom of God's plan is illustrated by the constant biblical theme that the heir of the promise is not necessarily the first born: thus, Isaac is chosen and not Ishmael. Man cannot take God to task for the free manifestations of his mercy or of his anger. Nor does his treatment of Pharaoh and of the Israelites conflict with his justice; while the mercy of God is manifest, in that the promises rejected by the Jews are now offered to the Gentiles—as the Scriptures had foretold (Rm. 9:6-29).

2) Next, Paul stresses human responsibility in the mystery of Jewish infidelity. Israel, in fact, has stumbled over Christ, a stumbling block for them, and has taken a wrong course. They have not submitted to God's plan; rather, seeking their own justification in works of the Law, they have missed the justification that Christ

---

[37]Dodd, *op. cit.*, p. 160.

has brought. Salvation is won through profession of faith in the Lord Jesus (Rm. 9:9 f.); this gospel has been proclaimed, and if the Israelites as such have not called upon the Lord, it can be only because they are "a disobedient and contrary people" (Rm. 9:30–10:21).

3) Finally, it follows from God's free choice of his people and his own faithfulness that Israel cannot be rejected by him. All is not lost: although the Chosen People as a whole are now unfaithful, they will yet enter upon their true destiny. As it is, some Jews—the "Remnant" of which the prophets spoke—have attained the promise, and this Remnant is the guarantee of a future restoration. The Jews' actual rejection of Christ has opened the way to the conversion of the Gentiles; and if the latter, branches of a wild olive, have been grafted on to the parent stock of Israel, how much easier it will be to graft on the converted Jews. The Gentiles can take salutary warning: they must realize that they, by the divine mercy, have won the inheritance that should have been Israel's; and they can learn from Israel's sad history that they too can be cut off if they prove unfaithful. But the Chosen People has not been rejected, and the Apostle announces the eventual conversion of Israel (Rm. 11:1-32). As he contemplates the final return of his people, Paul breaks into a hymn in praise of the great mercy of God (Rm. 11:33-36).

The great dogmatic themes of the Epistle now stand in the background as Paul takes up the moral demands of the Christian life (Rm. 12:1–15:13). It is his own person, not the animal sacrifices of Judaism or paganism, that the Christian offers to God (Rm. 12:1 f.). Charisms are to be used properly, for the common good of the whole Body (Rm. 12:3-8). Charity, love of the brethren and love of enemies, is the principle of Christian living (Rm. 12:9-21). Christians owe allegiance to the state, for civil authority is of divine origin; presuming, of course, that it is legitimate and has the common good in view (Rm. 13:1-7). Again charity is stressed: it is the fulfilling of the Law (Rm. 13:8-10). Awareness of the Parousia will remind the Christian that he is a child of light and should live in the light (Rm. 13:11-14).

In the long passage, Rm. 14:1–15:13, the Apostle considers a concrete moral problem (cf. 1 Cor. 8-10). The "strong" are those who can judge things in the light of Christian liberty; the "weak" are Christians with an insufficiently enlightened faith and who lack the conviction that would enable them to act with a sure conscience. Such a one, following a Jewish or pagan custom, will believe that he is bound to abstain from meat or to observe certain days as solemn festivals. Paul points out that there is room for both "strong" and "weak" in the Christian community (Rm. 14:1-12). The "strong" however, are bound, in charity, to take cognizance of the troubled conscience of the weak; he invokes (Rm. 14:15) the very highest motive for avoiding scandal (Rm. 14:13-23). All should take example from Christ (Rm. 15:1-13). The verse 15:13 gives the central themes of the first part of the Epistle and the conclusion of the writing; the rest is epilogue.

Paul again justifies his writing to Rome, a church he had not founded (Rm. 15:14-21). He plans soon to make a journey to Spain and will visit the Romans en route; he asks their prayers (Rm. 15:22-33). The recommendation of Phoebe—very likely the bearer of the letter (Rm. 16:1 f.)—is followed first by a long litany of personal greetings (Rm. 16:3-16) and then, unexpectedly, by a warning against those who create dissension and difficulties, probably Judaizers (Rm. 16:17-20). Then come the salutations of Paul's companions—Tertius is named as the secretary who wrote the letter (Rm. 16:21-23)—and the closing doxology (Rm. 16:24-27).

DOCTRINE   1. *The Justice of God, Faith, and the Law.* If we are to follow the argument of Paul in Rm. we must understand what he means by justice, faith, and Law.

The justice (or righteousness) of God, of which Paul speaks in Rm. 1:17 and throughout the Epistle, is not the vindictive justice which punishes sinners. In the Bible, this is termed the "anger" of God. Nor is it the distributive justice which rewards or chastens men according to their works: it is the saving justice of God. The Old Testament, which here as everywhere has influenced Paul, associates the justice of God with his fidelity to his promises and with his merciful will to save his people. God is just because, in spite of the infidelity of man, he has remained faithful to his promises. For the Apostle, then, "justice" is not primarily an attribute of God, but rather his saving activity, the deliverance of man from the power of evil. It will be of profit to examine more closely this Pauline usage and its background.

Like the Hebrew verb *sadhaq,* the Greek verb *dikaioun* in the LXX has a legal connotation: "to do a man justice"; "to declare a man innocent." But, and especially when used of God's action, *dikaioun* took on a wider meaning. Thus, for instance, Is. 45:25, where, in the LXX text, "to be justified" and "to be glorified" stand in parallelism; here, *dikaiousthai* means "to find salvation." And, in the New Testament we can point to Lk. 18:14: "I tell you, this man went down to his house justified, and not the other." Here, "justified" has the meaning "to find God's good pleasure." Accordingly, there is in the Bible a use of *dikaiousthai* which is not forensic but rather "soteriological." It is in this second sense that Paul understands "to justify" or "to be justified" (cf. Rm. 4:2; 5:1; 8:33 f.). Thus, Rm. 1:17 ("In it [the gospel] the justice of God is revealed") may be rendered: "In the Gospel, God's salvation is revealed." In short, we may say that, in the Pauline writings, the phrase *dikaiosynē (tou) theou* may be rendered "God's salvation," and *dikaiousthai,* "to find God's grace."[38]

In biblical language, faith does not mean the acceptance of a body of truths, it is not an assent given to "mysteries." It is an act by which a man trusts himself to God and looks to him as to the source of revelation. Faith is based on the truth of God, on his fidelity to his promises and his ability to carry them out. It is not seen primarily as an intellectual assent—as we tend to regard it—but involves the consecration of one's whole being to God, a commitment. For Paul, faith is that attitude in which, acknowledging one's complete insufficiency and relying utterly on the sufficiency of God, one accepts the revelation of divine justice in Jesus Christ.

Paul fully understood and appreciated the truth that the coming of Christ had brought in an entirely new phase of God's dealing with men. The new divine economy is not a continuation of the old along the same plane; although Christianity strikes its roots deep in Judaism, it moves on another level of reality: Christ has made all things new. The fundamental principle that Christ is all-sufficient determined Paul's appraisal of the Law. Although incontestably from God, holy and spiritual, a privilege of Israel, its role was transitory;

---

[38]See J. Jeremias, *The Central Message of the New Testament* (New York: Scribner's, 1965), pp. 51-55.

it marked a time and regime of preparation and education. More-over, the Law itself was powerless to justify men. Paul not only points to the uselessness (in the Christian Era) of the cultic observ-ance of Judaism, but also argues that, in its moral aspect, the Law gives the knowledge of good, not the means of accomplishing it (Rm. 7:16 ff.), the knowledge of sin but not the power of escaping from it (Rm. 3:20; 7:7); the moral precepts carry with them no power of justification. On the other hand, the "law of Christ" (Gal. 6:2) fulfills the promise of a covenant written on the hearts of men (2 Cor. 3:3). But the basis of all Paul's reasoning is that we are saved by Christ, while no one was ever saved by virtue of the Law. And to maintain that it was still obligatory would be to misunder-stand that God had given it only for the time between the promise and the fulfillment of the promise.

2. *Justification by Faith.* We have noted that the saving justice of God is the act by which he justifies men in accordance with the promises he himself has made; essentially positive, it turns man back to his Creator, restores him to his divine inheritance, and makes him a son of God. The life and death of Jesus Christ and his resur-rection constitute the decisive act of God which achieves all this; for, by his death, Christ has delivered men from sin, and by his resurrection he has won for them life in the Spirit.

Paul argues at length that justification cannot be won by observ-ance of the Law. The Law itself has, beforehand, rendered testi-mony to the justice won by faith in Jesus (Rm. 3:21); it was therefore subordinated to that justice as a regime of law to a regime of grace (Rm. 6:14). Still to seek justice in the Law would be to hold that Christ had died in vain (Gal. 2:21). Not only is the Law not necessary for salvation, but to place one's confidence in the Law is to reject salvation. How, then, is salvation achieved? Paul's answer is unhesitating: "We hold that a man is justified by faith apart from works of Law" (Rm. 3:28).

It is true that this doctrine of justification is directed against the basic concept of Judaism and Judaizing Christianity, according to which one finds grace by the observance of God's law, that is, by "works of the Law." But, the teaching itself is wider than this. Justification cannot be won by works of the Law—or by any works;

it cannot be merited. For, justification by faith is justification by faith *alone,* meaning the utter incapacity of man for any sort of self-justification. We are justified by God's grace; therefore, every human achievement is excluded when justification is in question. Yet, we may say that God does grant his grace on the basis of achievement. "But now it is not my achievement, but the achievement of Christ on the cross. Faith is not an achievement in itself, rather it is the hand which grasps the work of Christ and holds it out to God. Faith says: Here is the achievement—Christ died for me on the cross (Gal. 3:20). This faith is the only way to obtain God's grace."[39]

Justification is a manifestation of the divine mercy: "God shows his love for us in that while we were yet sinners Christ died for us" (Rm. 5:8); it is forgiveness for Christ's sake. But it is not only negative, it is an "antedonation" (a donation made in advance) of God's final salvation. It is the beginning of a movement toward a goal, toward the hour of definitive justification. Sanctification will be the development, in the course of a Christian life, of the seed planted at the moment of justification. And that gift can be lost. Justification places an obligation on the believer and leaves room for salutary fear and hope—a hope that is firmly grounded (Rm. 5:8 f.). Justification is not a mere covering of the past: it is forgiveness; it is an antedonation of the full salvation; it is a new creation; it is the new life in Christ.[40]

3. *Baptism.* The bestowal of justification takes place in baptism (cf. 1 Cor. 6:11; Gal. 3:24-27; Rm. 6:7; Ti. 3:5-7). Does not this conflict with the notion of justification by faith? The fact of the matter is that the term "by faith" implicitly includes baptism. "The connection of justification with baptism is so obvious to Paul that he feels no necessity to state in so many words that it is in baptism that God saves him who believes in Jesus Christ."[41] The formula, "justification by faith," should not be taken in isolation, but should be seen as one expression of the meaning of the rite of baptism; it stresses that God's grace in baptism consists in his undeserved par-

---

[39]*Ibid.,* p. 56.
[40]See *ibid.,* pp. 64-66.
[41]*Ibid.,* p. 69.

don. Faith and baptism are not in conflict, but are closely associated. There is no baptism without faith—not inner assent only, but faith in the heart and outward confession in the baptismal rite (cf. Rm. 10:8-10).

It is not at all surprising that Paul, again and again—if often only in passing—comes back to the meaning of baptism and its place in the Christian life.[42] As symbolized by the water rite, baptism is a "washing away" of the stain of sin, and hence a justifying and sanctifying of the former sinner (1 Cor. 6:11). The person to be baptized is baptized "in the name of the Lord Jesus Christ" (Rm. 6:11) and hence belongs to Christ (Gal. 3:29; 5:24; 1 Cor. 15:23). Described in terms of the initiation rite into the former people of God, baptism is a "circumcision" whereby the whole "body of flesh" is put off (Col. 2:11; cf. Rm. 6:6). On the positive side, baptism is a "putting on of Christ" (Gal. 3:27); the baptized person is so clothed with Christ that he is "in Christ," thereby becoming a "new creation" (2 Cor. 5:17). In Christ he finds a new existence (Gal. 3:28; Col. 3:11), a participation in the life of the Risen Lord (Rm. 6:5, 8; 8:11), for by sacramental union with Christ in baptism, the believer is "crucified with" and "buried with" Christ in order to be united with his resurrection and to live with him (Gal. 2:19 f.; Rm. 6:4-8; Col. 2:12 f., 20; 3:1; Eph. 2:5 f.). The basis for these declarations is found in the Adam-Christ parallel (1 Cor. 15:20-22, 45-49; Rm. 5:12-21): Christ is the head of the new, redeemed humanity; as the "first-fruits of the dead" (1 Cor. 15:20) and the "first born among many brethren" (Rm. 8:29), he draws to himself, by baptism, new members. Since, however, all Christians share the same baptismal experience and are filled with the same divine Spirit, baptism is essentially related to a community: all become "one in Christ Jesus" (Gal. 3:28); all become the "body of Christ" (1 Cor. 12:27; Rm. 12:5).

From the rich baptismal doctrine, Paul draws important moral conclusions, rules for Christian living. A right understanding of baptism necessarily excludes any magical conception of the sacrament

---

[42]We may conveniently give a brief summary of Paul's teaching on baptism. See R. Schnackenburg, BW, pp. 1089-1092.

and its effects (cf. 1 Cor. 10:1-13). It guards against the abuse of
the generous grace of God (Rm. 6). It demands a bold fight against
sinful desires and passions (Gal. 5:24; Rm. 6:12-14, 19) and looks
to the purifying of the community (1 Cor. 5:6-8). And, in this world
surrounded by evil, the reality of baptism and its significance stand
as sound motives for virtuous conduct (1 Thes. 4:3-8; Phil. 2:15 f.;
Col. 3:12-17; Eph. 5:6-14).

4. THE CAPTIVITY EPISTLES

The four letters, Philippians, Colossians, Philemon, and Ephesians,
are called the "Captivity Epistles" because Paul informs us that he
wrote them in prison (Phil. 1:7, 12-17; Col. 4:3, 10, 18; Phm. 1:9 f.,
13, 23; Eph. 3:1; 4:1; 6:20). Although 2 Tm. was also written during an imprisonment (2 Tm. 1:8, 16; 2:9), it is grouped with the
Pastoral Epistles. We learn from Acts that Paul was a prisoner for
two years in Caesarea, 58-60 A.D. (Acts 23:33—26:32), and again in
Rome (Acts 28:16, 30), apparently also for two years (61-63 A.D.).
But Acts does not give a complete picture of Paul's missionary activities and, indeed, tells us little of his three-year stay in Ephesus.
Hence, in recent times, many scholars have postulated a captivity
of the Apostle in that city. This hypothesis, however, applies more
directly to Phil. alone which, on several grounds, stands apart from
the other three.

It does seem clear that Col., Phm., and Eph. were written about
the same time, and tradition points to the Roman captivity. The first
two refer to the return of Onesimus (Col. 4:9; Phm. 12)—the
presence in Rome of this runaway slave is readily intelligible—
and list the same companions of Paul (Col. 4:10-14; Phm. 23 f.),
while Col. and Eph. are obviously closely associated. A date during the Roman captivity, some four to six years later than the writing of the Major Epistles, satisfactorily accounts for the notably-
developed doctrine of Col.-Eph. Paul's promise of a proximate visit
to Colossae (Phm. 22) does not really conflict with his intention
of passing from Rome to Spain (Rm. 15:28). His original plans—
and they were mapped out several years before—had been upset
by his arrest at Jerusalem and his imprisonment at Caesarea and
Rome; now, a visit to the churches of Asia might well be his most
pressing concern. Thus, there is no serious difficulty in maintain-

ing the traditional view that Col., Phm., and Eph. were written at Rome during Paul's first captivity (61-63 A.D.).

1) Philippians

THE PHILIPPIAN   Philippi was built by Philip of Macedonia, father
CHURCH   of Alexander the Great, on the site of the ancient Krenides. In 42 A.D., it became a Roman military colony and received from Augustus the title of *Colonia Iulia Augusta Philippensis.* Its population was made up principally of Roman veterans and the town was administered in the Roman fashion (Acts 16:21). The Jewish element was evidently very small, since there was no synagogue (Acts 16:13). Paul visited Philippi for the first time in 50 A.D., during his second missionary journey; he was accompanied by Silas, Timothy, and Luke. It seems likely that the first community assembled in the house of Lydia, a native of Thyatira in Asia Minor, who was profitably engaged in the purple dye trade. The church of Philippi—inevitably in view of the small Jewish population—was predominantly Gentile in composition (cf. Acts 16:12-40; Phil 2:15 f.; 3:3 f.; 4:8 f.). The Apostle visited the city again on his third missionary journey (57 A.D.)—Luke had been in charge of the community in the meantime—and, for a third time, on his way back from Corinth (58 A.D.), when he took Luke with him to Jerusalem (Acts 20:1-6). We gather that the church of Philippi was especially dear to Paul. This is the reason he made an exception in the case of the Philippians and, for once waiving his rigidly-maintained independence, accepted material help from them (Phil. 4:16; 2 Cor. 11:19).

INTEGRITY   The authenticity of Phil. is not in question; the internal evidence is so clear as to put the matter beyond reasonable doubt. But, since the beginning of critical study of the Epistle, its unity has been seriously in doubt. A reading of the letter reveals breaks in tone and subject matter at the beginning of chapter 3 and again at Phil. 4:10. The hypothesis that most satisfactorily accounts for these facts is that Phil. is a collection of letters—all emanating from Paul and all addressed to the church at Philippi.[43]

---

[43]See J. Murphy-O'Connor, "Paul: Philippiens (Épître aux)," DBS, VII, cols. 1211-1233. My treatment of Phil. keeps very close to the lines of this study.

Recent studies distinguished three letters, although there is not always agreement in defining the limits of each letter. For our purpose we may designate them as follows:

A. 4:10-20; B. 1:1–3:1 + 4:2-9; C. 3:2–4:1.

While there is agreement that letter A is earlier than the others, both the relative dates and the extent of B and C are uncertain.

Apart from the break between verses 9 and 10 of chapter 4, the claim of A to be an independent letter (or part of one) rests on two considerations:

1) Its place at the very end of the letter. In this section, Paul thanks the Philippians for their generosity in his hour of need. He shows himself so deeply grateful that it is highly unlikely that this sentiment would not have manifested itself earlier in the Epistle (but all we find are two allusions, Phil. 1:5; 2:30).

2) To suppose that the section belonged to the letter carried by Epaphroditus on his return to Philippi is to assume that Paul had neglected to thank the Philippians promptly and had even failed to avail of the earlier messengers to the community who could so easily have conveyed his letter. In view of the close bond of friendship that bound Paul to the Philippians, this assumption is unlikely. Hence the passage (A) should be considered as the letter—or part of one—which the Apostle sent on receipt of the gift.

C is considered a separate letter because it presupposes a situation other than that implied in A and B. In A and B, although we gather that all is not perfect in the church at Philippi, we are given no hint that matters are as serious as C would suggest. Paul's attitude toward his adversaries in Phil. 1:28 (B) is almost magnanimous, but in Phil. 3:2, 18 f. (C), it is harsh, and the terms he uses are deliberately insulting. The impression that he is not dealing with the same opponents is confirmed by other indications.

In Phil. 1:28 he exhorts the Philippians not to be "frightened" by their adversaries, thus suggesting that they operate by means of threats. When confronted by Jewish opponents, Paul is never worried that his Christians will be terrified into compliance, but rather that they will be seduced from the true faith. Hence, it is legitimate to conclude that the allusion in Phil. 1:28 is to persecution by *pagans*. This accords with what we know of the historical situation at Philippi, for it would appear that the pagan community there was particularly devout. Reference to circumcision in Phil. 3:2 (C), makes it certain that the second group of adversaries was Jewish in origin and upheld this central demand of the Law. The violence of Paul's reaction is readily explained by the insidious nature of the propaganda of this group.

These considerations do seem to establish a basic difference between C and A + B. In conclusion, we may suggest that Phil. is a collection of three letters, to any of which the ending Phil. 4:21-23 may belong. When the fusion of these letters took place is a matter of conjecture. It may have been at the moment when the Philippians passed on their Pauline correspondence to another church. In fairness, however, we must observe that the distinction of three letters rests on internal criticism alone: the manuscripts of Phil. show no variation in their presentation of the Epistle.

PLACE OF ORIGIN   Phil. was written from prison (Phil. 1:14, 17) AND DATE   and, until the end of the nineteenth century, it was taken for granted that the first Roman captivity of Paul (61-63 A.D.) was in question. Reference to the "praetorium" (Phil. 1:13) and to "Caesar's household" (Phil. 4:22) seemed to clinch the issue. But there are serious difficulties involved in this identification. Before considering these, a point or two must be clarified. First, the assertion of Roman origin can be traced back, not to an historical tradition received and accepted as such by the Fathers, but to a conclusion drawn from the data of the New Testament. Then, too, we now realize that neither "praetorium" nor "Caesar's household" necessarily indicate Rome. The term "praetorium" signifies properly "the general's tent," "the headquarters in a camp." From this we have the derived meaning common in the New Testament: "the official residence of a governor or prince" (Mk. 15:16; Acts 23:35). We must suppose that there was a praetorium at Ephesus, since that city was the seat of the Proconsul of Asia (for that matter Caesarea, seat of the Roman Procurator of Judaea, would qualify) and, indeed, inscriptions at Ephesus make the presence there of a praetorian cohort certain. Similarly, "Caesar's household" was, in fact, understood of the personnel employed in the emperor's service;

furthermore, inscriptions support the presence in Ephesus of members of the imperial household.

Since the beginning of the century, Caesarea and Ephesus have been proposed as alternatives to Rome. Caesarea, however, has found few supporters, because all of the reasons adduced in its favor may be applied with greater cogency to Ephesus. We may limit ourselves to a consideration of the rival claims of Rome and Ephesus. The problem is complicated by the fact that we feel justified in distinguishing three letters and hence must allow for the possibility that they were not all written in the same place or at the same date.

An imprisonment of the Apostle in Rome is formally attested (Acts 28:16, 30). Dependable, direct evidence in favor of an imprisonment at Ephesus does not exist. However, the Epistles to Corinth prove that Paul was imprisoned more frequently than Acts has recorded (2 Cor. 11:23) and that his ministry in Ephesus was much more troubled by persecution than Acts permits us to see. The brevity of the account of an Ephesian ministry that lasted nearly three years is accounted for by the fact that Luke was apparently not with Paul: he is not mentioned in Phil. and a "we-passage" terminates at Philippi in the narrative of the second missionary journey (Acts 16:10 f.), while the next "we-passage" commences with a mention of Paul's visit to Philippi on the return stage of his third journey (Acts 20:6). Therefore, despite the silence of Acts, it is possible that Paul was imprisoned at Ephesus.

According to Phil. 1:13, Paul was imprisoned because he was a minister of the Gospel, and not on any other specific charge; but the ostensible reason for his imprisonment at Rome was the violation of a Temple ordinance (Acts 21:28; 24:6; 25:8). However, this was obviously a pretext to cover a radical aversion to his teaching. On the other hand, Paul's imprisonment could end in his execution (Phil. 1:20; 2:17, 23), and this is a factor that seems to point to Rome because, as a Roman citizen, he could always have appealed from a provincial court to Caesar, as he actually did at Caesarea (Acts 25:11 f.).

Paul planned to send Timothy to Philippi as soon as possible (Phil. 2:19) and to come himself shortly (Phil. 2:24; cf. 1:26). Here the Ephesian hypothesis has the advantage, because we know that, while he was at Ephesus, Paul had formed the intention of going to Corinth via Macedonia (1 Cor. 16:5-9; Acts 19:21) and that he did send Timothy on ahead (Acts 19:22). Furthermore—another point in favor of Ephesus—the Epistle presupposes frequent contact between Philippi and the place of the Apostle's imprisonment. At the time of writing there had been at least four recent journeys: (1) a message to Philippi of Paul's imprisonment; (2) Epaphroditus brought gifts to Paul; (3) news of Epaphroditus' illness was sent to Philippi; (4) Epaphroditus had learned of the Philippians' concern on his behalf. Paul, moreover, plans to send Timothy (while hoping for his speedy return) and Epaphroditus to Philippi. The journey between Rome and Philippi would take a month, while the distance between Ephesus and Philippi could be covered in about ten days. Frequent journeys would certainly be more understandable if Paul were in Ephesus, but the argument is manifestly not conclusive. Still in favor of Ephesus is the fact that, what Paul says of the Philippian gift, can be reconciled with the Roman hypothesis only if we suppose that Phil. 4:10b is a bitterly sarcastic rebuke, because the Apostle had been in Philippi twice during his third missionary journey (Acts 20:2, 6).

We may present our conclusion by relating the evidence to the individual letters. Letter A contains only one feature capable of localizing it: the Philippians' gift. The terms in which Paul expresses his gratitude exclude the probability of Rome as the place of composition, while the Ephesian hypothesis fits the facts perfectly. Hence, A may be dated during the Apostle's stay there (54-57 A.D.) and likely toward its close. Letter B provides several points of reference, but no definite orientation either way. However, we may surely assume that the gift brought by the messenger Epaphroditus, mentioned in B, is the same gift with which A is concerned. This links B to the same place and date as A. The only element that permits us to date letter C is the ideas it expresses; it will be seen that these set it squarely in the period of the Major Epistles. It is well to consider some of the ideas of the Epistle as a whole.

If Phil. was written at Ephesus, we should expect to find in it some echo of the problems of the Corinthian church that preyed so much on Paul's mind at the time. Of these, the gravest was certainly caused by the presence of opposing factions in the church (1

Cor. 1:11 f.). Perhaps we may see it reflected in the intensity of the Apostle's appeal for unity at Philippi (cf. Phil. 1:27 f.; 2:1-5). The period between death and Parousia is mentioned by Paul only in Phil. 1:23 and 2 Cor. 5:8. These two passages exhibit precisely the same delicately-balanced attitude toward the future, and no great interval of time can separate them. Their perspective is very different from the realized eschatology[44] of Col. and Eph. A characteristic element of the teaching of Phil. is its formal assertion of the apostolic value of the Christian life (Phil. 2:14-16); this is closely paralleled by 1 Cor. 10:32 and Rm. 12:17. The cultic metaphor employed in Phil 2:17 is striking: the tribulation of the Apostle is presented as the libation completing the daily and perpetual sacrifice of the Christian faith. Similar cultic metaphor, drawn from the cult of the Old Testament, is proper to the Major Epistles: 2 Cor. 2:14-17; Rm. 15:16 f. All the points hitherto discerned pertain to letter B, and all, insofar as they manifest a closer affinity with the teaching of the Major Epistles rather than with the other Captivity Epistles, serve to confirm the date assigned to that letter.

At the end of letter C Paul introduces the theme of the city of God (Phil. 3:20); the closest parallel is the development on the two Jerusalems in Gal. 4:25 f. Two other passages in Phil. 3 also turn our minds toward Gal.-Rm. In Phil. 3:9, we find contrasted the justice which comes from the Law and that which comes from God through faith in Christ. And in Phil. 3:10 f., Paul singles out the resurrection as the ultimate gain which he has won for the surrender of the privileges of Judaism. However, he does not yet possess it and he realizes that, without continued labor and suffering in union with Christ, he might not in the end attain it. This is the perspective of Rm., and there is no trace of the evolution perceptible in Col.-Eph. (cf. Rm. 6:5; 7:14 f.; 8:17; Col. 2:12; Eph. 2:6). These three doctrinal themes of letter C point to the period of the Major Epistles as its date of composition.

---

[44]The decisive intervention of God on the stage of human history for man's salvation has already taken place; in the person of Jesus and in the saving event of his death and exaltation the last age has begun. The Parousia marks the term of this age. This "realized eschatology" is particularly evident in Col., Eph., and the Fourth Gospel.

In conclusion, we may point to approximately the same date for all three letters that make up the Epistle, and the indications are that this date is in the period of the Major Epistles. We have found, too, that the Ephesian hypothesis, although lacking external support, is confirmed by a study of the writing. With some confidence, then, Phil. may be dated in 56-57 A.D. and Ephesus put as its place of origin.

PLAN   While we may not ignore the form in which Phil. has come to us, it is important to have in mind, too, the probable genesis of the Epistle; hence, we give two plans of the writing.

1. ADDRESS (1:1 f.)	
THANKSGIVING AND PRAYER (1:3-11)	
1) Paul's situation	1:12-36
2) Exhortation	1:27—2:18
3) Apostolic ministers	2:19—3:1
4) The way of Christian salvation	3:2—4-1
5) Peace in the Church	4:2-9
6) Paul's acknowledgment of gifts received	4:10-20
FINAL GREETING (4:21-23)	
2. LETTER A (4:10-20)	
LETTER B (1:1—3:1 + 4:2-9)	
LETTER C (3:2—4:1)	
CONCLUSION (4:21-23)	

SUMMARY   The address (Phil. 1:1 f.) is very simply expressed. Timothy is named out of courtesy (the writer is Paul alone) and the "bishops" (rather, overseers) and deacons of the Philippian church are mentioned. Paul's remembrance of the Philippians leads to thanksgiving on their account: for the fervor with which they have accepted the Gospel from the beginning. He is confident that God will bring to perfection the good works he has begun in them. Love for his converts is based on the common grace they have shared in defense of the Gospels: they suffered with him (cf. Phil. 1:29 f.). He prays that their love may never cease to grow, that they may possess the true Christian wisdom, and be filled with the fruits of righteousness (Phil. 1:3-11).

Paul describes his present situation. The Philippians were obviously concerned at his imprisonment; he assured them that the preaching of the Gospel has not suffered. Indeed, the cause of the Gospel has been advanced, for the name of Christ was now known throughout the whole praetorian guard and beyond, and the brethren now preach more confidently. True, the motives of the preachers may differ, but Christ is proclaimed; Paul's desire is to serve Christ: if released, in the Gospel; if condemned, by martyrdom. For himself, he would welcome death in order to find life with Christ, but, for the sake of his converts, he is prepared to live on. In fact, he is convinced that God will send him to them again (Phil. 1:12-26).

He turns to exhortation. The Philippians should stand firm in the Spirit and present a united front to the opponents of the Gospel who seek to break them by persecution; let them bear in mind that suffering for the sake of Christ is a privilege. Unity is to be founded on humility and concern for others. The example has been given by Christ, whose humiliation and exaltation are celebrated in an early hymn (Phil 2:6-11). They must achieve salvation, the fulfillment of the Christian vocation, which is entirely the work of God. (The mystery of grace and free will is stated starkly in Phil. 2:12 f.) Thus, they will be lights in a dark world and will be Paul's pride and joy on the day of the Parousia. Their faith is a sacrifice pleasing to God, and Paul rejoices even if his lifeblood is to be poured out as an accompanying libation (Phil 1:27–2:18).

When he has ascertained the outcome of his imprisonment (liberty or death), he will send Timothy to Philippi: he has warm words for this faithful "son" of his. Paul really feels that he will be set free and will come to them soon after Timothy. In the meantime, he is sending back to them their own delegate, Epaphroditus. This man had been gravely ill; they must receive him with honor, a worthy minister of Christ who has risked his life in their service (Phil. 2:19–3:1).

It is clear that the opening part (Phil 3:2-11) of the next section is directed at Jews or Judaizers. In referring to them as "dogs," Paul turns back on them their own insulting estimate of Gentiles. He, Hebrews of Hebrews, a Pharisee by training, a flawless observer of the Law, is no less a Jew than any of them. But all this—which those others see as grounds of self-justification—he has sacrificed for Christ and for the justification that comes from God and the hope of resurrection. But he is not presumptuous. Like a runner at the last stage of a race, he keeps his eyes on the winning tape and does not look back: the prize is yet to be won. He does not hesitate to propose himself to his children as a model to be imitated, for he is conscious of being a faithful imitator of Christ (cf. 1 Cor. 11:1). The "enemies of the cross of Christ" (Phil. 3:18) may be Christians who fail to live up to their calling; more likely, however, they are the same Jewish adversaries as before. Christians, followers of Christ, are citizens of heaven where Christ is. He, at his Parousia, will establish his faithful in the universal kingdom of God (cf. 1 Cor. 15:23-28). In view of this hope, only one thing matters: "Stand firm in the Lord" (Phil. 3:2—4:1).

In urging peace in the Church (Phil. 4:2-9), Paul addresses a reprimand to two women of the Philippian community, Evodia and Syntyche. It seems that each of the two was overconcerned with her place in the community and jealous of her rival. Then he calls on the Christians to rejoice in the Lord; "joy" is a key-word of the Epistle (Phil. 1:18, 25; 2:2, 17 f.; 28 f.; 3:1; 4:1, 4, 10). They must be free from anxiety and live in a spirit of prayer and thanksgiving; in this way they will win the peace of God. Thus too their lives will appear honorable and gracious in the eyes of men, lives inspired by the Christian message and the example of the Apostle.

Paul goes on to thank the Philippians for the generous gift he has received from them. His courtesy is manifest, but so also is his embarrassment. He points to the unique relationship between him and the Philippians: they alone, of all his churches, are permitted to contribute to his material needs. But he wants to make it clear that he is in fact unconcerned about these needs, while at the same time expressing his genuine appreciation of their solicitude. This is one of the most delightfully human passages in the Pauline writings (Phil. 4:10-20). The final greeting (Phil 4:21-23) is addressed to all the Christians (the "saints") at Philippi from all the Christians of Ephesus (or Rome).

If we wish to take the three (hypothetical) letters separately we may summarize their contents as follows:[45]

1) Letter A (Phil. 4:10-20) was sent on receipt of the gift brought by Epaphroditus; it is simply an expression of the Apostle's gratitude.

2) Letter B (Phil. 1:1–3:1 + 4:2-9): the central message is a call for unity and perseverance and for unwavering witness to the truth. Permeated by the deep affection that bound him to Philippi, it is, with Philemon, the most personal of all Paul's letters. A report on his present situation follows Paul's assurances of his affection (Phil. 1:3-9). He tells of the effect of his imprisonment on the local church (Phil. 1:12-17) and of his own state of mind (Phil. 1:18-26). In the body of the letter (Phil. 1:27–2:18), three exhortations enshrine the hymn to Christ the glorified Servant (Phil. 2:6-11). Drawing his letter to a close, Paul announces his plans for the future (Phil. 2:19-30). He begins the postscript, but suddenly addresses a further appeal for unity to specific individuals, rounding it off with a number of general counsels (Phil. 4:2-9).

3) Letter C (Phil. 3:2–4:1): this is a sharp polemic against Jews or Judaizers, but includes a moving passage of spiritual autobiography (Phil. 3:7-10). Its destination is not specified, but if it had not originally been addressed to Philippi, there would appear to be no sufficient reason for combining it with letters A and B.

THE CHRISTOLOGICAL HYMN[46]   It is now universally recognized that Phil. 2:6-11 is a hymn to Christ. Its structure presents two almost equal parts, in the first of which (Phil. 2:6-8) Christ appears as subject, and in the second (Phil. 2:9-11) as object; each part consists of a single Greek period. It will be seen, however, that the near equality of the parts is due to additions in the second part; and on application of the rules of parallelism it is found that the hymn falls into three strophes. We may present it in the following manner:

---

[45]See Murphy-O'Connor, *art. cit.*
[46]See J. Jeremias, "Zu Phil. 2:7—EAUTON EKENOSEN," *Novum Testamentum,* 6 (1963), 182-88.

1. v. 6   1. He who was in the form of God
          2.   did not think to snatch at equality with God
  v. 7   3.   but emptied himself,
          4.   taking the form of a slave;

2.   1. Having come in human likeness
          2.   and being found in human shape,
  v. 8   3.   he humbled himself,
          4.   becoming obedient unto death
             (even death on a cross).

3. v. 9   1. Therefore God has highly exalted him
          2.   and bestowed on him the name above all names
  v. 10 3.   that at the name of Jesus every knee should bow
             (in heaven, on earth and under the earth),
  v. 11 4.   and every tongue confess: *Jesus Christ is Lord*
             (to the glory of God the Father).

It may be seen that strophes 1 and 2 are exactly similar in structure. The Greek text of each begins with the preposition *en* followed by a participle, while in the second line the thought of the first is continued by means of a comparative particle. The third line contains the key-verb ("emptied," "humbled"), whose object is in each case the reflexive pronoun ("himself"), and the fourth line develops the key-verb. The structural similarity is reinforced by the repetition of one term from the first line in the second ("God," "human") and of another in the fourth ("form," "becoming"). This careful structure supports a double parallelism: the repeated "God" stands in antithetical parallelism to the repeated "human," while the second parts of both strophes stand in synonymous parallelism.[47] Strophe 3 is constructed on exactly the same principles. Lines 1 and 2 stand in synonymous parallelism, as do lines 3 and 4. The unity of the strophe is assured by the correspondence between its two parts, for "exalted" is reflected in "bow," and "confess" evokes "name."

A number of elements in the actual text of Phil. 2:6-11 disturb this structure. It is clear that the three bracketed phrases fall outside the strict parallelism we have described; it is significant that all are

---

[47]See Murphy-O'Connor, *art. cit.*

found at the end of a line. It seems that they are Pauline additions to the original form of the hymn; for, indeed, the majority of commentators consider that Paul is here making use of a pre-existent hymn. They recognize that, while the ideas are perfectly apt, the solemn hieratic tone contrasts with the context. Some, however, would hold that Paul himself had composed the hymn at an earlier date and then has incorporated it in Phil. The others deny Pauline authorship. At any rate, even if Paul did not write this hymn, his adoption of it indicates that it perfectly expressed his thought. There is no doubt that the additions ("even death on a cross"; "in heaven, on earth, and under the earth"; "to the glory of God the Father") are all characteristically Pauline. It is surely more probable that he made these additions to a familiar hymn than that he would have disturbed the balance and parallelism of a hymn written by himself.

The hymn is obviously important for Christology, all the more so if its pre-Pauline origin is accepted, for in it we have, at a very early date, a clear declaration of the divine pre-existence of Christ. While there is not complete agreement concerning its interpretation, we present its more assured teaching.

The subject ("he who") is Christ Jesus (Phil. 2:5), the historical Christ, God and Man. He is in "the form of God": the word "form" designates the essential attributes of God; Christ, from eternity, had a right to all the divine prerogatives. But Jesus, as man, did not snatch at and jealously guard the glorious condition that was his by right of his divine origin. Instead, he "emptied himself" by the manner of his Incarnation. "The nature of this 'kenosis' (emptying) is explained by the clauses that follow. While theologians may legitimately consider its implications, the term has no metaphysical intention, but indicates the abyss of humiliation to which renunciation led the Christ."[48] What he freely set aside was not his divine nature, but the glory that was his (cf. Jn. 17:5) and which otherwise would normally radiate from his person (cf. the transfiguration [Mt. 17:1-8]). He had chosen to strip himself of it in order to receive it again from his father as the reward of his sacrifice (Jn. 8:50, 54; Phil. 2:9-11). Freely he took the form of a slave—in contrast to his true rank of "Lord." Christ made man has chosen the way of submission and

---

[48]G. R. Beasley-Murray, PCB, n. 861 d.

humble obedience. The passage surely has in mind the "Servant of Yahweh" of Isaiah.

Jesus is not only true man, he wished to share the weakness of human condition, except for sin (Gal. 4:4; Rm. 8:3; Heb. 2:17). Like the slave he had chosen to become, he was obedient unto death; and the utter abasement of Christ is emphasized by reference to the form of his death, that of a common criminal. But from the depths attained by his self-renunciation, God has exalted his Servant to unparalleled heights by his resurrection and ascension. And he has granted him the title of "Lord."

> The contrast between "Lord" and "Servant" is certainly deliberate.· At the term of his earthly journey, made in conformity with the will of his Father, but freely chosen, Christ recovers, but this time for his whole being, including his humanity, the plenitude of divine glory. He chose to arrive at glory not by glory but by humiliation. And this is the parenetical lesson that Paul proposes to the Philippians.[49]

2) *Colossians*

THE COLOSSIAN CHURCH   The town of Colossae lay in the Lycus valley about one hundred miles east of Ephesus and very close to the more important towns of Laodicea and Hierapolis; there was close contact between these three neighboring towns (Col. 4:15 f.). It is practically certain that Paul had never visited the towns (cf. Col. 2:1) and that he knew of their Christian communities only by hearsay (Col. 1:4, 9). We learn that a disciple of Paul, Epaphras, a native of Colossae (Col. 4:12), had evangelized Colossae (Col. 1:7) and Laodicea (Col. 4:12). The community at Colossae was mainly Gentile in origin (Col. 1:21, 27; 2:13). We know, however, that Jews were numerous in these towns of Phrygia and that here, as elsewhere, they tried to stifle the growth of the churches. Their propaganda had brought about a crisis: a dangerous error had won some acceptance and constituted a threat to the community. When Paul had become aware of the state of affairs, he dispatched Tychicus with a letter dealing with the problem (Col. 4:7 f., 16).

AUTHENTICITY   The traditional attribution of Col. to Paul is unhesitating. Although the authenticity of the Epistle was seriously

---

[49]Murphy-O'Connor, *art. cit.*

challenged by nineteenth-century criticism, in recent times there has been a decided switch in favor of Pauline authorship, which few modern scholars question. Arguments against Pauline authenticity were based on considerations of language and style and on the Christology of the Epistle. Col. has a large number of words not encountered elsewhere in Paul. But this means nothing more than that the Apostle is facing a new problem and develops new ideas. Besides, Phil.—whose authenticity is not in question—shows a proportionally distinctive vocabulary. The style of Col. does differ from that of the earlier Epistles: it is less spontaneous and rather more involved. This feature may find a ready explanation: Col. was certainly written by a secretary (cf. Col. 4:18), one who, we may presume, enjoyed a good measure of freedom in his composition.[50] Furthermore, the notably-developed doctrine (by comparison with the Major Epistles) of Col. is accounted for by our dating of the Epistle, possibly as much as six years later than the others. From what we know of him, we can be very sure that Paul's theological development had not come to a full stop in 57 A.D.

PLAN

ADDRESS (1:1 f.)	
THANKSGIVING AND PRAYER (1:3-12)	
CHRISTOLOGY (1:13-23)	
1) Transition	1:13 f.
2) Primacy of Christ	1:15-20
3) Reconciliation	1:21-23
POLEMIC (1:24—3:4)	
1) Paul and the Colossians	1:24—2:5
2) Error at Colossae	2:6—3:4
PRACTICAL ADMONITIONS (3:5—4:6)	
1) General admonitions	3:5-17
2) Particular admonitions	3:18—4:6
PERSONAL MESSAGES (4:7-17)	
FINAL GREETING (4:18)	

---

[50]See p. 302.

SUMMARY   The address (Col. 1:1 f.) presents Paul as an "apostle of Jesus Christ" and makes mention of Timothy. The Apostle thanks God for the faith, hope, and charity of the faithful and for the steady growth of the community founded by his disciple Epaphras. His prayer is that they may have the understanding that will promote their further progress and the patient endurance that will win for them a share in the inheritance of the saints (Col. 1:3-12). The "saints" may, perhaps, designate the angels (Jb. 5:1; Zech. 14:5; Dn. 4:10) with whom the elect will be associated (Mt. 22:30) in the eschatological light or brightness (Dn. 12:3; Mt. 13:43; Ap. 22:5). This interpretation is recommended by the Qumran writings with which Col. 1:12 f. presents striking literary analogies.[51] God is the one who has delivered us from the dominion of darkness and who has brought us into the kingdom of light, the kingdom of his Son who has won redemption for us (Col. 1:13 f.). For, Christ holds the primacy in the order of creation and in the order of salvation (Col. 1:15-20). And the Colossians, once enemies of God, have been reconciled to him by his Son; now they must stand firm in the faith (Col. 1:21-23).

Paul, the prisoner, suffers for his converts: he has his share in the reconciling work of God in Christ. As Apostle of the Gentiles, he is a minister of that "mystery hidden for ages": the calling of the Gentiles to salvation and to heavenly glory through union with Christ. His solicitude reaches to the Phrygian communities he has never seen; he prays that they may be granted confidence and unity, and that they may be given understanding to penetrate the mystery of God, so that they may not be led astray (Col. 1:24–2:5).

Possessing Christ, they must live in him and not follow a human wisdom that would enslave them once more (Col. 2:6-8). He is the one true head of men and angels; in him alone God is revealed. Joined to him in his death and in his resurrection, the Christian, in Christ, is superior to the heavenly powers and he must never submit to them. The Law had made man conscious of sin and had

---

[51]See P. Benoit, *Les Épîtres de Saint Paul aux Philippiens, à Philémon, aux Colossiens, aux Éphésiens*, (BJ), p. 56.

stood in accusation against him; this incriminating document has "died"; it has been cancelled by the sacrificial death of Christ. According to Jewish tradition, angelic powers stood behind the Law (cf. Acts 17:53; Gal. 3:19; Heb. 2:2), which became for them an instrument of domination over men. Now they are seen in their true role, intermediary creatures subject to Christ, captives in his triumph (Col. 2:9-15). To follow the practices and to accept the beliefs of Jewish false teachers would mean to come again under the influence of the heavenly powers. This is because the ascetical and cultic practices in question give too much importance to the elements of the material world and thereby to the heavenly powers that control them. In Christ, the Christians have died to the elemental spirits and hence are free of human prescriptions and doctrines (Col. 2:16-23). Since they have been raised by Christ, then all the more reason they should turn away from the things of earth and seek the things that are above. As it is, their life in Christ, although real, is hidden, but at the Parousia it will be manifest and glorious (Col. 3:1-4).

This is followed by the moral part of the Epistle. The Colossians must flee the vices of paganism which incur the divine anger for, indeed, they have put on the new nature of those who have been re-created in Christ. Therefore, they must practice Christian virtues and be grounded in charity. Peace should reign and they should live in an atmosphere of thanksgiving, doing everything in the name of the Lord Jesus (Col. 3:5-17). Next come particular instructions (Col. 3:18—4:1) relating to family life, including the master-slave relationship (significant in view of Onesimus, the fugitive slave [Col. 4:19; cf. Phm.]). Assiduous prayer is urged and the Apostle recommends himself to the prayers of his faithful (Col. 4:2-4). He asks that they show wisdom and courtesy in their relations with non-Christians (Col. 4:5 f.).

Paul is sending Tychicus and Onesimus to Colossae. He sends the greetings of his companions. The Colossians are bidden to greet the brethren at Laodicea and the two communities are to exchange letters (Col. 4:7-17). Paul authenticates the Epistle by adding the final greetings (Col. 4:18) in his own hand.

THE COLOSSIAN
ERROR

Paul wrote this Epistle because of a dangerous error which threatened to disrupt the Colossian community. Since the concrete situation was well known to his correspondents, his references to it are vague and, to us, obscure. It is widely held today that what was involved was a syncretistic movement of Jewish-Gnostic character or, rather, the infiltration of ideas from such a milieu.[52] However, it can be argued that this understanding of the situation does not, after all, stand on very firm ground. The alleged Gnostic or pregnostic nature of the ideas combated by Paul follows from an interpretation of certain expressions of the Epistle in the light of second-century Gnostic writings. It seems that the "Colossian error" should be sought in another direction.[53]

What the disturbers propose to the Colossians, in the first place, are observances touching the calendar (Col. 2:16b), dietary laws (Col. 2:16a, 21-23), and circumcision (Col. 2:11-13); the Jewish character of these observances is manifest. Paul lets it be clearly understood that, behind all this, is the Jewish Law (Col. 2:14) with its obsolete character and its air of "shadow of things to come" (Col. 2:17). It is true that the other traits, like excessive asceticism (Col. 2:23) and the pursuit of a human "philosophy," are less at home in orthodox Judaism, but may well mark the esoteric aspect of a particular Jewish sect.

The "cult of angels" (Col. 2:18) raises a more delicate problem. That the Colossian agitators showed excessive interest in the heavenly powers is obvious from Paul's care to place these powers under the Lordship of Christ (Col. 1:16; 2:10, 15). It is a long step, however—and in view of Jewish monotheism an unlikely one—to postulate a true "cult" of the powers. What does appear is that Paul so chose to interpret the liturgical and food observances of Judaism. It is significant that he substitutes the term "angels" for those of "principalities" and "powers" (Col. 2:15), thus passing from the astral and cosmic forces of the Hellenistic world to a purely biblical

---

[52]See Wikenhauser, *op. cit.*, pp. 296 f.; Eng. trans., pp. 415 f.; L. Cerfaux, IB, pp. 495 f.

[53]Benoit has reacted against the commonly-accepted view, with justification I believe. I give an outline of his position. See Benoit, *op. cit.*, (BJ), pp. 50 f.; "Paul: Colossiens (Épître aux)," DBS, VII, cols. 159-63.

angelology. The Jewish syncretists he had in mind speculated on these heavenly agents and, on the other hand, stressed the importance of Jewish observances. It was Paul himself (or so it would appear), however, who linked the speculation and the observances; he did so in accordance with the view already underlying Gal. 3:19; 4:8-10, that the Mosaic Law, given on Sinai by angels, leads to submission to the "elemental spirits," that is, to the material elements of the world and the spirits who administer them. Hence, to set religion in material observances is, in fact, to render a cult to the angels who rule the cosmos—but, this inference is Paul's.

It does not follow, either, that the syncretists assuredly assigned to Christ a determined place among these "angels" within the divine "pleroma." Here again it was Paul who pointed to the logical consequences of their views. And these views are erroneous because Christ has become, by his Cross and his triumph over death, the only Lord of the new world: all the angelic powers are necessarily subject to him. The Apostle's one concern is to maintain the absolute primacy of Christ; his interest in the "powers" is secondary. He treats of them only because of the misleading speculation about them. One thing he is sure of: the powers in no way compromise the role and rank of Christ. For the rest, he is content to speak in vague terms. We cannot say with confidence how he would regard these heavenly spirits, whether as good or bad, angelic or demonic.

In conclusion, we may observe that the Epistle's description (such as it is) of the error at Colossae lacks the specific elements of Gnosticism: the ontological dualism of spirit (good) and matter (evil) and the emanations of eons from the divinity to material creation. We may add that, side-by-side with orthodox Judaism, there existed, notably toward the beginning of our era, a Judaism that was more or less heterodox. We know of one such sect in Palestine itself—Essenianism—which went further than the Law in ritual observance and professed a special interest in the angelic hierarchies. The Qumran discoveries have thrown fresh light on this situation. It is not at all beyond the bounds of probability that a syncretistic Judaism was to be found in Asia Minor, and especially in Phrygia which was a utopia for esoteric cult and speculation. Such a Jewish milieu was the breeding ground of the "Colossian error."

3) *Philemon*

Philemon was a Colossian who had been converted by Paul himself (Phm. v. 9). His slave Onesimus had run away—having stolen some of his master's goods (vv. 15, 18)—and had somehow reached Paul in prison (v. 10). The Apostle converted him. Paul wants to send him back to his master (he will return with Tychicus [Col. 4:9]), and he provides him with a letter for Philemon.

The introductory greeting (vv. 1-3), as in Col., associates Timothy with Paul. Apphia and Archippus are very likely Philemon's wife and son; we learn that their house was a place of Christian assembly. The thanksgiving (vv. 4-7) lauds the charity and faith of Philemon.

In the body of the letter (vv. 8-21), Paul, "an old man and prisoner for Jesus Christ," appeals to that charity of Philemon on behalf of Onesimus, the Apostle's spiritual son. In parenthesis, and with a touch of humor, he plays on the name "Onesimus," which means "profitable." Regretfully, he sends away such a dear and valuable disciple; nothing but a sense of justice would make him part with his child. We seem to detect a hint that Philemon should let Onesimus return (v. 15). Paul suggests that the whole episode was providential: Philemon had lost a slave only to gain a brother (vv. 15 f.) —surely a hint that the slave should be set free. Then, the Apostle, who writes this letter with his own hand, appeals to their mutual friendship; for that matter, Philemon, who had been converted by Paul, owes him more than this! He is confident, however, that Philemon will do even more than he asks, again hinting at the release and probably at the return of the slave. In conclusion (vv. 22-25), Paul expresses the hope that he himself will soon visit Phileman. The five fellow workers of Col. 4:10-14 are again listed.

Philemon formed part of the Pauline corpus from the beginning. Some elements in the early Church questioned its authenticity because of its brevity and because it was a private letter. In the last century, some critics maintained that Phm. was the work of a second-century forger who wanted to provide a Pauline ruling on slavery. Both contentions are irrelevant; nothing short of a lamentable lack of literary feeling would permit one to doubt for an instant the Pauline character of this charming letter. And because it is Pauline, we do not look in vain for an important doctrinal contribution: it puts before us the fundamental attitude of the primitive Church to slavery. In the social pattern of the age, the abolition of slavery was impossible; but the Christian slave should be regarded and treated as a brother and not as a chattel. For that matter, Paul would welcome the freeing of Onesimus (Phm. 14-16, 21). In time, the leaven of the Gospel would create such relations between master and slave that the system of slavery would become obsolete.

1) Ephesians

DESTINATION   Ephesus, capital of the province of Asia, was a natural center of missionary activity. Paul visited the city for the first time toward the close of 52 A.D. on his way to Jerusalem at the end of the second missionary journey (Acts 18:19-21). He was back during his third journey for a long stay of almost three years (Acts 19-20). From there he sent his disciples to the other cities of Asia. It is obvious that none of his churches could have been so well known to Paul as that of Ephesus. This being true, it is highly improbable that the letter "to the Ephesians" was written to Ephesus. (Perhaps we should say that it cannot have been written to the Ephesians alone, as the title implies, but they may have shared it with others.) Internal evidence is conclusive, and the external evidence cannot be said to run counter to it.

In the first place, the Epistle is quite impersonal, so impersonal that it cannot have been written exclusively to a community founded by Paul and in which he had lived for three years. From Eph. 1:15 and 3:2 f., we may gather that he had never met those to whom he writes. He addresses converts from paganism (Eph. 2:1 f., 11 f.; 3:1; 4:17 f., 25 f.; 5:3 f.), while there was a strong Jewish element in the Ephesian church (Acts 18:19 f.; 19:8, 13-17, 34; 20-21). In striking contrast to Col. and Phm., written about the same time, Eph. contains no greetings from Paul's companions, although both Timothy and Aristarchus were personally known to the Ephesians (Acts 19:22, 29; 1 Cor. 4:17).

We can base no argument on the title "to the Ephesians," because this is neither original nor canonical, although it does reflect a tra-

ditional attribution. The really important factor is the words *en
Ephesō* in the address (Eph. 1:1). And these, although found in
the great majority of Greek manuscripts, are significantly absent from
some important witnesses: P[46], B, S, 424, 1730; Origen, Basil, and
probably Marcion and Tertullian. Thus, the textual evidence suggests that originally no place was mentioned in the introductory
greeting, which would have read: "To the saints and faithful in
Christ Jesus." It is true that the address as attested by the manuscripts reads: "To the saints who are [at Ephesus] and faithful in
Christ Jesus"; and where the name is omitted (as in the witnesses
listed), the words "who are" are left hanging in the air. It has been
suggested that originally they were followed by a blank space left
for the insertion of the name of one of a number of churches to
which copies of the letter were to be sent. It is also possible that
the addition of the words (together with "in Ephesus") happens
to be earlier than any of the witnesses known to us. Evidently,
there is no ready solution and we have a choice of two hypotheses:[54]

1) The Epistle was really written to the Laodiceans: it is the
letter referred to in Col. 4:16. Marcion is cited in support of this
view. However, the impersonal tone of the letter is not accounted
for. It is not enough to say that Paul had never visited Laodicea,
for he had never visited Colossae either and still Col. is quite personal. It seems, too, that Marcion's title, "To the Laodiceans," is
no more than a conjecture, one challenged by Tertullian. Harnack
explained the substitution of Ephesus for Laodicea in the address
on the grounds of the censure of Laodicea in Ap. 3:14 ff.—an ingeni-
ous but doubtful theory, especially as Laodicea quickly regained
favor.

2) The Epistle is an encyclical or circular letter to a group of
churches, near together, and not personally known to Paul. Because
of their close relationship, Eph. must have been written soon after
Col. and have been delivered by Tychicus (Eph. 6:21 f.; cf. Col.
4:7 f.). We should, then, seek these churches in the neighborhood

---

[54]See Wikenhauser, *op. cit.*, pp. 302-4; Eng. trans., pp. 423-26; P. Benoit,
"Paul: Éphésiens (Épître aux)," DBS, VII, cols. 195-97.

of Colossae, which would certainly include Laodicea and Hierapolis. Since it was a circular letter, a space for the name of the recipient was left blank. Later, because of its known Ephesian connection, it became known as an epistle *to* the Ephesians.

It seems that these hypotheses are not mutually exclusive and that, by taking them together, we may arrive at a more satisfactory theory. Eph. was indeed written as a circular letter, but when the Pauline letters were being collected, the manuscript of our Epistle bore the words *en Laodikeia* in its address; it was, in fact, one copy of that circular letter. (In this sense, Col. 4:16 may be taken as referring to Eph.) When this copy was itself recopied, the name Laodicea yielded to that of Ephesus, a more important city and the place where the collection of the Pauline letters was made.

In conclusion, if we cannot, with confidence, point to the destination of Eph., we can at least be sure that the letter was not written exclusively to the Ephesians.

DATE AND OCCASION   If we had to go on the evidence of Eph. alone, it would not be easy to determine the place of origin and the date of the Epistle, but its close relationship with Col. comes to our aid. We learn that Paul is a prisoner (Eph. 3:1; 4:1; Col. 4:3, 10, 18), and we find that the same messenger, Tychicus, carries both letters to their destination (Eph. 4:21; Col. 4:7; cf. Eph. 6:22; Col. 4:8). Similarities in style, and especially in doctrine, are maintained throughout the Epistles. Unless we are prepared to deny the Pauline authenticity of Eph., regarding it as the work of a plagiarist—a drastic step that is scarcely demanded—we must acknowledge that the two letters were written in the same place and about the same time. We have already agreed that Col., Phm., and Eph. were written in Rome, during Paul's first captivity (61-63 A.D.) and, most likely, toward its close.

We have seen above that Rm. followed on Gal. and was inspired by it; here we meet with an analogous situation. When Paul had learned of a crisis in the Colossian church, he wrote Col., which dealt with the problem and, in view of the error in question, presented the salvation of Christ in a cosmic setting. Then he wrote another Epistle, practically contemporaneous with Col., in which he set out more calmly, and developed, the ideas suggested to him by the polemic. Now he regards the Church, the Body of Christ, reaching out to the limits of the new Universe, and he also considers the problem of the union of Jews and Gentiles raised in Rm. This second letter, destined for a number of churches, and hence deliberately impersonal, was carried by Tychicus; it is probable that Col. 4:16 is an allusion to it.

> At any rate, Ephesians appears as a more developed and more systematic exposition of the ideas which the crisis at Colossae had suggested to Paul. It takes up and treats again many earlier ideas in a new light and brings them to fruition. A synthesis of the foregoing Epistles, notably of Romans and Colossians, it represents the apogee of Pauline thought.[55]

PLAN

ADDRESS (1:1 f.)	
DOGMATIC PART:	
THE MYSTERY OF SALVATION AND OF THE CHURCH (1:3—3:21)	
1) The divine plan of salvation	1:3—2:10
a. Contemplation of the plan	1:3-14
b. Realization of the plan	1:15—2:10
2) Union of Jews and Gentiles in one body	2:11-22
3) Revelation of the mystery	3:1-13
4) Prayer and doxology	3:14-21
MORAL PART (4:1—6:20)	
1) General principles	4:1-24
2) Particular applications	4:25—6:20
a. Individual morality	4:25—5:5
b. Social relations	5:6-20
c. Domestic morality	5:21—6:9
d. Spiritual warfare	6:10-20
CONCLUSION (6:21-24)	

---

[55]Benoit, *ibid.*, DBS, col. 198.

SUMMARY   The address (Eph. 1:1 f.) is much like the address of Col. except that Timothy is not mentioned and no church is designated by name. Instead of the customary thanksgiving, a hymn (Eph. 1:3-14)—which reads like a baptismal hymn—introduces the divine plan of salvation, a plan which is unfolded in six stages: election, adoption, redemption, revelation, call of the Jews, and call of the Gentiles. The introductory verse of the hymn (Eph. 1:3) characterizes the stages as so many "spiritual blessings." God's choice of his elect is an act of his love ("in love" should be attached to verse 4 as in the RSV margin), a choice that obliges them to live holy and blameless lives (Eph. 1:4). Through Christ, the elect become sons of God; and this divine filiation, like the other blessings of God, has its source in the divine goodness and its end in the exaltation of his glory by his creatures. In this plan everything comes from him and returns to him (Eph. 1:5 f.).

Redemption is achieved by the blood of the Beloved Son shed on the Cross (Eph. 1:7 f.). The fourth blessing is the revelation to the Apostles, and by them to all men, of the "mystery" of the universal supremacy of Christ. And in the "fullness of time," the Messianic Age, the whole of creation, the world of men and the world of angels, is drawn under the authority of Christ (Eph. 1:9 f.). In him, Israel, a Chosen People, had been set apart in order to keep alive in a fallen world the expectation of a Messiah and the hope of salvation through him (Eph. 1:11 f.). The sixth stage is the call of the Gentiles to share the salvation formerly reserved for Israel, a salvation assured by the gift of the Holy Spirit long ago promised by the prophets (Eph. 1:13 f.).[56]

Then, Paul turns to the realization of the divine plan (Eph. 1:15– 2:10). First (after the introductory verses, 15 f.) he considers the great wisdom and efficacious power of God's plan (Eph. 1:17-19). That power is revealed in his raising of Christ, in his placing him over all the angelic spirits, and in his making him the Head of the Church. The Church is the Body of Christ because it contains all the saved, who are united to him; it is his Fullness because it indirectly embraces the whole new world, the setting of saved human-

---

[56]See Benoit, *op. cit.*, (BJ), pp. 85-88.

ity, the world which shares in universal regeneration under the authority of Christ, Lord and Head (Eph. 1:20-23).

Formerly, not Gentiles only (Eph. 2:1 f.), but Jews too (Eph. 2:3) —subject to Satan, dead in sin—were objects of the divine anger. Now all of them, through God's love, have been brought back to life and reconciled in Christ. The baptized Christian is united to Christ dead and risen in a manner so real and intimate that he can be said to have shared in Christ's heavenly triumph. This sharing in the resurrection of Christ which Rm. 6:3-11 sees as something lying in the future is here presented as a reality already come to pass: it is realized eschatology, a characteristic trait of Eph. (2:1-6). In words that summarize the great thesis of Rm., Paul insists on the absolute gratuitousness of salvation (Eph. 2:7-10).

We pass to the theme of the reconciliation of Jews and Gentiles among themselves and with God (Eph. 2:11-22). The immeasurable grace of God has indeed reached to the Gentiles who, in Christ, are made inheritors of God's promises to his people, thus fulfilling Is. 57:19. Christ has broken down the "dividing wall of hostility" (an allusion to the barrier that marked off the court of the Gentiles from the Temple proper) by bringing to an end, on the Cross, the reign of the Mosaic Law that kept the Jews apart, and by substituting for it the universal regime of grace. Now, both peoples are joined together in the one Body of Christ that is the Church. This is the great Mystery known to Paul and of which he is the minister; this is why he is Apostle to the Gentiles.

Paul begins a prayer in Eph. 3:1, but then abruptly breaks into a long parenthesis (Eph. 3:2-13) which treats of his vocation and mission (Eph. 3:2-4, 7 f.), the revelation of the Mystery (Eph. 3:5, 9 f.), and the content of the Mystery (Eph. 3:6, 11 f.). We learn that the Mystery was made known to the Apostle by revelation and that he was especially commissioned by God to preach to the Gentiles. At best vaguely known to the prophets of the Old Testament, the Mystery is revealed to Christian apostles and prophets; hidden even from the heavenly spirits, it is now made known through the Church. The Mystery is this: the Gentiles are fellow heirs with Judaeo-Christians, members of the same Body. Then, the interrupted prayer is resumed and closes with a doxology (Eph. 3:14-21), a prayer for a better understanding in the Church of the Mystery; in effect, for a deeper knowledge of the love of Christ, the source of the Mystery.

The moral part of the Epistle (Eph. 4:1–6:20) is still bathed in the light of the sublime doctrine that went before. Paul first of all makes an appeal for unity (Eph. 4:1-16). Discord among Christians (Eph. 4:1-3) is opposed to the unity that should flow from the one Spirit, the one Body, the one Lord, the one faith and baptism, the one Father of all (Eph. 4:4-6). The necessary divisions of ministry (Eph. 4:7-11) are aimed at the building up of one Body into the fullness of Christ (Eph. 4:12 f.). Heretical doctrine (Eph. 4:14) is to be combated by means of close union with Christ, the Head who draws the whole Body together (Eph. 4:15 f.). Christian converts are called upon to put aside their former way of life and to live the new life in Christ (Eph. 4:17-24). Then follows a series of admonitions in the field of individual morality, all centered in charity (Eph. 4:25–5:5). Next come rules for social relations: contacts with non-Christians (Eph. 5:6-17) and the liturgical life (Eph. 5:18-20). Rules for family living (Eph. 5:21–6:9) comprise the magnificent passage on Christian marriage (Eph. 5:22-33). Finally, we have a description of the spiritual arms worn and used in the fight against the devil and evil spirits, especially the mighty weapon of prayer (Eph. 6:10-20). The Epistle ends abruptly with the recommendation of Tychicus and a closing salutation (Eph. 6:21-24).

AUTHENTICITY   From the early Christian centuries onward, the Pauline authenticity of Eph. was taken for granted. Doubts were first raised at the end of the eighteenth century and denial of Pauline authorship became widespread in the following century— although Roman Catholic scholars continued to defend it. Now again there seems to be a certain reaction in favor of authenticity. However, it is still widely held that Eph. is the work of an immediate disciple of Paul who wished to develop the ideas of his master in a more markedly ecclesiological sense. It is agreed that the writing cannot be by Paul himself, because of its developed theology, its overcrowded style, its unusual vocabulary, and its curious literary contacts with the other New Testament epistles in general and with Col. in particular.

Objections to Pauline authorship on grounds of doctrinal content are not formidable. The new themes or points of view are related to the Colossian crisis and do not go beyond the limits of a perfectly credible evolution in the Apostle's thought. However, certain ideas, certain patterns of thought, do seem to indicate that somebody as well as Paul had a hand in the writing of the Epistle.

The difficulties of a literary order appear more serious. The style is labored and redundant; long periods (e.g., Eph. 1:3-14) are encountered which contrast strikingly with passages like Rm. 4:1-10. Note, however, that Col.—although accepted as authentic—has examples of the same style (Col. 1:3-8, 9-20) which, even more significantly, can be traced in other Epistles (Rm. 3:21-26; 2 Cor. 9:8-14). Its prevalence in Col. and Eph. may be explained by the subject matter of these Epistles. It follows—and this is merely a common-sense assumption—that Paul has different styles. In discussion he sounds alert, staccato, rather like the Stoic "diatribe." In his dogmatic expositions, and especially in Eph., he adopts a contemplative, "liturgical" style, in the manner of liturgical hymns. Besides, if we accept the view that the letter was written, under his direction but with some freedom, by a disciple, then even uncharacteristic traits may be accounted for.

However, the most serious objection raised against Paul's authorship of Eph. always has been its literary relationship to Col. A comparative study of the two Epistles reveals numerous similarities both in style and vocabulary, contacts of a very special nature. They make it appear that Eph. is a meticulous, imitative adaptation of Col. This procedure may even be quite awkward at times and one hesitates to attribute it to Paul. It is not easy to imagine him, of all people, at work, laboriously dissecting and reassembling passages from Col. And yet, his genius permeates Eph. Hence, the hypothesis that the letter in its present form is the work of a secretary working at the direction of Paul seems very reasonable.

Literary dependence of Eph. on Col. cannot be doubted. We may note, for instance, the following passages: (1) citations: Eph. 3:2 = Col. 1:25; Eph. 4:16 = Col. 2:19; Eph. 4:22-24 = Col. 3:9 f.; Eph. 6:21 f. = Col. 3:7 f.; (2) the conflating of two (or more) passages of Col. in one of Eph.: Col. 1:14 + 1:20 = Eph. 1:7; Col. 1:25 + 1:20

+ 1:12 = Eph. 1:10 f.; (3) a rather artificial reproduction in Eph. of expressions of Col.: Eph. 3:1-13 = Col. 1:24-29.

This last example serves to highlight the problem. Four principal ideas occur in Col. 1:24-29: the sufferings of Paul; his vocation; the manifestation of the divine Mystery; and the content of the Mystery. Eph. 3:1-13 has the same ideas, but tends to repeat them. Thus, for example, Col. 1:15 is found once in Eph. 3:2 and a second time in Eph. 3:7. It happens that a formula has been broken up, so that the *ages and generations* of Col. 1:26 furnish the *generations* of Eph. 3:5 and the *ages* of Eph. 3:9. Words have changed meaning. Thus, *oikonomia*, which in Col. 1:25 has the normal Pauline sense of "office," "administration," receives in the parallel passage Eph. 3:2 the sense of "plan," "disposition" (cf. Eph. 1:10; 3:9). The "holy (*hagioi*) apostles and prophets" of Eph. 3:5 is a combination of "the saints" (*hagioi*) of Col. 1:26 with the "apostles and prophets" (cf. Eph. 2:20).

It seems impossible to attribute to Paul himself these laborious imitations; one senses the zeal of some disciple. But, it is equally impossible to deny the Pauline stamp of an Epistle whose doctrine carries the imprint of his genius and crowns his former work.

> One can see no other way out of the impasse than by admitting the significant literary intervention of a disciple-secretary. It is well known that Paul employed such helpers who were not always simple copyists. In the case of Ephesians, the Apostle would have expound- ed all the doctrine, may even have dictated certain passages, but would have left to another the task of making the final redaction with the aid of Col. and earlier Epistles—which must surely have been avail- able in Paul's immediate circle. So, even though it did not receive its final form from the Apostle, the Epistle to the Ephesians is no less his work, conceived and approved by him—the profound develop- ment and synthesis of his thought.[57]

Can we hope to know who the secretary was? We cannot expect to name him, but we may be able to determine his thought patterns and to discern the intellectual and religious atmosphere in which they were formed. Recent studies have shown that Eph. has numer- ous contacts with the Qumran literature which cannot be explained

---

[57]P. Benoit, "Paul: Éphésiens (Épître aux)," DBS, VII, col. 210.

on the basis of common dependence on the Old Testament.[58] There
is, for instance, the theme of *truth*. It plays a very important role
in the Qumran writings as the characteristic quality of the community and its members. It is applied in the same way in Eph.—
a feature that makes this letter unique among the letters of Paul.
In view of this and other contacts with Qumran, it is only reasonable to assume direct acquaintance with the writings of the Essenes
either on the part of Paul or of his secretary. If Paul had such acquaintance we would expect it to show at least as frequently in
other Epistles. This, however, is not the case. The passage, 1 Cor.
6:14–7:1, provides an exception, but it had been recognized as an
interpolation even before the discovery of the Dead Sea Scrolls.[59]
In view of the strict prohibition of the *Rule of the Community*
against the communication of the doctrines of the sect to outsiders
(e.g., 1QS 9:16 f.), we are led to believe that the writer of Eph.,
who evidently is familiar with these doctrines, must have been, at
one time, a member of the sect. We suggest, then, that Paul's secretary, on this occasion, was a converted Essene. But we must acknowledge that his conversion was profound and his assimilation
of the Apostle's teaching thorough.[60]

DOCTRINE[61]   The leading themes of Eph. are the cosmic dimension of Christ's salvation, the Church, and the divine Mystery. But
these are also the themes of Col. and, in view of the close relationship of the writings, it is well to outline their treatment in the earlier
Epistle. This will also help to highlight the notable theological
advance made in Eph..

1. *The Cosmic Supremacy of Christ*. In Col., the person and
work of Christ are considered from a point of view that is not only
soteriological but cosmic as well. Now Christian salvation takes on
the dimensions of the universe. Christ is not only head of the
Church, whose members are his members and build up his Body;

---

[58]See J. Murphy-O'Connor, "La 'Vérité' chez saint Paul et a Qumrân," *Revue
Biblique*, 72 1965), 29-76.

[59]See p. 251.

[60]See J. Murphy-O'Connor, "Who Wrote Ephesians?" *The Bible Today* (April,
1965), 1201-1209.

[61]I am content to summarize the splendid synthesis of Benoit, *op. cit.*, (BJ),
pp. 52 f., 78-80; "Paul: Éphésiens (Épître aux)," DBS, VII, cols. 199-204.

he is the head of all creation. To designate this situation Paul uses the term *plerōma*; and he finds the basis of Christ's universal supremacy in his divine pre-existence as Image of the Father and sees him as the source and end of creation.

The cosmic supremacy of Christ, head of the whole universe and even of the angels, has been so firmly established in Col. that Eph. does not have to dwell on it at length. At most, the theme is recalled in some striking formulas. Thus, the term of the divine plan is to "recapitulate" the universe under one sole Head, Christ (Eph. 1:10). He is superior to all the heavenly powers (Eph. 1:21) because he has mounted above the heavens (Eph. 4:10). What is truly specific in Eph. is that the idea of Christ's cosmic supremacy has influenced the notion of the Church.

2. *The Church.* Col., with its cosmic view of the heavenly Christ, clearly distinguishes the Church from him who is its Head. Its character of "Body of Christ," which was already met with in the earlier Epistles, takes on a new relief and a stronger realism. The Church is the Body of Christ because it is made up of all Christians whose bodies are joined, by baptism, to the physical body of the Risen Christ and receive from him the new life of the Spirit.

Paul's horizon was broadened by his consideration of the Colossian error and by the need to refute it. Now that he has established the universal supremacy of Christ, he realizes that the Church, the Body of Christ, must be seen in a wider perspective. But what has struck him most forcefully is the idea of the collective salvation of humanity in Christ. And so his thought is concentrated on the Church which has grouped in one Jews and Gentiles; the Church which is a Body with Christ as its Head, or again which is the Spouse of Christ, and which ultimately so fills the renewed cosmos that it is to be identified with the "Pleroma" of Christ.

In Rm. 9-11, Paul had faced the problem of the reunion of Jews and Gentiles and had to be content with regarding it as a "secret" of the divine plan: the rejection of the Gospel by the Jews was necessary for the access of Gentiles to salvation, but ultimately Israel would return to the fold. Eph. takes up the problem anew. Already the two last strophes of the initial hymn (Eph. 1:11-14) suggest that Jews and Gentiles correspond to two stages of the divine plan, that of hope and that of faith in the Gospel. Then, in Eph. 2:11-22, the matter is explicitly and confidently treated. Separated formerly during the time of the old economy in which Israel was the bearer of the Promise (Eph. 2:11-13), the two peoples have been drawn together and have been reconciled with God by the blood of Christ which has suppressed the old economy (Eph. 2:14-18); henceforth, they are united as the component parts of a spiritual Temple where God dwells among men (Eph. 2:19-22). Gentiles and Jews have won the same salvation and form the same Body (Eph. 3:6).

The gathering together of the saved is made "in one Man" (Eph. 2:15), who is Christ, prototype of the new humanity; "in one Body" (Eph. 2:16), which is his body, crucified and dead to sin; and "in one Spirit" (Eph. 2:18), which is the Spirit of the Risen Christ. Here we have the theme of the Body of Christ at its most profound. And here, less than ever, can it be a metaphorical application of the profane image of the "social body." It is something very different: the expansion of the individual body of Christ, dead and risen, by the joining to it, through baptism, of the bodies of Christians; and hence it reaches out to the dimensions of the great Body of the Church. And, at the same time, a distinction is maintained between the Body which is built up on earth and the Head which directs its growth from heaven (Eph. 4:15 f.; cf. Col. 2:19). The whole structure of the Church is founded in unity and leads to unity (Eph. 4:1-16). Finally, Paul has brought out even more clearly the distinction of Head and Body (seen in the subjection of one to the other) and their union (achieved through love) when he presents the Church as the Spouse of Christ (Eph. 5:23-32).

The Church is not only the Body of Christ, it is his "pleroma" (Eph. 1:23). Beyond the Christians who are the "Body" properly so called, the Church embraces, in some manner, all the forces of the new creation that is filled by the power of the Risen Lord. For the Risen Christ is the initial cell of the new world; in him, God has created humanity anew (Eph. 4:24) and "united" the universe (Eph. 1:10). He thus contains in himself all the fullness of God and of the new cosmos (cf. Col. 2:9); and those who are united to Christ are, by that fact, plunged into this fullness (Eph. 3:19; 4:13; cf. Col. 2:10). The cosmic breadth of view of Col. is indeed maintained in Eph., but always in relation to the concept of the Church.

3. *The Mystery.* His contemplation of cosmic salvation, which embraces Jews and Gentiles alike and touches the whole of creation, filled Paul's soul with admiration. He sees here a "Mystery," that is, a secret long hidden in God but now revealed; and he insists on the need for supernatural wisdom in order to attain true knowledge of the divine plan (Col. 1:26-28; 2:2 f.). In Eph., too, the divine plan of salvation is presented as the "Mystery." Fundamentally, it is still the incorporation of the Gentiles into the salvation of Israel: thus, in Eph. 3:3-6, 8 f. (a developed parallel of Col. 1:25-27), and in Eph. 6:19 (a parallel of Col. 4:3). Yet, we may say that the splendor of the Mystery of Christ and of the spiritual wisdom required for its understanding, are more firmly and explicitly affirmed in Eph. Here, Paul's wonder at the divine plan finds more moving expression (Eph. 1:3-14). Here, too, he speaks with pride of his own grasp of the Mystery and of his vocation in its service (Eph. 3:1-12). And he calls more urgently on his faithful to contemplate it and to pray to God for the light of his Spirit that they may understand it (Eph. 1:17 f.; 3:16-19).

5. THE PASTORAL EPISTLES

The two letters to Timothy and the letter to Titus form a distinctive group among the Pauline writings; since the eighteenth century they have been known as the Pastoral Epistles. Because all three of them are concerned with the qualities and responsibilities of those who administer to the Christian people, the designation is a happy one. But the three Epistles are closely related not only in their common interest and content but also in vocabulary and style. Hence, we may treat them as a group, rather than take them individually.

1) *The Epistles in General*

THE RECIPIENTS Apart from the very brief Phm., the Pastorals are the only letters of the Pauline *corpus* to be addressed to individuals. In this case, both recipients are close collaborators of the Apostle.

Timothy was a native of Lystra in Lycaonia. His father was a Greek, but his mother Eunice was a Jewess who had become a Christian (as had his grandmother Lois). He joined Paul at the beginning of the second missionary journey—the Apostle first had him circumcised (Acts 16:1-3; cf. 2 Tm. 1:5). Henceforth, he was the Apostle's constant companion and his name figures beside that of Paul in the address of many of the Epistles (1, 2 Thes., 2 Cor., Phil., Col., Phm.). During the second journey, Paul sent Timothy from Athens to inspect the Thessalonian church and was greatly relieved by his envoy's report (1 Thes. 3:2-6). Later, on the third missionary journey, Timothy was sent on a similar mission from Ephesus through Macedonia to Corinth (1 Cor. 4:17; 16:10; Acts 19:22). If one accepts the authenticity of the Pastorals, one may say that Timothy was still associated with Paul in his later missionary activity (1 Tm. 1:3), while at the end, the thoughts of the Apostle, now in prison and awaiting execution, still turned to his "beloved child" (2 Tm. 1:2) whom he longed to see again before he died (2 Tm. 4:9). Timothy held among the companions of Paul the place that Philippi occupied among his churches. It may be that, because of Timothy's youth (1 Tm. 4:12), a father-son relationship had replaced one of master and disciple.

Unlike Timothy, Titus is not mentioned in Acts. However, we learn from Gal. 2:1-5 that he was a Gentile and so uncircumcised. This is precisely why Paul took him along when he and Barnabas went to Jerusalem to vindicate the freedom of Gentile converts from observance of the Mosaic Law. Titus accompanied the Apostle on the second missionary journey; toward the end of it he was sent from Ephesus to Corinth to restore order in that turbulent church (2 Cor. 2:13; 7:6); a delicate mission which he successfully accomplished (2 Cor. 7:6-13). Later he was sent back to organize the collection in Corinth (2 Cor. 8:6-17). We learn from Ti. (again assuming the authenticity of the writing) that Paul, during the final phase of his missionary work, left Titus in charge of the church in Crete (Ti. 1:5); but, the disciple was to join him later at Nicopolis (Ti. 3:12).

COMMON CHARACTERISTICS[62]   The Pastorals, we have seen, are addressed to two of Paul's most faithful disciples, and are almost exclusively concerned with the organization and direction of the churches which the Apostle committed to their care. The interest centers in consolidation, and no fresh doctrine is expounded as in the earlier Epistles. In style and vocabulary, too, there is a notable difference. Gone is the rich variety, the not unusual lack

---

[62]See L. Cerfaux, IB, pp. 521-23; BJ, pp. 1488 f.

of coherence, of the other letters; instead, these letters flow smoothly, even sedately.

The Apostle charges his disciples to administer the churches founded by him, and for that purpose to set up overseers, elders, and deacons. Significantly, the first responsibility of the leaders is to teach: they must teach doctrine that is sound and, largely, of practical moral interest—prayer, good works, relations of family life. This doctrine, firmly set on the basis of the Old Testament, of Christ, and of the Apostles, is something that has been received and which must be safeguarded. The lines of transmission are clearly marked: from Christ to Paul who had confided the doctrine to his disciples; in their turn, they must pass it on to those whom they establish as teachers and guides of the churches.

True doctrine is recognized by its apostolic origin and by the sound piety which it engenders. There is no place here for sterile discussions concerning the Law, and for the venturesome speculation of doctors without mandate. It is noteworthy, too, that the charisms have slipped into the background. Nor is the concern with the Parousia so marked as in many of the earlier Epistles, and eschatological tension is almost absent. Indeed, Christianity is regarded as firmly installed in this present age, and as demanding from the world the conditions necessary for the expression and expansion of its own life. The Church has come of age.

The most pressing danger is from within. There are Christians who do not respect the solid traditional doctrine and who propagate false views; these Epistles have some harsh things to say about them. They are self-appointed—and self-opinionated—teachers, giving themselves the airs of deeply religious men, who win introduction into private homes and, apparently without much difficulty, win over to their views certain of the less enlightened faithful; women were particularly susceptible (2 Tm. 3:6 f.). These false teachers are boastful, controversialists tirelessly discussing vain problems (1 Tm. 1:4), mentally undisciplined, superficial, busy only with futile things (1 Tm. 6:4; Ti. 3:9; 2 Tm. 2:23), with fables and genealogies (1 Tm. 1:4; 4:7; Ti. 1:14; 3:9). Besides, they are self-interested, venal (Ti. 1:11), seeing in religion a "good thing" (1 Tm. 6:5). Hypercritical, disobedient, it can be said that they have made shipwreck of the faith (1 Tm. 1:19).

The Pastorals point to the existence of a local hierarchy in individual churches and name *episkopoi*, elders, and deacons. This is a matter that must be taken up again, in another context, and examined more closely. But, the fact is that the hierarchical organization of the churches is a common concern of these writings.

At the same time, although much is new and distinctive, the principal themes of Pauline teaching do occur, notably the doctrine of salvation by the gift of God and not by means of works, and the efficacy of the death and resurrection of Christ. So, too, the Christology of 2 Tm. 2:8 f. recalls that of Rm. 1:3. Perhaps it is not surprising that contacts would be particularly close where the person and work of Paul are in question. Thus, the description of Paul's vocation and of his mission (1 Tm. 1:11-14) seems to be made of reminiscences from the earlier Epistles, and the passage on the sufferings of Paul (2 Tm. 2:9-12) is distinctively Pauline. Finally, we must keep in mind that the practical interest of the Pastorals seriously modifies an initial impression of marked difference; here, considerations of church organization and Christian morality have taken the place of the great dogmatic themes.

2) *Analysis of the Epistles*

1 TIMOTHY

1. *Plan.*

ADDRESS (1:1 f.)	
THE GOOD WARFARE (1:3-20)	
1) False teaching	1:3-7
2) The role of the law	1:8-11
3) The vocation of Paul	1:12-17
4) The responsibility of Timothy	1:18-20
GUIDANCE OF THE CHURCH (2:1–3:16)	
1) Public worship	2:1-15
2) The ministers	3:1-13
3) The mystery of Christ	3:14-16

THE FALSE TEACHERS (4:1-16)	
TIMOTHY AND THE FAITHFUL (5:1—6:2a)	
1) In general	5:1 f.
2) Widows	5:3-16
3) Elders	5:17-25
4) Slaves	6:1-2a
CONCLUSION (6:2b-19)	
1) False teaching and money	6:2b-10
2) Challenge to Timothy	6:11-16
3) True riches	6:17-19
4) Final charge	6:20 f.

2. *Summary.* The greeting (1 Tm. 1:1 f.) presents Paul as an "apostle of Jesus Christ by command of God our Savior"; the title of "Savior" applied to God is frequent in the Old Testament and occurs six times in the Pastorals (1 Tm. 1:1; 2:3; 4:10; Ti. 1:3; 2:10; 3:4), but not elsewhere in the Pauline Epistles. He addresses Timothy, his "true child in the faith."

Timothy is urged to remain in Ephesus in order to combat false teaching. The "myths" and "endless genealogies" that formed part of the false doctrine are Jewish legends, based on the Old Testament narratives, and elaborate pedigrees, as we find them in the apocryphal literature; the self-styled doctors founder in their own sterile discussions. Timothy must inculcate charity, purity of conscience, and sincere faith (1 Tm. 1:3-7). The Jewish Law (abused by the false teachers) is good, although limited in its scope. Under its penal aspect, it is concerned with those who break the law, those who act contrary to the sound doctrine that is in conformity with the "glorious gospel" (1 Tm. 1:8-11). The idea of "soundness" of doctrine is found only in the Pastorals (1 Tm. 1:11; 6:3; Ti. 1:9, 13; 2:1, 8; 2 Tm. 1:13; 4:3).

Reference to the Gospel entrusted to him (1 Tm. 1:11) moves Paul to thanksgiving for the great mercy and magnanimity Christ had shown in calling a persecutor of the Church to his service. The Apostle is a living proof of the truth of the claim that Christ had come into the world to save sinners; he closes with a solemn doxology (1 Tm. 1:12-17). Timothy is again commissioned to wage war against the false teachers, this in accordance with the "prophetic utterances," that is, the testimony of Christian prophets which accompanied Timothy's ordination. Already some have made shipwreck of their faith; Paul has excommunicated two of them (cf. 1 Cor. 5:5); one of the two, Hymenaeus, is named again in 2 Tm. 2:17.

Paul then puts forward recommendations for the ordering of the public worship of the community. Prayer is to be offered for kings and for all who are in high administrative positions, in order that Christians may be able to lead peaceful and godly lives and that all men may arrive at a knowledge of the truth; for God desires all men to be saved (1 Tm. 1:1-4). The object of Christian faith is this: one God, and one Mediator, Christ, who has died for all. Paul, preacher and Apostle of the Gentiles, is the herald of the testimony to the saving will of God made by Christ (1 Tm. 2:5-7). In the communities, men alone should recite public prayers; women will remain silent in church. It is their place to live modestly, to perform good deeds, and to be submissive to their husbands (cf. 1 Cor. 14:34 f.; 1 Pt. 3:3 f.). Woman's vocation, in conformity with Gn. 3:16, is to be a mother; this declaration is directed against a false doctrine (1 Tm. 4:3) that depreciated marriage (1 Tm. 2:8-15).

The office of *episkopos* ("bishop") is a noble task, demanding sterling qualities (cf. Ti. 1:7-9). Much the same qualities are demanded of deacons (1 Tm. 3:1-13). Paul hopes to come to Ephesus soon, but the instructions contained in this letter will serve in case he is delayed. Meanwhile, Timothy is in charge of the "household of God"—a "pillar and bulwark of the truth."[63] The theme of "truth" keeps recurring in the Pastorals: 1 Tm. 2:4; 3:15; Ti. 1:1, 14; 2 Tm. 2:15, 18, 25; 3:7 f.; 4:4. The "mystery of our religion" (cf. 1 Tm.

---

[63]Certain Fathers had referred the image "bulwark of the truth," that is, of the Christian revelation, not to the Church but to Timothy, an interpretation that is in harmony with the role of Timothy in the Pastorals. This interpretation seems to be supported by evidence from Qumran. See Murphy-O'Connor, *art. cit., Revue Biblique*, 67-76.

3:9)[64] is great indeed: it is nothing other than Christ. This idea is developed in a quotation from an early Christian hymn which sings of the triumph of Christ's glorious resurrection and ascension (1 Tm. 3:14-16).

The latter days will be marked by apostasy from the faith (cf. 2 Thes. 2:3-11), brought about by deceitful spirits who turn men against the good things given to them by God. Condemnation of marriage (if not necessarily abstinence from certain foods) appears to point to Gnostic dualism; yet, the errors may be those of an esoteric Jewish sect (cf. Col. 2:16-21).[65] The true doctrine is that everything created by God is good, and its use is consecrated by prayer (1 Tm. 4:1-5). Timothy, faithful disciple, will instruct the brethren along these lines; he will have nothing to do with godless and foolish fables (1 Tm. 4:6-10). Although young in years, he must set a good example to all. He will attend to the public reading of the word of God and comment on the sacred text in the public assemblies. He was consecrated for the ministry by the imposition of hands: let him exercise the divine charism he has received. If he is faithful to his ministry of the word, he will save himself and those who hear him (1 Tm. 4:11-16).

Timothy must be circumspect in his dealing with the faithful—there is no place for self-assertion (1 Tm. 5:1 f.). Then, his attitude toward different classes within the community is specified (1 Tm. 5:3—6:2a). Three categories of widows (1 Tm. 5:3-16) are distinguished: those who are cared for by their own families (v. 4); those who are "real widows," that is, really dependent (vv. 2-8, 16); those who have official standing and render special service in the churches (vv. 9-15). The elders are to be treated with honor, especially those who have acquitted themselves well as preachers and teachers. But Timothy is not to be hasty in appointing men to office in the Church (1 Tm. 5:17-22). Among sundry remarks (1 Tm. 5:23-25), he is advised to moderate his own asceticism. Finally, there are instructions for slaves and masters. Christian slaves owe respect to their pagan masters, so that Christian teaching will not be brought into

---

[64]See p. 307.
[65]See pp. 293 f.

dishonor. And they must not take advantage of Christian masters, but should respect them even more (1 Tm. 6:1-2a).

Timothy is urged to be mindful of the instructions he has been given and receives another warning against false teachers (1 Tm. 6:3-5). Their erroneous view that godliness is a means of gain leads to a statement on the contrast between false and true riches (1 Tm. 6:6-10). A moving exhortation to Timothy to fight the good fight of the faith (1 Tm. 6:11-14) closes with a solemn doxology (1 Tm. 6:15 f.), reminiscent of 1 Tm. 3:16. In 1 Tm. 6:17-19—a passage which should come, logically, after 1 Tm. 6:6-10—there is a return to the theme of riches and the dangers of wealth. The final charge to the disciple reminds him yet again of his obligation to defend the true faith against the attack of false teachers (1 Tm. 16:20 f.).

TITUS

1. *Plan.*

ADDRESS (1:1-4)	
DUTIES OF TITUS (1:6-16)	
1) Appointment of elders	1:5-9
2) Opposition to false teachers	1:10-16
EXHORTATIONS (2:1–3:11)	
1) Christian conduct in the Church	2:1-10
The ground of this conduct	2:11-15
2) Christian conduct in the world	3:1 f.
The ground of this conduct	3:3-7
3) Final advice to Titus	3:8-11
CONCLUSION (3:12-15)	

2. *Summary.* The address (Ti. 1:1-4) is long and unusually solemn in tone. The mission of Paul, Apostle of Jesus Christ, is, by means of his preaching, to lead the elect, by faith, to the eternal life promised by God in the Old Testament.

Titus is reminded that he was left in Crete to organize the Church, specifically by appointing elders in the local churches. The qualities and duties of an elder—an overseer ("bishop"), God's steward—are listed; his principal concern is the teaching and defense of sound doctrine (Ti. 1:5-9). False teachers—patently Jews or Judaizers—have been disturbing the communities; they must be refuted (Ti. 1:10-16). The saying (v. 12) of the sixth-century Cretan poet Epimenides fits these people exactly; Cretans had a reputation for lying (as Corinthians had for sexual immorality).

Then comes a series of exhortations to Titus. In the first place it should always be his concern to teach sound doctrine. He must instruct Christians in their duties. Five groups are distinguished, with specific counsels for each: older men, older women, young women, young men, slaves (Ti. 2:1-10). The ground of Christian conduct is the revelation of God's saving grace in Christ. Although they live in this world, the eyes of Christians are (or ought to be) turned to the Parousia of "our great God and Savior Jesus Christ" —a straightforward affirmation of the divinity of Christ—who by his death has won for himself the new people of God (Ti. 2:11-15).

Christians are reminded of their duty of submission to lawful civil authority and are exhorted to show gentleness and courtesy to all men (Ti. 3:1 f.). The ground of such conduct is presented in a statement that develops the teaching of Eph. 2:3-10 and summarizes the doctrine of Rm.: the goodness and loving kindness of God our Savior who has saved us not by works but, through Jesus Christ, by the gift of baptism, renewal in the Holy Spirit. And once justified by the grace of Christ, we are heirs to eternal life (Ti. 3:3-7).

In conclusion, Titus is urged to insist on the matters that have been drawn to his attention. He must inculcate the practice of good works and, on the other hand, avoid futile controversies and shun entanglement with the factious (Ti. 3:8-11). When Artemas and Tychicus arrive in Crete, Titus is to join Paul at Nicopolis (in Epirus); also, he is to make arrangements for the journey of Zenas and Apollos (Ti. 3:12-14). The closing greeting (Ti. 3:15) is brief and conventional.

2. TIMOTHY

1. *Plan*

ADDRESS (1:1 f.)	
THANKSGIVING (1:3-5)	
THE CALL TO SUFFER (1:6—2:13)	
1) Fearless profession of faith	1:6-14
2) Disloyal and loyal friends	1:15-18
3) The will to suffer	2:1-13
FALSE TEACHERS (2:14—4:5)	
1) Advice to ministers	2:14-19
2) Personal advice	2:20-26
3) Perils of the Last Days	3:1-17
4) Solemn adjuration	4:1-5
CONCLUSION (4:6-22)	
1) Paul's testament	4:6-8
2) Paul and his friends	4:9-18
3) Personal greetings	4:19-23

2. *Summary.* The address (2 Tm. 1:1 f.) is the same as in 2 Cor. and Col. Paul thinks lovingly of his beloved "son" and thanks God for Timothy's faith, a faith like that of his grandmother and mother (2 Tm. 1:3-5).

Timothy is called upon to rekindle the gift of God within, the grace of consecration which he received when he was officially invested as an apostle, a grace of courage and of power. He is urged to accept his share of suffering for the Gospel and to bear these sufferings cheerfully as Paul did (2 Tm. 1:6-8). For, God has called us not because of our deeds but freely, in virtue of his grace, now manifested through the appearance of our Savior Jesus Christ who has destroyed death and brought life and immortality to light (2 Tm.

1:9 f.). Paul suffers for the Gospel, but he is not ashamed of his sufferings (so neither should Timothy). He had been appointed preacher and apostle and teacher of the Gospel and he is confident that he will stand firm in his charge to the end; Timothy, too, with the help of the Holy Spirit, will be faithful to the Gospel (2 Tm. 1:10-14). Paul's Asian friends have deserted him. By contrast, the fidelity of Onesiphorus is all the more welcome, and the Apostle expresses his gratitude with warmth (2 Tm. 1:15-18). At his inauguration as an apostle ("before many witnesses" [cf. 1 Tm. 4:14; 6:12]), Timothy had been entrusted by Paul with the sound tradition of the faith; in his turn he is to entrust it to dependable men who will instruct others. But, he must be prepared to shoulder his share of suffering, like the soldier or athlete or farmer who earns his reward only by facing up to the demands of the task in hand (2 Tm. 2:1-7). Faithful service will win fellowship with Jesus Christ. Again Paul points to the example of his own sufferings. The passage closes with a quotation (2 Tm. 2:11-13) from a baptismal hymn: at baptism the Christian dies and rises with Christ, but the sacrament imposes the obligation of endurance and fidelity (2 Tm. 2:8-13).

The central part of the letter (2 Tm. 2:14—4:5) is dominated by a concern for the dangers that false teachers and corrupting doctrine can give rise to in the communities. Timothy must remind his faithful of the demands of their Christian calling and get them to cease from futile discussions; he himself must set the example. Two false teachers, Hymenaeus and Philetus, are mentioned by name; the former had already been excommunicated by Paul (1 Tm. 1:20). Their teaching was that the resurrection is already past. We know that the Greeks had difficulty in accepting the idea of bodily resurrection (Acts 17:32; 1 Cor. 15:12), and these teachers interpreted it in a spiritual fashion, as referring to postbaptismal life in the Spirit (cf. Rm. 6:1-11; Col. 2:12; 3:1; Eph. 2:5). But the Church—which upholds the reality of the resurrection—stands on solid foundations that bear the inscription of God (2 Tm. 2:14-19). The metaphor of the Church as a building leads, naturally enough, to the further image of the utensils of a house, some for noble, some for ignoble, use; here, the ignoble utensils are false teachers, who must be avoided. Once again, Timothy is warned to abstain from sterile controversy. It is pointed out that, if he must oppose the false teachers, he must do so patiently and gently, for God may yet bring them to their senses (2 Tm. 2:20-26). "The true apostle does not condemn. He knows that the Lord can always straighten up the bruised reed and light the smouldering wick (Is. 42:3; Mt. 12:20)."[66]

If there is to be a final wave of evil before the Parousia (2 Tm. 3:1-5a), it is implied (v. 5b) that the false teachers are already enemies of true religion. They may be able to lead astray silly women, but they will be no more successful in the long run than Pharaoh's magicians (cf. Ex. 7:11 f., 22; 8:7)—the names Jannes and Jambres come from late Jewish tradition (2 Tm. 3:6-9). Timothy, however, has been the faithful disciple of Paul from the beginning and knows what the Apostle has suffered. He had been well instructed in the Old Testament by his mother and grandmother (cf. 2 Tm. 1:5). In 2 Tm. 16 f., we have an attestation of the inspired character of Scripture,[67] while the whole passage is an important statement on the importance and profit of the reading of Scripture (2 Tm. 3:10-17). There follows a very solemn adjuration to Timothy: he must continue to preach the Gospel "in season and out of season." The fact that people will refuse to listen to the word, and turn to novelties is, paradoxically, a further reason for more earnest preaching still. In these difficult times and circumstances, the utmost loyalty is demanded of the disciple (2 Tm. 4:1-5).

Paul realizes that this, his second Roman captivity, will end with his execution; hence, he can speak of his blood about to be poured out as a libation to God (cf. Phil. 2:17). And he can declare in all sincerity that he has been faithful to his charge and that he is confident of the victor's wreath (2 Tm. 4:6-8). Demas—a companion of the first captivity (cf. Col. 4:14; Phm. 24)—has now deserted Paul, while Crescens, Titus, and Tychicus are absent on missionary work. Only Luke is with the Apostle, and now he dearly wishes to have Timothy and Mark come to him—these three are like that choice inner circle of Jesus' disciples, Peter and James and John. He wants Timothy to bring a cloak, books, and parchments left at Troas, and the disciple is warned against a certain Alexander. Paul feels all

---

[66]P. Dornier, Les épîtres de Saint Paul à Timothée et à Tite, (BJ), p. 58.
[67]See Wilfrid J. Harrington, Record of Revelation: The Bible (Chicago: The Priory Press, 1965), p. 26.

the more lonely and abandoned because, at a recent appearance before the tribunal, there was not one voice raised in his defense; but the Lord saved him (2 Tm. 4:9-18). The letter closes with an exchange of personal greetings (2 Tm. 4:19-22).

3) *Authenticity and Date of Composition*[68]

AUTHENTICITY   On the ground of external criticism, few of the New Testament writings are as well attested as the Pastorals. Eusebius, who was acutely aware of doubts relative to certain inspired books, accepted them without hesitation. Irenaeus (c. 185 A.D.) referred to 1 Tm. 1:4 and attributed to Paul several quotations from the Pastorals, in particular 2 Tm. 4:10 f. Clement of Alexandria cited the Pastorals, which he attributed to Paul, more than forty times. Tatian acknowledged Ti. as Pauline, and the Muratorian Canon has the three writings in its list of Pauline letters. Polycarp was very familiar with them and Clement of Rome knew them. We may be quite sure that the Pauline *corpus,* constituted before the end of the first century, contained these Epistles. At that date, however, many contemporaries of the Apostle were still alive; it is improbable that a forger would have succeeded in having adopted, especially in Ephesus, letters "of Paul" which he had not written.

Yet, despite the strong traditional witness to the Pauline origin of the Epistles, ever since the beginning of the nineteenth century their authenticity has been more and more assailed on critical grounds, and today very many scholars tend to accept their inauthenticity as an established fact. These scholars take their stand on the nature of the errors combated and on the hierarchical organization of the churches, both of which (they say) point to the second century, and also on the language and style which (they claim) are quite unlike those of Paul. We shall examine these arguments more closely.

1. *The Errors.* Here the onus is surely on those who would argue that the errors envisaged are characteristic of second-century Gnosticism. It does seem that the incomplete and passing references to false teaching which the Pastorals provide are a fragile ground for such

---

[68]See Dornier, *op. cit.*, pp. 7-17; C. Spicq, "Paul: Pastorales (Épîtres)," DBS, VII, cols. 50-65.

an assured assertion. In fact, the indications, such as they are, do not require us to move outside a first-century setting.

Besides, we have the impression that the danger threatens, not from a movement opposed to the Church, but from within the Christian communities. We may, however, look to Judaism for the *source* of these errors. The preaching of the adversaries is the occasion of disputes on the subject of the Mosaic Law (Ti. 3:9; 1 Tm. 1:7); these false teachers distinguish between clean and unclean foods (1 Tm. 4:3; Ti. 1:15); their teaching is nothing more than "Jewish fables" (Ti. 1:14). Titus is put on his guard especially against "the circumcision party" which he must silence (Ti. 1:10 f.). It appears, then, that the false teachers are Judaizers. But, since 2 Tm. 3:8 seems to make a discreet allusion to magic practices, and the condemnation of marriage (1 Tm. 4:3) is certainly not in the line of orthodox Judaism, we may look to a syncretistic Judaism—as in the case of the Colossian error.[69] This heterodox Judaism may be on its way toward the Gnosticism of the second century, but the Pastorals give no hint of the characteristic traits of Gnosticism: dualism, the emanation of eons, opposition between the God of the Old Testament and the God of the New Testament. We find, then, that the evidence, far from demanding a second-century date for the Pastorals, points rather to a time not much later than the writing of Col.

2. *Church Organization.* Again it is maintained that the hierarchical organization of the churches, as it is presented to us in the Pastorals, demands a date considerably later than Paul's time. To appreciate the value of this argument, and to estimate the weight of it, we must look to the New Testament evidence of an evolution in community organization. We find that the primitive Palestinian community, at its earliest stage, had, as hierarchy, Apostles and deacons. Communities outside Palestine were under the direction of the Apostle who had founded them; when absent, the same Apostle would guide them by letter or by fully-accredited representatives. A local organization also began to take shape. It was modeled on the Jewish synagogue and especially on the synagogue's system of elders. Hence, already in Acts 11:30 we find "elders" in the Jerusalem church

---

[69]See pp. 293 f.

itself, and in Acts 15 "apostles and elders" are named together. There is no evidence that, in the communities, one elder held pre-eminence over the others. (James' position was due to his unique standing as "brother of the Lord.") At this stage, the hierarchy comprised: the Apostles and their delegates, the elders and the deacons.

As time passed and the Apostles disappeared, one figure began to assume a special position in the local churches. This was the *episkopos*, who exercised authority over the elders, deacons, and faithful. We know from Ignatius of Antioch that such was the situation in the churches of Asia Minor at the beginning of the second century. At that date, the *episkopos* is the bishop and the *presbyteroi* are priests.

But the term *episkopos* was already used in the first century, although in a much less precise sense, and was the equivalent of *presbyteros* (elder). Thus, for instance, Paul summoned to Miletus the "elders" of the church of Ephesus (Acts 20:17) and assured them that the Holy Spirit had constituted them "guardians (*episkopoi*) to feed the church of the Lord" (Acts 20:28). Similarly, in saluting the dignitaries of the church of Philippi, Paul names "the overseers (*episkopoi*) and deacons" (Phil. 1:1); unless the elders are included among the "overseers," their omission is inexplicable. Thus, in the middle of the first century, *prebyteros* and *episkopos* are, for all intents and purposes, synonymous. We may, at most, discern certain nuances rather than real differences. The first term, of Jewish origin (at least, the primitive Church borrowed it from Judaism), refers to the maturity and dignity of the person; the other was used in the Greek world to indicate an inspector or guardian. We must also acknowledge that the *episkopos*, especially as the office became more clearly defined, is strangely like the *mebaqqer* or president of the Qumran "camps" or groups. "Each camp had a 'superintendent' (*mebaqqer*) who was also responsible for instructing and guiding candidates for admission. This curious combination of religious and administrative functions is met with again in the *episkopos* of the early Church."[70]

---

[70] J. T. Milik, *Ten Years of Discovery in the Desert of Judaea* (Naperville, Ill.: Allenson, 1959), p. 100.

Regardless of the background of the terms, we find that the Pastorals reflect the historical situation of the first century. Although we meet with the terms *episkopos*, elder, and deacon, they are never used with the precise technical meaning they have in the letters of Ignatius of Antioch. Thus, in 1 Tm. 3:2, the author begins to outline the qualities and duties of an *episkopos* and then passes to those of a deacon, with no mention of elders. And in Ti. 1:7 (the only other passage where *episkopos* occurs), the argument runs like this: Verse 5: Titus will establish "elders" in the towns of Crete; verse 6: each of them must be blameless; verse 7: "for an *episkopos*," etc. These texts show that *episkopos* and *presbyteros* do not yet stand for two clearly-distinguished degrees of the hierarchy. Therefore, the hierarchical organization presupposed in the Pastorals, far from demanding a second-century date, is more likely to be an effective argument of their Pauline authenticity.

3. *Style and Vocabulary*. The most serious objections to the Pauline authenticity of the Pastorals come under this heading. It is maintained that the style is quite unlike that of Paul; and, with regard to the vocabulary, it comprises very many words not found in the other letters.

This sort of argument needs to be handled with great delicacy and is notoriously open to subjective interpretations. Our study of the other Epistles should have convinced us that Paul is versatile and has different styles. Again, new problems are faced in the Pastorals. The imposing total (306) of *hapax legomena* may be significantly reduced when we exclude certain words that have nothing characteristic about them (for example, stomach, grandmother), or which derive from a root already used by Paul, or which are demanded by the subject matter (references to the errors, and so forth). Furthermore, they must be balanced by the presence of words and expressions of authentically Pauline stamp. What we meet with, however, is not only a change of vocabulary and accent, but also, and more fundamentally, a new manner of expression. We are faced with thought patterns and notions that are properly Hellenistic and that are not represented by the earlier New Testament writings. At the same time, the Jewish and rabbinical substratum of the Pastorals remains preponderant.

The result seems to be Pauline thought in Hellenistic dress. Until now, the Apostle, heir to the prophets of Israel, had elaborated his theology in Jewish terms and in Old Testament terminology. Now, at the close of his days, he sees that—thanks mainly to himself—Christianity has taken root in another culture and has become a universal religion. Hence, it has become urgent to present the new faith in terms more accessible to the Greek mentality. This he proceeds to do in the Pastorals.

An old man, Paul is again the rabbi confiding to his disciple the doctrine that is to be faithfully preserved by him. Thus, the Pastorals are concerned primarily with the transmission of the Christian doctrine, with its passage from the age of the Apostles to the next generation.

> Paul not only wishes to perpetuate his teaching, but he wishes to give an official, "authoritative" character to the institutions and to the content of a preaching which he henceforth considers as a *parathēkē* (deposit) (2 Tm. 1:14). In 67, the believers are the heirs of a sacred and immovable tradition: *Pistos ho logos* (the saying is sure) (1 Tm. 1:15; 3:1; 4:9; Ti. 1:9; 3:8; 2 Tm. 2:11).[71]

Yet, much of what was written above concerning the authorship of Eph. applies here too, and with even greater force. While nothing compels us to deny substantial Pauline authenticity, it is not easy to accept that the author of Thes. and Gal. and Phil. penned these pages. Here, more than ever, do we need to postulate the hand of a responsible secretary. But, who he was we cannot say. Perhaps "a professional rhetorician, a sort of Christian Tyrannos (cf. Acts 19:9) of Jewish origin"?[72] Or, a converted Essene, for the theme of "truth," characteristic of Qumran, is also characteristic of the Pastorals.[73]

DATE AND PLACE   The relationship of the Pastorals is such that
OF COMPOSITION   all three must have been written within a short
space of time. No more than a month or two, perhaps only a few weeks, separate 1 Tm. and Ti. And it seems that, of the two, 1 Tm. was written first and Ti. is a résumé of it; it cannot be doubted that both come before 2 Tm. The latter was written when the Apostle

---

[71]Spicq, *art. cit.*, DBS, cols. 69 f.
[72]*Ibid.*, col. 64.
[73]See Murphy-O'Connor, *art. cit.*, *Revue Biblique*, 61-76.

was a prisoner in Rome for the second time (2 Tm. 1:17). He speaks
of his imminent trial (2 Tm. 4:16-18) and, with no illusions as to
the outcome, he prepares for death (2 Tm. 4:6 8). Consequently,
2 Tm. was written in Rome, in the year 67 A.D.—the traditional date
of Paul's death. The others were written shortly before, in 66-67 A.D.,
doubtless from Macedonia.[74]

4) *Doctrine*[75]

It is in the *Church,* with its preaching, its sacraments, and its
ministers that the salvation of believers is realized. The Church is
comparable to a house (1 Tm. 3:15; 2 Tm. 2:19-21), with God's
stewards as caretakers (Ti. 1:7). It is the assembly which takes the
place of the people of God of the Old Testament; the assembly is
the new people of God which Christ has won for himself (Ti. 2:14).
It is the "Church of the living God," for the "living God" of Israel
has become the God of Christians; hence, the Church has become the
one sanctuary of the true God.

This Church is served by *ministers*: apostolic delegates, elders or
overseers, and deacons. The envoys of the Apostle—who is the ultimate head of the church founded by him—continue to consolidate
the work which Paul had started (Ti. 1:5). They are teachers who
must speak without tiring (2 Tm. 4:2), expounding the sound doctrine they themselves have received (1 Tm. 6:20; Ti. 2:1; 2 Tm. 1:13;
3:14), vigorously taking issue with unsound doctrine (1 Tm. 1:3; Ti.
1:10-13), demanding thorough doctrinal formation in those whom
they appoint to office (Ti. 1:9; 2 Tm. 2:2). They are pastors who
guide the faithful and carefully instruct them in the duties of their
state (1 Tm. 6:1 f.; Ti. 2:1-10). They are responsible for organizing
the cult (1 Tm. 2:8-11). The elders, or *episkopoi,* are the adminis-
trators of the local communities (1 Tm. 3:2; Ti. 1:7), who preside
over the liturgical assemblies, preach, and teach (1 Tm. 3:2; 5:17;
Ti. 1:11), and who, with the Apostle or his delegates, impose hands
on others (1 Tm. 4:14). The portrait of the perfect *episkopos* is
drawn in two parallel passages (1 Tm. 3:1-7; Ti. 1:6-9). The precise

---

[74]For the journeys of Paul between 63 A.D. and 67 A.D. see pp. 65 f.
[75]See Spicq, *art. cit.,* DBS, cols. 45-50; Dornier, *op. cit.,* pp. 17-20.

function and duties of deacons are not clear; instead, we learn of
the qualities demanded of them, almost the same as those required
for elders (1 Tm. 3:8-10, 12 f.).

The *moral virtues* figure largely in the Pastorals. Christians are
called upon to live "godly lives" (1 Tm. 2:2; Ti. 2:12). *Eusebeia*
("piety," "godliness") goes far beyond the meaning of the English
word *piety*: it is at the same time the adoration of God and the
accomplishment of his will; it embraces the totality of our relations
with God. For, by associating reverential fear, gratitude, and love,
it commands all the duties of religion and the exercise of the moral
virtues. Thus, in fact, the Christian can be urged simply to "train
yourself in godliness" (1 Tm. 4:7). Insistence on the practice of
the moral virtues is doubtless an answer to the adversaries who, by
their aimless speculations, would lose themselves and others in a false
mysticism. Quite apart from the combating of error, however, there
is the realization that sublime doctrine must become a reality, that
Christianity is not vague; and thus, like 1 Jn., the Pastorals bring Christians back to the concrete living of daily life in Christ.

This is the reason the *Christian* will do his best to fulfill the duties
proper to his age and condition. The father of a family will govern
his household with authority (1 Tm. 3:4 f.); wives will love their
husbands and mothers their children (Ti. 2:4 f.); slaves will be
docile and conscientious in their service (Ti. 2:9 f.). All must obey
the lawfully-constituted authority (Ti. 3:1). Christian education,
based on Scripture, is not superficial; rather, it aims at the formation
of the complete man (2 Tm. 3:16 f.). Whether the believer is compared to a soldier, an athlete, or a farmer (2 Tm. 2:3-6), the accent
is on personal effort, the practice of virtue, training in godliness
(1 Tm. 4:7). Good deeds will be his constant preoccupation (Ti.
3:8, 14), that is, virtue in all its forms (Ti. 2:7; 1 Tm. 5:25), or, more
precisely, the service of one's neighbor (1 Tm. 5:10; 6:18). The truth
of the doctrine of the faith will be demonstrated and adorned by the
virtuous lives of Christians (Ti. 2:10). And, all the while, the good
fight of the faith is a permanent homage rendered to the efficacy
of the grace of God (1 Tm. 6:12; Ti. 3:3-8).

6. HEBREWS

1) Generalities

LITERARY FORM   The Epistle to the Hebrews differs from the other New Testament Epistles in that it ends like a letter (Heb. 13:18-25), although it does not begin like one and lacks the customary opening address with the names of the writer and recipients. Although 1 Jn., which also begins without an epistolary formula, quickly manifests (1 Jn. 1:4) its proper character of letter, Heb. presents the first formally epistolary expression only in 13:22: "I have written to you." But, references throughout the work suggest that it is a letter. The apostrophes: "brethren" (Heb. 3:12; 10:19), "holy brethren" (Heb. 3:1), "beloved" (Heb. 6:9) would be out of place if Heb. were a treatise, and therefore impersonal in tone. The recipients are well known to the writer with regard to their spiritual condition (Heb. 5:11-14; 6:9-12), the dangers to which they are exposed (Heb. 2:1 ff.; 3:12 f.; 4:1, 11; 10:25 ff.), and the merit of the good works which they have done (Heb. 6:11; 10:32 ff.). In short, it does seem that Heb. is indeed presented as a letter; the writer is at a distance from his addressees and he intervenes in a concrete situation.

All the same, Heb. has a distinct solemnity about it. Its author describes it as a "discourse of exhortation" (Heb. 13:22) and uses expressions proper to oratorical style (Heb. 2:5; 5:11; 6:9; 7:9; 9:5; 11:32). Hence, it has been regarded as a homily cast as a letter, or a writing which is part homily and part letter. However, the presence of undoubted homiletical elements does not prove that this was originally a homily, afterwards set down in letter form. This impression is due to the notable oratorical gifts of the writer, which show themselves even in the framing of his letter. Again, it has been suggested that Heb. is an epistle rather than a letter, but, perhaps, it would be better not to overstress the differences between these two literary categories, as though there could not be a varied form. And this seems to be just the case of Heb.: it is a letter because of its setting, which never loses sight of a clearly-determined group of readers; and it is an epistle because of the loftiness of the subject treated and because of its style.[76]

OCCASION   The author of Heb. addresses Jews who have renounced their former religion and who have abandoned the Mosaic rites and observances (cf. Acts 21:21). They have joined the Church and confess Jesus as Messiah and Savior (Heb. 13:8). But, the change from the old order of things to the new is psychologically difficult. It is not easy for them to turn their backs on ingrained habits and on national and religious traditions and prejudices. These converts are more keenly aware of what they have lost in renouncing the Temple than in what they can find in the Christian assemblies. They miss the splendid liturgy they had known so well; the new cult has so little to offer by way of tangible support for their faith.

Branded by them as renegades, they find themselves ostrasized by their former coreligionists and feel themselves quite isolated and like exiles. They have suffered persecution, they have been despoiled of their goods, and some of them have been imprisoned (Heb. 10:32-36). Their Jewish mentality tended to see in this misery a sign that they had been abandoned by God (cf. Heb. 6:10). Had their conversion been a mistake? Their spiritual life had suffered: they had grown sluggish and hard of hearing (Heb. 6:12; 5:11); they had been tempted (Heb. 2:18); they faced a real possibility of martyrdom (Heb. 12:14); hence, some had become discouraged (Heb. 12:12).

All this explains the tone of the Epistle and its repeated exhortations. The readers are first of all called upon to cling to the Word of God as revealed by Christ, lest they should stray from the truth (Heb. 2:1). They must continue on their way perseveringly, like athletes (Heb. 12:1). They must not be deceived (Heb. 13:9), nor overcome by weariness (Heb. 12:3); they must resist sin (Heb. 12:4). On the positive side, they must look to the joyful certainty of salvation (Heb. 10:35); they must remain steadfast in hope (Heb. 10:39). In a word, they must at all times preserve *pistis* ("faith")

---

[76]See Teodorico da Castel San Pietro, *L'Epistola agli Ebrei* (Rome: Marietti, 1952), pp. 4-6.

in its triple sense of docile acceptance of the revealed word, of confidence in Providence, and of persevering fidelity to the divine will (Heb. 3:7; 4:13; 11). "Just as Rm. is the Epistle of salvation, Gal. of liberty, 1 Cor. of fraternal charity, Heb. is the Epistle of confident and courageous faith, attachment of mind and of all one's being to the Savior (cf. Heb. 10:39; 13:6)."[77]

AUTHORSHIP   External evidence for the Pauline authenticity of Heb. shows a difference in attitude between the Eastern and Western Church. In the East, the first clear attribution of Heb. to Paul is that of Pantaenus (c. 180 A.D.), and from his time all the Eastern churches included Heb. among the Pauline Epistles. This is not to say that there was not some hesitation. Critics like Origen, taking their stand on literary grounds, inclined to the view that the Apostle had not himself written the Epistle. But, these were lone voices, and the bishops and councils maintained strict Pauline origin. Belief in the canonicity of the writing was unwavering.

The situation in the Western Church was not the same. Before the end of the first century, Clement of Rome knew Heb. and had a high estimation of it. Clement, however, does not mention the name of Paul in connection with it. Tertullian attributed it to Barnabas; no other writer of the Roman church refers to the Epistle until the middle of the fourth century. Jerome attests that the authenticity of Heb. was quite eclipsed in the West. The African churches do not appear to have known it until the end of the fourth century. But, Jerome and Augustine treated it as Pauline, and from the fifth century it was accepted as such in the West.[78]

Although the Western Church, like the East, did eventually come around to the view of the Pauline authorship of Heb., it is clear that the matter was in serious doubt from the beginning. Today there is scarcely a scholar who would attribute the writing to the Apostle. The arguments against Pauline authenticity, which are decisive, may be listed:

---

[77]C. Spicq, "Paul: Hébreux (Épître aux)," DBS, VII, cols. 227 f. This understanding of the occasion of Heb. is the traditional view, by no means accepted by all.

[78]See Harrington, *op. cit.*, pp. 68-72.

1) The Epistle has no address giving Paul's name; all thirteen Pauline Epistles do have such an address.

2) Language and style differ notably: there are 168 New Testament *hapax legomena* and 124 words not found in Paul, while perfect Greek periods manifest a carefully polished style.

3) The manner of citing Scripture is different. Paul's formulas are: As it is written; Scripture says; Moses, David, etc., says. Heb. has: God, the Son, the Holy Spirit, speaks; "It has been testified somewhere."

4) The arrangement differs: in Paul, a dogmatic part is followed by a didactic or exhortatory part; in Heb., doctrine and exhortation alternate throughout.

5) Heb. 2:3 describes its author as one who learned from hearers of Christ, that is from Apostles; contrast Gal. 1:1, 11 ff.

6) The central theme of the Christology of Heb., the Priesthood of Christ, nowhere occurs in the Pauline Epistles.

7) Heb. has no reference to the doctrine, so important in Paul's eyes, of justification through faith and not by works of the Law— even though the letter is addressed to Judaeo-Christians.

Wikenhauser, to whom the preceding summary is due, thus sums up the position:

> The differences are so numerous and so sharp that the Epistle cannot have been written by Paul. The religious ideas, the style, and the mode of expression of Heb. point to another author than the Apostle. Yet, agreements with Paul show that the writer was an intellectual disciple of the Apostle. He was, however, a thoroughly original thinker, and the Epistle was neither commissioned nor directed by Paul.[79]

Indeed, undoubted similarities with Pauline doctrine, allied to such marked singularity of thought and style, are readily accounted for by the reasonable assumption that the author of Heb. was a disciple of Paul.

It is not surprising that scholars have sought to identify the author of this outstanding work. In fact, almost every person named in Acts or the Pauline Epistles as a disciple or even acquaintance of the

---

[79]Wikenhauser, *op. cit.*, p. 334; Eng. trans., p. 467.

Apostle has been suggested at some time or other. The strongest claim to authorship seems to be that of Apollos.[80]

From the very favorable description of him in Acts 18:24-28, we gather that Apollos was a Jew, an Alexandrian by birth, an eloquent man, exceptionally well versed in the Scriptures; he was an apologete, fervent in spirit, who strenuously refuted the Jews, "showing by the scriptures that the Christ was Jesus."

1) Apollos was a Jew; a reading of Heb. will convince one that its author was a Jew.

2) He was a native of Alexandria, the home of Philo. One of the most characteristic traits of the Epistle is not only its Alexandrian language and culture, but its extensive and precise knowledge of the Philonian writings.

3) Apollos was at once an erudite man and an orator; this combination, rarely met with, is verified in the author of Heb.

4) Apollos was a Scripture scholar; his ability must have been outstanding when Luke mentioned this specialty in an age and milieu nourished on the Old Testament. Heb. is the work of a master of Scripture.

5) Apollos was an apologete; Heb. is a masterpiece of scriptural apologetics.

6) Every orator has his favorite theme. Apollos "spoke and taught accurately the things concerning Jesus" (Acts 18:25); the theme of Heb. is the exaltation of the person of Christ under his different aspects of King, Prophet, and Priest.

7) The eminent personality of the author of Heb. corresponds exactly to the character of the orator who in Corinth was placed on an equal footing with Cephas and Paul (1 Cor. 1:12; 3:4 f.; 4:6). At the same time, Apollos was so affected by the Corinthian party strife that, although earnestly invited by Paul to return to Corinth, he firmly refused (1 Cor. 16:12); the sensitivity of its author is obvious in Heb.

8) Although Acts indicates the Alexandrian origin of Apollos, it also tells us that his Christian instruction was completed at Ephesus (Acts 18:26), which apparently became his home for some time

---

[80]See C. Spicq, "Paul: Hébreux (Épître aux)," DBS, VII, cols. 248 f.

(cf. 1 Cor. 16:12). It is known that the Christian community of that city was preoccupied with priestly and cultic matters, and Asia Minor was a natural milieu for the origin and growth of speculation on the Priesthood of Christ. At Ephesus, too, the author could have come to know the Johannine tradition and the Captivity Epistles.

9) When Apollos had arrived at Ephesus about the year 53 A.D., he had received only the baptism of John and did not know of the Holy Spirit (Acts 18:25; 19:2 f.). Heb. happens to be exceptionally poor in doctrine of the Holy Spirit (in sharp contrast to Paul). It seems that Apollos had never really integrated this doctrine into his theological synthesis.

This accord between the personality and gifts of the author of Heb. and those of the Alexandrian Jew is certainly very remarkable. The principal objection raised against the attribution of the Epistle to Apollos is that it is too recent; he was not mentioned in this connection in the early Church. But, there is no tradition in this matter. Even the names mentioned at an early date—those of Clement of Rome, Luke, and Barnabas—are put forward hypothetically and not on the grounds of traditional data.

PLACE AND DATE   We have suggested that Heb. was written to
OF COMPOSITION   a community of converts from Judaism situated, perhaps, in Caesarea or even in Antioch. This remains likely, even though a sizable number of exegetes opt for a Gentile-Christian community. Not much weight can be placed on the title "To the Hebrew" which dates from the middle of the second century.

The place of origin of the writing is uncertain. The final salutation of Heb. 13:24 suggests Italy. But *hoi apo tēs Italias* may mean: "those who have come from Italy" (more simply "the Italians"— whether still in Italy or not). Hence, some have argued from this text that the letter was written *to* Italy.

The Epistle is cited by Clement of Rome (c. 95 A.D.); hence, it cannot be later than that date. The majority of scholars believe that it was written between 85 and 90 A.D. Others, because of its affinity with the Pauline writings, would put it before the death of the Apostle. Internal criticism does not exclude a date before 70 A.D. It is true that the author's treatment of sanctuary and cult is meant to be scriptural rather than a description of contemporary worship, and he has in mind the desert tent rather than the Herodian Temple (hence, it cannot be argued from Heb. 8:13 and 9:2-5 that the Temple still stood)—but would he have passed in silence the catastrophe of 70 A.D.? This would have clinched his case for the contemporary nature of the Old Testament cult. At any rate, a date before 70 A.D. is not improbable.

INFLUENCES[81]   Whether or not the Alexandrian Apollos was the author of Heb., it is admitted by many scholars that the Epistle was written by an Alexandrian Jew. Some would go so far as to say that he was very familiar with the works of Philo.[82] Traces of Philonian influence may be discerned throughout the writing (such as the ideas of *teleiōsis* ["perfection"], of two revelations [Heb. 1:1], of messianic intercession, and of two sanctuaries, while the Christ of Heb. is the antitype of the Philonian Moses), but they are most marked in the apologetic and exhortatory sections. Thus, for instance, the literary structure of the eulogy of faith (Heb. 11) is identical with a eulogy of hope in Philo's writings. Heb. is marked by Philo's philosophy and by his biblical apologetic; it does seem that the author of the Epistle must have studied the works of the Alexandrian philosopher. And when he became a Christian, he did not thereby reject the ideas and technical terms he had assimilated. Yet, these words and these ideas are no longer exactly those of Philo. They have evolved, they have been enriched, they are related to other realities; but, it remains possible to identify their origin.

We do not need to insist on Pauline influence in Heb. The fact that the Pauline authenticity of the writing was defended until recently—especially by Catholic scholars—with some plausibility, is enough to indicate that the author must have been a disciple of the Apostle, one who had, in particular, assimilated the theology of the Captivity Epistles. What is rather unexpected is that no other New Testament writing has such affinities with the Johannine writings. We may go so far as to say that Heb. seems to depend, to some extent, on the Johannine catechesis which was later fixed in the Fourth Gospel and Epistles. The contacts are such that they seem

[81]See *ibid.*, cols. 233-47.
[82]See p. 32.

to presuppose a common theological school, or, at least, the same cultural milieu. We shall point to some of these contacts in our summary of the Epistle.

USE OF THE   Although the author of Heb. did not disdain
OLD TESTAMENT[83]   literal exegesis (thus, e.g., the exegesis of Ps. 110 [109]:4; Heb. 5:6; 7:21; 5:10; 7:3, 16 f., 24), more often his method is strange to us. We must understand that his exegesis presupposes that the whole of Scripture is messianic, a constant and harmonious prophecy of Christ and of the Covenant which he has sealed between regenerated humanity and God. In other words, the economy of the Old Testament is already orientated toward the New to such an extent that persons (Melchizedek and the Israelites of the Exodus) and institutions (the Mosaic ritual) are properly seen in terms of their messianic prefiguration. The two economies, expressions of one divine plan, speak the same language and reveal the same object to believers. Although the Old must give way to the other, it has prepared it and, in a manner, contained it. This is why, for instance, 2 Sm. 7:14, which is in its obvious sense a divine declaration of fatherhood with regard to Solomon, is in Heb. 1:5 referred directly to the most illustrious scion of the Davidic line, the Messiah. In the same way, the crossing of the desert by the Iraelites represents the conditions of the life of the people of God: called to a place of rest and submitted to temptation, it must accomplish its pilgrimage in fidelity to the word of God. The example of the generation of the Exodus is therefore valid for all future generations.

Again, to describe the redemptive work of the High Priest of the New Covenant, Heb., by an argument of analogy and typology, exploits and transposes the rite of the Day of Expiation, and thus the Mosaic cult is seen as a prophetic image of the cult of God by Christ. In short, Heb. is largely the exegesis of the *mashal* ("parable") which the Old Testament constitutes; hence, the literal interpretation yields to midrashic exegesis[84] or to allegory; for example, Heb. 3:12–4:10 is a midrashic interpretation of Ps. 95 (94):7-11.

---

[83]See C. Spicq, "Paul: Hébreux (Épître aux)," DBS, VII, cols. 269-71; J. Cambier, IB, pp. 540-42.

[84]See Wilfrid J. Harrington, *Record of the Promise: The Old Testament* (Chicago: The Priory Press, 1965), pp. 323-26.

The worth of an exegesis based on such procedure is not to be evaluated on grounds of modern biblical criticism, but insofar as it is the affirmation of an inspired author. The author of Heb. is a charismatic. Reading the Old Testament in the light of the new economy, he discerns in the "shadow" of the Old Law the "true form" brought by Christ (Heb. 10:1), and in the "parable" of the Old Testament he reads a message for the present (Heb. 9:9). Therefore, he must be taken at his word when he writes that Moses, by choosing to share ill-treatment with the people of God rather than to enjoy the fleeting pleasures of sin, had chosen, in fact, to suffer for Christ (Heb. 11:25 f.); or, when he assures us that Christ himself speaks to Christians in Ps. 95 (94) (cf. Heb. 3:7-11). For, only the Spirit of God who has guided the history of the people of God and inspired the Old Testament can fully declare the sense of the one and of the other; and the author of Heb. is also inspired by the same Spirit.[85]

2) Analysis

The structure of Heb. has been much discussed in this century; it is, obviously, an important factor in our understanding of the writing. In this matter, the contribution of L. Vaganay has proved significant.[86] Working on the technique—present in the poetical and prophetical books of the Old Testament—of *inclusio*, the repetition of certain words which mark off a literary unit, and of *concatenatio*, the linking of strophes by identical or similar words, he discovered in Heb. an intricate system of catchwords. The conclusions of Vaganay have been accepted, with some reservations and modifications, by Ceslaus Spicq.[87] The theory has also served A. Vanhoye, whose remarkable analysis is the most detailed study of the literary structure of Heb. yet to appear.[88]

---

[85]See Harrington, *Record of Revelation: The Bible, op. cit.,* pp. 54-62.

[86]See L. Vaganay, "Le plan de l'Épître aux Hébreux," in *Memorial Lagrange* (Paris, 1940), pp. 269-77.

[87]See p. 342.

[88]See A. Vanhoye, *La Structure Littéraire de l'Épître aux Hébreux* (Paris/Bruges: Desclée de Brouwer, 1963).

PLAN I   1. *The Literary Structure.*[89] The technique of catch-words as a linking device has not quite the importance that Vaganay attached to it; instead, the indication of a subject to be treated is more constant and has greater significance. This is done regularly before each of the five parts of the Epistle and points, according to the part in question, to its one, two, or three sections. Thus, for the central part, which has three sections preceded by a preamble, the indication of the subject is made in a single phrase before the preamble; it is then repeated, piece by piece, before the start of the three respective developments. For parts II and IV, each composed of two sections, the indication of these two sections is presented in an order that is the inverse of the two subsequent developments, thus enabling the author to introduce the first section by using as catch-words the very terms of the title. With regard to the second sections of the two parts, he judged it unnecessary, both times, to announce the subject again before going on to treat of it: he could hope that the reader would still remember it.

This structure gives a concentric symmetry that is clearly apparent. Corresponding to the number of sections in each, the parts are symmetrically arranged around a central part: part III. Parts I and V have one section each, while parts II and IV have two each, and the central part has three. This part III, in its turn, is built around a center—its second section—which is preceded by a preliminary exhortation and a first section, and followed by a third section and a final exhortation.

The whole Epistle is a combination of doctrinal exposition and parenesis (admonition, exhortation):

1) The single section of part I (Heb. 1:5–2:18) is doctrinal (apart from Heb. 2:1-4).

2) Part II has one section of parenesis (Heb. 3:1–4:14) and one doctrinal section (Heb. 4:15–5:10).

3) In part III, the two exhortations or pareneses (Heb. 5:11–6:20 and 10:19-39) frame the three sections (Heb. 7; 8-9; 10:1-18), all doctrinal, which together form one great exposition.

---

[89]See *ibid.*, pp. 49-59.

4) Part IV has one parenetical section (Heb. 11:1-40) and one doctrinal section (Heb. 12:1-13).

5) Part V has clearly the character of an exhortation (Heb. 12:14 —13:19), although there are some doctrinal traits (e.g., Heb. 12:8-24; 13:11 f.).

It may be seen that the symmetry is not perfect; thus, for instance, part V, like part I, should be doctrinal. On the other hand, the actual arrangement gives a better over-all balance: six sections of doctrine and five of parenesis. Besides, it is fitting that this "word of exhortation" should close with practical exhortation.

2. *Plan.*

		1:1-4	Introduction	
I		1:5—2:18	The name more excellent than the angels	Doctrine
II	A.	3:1—4:14	Jesus, faithful	Parenesis
	B.	4:15—5:10	Jesus, compassionate High Priest	Doctrine
III		5:11—6:20	Preliminary exhortation	Parenesis
	A.	7:1-28	Jesus, High Priest according to the order of Melchizedek	Doctrine
	B.	8:1—9:28	arrived at fulfillment	Doctrine
	C.	10:1-18	cause of external salvation	Doctrine
		10:19-39	Final exhortation	Parenesis
IV	A.	11:1-40	Faith of the elders	Doctrine
	B.	12:1-13	Necessary endurance	Parenesis
V		12:14—13:19	The peaceful fruit of justice	Parenesis
		13:20 f.	Conclusion	
		(13:22-25	Final Greeting)	

3. *The Thought Pattern.*[90] 1) The central point: The structure of
Heb. is designed to set the central elements in relief. Hence, part III
(which is central [Heb. 5:11–10:39]) must be regarded as the most
important of the five parts of the Epistle. In this third part, the section
B (Heb. 8:1–9:28) is central; in this section, the subdivision Heb.
9:1-10 + 9:11-14 is central; and, finally, the first word of Heb. 9:11 is
the very center of the whole Epistle. This word (in the Greek
text) is the name *Christ.* Hence, Heb. is seen to be "Christocentric"
in the most literal sense. This external trait corresponds to a profound reality: the doctrine expounded in the Epistle is essentially
a *Christology.*

2) The three themes: A study of the plan of the central section
provides the key to the Epistle.

(8:1 f.) Introduction	
8:1-9:10:	Insufficiency and Replacement of the Old Cult.
c 8:1-6:	the old cult, earthly and figurative
b 8:7-13:	the first covenant, imperfect and provisional
a 9:1-10:	the old, powerless cultic institutions
9:11-28:	The Sacrifice of Christ, Efficacious and Definitive.
A 9:11-14:	the new efficacious institutions
B 9:15-23:	the new covenant
C 9:24-28:	access to heaven
(9:27 f.) Conclusion—transition	

We may recognize in the three couples of subdivisions (*a* + A;
b + B; *c* + C) three different themes. The theme of the central
subdivision (*a* + A [Heb. 9:1-14]), and therefore the most important
of the three, is that of *sacrifice*: the Jewish rites, culminating in the
liturgy of the Day of Expiation (Heb. 9:1-10), give way to the sacrifice of Christ (Heb. 9:11-14). From the central place given to this
theme, it follows that the Christology of the Epistle is not meant to

---

[90]See *ibid.,* pp. 237-58.

be a timeless speculation; rather, it is the revelation of an event. It is by his sacrifice that Christ has been manifested (Heb. 9:26); and not only manifested, but "made perfect," as the title of the section (Heb. 7:28) has it. The other subdivisions do no more than develop certain implications of this decisive affirmation. In the first and last of these (*c* [Heb. 8:1-6] and C [Heb. 9:24-28]), the author defines the level of the reality which is attained. While the old liturgy was confined to an earthly world which was only figurative (*c*), the sacrifice of Christ reached heaven itself. Thus, it is unique and definitive; it marks the end of time (Heb. 9:26) and will be followed only by the Parousia (Heb. 9:24-28). We recognize the *eschatological* perspective; it is the second theme.

The intermediary subdivision (*b* [Heb. 8:7-13] and B [Heb. 9:15-23]) expound a third theme, which is also in direct relationship with that of sacrifice, the theme of the Covenant. The old rites, powerless, belong to a Covenant destined to disappear; the fruit of the sacrifice of Christ, on the contrary, is the establishment of a new and better Covenant. We may call this the *ecclesial* theme.

Thus, in this central section we obtain the following concentric arrangement of themes:

c	Eschatology
b	Ecclesiology
a $\Big\}$ Sacrifice	
A	
B	Ecclesiology
C	Eschatology

This trilogy of themes is found throughout Heb. and is indeed the key to its composition:

a) Part I, whose subject is "the name more excellent than that of the angels," speaks especially of the heavenly glory of Christ; it is predominantly *eschatological*.

b) Part II, which presents Jesus as the "faithful and merciful high priest," is predominantly *ecclesiological* (fidelity and mercy are essential aspects of the Covenant).

c) Part III is predominantly *sacrificial*.

d) Part IV, like the second part, is predominantly *ecclesiological*.

e) Part V: its very title, "the peaceful fruit of righteousness" (Heb. 12:11), has an undeniable *eschatological* coloring (cf. Heb. 12:14, 22-27; 13:4, 14).

We find, then, that the succession of the dominant themes in the five parts of the Epistle corresponds to the following schema:

I   Eschatology
II   Ecclesiology
III   Sacrifice
IV   Ecclesiology
V   Eschatology

Also note that, while one theme *predominates* in each part, the whole trilogy is present in each part.

3) The present age and the age to come. The subdivisions of the central part bring out another fundamental trait of the author's thought, a characteristic which also marks the whole of Heb.: the distinction of two phases of salvation history. This distinction is applied to each of the themes and enables one to penetrate them more deeply. Whether it is a question of sacrifice, Covenant, or eschatology, it is the comparison of these two phases that can shed full light on the theme.

In the opening lines of Heb., two periods are set in parallelism: *of old*, the period of multiform revelation; and *in these last days*, revelation "in the Son." The central section also notes that the sacrifice of Christ is situated "at the end of the age" (Heb. 9:26), and underlines the fact that it has opened the second phase. But, consideration of the unique role played by the sacrifice of Christ, affirms the fundamental weakness of the Old Law; while, at the same time, the Old Law retains its value of prefiguration. Hence, a comparison of the two phases leads to the identification of three kinds of relations: *resemblance*, *difference*, and *superiority*.

In the central part, it is, in a particular way, the value of the sacrifice that is defined in this fashion:

a) The sacrifice *resembles* the old sacrifices: something is "offered" (Heb. 8:3); a death was necessary (Heb. 9:15 f.); blood was shed (Heb. 9:7, 14, 18, 22); there is question of "entering the sanctuary" (Heb. 9:7, 12).

b) Essential *differences* appear: between "offering gifts and sacrifices" (Heb. 9:9) and "offering himself" (Heb. 9:14); between the blood of victims and the blood of the priest (Heb. 9:12, 19, 25); between an entry "once a year" (Heb. 9:7, 25) and entry "once for all" (Heb. 9:12, 26); between access to the type-sanctuary and to the true sanctuary (Heb. 9:24).

c) There is evident *superiority*: Christ offers "better sacrifices" (Heb. 9:23); he has passed through "the greater and more perfect tent" (Heb. 9:11); the efficacy of his sacrifice is not in the realm of ritual purity, but purifies consciences (Heb. 9:13 f.); he wins an "eternal redemption" (Heb. 9:12).

The same relations exist between the Covenants: *resemblance* (Heb. 8:4, 6, 8-10; 9:1, 19-21); *difference and superiority* (Heb. 8:6-9). And, in the third theme, the old order is modeled on the heavenly: *resemblance* (Heb. 8:5). But, there is a greater *difference* between the tent "made with hands'" and the tent "not made with hands" (Heb. 9:11, 24), between the earthly and the heavenly (Heb. 8:4; 9:23 f.), between the provisional and the eternal (Heb. 9:10, 12, 15). The *superiority* of the New Testament over the Old is shown in a decisive manner: only the New Testament gives access to the ultimate realities. The three kinds of relationship may be discerned throughout the Epistle.

4) Christ and Christians. Although Christians are situated in the same phase of salvation history, they are not there on the same title as Christ. This is brought out in Heb. In the matter of eschatology, for instance, part I treats only of Christ: it speaks of "the first-born" (singular) (Heb. 1:6); of the sceptre of *his* kingdom (Heb. 1:8); and *his* kingship (Heb. 1:6; 2:5). In the corresponding part V, there is question of the first-born (plural) (Heb. 12:23); the kingdom which *Christians* receive (Heb. 12:28); the city to come which will receive *them* (Heb. 13:14).

On the sacrificial theme, part I describes the movement which the Son has accomplished to place himself on the same rank as his brethren (Heb. 2:10-18); part V indicates the path which we take to find ourselves beside him (Heb. 13:11-13). The parallelism of parts II and IV takes the same line: part II has as subject the fidelity of Christ and his priestly compassion; part IV gives to Christians the example of faith and appeals to their endurance.

In a general way, we may say that the entire first half of Heb. is more concerned with Christ and the second half more with Christians. Thus, the relative positions of Christ and of Christians are not confused, even though they are comprised on the same plane of salvation history.

5) Exposition and parenesis. The author has used two literary forms, doctrinal exposition and parenesis, which alternate. It is more than a simple stylistic procedure, however, and has, in fact, a profound significance. It shows that Christian salvation is not a matter of knowledge alone, but demands a conversion (cf. Heb. 12:1-3). This is the reason the Christian apostle cannot limit himself to expounding the mystery of Christ; he must at the same time incite his hearers to receive this mystery into their lives by an ever-deeper commitment.

Although exposition and parenesis has each its proper consistency, their multiple and essential links will not permit us to present each as a separate organism; but we may consider them as two "systems" (in the sense in which we speak of the nervous system and the blood system) forming part of one same organism. The ensemble of the different exposés forms the "doctrinal system" of Heb., and the ensemble of exhortations forms its "parenetic system." If the summit of the one (Heb. 8:1–9:28) is like the head of the whole work, the vital core of the other (Heb. 10:19-39) is its heart.

PLAN II[91]

PROLOGUE: CHRIST AS KING, PRIEST, REVEALER, AND REDEEMER (1:1-4)	
First Theme: The Incarnate Son of God as King of the Universe	1:5–2:18
Second Theme: Jesus, Faithful and Compassionate High Priest	3:1–5:10
Third Theme: The Authentic Priesthood of Jesus Christ	5:11–10:18
Preamble	5:11–6:20
1) The superiority of Christ over the Levitical Priests	7:1-28
2) The superiority of the Cult, Sanctuary, and Sacrifice of Christ	8–9
3) Recapitulation: the Sacrifice of Christ superior to the Mosaic sacrifices	10:1-18
Fourth Theme: The Persevering Faith	10:19–12:29
APPENDIX (13:1-21)	
CONCLUSION (13:22-25)	

SUMMARY   The practical purpose of Heb., the encouragement of its hearers, is achieved by means of a great contrast. The superiority of the New over the Old is really the one lesson of the Epistle, and it is taught by insisting on the superexcellence of Christ from every point of view; this concern is present from the beginning. The prologue (Heb. 1:1-4)—reminiscent of Jn. 1:1-18—presents the person and work of Christ in terms of the two Covenants—God's plan of salvation. He is the Son, heir of all things, through whom the world was made (cf. Prv. 8:22 f.; Jn. 1:3). He is the reflection of God's glory and bears the very stamp of his nature—ideas suggested by

---

[91] For this plan and summary see C. Spicq, *L'Épître aux Hébreux*, (BJ); *L'Épître aux Hébreux* (Paris: Gabalda, 1953), II; "Paul: Hébreux (Épître aux)," DBS, VII, cols. 230-33. Since Vanhoye's theory has yet to prove itself and awaits a commentary on Heb. along the lines traced by him, the summary of the Epistle follows the competent guidance of Spicq.

Wis. 7:25 f.; he is the adequate expression of the Father (cf. Jn. 14:9), who alone knows the Father and can make him known (cf. Jn. 1:18; 4:25; 14:9). By him, God has spoken his definitive word: "in these last days." High Priest of the New Covenant, he has made purification for sins by the offering of himself, and now takes his proper place at God's right hand. The name he has received— Son of God—and his exaltation to the throne of God, place him immeasurably above the angels.

The first theme (Heb. 1:5–2:18) is the presentation of Christ as King of the universe; it is sufficient to show his superiority over the highest of creatures, the angels. This is established by a catena of Old Testament texts; the conclusion is that, after all, the angels themselves are ministering spirits who, in God's saving plan, serve Christians (Heb. 1:5-14). Although they were God's agents in the promulgation of the Law (cf. Gal. 3:19), that Law is manifestly inferior to the Gospel inaugurated by the Son (Heb. 2:1-4). Christ is the "pioneer" (*archēgos* [cf. Heb. 12:2]), the pathfinder, who opens up the way and leads those who follow him into the glory of God. If he has suffered, it is because he was one with men. He was glorified because he had suffered, and his triumph consecrated the redemptive value of his death (cf. Jn. 12:23; 13:31) and won the sanctification of his brethren (cf. Jn. 17:17); he can, indeed, call them his brethren (Heb. 2:5-13). For, Christ is concerned not with angels but with men whom he desires to deliver from the power of the devil. He became man that he might, by his priestly expiation, achieve their redemption; he suffered and was tempted that he might be a compassionate priest (Heb. 2:14-18). In Heb., the Incarnation is set forth in a specifically sacerdotal manner; if the Son were not man, he would not be a priest (cf. Heb. 5:1).

The second theme presents Jesus as a faithful and compassionate High Priest (Heb. 2:1–5:10). First, it is shown that Jesus—the "apostle," that is, the one sent by God (cf. Jn. 3:17, 34; 5:36; 9:7) to transmit to men the divine call to faith and salvation and to be their mediator before God—is greater than Moses (Heb. 3:1-6). Verses 1 and 2 show Christ and Moses in their respective roles as mediators. The superiority of Christ is proved by two arguments: the builder is greater than the house, and Christ is the builder (of the people of God [v. 3 f.]); the Son is greater than the servant

(vv. 5 f.). The argument is in terms of fidelity, so that Christ is, pre-eminently, our faithful High Priest. An exhortation to fidelity (Heb. 3:7—4:11) follows naturally on the previous passage, since the comparison between Christ and Moses leads to a comparison between their respective disciples. The infidelity of the Jews in the desert serves as an eloquent warning to Christians. The whole is a *midrash* on Ps. 95 (94):7-11: under Moses, an unfaithful generation was punished by exclusion from the temporal rest of Canaan; much more must Christians fear the apostasy which would exclude them from eternal rest.

Verses 4:12 f. form a peroration to the preceding exhortation, but also recall the supremacy of Christ over Moses (Heb. 3:1-6). They express one of the main themes of Heb.: the comparison of the two Covenants in terms of their mediators; but even if the ministers of the Old Testament are inferior to Christ, nevertheless it is the same God who speaks in both Covenants. The qualities of the word of God are such that there is no escape from its authority, no hope of shirking our responsibility toward it. The passage, Heb. 4:14-16, serves as a transition to the consideration of the compassionate High Priest (Heb. 5:1-10); it is at the same time a conclusion of the preceding exhortation. Moses and the Israelites were unable to enter the Promised Land, but our High Priest has already attained his rest; and through him we have access to the mercy of God. He has entered heaven, but he is united to us still in his perfect understanding of our trials and difficulties. The distance between us, abolished by the Incarnation, has not been broadened again by the ascension; he is always ready and able to help us because he is always our compassionate High Priest.

The passage Heb. 5:1-10—Jesus, compassionate High Priest—shows that Christ has perfectly fulfilled the requirements of priesthood. It falls naturally into two parts: (1) the qualities necessary for the priestly office (Heb. 5:1-4); (2) Christ possesses these qualities (Heb. 5:5-10). A high priest is a man officially instituted as a mediator between God and men, who defends the cause of men before God, and who offers the gifts of men to God, especially sacrifice for sin. But, a true high priest must be compassionate, showing great benevolence and indulgence to sinners, and he must be chosen and called by God (Heb. 5:1-4). In proving that Christ possesses these qualities, the author proceeds in inverse order, dealing first with Christ's vocation and then with his fellowship in human suffering. Christ did not take that dignity of high priesthood upon himself, for God who, in Ps. 2:7, hails the Messiah as his Son (cf. Heb. 1:5), declares him in Ps. 110 (109):4 to be a High Priest forever after the order of Melchizedek. This second text is the explicit and solemn declaration of the Priesthood of Christ as the former text established its fundament (Heb. 5:5 f.). If Christ possesses the premier condition of priesthood, the divine vocation, he also possesses the fundamental quality of the priest, compassion toward sinners (Heb. 5:7-10). These verses present Christ in an attitude of supplication before the Father. At once priest and victim, he learned the difficulty of obedience; and, at last, being perfected, he brought salvation to those who obey him. This long period falls into two principal propositions: the first (vv. 7 f.) indicates the means (suffering) by which the saving mission of Christ is effected; the second (vv. 9 f.) indicates the result for himself and for those who trust in him. Through his obedience, Christ, as man, gained an enriching psychological experience, a practical comprehension and appreciation of suffering which would enable him fully to sympathize with his brethren. Thus, Christ possesses perfectly the second quality requisite for priesthood: the faculty of compassion. As a result, he is consummated in perfection, author of eternal salvation, a high priest according to the order of Melchizedek.

The central section of the authentic Priesthood of Christ (Heb. 5:11–10:18) opens with a long preamble (Heb. 5:11–6:20). In Heb. 5:1-10, the author has defined the Priesthood of Christ. It is obviously his intention to develop this theme; but, because of the difficulty of the subject and the dullness of his hearers (Heb. 5:11), he finds it necessary to rouse them, to gain their full attention, before he launches into the exposition of this sublime doctrine. He addresses them as backward pupils and reproaches them for their laziness in the study of the Christian religion (Heb. 5:11-14); he urges them to a deeper understanding of their faith and warns them with severity of the dangers of apostasy (Heb. 6:1-8); he reminds them of the promises attaching to their good deeds and encourages them to persevere in the faith, ending, as always, on a note of hope (Heb. 6:9-20). The hope of Christians is indeed well

founded, for it is centered in Christ who has entered beyond the
veil to heaven, always in his quality of High Priest forever according
to the order of Melchizedek (Heb. 6:20). Thus, once again the
author, a master in the art of transition, effortlessly resumes his
main theme, the High Priesthood of Christ.

The author intends to prove the superiority of Christ over the
Levitical priests (Heb. 7:1-28). He begins by showing the excellence of the type of this priesthood, that of Melchizedek, although
he soon concentrates completely on the antitype, Christ. Melchizedek,
who appears in the Bible like a meteor (Gn. 14:17-20), interests
the author of Heb. only as a type of Christ. Three circumstances
impress him: the etymology of the names; the conduct of Abraham
in regard to the priest-king of Salem; and the silence of Scripture
concerning his origin. Melchizedek "continues a priest forever" because his priesthood, being personal, not subject to the laws of human heredity, and scripturally without beginning or end, enjoys
a "negative" eternity. The Priesthood of Melchizedek and Christ is
distinguished from all other priesthoods in that it has no human
origin nor any human succession (Heb. 7:1-3). In showing Melchizedek's superiority over Abraham and the Levitical priesthood,
the author develops two arguments: Melchizedek is superior to Abraham since he received tithes from the latter and blessed them (Heb.
7:4-7); he is superior to the Levites because they are mortal and
because, in the person of Abraham, Levi himself paid tithes to
Melchizedek (Heb. 7:8-10).

The excellence of Melchizedek has been proved, but, since his
priesthood was anterior to the Law, may not one conclude that
Aaron and the Aaronitic priesthood have taken its place or at least
inherited its privileges? This inference is based on the hypothesis—
a dogma, in fact, of Judaism—that the Law was the definitive expression of God's will. The author points out that the Levitical priesthood was in need of a radical reform; the whole Mosaic system is
imperfect. But this necessary change has been effected and the new
Priest has risen according to the order of Melchizedek (Heb. 7:11-14).
The transitory nature of the Levitical priesthood is marked by its
suppression; the new Priesthood is eternal (Heb. 7:15-19). The
superiority of the Priesthood of Christ is demonstrated by a new
argument: Christ alone is invested with the priesthood by a solemn

oath of Yahweh; the Levitical priests were inaugurated without an
oath (Heb. 7:20-22). Just as unending life was contrasted with
fleshly succession in Heb. 7:15-17, the oneness and permanence of
Christ's Priesthood is finally set against the multiplicity of priests
whom death prevented from continuing in office (Heb. 7:23-25).
Verse 25 forms a transition: it concludes the argument of Heb.
7:20-24 and introduces the peroration, Heb. 7:26-28. It is an excellent definition of the priestly office of Christ. Because of his
eternal Priesthood (Heb. 7:24), he can save his own with a salvation
perfect in every respect; he saves all who come to God through him,
the Pontifex and Mediator, for he is always living to make intercession
for them (cf. Jn. 12:34; 1 Jn. 2:1 f.).

The passage, Heb. 7:26-28, is something very like a hymn to the
High Priest. In concluding his doctrine on the priesthood according
to the order of Melchizedek, the author stresses the holiness and
perfection of Christ which place him above all priests, even Melchizedek himself. The last verse sounds a note of triumph: the
Law sets up men as high priests, men subject to sin and mortality,
but the word of the oath announced through the mouth of David,
long after the Law, sets up one who is Son and whose perfection
is consummated forever in priestly achievement and in glory.

Chapters 8 and 9 consider the superiority of the cult, sanctuary,
and sacrifice of Christ. The superiority of the high priest according
to the order of Melchizedek can be measured by the excellence of
the sanctuary in which he ministers. The Mosaic Law had instituted a place of cult, the tabernacle set up in the desert, of which
Levi and his posterity were the privileged ministers; there was no
place left (under the Law) for another priesthood. But the Law
itself had prescribed that the earthly tent was to be a copy, and
therefore a shadow, of the heavenly sanctuary. Christ, however, had
access to the heavenly Holy of Holies (Heb. 7:26). Just as priestly
power is ordained to the offering of sacrifice (Heb. 5:1; 8:3), it is
in the heavenly sanctuary, in the presence of God, that Christ ministers and offers himself as victim (Heb. 8:1-5). A verse of conclusion and transition (Heb. 8:6) states that Christ has obtained
a more excellent ministry (*leitourgia*), inasmuch as he is the mediator of a better Covenant established on better promises. The occasion and need for a New Covenant are found in the imperfection

of the Old (Heb. 8:7). This fact is set in relief by a citation of
Jer. 31:31-34 which predicts a New Covenant based on the highest
and most sure promises (Heb. 8:6-13).

Throughout chapter 9 the supreme importance of the sacrifice of
Christ is established in terms of the most solemn sacrificial ceremony
of the Old Law, that of the Day of Atonement or Expiation (cf. Ex.
25-26; Lv. 16). There is no religious regime without a sacrifice; and
what is of supreme importance in this New Covenant is the sacrifice
on which it is based (Heb. 9:1-14). In Heb. 9:2-5, the author
describes the tent set up by Moses. Although he does not intend to
enter into details about liturgical symbolism (v. 5), he wishes to
note one important fact. Officiating priests go into the Holy Place
at all times, but entrance into the Holy of Holies is permitted once a
year, to the high priest alone, who enters "not without taking blood"
(Heb. 9:6 f.). In Heb. 9:8-10, he declares the symbolic signification, intended by the Holy Spirit, of this rigid separation between
the two parts of the sanctuary and of the complex ceremonial imposed on the high priest in view of his entry into the Holy of Holies.
This symbolism is twofold: the way to the true sanctuary is inacces-
sible—the people cannot go to God; on the other hand, consciences
have not been purified from sin. But Christ has arrived before God
in the heavenly Sanctuary; he has entered once for all, by virtue of
his own blood, and by that same means he has won for us eternal
redemption (Heb. 9:11 f.). The verses 9:13 f. constitute an argument *a fortiori*: the blood of animals had a certain efficacy in the
sphere of ritual purity; but how much more in the spiritual order can
the blood of Christ purify souls! The remission of sin, announced
in Heb. 8:12, is achieved by the sacrifice of Jesus and his heavenly
oblation. Hence, the emphasis is on blood. The blood of animals
with which the high priest sprinkled the Holy of Holies is set in
contrast to the Blood of Christ which he himself has poured out:
it alone purifies souls.

The Redeemer is a Mediator. What he mediates is the New
Covenant of friendship between God and mankind, a Covenant that
has been sealed in his own blood (Heb. 9:15-28). By a play of
words on *diathēkē*, which signifies "covenant" in the LXX (Heb.
9:15, 18-20) and "testament" in profane Greek (Heb. 9:16 f.), and
by noting the need for an effusion of blood in either case (sacrifice

is necessary for a covenant—and the death of the testator in the case of a testament), the author establishes that Christ must die to found the New Covenant and to make it bear fruit (Heb. 9:15-22). The purifications of the Old Law were shadows, effecting only shadow types of heavenly things; but, by the blood of the Son of God poured out in sacrifice, heaven, the dwelling place of God, became a sanctuary apt for the liturgy of which Christ is the great High Priest. He does not offer himself again and again to effect a periodical expiation, like the annual expiation made by the Israelite high priest; now, once and once only, at the consummation of the age, he has appeared for the destruction, through the sacrifice of himself, of sin and the power of hell. According to the law common to all men, Christ could sacrifice himself and die only once; on death follows the judgment (general [cf. Heb. 6:2; 10:27]). When Christ will appear a second time (the first time, by the Incarnation, he came to redeem mankind), he will have nothing to do with sin, for it has been radically abolished by the unique offering on Calvary. The salvation of the faithful will be total and definitive—all has been effected through the redemptive blood presented to God by his Son (Heb. 9:23-28).

By way of recapitulation, the author again insists on the superiority of the sacrifice of Christ over the Mosaic sacrifices (Heb. 10:1-18). Jesus, having poured out his blood for the remission of sins and having entered into heaven to intercede for men (chap. 9), is the author of a real sanctification and of eternal salvation. This peerless sacrifice is set in contrast to the sacrifices of the Old Law (Heb. 10:1-4). Christ is a human victim and offers himself; hence, his sacrifice is most agreeable to God; this is worked out by a quotation and exegesis of Ps. 40 (39):7-9 (Heb. 10:5-10). The divine acceptance, sanctioned by the session of Christ at the right hand of God, gives its special efficacy to this unique sacrifice. Its fruits are: spiritual purification (Heb. 10:2, 10, 14); remission of sins and salvation (Heb. 10:12, 17 f.); and union with God (*teleiōsis* [Heb. 10:1, 14]). Again the text of Jer. 31:34 is cited (cf. Heb. 8:8-12) to show that the New Covenant brings the remission of sins. The author concludes the theme of the Priesthood of Christ by an exegetical gloss: "Where there is forgiveness of these [sin and misdeeds: v. 17], there is no longer any offering for sin" (Heb. 10:18). The complete remission of sin, won by a unique oblation, is the characteristic note of the New Covenant sealed in the blood of Christ (Heb. 10:11-18).

Christ has opened the way to heaven; it is necessary, then, to support the trials of this life patiently—to have persevering faith (Heb. 10:19–12; 29). The passage, Heb. 10:19-25, is a transition, a call to confidence in the High Priest. The way to God (Heb. 10:20) is Christ himself (cf. Jn. 14:6). A fresh warning is sounded against apostasy. One who has turned his back on the sacrifice of Christ is in a hopeless state, for he can find no other sacrifice to help him (Heb. 10:26-31). But, the readers must recall their earlier steadfastness in face of persecution; now again there is need of that patient endurance and a firm faith (Heb. 10:32-39; cf. Ap. 13:10).

Faith is described in Heb. 11:1: it is the firm assurance of the fulfillment of our hope. For, faith is orientated toward the future and reaches out to the invisible. Grounded on the word of God, it is a guarantee of the possession of heavenly beatitude; it persuades us of the reality of what is not seen as yet and enables us to act upon it. The splendid eulogy of faith (Heb. 11:1-40) is worked out in terms of the example offered by the just who had lived before Christ; this will be followed (Heb. 12:1-4) by the supreme example of Christ himself. The chapter falls into three parts, each covering a definite period of Old Testament history: the patriarchal period, the example of faith given by the patriarchs (Heb. 11:1-22); the Mosaic period, the example given by Moses and Joshua and by those who followed them with docility (Heb. 11:23-31); the faith of the heroes of Israel from the Judges to the Maccabees (Heb. 11:32-38). The chapter closes with a consideration of the relationship, in God's providential plan, between the just of the Old Testament and Christians (Heb. 11:39 f.).

The realization that the saints of the Old Testament, their noble ancestors in the faith, are witnesses of the great race which Christians must run, will give them heart and encourage them to persevere. But the example that is best calculated to sustain the patience and courage of Christians is that of their Lord who was humiliated and crucified only to rise again and enter into his glory (Heb. 12:1-4). Suffering is a part of the Christian life, a factor of the divine pedagogy. When God punishes his children, he does it as a Father, for their good (Heb. 12:5-13). For their part, let them strive after peace with all men, and holiness; they must not imitate Esau (Heb. 12:14-17).

Sinai and Sion, symbols of two religious economies, the new superior to the old—this is the dominant idea of the passage Heb. 12:18-29, a passage that blends parenesis and doctrine and is the true conclusion of the Epistle. The argument, worked out with respect to the City of God (Heb. 12:18-24) and the kingdom of God (Heb. 12:25-29), is, in brief, the following: You no longer belong to the Sinai Covenant, founded on fear, imperfect and transitory, but to the New—the Christian—Covenant, founded on confidence and love, perfect, definitive, eternal. Look no more to Sinai, grandiose, awesome, but to Sion and to the heavenly Jerusalem and its atmosphere of assurance and hope. More than hope, for you already possess, initially, the good things of the new economy; you are already citizens of the heavenly Jerusalem, of the kingdom that cannot be shaken—on condition that you hear him who now speaks to you from heaven, the same who one time spoke on earth.[92] And you will hear the voice of God, the voice of the blood of Christ; you will be established in that unshakable kingdom, possessing grace, that is, the love of God and his gifts. You will enter into the divine rest, following Christ (Heb. 12:2).

An appendix (Heb. 13:1-21) rounds off the Epistle. Here, the moral and practical character is most marked; yet, even here we find an important doctrinal passage (Heb. 13:7-16). First, there is an exhortation to fraternal charity, in the practice of hospitality and in generosity to prisoners and those suffering ill-treatment (Heb. 13:1-3). Then follows an admonition on marriage (Heb. 13:4) and a warning against avarice which is to be ousted by full confidence in God (Heb. 13:5 f.). The passage, Heb. 13:7-16, has as its theme fidelity to the sanctifying Christ, involving a radical detachment from the Mosaic cult and attachment to the doctrines and example of the leaders of the community. And if these human leaders must pass away, Jesus Christ, the supreme object and subject of their preaching, remains, and remains the same (Heb. 13:8); he will preserve the believers from false doctrine. Our sacrifice is that of

---

[92]Teodorico da Castel San Pietro, *op. cit.*, p. 217.

Christ, our altar is the Cross; the Jews who cling to the Mosaic rites cannot participate in the sacrifice of salvation. And Christians, on their part, remembering that their Lord had suffered outside the camp of Israel—the walls of Jerusalem—must cut themselves off definitely from the Mosaic cult and, looking only to the city that is to come, regard themselves as exiles and pilgrims on earth (Heb. 13:7-16).

Obedience to the community leaders is inculcated and the author asks for the prayers of the community (Heb. 13:17-19). A wish for peace and for progress in virtue reminds the readers that they are in the care of "our Lord Jesus, the great Shepherd," and concludes with a doxology that is Pauline in tone (Heb. 13:20 f.). In a sort of postscript (Heb. 13:22-25), the author excuses himself for his boldness in writing the letter, adds some information regarding Timothy, and sends his greetings.

| EIGHT | *The Catholic Epistles* |

1 PETER
JAMES
JUDE
2 PETER

In addition to the collection of Pauline letters, the New Testament contains another group of seven epistles: James; 1, 2 Peter; 1, 2, 3 John; Jude. But these writings differ so widely among themselves that the mere fact of not being Pauline seems to be the only reason for grouping them together. The existence of this group was attested to by Eusebius early in the fourth century.

The seven writings are known as the Catholic Epistles. Although there is some doubt about the meaning of *katholikos* in this context (it was first used by the anti-Montanist writer Apollonius [c. 197 A.D.] with reference to 1 Jn.), it seems likely that it is meant to imply the "general" as opposed to the "particular" nature of these writings: the Catholic Epistles were addressed to Christians in general, in contrast to the Pauline Epistles which—for the most part—were addressed to individual churches. The adjective is appropriate in the case of Jas., Jude, 2 Pt., and 1 Jn.; while 2, 3 Jn., although each is addressed to a particular church, were, naturally enough, grouped with the first Epistle and perhaps, in view of their brevity, may have been regarded as appendices. Although 1 Pt. is addressed to the churches of a definite region, it is at least general in comparison with the Pauline writings.

In the Eastern Church—the practice is reflected in the Greek New Testament—the Catholic Epistles come between Acts and Paul, while in the West they stand after the letters of Paul, as in the Vulgate. A matter of greater significance is that five of the Catholic Epistles (Jas., Jude, 2 Pt., 2, 3 Jn.), with Heb. and Ap., form the "deutero-canonical" books of the New Testament.[1] It is clear, then, that the group has no real homogeneity and that their classification is a matter of expediency. In view of their close relationship with the Fourth Gospel, we are justified in considering 1, 2, 3, Jn. in the following chapter, with the other Johannine writings. Here we shall treat of the remaining four Catholic Epistles.

1. JAMES

1) Literary Form[2]

Apart from the address (Jas. 1:1), Jas. has none of the characteristics of a letter and is much more like a homily or sermon. It ends abruptly without the slightest trace of an epistolary formula. In form, it is a series of moral exhortations without obvious links and without doctrinal exposition. In short, the writing is akin to the Old Testament wisdom literature, especially Prv. and Sir. Nor is this influence one of form only; Jas. is clearly inspired by the themes of the wisdom writings. Thus, he takes up the notion of the divine origin of wisdom (Jas. 1:5; cf. Prv. 2:3-6; 8:22-36; Sir. 1:1; 51:13; Wis. 7:7; 8:21-29); he recalls the universality of sin (Jas. 3: 2; cf. Prv. 20:9; Sir. 19:16), the fragility of human life (Jas. 4:13 f.; Prv. 27:1; Sir. 11:16 f.), faults of the tongue (Jas. 3:3-12; cf. Prv. 16:27; 18:21; Sir. 5:13; 28:13-36). But, if the ideas reappear, the Old Testament text is rarely quoted. In fact, Jas. is more directly inspired by the paraphrases and commentaries of the synagogue homiletic.

This Jewish influence, however, is balanced by the Christian spirit of his exhortation and, more strikingly, by a close affinity with the teaching of Jesus, as this is found in the synoptic tradition. Hence,

---

[1]See Wilfrid J. Harrington, *Record of Revelation: The Bible* (Chicago: The Priory Press, 1965), p. 64.

[2]For the literary form and our whole treatment of Jas. see R. Leconte, *Les Épîtres Catholiques de saint Jacques, saint Jude, et saint Pierre*, (BJ), pp. 9-52; J. Cantinat, IB, pp. 559-76; A. Wikenhauser, *Einleitung in das Neue Testament* (Freiburg: Herder, 1956²), pp. 339-49; English translation by J. Cunningham (London: Herder/Nelson, 1958), pp. 472-87; L. E. Elliot-Binns, PCB, nn. 893-96.

in Jas. and in the Synoptics, we encounter the themes of joy in suffering with the hope of heavenly recompense (Jas. 1:2, 12 = Mt.
5:11 f.), of the poor who inherit the kingdom (Jas. 2:5 = Mt. 5:3),
of the merciful who will obtain mercy (Jas. 2:13 = Mt. 5:7), of
the forgiveness of sins (Jas. 5:15 = Mt. 12:32), of swearing (Jas.
5:12 = Mt. 5:34), and so on. Again, the eschatology is the same
(Jas. 5:1-11 = Mt. 24), the world is an object of reprobation (Jas.
1:27 = Mt. 18:7), charity has the same importance (Jas. 2:1-13 =
Mt. 25:31-46), the abuse of riches receives the same censure (Jas.
2:5-7; 5:1-6 = Lk. 6:24 f.). Here again, however, there is no quotation
of a Gospel text. Clearly, Jas. is inspired by the oral tradition and
the first written accounts.[3]

2) Author and Date

It is widely acknowledged that the James named in the address as
author of this writing is James "the brother of the Lord," leader of the
Jewish Christian community of Jerusalem.[4] Internal evidence supports this view. The author of Jas. writes with authority (Jas. 3:1).
Knowledge of the synoptic tradition is not surprising in one who was
a close relative of Jesus and became his disciple. A profound influence of the Old Testament is inevitable in the James whom we know
from Acts. So, too, his Palestinian origin and background account
for his familiarity with Jewish synagogal paraphrases of Scripture
and commentaries on the biblical writings and with apocryphal literature. It seems that Jas. may be regarded as an expression of the
catechesis of the Jewish-Christian milieu of Jerusalem. And we may
add that the writing was directed to Christian Jews; but the impersonal style provides no clue that might enable us to determine
where these recipients had their home.

An argument against authenticity is constituted by the Greek style
of the writing, although the Semitic basis of the author's thought
always remains perceptible. Yet, it is not easy to accept that a man
of James' background, with his necessarily superficial contacts with
Hellenism, could write such good Greek; in this respect the author

[3] See p. 110.
[4] See p. 46.

of Jas. is not surpassed by any other New Testament writer. Again we have recourse to the intervention of a gifted and trusted secretary. The assumption is all the more reasonable if, as we have presumed, James was not at home in Greek. We suggest, then, that a close disciple had worked over the catechesis of his master and had given it the form that we know.

Some of those who accept the authenticity of Jas. date it quite early, between 35 A.D. and 50 A.D., because they believe that the writing bears the marks of primitive Christianity, particularly in its teaching. Thus, for instance, traces of a Christology are few (Jas. 1:1; 2:1; 5:6 f.), the doctrine is pre-Pauline in tone (Jas. 2:14-26), and there is no awareness of a Judaizing crisis (cf. Acts 15). Many more scholars feel that these conclusions are not justified; the literary form employed and the end in view sufficiently account for the apparent ignoring of issues and for the doctrinal omissions. Consequently, they suggest that James composed his Epistle toward the end of his life, between 57 A.D. and 62 A.D. Close contacts with 1 Pt. appear to support this dating. On the other hand, those who reject authenticity tend to place the writings of Jas. at the end of the first century. An argument in favor of this view is the remarkable affinity of Jas. with the first epistle of Clement (c. 96-98 A.D.). Rather than claiming mutual dependence in either direction, however, scholars now prefer to admit the existence of a common source. In short, like many of the New Testament writings, the date of Jas. cannot be determined with any real measure of confidence.

3) Occasion

Jas. is addressed to a milieu in which social differences are marked. There are the rich, who expect, and receive, deferential treatment even in the liturgical assemblies (Jas. 2:1-3), men who are prodigal of generous words that cost them nothing (Jas. 2:16). Entirely absorbed in their business affairs (Jas. 4:13-17), they do not hesitate to cheat their workers and to squeeze the poor (Jas. 5:1-6). These same poor receive scant attention even from those who are supposed to be their shepherds and ought to be their servants (Jas. 2:2-6). Such conduct cannot but give rise to dissension: jealousy (Jas. 3:14; 4:2); anger (Jas. 1:19); murmuring (Jas. 5:9); and cursing (Jas. 4:11). The exasperated poor may be driven to rebel against their lot (Jas. 4:2), or they may, enviously, be seized by the desire for worldly possessions.

All James' sympathy goes to the afflicted and to the weak; he has written mainly for them. Like the Old Testament prophets, he takes issue with social injustice; at the same time, however, he considers poverty to have a religious value which makes of the unfortunate the privileged friends of God—the 'anāwîm.[5] And if he could, and did, turn to the sages and the psalmists to find expression of this outlook, his words have a fresh vigor from the practice and teaching of Jesus.

4) Analysis

In Jas. there is no real co-ordination of ideas and no discernible plan. The different moral exhortations which make up the Epistle are so independent of one another that each of them could stand on its own, not unlike the *meshalim* of Prv.[6] Nevertheless, an underlying truth confers a certain measure of cohesion and a unity on the whole. And this truth is that the Christian must bring his practical daily living into conformity with his religious beliefs; he may not take refuge in double-think and must not seek to lean on both God and the world at the same time.[7]

---

[5]See Wilfrid J. Harrington, *Record of the Promise: The Old Testament* (Chicago: The Priory Press, 1965), pp. 192 f.

[6]See *ibid.*, pp. 244-48.

[7]See J. Cantinat, IB, p. 560.

DIVISION

ADDRESS (1:1)
THE VALUE OF TRIALS (1:2-4)
CONFIDENT PRAYER (1:5-8)
POOR AND RICH (1:9-11)
CONSTANCY (1:12)
TEMPTATION (1:13-15)
REBIRTH (1:16-18)
DOERS OF THE WORD (1:19-25)
GENUINE RELIGION (1:26 f.)
RESPECT FOR THE POOR (2:1-13)
FAITH AND WORKS (2:14-26)
CONTROL OF THE TONGUE (3:1-12)
TRUE WISDOM (3:13-18)
DISCORD (4:1-12)
SINS OF THE RICH (4:13—5:6)
THE PAROUSIA (5:7-11)
FINAL EXHORTATIONS (5:12-20)

SUMMARY   James writes to the "twelve tribes in the dispersion," that is, either Jewish Christians "dispersed" throughout the Greco-Roman world, or all Christians, the new people of God, exiles from their true fatherland. In the Christian view, trials should be a source of joy, for they are the testing-ground of faith (in the sense of confidence in God and perseverance in action) and give rise to stead-fastness (Jas. 1:2-8).

While the poor man (one of the 'anāwîm) may exult in his dis-cernment of true spiritual realities, the wealthy Christian must ponder on the precarious nature of riches (Jas. 1:9-11). From trials in general the author passes to a special trial: temptation (Jas. 1:13-15). While God permits temptation, he himself does not tempt; hence, one who succumbs cannot cast the blame on him. It is a man's own desires that set him astray, conceive sin, and lead to death (cf. Rm. 6:21-23). God sends, not temptation, but good and perfect gifts (Jas. 1:16 f.). His greatest gift to men is rebirth through the Gospel; verse 18 (cf. 1 Pt. 1:22 f.) seems to refer to a baptismal liturgy (Jas. 1:16-18). Nevertheless, one must be prepared to listen, to check hasty speech, to put away wickedness, and to attend with docility to the word of the Law written on the heart (Jas. 1:19-21). In Judaism, the Law was not regarded as a burden; in a much truer sense, the Gospel, fulfillment of the Old Testament, is a law of liberty which is gladly obeyed (Jas. 1:22-25). It is all too easy to imagine oneself a "religious" person; failure to control one's tongue (cf. Jas. 3:1-12) gives the lie to such an illusion. Genuine religion manifests itself in the service of those in need and in aloofness from the de-filement of the world (Jas. 1:26 f.).

The passage, Jas. 2:1-13, is concerned with class distinction: it deplores favoring the rich and slighting the poor. This is the only passage (apart from the address) in which Jesus is named, and his title is solemn: "Our Lord Jesus Christ, the Lord of glory" (Jas. 2:1). The different treatment meted out to rich and poor is particularly reprehensible in the liturgical assemblies (cf. 1 Cor. 11). Besides, the 'anāwîm are the truly rich. Christians must be ruled by the "royal law" of fraternal love; partiality and discrimination are sins against Christian love. But since the law is a unit, the breaking of one com-mandment (a fortiori, the "royal" commandment) is a violation of the law as such—an indication of the gravity of sin. Therefore, Christians must be mindful of the law under which they will be judged. One who does not show mercy cannot expect to be shown mercy at his judgment (cf. Mt. 6:14 f.); the merciful will meet with mercy.

When Paul uses the word "faith," he implies a trust in God, a personal commitment; for James, however, "faith" is a set of beliefs, a "creed." The profession of Christianity is of no avail unless one lives up to it; significantly, the works in question are works of charity. Whereas Paul (Rm. 4:2 f.; cf. Gn. 15:6) argues that Abraham was justified by faith and not by works, Jas. (2:21)—referring to the sacrifice of Isaac (Gn. 22:4), the culminating point of the trial of Abraham—argues that the patriarch was justified by his good works. Similarly, it was the action of Rahab (cf. Jas. 2) that won her justification (Jas. 2:14-26).

Control of the tongue, already referred to in passing (Jas. 1:19, 26), is now treated at length (Jas. 3:1-12). The brethren should not be overanxious to be teachers (cf. 1 Cor. 12:8, 28), unless they are prepared to be judged in the light of the greater obligation thereby incurred. Only a mature Christian can really control his tongue, for such control points to mastery of one's whole conduct. True wisdom, like faith, finds expression in works (cf. Sir. 19:20). Jealousy and ambition can lead to betrayal of the truth; this is not the "wisdom" of God, but of the devil, and entails disorders of all kinds. The wisdom from above (cf. Prv. 2;6; 8:22-31; Sir. 1:1-4; 24:3 f.; Wis. 7:22–8:21) is pure, peaceable, merciful; a rich crop of righteousness is sown by the peaceful who possess wisdom (Jas. 3:13-18).

By contrast, Jas. turns from peace to warfare (Jas. 4:1-12). Strife is caused by unruly passions and uncontrolled desires; even prayer can be wrongly motivated (Jas. 4:1-3). Friendship with the world is "adultery," unfaithfulness to God, who is a jealous God and who opposes the proud (Jas. 4:4-6). Hence, the Christian must resist the devil, draw near to God submissively with sincere contrition, and be humble (Jas. 4:7-10; cf. 1 Pt. 5:5-9). He must not speak evil against or judge his neighbor (Jas. 4:11 f.).

The passage, Jas. 4:13–5:6, is a warning to the wealthy. First, boastful self-confidence is censured (Jas. 4:13-17; cf. 1:10 f.; 2:9). The denunciation, Jas. 5:1-6, unlike the preceding verses, is eschatological in tone and the language is reminiscent of the Old Testament prophets (cf. Am. 5:11; Mi. 2:8 f.; Is. 5:8-10; Jer. 22:13 f.): judgment is stored up for the godless rich who have laid up treasure, kept back the wages of their workers (cf. Dt. 24:15), and lived in luxury. The brethren are to be patient, looking to the endurance of the prophets and the steadfastness of Job. Verse 9, summing up the ideas of 4:11 f., seems to be an isolated saying not quite in its context.

The letter closes with various admonitions (Jas. 5:12-20). A warning against swearing is in the spirit of Sir. 23:9-11 and, very close to Mt. 5:34-37, doubtless echoes the synoptic tradition. In the spirit of the Psalter—psalms of supplication and of thanksgiving—prayer is recommended both in suffering and in joy (Jas. 5:13). The scriptural basis for the sacrament of the anointing of the sick is found in Jas. 5:14 f.; the elders of the (local) church, summoned to a sick person, will anoint him with oil (cf. Mk. 6:13), while invoking the name of the Lord Jesus (cf. Mk. 2:7), and will pray over him. This rite, inspired by faith, will comfort the sick man and forgive sin. Then, by association of ideas, the author passes to (public) confession of sin and to prayer. Elijah is presented as an example of the efficacy of the prayer of a righteous man (Jas. 5:16-18). The Christian who guides an erring brother back on the right road will save a soul from death and cover a multitude of sins (Jas. 5:19 f.; cf. Prv. 10:12). And thus the writing ends abruptly.

5) Faith and Works[8]

"You see that a man is justified by works and not by faith alone" (Jas. 2:24). "We hold that a man is justified by faith apart from works of law" (Rm. 3:28; cf. Gal. 2:16). So speak James and Paul, and, at the same time, offer apparently diametrically opposed interpretations of the justification of Abraham. James asks: "Was not Abraham our father justified by works, when he offered his son Isaac upon the altar?" (2:21); and Paul flatly asserts that Abraham was justified not by works but by his faith (Rm. 4:2 f.; Gal. 15:6). To claim that there is no contradiction here would seem to ignore the plain meaning of words. In fact, these texts of Paul and James bring home to us the necessity of grasping the purpose and preoccupations of a writer if we are to read him aright. And each of these writers is treating a different question. The same words are used, but the meaning of the words is different in each case.

---

[8]See R. Leconte, (BJ), pp. 14-19.

When Paul puts his readers on their guard against a vain confidence in works, he has in view specific works, obsolete works: those of the Mosaic Law. He is engaged in polemic against Judaizers and wants to show that circumcision and the other ritual practices to which Jews attached excessive importance were of no use to a Christian. More than that, he states emphatically that justification is an absolutely free gift of God which cannot be merited by works of the Law—or by any works.[9] The works envisaged by Jas. are of a different order; they are good actions which sanctify Christian life: charity toward one's neighbor (Jas. 2:15-17); hospitality (Jas. 2:25); obedience to God's commands (Jas. 2:22). Paul sets just as much store by the practice of these virtues (cf. Rm. 11:9-12; Gal. 5:22). And when James seems to minimize faith to the profit of works, he has in view a merely speculative assent without repercussion on daily living, a faith that is incapable of saving (Jas. 2:14), that is dead (Jas. 2:17 f.); the demons believe in this manner (Jas. 2:19). But he also speaks of a living and active faith (Jas. 1:3 f.; 2:22). On the other hand, unlike Paul, he does not consider the gratuitousness of faith. He is not engaged in polemic; rather, he encourages Christians to observe the Commandments and to lead lives that conform to the divine will. The Apostle, we have remarked, is concerned with demonstrating that, at the moment of his conversion, the unjustified man is justified independently of the practice of the Jewish Law or of his personal merits.

We may view the arguments from Gn. in a similar light. Paul wishes to show that Abraham could not be justified by the practice of the legal observances of Israel, but only by the free divine choice; while James presents the patriarch long after he had been justified and recalls how his heroic conduct had helped to maintain him in the divine friendship. In short, James and Paul, in view of distinct concerns, had each been led to draw a different application from the same fundamental ideas. Besides, the points of contact in their treatment of faith and works may be explained by reference to a common ground. Thus, for instance, the wisdom theme of constancy in trial is traced in Jas. 1:12 and Rm. 5:3-5 in an identical order: constancy or endurance; the bearing up under trial; eschatological

---

[9]See pp. 270-73.

glory as the reward of proved virtue—the whole motivated by love of God. The same sequence is found in 1 Pt. 1:6-9 (and secondarily, in Jas. 1:2-4); perhaps all these passages are reminiscences of a baptismal hymn.

Although there is no conflict with Paul, the fact remains that James does insist on the value and necessity of works. Authentic religion consists just as much in help given to orphans and widows in their need, or in keeping oneself spotless from the world (Jas. 1:27), as in cultic practices; otherwise, ritual observance is a vain and empty thing. James wants to prevent just that. He is concerned with the liturgy and with the common life of the Christian assembly: this is the reason he insists on the necessity of social justice and works of mercy. An economic gulf divides the members of the community; hence, the need for insisting on the dignity of the poor before God (Jas. 2:5) and for censuring the attitude of the rich (Jas. 2:6 f.)—all in a liturgical context. Similarly, the liturgical salutation, "Go in peace," is cruel derision when not accompanied by effective help (Jas. 2:14-16). It is a fundamental aspect of Christian life, a lesson that cannot be driven home too often. It is a message that John has formulated with characteristic simplicity and force: "Little children, let us not love in word or speech but in deed and in truth" (1 Jn. 3:18).

2. 1 PETER

1) *Literary Form*

The address and conclusion of 1 Pt. are indeed those of a letter; and, in general, the epistolary form of the writing is much more marked than in Jas. On the other hand, we learn few personal details of the author or of his addressees. The author is an elder, but differs from his colleagues in being a witness of the sufferings of Christ (1 Pt. 5:1). The addressees live in a pagan milieu (1 Pt. 2:12; 4:4) which, indeed, is their own background (1 Pt. 1:14, 18; 2:19 f.; 4:2-5); they experience trial and persecution (1 Pt. 1:6 f.; 3:13-17; 4:1, 12-19); many of them are slaves (1 Pt. 2:18-25). Yet, the writing gives no hint of any personal relationship between author and recipients. We cannot say, then, that it is a familiar letter—like so many of Paul's—and, of course, it is addressed to a wide grouping of churches (Jas. 1:1).

The writing is markedly parenetic in tone (cf. Jas. 5:12). It has the air of a homily, cast in epistolary form, and destined for a wide audience. At the same time, there are many passages of significant doctrinal content. This combination of parenesis and doctrine is reminiscent of Heb. Although there are certain resemblances between 1 Pt. and Jas., their main characteristics are not the same; the former has a certain basic plan and its Christian aspect is much more manifest.

2) Sources[10]

Analysis of 1 Pt. has enabled scholars to discern certain underlying sources. Although these have been differently delineated and evaluated, there is a large measure of agreement, at least on broader lines. Thus, for instance, it seems undeniable that the author was influenced by a baptismal liturgy, or a baptismal catechesis, even if we cannot determine to what extent. We may distinguish, with some confidence:

(1) a prayer of introduction to the baptismal liturgy (1 Pt. 1:3-12);
(2) the baptismal catechesis: before baptism (1 Pt. 1:13-21) and after baptism (1 Pt. 1:22—2:10);
(3) a baptismal credo (1 Pt. 3:18—4:6);
(4) a parenetic section concerning the Christian vocation (1 Pt. 2:11—3:7 + 5:5-9);
(5) a series of recommendations in view of a period of persecution (1 Pt. 3:13-17; 4:12—5:4; 5:10 f.).

A means of ethical instruction well known in antiquity was the social code; Old Testament examples are Tb., chapters 4 and 12; Sir. 7:18-35. In the New Testament, 1 Pt. 2:13—2:12 follows closely the pattern of such a social or "household code," and finds close parallels in Eph. 5:22—6:9; Col. 3:18—4:1; 1 Tm. 2:8-15; 5:3-8; 6:1 f.; Ti. 2:1-10.

This discernment of sources is obviously important for an understanding of our Epistle. But, it also suggests to us that contacts between 1 Pt., Jas., and some of the Pauline Epistles can be best explained by the use of common sources; it also forestalls the problem of apparent Pauline influence on 1 Pt. The Epistle reflects the corporate tradition of the primitive Church.[11]

---

[10]See R. Leconte, (BJ), pp. 83-86.
[11]See E. G. Selwyn, *The First Epistle of St. Peter* (London: Macmillan, 1946), pp. 17-24.

3) Occasion

In the concluding greeting (1 Pt. 5:12-14), written in his own hand, the author indicates the purpose of his work: to strengthen the recipients in their faith. Like Heb., it is a "word of exhortation" (cf. Heb. 13:22), and, in a similar manner, builds its parenesis on doctrine. Peter addresses to Christians, recruited in large measure from the ranks of the poor (1 Pt. 2:18 f.), a letter of consolation and of encouragement. The readers are called upon to endure with steadfastness, and even cheerfully, the sufferings and trials that have come upon them and which will continue. They have to contend with slander (1 Pt. 2:12; 3:16), and they suffer simply because they are Christians (1 Pt. 4:16). The best answer to such charges and hostility is the leading of blameless lives (1 Pt. 2:12, 15; 3:2, 13-17). They will be comforted and strengthened by the example of Christ, of his meekness in the face of suffering unjustly inflicted (1 Pt. 2:21, 23 f.).

4) Author and Date[12]

The Epistle certainly purports to be the work of Peter (1 Pt. 1:1; cf. 5:1 f., 13). The writing was well known in the early Church: 2 Pt. 3:1 refers to it; Clement echoes it; and Polycarp and Papias were aware of it. Irenaeus tells us that the patristic tradition had always regarded the head of the Apostles as the author of this Epistle.

Many modern exegetes, and not all of them Roman Catholic, accept the traditional attribution because they feel that it is well supported by internal criticism of the writing. Hence, for instance, Petrine authorship readily accounts for the many allusions to the expiatory sufferings of Jesus (1 Pt. 1:18 f.; 2:21-24; 3:18; 4:1); the frequent quotations and reminiscences of the Old Testament; the echoes of the words of the Savior (1 Pt. 1:6 f.; 10 f., 13, 21; 2:4 f., 8-10; 3:14 f.; 4:3, 7, 13, 17 f.; 5:4, 8-11); the parallels to the discourses of Peter in Acts (cf. 1 Pt. 1:10 and Acts 3:18; 1 Pt. 2:4 and Acts 4:11; 1 Pt. 3:22 and Acts 2:33 f.); and the sentiments of humility (1 Pt. 5:5 f.),

---

[12]See *ibid.*, pp. 7-63; J. Cantinat, IB, pp. 582-87; R. Leconte, (BJ), pp. 93-95.

of joy and of confidence (1 Pt. 1:3; 2:22-25; 5:10 f.) that are characteristic of the writing.

On the other hand, the Greek style of the Epistle is comparable to that of Jas.; clearly, the author thinks in Greek and quotes from the LXX. We know that Peter's mother tongue was Aramaic (cf. Mt. 26:73), and Papias' reference to Mark as his "interpreter" suggests that his knowledge of Greek was deficient. However, we are told explicitly (1 Pt. 5:12) that 1 Pt. was written down by a secretary. In the circumstances, it is not unreasonable to assume that Peter would have allowed Silvanus—"a faithful brother as I regard him"—a rather free hand in the composition of the letter. Thus, the unexpected Greek style may be reconciled with a real Petrine authorship of the Epistle.

It is generally accepted that the "Babylon" of 1 Pt. 5:13 is Rome; it was a current designation in first-century apocalyptic (cf. Ap. 14:8; 16:19; 17:5; 18:2, 10, 21). The traditional date of Peter's martyrdom is 64 A.D.; he was a victim of Nero's persecution.[13]

Since the writing gives no indication that a violent persecution of the Roman Church was in progress or had taken place, a date of 64 A.D., before the offensive against the Christians, is intrinsically probable. It must be acknowledged that a considerable body of critical opinion regards the Epistle as pseudonymous and sets its composition in the reign of Domitian (81-96 A.D.) or of Trajan (98-117 A.D.).

5) *Analysis*

DIVISION

ADDRESS (1:1 f.)	
INTRODUCTION: THANKSGIVING FOR NEW BAPTISMAL LIFE (1:3-12)	
1) Rebirth	1:3-5
2) Joy in Christ	1:6-9
3) Testimony of prophecy	1:10-12

---

[13]For a biographical sketch of St. Peter see pp. 45 f.

DEMANDS OF THE NEW LIFE (1:13—2:10)	
1) Holiness	1:13-21
2) Love	1:22—2:3
3) Priesthood	2:4-10
DUTIES OF CHRISTIANS (2:11—4:6)	
1) Toward pagans	2:11 f.
2) Toward the state	2:13-17
3) As slaves	2:18-25
4) In marriage	3:1-7
5) Of fraternal love	3:8-12
6) In persecution	3:13—4:6
VARIOUS EXHORTATIONS (4:7—5:11)	
1) Imminence of the end	4:7-11
2) Fiery ordeal	4:12-19
3) The elders	5:1-4
4) The faithful	5:5-11
CONCLUDING GREETINGS (5:12-14)	

SUMMARY   The address (1 Pt. 1:1 f.) explicitly names the Apostle Peter as the author of the letter. He writes to "the exiles of the dispersion" (cf. Jas. 1:1), that is, to the new Diaspora, Christians exiled from their true homeland. The five provinces named cover the whole of Asia Minor except Cilicia. A trinitarian formula states the situation of Christians: called by the Father, sanctified by the Holy Spirit, for obedience to Christ and for salvation through him; the action of the Trinity is developed in 1 Pt. 1:10-12.

God in his great mercy has begotten Christians anew (cf. Jn. 3:3; Ti. 3:5) through the resurrection of his Son, that is, by means of baptism (1 Pt. 3:21; cf. Rm. 6:3-11), to a living hope (cf. 1 Pt. 1:13, 21; 3:5, 15) of salvation in Christ and of an imperishable inheritance (1 Pt. 1:3-5). That heavenly inheritance, although it is an object of hope, is yet seized by faith; even in the midst of trials, such faith and hope are the source of Christian joy. The basis of the faith of Christians and the object of their hope is one: Jesus Christ. Although they have not seen him, they love him; their faith in him is the source of "unutterable and exalted joy," for it is the guarantee of salvation (1 Pt. 1:6-9). The role of the prophets of the Old Law, inspired by the Spirit of Christ, was to announce the Christian mystery (cf. Acts 3:18; 7:52; Mt. 13:17; Lk. 10:24; 24:26 f.; Heb. 11:13, 39 f.) which is characterized by "suffering" and "glory" (cf. Lk. 24:26; Acts 17:3; 1 Cor. 15:3 f.). That gift of salvation, looked forward to by the prophets and not yet revealed even to the angels, has been made known to Christians, by the Holy Spirit, through the Gospel preaching (1 Pt. 1:10-12).

But, Christian faith makes demands for holiness, charity, and closer attachment to Christ (1 Pt. 1:13—2:10); the typology of the Exodus is in view throughout this passage. In the first place, Christians must set their hearts fully on the living hope and order their conduct accordingly. The God who has called them is holy (cf. Lv. 19:2); they cannot go back to their former way of life. They must recall that their heavenly Father is also a Judge and that they have been ransomed from the old ways by the blood of Christ (cf. Ex. 12:5). In short, their life must be lived, in faith and hope, in the God who raised Jesus Christ from the dead (1 Pt. 1:13-21). The way of holiness is a way of fraternal love, a characteristic of the new life into which they have been born, a life sustained by the abiding word of the Good News (cf. Is. 40:6-8). The newly baptized (a baptismal liturgy seems to be in view) must put aside malice and insincerity, and should desire the spiritual food that will enable them to grow as Christians. Reference to milk seemingly has in mind the ancient custom of giving milk and honey to the newly baptized; the quotation of Ps. 34 (33):9 probably refers to the Eucharist, received at baptism (1 Pt. 1:22—2:3).

Christians must come to Christ that they may be built, living stones, into the spiritual temple founded on him (cf. Eph. 2:20-22; Mt. 21:42 f.), that, as a holy priesthood, they may offer to God a true cult (cf. Jn. 4:23), and that they may become the new

Israel (cf. Eph. 1:14). The gist of the whole passage (1 Pt. 2:4-10) is found in verses 4, 5, and 9: to come to Christ means incorporation into his community of the new Israel whose function is to offer cult to God through Christ and to manifest the saving mercy of God.

The principles have been established, and what follows (1 Pt. 2:11—4:6) is largely their application in daily living. Christians, as exiles in this world (cf. Phil. 3:20; Heb. 11:8-10, 13; 13:14), must first subdue in themselves the attraction of the alien world. Their good conduct toward pagans will be, at the Parousia, a reproach to their slanderers (1 Pt. 2:11 f.). Since it is God's will that Christians should live in harmony with all men, then, by that will, they are obliged to respect the laws and functionaries of Rome, their land of exile; but, if they honor the emperor they must fear God—their ultimate allegiance is to him.

Christian slaves should be submissive and respectful even toward overbearing masters; the patient acceptance of punishment unjustly inflicted is especially salutary in God's eyes. It is, however, the example of Christ that will enable the Christian slave to transform a degrading state into something noble and to attain an inner freedom (1 Pt. 2:18-25). The passage, 1 Pt. 2:21-25, is a Christian interpretation of the Servant of Yahweh theme (cf. Is. 53:5-12; Acts 3:13, 16; 4:25, 30).

Next, marriage is considered, with exhortation for wives (1 Pt. 3:1-6) and husbands (1 Pt. 3:7). Wives are to be subject to their husbands (cf. Col. 3:18; Eph. 5:22); this is all the more important in the case of an unbelieving husband (one who does not obey the word of the Gospel [cf. 1 Pt. 1:25]) who may be won by the conduct of his wife. Christian wives must not set store by external adornment (cf. 1 Tm. 2:9 f.), but in the interior beauty of a quiet and gentle spirit; they must look to the holy women of Israel: Sarah obeyed her husband and called him "lord" (Gn. 18:12). By following her example, they become the true children of Sarah. Christian husbands are urged to treat their wives with great consideration and gentleness and to show them honor as coheirs of the gift of eternal life; husbands and wives are on terms of complete spiritual equality. The admonition to husbands closes with the words: ". . .

that your prayers may not be hindered." This seems to mean that, "where hardening of heart is caused by lack of understanding in the highest and most delicate of all human relationship, the relationship with God expressed in prayer is subject to serious impediment. At the same time access to God in prayer is at once the goal and the test of human affection."[14] All Christians are again urged to live in unity of spirit, in fraternal charity (cf. 1 Pt. 3:8-12; 4:7 f.); the exhortation is supported by the quotation of Ps. 34 (33):13-17.

The passage, 1 Pt. 3:13–4:6, has to do with the conduct of Christians in face of persecution; but the development of the argument covers the most difficult part of the Epistle: the descent of Christ into hell (1 Pt. 3:18–4:6). No hurt can come to Christians who are zealous for good; even suffering in such circumstances is a blessing. Let them cling to the Lord Christ and not be troubled by those who persecute them (cf. Jn. 8:12 f.). They must be prepared, when challenged, to defend their Christian hope—but gently and respectfully; they must not descend to the level of their adversaries who revile them (cf. 1 Pt. 2:12), but should act in accordance with the will of God, in this way maintaining a clear conscience (cf. 1 Pt. 2:20). The practice of goodness will triumph over suffering (1 Pt. 3:13-17).

Christ himself suffered unjustly (cf. 1 Pt. 2:21-24), but his death saved us. It seems that 1 Pt. 3:18–4-6 preserves different elements of a baptismal Credo:[15] death of Christ (1 Pt. 3:18); descent into hell (1 Pt. 3:19); resurrection (1 Pt. 3:21); session at the right hand of God (1 Pt. 3:22); judgment of the living and dead (1 Pt. 4:5). Christ died, but has made us alive in the Spirit (1 Pt. 3:18), the principle of his resurrection (cf. 1 Pt. 1:2; 3:21; Rm. 1:14). In the state of spirit quickened after physical death or, better, in the course of the process of death and resurrection described in verse 18 (for this seems to be the meaning of *en hō* ["in which"]),[16] Christ "went and preached to the spirits in prison" (1 Pt. 3:19). This may mean (especially if taken in conjunction with 1 Pt. 4:6) that, in the in-

---

[14]Selwyn, *op. cit.*, p. 188.

[15]See M. E. Boismard, *Quatre Hymnes Baptismales dans la Première Épître de Pierre* (Paris: Cerf, 1961), pp. 57-109.

[16]See Selwyn, *op. cit.*, p. 197.

terval between his death and resurrection, Christ preached to the spirits of the dead in Sheol. On the other hand, verse 20 seems to have in mind "those who did not obey"; it is these who are the spirits "in prison"—the just are not in question. On the whole, it seems better to interpret 1 Pt. 3:19-20a in the light of Gn 6:1-6: the spirits in prison are the "sons of God" whose union with the "daughters of men" was the final wickedness that occasioned the Flood.[17] They are the fallen angels who received notification of the domination of Christ over them (cf. Eph. 1:21 f.; 3:9 f.; Col. 2:15; Phil. 2:8; 1 Cor. 2:6 ff.; 1 Tm. 3:16),[18] just as the heavenly powers were subject to the ascended Christ (1 Pt. 3:22). In 1 Pt. 3:20b-21, the ark of Noah is presented as a type of baptism: just as the family of Noah, thanks to the ark, passed unscathed through the waters of the Flood which buried sinful humanity, so also the baptized person passes safely through the waters of baptism, which bury his sins, to find a new life with Christ.

The theme of 1 Pt. 3:18 is taken up again in 1 Pt. 4:1 f.—the example of the suffering Christ. Christians have died to sin with Christ and now must live the new life in Christ (cf. Rm. 6:1-14). Let their pagan past be indeed a thing of the past. Gentiles, too, for that matter, will have to render an account to him who judges the living and the dead (1 Pt. 4:3-5). The preaching of the Gospel to the dead (1 Pt. 4:6) most likely refers to the descent of Christ. Yet, it does not necessarily follow that "the dead" of 1 Pt. 4:6 are "the spirits" of 1 Pt. 3:19. Hades was not the same for all: the place of rest and the place of torment were separate worlds (cf. Lk. 16:23, 26).

The imminence of the Parousia (1 Pt. 4:7-11)—a theme that recurs in 1 Pt. 4:17 and 1 Pt. 5:10—is brought forward as a motive for virtue and watchfulness (cf. Phil. 4:5; Jas. 5:8; 1 Jn. 2:19), and especially for the love that covers a multitude of sins (cf. Jas 5:20) and which can find expression in hospitality. Charity, too, must order the use of the charisms that manifest themselves in the course of divine worship (cf. 1 Cor. 12:4-11; Rm. 12:6-8). Persecution and

---

[17]See K. H. Schelkle, *Die Petrusbriefe, Der Judasbrief* (Freiburg: Herder, 1961), pp. 106 f.

[18]See J. Cantinat, IB, p. 579.

suffering are taken up again in 1 Pt. 4:12-19, a passage which might be regarded as a synthesis of the Epistle. The "fiery ordeal" (cf. 1 Pt. 1:7) of persecution should not come as a surprise, for it is a feature of Christian life in this world. It not only tests the genuineness of the faith of Christians, but also is a sharing in Christ's sufferings; it is even a cause for joy as a pledge of a part in his glory (cf. 1 Pt. 1:21; 5:1, 10). The Spirit of God rests on those who bear reproach for Christ (1 Pt. 4:12-14). While they should do nothing that merits punishment, to suffer simply because one is a Christian (the name occurs elsewhere only in Acts 11:26; 26:28) is not something to be ashamed of. Judgment begins with the household of God (cf. Jer. 25:29; Ezek. 9:6)—persecution is a purifying trial—but it will be much more severe for unbelievers (cf. Prv. 11:31 [LXX]). Those who patiently endure suffering are in the care of a faithful Creator—only in this place in the New Testament is God so designated (1 Pt. 4:15-19).

The author, an elder of the Church, has a word of advice for his fellow elders (1 Pt. 5:1-4). Leadership in the Church must not be regarded as a road to profit or to power; true leadership is not achieved by brandishing authority, but by example, following the lead of the Chief Shepherd.

Next, the author turns to the faithful (1 Pt. 5:5-11) in a passage that is very close to Jas. 4:6-10. For the younger members of the community (cf. Ti. 2:6; 1 Jn. 2:12, 14) there is an admonition to obey the elders; all are to be humble (cf. Prv. 3:34). They must accept, as coming from God, the trials that humiliate them, but which will cause their greater glory (cf. 1 Pt. 1:6 f.); and they must trust absolutely in him (cf. Ps. 55 (54):22; Mt. 6:25-34). They must be sober and watchful (1 Pt. 1:13; 4:7), because the devil is at work; their resistance will be helped by the knowledge that they do not suffer alone, but share the common lot of Christians. Besides, God himself will speedily establish them in eternal glory. Another doxology (cf. 1 Pt. 4:11) concludes the Epistle proper. The final greeting (1 Pt. 5:12-14) was probably added in the author's own hand; Silvanus is presented as the secretary who has written the letter. The faithful of Asia receive the greeting of the Roman church (the "elect of Babylon"); Mark is mentioned specifically.

The "kiss of love" may be a liturgical rite (cf. Rm. 16:16; 1 Cor. 16:20), and the very last word is an echo of the address (1 Pt. 1:2), the wish of peace.

3. JUDE

1) *Literary Form and Sources*

Apart from the address (Jude 1 f.), Jude has little to mark it as a letter, although it was written to a community well known to the writer. It is an exhortation to the faithful, but at the same time, and more obviously, it is an antiheretical polemic.

While Jude's borrowings from the Hebrew Bible or from the LXX are rare, his knowledge of the apocryphal literature, especially the Book of Enoch, is evident. He cites, almost literally, a passage of Enoch (Jude 14 f.; Enoch 1:9), and the manner in which he speaks of wandering stars (v. 13) or of the guilty angels provisionally punished by imprisonment in darkness until their final fate at the day of Judgment (v. 6) strikingly recalls Enoch 18:13-16; 10:4-13. Nor is this the only link with the apocrypha. According to Origen, the author is indebted to the Assumption of Moses for his theme of the altercation between Michael and the devil over the body of Moses (v. 9). Like the Testament of the Twelve Patriarchs (Naphtali 3), Jude associates the sin of the angels with that of Sodom (vv. 6 f.). And his description of the sin of the "sons of God" (Gn. 6:2-4), according to which they had sexual relationship with women, is also found in Enoch (9:8; 10:11; 12:4), in the Book of Jubilees (4:15; 5:1-10), and in the Testament of the Twelve Patriarchs (Reuben 5; Naphtali 3). With the Targum of Jonathan (in Gn. 4:7), he seems to make Cain the type of the unbeliever (v. 11); and his reference to Balaam (v. 11) has been colored by the midrashic literature.

This factor reveals Jude's understandable, even inevitable, dependence on the milieu to which he belonged. He does no more than betray his familiarity with contemporary Jewish literature; there is no question of his elevating the apocrypha to the status of Scripture. Besides, even Paul has referred to these writings (cf. 1 Cor. 10:4; 2 Tm. 3:8).[19]

---

[19]See R. Leconte, "Jude (épître de saint)," DBS, IV (1949), cols. 1295-1297.

2) Purpose[20]

Although it certainly takes issue with false teaching, this short writing does not offer us sufficient data to determine what form of heresy is in view. However, the indications are that it is incipient Gnosticism.[21] The writer unmasks some—seemingly a small number— who pervert the traditional doctrine of the Church (v. 3) and put the faith of the community in peril. These men create divisions among the faithful (v. 19). They act as Cain the unbeliever or Korah the rebel (v. 11): they are like unreasoning animals (v. 10). They are like trees which, at the end of autumn, are still without fruit; rather, they are uprooted and dead trees (v. 12). Or they may be compared to wild waves of the sea (v. 13), to wind-driven clouds which shed no beneficent rain (v. 12), to wandering stars which have turned from their true course (v. 13). They were long ago marked down for judgment (v. 4) and they will be punished like the rebellious Israelites in the desert, like the guilty angels or like the inhabitants of Sodom and Gomorrah (vv. 5-7). According to the word of Enoch, the Lord himself, surrounded by his heavenly court, will come to judge them (vv. 14 f.).

Jude castigates them for immorality. They walk according to their passion (v. 16) and ungodly desires (v. 18), giving themselves to debauchery (v. 4) and perhaps unnatural lust (v. 7), and defiling the flesh (v. 23). They disseminate their false teaching for gain and court the favor of the wealthy (v. 16). And all the while they justify their conduct by appealing to the grace which God has given them (v. 4). These false teachers bear a marked resemblance to the Nicolaitans of Ap. 2:6, 14 f., 20-23.

It does not seem likely that they—or for that matter the addressees —were former Jews. The emphasis is on moral misconduct, especially in sexual matters; this would have been a greater danger for Gentiles than for Jews with their rather puritanical background. The error seems to have been a gnostic type of antinomianism (that is, the view that the moral law was not binding on Christians, who had been liberated by grace).

---

[20]See *ibid.*, cols. 1286-1288; (BJ), pp. 66-70; J. Cantinat, IB, pp. 606 f.
[21]See pp. 444 f.

3) *Authorship and Date*[22]

The Epistle of Jude, used by the author of 2 Pt., was probably known to Polycarp and to the author of the Didache. Tertullian attributed it to "Jude the Apostle"; Clement of Alexandria expounded it; and it figured in the Muratorian Canon. By about 200 A.D., it was widely esteemed as Scripture. Later, Origen attributed it to Jude the "brother of the Lord," but records the doubts of some in its regard; Eusebius classed it as "disputed"; Jerome accepted it, but admitted that many rejected it; Athanasius, Augustine, and Cyril of Jerusalem approved of it. The Council of Carthage (397 A.D.) declared it canonical.

The author of the Epistle names himself "Jude, a servant of Jesus Christ and brother of James" (v. 1). He has been identified with the "Judas of James," that is, the Apostle Jude (Lk. 6:16; Acts 1:13). Although, grammatically, "of James" might be rendered "brother of James," it is more likely that Luke intends the normal meaning "son of James." A more probable identification is with the Jude named together with James in Mk. 6:3; Mt. 13:55 as brothers of the Lord. The author of the Epistle (v. 1) does not name himself an Apostle; and in verse 17 he seems to distinguish himself from "the apostles of our Lord Jesus Christ." James and Jude, brothers of the Lord, were not Apostles.

Jude is written in good Greek, although it is not without Semitisms. The style may be too polished for one with the Galilean peasant background of St. Jude, but a Jewish-Christian secretary with a Hellenistic formation could account for it. Some scholars have dated the writing to the second century because of the alleged late Gnostic errors combated in it; but we have seen that this Gnosticism, such as it is, is at an embryonic stage. Still, verse 17 gives the impression that the first generation of Christians has passed away and verse 3 speaks of the Christian faith as a traditional and unchangeable deposit. Consequently, many scholars hold that the Epistle is pseudonymous and was written in the decade 80-90 A.D., or perhaps even later. Although a date after 70 A.D. seems indicated, it does not appear necessary to descend much later, and Jude, brother of the Lord,

---

[22]See G. H. Boobyer, PCB, n. 911 a; J. Cantinat, IB, pp. 604-8.

could well have lived long enough to be its author. We may add
that intrinsic evidence does not make the traditional attribution un-
tenable, and it is not unreasonable to suggest that Jude was written
to a community of Gentile-Christians about 80 A.D. We have no means
of determining the place of writing or the home of those to whom it
was sent.

4) Analysis

DIVISION

ADDRESS (vv. 1 f.)

OCCASION (vv. 3 f.)

THE FALSE TEACHERS (vv. 5-16)	
1) The punishment which awaits them	vv. 5-7
2) Their blasphemies and perversity	vv. 8-16

EXHORTATION TO THE FAITHFUL (vv. 17-23)	
1) Teaching of the Apostles	vv. 17-19
2) Christian obligations	vv. 20-23

DOXOLOGY (vv. 24 f.)

SUMMARY   In the address (Jude 1 f.), the author names himself
Jude and describes himself as a servant of Jesus Christ and a brother
of James. He was desirous to write to the faithful on the subject
of Christian salvation; now, instead, he must appeal to them to contend for their traditional faith. He writes as he does because he
has become aware that certain heretical teachers have found their
way into the community (vv. 3 f.).

In verses 5-7, the author brings forward, as a threat to these false
teachers, three Old Testament instances of sin and its punishment.
The false teachers are blasphemers (vv. 8-11; cf. 2 Pt. 2:10-12).
Their "dreamings" may be the alleged revelations of Gnostics. They
"defile the flesh" by unnatural lust (cf. v. 7). They reject *kyriotēs*

("lordship," "authority"), either the lordship of their Master and Lord, Christ (v. 4), or authority as such. They revile the angels (cf. 2 Pt. 2:10 f.). Even their instinctive knowledge has been morally perverted (vv. 8-10). They are compared with traditional representatives of evil known to the Bible (Gn. 4:3-15; Nm. 16:22-24; Dt. 23:5) and in Judaeo-Christian tradition. The presence of the false teachers was a blemish on the *agapē* of the community, the common cultic meal which was accompanied or followed by the Eucharist. Their deceitful and useless character is illustrated by a series of examples. A catalogue of their vices closes this polemic against the false teachers (vv. 11-16).

The faithful must not be led astray by error, but should cling to the teaching of the Apostles (vv. 17-19). Verse 17 implies that the writer is not an Apostle; verse 18 is a summary of the warnings of the Apostles. The faithful must build themselves up on the sure foundation of the Christian religion they profess. By prayer in the Holy Spirit, they must maintain themselves in the love of God, looking to the mercy of Christ that leads to eternal life (vv. 20 f.). Their attitude toward the false teachers is outlined: some, the waverers (cf. Jas. 1:7; 4:8), they should seek to convince; they should seek to snatch others, as at the last moment, from the "fire," the eschatological punishment (cf. 2 Pt. 3:7; 10, 12). They should look with eyes of mercy on those who have been won by the heresy, while abhorring the sin and entertaining a salutary fear of contamination (vv. 22 f.). The closing doxology (vv. 24 f.), which resumes the trinitarian formula of verses 20-21, resembles that of Rm. 16:25-27 (cf. 2 Pt. 3:14).

5) Doctrine

The only God to whom "glory, majesty, dominion, and authority belong" (v. 25) is Father (v. 1), Savior (v. 5), source of grace (v. 4), of charity (v. 21), and of justice (vv. 5-7). The Trinity of persons is affirmed (vv. 20 f.). Jesus Christ, Master and Lord of Christians, is he whom the Father has sent to achieve the work of our salvation (vv. 4 f., 25). Christians are being guarded by God for him who has mercy on them unto eternal life (vv. 1, 21). The Holy Spirit is present in the soul of the faithful and prayer must be made in him (v. 20).

The Christian is one called, one loved, by God. Faith, which is the adhesion to truths transmitted by the Church, is the foundation of the Christian life (vv. 3, 20); its orthodoxy is measured by its conformity with the teaching of the Apostles (vv. 17 f.). But, it is inseparable from charity, and one must remain firm in the love of God (v. 21); here the thought of Jude joins that of the Fourth Gospel and Johannine Epistles. The Christian can look to the day of judgment without apprehension, conscious of the mercy of Christ (vv. 21, 24). But the impious, and the rebellious angels, will find inexorable chastisement (vv. 4-6, 13). The closing doxology (vv. 24 f.), which seems to reproduce a liturgical formula, stresses the necessity of grace: the Christian cannot live without fault, nor arrive at blessedness, if God himself does not take the initiative in helping him (v. 24). If he gives way to licentiousness (vv. 4, 8, 10), and becomes self-centered (vv. 12, 16) on the pretext that grace sets him free from restraint (vv. 4, 19), he will make shipwreck of the faith (vv. 4, 8) and undergo divine punishment (vv. 4, 11, 14).

4. 2 PETER

1) *Literary Form and Purpose*

An address (2 Pt. 1:1 f.), conclusion (2 Pt. 3:17 f.), and some personal indications give an epistolary form to this writing. Yet, there is no clue to its destination and we do not know who the addressees were. The writing strikes one as being more like a homily decked out as an epistle than a letter properly so called.

The author is concerned that his readers should not lose their promised entry into the eternal kingdom of Jesus Christ (2 Pt. 1:11) and he writes to strengthen them in the traditional faith (2 Pt. 1:12 f.; 3:2), in a special way taking issue with false teachers who might lead them astray. Especially in chapter 2 the antinomianism of these false teachers appears; in this respect they are quite like those envisaged in Jude. But 2 Pt., later than the other writing, gives us to understand that they have progressed in error and have now become deriders of the hope of the Parousia. From their fundamental error others flowed: the Lord of the Parousia is denied (2 Pt. 2:1,

10), and, ignoring the expectation of judgment, they also set the moral order aside (2 Pt. 3:3). Against these false views, 2 Pt. insists on the expectation of the Parousia (2 Pt. 1:4, 8, 11; 3:10, 14). It teaches the divine Lordship of Jesus (2 Pt. 1:2, 16 f.; 3:18) and insistently exhorts them to moral living (2 Pt. 1:4-11; 3:11, 14, 17).

2) 2 Peter and Jude[23]

There is undeniable correspondence between 2 Pt. and Jude; the most satisfactory explanation, not only of similarities, but also of divergences of wording in substantially parallel verses, is the dependence of 2 Pt. on Jude. In the first place, both writings have a common structure: address (2 Pt. 1:1 f.; Jude 1 f.); reminder of traditional teaching (2 Pt. 1:12; Jude 5); polemic against heretics (2 Pt. 2:3-22; Jude 5b-16); another reminder (2 Pt. 3:2; Jude 17); another allusion to the scoffers (2 Pt. 3:3; Jude 18); a closing doxology (2 Pt. 3:18; Jude 25). Note that the verses 2 Pt. 1:1 f.; 5:12; 3:2 f., 14, 18, have parallels in Jude 1 f., 3, 5, 17 f., 24 f., and, in particular, that the passage 2 Pt. 2:1-18 closely resembles Jude 4-16.

The retouches that 2 Pt. has wrought on its source are readily understandable. Thus, 2 Pt. 2:4-7 rearranges the examples of Jude 5-7 to correspond with biblical chronology. In general, 2 Pt. has sought to remove the traces of apocryphal documents. References to Enoch in Jude 14-16 and those to the Assumption of Moses in Jude are suppressed. Unlike Jude 7, 2 Pt. 2:4 does not specify the sin of the angels. References to the Exodus (Jude 5, 11) do not appear in 2 Pt. 4-8. 2 Pt. 3:2 adds the authority of the prophets to the Apostles proposed by Jude 17. In short, the author of 2 Pt. has freely-adapted and incorporated the short writing of Jude.

3) Authorship and Date[24]

The author of the Epistle names himself Symeon Peter (2 Pt. 1:1); he claims to have been present at the Transfiguration (2 Pt. 1:16-18); he refers to an earlier letter of his, meaning 1 Pt. (2 Pt. 3:1); he recalls that Jesus had predicted the time of his death (2 Pt. 1:14);

---

[23]See R. Leconte, (BJ), pp. 124-27; Schelkle, *op. cit.*, pp. 138 f.
[24]See Schelkle, *ibid.*, pp. 179-81; R. Leconte, (BJ), pp. 132 f.

and he speaks of Paul as his beloved brother (2 Pt. 3:15). But, at the same time, we gather that the first Christian generation has passed away—"The fathers have fallen asleep" (2 Pt. 3:4)—and the author can speak of the Apostles as though he were not one of them (2 Pt. 3:2). Even if all the Pauline Epistles had not yet been gathered together, there was already a collection of these writings (2 Pt. 3:15 f.). We have seen that 2 Pt. is later than Jude.

Furthermore, there are notable differences between 1 Pt. and 2 Pt., differences of vocabulary, style, and thought. In 1 Pt., Christology is a dominant theme and Christ is the model of Christians, while in 2 Pt. he is simply the object of Christian profession. Although both Epistles claim the proximity of the Day of the Lord, they use different terminology: 1 Pt. (1:7, 13; 4:13) speaks of *apokalypsis* ("revelation") and 2 Pt. (1:16; 3:4, 12) of *parousia*. Besides, in 1 Pt. the proximity of the Coming is unquestioned, while in 2 Pt. the hope faces grave opposition. Again, 1 Pt. frequently and confidently uses the Old Testament, while 2 Pt. has scant reference to scriptural texts. The short 2 Pt. has 23 New Testament and 33 biblical *hapax legomena;* it has a more stilted style than the other writing and reflects, to some extent, the religious and philosophical language of Hellenism. In short, both Epistles cannot have been written by the same author.

In addition, when we note that there is no sure sign of the use of 2 Pt. in Christian literature earlier than the middle of the second century, and that in the third and fourth centuries its authenticity was widely questioned, it is not easy to regard it as the work of Peter. It seems at home among the later New Testament writings; we may suggest the decade 80-90 A.D.; thus, it is a pseudonymous epistle—conforming to a common literary convention of the ancient world. In this case, the writer, by identifying himself with Peter, shows that his intention is to transmit apostolic teaching. It is in the same spirit that he has made use of the letter of Jude and appealed to the authority of Paul.

4) Analysis

DIVISION

ADDRESS (1:1 f.)	
CALL TO HOLINESS (1:3-21)	
1) God's gifts and the practice of virtue	1:3-11
2) Security of Christian hope	1:12-21
FALSE TEACHERS (2:1-22)	
1) False teachers to be expected	2:1-3
2) Lessons of the past	2:4-10a
3) Further description of false teachers	2:10b-22
THE DAY OF THE LORD (3:1-13)	
1) Testimony of prophets and Apostles	3:1 f.
2) Scepticism of the false teachers	3:4-13
ANOTHER CALL TO HOLINESS (3:14-18)	

SUMMARY   The address (2 Pt. 1:1 f.) names Symeon Peter as the writer of the Epistle; he is a "servant and apostle of Jesus Christ" (cf. Rm. 1:1; Ti. 1:1). Growth in the knowledge (*gnosis*) of Jesus Christ is a wish repeated in the conclusion (2 Pt. 3:18; cf. 1:5 f., 8; 2:20).

The first part of the writing (2 Pt. 1:3-11) reminds the readers of the wonderful gifts they have received along with God's call and the promises he has made them. The divine power of Christ has enabled him to give to Christians hope and the knowledge of him and entry into his kingdom, by making them partakers in the divine nature (2 Pt. 1:3 f.). In gratitude for this divine liberality, they must practice virtue (2 Pt. 1:5-11). In 2 Pt. 1:12-18, the author, in the name of Peter, makes a personal appeal. Verse 14 is a witness to the tradition that Peter's death was foretold by Jesus (cf.

Jn. 21:18 f.). As in 2 Pt. 1:9, he warns against Gnostic errors by assuring them that he did not follow "cleverly devised myths" (2 Pt. 1:16), but recalls his presence as eyewitness on the Mount of Transfiguration; hence, he can bear testimony to Christ's power and to his Second Coming because he had seen the anticipated glory of his Parousia (cf. Mk. 9:2-8 parr.). Besides, there is the "prophetic word," the oracles of the Old Testament relative to the Parousia, and confirmed by the Transfiguration experience. The false teachers' interpretation of Scripture is arbitrary; God alone, by his Spirit, makes known the true sense of his Scripture (2 Pt. 1:20 f.).[25]

2 Pt. 2 is very like Jude 4-16, which it has used as a source. Both passages condemn false teachers in similar terms and bring forward Old Testament examples of transgressors. False teachers are to be expected because false prophets arose even in Israel (for example, Dt. 13:1-6; Jer. 3:31). Many will be deceived by their immorality and the Christian way will be discredited because of them (2 Pt. 2:1-3). Inevitable judgment is illustrated by examples from the Old Testament which show that the Lord knows not only how to punish the wicked but how to rescue the godly (2 Pt. 2:4-10a; cf. Jude 6-8).

These false teachers do not hesitate to revile the fallen angels, whereas the superior angels do nothing of the kind (2 Pt. 2:10b-11; cf. Jude 9 f.). They are like brute beasts, given over to debauchery and avarice; they follow the way of Balaam (2 Pt. 2:2-16; cf. Jude 11 f.). They are waterless springs or useless mists (2 Pt. 2:17; cf. Jude 12 f.). Their immorality seduces the weak, "unsteady souls" (cf. 2 Pt. 2:14), by promising a freedom from the moral law (cf. Jude 4), while they themselves are slaves of sin (cf. Jn. 8:34; Rm. 6:16 f.) (2 Pt. 2:18 f.). The warning of 2 Pt. 2:20 f. is in the line of Heb. 6:4-8; 10:26 (cf. 1 Tm. 6:3-5; 2 Tm. 14-18). The first proverb in 2 Pt. 2:22 is from Prv. 26:11.

The author returns to his vindication of hope in the Parousia. In this second letter (a deliberate reference to 1 Pt.), he again reminds his readers of the prophecies referring to the Coming and of the apostolic teaching founded on the authority of Christ (2 Pt.

---

[25]See Harrington, *Record of Revelation: The Bible, op. cit.*, p. 26.

3:1 f.; cf. 1 Pt. 1:12-21; Jude 17 f.). The skepticism of the false teachers is refuted (2 Pt. 3:3-7); and the nature of the Parousia, with its implications for Christian living, is explained for the faithful (2 Pt. 3:8-13). In 2 Pt. 3:15 f., the author refers to a collection of Pauline letters regarded as authoritative (the "other scriptures"); the heretics had misinterpreted the difficult Pauline texts relative to the Second Coming. The closing admonition sets the faithful on their guard, and the final doxology (2 Pt. 3:18) is a condensed form of Jude 25.

5) *Eschatology in 2 Peter*[26]

The perspective of the author of this Epistle is that, since the resurrection, humanity lives in the last phase of its history and awaits the "Day of the Lord," which will mark the end of this present world; he takes issue with scoffers who openly ridiculed the expectation of the Parousia (2 Pt. 3:3 f.). Against their argument that the changeless nature of the universe forestalled the radical change demanded by the Christian hope, he shows from the Old Testament that once before the world had been destroyed—by the Flood—and that God could just as easily once again destroy it by fire (2 Pt. 3:4-7). Turning then to the faithful, he points out that the apparent delay of the Parousia may be explained in part by the fact that God's measure of time differs from ours (cf. Ps. 90 [89]:4) and in part because of his forebearance (2 Pt. 3:8 f.). But, the Day of the Lord will come, like a thief (cf. Mt. 24:43). Thus, while the delay of the Parousia is explained, the expectation remains that of the synoptic tradition (Mt. 24:37-44; Lk. 12:39; cf. 1 Thes. 5:2; Ap. 3:3; 16:15). This world will disappear in a conflagration (2 Pt. 3:10), as found in the Qumran writings (cf. 1QH, 13-36) and Jewish apocalyptic.

The Day of the Lord will mean the final punishment of the wicked (2 Pt. 2:9; 3:7; 10-12) and of the rebellious angels (2 Pt. 2:4; cf. Jude 6). On the other hand, the just have nothing to fear (2 Pt. 3:11, 14). Realization of the end will inspire them to live lives of holiness and godliness (2 Pt. 3:11). Developing a Jewish idea that sin could delay the Coming (cf. Acts 3:19 f.), the author

---

[26]See Schelkle, *op. cit.*, pp. 240 f.

suggests that righteousness can hasten the Parousia (2 Pt. 3:11 f.), thus providing an added incentive for virtuous living. And the fiery end of this world of ours is not really destruction; it will mark the emergence of the "new heavens and a new earth in which righteousness dwells" (2 Pt. 3:13; cf. Is. 65:17; 66:22; Ap. 21:1, 5).

NINE

The Johannine Writings

THE FOURTH GOSPEL

THE THREE EPISTLES OF ST. JOHN

THE APOCALYPSE

The Fourth Gospel, the three Epistles of St. John, and the Apocalypse—despite notable differences—represent a distinctive current of New Testament thought and are best considered together. We shall take the writings in the order indicated.

1. THE FOURTH GOSPEL

1) The Authorship of the Gospel

The problem of the authorship of the Fourth Gospel is very involved, particularly because even the traditional evidence is not unanimous. However, the weight of tradition is unquestionably in favor of attributing the Gospel to St. John the Apostle, and, despite sustained criticism of this view in recent times, it has not been disproved. Indeed, when all the aspects of the case are taken into account, Johannine authorship in some shape or form would seem to be demanded.

THE TESTIMONY   According to the main stream of early Church
OF TRADITION   tradition, John the Apostle, the son of Zebedee and brother of James, wrote, in his old age, the Fourth Gospel, at Ephesus. The principal witness of this tradition is Irenaeus.

Irenaeus in his *Adversus Haereses* (c. 180) writes: "Afterwards [that is, after the other Gospels had appeared] John, the disciple of the Lord, who also reclined on his breast, published his Gospel while staying at Ephesus in Asia." He also says that John lived in

Asia until the reign of Trajan (98-117 A.D.). The testimony of Irenaeus gains in weight when one remembers that, according to himself, he had in his youth known Polycarp, bishop of Smyrna, and that the latter had known John personally.

Other witnesses are: 1) *Polycrates* of Ephesus, in a letter to Pope Victor (c. 190 A.D.), mentions "John, who was both a witness and a teacher, who leaned upon the breast of the Lord, and being a priest wore the *petalon* [priestly insignia]; he also sleeps at Ephesus."

2) *Clement of Alexandria* (d. c. 211-216 A.D.) says that, after the death of Domitian (81-96 A.D.), John returned to Ephesus from the island of Patmos. Elsewhere Clement states: "Seeing that other gospels set forth only the material story, John, the last of all, entreated by his familiar friends and divinely upheld by the Spirit, wrote the spiritual Gospel."

3) *The Anti-Marcionite Prologue* (160-180 A.D.): "The Gospel of John was revealed and given to the churches by John while still in the body, as one Papias of Hierapolis, a dear disciple of John, recorded in his last five books."

4) *The Muratorian Canon* (180-200 A.D.): "The fourth gospel is that of John, one of the disciples."

Some in the early Church, however, would not accept this tradition. Irenaeus testifies that it was rejected by some anti-Montanists, and, according to Eusebius, it was discounted by the Roman priest, Gaius. From Epiphanius of Salamis we learn that it was opposed by an heretical sect called the Alogi. However, this opposition was confined, soon disappearing altogether, and from the beginning of the third century the apostolic origin of the Fourth Gospel was universally accepted.

In the nineteenth century, however, the tradition was again questioned. Since that time, many scholars have denied that the Apostle was the author of the Gospel. They attribute it to a certain "John the Presbyter," or claim that the writer is unknown. They question the traditional evidence on the following grounds:

1) The John mentioned by Polycrates and Irenaeus is not the Apostle, but a "presbyter" of the same name, who was also an eyewitness and a disciple of the Lord. The weight of the testimony of

Irenaeus rests on the authority of Polycarp, but neither an extant *Life* of Polycarp nor his epistle to the Philippians mentions his close connection with the Apostle; the omission of any reference to St. John in the letter is all the more surprising because St. Paul is eulogized in it. It appears, then, that the John whom Polycarp had known was not the Apostle, and Irenaeus was mistaken in thinking that he was. This is all the more likely since Irenaeus is certainly in error when he makes Papias a hearer of the Apostle John. In this he is corrected by Eusebius who points out that Papias, in his prologue, makes it quite clear that he was no eyewitness or hearer of the Apostles.

Besides, Papias himself names a "John the Presbyter" or Elder, who is certainly not the Apostle. He writes:

> If, then, anyone came who had been a follower of the elders, I enquired into the sayings of the elders—what Andrew or what Peter *said*, or what Philip or Thomas or James or John or Matthew or any of the disciples of the Lord *said*—and the things which Aristion and the Elder John, the disciples of the Lord, *were saying*. For I did not think that what was to be had from books would profit me as much as what came from the living and abiding voice.

It should be noted that this whole argument at most suggests the possibility that Irenaeus and Polycrates may have confused a disciple of the Lord named John with the Apostle of the same name. Besides, although Irenaeus has erred with regard to Papias, the case is surely different when he gives his own reminiscences. "On this point it is impossible to doubt Irenaeus' veracity," remarks C. H. Dodd.[1]

2) Another objection raised is that John the Apostle never went to Ephesus but died a martyr's death in Palestine, either in 44 A.D., with his brother James, or later, between 64 A.D. and 70 A.D.

    a) Mk. 10:39. This is, apparently, a prophecy that the sons of Zebedee would share the suffering of their Lord, and, probably that they would be martyred; it would not have been recorded had it not been fulfilled by the time Mark was written. In fact, however, Mk. 10:38 f. is not necessarily a prophecy of a

---

[1] *Historical Tradition in the Fourth Gospel* (New York: Cambridge University Press, 1963), p. 11.

violent death; even if it is so interpreted there is no reason why Mark should not have recorded it even though, as regards one of the brothers, the prophecy had not yet been fulfilled.

b) An epitomist of the historian Philip of Side (430 A.D.) gives the following quotation: "Papias, in his recent book, says that John the Theologian, and James his brother, were martyred by the Jews."

c) The monk Georgios Hamartolos (ninth century) gives a similar reference to Papias: "Papias, who was an eyewitness of him [John], in the second book of the Sayings of the Lord, says that he was killed by the Jews."

d) Two martyrologies (liturgical calendars giving the names of martyrs and the date of their martyrdom) suggest that James and John suffered a similar fate, apparently at the same time: A Syrian martyrology, drawn up at Edessa about the year 411 A.D., commemorates on December 27: "John and James the Apostles, in Jerusalem." The Calendar of Carthage (c. 505 A.D.) contains two references to John the Baptist, one of which must certainly be a mistake for John the Apostle. Probably the error is in the entry under December 27: "Commemoration of St. John the Baptist and of James the Apostle whom Herod slew."

What is the value of these arguments? We may surely accept, as patently objective, the judgment of a modern scholar who, while not accepting the tradition of Johannine authorship, nevertheless discounts the evidence of the sources just indicated.

> It is impossible to feel confidence in the witness of the epitomist of Philip and of George to the text of Papias. Neither was an accurate historian. . . . The martyrologies can hardly stand as independent witnesses. . . . It is true that the tradition of John's martyrdom solves some problems; but it is not the only possible solution, and in any case we cannot martyr the apostle for our convenience in handling critical problems. The martyrdom tradition may have arisen simply on the basis of Mark 10:39.[2]

3) Also to be noted is the silence of some who would have been expected to have known of the stay of St. John at Ephesus. On this

---

[2]C. K. Barrett, *The Gospel according to St. John* (New York: Seabury Press [S.P.C.K.], 1955), p. 87.

ground, it is held that the statement of Irenaeus to the effect that Polycarp had known John seems to be erroneous. A *Life* of Polycarp is extant, but it says nothing of the relation between him and John, and Polycarp shows no knowledge of the Fourth Gospel.

However, this last point, at least, can be contested. The letter of Polycarp to the Philippians has a citation that is a fusion of two texts found in the Epistles of St. John (1 Jn. 4:2-3 and 2 Jn. 7). The citation expresses one of the major themes of the Fourth Gospel: the coming of Jesus Christ in the flesh.[3]

Ignatius, bishop of Antioch, was martyred in Rome in 115 A.D. In his letter to the Ephesians, written on his way to martyrdom, he emphasized their close relationship with Paul, but he never refers to John—nor does he in any other Epistle. This objection, however, is not as serious as it appears, because, in the context, it is easy to understand that Ignatius was preoccupied with St. Paul, and, more especially, with the latter's journey to Rome which ultimately led to martyrdom. With the prospect of a violent death in sight, Ignatius had no occasion to recall St. John who had died peacefully at Ephesus, at an advanced age, some years previously.

In conclusion, then, it would appear that the traditional attribution of the Fourth Gospel to St. John the Apostle, and the tradition of its composition in Ephesus, are by no means unassailable. At the same time, it is clear that the tradition which attributes the Gospel to John is still in possession; it may have been questioned, but it has not been disproved. It should be noted, moreover, that, even if the tradition of an early martyrdom of the Apostle is accepted, the Gospel can still be attributed to St. John. Many eminent scholars believe in the existence of a "Johannine school"—a group of disciples of the Apostle. In this view, the Gospel is substantially the work of St. John, but its present form may be due to the disciples, preferably to a disciple who published it after the death of the master.[4] This theory not only safeguards the Johannine origin of the Gospel, but also seems most reasonable in the light of both external and internal evidence.

_____.

[3]See A. Feuillet, IB, pp. 651 f.
[4]See M.-E. Boismard, BJ, p. 1396.

THE NEW TESTAMENT   Since it seems reasonable that the Johan-
WITNESS TO ST. JOHN   nine authorship of the Fourth Gospel should
be accepted, we may view briefly what the New Testament has to
tell us about the Apostle.[5]

John and James form the second pair of brothers called by Jesus
to be his Apostles (Mk. 1:19 f.). Their father was named Zebedee
(Mk. 1:20) and their mother was Salome (Mk. 15:40; Mt. 27:56).
Like their father, the "sons of Zebedee"—as they are frequently called
in the Gospels (for example, Mk. 10:35; Mt. 20:20)—were fishermen
on the lake of Gennesareth. Because of their impulsive temperament, Jesus called them "sons of thunder" (Mk. 3:17; Lk. 9:54).
With Peter they formed the inner circle of the three privileged disciples (Mk. 5:37; 9:2; 14:33). They wished to receive the places of
honor in the kingdom (Mk. 10:33). John is named alone in Mk.
9:38 and Lk. 9:49. In Acts, he stands next to Peter (Acts 1:13;
3:1 f.; 4:13, 19; 8:14). In Gal. 2:9, Paul designates him as one of the
"pillars" of the early Church. There is no further mention of him
in the New Testament, apart from Ap. 1:1, 4, 9; 22:8, although some
would deny that the John named here is the Apostle.

The Fourth Gospel does not name its author—at least, not directly.
In the Appendix (chap. 21)—probably not written by the author of
the Gospel—the "disciple whom Jesus loved" (Jn. 21:20-23) is introduced as a trustworthy authority for the content of the Gospel,
and, indeed, as its author (Jn. 21:24). Who is this "beloved disciple"?
At the Last Supper he lay on the breast of Jesus (Jn. 13:23). At
the foot of the cross the Mother of Jesus was confided to his care
(Jn. 19:26). On Easter Sunday he went with Peter to the sepulchre
and believed in the resurrection (Jn. 20:3). At the lake of Tiberias
he recognized the Lord sooner than the other disciples and heard
from him a mysterious prophecy (Jn. 21:7, 20-23). In two other
places, an unnamed disciple appears (Jn. 1:40; 18:15 f.); this is
possibly, but by no means necessarily, the "beloved disciple."

The "beloved disciple" is certainly an Apostle since, according to
the Synoptics, only Apostles were present at the Last Supper. As
"beloved disciple," he surely belongs to the privileged inner circle of

---

[5]See A. Wikenhauser, *Einleitung in das Neue Testament* (Freiburg: Herder,
1956[2]), pp. 208-10.

Peter, James, and John. He cannot be Peter—who is named with the beloved disciple (Jn. 13:23 f.; 2:2 f.; 21:20 f.). He cannot be James —who was martyred in 44 A.D. (Acts 12:2), while the beloved disciple reached an advanced age, for this would seem to be the obvious meaning of Jn. 21:20-23. John alone remains. It is noteworthy that neither James nor John are mentioned by name in this Gospel (except in the Appendix, Jn. 21:2). All goes to support the view that the beloved disciple is St. John; hence, Jn. 21:24 would indicate that the Gospel was written by an Apostle.

2) *Place of Origin and Date*

Where was the Fourth Gospel written? The Anti-Marcionite Prologue, Jerome, and Ephiphanius speak of its place of origin as Asia Minor. Irenaeus names Ephesus, and the Ephesian origin of the Gospel is widely accepted, even by scholars who doubt that it was written by John the Apostle. On the other hand, St. Ephrem affirms that the Gospel was written in Antioch, and the letters of Ignatius of Antioch bear the mark of this influence. It is likely, as we shall see, that the work of John is the term of a long ministry which could well have been carried on, to a large extent, in Antioch, and this is how the Gospel may have grown. It is not improbable that the tradition of John's sojourn at Ephesus is the reason why the writing of the Gospel has been set in that city.

It is now beyond question that the Fourth Gospel was known in the first half of the second century. About 150 A.D., St. Justin (*Apol.* 61, 4) cites Jn. 3:3-5, and elsewhere shows clearly the influence of the Gospel—as does the *Pastor of Hermas* (c. 140 A.D.). Polycarp, as we have noted, in his letter to the Philippians (c. 110 A.D.), echoes phrases of the Gospel and cites 1 Jn. 4:2 f.; 2 Jn. 7. The letters of St. Ignatius of Antioch (c. 110 A.D.) show frequent contacts with the Gospel—or, at least, with the Johannine tradition. The *Odes of Solomon*, a Christian work of the first half of the second century,[6] seems to betray an unmistakable influence of the Gospel.

More striking, and indeed decisive, evidence, is provided by the *Papyrus Rylands*. This fragment, which contains Jn. 18:31-33, 37 f., was found in Egypt and is dated to the early part of the second

---

[6]See p. 37.

century. If we allow time for the diffusion of John to Egypt, a date after 100 A.D. would appear to be ruled out. According to Irenaeus and Clement of Alexandria, the Apostle lived until the time of Trajan (98-117 A.D.), and hence may have died about the year 100 A.D. In this case, the Gospel was written before the turn of the century, perhaps about 90 A.D.—although parts of it may have been written earlier. Thus, as far as the evidence goes, the decade 90-100 A.D. is a likely date for the composition of the Fourth Gospel, at least in its present form.

3) *Literary Construction of the Gospel*

LANGUAGE AND STYLE   The Greek style of the Fourth Gospel is highly individual, having no parallel in the New Testament, apart from the closely-related Johannine Epistles. It remains distinctive even in translation, so that if one is at all familiar with the Gospels, one can straightway identify a passage from John. The language, although not literary Greek, is far from being merely popular, and the vocabulary, although remarkably limited, is adequate. One cannot really speak (as is sometimes done) of the poverty of St. John's language, because the style is deliberately repetitive, and the effect produced is one of solemn dignity.

The more one studies this Gospel the more convinced one becomes that it is a work of genius. Yet, it remains true that the overall dramatic effect, which is so striking, appears to have been achieved without deliberate effort and without any studied technique. The art of the Fourth Gospel is largely unconscious art; the work seems to have grown spontaneously—one might say inevitably—out of the genius of the evangelist and the sublimity of his subject.

The vocabulary (and style) of John shows an undeniable Aramaic influence; thus, for example, a number of Aramaic words appear in transliteration, with translations or equivalents: Jn. 1:38, 41, 42; 4:25; 9:7; 11:16; 19:13, 17; 20:16; 21:2. It is noteworthy that, in passages closely related to passages in the Synoptics, John sometimes introduces Aramaic terms not present in the others. Thus, where they speak of *Christos* and *Petros,* John alone has *Messias* and *Cephas.* Again, he uses different Greek words to translate Aramaic terms which must have been common to all of them; for instance, *paroimia* ("figure") for *mathla,* where they have *parabolē* ("parable"), and *sarx* ("flesh") for *bisra* where they have *sōma* ("body").[7]

In tracing the extent of this influence, critics are not agreed. Some scholars have argued that our present Gospel was translated from an Aramaic origin. An interesting supporting argument for this view is that some Greek manuscripts of the *Gospel* have variant readings, which may very easily be explained as different translations of the same Aramaic expression.[8] However, the majority of scholars are not inclined to accept the Aramaic origin of John. It is held that the Aramaisms are too few to prove that the Greek was translated from an Aramaic original, and that they can be accounted for on the ground that the author of the Gospel was accustomed to think and speak in Aramaic as well as in Greek.

The undoubted Semitic background to the Gospel is of capital importance for the understanding of it, and it is essential to have in mind what we have said elsewhere about the Semitic way of thought.[9] Our manner of thought is abstract, a process of reasoning, and follows a direct line from principles to conclusion. We should realize that this is not the method of the fourth evangelist. St. John does not work with abstract concepts, but with representations, with imagery that has something concrete about it.[10] Where we say: "God is infinite perfection," St. John says: "God is light and in him is no darkness at all" (1 Jn. 1:5). Where we say that Christ is the source of all grace—and the word "source" has ceased to be an image—Jesus says, in the Fourth Gospel: "I am the vine, you are the branches" (Jn. 15:5).

We tend to regard this last statement as a figure of speech; quite spontaneously (for this is our way of thinking) we interpret the declaration about the vine as meaning that the union of Christ with his own is *like* the union of branches with the vine. What John means is precisely the opposite! For him, the intimate union of vine and branches is only a *symbol* of the infinitely closer union of Jesus

---

[7]See Dodd, *op. cit.,* pp. 424 f.

[8]See M.-E. Boismard, *Du Baptême à Cana* (Paris: Cerf, 1956), p. 7.

[9]See Wilfrid J. Harrington, *Record of Revelation: The Bible* (Chicago: The Priory Press, 1965), pp. 21-24.

[10]See W. Grossouw, *Revelation and Redemption,* trans. M. W. Schoenberg (London: Chapman, 1958), pp. 11-17.

with his disciples. This is the reason Jesus can speak of himself as the *true* vine (Jn. 15:1)—the supreme truth that the vine symbolizes is fully realized only in him.

We must beware of misunderstanding these passages in which St. John's thought seems unquestionably to be contained in abstract expressions. Thus, Pilate's question, "What is truth?" is not at all the key to Jn. 18:37 f., for, by taking the word in a philosophical sense, he showed that he had not grasped what Christ meant. The truth to which Jesus has borne witness (Jn. 18:37) is no metaphysical abstraction, it is religious truth, the revelation of God in his person, for, indeed, Jesus *is* Truth (Jn. 14:6).

Similarly, the expression, "God is love" (1 Jn. 4:8), is not a definition of God.[11] It is to be taken in just the same way as the declarations: "God is spirit" (Jn. 4:24) and "God is light" (1 Jn. 1:5), where John indicates an essential property of God. However, love is the most manifest divine attribute, the one that is most emphatically revealed, as is clear from 1 Jn. 4:9: God is love because, "in this the love of God was manifested among us, that God sent his only Son into the world, so that we might live through him." This is the key to the interpretation of the sentence. John is not speculating about the nature of God, and the pronouncement, "God is love," really means that God is the manifestation of love insofar as his self-revelation is motivated and characterized by love. His revelation and his love both find their perfect and concrete expression in Christ.

If our abstract modes of thought are absent from the Fourth Gospel, so also is our process of reasoning. John does not reason, he testifies, he affirms. He does not set out to prove a thesis by building up consecutive arguments until the conclusion is reached. Instead, his thought moves around a central point, a point that is no abstract idea, but Christ himself. He takes the various facets of this Reality one by one. He understands very well that human language is incapable of ever conveying the full meaning of Christ, still less of confining that plenitude within the limits of a formula. For him, then, Christ is light, life, truth. Each of these images stands for the

[11]See C. Spicq, "La charité est amour manifeste," *Revue Biblique*, 65 (1958), 363.

whole Christ, and not just for any attribute of his, and hence they are interchangeable. Christ is Life, Christ is Truth, Christ is Light—he is each of these and he is all of them together.

We may illustrate this manner of thought by taking, in the discourse on the Bread of Life, the passage Jn. 6:53-58. The Jews' question: "How can this man give us his flesh to eat?" (Jn. 6:52) cannot be fully answered at this stage in the Gospel, but the response of Jesus (Jn. 6:53-58) is not just a mere repetition of the same idea. The thought moves around the reality: Christ, the Bread of Life. Already, in verse 51, this reality is set forth, and the objection of the Jews (v. 52) does not interrupt the movement of the thought. There is, in fact, a certain development, for the notion of life in verse 53 can be more clearly understood in the light of the teaching on the resurrection of the body (v. 54); and union with Christ (v. 56) is shown to be based on the union of Father and Son (v. 57). But all the while, the central idea remains: Bread of Life.

In reading John, we must come up against parallel situations at every turn. We should take care not to judge such passages by our standards; rather, we should strive to understand them in the same way that the first readers of the Gospel did. This may not be easy for us, but if we keep in mind the points made above—St. John's imagery is concrete rather than abstract; his thought moves in concentric circles rather than in straight lines—we should be able to make the necessary readjustment.

UNITY OF THE GOSPEL   The construction of the Fourth Gospel is complex, a fact that will be readily apparent when we come to study its plan. In spite of a general impression of unity, it is also true that, as one reads the Gospel, certain indications of an apparent lack of unity are met with. The narrative does not always proceed evenly and sometimes a passage seems to be out of its proper setting. In order to rectify this seeming lack of cohesion, many modern scholars have put forward theories of displacement; this is to say, they presume that, due to accidental circumstances, certain parts of the Gospel are out of their proper context, and they rearrange the present order of the work in order to accommodate, in a more logical manner, these presumably displaced passages.

The proposed displacements which have won the greatest measure of agreement are the following:[12]

1) Jn. 3:22-30, which seems to interrupt the Nicodemus discourse (Jn. 3:31 would appear to follow logically on Jn. 3:21), should be placed between Jn. 2:12 and 2:13. This change would improve the itinerary, since Jesus, in Galilee in Jn. 2:1-12, next comes into Judaea (Jn. 3:22) before going to Jerusalem (Jn. 2:13).

2) Chapter 6 should stand between chapters 4 and 5. Again the itinerary is improved. As the Gospel stands, Jesus is in Galilee (Jn. 4:54), goes up to Jerusalem (Jn. 5:1), crosses the Sea of Galilee (Jn. 6:1)—no mention being made of his return from Jerusalem—and moves about in Galilee since he is unable to move freely in Judaea (Jn. 7:1). If chapter 6 is taken before chapter 5, the course of events is as follows: Jesus is in Galilee (Jn. 4:54), crosses the lake (Jn. 6:1), goes up to Jerusalem (Jn. 5:1), and returns to Galilee (Jn. 7:1).

3) Jn. 7:15-24 should be read after Jn. 5:47, for the passage continues the argument of chapter 5 and interrupts the natural connection between Jn. 7:14 and Jn. 7:25.

4) Jn. 10:19-29 should be read after Jn. 9:41. The "division" of Jn. 10:19 follows naturally on the miracle of chapter 9, as does the remark of Jn. 10:21. Jn. 10:18 is admirably taken up by Jn. 10:30.

5) Chapters 15 and 16 should be fitted in somewhere before Jn. 14:31, which closes the farewell discourses.

A weighty argument against all such proposed changes is that there is no textual evidence in favor of any of them. All manuscripts of John give the Gospel in an order which—apart from insignificant details—is invariable; consequently, any rearrangement cannot avoid being, in some degree, subjective. The exegete who seeks to rearrange certain passages which he has judged to be out of place, in fact reshapes the Gospel according to his way of thinking. If such manipulation of the Gospel is admitted as a principle in the interpretation of John, much will inevitably depend on the literary tastes and discernment of each interpreter. It is understandable that many outstanding scholars refuse to accept any of the proposed changes. C. H. Dodd speaks for such scholars:

---

[12]See Barrett, *op. cit.*, pp. 18-21.

I conceive it to be the duty of an interpreter at least to see what can be done with the document as it has come down to us before attempting to improve upon it. This is what I shall try to do. I shall assume as a provisional working hypothesis that the present order is not fortuitous, but deliberately devised by somebody—even if he were only a scribe doing his best—and that the person in question (whether the author or another) had some design in mind, and was not necessarily irresponsible or unintelligent. If the attempt to discover any intelligible thread of argument should fail, then we may be compelled to confess that we do not know how the work was originally intended to run. If, on the other hand, it should appear that the structure of the Gospel as we have it has been shaped in most of its details by the ideas which seem to dominate the author's thought, then it would appear not improbable that we have his work before us substantially in the form which he designed.[13]

This is an eminently reasonable view, and it does seem that any study of John should be undertaken in a like spirit; transpositions should be regarded as a last resort. In this matter, it would be well to recall what has been said about the author's manner of thought. Since the composition of the book has not been governed by our concept of logical sequence, it should not surprise us if at some points the development, to our way of thinking, appears strained. It will be noted, too, that many of the emendations have been suggested on the ground of improving the order of the journeys of Jesus; but this is a criterion that has little weight in a Gospel whose movement is dictated by theological rather than by chronological and topographical considerations. On the whole, it is best to regard the Fourth Gospel as a deliberately planned writing, the work of an author of genius, while at the same time one recognizes that it cannot altogether be measured by our Western standards of logical thought and literary style.

However, our position on the overall unity of the Gospel does admit of exception. There are a few passages which, on weighty literary and textual grounds, can be shown to fall outside the main Gospel plan.

1. *Chapter 21.* Quite clearly, the Gospel ends at Jn. 20:30-31—chapter 21 is an *appendix.* This is the view held by almost all

---

[13]*The Interpretation of the Fourth Gospel* (New York: Cambridge University Press, 1955), p. 290. See A. Feuillet, IB, pp. 640-43.

modern scholars. The position, as summed up by A. Wikenhauser,[14] is as follows: Very probably, chapter 21 was not written by the Apostle, but was composed by his disciples soon after his death—at any rate before the circulation of the Gospel, since it is present in all manuscripts. The arguments for this view are:

a) The impression that Jn. 20:30 f. is, and was meant to be, the conclusion of the Gospel.

b) Chapter 21 speaks of the death of the beloved disciple—this, at least, would be the natural interpretation of verses 22-23.

c) Only in this chapter is there mention of the "sons of Zebedee" (v. 2), whereas there seems to have been a deliberate effort to avoid naming them throughout the Gospel.

d) In language and style, this chapter is clearly related to the rest of the Gospel, yet there are so many differences that it can scarcely have come from the same hand.

The status of appendix does not, in any way, detract from the value or beauty of chapter 21 which remains an integral part of the Gospel; but the recognition that it is an appendix enables us to appreciate the natural climax of the Gospel.

2. *The Woman Taken in Adultery* (Jn. 7:53—8:11). This passage is omitted by the very best early manuscripts and, indeed, the textual evidence in support of it is much less favorable than that for the Marcan ending.[15] The passage is not in context in John, while in form and style it closely resembles the synoptic tradition, and is quite like the style of Luke (a few manuscripts have it after Lk. 7:36). It seems to have been inserted in John because of the reference to judgment according to the Law in Jn. 7:51. Since it has been accepted by the Church as an integral part of Scripture, Jn. 7:58—8:11, although not really part of the Gospel of John, is most certainly inspired.

3. *Jn. 5:3b-4.* These verses are omitted by many important manuscripts. It is now almost universally accepted that they constitute a gloss, or note, added to the Gospel (and not forming part of it)

---

[14]See *op. cit.*, p. 219.
[15]See M.-J. Lagrange, *Évangile selon saint Jean* (Paris: Gabalda, 1925), p. 222.

in order to explain the reference to the "troubling" of the water in verse 7.[16]

PLAN OF THE   Plans of the Fourth Gospel are manifold and
GOSPEL   diverse; there would be little profit in outlining
or summarizing them. The following has been chosen because its chief merit is that it brings out, in striking fashion, the theological richness of the Gospel. It has also seemed well to indicate another which draws attention to a liturgical preoccupation of the evangelist.

1. *Division A.*[17]

A. THE INTRODUCTION (1:1-51)	
1) The Prologue	1:1-18
2) The Testimony	1:19-51
B. THE BOOK OF SIGNS (2–12)	
Section 1: Jesus is the Founder of a new religious economy superior to the old	2:1–4:42
1) Narrative: Miracle of Cana	2:1-12
2) Narrative: Clearing of the Temple	2:13-25
3) Dialogue: Rebirth	3:1-21
Testimony of the Baptist	3:22-36
4) Dialogue: a) Living Water	4:1-15
b) True Worship	4:16-26
c) The Will of God	4:27:38
Testimony	4:39-42

---

[16]See *ibid.*, p. 135. Lagrange accepts verse 3b as authentic, but the growing tendency is to exclude it also.

[17]See Dodd, *The Interpretation of the Fourth Gospel, op. cit.*, pp. 289-443; A. Feuillet, IB, pp. 625-38.

Section 7: Life through Death	12:1-36
1) Narrative: a) Anointing at Bethany	12:1-11
b) Triumphal Entry into Jerusalem	12:12-15
Reflections of the Evangelist	12:16-19
2) Discourse: Glorification through Death	12:20-36
Epilogue to the Book of Signs:	
a) Comment of the Evangelist	12:37-43
b) Résumé of Leading Ideas	12:44-50

C. THE SUPREME MANIFESTATION OF CHRIST (13–20)

I. THE FAREWELL DISCOURSES (13–17)

1) Opening dramatic scene	13:1-30
2) Dialogue on Christ's departure and return	13:31–14:31
3) Discourse on Christ and his Church	15–16
4) The Prayer of Christ	17

II. THE PASSION (18–19)

III. THE RISEN CHRIST (20)

APPENDIX: APPARITION BY THE LAKE (21)

ADDITION: THE WOMAN TAKEN IN ADULTERY (7:53–8:11)

The plan given above takes for granted that the fourth evangelist is primarily interested not in chronology or topography but in *ideas;* consequently, it aims at bringing out the theological development of the Gospel. It is apparent that the significance of the plan cannot be appreciated at a cursory glance; indeed, a rather detailed explanation of it is called for. This is attempted in the analysis of the ideas of the Gospel given in the following section.

2. *Division B.*[18]

PROLOGUE: "IN THE BEGINNING . . ." (1:1-18)	
I. The events which gravitate around the first Pasch—the *Pasch of the New Temple*	1:19—2:12
A. The week of inauguration: Jesus is manifested as Messiah	2:19—2:12
B. The first Pasch at Jerusalem	2:13-35
C. The new birth in the Spirit	3:1-21
D. Journey in Samaria and Galilee	3:22—4:54
II. *The sabbath of the paralytic:* Jesus cures a sick man at the pool of Bezatha	5:1-47
III. *The Pasch of the bread of life:* Jesus multiplies the loaves and presents himself as the bread from heaven	6:1-71
IV. *The Feast of Tabernacles and the sabbath of the man born blind:* Jesus is the light of the world and the Good Shepherd	7:2—10:21
V. *The Feast of Dedication:* Jesus declares himself Son of God and raises Lazarus	10:22—11:54
VI. *The Pasch of the crucifixion:* The Lamb of God, rejected by his people, is "raised" on the Cross	11:55—19:42
VII. *The Day of the Resurrection:* Jesus confides his mission to the disciples and gives them his Spirit.	20
APPENDIX: THE LIFE OF THE CHURCH AND THE EXPECTATION OF THE RETURN OF JESUS (21)	

---

[18]See D. Mollat, *L'Évangile selon Saint Jean,* (BJ), pp. 32-36.

4) John the Theologian

The Fourth Gospel is often characterized as the *theological* Gospel, and St. John is traditionally known as the *Theologian*. We should realize, however, that these terms are not to be understood in a modern technical sense, for the Gospel is not a manual of systematic theology and the evangelist is not a dogmatic theologian. Theology, according to the original meaning of the word, is nothing else than knowledge of God and of divine things, and St. John is the Theologian *par excellence* because he has penetrated, more deeply than the other evangelists, the divine mystery of salvation; his Gospel is theological because it reveals to us, more intimately, the meaning of Christ.

St. John's literary method and his style have been influenced by his own vision of Christ and by his effort to share that experience with others. In the foregoing section, we considered only the material, merely technical, aspect of his style; now we have to see the deeper, the far more important, aspect that lies beneath the surface. It is only at this level that we can make contact with the real St. John, because, in a true sense, this writer begins where all others, whether inspired or not, leave off.

SYMBOLISM   The wide use of symbolism is an obvious characteristic of the Fourth Gospel. Such symbols are, for example, living water, bread of life, the vine, the good shepherd; but the method is best illustrated by a study of the term "sign" as used by the evangelist.

"Sign" (in Greek, *semeion*) does not necessarily connote a miraculous event. Although on the four occasions when the evangelist refers to a particular action of Jesus as a sign (Jn. 2:11; 4:54; 6:14; 12:18), such action is, in fact, miraculous, yet it is certain, in the context of the Gospel, that other actions, where there is no miraculous element, are equally signs. This is true, for instance, of the clearing of the Temple (Jn. 2:13-25) and the washing of the disciples' feet (Jn. 13:1-20). We are obviously not meant to look for a deeper significance only in those actions that are expressly described as "signs"—the whole range of symbolism must be exploited.

Still, it is by contrasting "miracle" and "sign" that we can best understand John's intention. The restoring of sight to a blind man at Siloam (Jn. 9:1-12) is indeed a miracle, just like similar miracles in the other Gospels (cf. Mt. 9:27-31). The synoptists related such miracles for their own sake, or, at most, because they manifested the messianic power of Jesus. But John is not interested in these miracles as such; his interest is in their symbolism, their signification. For him, the giving of sight to a blind man is a sign of the spiritual light that Christ, who is Light, can give, because he viewed such actions of Jesus as visible pointers to a deeper, spiritual truth. Fortunately, we are not always left to work out these hidden meanings by ourselves, for, in many cases, they are brought out in the discourses that accompany the signs; we are also thereby provided with a criterion for judging other passages where such comment is lacking.

Perhaps it may seem that the emphasis on the symbolism of gospel events would mean, or at least could mean, that these events are not historical. To put it bluntly, it may appear that John has contrived the events in view of the symbolism he wished to bring out. We have only to remember that the evangelist is intent on showing that Jesus of Nazareth—a real, historical Person—is the Messiah, the Son of God (Jn. 20:30-31); his argument would lose all its force if he were suspected of inventing the facts he relates.

Yet, undoubtedly he has paid special attention to the symbolism of these facts, and, although he has by no means invented them, he has certainly *chosen* them, and that precisely because of their symbolism. For instance, in giving sight to the blind man, Christ is manifested as the Light of the world, and in the raising of Lazarus he is the Resurrection and the Life—thus, these two miracles find a place here. The symbolism of these facts is all the more striking because the facts are historical. We may admit, however, that the evangelist has modified details in order to emphasize the symbolism and thus bring out the theological teaching that is his first concern.

DOUBLE   Another notable feature of John is the frequent use
EXPRESSIONS   of double or ambiguous expressions;[19] this practice involves a whole technique. Such expressions, when spoken by Jesus, are first understood by his interlocutors in the obvious or

---

[19]See O. Cullmann, *Early Christian Worship* (Naperville, Ill.: Allenson, 1956), pp. 50-56.

natural sense, and he then goes on to explain the deeper spiritual
meaning. For example, in Jn. 2:19, the Temple of which Jesus
speaks is not the building—as the Jews believed—but, in reality, the
temple of his body (Jn. 2:21).

More characteristic, however, are such words as the adverb
anōthen (Jn. 3:3, 7) which means "again" (and was so understood
by Nicodemus) and also "from above" (the meaning really intended by Christ). The rendering of the adverb qualifies the meaning of "birth" (Jn. 3:3, 7) and this is also misunderstood by Nicodemus. In Jn. 3:14, we read of the Son of Man being "lifted up."
The same expression occurs in Jn. 8:28 and Jn. 12:32 f.; in the latter
case, a note makes it clear that crucifixion is meant. The evangelist
regards the "elevation" of Christ on the cross as a symbol of his "elevation" to heaven by his resurrection and ascension. In John's eyes,
the death, resurrection, and exaltation of Christ are all aspects of
one and the same mystery; hence, he can regard the exaltation on
the cross and the exaltation in glory as one movement.

The "living water" in Jn. 4:10 signifies first of all running or spring
water in contrast to stagnant water (and was so understood by the
Samaritan woman); Jesus has used the expression in a spiritual sense,
to signify a free gift of God. In Jn. 7:38 f., it is further specified
that "living water" symbolizes the Holy Spirit. Much the same is
true of "living bread" in chapter 6. The starting point is the theme
of material bread given to the crowd. Then, the line runs to the
miraculous bread of the Old Testament, the *manna*, and its signification is further extended to take in the person of Christ and the
Eucharistic Bread. Other examples, where a word with a double
signification is first taken in the more obvious or material sense, are
the following: "to go" (Jn. 7:33-36); "bondage" (Jn. 8:33-36); "fallen
asleep" and "to awaken" (Jn. 11:11-14). Even a whole sentence can
be understood in two ways (Jn. 11:50).

In all of these, and in similar, cases, Jesus intends the full meaning from the beginning; it is only the interlocutors who misunder-
stand; this is an important observation. Even in such places as Jn.
3:8, where there is a word-play on *pneuma*, meaning "wind" or
"spirit" (so that the first part of the verse should read: "The wind
blows where it wills"), we cannot absolutely rule out the Vulgate
rendering: "The Spirit breathes where he wills"; for John, ever as

he devised the word-play, was aware of the ambiguity of the word.

In interpreting the Fourth Gospel, we must be careful to give full weight to this technique of the evangelist. We should realize that he has chosen these expressions precisely because they have more than one signification, and that he clearly intends the two (or more) significations of each expression. We would not be true to his mind if we were to narrow his meaning to one or other alternative. Indeed, speaking generally, it would be unwise to feel that we had ever fully exhausted the meaning of any passage of this Gospel.

If John uses ambiguous words, it is not because he wants to be obscure or wishes to hide something. Quite the opposite is true, because what he does is to look beyond the superficial signification of an expression to a deeper, spiritual meaning. This method is to be understood in much the same way as his presentation of signs; not only the actions of Jesus, but his words too are "signs." It is because they are words of Christ—"words of eternal life" (Jn. 6:68)—that they have a deeper meaning, and this truth can be effectively symbolized by the use of double expressions.

THE
DISCOURSES
Nowhere does the difference between John and the Synoptic Gospels strike one more forcefully than in the discourses of Jesus. In the first three Gospels, the language of our Lord, in his sayings and parables, is very much the same in each Gospel; even where there is a notable difference in parallel passages, it has to do with words and not with style. With John it is another matter. In the first place, there are no developed parables here, and the allegories of the Good Shepherd and the True Vine are unlike anything in the Synoptics. The discourses of the Fourth Gospel are quite distinctive.

It is often urged that the differences can be explained on the ground of a change of audience: in the Synoptics, Jesus was addressing the simple folk of Galilee, whereas in John his audience is composed of the cultured elite of Jerusalem. Like all *simpliste* solutions this argument is not even true to the facts. Even in the Synoptics we find accounts of controversies with the leaders of the people (cf. Mt. 21:23–22:46), yet, these are not at all like the disputes of John (7:14–8:59). On the other hand, the discourse in Jn. 6, addressed mainly to Galileans, and the conversation with the Samaritan woman (chap. 4) are as distinctly Johannine as any other passage in the Gospel.

A significant aspect of the problem is that the Baptist speaks in just the same way as Jesus (Jn. 1:29-31; 3:27-30); and the style of the evangelist himself, in the prologue and in the passages that are generally regarded as personal reflections of his (Jn. 3:14-21, 31-36; 12:16-19), is no different. Most striking of all, the style of 1 John is remarkably close to that of the Gospel. Some would explain this phenomenon by supposing that St. John, through long familiarity and loving contemplation, has acquired the style and expression of his Master. This may be a pious, and perhaps consoling, consideration, but it cannot be sustained as a serious explanation. All competent scholars are agreed that in the Synoptics we find the closest approximation to the manner of speech of our Lord; the words of the Sermon on the Mount, for instance, reflect the actual style of Jesus.

What, then, are we to say about the Fourth Gospel? The verdict, the only possible one, can scarcely be better expressed than in the clear, yet finely-nuanced, conclusion of Dr. Grossouw:

> John treated his material very freely, particularly the words of Jesus, and this to such an extent that we must perhaps say that we can no longer call them literal. He has faithfully preserved their substance, but they have been completely recast. One may compare it to an old theme that has been reworked; to some classic motif that has been adapted by a modern writer. The transposition may have the appearance of a new work, but an experienced ear will detect the original theme immediately. This is true in a higher sense of the way in which St. John transmits the words of Jesus.[20]

The evangelist himself has intimated that he has indeed adapted and interpreted the teaching of Christ. For instance, he remarks that a saying of Jesus was not fully understood until he had risen from the dead (Jn. 2:22), just like some of his signs (Jn. 12:16; 13:7) and even the predictions of his resurrection (Jn. 20:9). John knows that the Spirit, whom Christ gave to his disciples, would remind them of his teaching (Jn. 14:26). But this was to be no mere recalling of the words of Jesus—he would lead them into "all the truth" (Jn. 16:13), that is, into the full meaning of the life and death and resurrection of the Lord, for the office of the Spirit is to render testimony

---

[20]*Op. cit.*, pp. 22 f.

to Christ (Jn. 15:26). It was with full confidence in these promises of his Master, and with the tranquil assurance that he was being guided by the Spirit of truth, that St. John wrote his Gospel.

ANALYSIS OF THE IDEAS   *The Prologue (1:1-18).* The prologue,
OF THE GOSPEL[21]   an opening quite unlike that of the other
Gospels, introduces the fundamental themes (life, lights, darkness, truth, witness, glory, the world) which will be subsequently developed. Since, however, it merely indicates these, it cannot be fully understood until the Gospel as a whole has been read. It seems likely that the prologue is a pre-existing Christian hymn which has been taken over and adapted by the evangelist; the verses 6-8, 12b-13, and perhaps, 17 f. constitute his comments. It is a hymn in praise of Christ and as such is not primarily a dogmatic passage or Christological speculation about Christ's pre-existence, his part in creation, and his Incarnation.

> The community of faith, so to speak, can no longer be satisfied with the prose-version of the incarnation—it falls on its knees and worships with a hymn of praise: "We have seen it, we have experienced it, 'we have beheld his glory'." We now have the answer to our question how the strange beginning of the Gospel of John is to be explained. The evangelist begins his book on an exalted note. Apparently, he has the feeling that the pronouncement of the Gospel is incompatible with the usual sober pattern of the beginning of a book. Therefore, he starts with the powerful Logos-hymn, teaching us that the proclamation of the Gospel can never strike too high a note.[22]

The concept of the "Word" figures prominently in the prologue. A sharp contrast is set up between this Word of God—who is Christ—and the Law (which is also God's word). It is affirmed that the Law did not in any real sense bring grace and truth; this is the work of Christ (Jn. 1:17). The Law is, therefore, only a shadow of the true Word of God, the Word who "became man and pitched his tent among us" (Jn. 1:14). In the world but not recognized by the world, rejected by his own people, he yet grants the divine sonship to those who believe in him (Jn. 1:10-13).

---

[21]See Dodd, *The Interpretation of the Fourth Gospel, op. cit.,* pp. 289-443. Throughout this analysis I am constantly in debt to the eminent Cambridge scholar. See A. Feuillet, IB, pp. 626-38.

[22]J. Jeremias, *The Central Message of the New Testament* (New York: Scribner's, 1965), pp. 78 f.

The Testimony (*Jn. 1:19-51*). Before embarking on his Gospel proper, John brings forward a series of witnesses who bear testimony to the Messiah in a variety of messianic titles. John the Baptist calls him the "Lamb of God" (Jn. 1:29-36) and the "Elect[23] of God" (Jn. 1:34). Andrew speaks of him as the "Messiah" (Jn. 1:41). For Philip, he is "he of whom Moses in the Law and also the prophets wrote" (Jn. 1:45); and Nathanael exclaimed: "You are the Son of God; you are the King of Israel!" (Jn. 1:49). Jesus himself rounds off the list by adding his own special designation: Son of Man (Jn. 1:51).

The title used by the Baptist, "Lamb of God," is one that is variously interpreted. Many would argue that the Paschal lamb is meant. Some would see here a reference to the divinely-appointed leader of the people of God—God's flock—in much the same way that the lamb of Apocalypse is also a leader (Jn. 7:17). These identifications have much in their favor, and John probably had them in mind, but they do not sufficiently explain the "taking away" of the sin of the world. Consequently, another explanation, which has gained some acceptance, is that "Lamb of God" stands for "Servant of Yahweh." In Is. 53:7, the Suffering Servant is likened to a "lamb led to slaughter," and it is noteworthy that the Aramaic term *talya* can be translated "lamb" or "servant." The Baptist, then, points to the Lamb that is the Servant who suffers and dies for the sins of the world.

A further argument in favor of this interpretation is that another passage of Isaiah, which also treats of the Servant, lies behind the testimony of John.[24] In Is. 42:1-2, we read: "Behold my *Servant*, whom I uphold;/My *Elect* in whom my soul delights;/I have put my *Spirit upon him*." In Jn. 1:29-34, this text is manifestly in mind: "Behold the Lamb [= *Servant*] of God" (Jn. 1:29); "This is the *Elect* of God" (Jn. 1:34); "I saw the *Spirit* descend and remain *on him*" (Jn. 1:32 f.). It appears that here too, as in the Synoptic Gospels, these important texts of Isaiah are very much to the fore.

---

[23]In Jn. 1:34, instead of "Son of God," some important manuscripts have "Elect of God"; this reading is accepted as the better one by a great number of scholars.

[24]See Boismard, *Du Baptême à Cana, op. cit.,* pp. 56 f.

The Book of Signs. 1. *The New Beginning.* The first episode or section of the Gospel (Jn. 2:1–4:42) may be regarded as an inauguration, a new beginning: Jesus the Messiah founds a new religious economy.

The miracle of Cana is solemnly described as the "beginning of signs" (Jn. 2:11); by that fact, we are sufficiently warned that we are not to take it merely at its face value. The water ("for the Jewish rites of purification"), turned into wine, symbolizes the old and imperfect order which yielded place to the new. In view of the author's interest in the sacraments, the wine of the Supper is also indicated. The narrative then turns to the clearing of the Temple, and there is an explicit reference to the perfect temple that will be constituted by the glorified body of the Savior (Jn. 2:21-22).

The meaning of these "signs" is brought out in the discourses. The dialogue with Nicodemus (Jn. 3:1-21) treats of a new birth. The phrase rendered "born anew" (Jn. 3:3, 7) can, as we have seen, equally well mean "born from above," and, typically, John intends both meanings. True to the procedure of this Gospel, Nicodemus understands the statement of Christ in a material sense (Jn. 3:4); Jesus then explains that he means spiritual rebirth from above; his Baptism, which brings about this rebirth, is not in water only—as was the baptism of John—but in "water and the Spirit" (Jn. 3:5). Then follow an enigmatic reference to the death of Christ (Jn. 3:14 f.) and a clear statement of the marvelous love of God (Jn. 3:16-18). Finally, the Baptist again bears witness to Christ and to the same great love (Jn. 3:22-36).

Baptism would still appear to be in mind in the discourse with the Samaritan woman (Jn. 4:1-15). The "living water" (at first understood by the woman in the sense of running water) which Jesus gives, stands for the Spirit (Jn. 7:39), and the rebirth of Baptism is in "water and the Spirit" (Jn. 3:5). But there is a wider context, for the conversation with the woman now switches to the idea of worship. The scene is highly dramatic, for the meeting took place in the shadow of Mt. Gerizim, and the woman could point to the schismatic temple on top of "this mountain" (Jn. 4:21). We now understand that the water of the cistern dug by Jacob—like the water of Jewish purification (Jn. 2:6)—will be replaced by the regime of the Spirit; and worship, both on Gerizim and in Jerusalem, will give place to the new Christian worship (Jn. 4:21-24).

In the subsequent brief conversation with his disciples, our Lord summarizes his mission as a doing of the will of his Father (Jn. 4:27-38). This is a truth that will be emphasized more and more as the Gospel proceeds, and the program traced here: "My food is to do the will of him who sent me, and to accomplish his work" (Jn. 4:34), will find its fulfillment only in his last words on the cross: "It is accomplished" (Jn. 19:30).

The woman had recognized Jesus as the Messiah (Jn. 4:29), and the other Samaritans, who came to meet him and hear his words, were convinced that here indeed was the "Savior of the world" (Jn. 4:42). This faith and this acceptance should be viewed against the unbelieving attitude of the "Jews" throughout the Gospel.

2. *The Life-giving Word* (*Jn. 4:43–5:47*). Chapter 5 marks a turning point in the Fourth Gospel. Up to now (apart from the prologue, of course), the messianic character of Jesus was in question, as well as the superiority of the Christian economy over the old regime; henceforth, the properly divine dignity of Jesus is stressed. At the same time, the opposition that, until now, was latent comes into the open, and becomes more and more pronounced.

The suggestion, very often put forward, that chapter 6 should come before chapter 5 is, doubtless, attractive, but, apart from the fact that it has no support at all in any of the manuscripts of the Gospel, the theological development would seem to demand the present order.[25] In chapter 5, the reader is told of the identity, in will and work, of the Father and the Son, through the love of the Father and the perfect obedience of the Son; this teaching seems to prepare the way for the teaching of chapter 6. Although it has been shown in chapters 2 and 4 that Christ gives life, the way in which he does so is not considered until chapter 6; for, with the declaration: "I am the living bread," we learn for the first time that he himself is the gift which he brings (Jn. 6:35, 48), and that the bread which he will give is his flesh for the life of the world (Jn. 6:51). But, the life which Christ gives is that life which he eternally

---

[25] See R. H. Lightfoot, *St. John's Gospel: A Commentary* (New York: Oxford University Press, 1956), p. 9.

shares with his Father—a truth that is expressed in chapter 5. We find too that certain verses of chapter 6 (for example, vv. 38-40, 57a) echo the teaching of Jn. 5:23-30, for when we examine the texts we see that the doctrine concerning life and resurrection is expressly propounded in chapter 5, whereas in chapter 6 the same ideas are subordinate to the main theme of that chapter, which is that Christ himself is the life-giving Bread.

The two narratives of this section—the cure of the Nobleman's son (Jn. 4:43-54) and of the sick man at the pool of Bezatha (Jn. 5:1-18)—have in common the fact that it is by his word that Christ effected the cures. He told the nobleman: "Go; your son will live," and the man believed in the *word* of Jesus (Jn. 4:50). In the other case, he merely said to the infirm man: "Rise, take up your pallet and walk," and the man was cured (Jn. 5:8 f.). That life-giving word restored to life the son who was on the point of death and the man who had been helpless for thirty-eight years.

The accompanying discourse (Jn. 5:19-30) explains why the word of Jesus is so efficacious: "As the Father raises the dead and gives them life, so also the Son gives life to whom he will" (Jn. 5:21). We now perceive that he can restore to life precisely because he *is* the life-giving Word. And if the Jews now accuse him of healing on the sabbath, the day will come when it is Jesus who will pass judgment; for the Father has given him authority to execute judgment, because he is the Son of Man (Jn. 5:27). Yet, Jesus will not need to judge the unbelieving Jews: Moses himself will accuse them because they have not believed in the Scriptures which tell of Christ (Jn. 4:39-42).

3. *The Bread of Life (chapter 6).* This section is composed after much the same pattern as the previous one: two miracles are followed by a discourse which explains the significance of the miracles. The narrative of the multiplication of loaves lends itself incontestably to a Eucharistic interpretation. The account of the walking on the waters, which presents Jesus as being in some way beyond the laws of nature, is meant to clarify the close of the discourse (Jn. 6:60-71) where he replies to the difficulties of those who refused to accept his Eucharistic doctrine.[26]

---

[26]See Dodd, *The Interpretation of the Fourth Gospel, op. cit.,* pp. 344 f.; A. Feuillet, IB, p. 631.

In the first part of the discourse (Jn. 6:22-34), Jesus points out the difference between a "miracle" and a "sign": the multitudes may have eaten the miraculous bread, but unless they realized its underlying signification it had no lasting effect for them. Just like the "living water" (Jn. 4:13 f.), the bread is "food of eternal life" (Jn. 6:27); and exactly as the Samaritan woman understood the words of Jesus in the most material sense (Jn. 4:15), so here the crowds take him up quite literally (Jn. 6:34).

Jesus corrects the misapprehension by pointing out that he himself is the Bread of Life (Jn. 6:35-50). Once again he is presented as the life-giver: "This is the will of my Father, that everyone who sees the Son and believes in him should have eternal life" (Jn. 6:40); for, he who believes in the Son of God has life here and now. But, just as Jesus himself has come to do the will of his Father and is entirely subject to that will, it is also necessary that he who comes to Christ should be led to him by the Father: "No one can come to me unless the Father who sent me draws him" (Jn. 6:44).

The teaching of Jesus becomes more emphatic still in Jn. 6:51-58. (It should be noted that the passage is welded into a unit by the phrase: ". . . whoever eats this bread will live forever," occurring in verses 51 and 58.) This passage is the logical conclusion of the earlier parts of the discourse, for if Christ is both Bread and the Giver of bread, it follows that what he gives is himself, his own body and blood. The Jews ask: "How can this man give us his flesh to eat?" (Jn. 6:52); this question is not answered at this stage, any more than the question of Nicodemus was answered: How can a man be born again (Jn. 3:4). These questions cannot be fully answered until the close of the Gospel, but at least it is abundantly clear that the Eucharist is envisaged here, as Baptism was in chapter 3.

The emphatic declaration of our Lord is undoubtedly a "hard saying"; as a result, many of his disciples deserted him. Yet, he had not left them entirely mystified, but had given them a key to its meaning in a reference to the ascension and in the significant opposition between the Spirit who vivifies and the flesh that is of no avail (Jn. 6:62 f.). For, it is by the ascension that the body of Christ entered fully into that spiritual state when, penetrated by the Spirit, it can be dispensed under the form of the Eucharist. Before Jesus was glorified, the Spirit had not yet been given (Jn. 7:39); but, after his resurrection and his return to his Father, he will possess even in his body the fullness of the Spirit which he will dispense by means of the sacraments.[27]

When the many disciples, scandalized by this teaching, had gone away, Jesus turned to the Twelve. This is John's parallel to the Synoptics' scene at Caesarea Philippi. Here too Peter is the spokesman and professes his faith in the Messiahship of his Master: "We have believed, and have come to know, that you are the Holy One of God" (Jn. 6:69). In the Synoptics, the confession of Peter is followed by the first prediction of the passion; here too the foretelling of the betrayal by Judas opens up the same perspective.

Chapters 7-12 really form a unit. The center of interest is Jerusalem; the leading ideas of light and life occur throughout these chapters and are always closely associated. The ground for the subdivisions we have made in this long section lies in the mounting opposition to Christ and the growing certainty that he is going to his death. At the same time, however, there is a corresponding development in his self-manifestation.

4. *Light and Life of the World* (*chapters 7-8*). The scene is set at the feast of Tabernacles to which Jesus had gone privately. Right at the outset we are told that his very presence was a cause of dissension, and so the way is prepared for the series of controversies (Jn. 7:1-13). The discourse that follows is unlike any other in the Gospel. All the others follow the usual Johannine pattern of dialogue rapidly yielding to monologue, but here it is dialogue right through. This causes a mounting tension, and there is a constant harping on hostile action against Christ (Jn. 7:1, 13, 19, 25, 30, 32, 44; 8:37, 40, 59).

It is probably the setting at the feast of Tabernacles which has prompted a memorable saying of our Lord. During the seven days of the feast, water was taken from the pool of Siloam and was solemnly carried to the Temple to be poured over the altar of holocausts. We are, doubtless, meant to have this in mind when we read that, on the last day of the feast, Jesus proclaimed: "If anyone thirst, let

---

[27]See P. Benoit, *Exégèse et Théologie* (Paris: Cerf, 1961), I, p. 389.

him come to me,/And let him who believes in me drink./As the scripture has said, 'Out of his heart shall flow streams of living water'" (Jn. 7:37 f.). This, and not the other, perhaps more frequent reading (the difference is one of punctuation), gives the true sense, and Christ himself is indicated as the source of living water. The evangelist explains (v. 39) that this water symbolized the Spirit which, however, would not be given until Jesus had been "glorified," that is, had passed through death to his resurrection and exaltation.

The idea of judgment runs through this section. It is in this context that we can grasp the significance of the declaration of Jesus that he is the Light of the World (Jn. 8:12). It is a feature of the Fourth Gospel, to be met with again and again, that Christ, by his very presence, causes division: men must be for or against the light, they cannot ignore it, for light shows up, light judges. But those who follow him will be guided surely, and in that Light will find life (Jn. 8:12).

The mounting opposition to Jesus means that the passion is not far from sight. Again he refers to it cryptically; he tells the Jews: "When you have lifted up the Son of Man, then you will know that I AM" (Jn. 8:28). The "lifting up" of the Son of Man was already mentioned in Jn. 3:14 (what is meant by it will be made clear in Jn. 12:32 f.). The "I AM" is an echo of the divine name of Ex. 3:14 (repeated in Is. 43:10, 13); by applying that Name to himself, Jesus claims to be divine. At the very end of the discourse, he makes this claim again, and the reaction of his hearers was immediate. "Truly, truly, I say to you, before Abraham was, I AM. So they took up stones to throw at him" (Jn. 8:58 f.). They understood very well what he meant and judged him guilty of blasphemy. This is the climax of the long series of conflicts, and it is evident now that the struggle will be resolved in the death of Jesus.

5. *Judgment by the Light* (*chapters 9-10*). This episode is highly dramatic. There is an obvious contrast between the Jewish authorities—blind guides—and Jesus, the good shepherd.

We have seen that Christ can give life by his word because he is the life-giving Word; here he restores sight to a blind man because he is the Light of the World (Jn. 9:5). The restoring of sight is a typical Johannine "sign" of something much more profound. The deeper significance is hinted at by the evangelist's interpretation of Siloam as "Sent," for, throughout the Gospel, Jesus is characterized as the one sent by the Father. It is clear that we are meant to look beyond the surface meaning of the miracle to the further meaning that lies beneath.

The cure took place on a sabbath and the Jews were immediately up in arms; the man whose sight had been restored was dragged before the Sanhedrin and was eventually excommunicated (Jn. 9:34). The drama of the situation is that, in his person, it is Christ who has been judged and rejected. Ironically, however, it turns out that the judges have, by their action, been judged; inexorably, the Light has shown them up: "For judgment I came into this world, that those who do not see may see, and that those who see may become blind" (Jn. 9:39).

The discourse on the Good Shepherd is to be understood against the background of Ezekiel 34. There the rulers of Israel are condemned as false shepherds and God declares: "I myself will be the shepherds of my sheep" (Ezek. 34:15). In Jn. 10, the hirelings are the Jewish leaders who have just cast out the sheep they should have sheltered; Jesus, however, sought out the one who had been rejected; once again the judges are judged by their very conduct. But John goes beyond Ezekiel, for this Shepherd will lay down his life for his sheep (Jn. 10:11, 15).

The epilogue (Jn. 10:22-39) centers on the messianic claims of Jesus. In Jn. 10:24, he is urged by the Jews to tell them plainly if he is the Messiah, and he does answer them plainly: "I am the Son of God" (Jn. 10:36). In their eyes he thereby was guilty of blasphemy, and an attempt was made on his life (Jn. 10:33). It becomes more obvious still that the Good Shepherd must indeed lay down his life.

6. *Victory of Life Over Death (Jn. 11:1-53)*. Instead of following the usual pattern of narrative leading to discourse, this section is formed of narrative plus discourse. Jesus is in Transjordan when he is informed of the illness of Lazarus, but he does not depart from there until he knows that Lazarus has died. Quite explicitly, the journey to Jerusalem is presented as a journey to death. The disciples point out that the Jews had tried to stone him (Jn. 11:8), and

Thomas says to the others: "Let us also go, that we may die with him" (Jn. 11:16).

In the ensuing dialogue, Martha at first believes that Jesus is referring to the general resurrection (Jn. 11:23 f.). He gives her to understand that he himself is the resurrection, as he is life; he can give life and restore it at any time. Martha's profession of faith in the Messiahship of Jesus is exceptionally solemn: "I believe that you are the Christ, the Son of God, he who is coming into the world" (Jn. 11:27). The miracle dramatizes the claim of Jesus: at his life-giving word the dead man rose up and came out of the tomb (Jn. 11:43 f.).

The Jewish authorities reacted at once to the raising of Lazarus. Perturbed by the influence of Jesus and the compelling evidence of his "signs" (Jn. 11:47), they debated on what action should be taken. The high priest spoke: "It is expedient for you that one man should die for the people" (Jn. 11:50). This is a striking example of "Johannine irony." The advice of Caiaphas, if utterly unscrupulous, was sound political commonsense, but the evangelist is aware that the words had a deeper meaning of which Caiaphas himself was quite unaware. However unworthy, he was high priest, and as such had uttered a prophecy: "He prophesied that Jesus should die for the nation, and not for the nation alone, but to gather into one the children of God who are scattered abroad" (Jn. 11:51 f.). This is an echo of chapter 10: the Good Shepherd must gather his sheep, even those not of the fold of Israel, so that there may be one flock and one shepherd (Jn. 10:16); but, in order to do that, he must lay down his life. Thus, here too he is given over to death: ". . . from that day on they took counsel how to put him to death" (Jn. 11:53). By coming to raise Lazarus, Jesus had indeed come to his death; it is in view of his own self-sacrifice that he is manifested as Resurrection and Life.

7. *Life Through Death* (*Jn. 12:1-36*). Jesus has now been marked down for death by the Jewish authorities (Jn. 11:53), and the narrative of the anointing at Bethany follows with dramatic appropriateness. This anointing is explicitly associated with his burial by Christ himself (Jn. 12:7). Symbolically, then, we are to understand that he is already dead (Jn. 11:53) and buried (Jn.

12:7). In this context, the triumphal entry into Jerusalem must have the signification of his triumph, his glorification (Jn. 12:12-15). The evangelist indicates that there is indeed a deeper meaning in these things when he notes: "His disciples did not understand this at first; but when Jesus was glorified then they remembered that this had been written of him and had been done to him" (Jn. 12:16). On the occasion of the triumphal entry, we meet another example of Johannine irony. Annoyed by this popular demonstration, the Pharisees petulantly exclaimed: "The world has gone after him" (Jn. 12:19); this was true to a degree that they did not suspect.

We have noticed that, in the Gospel, there is a definite movement toward a climax. It has become increasingly apparent that a violent death is in store for Jesus, and in this last section the point is made quite explicitly. The hour has now at last come for the Son of Man to be glorified (Jn. 12:23), but this glory will spring from his death as the ear of corn comes forth from the seed that has perished in the ground (Jn. 12:24). He can speak of his death as his "glorification" because his one purpose is to do the will of his Father, and the laying down of his life is the supreme expression of his loving obedience (Jn. 12:27 f.). It is in his death too that the burning desire of the Good Shepherd will find fulfillment: "I, when I am lifted up from the earth, will draw all men to myself" (Jn. 12:32). After this, Jesus withdrew (Jn. 12:36b); the public ministry was at a close.

The evangelist, in his reflections on the ministry of Jesus, is struck by the sad failure of the Jews to accept their Messiah: "Though he had done so many signs before them, yet they did not believe in him" (Jn. 12:37). He rounds off the Book of Signs by an epilogue (Jn. 12:44-50), where the leading ideas of the preceding chapters recur. Jesus had clearly ended his ministry at Jn. 12:36, and it seems strange that he should begin to speak again in this passage. We should recognize here a literary convention. It is indeed a summary, and we should not be misled by the use of direct speech, for, in ancient writings, this style is often employed where we would have indirect speech (see, for example, Mk. 1:14 f.; Acts 2:40). It is appropriate that the story of the ministry of our Lord should end with a summary of his teaching.[28]

The Supreme Manifestation of Christ. Our analysis of this third part of the Gospel can be rather brief, not, by any means, because it is of less importance, but simply because it is less involved than the Book of Signs.

1. *The Farewell Discourses (chapters 13-17).* Before the Passion-narrative, St. John has given us a long discourse of our Lord followed by a prayer. We are to take it that the discourse presents to us, rather in the style of Matthew, a synthesis of Christ's teaching. We do not doubt that our Lord did engage in intimate conversation with his disciples on the solemn occasion of the Last Supper, but we are justified in believing that the evangelist took advantage of this fact in order to give a fuller account of related teachings of his Master. When we examine the text, the truth of this observation becomes apparent. The sentence: "Rise, let us go hence," at the end of chapter 14 is understandable only if the Passion-narrative were to follow immediately. It may be seen that chapters 15 and 16 are, to a large extent, a repetition of chapters 13 and 14; it would seem that chapters 15 and 16 form a second version of the last discourse, or, perhaps, they are meant to complement it.

The washing of the feet (Jn. 13:1-11), which precedes the discourses, has been variously interpreted, but it seems best to regard it as symbolizing the great humiliation of the passion. This incident is followed by the prediction of the betrayal by Judas and his withdrawal (Jn. 13:21-30). The phrase, "and it was night" (Jn. 13:30), is dramatic in the fashion of John—Judas is one of those who loves darkness rather than light (Jn. 3:19).

In chapters 1-12, the leading ideas were "life" and "light," whereas in chapters 13-17 these scarcely occur at all and the new theme is "love." With love are associated two other fundamental themes: consolation and union.[29] Jesus gives the supreme example of love as

---

[28]For another, different, explanation of this passage (Jn. 12:44-50) see A. Feuillet, *Études Johanniques* (Paris: Declée de Brouwer, 1962), pp. 149 f. He regards it as a commentary on the entry into Jerusalem (Jn. 12:12-19).

[29]See A. Feuillet, IB, p. 636.

the Good Shepherd laying down his life for his sheep. The disciples must love him as he loves them, and they must love one another because he loves each of them. He gives them only one commandment: "This I command you, to love one another" (Jn. 15:17).

As he takes leave of his own, the Lord seeks to console them, and he gives them three grounds for consolation: 1) They are not left as orphans, because he will come again to them (Jn. 14:3, 18). 2) He will send them another Advocate, a Consoler, who will remain with them and dwell in them (Jn. 14:16). Above all, 3) he gives them the assurance that the Father will regard them with special solicitude. It is the Father who will send the Paraclete (Jn. 14:16), and it is he who will grant whatever they ask in the name of Christ (Jn. 16:23); and he does all this for the reason that "the Father himself loves you, because you have loved me and have believed that I came from the Father" (Jn. 16:27).

Finally, there is the theme of union: the union of Jesus and those who believe in him, in the allegory of the vine; the union of the disciples among themselves, in the concluding prayer. The followers of Christ are branches of that Vine planted by the Father himself; they live by the life of the Vine and, apart from him, they count for nothing and can do nothing (Jn. 15:1-8). The idea of unity is emphatically stressed in the prayer of Christ (chapter 17). In the serene awareness that he has accomplished his work (Jn. 17:14), the great Priest of the New Alliance asks for the sanctification of his own. He is leaving them in the world and he prays that, closely-linked together in love, they may be kept in the Father's name, preserved from evil and steadfast in the truth (Jn. 17:11-19). The prayer includes not only his immediate disciples but reaches out to all future believers (Jn. 17:20-26). He prays that all may be brought into the perfect unity of the divine life as shared by Father and Son.

Throughout these last discourses, although the setting is the eve of the passion, yet, in a real sense, it is the glorified Lord who speaks. This is especially true of the final prayer. Thus, the Father has given all things into his hands (Jn. 13:3), has given him power over all flesh (Jn. 17:2): the prerogative of the Risen Christ (Mt. 28:18). He has overcome the world (Jn. 16:33); he has finished the work that the Father has given him to do (Jn. 17:4); the Son of Man has been glorified (Jn. 13:21). Jesus can speak in this way, within the atmosphere of fulfillment, because by his full acceptance of the will of his Father he was already glorified on the spiritual plane; but the death and resurrection remain to be accomplished on the historical plane. It is only on the cross that he can finally say: "It is accomplished" (Jn. 19:30).

2. *The Passion (chapters 18-19).* The story of the passion as told by John is essentially the same as the synoptists' account—it is closest to Luke—but it also has some specifically Johannine differences. An interesting source of many of these differences is the fact that the Passion-narrative in John has many links with the Book of Signs. A study of some of these will, incidentally, shed much light on the evangelist's method.

Earlier in the Gospel it had been pointed out that the Good Shepherd will lay down his life of his own accord (Jn. 10:18); this is dramatized at the moment of arrest when, at the mere presence of Jesus, those who had come to take him became quite helpless (Jn. 18:6). Before giving himself up, he insisted that his disciples should go free (Jn. 18:8 f.), in order that the saying of his might be fulfilled: "Of those whom thou gavest me I lost not one" (cf. Jn. 17:12), which, in turn, refers back to Jn. 6:37-40 and recalls also the words of the Shepherd: "No one will snatch them out of my hand" (Jn. 10:27 f.). The Christ of John is always in full command of every situation and this characteristic is at its most striking in the Passion-narrative.

In Jn. 3:14 f., we were told that the Son of Man must be "lifted up," and in Jn. 12:32 Jesus declared: "I, when I am lifted up from the earth will draw all men to myself." The evangelist notes that he said this in order to indicate the kind of death he was to die. The same comment is added when Jesus was transferred from the jurisdiction of the Sanhedrin to that of Pilate (Jn. 18:31 f.). At last its meaning is clear: Jesus was not to die by stoning—the Jewish method of execution—but, in accordance with Roman law, on a cross. For the evangelist, this fact is highly significant: crucifixion is utterly humiliating—a criminal's death—and yet the victim on the cross is raised up toward heaven.

Thus, paradoxically in a sense and yet not illogically, the death of Christ is at once his descent and his ascent, his humiliation and his exaltation, his shame and his glory; and this truth is symbolized, for the evangelist, in the manner of his death—crucifixion, the most shameful death, which is, nevertheless, in a figure, his exaltation from the earth.[30]

In Jn. 9:13-41, we have the theme of judgment treated with Johannine irony: the Pharisees sat in judgment upon the claims of Jesus and at the end found the tables turned and sentence pronounced against them. The situation is very much the same in the trial scene before Pilate. Jesus claimed that he had come to bear witness to the truth (Jn. 18:37), for he himself is the Truth (Jn. 14:6). Truth and light are closely akin and it is the man that "does the truth" who alone can stand the scrutiny of the light (Jn. 3:21). Here the scornful question of Pilate: "What is truth?" (Jn. 18:38) marks him out as one who will not "come to the light" (Jn. 3:20). All the while it is Pilate who is being judged: this is explicit in Jn. 19:11.

The evangelist gives as the last word of Jesus, before he bowed his head in death: "It is finished" (Jn. 19:30); the task is done. In Jn. 4:34, we were told that his food is "to do the will of him who sent me, and to accomplish his work." In Jn. 5:36, Jesus can point to a greater testimony than even the Baptist has rendered: "The works which the Father has granted me to accomplish, these very works which I am doing, bear me witness." In his prayer to his Father, he can already say: "I glorified thee on earth, having accomplished the work which thou gavest me to do" (Jn. 17:4). At that moment, Jesus had, in spirit, completed even the part of his task that yet remained, but on the cross he can finally offer up that life-work with his life itself.

In Jn. 19:34 f., the evangelist draws very special attention to the fact that, after the death of Christ on the cross, water and blood issued from his side. The testimony is exceptionally solemn: "He who saw it has borne witness—his testimony is true, and he knows that he tells the truth—that you also may believe." Here, if anywhere, we are surely invited to look for a deeper meaning. In chapter 6, it was not stated how men can partake of the body and

---

[30]Dodd, *The Interpretation of the Fourth Gospel, op. cit.,* p. 435.

blood of Christ. Now it is made clear that the wine at Cana is a sign of the blood of the true Vine; now we know that the sustenance of the eternal life which men receive depends on Christ's self-immolation in fulfillment of the will of God. In Jn. 7:38 f., the water which will flow from the heart of Christ is explicitly said to symbolize the Spirit. At that stage the Spirit had not been given, because Jesus was not yet glorified; "exalted" at last on the cross, he can give that other great gift of God to men.

It now appears that the passion is the great sign which gives meaning to all the others; yet, it differs from all of them. The other signs, in themselves, even if they were miracles, had no lasting effect on history. The multitudes might eat of the loaves which Christ had provided for them, but they were soon hungry again. Unless they had "seen signs," the incident had no further relevance for them; it is the eternal reality that the event signified which really satisfies men's hunger. Lazarus was raised to life, but he must soon die again. The vital thing is what the raising signified: "Whoever lives and believes in me shall never die." The same is true of the other signs; the passion alone is different from all the others—the event of the cross is unique.

> Here is something that happened in time with eternal consequence. Though individual men may miss its significance, nevertheless the thing has happened and history is different: the whole setting of human life in this world is different. It is an "epoch-making" event; in history, things can never be the same again. But more: in it the two orders of reality, the temporal and the eternal, are united; the Word is made flesh. It is an event in both worlds; or rather, in that one world, of spirit and of flesh, which is the true environment of man, though he may fail to be aware of its twofold nature. Thus, the cross is a sign, but a sign which is also the thing signified. The preliminary signs set forth so amply in the Gospel are not only temporal signs of an eternal reality; they are also signs of this Event, in its twofold character as word and as flesh. They are true—spiritually, eternally true—only upon the condition that this Event is true, both temporally (or historically) and spiritually or eternally.[31]

It follows necessarily that, in this view, the story cannot end with the death of Jesus. His death on a cross, as we have seen, *signifies* his glorification and exaltation, but in reality it is the end of a

---

[31]*Ibid.*, p. 439.

struggle. What John sees is the deeper reality symbolized by the crucifixion: the death-and-resurrection as one complete event; this is the reason he can characterize the death of Christ as his "glorification." Consequently, he does not have to speak of the resurrection in itself (since in his view it is inseparable from the death of Jesus) and he is content to speak of some postresurrection apparitions.

3. *The Risen Christ (chapter 20)*. Quite like the Passion-narrative, the account of the postresurrection apparitions in John is very much the same as that of the Synoptics, yet with typically Johannine differences. We read, for instance, that the beloved disciple "saw and believed" when he entered the empty tomb, "for as yet they did not know the scripture, that he must rise from the dead" (Jn. 20:9). This observation, in some related form, is found at other points in the Gospel (Jn. 2:22; 16:16). The meeting with Mary Magdalene is highly significant. Jesus tells her that she must not now touch him, cling to his feet: there is not, for the moment, place for the intimate relations of the time just past, for he has not yet ascended to his Father. However, he is going to the Father without delay, and he sends Mary to tell his brethren so.[32]

That same evening he came from the presence of his Father and appeared to his disciples. It is because he was now fully "glorified" —by his death, resurrection, and exaltation—that he can give them the gift of the Spirit (Jn. 20:22), for the Spirit was not, in fact, given until then (Jn. 7:39). Eight days later he appeared to them again, and this time Thomas was with them.

It is remarkable that, in all these apparitions (and the same is true of chapter 21), the Risen Christ is presented without any suggestion of divine majesty, such as is present in Mt. 28:16-20. This

---

[32]See P. Benoit, "L'Ascension," *Revue Biblique*, 51 (1949), 161-203; A. Wikenhauser, *Die Apostel-Geschichte* (Regensburg: Pustet, 1956³), pp. 28-32. It is clear that, according to the New Testament itself and early ecclesiastical tradition, our Lord went to his Father on Easter Sunday. The ascension forty days later (mentioned by Luke in Acts 1:6-11) is the final leave-taking of Christ; now he will no longer come from the presence of his Father to appear to his disciples as he did during the short time after the resurrection. It should be made clear that, although the liturgical feast of Ascension Day commemorates his final ascension only, it is in no way opposed to the other tradition. In the course of time, emphasis fell altogether on this final ascension and the other aspect of the mystery was lost to sight.

procedure would seem to be closely linked to John's doctrine that Christ is glorified and exalted by his death, for, by dying, Christ is really "going to the Father" (Jn. 14:28; 16:10, 16).[33] This is the reason he has consistently shown that the crucifixion, which is obviously an event on the historical plane, is, at the same time and with more truth, an event on the spiritual plane, for this is the aspect that needs to be stressed. The resurrection, on the other hand, is first and foremost a reality on the spiritual plane, and the evangelist wants to show that it is also an event on the historical plane; this is the reason he stresses the reality of the postresurrrection appearances and, especially, Christ's renewal of personal relations with the disciples. Thus, he shows that the death-and-resurrection, while retaining its full spiritual significance, is of vital importance for men precisely because it happened as a matter of history, at a point of time, in this world.

The solemn profession of faith by Thomas brings us to the meeting place of the temporal and spiritual worlds. It is the true climax of the Gospel. Thomas sees the Jesus that he knew so well; he sees him in a given place and at a given time; then he takes a step beyond place and time, into the realm of faith, into the eternal world. When he confesses Jesus as God, he becomes one of those who has "seen his glory" (Jn. 1:14). The closing words of Jesus open up a vast perspective, for, all men, to the end of time, who, like Thomas, believe in this Lord and God, are included in the last solemn blessing: "Blessed are those who have not seen and yet believe" (Jn. 20:29). It is in order that these may, like Thomas, believe that Jesus is the Messiah, the Son of God, that this Gospel has been written (Jn. 20:31).

Appendix: Apparition by the Lake (*chapter 21*). Chapter 21, although an appendix, is at the same time a fitting postscript to the Gospel, for it is concerned not immediately with Christ, as is the Gospel, but with the Church which he left to carry on his work. The narrative of the miraculous draught of fishes (Jn. 21:14) symbolizes the conquests of that Church, founded on Peter (Jn. 21:15-17). The hyperbole of the conclusion (Jn. 21:25) is striking and effec-

---

[33]See Dodd, *The Interpretation of the Fourth Gospel, op. cit.,* pp. 441 f.

tive; however, even though it is clearly an echo of the other, it lacks the marvelous solemnity and finality of Jn. 20:30 f. To repeat an observation made earlier, the fact that it is an appendix does not derogate from the value of the last chapter of the Gospel: It remains an essential part of the Gospel.

5) The Historical Aspect of the Gospel

JOHN AND THE SYNOPTICS   The difference between John and the Synoptics, although more marked in the discourses, is not confined to these but extends also to the narrative, and indeed, to the whole plan and presentation of the Gospel. This difference has been noted from the beginning—it scarcely could have been overlooked—and various theories have been put forward to explain it. The two extreme views are that John wished to supplement the other Gospels and that he never really knew the Synoptics at all. The view of A. Wikenhauser, who strikes a mean between these two positions, is likely to be nearest the truth. He writes:

> Most exegetes acknowledge that John knew Mark, and admit the possibility of his knowing Matthew and Luke; but it is not at all certain that he did know all three Synoptics. . . . In fact, it is very difficult, often indeed quite impossible, to fit the synoptic material with any certainty into the Johannine plan of the life of Jesus. If the fourth evangelist had had the intention of supplementing the Synoptics, he would surely have taken care to harmonize his account with theirs. He presumes that the synoptic tradition is known to his readers, but he himself is quite independent of the other Gospels.[34]

This last point is of capital importance; neglect of it has too often hindered a more positive and rewarding approach to John. It has been far too easily taken for granted that the fourth evangelist, in writing his Gospel, must have had the other Gospels constantly in mind. Yet, this view is obviously unreasonable. St. John (who, even if one does not admit that he is the author of the Gospel in the strict sense, is certainly responsible for the tradition underlying it) was an eyewitness on his own right, and the actual author of the Gospel (whether the Apostle or another) was patently a most original thinker and writer. We have also seen that the framework

[34]*Einleitung in das Neue Testament, op. cit.,* p. 217.

of the Synoptic Gospels is largely conventional and, especially, that the choice of material was quite selective. Besides, it is clear that Luke, as a result of personal research, has made important additions to the original plan. Why then could John not have gone a step further and written his Gospel independently of the Synoptic Gospels? Surely an unbiased reading of his Gospel will convince one that this is just what he has done.

It follows that John ought to be interpreted by itself and for itself, since even the aim of the fourth evangelist is different from that of the others. It was St. John's special interest to give theological depth to the portrait of Christ. While the Synoptic Gospels tell of Jesus as he appeared to the eyes of his disciples during his ministry, John presents the picture of him that had taken shape before his own Spirit-enlightened gaze.

In the passage quoted above, Wikenhauser, significantly, refers to the synoptic *tradition,* for undoubted similarities between John and the Synoptics do not necessarily point to *literary* dependence on one side or the other. A common tradition, shaped by the living voice of the Church in *kerygma, didachē,* and liturgy can effectively account for such similarities. The situation is not the same as when the Synoptic Gospels are compared with one another; then the evidence indicates that the synoptic evangelists used common written sources in certain parts of their works. But the extent of agreement between the Fourth Gospel and any (or all) of the others does not demand common written sources.

In the Fourth Gospel, we can discern the main lines of the primitive gospel plan: the preaching of the Baptist; the ministry in Galilee; the last journey to Jerusalem; and the Passion-narrative. There are also a number of sayings of Jesus quite like those in the Synoptics (Jn. 2:19; 4:44; 12:25 f.; 13:16, 20; 15:20). On the other hand, there is the striking saying about the "knowledge" of Father and Son which turns up in the Synoptics (Mt. 11:27; Lk. 10:22). The language is typically Johannine, and the idea is central to the theology of the Fourth Gospel; yet, the saying occurs in one of the earliest strata of the tradition, namely, the common source which lies behind Matthew and Luke.

It will be helpful to consider at greater length the relationship between John and Luke.[35] We find in both the sequence: multiplication of loaves/Peter's confession (Lk. 9:10-20; Jn. 6:1-69); the friendship of Jesus with Martha and Mary (Lk. 10:38-42; Jn. 11:1 f.; 12:1 f.); the companionship of Peter and John (Lk. 8:51; 9:28; 22:8; Acts 1:13; 3:1 f.; 11; 4:13, 19; 8:14; Jn. 13:23 f.; 18:15 f.; 20:3-9; 21:7, 20 f.); the role of Satan in Judas' act of betrayal (Lk. 22:3; Jn. 13:2, 27). Contacts are particularly numerous throughout the Passion- and Resurrection-narratives. In both, the ascension is regarded as the term of Jesus' ministry (Lk. 9:51; 24:50 f.; Jn. 6:62; 13:1; 20:17), and both present the Spirit as a gift sent by the Father at the prayer of the glorified Christ (Lk. 24:48; Jn. 14:16; 16:12 f.; 20:22). Although it may be true that some of these contacts can be explained by the influence of Luke on the final form of John, the greater number are so distinctively Johannine that the influence must lie in the other direction. Luke's research (Lk. 1:1-4) turned up Johannine traditions and these he built into his work. This would point to the early formation of a Johannine tradition, long before the final edition of the Fourth Gospel.

In a wider perspective we may make the following comparison between the pre-Johannine tradition and that behind the Synoptics.[36] Certain forms of the oral tradition, identified by Form Critics in the synoptists, reappear in John. Thus, for instance, the sequence action-dialogue-pronouncement has been preserved by John in the Cleansing of the Temple passage (Jn. 2:13-19), while in Mk. 11:15-17 it has disintegrated. Other similar sequences in John may well be traditional and not the work of the evangelist. Again, the synoptic parables can be arranged, on the basis of form, in a varied series within a general pattern; three Johannine parables (The Grain of Wheat, The Benighted Traveler, and The Pains of Childbirth [Jn. 12:24; 11:9 f.; 16:21]) fit easily within the series. Thus, too, the sayings on harvest (Jn. 4:34-38) are closely akin to the frequent sayings associated with the mission of the disciples in the Synoptics. Similarly, the three healing narratives (at Cana [Jn. 4:43-53]; at

---

[35]See Mollat, *op. cit.*, pp. 38 f.
[36]See Dodd, *Historical Tradition in the Fourth Gospel, op. cit.*, pp. 427-29.

Bezatha [Jn. 5:1-9]; and at Siloam [Jn. 9:1-6]) are perfectly at home among the synoptic stories of healing.

At times, the Johannine tradition can clarify obscure passages of the Synoptics. For instance, the Marcan story of Peter's confession begins with the abrupt question: "Who do men say that I am?" (Mk. 8:27); there seems no obvious reason for the question. In John, on the other hand, widespread defections lead naturally to the question: "Will you also go away?" (Jn. 6:67); and Peter's profession of loyalty is a natural reply. Again, in Mk. 6:45, we are rather at a loss to understand why Jesus, immediately after the multiplication of loaves, "*made* his disciples get into the boat and go before him to the other side," while he went into the hills to pray, and also why we are told that "they did not understand about the loaves, but their hearts were hardened" (Jn. 6:52). All is explained in John's reference to an attempted messianic rising (Jn. 6:14 f.). He "compelled" his reluctant disciples—willing sharers of the popular enthusiasm—to embark, and he retired into the hills to frustrate any further attempts to force his hand. In both cases cited, John is surely following a fuller tradition.

Yet, these and other points of contact ultimately serve to emphasize the independence of John. Although he has followed the broad lines of the synoptic plan, he has not felt himself bound by the convention which seemed to fit the ministry of Jesus into one year and which indicated only one journey to Jerusalem,[37] for by his mention of three Paschs, he shows that the ministry lasted more than two years and he tells us that Jesus visited Jerusalem frequently. And although he has shown that he knows how our Lord framed his teaching, he has chosen to give that teaching in his own words. In short, he follows his own plan and pursues his own purpose, knowing that his own presentation of Christ and his teaching cannot clash with any true portrait of him or with any authentic outline of his message.

THE JOHANNINE   In our study of the formation of the Gospels,[38]
TRADITION   we stressed the importance of oral tradition and drew attention to the fact that we must not consider it only as the

---

[37]See p. 74.
[38]See p. 78.

basic stratum of the subsequent literary constructions. We saw that it was more correct to regard the oral tradition as keeping step with the written forms of the tradition, constantly modifying the latter along the way, and continuing even beyond the New Testament period. Thus, for instance, Papias, in the first half of the second century, still preferred oral tradition, where it was available.

> We have to think of the life of the Church as being nourished, and its faith and fellowship maintained, by a living tradition. This tradition served (among other purposes) to guard and hand on what was remembered or believed concerning that which Jesus had done, said, and suffered—in other words, the raw material of gospel composition; and it was still very much alive when the Fourth Gospel was written and in the region where (in all probability) it was written.[39]

Already, in comparing John and the Synoptics, we have implicitly acknowledged the existence of a Johannine tradition, in part parallel to the synoptic tradition and in part complementary. Now, we may indicate briefly the character and content of this Johannine tradition.[40] The distinctive Aramaic coloring, already noted, of the Fourth Gospel is relevant here, for a tradition that purports to go back to the beginnings of Christianity would reasonably show traces of Aramaic idiom. So, too, certain features of the pregospel tradition point to a Jewish-Christian setting (for instance, an allusion to the belief that the Messiah would remain unknown until Elijah had pointed him out [cf. Jn. 1:26 f.] and the belief in the high priest's gift of prophecy [Jn. 11:51]). The curious expression, "when you were under the fig tree" (Jn. 1:48), would seem to have point only in a Jewish environment (cf. Dn. 13:51-60 and some rabbinical evidence). And there are other contacts with Jewish tradition. John's date for the crucifixion, the eve of the Pasch, while differing from the synoptic dating, agrees with that of rabbinical tradition: "Jesus was hanged on the Eve of the Passover."[41] The discussion of the sabbath in Jn. 7:22-24, like similar discussions in the Synoptics, clearly points to a Jewish environment; while, in forecasts of persecution for the disciples, the threat of excommunication from the synagogue (Jn. 16:2) would hold terrors for none but a Jewish-Christian com-

---

[39]Dodd, *Historical Tradition in the Fourth Gospel, op. cit.,* p. 7.
[40]See *ibid.,* pp. 424-32.
[41]*Babylonian Talmud,* Sanhedrin, 43b.

munity. We may note, too, that the political situation reflected by the Johannine tradition fits the years before the outbreak of the Jewish rebellion in 66 A.D., a situation that had passed away when the Gospel itself was written.

So much for the Jewish-Christian character and setting of the tradition; now we may consider its contents, at least the salient points. The ministry of John the Baptist is treated more fully than in the Synoptics and his importance in preparing the way for Jesus is more in evidence. Yet, in his handling of the tradition, it does seem that the evangelist had in mind a false evaluation of John the Baptist by the "disciples of the Baptist." The existence at Ephesus of a group so designated is attested by Acts 19:1-8, and we know that some of them were still there in the third century. Thus, the Fourth Gospel is silent about the repentance preaching of the Baptist and presents him exclusively in his role as Precursor. He is not the light, but bears witness to the Light (Jn. 1:6-8); he is not the Messiah or Elijah or the Prophet (Jn. 1:20); he is only the friend of the Bridegroom, who must decrease while the Bridegroom must increase (Jn. 3:28-30). His great glory is that he had recognized the Lamb of God (Jn. 1:29). The evangelist was able to select the material that suited his polemical purpose.

We learn of an early ministry of Jesus in Judaea, parallel to that of the Baptist. The tradition preserved much topographical information; in particular, it contained many placenames of Judaea and Transjordan not found in the other Gospels. It is likely that the tradition, in great part—and not the evangelist only—is responsible for an overwhelming interest in the Judaean ministry. On the other hand, we learn from this Gospel of a threatened messianic rising in Galilee, followed by a widespread desertion of followers and the loyal adherence of the Twelve (Jn. 6:14 f., 66-69). The Passion-narrative is full and detailed, supplementing the synoptic accounts and even deviating from them. It stresses the political aspect of the charges against Jesus. It is difficult to define the content of the tradition in regard to the sayings of Jesus because the evangelist has consistently recast the teaching. But it is still possible to point to sayings and parables obviously drawn from a reservoir common to the four Gospels, and it is reasonable to believe that many more, now veiled in Johannine language, are from the same general source.

We may end this brief survey by noting that, in his introduction
to his study of historical tradition in the Fourth Gospel, Professor
Dodd asked the question: "Can we in any measure recover and describe a strain of tradition lying behind the Fourth Gospel, distinctive of it, and independent of other strains of tradition known to
us?"[42] And at the close of his work, he asserts that his investigation
had led him "to the conclusion that, behind the Fourth Gospel, lies
an ancient tradition independent of the other gospels, and meriting
serious consideration as a contribution to our knowledge of the historical facts concerning Jesus Christ. For this conclusion I should
claim a high degree of probability—certainly in such matters is seldom
to be attained."[43] It remains, then, to consider the historical character of the Gospel. Beforehand, since it has to do with source-
material, it would be well to consider the Fourth Gospel and the
Qumran writings.

JOHN AND THE
QUMRAN TEXTS
Among the manuscripts found at Qumran—the
Dead Sea Scrolls—there are some that have shed
light on the New Testament. It is notably with John and the Epistles
of St. Paul that the greatest number of points of contact, both
literary and doctrinal, have been discerned. Both John (and Paul)
and the Qumran sectarians were influenced by currents of thought
that were prevalent in certain circles of Judaism at that time. In
John, a form of dualism is expressed in contrasts: light-darkness;
truth-falsehood; life-death. The evangelist treats light, truth, and life
as kindred and often as identical images, and the same holds true
for darkness, falsehood, and death. The meaning of these expressions is very close to that of similar ones in the Qumran texts, where
they occur a number of times in practically the same sense. The
Johannine, like the Qumran dualism, is monotheistic, ethical, and
eschatological (expecting the victory of light) and hence differs
from Gnostic dualism.

In the *Manual of Discipline,* the Rule of the Essene community
of Qumran, we come across many of these ideas. For instance, the
opposition between light and darkness, and the link between them

---

[42]*Historical Tradition in the Fourth Gospel, op. cit.,* p. 8.
[43]*Ibid.,* p. 423.

and truth-falsehood: "The origin of truth lies in the fountain of Light, and that of perversity in the wellspring of Darkness. All who practice righteousness are under the domination of the Prince of Lights and walk in the ways of light; whereas, all who practice perversity are under the domination of the Angel of Darkness and walk in ways of darkness." There is mention of sons of light and sons of darkness: "Everyone who wishes to join the community must pledge himself . . . to love all the children of light . . . and to hate all the children of darkness." Just as in the Fourth Gospel, stress is laid on a spirit of unity, in fraternal charity: The members of the community are to "unite in a bond indissoluble forever," and each of them must pledge himself "to bring into a bond of mutual love all who have declared their willingness to carry out the statutes of God." Similar, if not so frequent, parallels are found in the Commentary on Habakkuk, the Hymns, and the Rule for the War, as well as in the Damascus Document.[44]

These ideas, in a similar dress, are frequent in John; yet, there are notable differences. Thus, the fraternal love so insisted upon in Qumran is limited to members of the sect; all other men are to be hated as enemies of God. This is not Christian charity. It is the word "Christian" that underlines the essential difference between the Scrolls and the Gospel. The occurrence of these various themes in the Fourth Gospel and in the Qumran writings points to a common Jewish background, but in John these same ideas have been transformed by the impact of Christian faith and Christian experience.

One positive result of these contacts is to emphasize further the essential Jewish background of the Fourth Gospel; they may even constitute another argument in support of the Johannine authorship of the work. We can put it like this: it does seem not unlikely that John the Baptist had some contact with the Qumran community, for the wilderness in which the Baptist sojourned (Lk. 1:80) was not far from Jericho (Jn. 3:2); it must have been in the neighborhood of Qumran, for there can be little doubt that the desert of Judah is meant. One of the two disciples of John who followed Jesus (Jn. 1:35-39) is likely the "beloved disciple." It is reasonable

---

[44]See p. 27.

to suppose that, through contact with his first master, the Apostle became familiar with the favorite themes of the men of Qumran. But he came to see these themes, as he came to gaze on all things, through the prism of his faith in Jesus Christ, and it is in this light that they appear in his Gospel.

THE HISTORICITY   In view of his predominantly theological inter-
OF THE GOSPEL   est, it is evident that it was not St. John's intention to write a work of scientific history. In fact, he handles his material rather freely and subjects it to his leading thought; he dominates his material—which is a very different matter from falsifying it in any way. He is interested in events and the meaning of events, but he is not unduly troubled with details, unless he finds some symbolism in them. The one fact that is of supreme importance for him is that Jesus of Nazareth, who really lived and died in Palestine, was the Son of God; or, to put it in his own way, that the Word did in very truth become flesh and tabernacle among us.

If we are to keep John's approach to the Gospel facts in proper perspective, it would be well to recall that the first three evangelists were in no way mesmerized by these facts. They did not feel that they had to give a verbatim account of the words and works of the Savior, for, when we compare these Gospels, it becomes apparent at once that Matthew and Luke especially permitted themselves considerable liberty in the presentation of the material. We are not, then, pleading for special treatment for the fourth evangelist; we merely stress the fact that, by temperament and by design, he was more individualistic than the others and more independent of the synoptic-type tradition.

But this is by no means to deny that he, too, was faithful to his sources. We have seen, sufficiently clearly for our purpose, that the Fourth Gospel, no less than the others, is solidly founded on tradition going back to the beginnings of Christianity. This is not only an *a priori* assertion—although such an assertion would find a valid basis in one's appreciation of the process of gospel-writing—but has emerged as a scholarly conclusion from a painstaking study of the Gospel. It is obviously true that John shows a marked individuality and his work is, to a degree unequalled by the other Gospels, an original literary composition. His work, in short, bears the hallmark of genius; but, the inference that he has shaped it at the expense of historical truth is surely unwarranted. Yet, some such line of reasoning seems to be implicit in certain treatments of this question.

The Fourth Gospel is essentially a theological work rather than a history, but it is presented in the literary form of a "gospel." A gospel is a recital of the historical narrative of the suffering, death, and resurrection of Jesus Christ, prefaced by an account of his ministry. The aim of an evangelist is to set forth the knowledge of God contained in the Christian revelation; this revelation, as clearly in the Fourth Gospel as in the others, is an historical revelation. Consequently, it is of vital interest for the evangelist that what he relates did really happen, that he is dealing with *facts*.

But the evangelist is not debarred from interpreting the facts with which he deals, and when he does so he is not being unhistorical, for history, in any real sense, includes interpretation of the facts related. And, as an evangelist, John, although not primarily an historian, is, nevertheless, dealing with history. The remark of Pierre Benoit is just as applicable to John as it is to the first Christian preachers: "The early Christians had not, perhaps, our regard for 'history,' but they had regard for the 'historical.' The preachers of the new faith did not intend to relate everything about Jesus, but they were careful to relate only what was solidly founded."[45] If, by long reflection, John was able to find a deeper significance in many actions of our Lord, he looked for that significance in solidly founded facts. If his carefully-composed discourses brought out the more profound aspects of the teaching of Jesus, these discourses are founded on that teaching and are true to the mind of our Lord.

When we get down to details of chronology and topography, we must never lose sight of John's essential independence of the Synoptics. We should not be perturbed by minor differences, nor even by apparent contradictions; there should be no question of smoothing out such differences by unjustifiable harmonization. For example, John has the clearing of the Temple at the beginning of the ministry (Jn. 2:13-21), while the Synoptics place it just before the last Pasch (Mk. 11:15-19; Mt. 21:12-17; Lk. 19:45-48). It would be a puerile

---

[45]*Revue Biblique*, 53 (1946), 501.

expedient to explain this discrepancy by supposing that the Temple was cleared twice, for both John and the Synoptics quite obviously relate the same event. Much more important are the points at which the two traditions meet, and by doing so emphasize the essential historicity of both. John and the Synoptics tell the same story; the main difference is that St. John the theologian is less interested in the facts than in their symbolism.

6) *The Logos*

The title of Logos (Word), which is applied to Jesus in the prologue of the Fourth Gospel, is found nowhere else in the New Testament except in the First Epistle of St. John (1 Jn. 1:1) and in the Apocalypse (19:11-13). *Logos* is a Greek word of many meanings; it signifies not only the spoken word, but also the interior word of the mind—the thought or idea. Hence, our rendering, "Word," does not fully translate the original term, which is wider, and can even designate the mind itself, as the faculty of thought, and also the philosophical *ratio* or reason of a thing.

In Greek philosophical speculation, especially within the Stoic system, the Logos represents a ruling principle, immanent in the world. This idea was adopted by Philo—a contemporary of Christ.[46] For him, the Logos became an intermediary between God and the world, an instrument employed by God in the work of creation and in his dealings with the world. In his writings, it can appear as an image of God and even as a divinity of lower rank.

St. John introduces the term Logos without explanation, thus intimating that it was familiar to his readers. The evangelist makes the term the vehicle of his own ideas, which owe little to Greek speculation and, most probably, nothing to Philo. It is not "Logos," but what John meant by it that is important. Today it is almost universally recognized that the evangelist's thought is to be explained (if not entirely, at least predominantly) in terms of the Old Testament and of Christian tradition.

Logos is, naturally, a word of frequent occurrence in the Greek Old Testament, and its use in two particular contexts is of special

---

[46]See p. 32.

interest here.[47] In one group of passages, the word of God is creative, for instance in the Creation story (Gn. 1:3, 6, 9), summarized in Ps. 33 (32):6: "By the word of the Lord were the heavens made." In another group of passages, the "word of God" is that spoken by the prophets, the word of revelation (for example, Am. 3:1; Jer. 1:4; Ezek. 1:3). It is significant that the ideas of creation and revelation are in evidence in the prologue of John (Jn. 1:3, 18); and it is surely reasonable to see here the influence of the Old Testament.

Another very important Old Testament concept, which must also inevitably lie behind John's use of Logos, is that of divine Wisdom.[48] (We should recall that *Logos* signifies not only the spoken word, but also the thought.) This Wisdom was with God "before he made anything from the beginning" (Prv. 8:22); it is "the brightness of eternal light, the unspotted mirror of God's majesty and the image of his goodness" (Wis. 7:26). The divine Wisdom is very often personified and, in general, it tended to be looked upon as a personal being, standing by the side of God and bearing some relation to the created world. As such, Wisdom appears as a foreshadowing of the Word of John and must have been immediately present to the evangelist's mind. It is noteworthy too that, in Wis. 18:15 f., God's Logos is depicted as a stern warrior with a sharp sword leaping down from the royal throne in heaven (cf. Ap. 19:11-16).

In Jewish thought, the Law was the Word of God *par excellence,* and the rabbis often personified the Law. Here too we can reasonably hope to find part of the background to the Johannine Word, if only by contrast. For, it does seem clear that John sets up an opposition between his Word and the Word of the Law: "The Law was given through Moses; grace and truth came through Jesus Christ" (Jn. 1:17)—who is the true Word of God.

The Christian background is certainly not less important than the Jewish. In the New Testament, the word of God is frequently the message of salvation, the Gospel (Lk. 8:11; 2 Tm. 2:9; Ap. 1:9; 1 Jn. 1:1). It was spoken by Paul (Acts 13:5; 1 Thes. 2:13) and by

---

[47]See Barrett, *op. cit.,* pp. 127-30.
[48]See Wilfrid J. Harrington, *Record of the Promise: The Old Testament* (Chicago: The Priory Press, 1965), pp. 240-45, 268 f.

the other Apostles (Acts 6:2) and by Jesus himself (Lk. 5:1; Mk. 2:2). But the Gospel that Paul and the Apostles preached was in reality Christ (1 Cor. 1:23; Gal. 3:1; Acts 2:36; 4:12). It is on the person of Jesus that John also focused his attention; he sees clearly that Jesus is himself the message of salvation, the Word.

In asking what the title "Logos" meant for the evangelist's contemporaries, we should observe that the notion of God's silence had emerged in Judaism—from an exegesis of Gn. 1:3: "And God said, 'Let there be light.'" The rabbis asked what there was before God spoke, and the answer was: God's silence. In the Hellenistic world, Silence became a symbol of the highest deity. Against this background, we can understand how Ignatius of Antioch (c. 110 A.D) presupposed that God was silent before the sending of the Word; he speaks of "Jesus Christ, who is the Word of God, which came forth out of silence" (*Magnesians*, 8.2).

> It is in a world which knew of God's silence as a token of his inexpressible majesty that the message of the Christian Church rings out: God is no longer silent—he speaks. It is true, he has already acted: he revealed his eternal power through the creation, he made known his holy will, he sent his messengers the prophets. But, in spite of all this, he remained full of mystery, incomprehensible, inscrutable, invisible, hidden behind the principalities and powers, behind tribulations and anxieties, behind a mask which was all that could be seen. Still, God has not always remained hidden. There is one point at which God took off the mask; once he spoke distinctly and clearly. This happened in Jesus of Nazareth; this happened, above all, on the cross.
>
> This is how the joyful confession of the psalm in praise of Christ at the beginning of the Gospel of John must have sounded in the ears of those who heard it for the first time: God is no longer silent. God has spoken. Jesus of Nazareth is *the* Word—he is the Word with which God has broken his silence.[49]

It would seem to follow that, although Logos is a Greek term and may possibly have been chosen as a concession to Greek mentality, nevertheless, the sources of St. John's thought are predominantly Jewish and Christian; and it follows, too, that the prologue is quite in line with the rest of the Gospel. John teaches that the Logos exists from eternity, that he is with God from eternity, that he is

---

[49]See Jeremias, *op. cit.*, pp. 89 f.

God and the creator of all things. Lastly, and most wonderfully, he teaches that this Word "was made flesh." For, it is in the person of Jesus alone that the pre-existing Logos is made known to men; and although the title "Logos" does not appear in the rest of the Gospel, yet the Gospel itself is comprehensible only in the light of the conviction that Jesus is the Incarnate Word, God's perfect self-revelation. But, in speaking of the Logos as the Word made flesh, in declaring that all things were made by him, by stressing his power to make men "sons of God," John underlines the truth that God's revelation in the Logos is *for us*.[50]

2. THE THREE EPISTLES OF ST. JOHN

The three Epistles of John show a striking resemblance among themselves and with the Fourth Gospel. In vocabulary, style, and doctrine all three writings stand so closely together as to suggest a common authorship; the problem, then, of the Johannine authenticity of the Epistles is related to that of the authenticity of the Gospel. Hence, it is fitting to study the Epistles immediately after the Gospel. It also seems best to consider the First Epistle separately, since it stands apart from the others.

1) The First Epistle of John

AUTHORSHIP[51]   The earliest reference to the First Epistle is by Polycarp who cites 1 Jn. 4:2 f. (*Philippians*, 7, 1). Eusebius states that Papias had known the Epistle; and it is likely that Justin, too, had known it. The Johannine authorship of the writing is attested by Irenaeus, Clement of Alexandria, Origen, and Denis of Alexandria. The Muratorian Canon lists it and Jerome noted that 1 Jn. was accepted everywhere.

In the early Church, then, the Epistle—like the Fourth Gospel— was attributed to John the Apostle; indeed, the writings are so closely related that their attribution to the same author is natural. We have

---

[50]For a treatment of the doctrinal aspects of Jn. see Wilfrid J. Harrington, *Explaining the Gospels* (New York: Paulist Press, 1963), pp. 172-78.

[51]See A. Wikenhauser, *New Testament Introduction*, trans. J. Cunningham (New York: Herder & Herder, 1958), pp. 525-29; A. Feuillet, IB, pp. 694-97; F.-M. Braun (Mollat-Braun), *L'Évangile et les Épitres de Saint Jean*, (BJ), pp. 197-210; R. Schnackenburg, *Die Johannesbriefe* (Herders Theologischer Kommentar zum Neuen Testament), (Freiburg: Herder, 1953), pp. 33-36.

studied above the problem of the authorship of the Gospel, and much of what has been said there is applicable here. Some modern scholars, however, deny that Gospel and Epistle have the same author. In fact, if resemblances are marked and constant, there are also notable differences between the writings.

A whole series of characteristic expressions is common to both writings: eternal life; the new commandment; perfect joy; to walk in the light; to do the truth; to pass from death to life; to see and testify; to know and believe; to abide in God. For that matter, a great number of identical phrases occur in both Epistle and Gospel (for example, 1 Jn. 1:6 and Jn. 12:35; 1 Jn. 1:8 and Jn. 8:44; 1 Jn. 2:11 and Jn. 12:35; 1 Jn. 2:15 and Jn. 5:42; 1 Jn. 2:27 and Jn. 16:30; 1 Jn. 3:14 and Jn. 5:24; 1 Jn. 4:16 and Jn. 6:69; 1 Jn. 5:9 and Jn. 5:34).

There is also close agreement in theological ideas. Christ is the Word (1 Jn. 1:1) and emphasis is placed on the Incarnation and on the fact that the Incarnate Word has taken away sin. He, the only-begotten Son, was sent by the Father into the world and his coming is a sign of the Father's love. Acceptance of Christ is a passage from death to life; it involves a rebirth and a new life. In both writings, we find opposition between light and darkness, life and death, truth and falsehood, the children of God and the children of the world, the disciples and the world. Love of God finds expression in the keeping of his Commandments, while fraternal love, the demand of the new commandment of Christ, is the hallmark of Christian life.

At the same time, differences between Gospel and Epistle are notable. Certain expressions which are characteristic of the Gospel do not appear in the Epistle; for example: Law; glory; glorification; seek; send; Holy Spirit; birth from above; to be from below; judge; judgment; save. On the other hand, the Epistle has certain expressions not found in the Gospel; for example: anointing; seed of God; fellowship (*koinōnia*); *parousia*; propitiation; pseudoprophet; antichrist; to have the Father; to have the Son; to deny Father/Son. The Epistle has none of the Aramaic coloring so obvious in the Gospel and it contains scarcely any reference to the Old Testament.

It should be admitted, however, that these differences, marked though they are, cannot outweigh the impressive contacts between the writings and the unanimous traditional attribution of the Gospel and Epistle to the same author. Nevertheless, the differences must be reckoned with and reasonably explained. An important factor is that, in the Epistle, the author is combating Gnostic tendencies. This would explain the particular emphasis of the writing and the use of such terms as "antichrist"; but it is not enough, by itself, to account for all the differences, or for most of them. It is not more helpful to appeal to different literary forms: gospel and letter.

The simplest solution is one that, at first sight, makes an unwarranted assumption and appears to beg the question: it suggests the use of a secretary.[52] We do know that this was common practice in antiquity and, more important for our purpose, we are assured that St. Paul employed secretaries (cf. Rm. 16:22; Col. 4:18; 1 Cor. 16:21; 2 Thes. 3:17; Gal. 6:11). Since writing on papyrus was an extremely slow business, it is understandable that, instead of dictating a letter, an author might carefully outline the plan to his secretary and be satisfied with revising the finished draft. In the present case, it is likely that the secretary was also a disciple of the Epistle's author, one who had assimilated his thought and who was familiar with his favorite expressions. The Epistle was, then, the result of the close collaboration of master and disciple.

In spite of the close relationship of Gospel and Epistle, it is not easy to say which preceded the other. The Epistle presupposes the main themes of the Gospel, but we have seen that, most likely, the Gospel took shape gradually. We shall see that something the same may be said of the Epistle. While it does seem that the Fourth Gospel, in its final form, is the later writing, it does not appear that the Epistle can be much earlier. A date toward the end of the last decade of the first century is reasonable.

LITERARY CONSTRUCTION   1. *Plan.* Analysis of 1 Jn. is not easy; for one thing, like the Fourth Gospel, we cannot find in it a strictly logical development of thought. Hence, we cannot hope to discern in the Epistle a logical plan. It seems that—again like the Gospel—we must reckon with the main theological ideas and allow them to be our guide. We follow a plan which, however hypothetical it may be, does indeed bring out effectively the striking message of the Epistle and its depth.[53]

---

[52] See F.-M. Braun, (BJ), pp. 206 f.
[53] See *ibid.*, pp. 210 f.

INTRODUCTION (1:1-4)	
FIRST PART (1:5–2:28)	SECOND PART (2:29—4:6)
Principle: To Walk in the Light (1:5-7)	Principle: To Live as Children of God (2:29–3:2)
1) To break with sin (1:8—2:2)	1) To break with sin (3:3-10)
2) To keep the commandments— especially that of love (2:3-11)	2) To keep the commandments— especially that of love (3:11-24)
3) To keep oneself from the world (2:12-17)	3) To keep oneself from the world (3:13; 4:1-5)
4) To be on guard against anti- christs (2:18-28)	4) To be on guard against false prophets (4:1-6)
THIRD PART (4:7–5:12)	
1) Love is of God (4:7–5:4) 2) Faith is of God (5:5-12)	
CONCLUSION (5:13)	
APPENDICES (5:14-21)	
1) Prayer for sinners (5:14-17) 2) Résumé of the Epistle (5:18-21)	

In a short introduction (1 Jn. 1:1-4), which recalls that of the Fourth Gospel, the author, who is conscious of his fellowship with the Father and Son by means of what he has seen, heard, and touched of the Incarnate Word, expresses his desire that the faithful, taking their stand on his testimony, may also enter into communion with the Father and with his Son, Jesus Christ. Then he proceeds, in the form of a diptych, to trace a parallel development of four themes: sin; fraternal charity; opposition to the world; and antichrists. In the first panel (1 Jn. 1:5–2:28), God is seen as Light—the utterly sinless One, the holy One; hence, the Christian must rid himself of sin and live a life worthy of that Light. Only in this way can he have fellowship with God and with his Son. In the second panel (1 Jn. 2:29—4:6), God is the loving Father whose children must walk in his ways. The emphasis is on the divine sonship of Christians.

The third part (1 Jn. 4:7–5:12) completes the other two by explaining more thoroughly the Christian's duty to love and to believe and by pointing to the source of love and faith. One must love because God is love. One must believe because God himself has borne testimony to his Son. The verse 1 Jn. 5:13—which echoes the conclusion of the Gospel (Jn. 20:31)—is manifestly the conclusion of the Epistle and sets out its purpose. It follows (again like the final chapter of the Gospel) that 1 Jn. 5:14-17 is an appendix—rather, two appendices—recommending prayer for sinners and giving a résumé of the Epistle.

2. *Literary Form*.[54] Unlike contemporary Greco-Roman letters and the other New Testament epistles (except Hebrews), 1 Jn. begins abruptly, without the customary prescript or greeting. The writer is not named and there is no final greeting. In other words, it has none of the usual epistolary formulas. It seems that the writing may be described as a homily addressed to the whole Church, or as a sort of encyclical addressed to the churches of the Roman province of Asia.

Yet, on closer study, it does show characteristics of a letter, that is to say, a writing composed on a particular occasion and addressed to a particular person or group of persons. The author of 1 Jn. addresses his readers as "little children" (1 Jn. 2:1, 18, 28; 3:7, 18; 4:4; 5:21) and "beloved" (1 Jn. 2:7; 3:2, 21; 4:1, 7, 11). He is well aware of their moral and spiritual state and shows a feeling of responsibility for them. He knows that false teachers are at work among them, and although he does not fear apostasy, he does think it well to emphasize the essential elements of Christianity. It is sufficiently clear, then, that he is addressing a definite group of readers, although these may have included several communities. So it is that, although 1 Jn. has certain homiletic characteristics, and

---

[54]See Wikenhauser, *New Testament Introduction, op. cit.*, pp. 522 f.; A. Feuillet, IB, p. 698; Schnackenburg, *op. cit.*, pp. 1-3.

lacks some of the more obvious traits of a letter, it may still be fairly described as a letter.

3. *Purpose.*[55] The occasion of the letter is the activity of false teachers: John has written to counteract it. Since, however, he is aware that his readers know the truth and have, in fact, effectively repulsed the false prophets (1 Jn. 2:20, 27; 4:4), his message is essentially positive. True, he does denounce the false teachers (1 Jn. 2:18, 28; 4:1, 6), men who had belonged to the Christian community—although they had never known its spirit (1 Jn. 2:19, 22 f.; 4:1)—and his tone can be polemical at times (1 Jn. 1:6-10; 2:3—6:9). Yet, the conclusion (1 Jn. 5:13) states unequivocally the purpose he had in mind: "I write this to you who believe in the name of the Son of God, that you may know that you have eternal life." He, conscious of his fellowship with the Word of life (1 Jn. 1:1), desires to share that experience. He is a witness, and he bears witness. This Epistle is his testament to his disciples. And if he does point to certain dangers, and if there is an element of exhortation, we learn once again—what the author of Hebrews has so effectively taught us—that the only effective way to counter error is to give men an ideal to live by, to hold up before them the Incarnate Son of God.

Who were the false teachers John had in view? They were not Docetists (for whom the Son of God did not become Incarnate, but had assumed the appearance of a human body)—as has sometimes been asserted—since they, on the contrary, appear to deny the Messiahship and divinity of Jesus (1 Jn. 2:22, 4:15; 5:5). It can scarcely be doubted that they were Gnostics of some sort (those who claimed a special *gnosis*—knowledge or wisdom—which often went hand-in-hand with an indifference to moral conduct). From the Epistle, we learn that the false teachers claim a knowledge of God (1 Jn. 2:4; 4:8), love for God (1 Jn. 4:20), and a fellowship with God (1 Jn. 1:6; 2:6, 9) superior to those of ordinary Christians. They deny that Jesus is the Messiah (1 Jn. 2:22), the Son of God (1 Jn. 4:15; 5:5), and that he has come in the flesh (1 Jn. 4:2).

---

[55] See Wikenhauser, *New Testament Introduction, ibid.,* pp. 523-25; A. Feuillet, IB, pp. 698-701; Schnackenburg, *ibid.,* pp. 13-20.

The assertion of 1 Jn. 5:6: "This is he who came by water and blood, Jesus Christ, not with the water only but with the water and the blood," which refers to the baptism and death of Jesus and demonstrates that he is no phantom but was baptized in the Jordan and died on the cross, is probably aimed at a denial of the reality of the Incarnation. The antichrists held that the Son of God dwelt in Jesus only from the moment of baptism and, before the passion, departed to the Father. The author's emphasis on the need of breaking with sin and his insistence on practical Christian living would have in mind the Gnostic view that sin is of no account in one who possesses the perfect knowledge of God—it does not touch that deepest reach of the spirit where one loves the Father. Similarly, they felt that, when one is occupied with God, one has no concern with others. John deals with both errors in a characteristic statement of devastating simplicity: "Whoever does not do right is not of God, nor he who does not love his brother" (1 Jn. 3:10).

4. *1 John and Qumran*.[56] We have noted above certain affinities between the Fourth Gospel and the Qumran writings; contacts of the latter with 1 Jn. are even more evident. The same themes crop up: the two ways of light and darkness (1 Jn. 1:6 f.; 2:9-11); the evil world subject to the devil (1 Jn. 3:8, 10, 13 f.; 5:19); the lawlessness which must be rigorously avoided (1 Jn. 3:3-6); and, most striking of all, the two spirits (1 Jn. 4:1-6). In the *Rule of the Community* (1QS), these two spirits come from God: he employs them to lead and direct men until the day of God's visitation. Both seem to be in his service, one for good and the other for evil. The author of the Epistle contrasts the two spirits (1 Jn. 4:6), but he also makes a clear distinction between the good spirit, who comes from God, and the spirit of antichrist, who is not of God (1 Jn. 4:3). Here Christ and Antichrist stand face to face, like the Prince of light and the Angel of darkness in the Qumran texts; while the children of God and the children of the devil (1 Jn. 3:10) are none other than sons of light and the sons of darkness of Qumran.

We do not know if John had firsthand contact with the Essenes of Qumran, but contact of some sort was certainly present. The

---

[56]See F.-M. Braun, (BJ), pp. 208 f.

Johannine writings and the writings of Qumran meet in a common literary and spiritual current which emerged in Palestinian Judaism. Having said this, however, we must acknowledge that the Fourth Gospel and the First Epistle, which present the Christian message in its most sublime form, by that very fact immeasurably surpass even the finest of the Essenian writings.

5. *The "Johannine Comma."* In 1 Jn. 5:7 f., the Clementine (or official) Vulgate reads: "Quoniam tres sunt qui testimonium dant *in caelo*: *Pater, Verbum et Spiritus Sanctus, et hi tres unum sunt. Et tres sunt qui testimonium dant in terra*: Spiritus et aqua et sanguis, et hi tres unum sunt." ["For there are three that bear witness *in heaven*: *the Father, the Word, and the Holy Spirit; and these three are one. And there are three that bear witness on earth*: the Spirit, and the water, and the blood; and these three are one."] The words in italics, the so-called Johannine Comma, are now universally admitted to be nonauthentic. Indeed, the case against them is decisive. They are absent from all (except four late) Greek manuscripts of the New Testament and from all ancient Eastern versions. Nor are they found in the best and oldest manuscripts of Old Latin and Vulgate. No Greek Father cites them, and Priscillian (380 A.D.) is the first Latin writer to cite them; in view of the great trinitarian disputes, this is a powerful argument.

The most likely explanation of the origin of the text is that it began—in Africa or Spain, if we may judge from the predominantly African and Spanish sources—as an allegorical exegesis of the three witnesses mentioned by John (the Spirit, the water, and the blood). First written as a marginal gloss (or note) in a Latin manuscript of 1 Jn., it ended by slipping into the text—a procedure that is by no means unparalleled. It does not appear in manuscripts of the Vulgate before 800 A.D.

2) *The Second and Third Epistles of John.*[57]

Unlike 1 Jn. which, we have seen, has something of the character of an encyclical, 2, 3 Jn.—which are much shorter than the other— are addressed, respectively, to a single Church and to an individual.

---

[57]See Wikenhauser, *New Testament Introduction, op. cit.,* pp. 530-33; A. Feuillet, IB, pp. 704-8; F.-M. Braun, (BJ), pp. 197-200; Schnackenburg, *op. cit.,* pp. 263-68.

Again, the First Epistle is anonymous, but the others are written by "the elder"—in the context one whom that title sufficiently identifies to his readers. Another point of difference is that there was some hesitation in certain quarters about accepting 2, 3 Jn. However, given the brevity of these writings and the marked personal tone of the third, hesitation is understandable.

More remarkable is the imposing early testimony in their favor. Polycarp (*Phil.* 7, 1) refers to 2 Jn. 7 as well as 1 Jn. 4:2 f. Irenaeus cites as Scripture the letter to the Elect Lady and regards it as the work of John, disciple of the Lord. The Muratorian Canon speaks of epistles of John (*in epistolis suis*), thus acknowledging at least two. According to Eusebius, Clement of Alexandria commented on all three Johannine Epistles. Origen and Denis of Alexandria attribute 2, 3 Jn. to John the Apostle—as does Eusebius.

Yet, Origen and Eusebius list them among the *Antilegomena*, because they are not accepted in every church. Jerome regarded 2, 3 Jn. as canonical and authentic, but he does admit that others had doubts in their regard. However, by the second half of the fourth century, both Epistles were accepted as canonical throughout the whole Greek and Latin Church. Their acceptance by the Syriac churches came later.

The author of both Epistles describes himself as "the Elder" (*ho presbyteros*). In the early Church, the communities were governed by elders (cf. Acts 11:30; 15:2; 14:23). Here it is a question of an Elder *par excellence,* one whose jurisdiction covers the local communities of a whole region. It is a title that could fittingly describe John, as tradition presents him, surveying from Ephesus the churches of Asia. It is generally admitted that 2, 3 Jn. were written by the same author as 1 Jn. Since we have noted that the First Epistle may reasonably be regarded as the work of the author of the Fourth Gospel (while admitting the use of a secretary), we may, logically, also attribute the other two to him. And, in the same way, they also may be dated to the last decade of the first century.

2 JOHN

PRESCRIPT (vv. 1-3)
THE COMMANDMENT OF LOVE (vv. 4-6)
THE ANTICHRISTS (vv. 7-11)
CONCLUSION (vv. 12 f.)

The Second Epistle is addressed to the "Elect Lady and her children." There is little doubt that the title designates a church (cf. vv. 1, 14, 13), probably a church of Asia Minor. This community, still faithful, is threatened by deceivers "who will not acknowledge the coming of Jesus Christ in the flesh" (v. 7). Hence, the Elder puts the faithful on their guard against the false prophets (vv. 7–10); he assures them that to abide in the doctrine of Christ (that is, the doctrine of the Incarnation [v. 7]) is to have fellowship with the Father and the Son (v. 9) and he forbids them to associate with the false teachers (v. 10). Typically, he insists on the love of one another in fulfillment of the new commandment of Christ (vv. 5 f.). This short letter is, in fact, a summary of 1 Jn., and may be regarded either as a first outline of it or as a brief résumé. In both writings, circumstances are similar and the purpose is the same.

3 JOHN

PRESCRIPT (vv. 1 f.)
EULOGY OF GAIUS (vv. 3-8)
CENSURE TO DIOTREPHES (vv. 9-11)
TESTIMONY OF DEMETRIUS (v. 12)
EPILOGUE (vv. 13 f.)

Very likely, the Third Epistle was written earlier than the others, before the emergence of the false teachers. The letter is addressed to Gaius, a faithful disciple of John (vv. 1 f.). His conduct is beyond reproach, and he is especially conspicuous for his generous hospitality to the brethren who visit his community. These are probably itinerant preachers (like Demetrius [v. 12]) sent out by John. On principle, they accepted nothing from the pagans to whom they preached (v. 7) and so were altogether dependent on the generosity of the faithful. Indeed, it was the duty of Christians to support such men (v. 8).

However, the Epistle is more directly concerned with a conflict between the Elder and Diotrephes, the head of a community (most likely that to which Gaius belongs). The authority of the Elder is being challenged: in practice, by refusal to accept the Elder's envoys and by the expulsion of those Christians who do receive them. Some, however, like Gaius, were not cowed by Diotrephes, and the Elder counted on them to have his orders carried out. Demetrius is obviously a trusted emissary. His commission may have been to replace Diotrephes as head of the community, or to install Gaius in that office.

From both Epistles, it emerges that the Elder claims considerable authority; his attitude to the churches is quite like that of Paul. Tradition names John the Apostle as the author of these writings —in that tradition, we have a ready explanation of their tone of authority. At the same time, the title of *the* Elder is explained; and the absence of a proper name fits in well with the practice of the author of the Gospel, the "beloved disciple."

THE MESSAGE   Unlike the Fourth Gospel, which is addressed
OF 1 JOHN[58]   even to non-Christians—"that you may believe" (Jn. 20:31)—the First Epistle is written for those "who believe in the name of the Son of God" (1 Jn. 5:13). The author's primary purpose is not to exhort his readers to practice virtue or to fly sin, but to make them understand the sublimity of their condition as Christians.

Christian existence is defined as a vital relationship to God. It is a matter of birth to the life of God, of fellowship with Father and Son: the faithful are born of God, they abide in God, they

---

[58]See F.-M. Braun, (BJ), pp. 200-203; A. Feuillet, IB, pp. 690 f.

know God. In short, they have "eternal life"; and, for John, eternal life is the very life of God. This life, possessed by the Christian, is a reality, but it is mysterious: what the faithful are now, as well as what they will be hereafter, is attested only by faith. Therefore, the author multiplies the criteria by which the believer may judge the genuineness of his Christian life; hence, the frequency of "by this" and the verb "recognize" (1 Jn. 2:3, 5; 3:10, 14, 19, 24; 4:2, 6, 13; 5:2, 13, 18, 20). Since it is a participation in the divine life, Christian life must reflect the very qualities of God; if we are children of God, in fellowship with him, it is impossible that we should not be conformed to him.

God is Light (1 Jn. 1:5) and Love (1 Jn. 4:8): *Light* because he is the absolute good and because our moral conduct should be modeled on his justice and holiness (1 Jn. 2:20; 3:7); *Love* because he is the source of all the tenderness and generosity that the verb "to love" suggests. The Christian is called to walk in the Light (1 Jn. 1:6 f.) and to abide in Love (1 Jn. 4:16) by observing the Commandments (1 Jn. 2:3-7; 3:22-24; 5:2 f.), summed up in the two precepts of faith in the name of Jesus and of fraternal charity (1 Jn. 3:23). To believe in the divine Love which is incarnate in Jesus and, in turn, to love their brethren—such is the message addressed by John to Christians.

But the Apostle does also intend to recall—by implication at least —the fundamental norms of the Christian life. In the realm of faith, his readers must readily accept the apostolic witness (1 Jn. 1:5; 2:21-24), as well as the testimony of God (1 Jn. 4:6, 9, 13) and the intimate word of the Spirit (1 Jn. 2:20, 27). Their relationship to their brethren is colored by their care to observe the Commandments, centered in the precept of charity (1 Jn. 2:3-11; 3:11-24; 4:7—5:4). They must take their stand against the unbelieving world and face up resolutely to its allurements (1 Jn. 2:12-17; 3:13; 4:1); similarly, they must adhere to the truth and combat the errors that are propagated around them (1 Jn. 2:18-23; 4:1-4). Their personal attitude must be characterized by the candid avowal of sin (1 Jn. 1:8-10; 2:1; 3:3 f.) and by confidence in the person of the Savior (1 Jn. 2:1 f.; 3:5, 8; 5:6 f.). The Christian life makes demands, and its sublimity is matched by a practicality that calmly accepts the realities of human existence.

John combats Gnostic tendencies, but it is true to say that the First Epistle is the fruit of an authentically Christian *gnosis,* at once knowledge and fellowship. Its spiritual teaching is basically the same as that of Paul, but it is more theocentric than Paul, and goes to the Father. Here the ideal is not to live "in Christ," but to "abide in God," in the "Father and Son." But this does not prevent John from emphasizing, just as strongly as Paul, the indispensable mediation of the Incarnate Son of God: it is through the Son that the believer receives the very life of God. All the while, let it be said again, a writing of such elevated spirituality, cast in the realm of Father and Son, keeps a close and constant grip on the world of men and testifies to a simple and demanding moral realism: fellowship with God, participation in the divine life, is impossible without absolute fidelity to the Commandments. This short writing has an abiding message for those far advanced in Christian perfection—and for all Christians.

3. THE APOCALYPSE

1) The Authorship of Apocalypse

THE TESTIMONY OF TRADITION   Four times (Ap. 1:1, 4, 9; 22:8) the author of Ap. names himself John, and Christian tradition has, on the whole, identified him with the Apostle John. The earliest witness is Justin (c. 150 A.D.), who, in his *Dialogue with Trypho,* declares: "A man of our number, by name John, one of the Apostles of Christ, prophesied in a revelation vouchsafed to him that those who believe in our Christ will dwell for a thousand years in Jerusalem" (cf. Ap. 20:4-6). About the turn of the second century, the identification was accepted by Irenaeus, the Muratorian Canon, Clement of Alexandria, Tertullian, and Hippolytus. Origen says explicitly that the Apostle had written both the Ap. and the Fourth Gospel.

Dissident voices were first heard in the third century; the earliest was that of the Roman priest Gaius (Irenaeus, *Adv. Haer.,* III, 28, 2). The Montanists were invoking Ap. in support of their doctrines, and the reaction of Gaius was radical: he attributed Ap. to the heretic

Cerinthus—a veritable cutting of the Gordian knot. Far more important is the view of Denis of Alexandria (d. c. 265 A.D.). On critical grounds, following a literary and theological analysis of both writings, he concluded that Ap. could not have been written by John the Apostle, the author of the Fourth Gospel; he did not question the canonicity of Ap. The opinion of Denis has been recorded by Eusebius (*H.E.* VII, 25) who seems to have accepted it (*H.E.* III, 39, 5 f.). But it is in the Eastern Church, especially, that there was some hesitancy about Ap.[59] Cyril of Jerusalem and Gregory Nazianzen did not number Ap. among the New Testament writings; John Chrysostom and Theodoret never used it. It does not figure in the Syriac versions.

Yet, the negative witness, however impressive, represents no more than a fraction of the patristic tradition. Furthermore, these dissident views were motivated by political preoccupations or by the findings of personal research and not by conflicting traditional data. "One may, in fact, affirm that the almost unanimous tradition of the Church has regarded the Apostle John as the author of Apocalypse."[60]

THE PROBLEM   Unfortunately, the virtual unanimity of tradition does not really solve the problem of authorship. It is an important factor which may not be set aside, but the whole matter is complicated by the impressive traditional attribution of the Fourth Gospel and the three Epistles to the Apostle John. Modern scholarship overwhelmingly supports the view of Denis of Alexandria that Ap. and the other writings—at least in their present form—cannot have been written by the same hand.

Certainly, there are linguistic and doctrinal contacts between Ap. and the Fourth Gospel, and these do justify the grouping of all the Johannine writings in one corpus. It can at least be said that they are of Johannine inspiration, written in the immediate entourage of the Apostle and penetrated by his teaching. Ap. and the Gospel show a common taste for allegory and symbolism and employ the same figures: living water; shepherd; Lamb; manna. They also em-

---

[59]See Harrington, *Record of Revelation: The Bible, op. cit.*, pp. 70 f.
[60]M.-E. Boismard, *L'Apocalypse*, (BJ), p. 17.

ploy the same characteristic themes: witness; the Word; both refer to Zech. 12:10—"They shall look on him whom they have pierced" (Jn. 19:37; Ap. 1:7). Yet, on the other hand, Ap. does not have most of the key-words of the Gospel or Epistles: light; darkness; truth; love; while for "world" (in a pejorative sense) Ap. has "the inhabitants of the earth." The doctrine of the Holy Spirit which appears in its most developed form in the final discourses of the Gospel barely emerges in Ap.

Most marked of all is a different conception of eschatology; or, at least, a different presentation of eschatological doctrine. In Ap., there is the vivid anticipation of the return of Christ. Here the Son of Man is the glorified Christ who will come to destroy the wicked, and Antichrist is a political power opposed to the establishment of the kingdom. In the Gospel and Epistles, Christ, in a real sense, has already come and abides in the hearts of his faithful. He has already brought about the separation between the faithful and others, between those who accept God's plan of salvation and those who reject it. Antichrists, heretical teachers propagating false Christological doctrines, are already active (1 Jn.). The Holy Spirit, abiding in Christians, has established the kingdom of God among us.

The Greek style of Ap. is certainly very different from that of the Fourth Gospel. This is not simply due to the fact that the former is the more markedly Semitic; the Greek of Ap., in contrast to that of the other Johannine writings, is often ungrammatical. The difference is too great to be explained on the ground of distinct literary forms. Finally, it is noteworthy that the author of Ap., who is aware of the distinction between Apostles and prophets (Ap. 18:20), fits himself into the category of prophet (Ap. 22:9) and makes no claim to be an Apostle (cf. Ap. 21:14).

Is there any hope of a positive solution to the problem of authorship? One cannot help agreeing with Father Boismard:

> We are faced with the following dilemma: if we wish to maintain the integral Johannine authenticity of the Fourth Gospel, we must attribute the redaction of Apocalypse to a disciple of the Apostle. If we prefer to maintain the Johannine authenticity of Apocalypse—taking our stand on the testimony of St. Justin and of St. Irenaeus—we must then admit that the Gospel, while giving, substantially, the content of the Johannine preaching, was edited by a disciple of the

Apostle, or by a group of disciples. As the problem stands at the moment, no definite solution is in sight and the way is wide open for further research.[61]

DATE   Regarding the date of Ap., the traditional evidence is not in agreement. The earliest testimony is that of Irenaeus (*Adv. Haer.*, V, 30, 3) who declared that Ap. appeared "not very long ago, almost in our own time, that is at the end of Domitian's reign." Since Domitian reigned between 91-96 A.D., this would date the writing about 95 A.D. The earliest Latin commentator on Ap., Victorinus of Pettau (d. c. 305 A.D.), states that John was relegated by Domitian to the island of Patmos (cf. Ap. 1:9). Eusebius follows Irenaeus, who also mentions the exile, and dates the book to the fourteenth year of Domitian. St. Jerome and most subsequent writers followed Eusebius. However, another tradition (the Muratorian Canon, the apocryphal *Acts of John*, and perhaps Tertullian) places the writing of the work under Nero (54-68 A.D.). Epiphanius dates it in the reign of Claudius (41-54 A.D.).

Most modern scholars accept the attestation of Irenaeus; indeed, there seems little doubt that, in its final form, Ap. is at home in the time of Domitian. However, the evidence pointing to Nero's reign cannot be shrugged off. The passage, Ap. 17:9-11, speaks of seven kings, that is, without doubt, seven Roman emperors. In Ap. 17:10, we are told that "five have fallen" and that "one is"—the sixth in whose reign the book is thus set. Since the list most probably begins with Augustus and leaves aside the three imperial competitors of 69 A.D. (Galba, Otho, and Vitellius), it turns out that the sixth emperor is Vespasian, Nero's successor.[62] This would seem to add weight to the tradition that John wrote earlier than the reign of Domitian. In fact, the indication of Ap. 17:10 can be explained on the ground of a well-known apocalyptic procedure, that of fictitious antedating. The author, of set purpose, has antedated his work to the reign of Vespasian (69-79 A.D.)—before the destruction of Jerusalem and the Temple—in order to bring out the theological signifi-

---

[61]IB, p. 741.
[62]The list is: Augustus, Tiberius, Caligula, Claudius, Nero, Vespasian, Titus. The eight (Domitian) "belongs to the seven" (Ap. 17:11); the author utilizes the current legend of *Nero redivivus*—the return of Nero. Domitian, like Nero, is a persecutor of Christians; he is Nero all over again.

cance of that event.[63] This is a factor that must be reckoned with in our interpretation of the work.

Besides, it is not unlikely that Ap., as we have it, is a combination of two writings, of different dates: one composed under Nero and the other under Domitian;[64] hence, the (apparently) conflicting traditional views. Perhaps, in the light of all the evidence, it is best to say that Ap., *in the form in which it has come to us,* dates from the close of Domitian's reign.

2) *The Literary Construction of Apocalypse*

THE LITERARY FORM   The word "apocalypse"—from the Greek *apokalypsis*—means "revelation," and an apocalypse is a revelation of hidden things known only to God, made by God himself or by an angel speaking in his name. The revelation is almost always concerned with the development of history, culminating in the end of this world and pointing to the mysteries of the future; thus, apocalypse is also prophecy. Indeed, as a literary form, it is a child of prophecy. Already the visions of Ezekiel, for instance, have something of the fantasy and exuberance of the apocalyptist's visions. It was when prophecy had ceased that the apocalyptic form really developed in Israel. It flourished in the last two centuries B.C. and the first two centuries A.D.: the Book of Daniel (more precisely, Dn. 7-12) is the earliest Jewish apocalypse.[65] The form was also cultivated in the early Church, but never to the same extent as among the Jews, and Ap. is the only New Testament apocalyptic work.[66]

In an apocalypse, the revelation of divine mysteries was made through the medium of visions which the seer describes in conventional language; thus, we have images and symbols and numbers. With regard to the latter, in Ap. for instance, the number 3 means God and 4 means the earth; their addition (7) and multiplication

---

[63]See A. Feuillet, *L'Apocalypse, État de la question* (Paris: Desclée de Brouwer, 1963), pp. 78 f.; English trans., *The Apocalypse,* trans. T. E. Crane (New York: Alba House, 1965), pp. 92 f.

[64]This is the view of M.-E. Boismard. See p. 460.

[65]See Harrington, *Record of the Promise: The Old Testament, op. cit.,* pp. 381-84.

[66]There are apocalyptic passages in the Synoptic Gospels: Mk. 13; Mt. 24:1-36; Lk. 21:5-33; 17:22-37.

(12) represents the perfect action of God in the universe, or God dwelling with men. Powers hostile to God are symbolized by incomplete numbers: 3½, which is half of 7; and 6, which is one less than 7. Everything, or nearly everything, in an apocalypse is symbolic, although the details of the symbols are not always significant and should not be unduly pressed. It is imperative that the procedure should be correctly understood.

> When the seer describes a vision, he translates into symbols the ideas which God had suggested to him; he accumulates things and colors and symbolic numbers without worrying about the form of his picture. His primary purpose is to convey the ideas he has received from God, not to describe a coherent vision, an *imaginable* vision. If we are to follow, without losing heart, the way he has traced, we must accept his terms, and translate into ideas the symbols which he describes, and not be disturbed by their lack of coherence. Thus, it would be wrong to strive to imagine *visually* the Lamb with seven horns and seven eyes (Ap. 5:6) and the Beast with seven heads and ten horns (Ap. 13:1), and to wonder how the ten horns should be shared among the seven heads. These visions are not plastically conceivable, but that fact should not disturb. One must be satisfied with understanding the symbols *intellectually* without lingering over their more or less surprising details: the Lamb enjoys the fullness of power and knowledge; the Beast represents the Roman Empire with its emperors (the heads) and vassal kings (the horns). If one does not take full account of such procedure—often disconcerting—it is impossible for one to understand the Apocalypse.[67]

The author of an apocalypse looks to the future not only when he describes the time of the end but also when he unrolls the course of history. His vantage point is in the past—an apocalypse is almost always pseudonymous—and he speaks as a prophet. In noncanonical apocalypses, description of the last things is a product of the author's unaided imagination; but the authors of Dn. and Ap. have been granted a vision of the end of time and the era of salvation; they are authentic prophets. The apocalyptic flourished in times of crisis and was designed to console and to encourage those undergoing affliction and distress and to fill them with confidence in God who guided human destiny and was master of history. Here Ap. is at one with the other apocalyptic writings.

---

[67]M.-E. Boismard, (BJ), pp. 8 f.

Yet, John's work is no imitation of earlier apocalypses and is, in many ways, a new departure:[68]

1) The Jewish apocalypses are pseudepigraphic, whereas this Christian apocalypse bears its author's name. This is significant, for John thus claims for himself the position of a prophet who, conscious of his own inspiration, has no need to shelter under the name of a notable biblical personage.

2) It is difficult to determine the date and provenance of Jewish apocalypses because these matters are left intentionally vague. The apocalypse of John makes no secret of its origin and destination: it is the work of a Christian undergoing exile on the Island of Patmos and it is addressed to the Christian congregations in seven of the chief cities of Asia Minor; its date can be set within definite limits.

3) Whatever may be said of his indebtedness to Jewish sources, John has produced a work which, taken as a whole, is profoundly Christian. "It breathes a religious spirit which is not that of its predecessors; it is marked with the sign of the Cross."

4) In Ap., the Messiah plays a role that is not his in Jewish apocalypses. In these, the New Age is brought about by God alone and not through his Messiah—in some, the Messiah does not figure at all. For John, it is Jesus Christ who, by opening the sealed book, sets in operation the plan of God. For Christ, by his sacrifice, has freed men from sin (Ap. 1:5; 5:9; 7:14; 12:11; 22:14) and he alone is worthy to open that book (Ap. 5:6-9; 13:8). His place is in heaven beside the throne of God (Ap. 3:21; 7:17; 22:1-3). At the end of time he will appear in judgment (Ap. 19:11 ff.) and he will manifest himself as the Lord of the world (Ap. 2:26 ff.; 12:5; 19:15). In the New Jerusalem, he is, with God, the source of eternal life and unending happiness for the elect (Ap. 21:22 f.; 22:1 ff.).

In short, although he has employed a current literary form, and although (as we shall see) he is much indebted to the Old Testament, John has written a work that is distinctive and ultimately original.

---

[68]See H. B. Swete, *The Apocalypse of St. John* (London: Macmillan, 1922³).

When we describe John's work as an apocalypse, taking that word in its proper sense, we leave aside the first three chapters, the "letters to the seven churches." Although an integral part of the whole Book, these are not apocalyptic in form. Even though we call them "letters," they are not, strictly speaking, letters, but prophetic messages. Primarily, they are judgments on the spiritual state of the churches and they stress the necessity of keeping the faith; hence, they are closer to the prophetical form than to the apocalyptic.

THE PLAN   In reaction to a trend of the recent past, modern scholars tend to accept the unity of Ap. Even the "letters to the seven churches" (chaps. 1-3), although in a different literary form, are an integral part of the Book; the whole bears the stamp of one hand. At the same time, there is an unevenness which can be put down, in part at least, to the apocalyptic form—where a strictly logical arrangement is not to be sought; but, it may also point to a complicated prehistory of the work. Consequently, we think it well to give two plans: Division I, which stresses the unity of Ap. (and which will be the basis of our interpretation of the work); and Division II, which brings out, in graphic manner, how the book may have grown.

1. *Division I.*[69]

PROLOGUE (1:1-3)	
A. THE LETTERS TO THE SEVEN CHURCHES (1:4–3:22)	
1) Introduction	1:4-8
2) The Vision of the Son of Man	1:9-20
I. Letter to Ephesus	2:1-7
II. Letter to Smyrna	2:8-11
III. Letter to Pergamum	2:12-17
IV. Letter to Thyatira	2:18-29
V. Letter to Sardis	3:1-6
VI. Letter to Philadelphia	3:7-13
VII. Letter to Laodicea	3:14-22

[69]This division will be justified and explained in our interpretation of Ap., pp. 467-85.

B. THE PROPHETICAL VISIONS (4:1–22:5)	
Part I. The Church and Israel	4–11

1) God gives to the Lamb the Sealed Scroll	
a) Vision of the Throne of God	4
b) The Lamb receives the Sealed Scroll	5
2) Opening of the Seven Seals	
a) The First Four Seals	6:1-8
b) The Last Three Seals	6:9–8:1
3) The Seven Trumpets	
a) The First Four Trumpets	8:2-13
b) The First Two "Woes" (5th & 6th Trumpets)	9
c) The Little Scroll	10
d) The Temple Measured; The Two Witnesses	11:1-13
e) The Last "Woe" (7th Trumpet)	11:14-19

Part II. The Church and Pagan Rome	12:1–21:8

1) The *Dramatis Personae*	
a) The Woman and the Dragon	12
b) The Two Beasts	13
c) The Companions of the Lamb	14:1-5
2) The Hour of Judgment	
a) Proclamation of the Hour of Judgment	14:6-13
b) The Symbolical Harvest and Vintage	14:14-20
c) Preparatory Vision of the Seven Plagues	15
d) Chastisement of the "inhabitants of the earth": The Plagues of Seven Bowls	16
3) The Chastisement of Babylon (Rome)	
a) The Great Harlot	17
b) Proclamation of the Fall of Babylon	18:1-8
c) Lament for Babylon	18:9-24
d) Triumphal Liturgy in Heaven	19:1-10
4) The End	
a) Victory over the Beasts	19:11-21
b) Blessedness of the Martyrs: The Reign of a Thousand Years	20:1-6
c) Victory over the Dragon	20:7-10
d) The Last Judgment	20:11-15
e) The New Creation	21:1-8

Part III. The Heavenly Jerusalem	21:9–22:5

EPILOGUE (22:6-21)	

2. *Division II.*[70] Ap., as it stands, appears to contain many doublets. An examination of these suggests that the properly apocalyptic part (chaps. 4-22) is composed of two different, originally independent, apocalypses which were later fused to form one text. Since both apocalypses show the same literary characteristics, however, they must both be attributed to the same author, who composed them at different dates.[71] A literary analysis of the writing enables us to discern and to isolate the two primitive texts.

PROLOGUE (1:1-3)		
A. LETTERS TO THE SEVEN CHURCHES (1:4—3:22)		
B. THE PROPHETICAL VISIONS:		
	TEXT I	TEXT II
Prologue: the Little Scroll		10: (1), 2a, 3 f., 8-11
Satan and the Church	12:1-6, 13-17	12:7-12
Proclamation and Signs of the Great Day of Wrath	4—9; 10:1, 2b, 5—7; 11:14-18	13—16
Presentation of Babylon	17:1-9, 15-18	17:10, 12-14
Fall of Babylon	18:1-3	(cf. 14:8)
The Elect Preserved		18:4-8
Laments for Babylon	18:9-13, 15-19, 21, 24	18:14, 22 f.
Triumphal Canticles	19:1-10	18:20 (cf. 16:5-7)
The Messianic Kingdom	20:1-6	
The Eschatological Combat	20:7-10	19:11-21
The Judgment	20:13-15	20:11 f.
Jerusalem of the Future	21:9—22:2 22:6-15	21:4; 22:3-5 21:5-8
Appendix: the Two Witnesses		11:1-13, 19

[70]See M.-E. Boismard, (BJ), pp. 9-15; "L'Apocalypse ou les Apocalypses de saint Jean," *Revue Biblique,* 56 (1949), 507-41.

[71]It seems possible, on internal evidence, to date Text II in the reign of Nero. Text I was undoubtedly written after the death of Nero (Ap. 17:8), perhaps at the time of Vespasian or in the beginning of Domitian's reign.

The letters to the seven churches (chaps. 1-3) present the same literary characteristics as the properly apocalyptic part and hence are the work of the same author. Although meant to be read with the two other texts, they originally existed independently of them. The state of the churches of Asia described in the letters suits very well the time of Domitian, before the persecution of 95 A.D. At that date, or a little later, Ap. took its final shape. The fusion of all three texts was probably the work of another hand; this final editor was responsible for minor retouches aimed at smoothing the joints of the texts and at harmonizing their data.

The plan of Text II (the earlier in date) is the simpler of the two. Cast out of heaven, Satan turns in his wrath against the earth and its dwellers (Ap. 12:7-12); to help him in his purpose he takes into his service the Beast with seven heads (the Roman Empire), which undertakes a violent persecution of the Church (chap. 13). But all is not lost; there are signs of hope: the vision of Christ's faithful ones (Ap. 14:1-5), the prophetic announcement of the fall of Babylon (Rome) (Ap. 14:6-13), the symbolic vision which foretells the extermination of the pagan nations (Ap. 14:14-20). A heavenly interlude serves to justify the rigor of the divine decrees (Ap. 15:1-4); then a series of plagues strikes Babylon, which is finally destroyed by an invasion of peoples coming from beyond the Euphrates (the Parthians) (Ap. 15:5—16:21); but the faithful, warned in time, have been able to flee (Ap. 18:4-8). A lament for Babylon, accompanied by cries of triumph, closes this first episode of the Great Day of Wrath (Ap. 18:14, 22 f., 20). Next, the pagan nations, assembled by the Beast, are exterminated (Ap. 19:11-21). Then comes the Judgment, which marks the triumph of Christ's faithful (Ap. 20:11 f.), the end of this world and the coming of the heavenly Jerusalem (Ap. 21:1-8).

Text I follows more or less the same plan. In an opening vision, God enthroned in heaven, hands over to the Lamb the sealed scroll which contains the decrees of extermination against the pagan and persecuting nations (chaps. 4-5). A series of visions proclaim the coming of the Great Day of Wrath (cf. Ap. 6:17; 9:15; 11:18) under the form of an invasion of Parthians (chaps. 6-11, minus the relevant passages of Text II). The whole of this part is inspired

mainly by Ezek. 5-14. Then Babylon, the Great Harlot, is exterminated (chap. 17, minus the passages of Text II [Ap. 18:1-3]), and
her fall is followed by a lament (Ap. 18:9-13, 15-19, 21, 24) and
triumphal canticles in heaven (Ap. 19:1-10). The fall of Babylon
marks an era of peace for the Church, the establishment of the
messianic kingdom (Ap. 20:1-6), preceded by the symbolic resurrection of the martyrs (Ap. 20:4). At the end of time, the pagan
nations (God and Magog) attempt a last assault on Jerusalem
(the Church) and are annihilated (Ap. 20:7-10). Finally comes
the Judgment (Ap. 20:13-15) and the description of the Jerusalem
of the future (Ap. 21:9–22:2; 22:6-15).

USE OF THE   The author of Ap. obviously knows the Old
OLD TESTAMENT   Testament thoroughly. It is not only that a
whole crowd of biblical images appear in his work, but the very
language is Old Testament language. He does not quote, formally,
but he uses familiar turns of phrase quite naturally. But he is not
slavishly tied to this style and vocabulary—he dominates them, just
as he can adapt the images to suit his purpose.

Although Old Testament phrases are used consistently, and perhaps even unconsciously, there are references in which it is clear
that a particular book and certain passages are in view; this occurs
most frequently in the visions. Almost all of the Old Testament
books make their contribution, but some of them are used with
special frequency. More than half of the author's references belong to the prophecies of Isaiah and Ezekiel, to Psalms and to Daniel;
in proportion to its length, Dn. yields by far the greatest number.

In many cases, if not in most, the author blends two or more
Old Testament contexts, whether from different books or from different parts of the same book; this is because his memory is charged
with biblical words and thoughts. His handling of the material is
always original and independent. Thus, in the first vision of Ap.,
while nearly every detail is drawn from Ezek. and Dn., the concept of the glorified Christ has no parallel in the Old Testament.
If the vision of chapter 4 owes much to Is., Ezek., and Zech., no
mere compiler could have produced it; and the same may be said
of every other vision throughout the book. "Though in constant
relation to the older apocalyptic, St. John's picture of the unseen

and the future are truly creations, the work of the Spirit of prophecy upon a mind full of the lore of the earlier revelation and yet free to carry its reminiscences into new and wider fields of spiritual illumination."[72]

The following table will give an impression of the very wide use of the Old Testament in Ap. The list is in no way exhaustive and includes those passages only whose influence can be readily discerned.

Vision of the Throne of God, Ap. 4	Is. 6:1-5; Ezek. 1:4-10, 25-27; Dn. 7:9 f.
The Sealed Book, Ap. 5	Ezek. 2:9 f.
The First Four Seals, Ap. 6:1-8	Zech. 6:1-5; (Mt. 24:6-8)
The Last Three Seals, Ap. 6:9—8:1	Zech. 1:12; (Mt. 24:9 f.); Is. 13:10; 34:4; (Mt. 24:29); Is. 27:13; Hos. 10:8; (Mt. 24:31); Ezek. 9:4, 6; Is. 49:10; 25:8
The First Four Trumpets, Ap. 8:2-13	Ezek. 10:2; 38:22; Jl. 3:3; Ex. 9:22 f.; 7:17; Is. 14:12; Ex. 15:23; Jer. 9:14; Ex. 10:21 f.
The First Two "Woes," Ap. 9	Ex. 10:12-15; 19:18; Jl. 1:6—2:5
The Little Scroll, Ap. 10	Dn. 12:7; Ezek. 2:8—3:3
Temple/Witnesses, Ap. 11:1-13	Ezek. 40:3; Zech. 4:13, 11-14
The Last "Woe," Ap. 11:14-19	Ps. 2:2; 115:13
The Woman and the Dragon, Ap. 12	Gn. 3:14-16; Is. 7:10, 14; 66:7; Dn. 10:13
The Two Beasts, Ap. 13	Dn. 7:2-8
The Little Apocalypse, Ap. 14:6-20	Jl. 3:13; Is. 63:1-6
Preparatory Visions, Ap. 15	Ex. 14:31—15:2; 15:11-14
The Seven Bowls, Ap. 16	1st, Ex. 9:10; 2nd, Ex. 7:20 f.; 3rd, Ex. 8:10; 5th, Ex. 10:21 f.; 6th, Ex. 8:2; 7th, Ex. 9:23 f.
The Great Harlot, Ap. 17	Jer. 51:7, 12b-13; Is. 25:15-17
Two Proclamations, Ap. 18:1-8	Jer. 51:8; Is. 21:9; Jer. 51:45; Is. 52:11; Is. 47:7 f.
Lament for Rome, Ap. 18:9-19	Ezek. 26:16 f.; 27:12, 22, 26-36

---

[72]Swete, *op. cit.*, p. clv.

Sorrow and Joy, Ap. 18:20—19:10	Jer. 25:10; Ezek. 26:13; Is. 24:8; Dt. 32:43; Ps. 22:24
Parousia/Victory, Ap. 19:11-21	Wis. 18:14-16; Ps. 2:2, 9; Is. 11:4; 63:1-3; Ezek. 39:17-20; (1 Cor. 15:25-26)
Millenium/Dragon, Ap. 20:1-10	Dn. 7:9, 21 f., 26
Last Judgment, Ap. 20:11-15	Dn. 7:9 f.; 12:1
The New Creation, Ap. 21:1-8	Is. 65:17; 52:1; 61:10; Lv. 26:11 f.; Zech. 8:8; Ezek. 37:27
The New Jerusalem, Ap. 21:9—22:5	Ezek. 40:1-3, 5; 48:30-35; 47:1, 5-7, 12; Is. 54:11 f.; 60:1-4; Zech. 14:11; Dn. 7:18

It is particularly instructive to see how John had modeled his plagues of Trumpets and Bowls on the plagues of Egypt, transforming the latter in the process.

Trumpets	Plagues of Egypt	Bowls
1) Ap. 8:6 f.	Ex. 9:23 f.	7) Ap. 16:17-21
Hail, fire, blood	VII	Thunder, earthquake, hail
2) Ap. 8:8 f.	Ex. 7:20 f.	2) Ap. 16:3
Sea into blood	I	Sea turned to blood
3) Ap. 8:10 f.	Ex. 7:20 f.	3) Ap. 16:4-7
Waters turned bitter	I	Waters turned to blood
4) Ap. 8:12	Ex. 10:21-23	5) Ap. 16:10 f.
Darkness	IX	Darkness
5) Ap. 9:1-11	Ex. 10:12-20	
	(Jl. 1:6—2:5)	
Locusts	VIII	
	Ex. 9:8-11	1) Ap. 16:2
	VI	Ulcers on men
	Ex. 8:2-6	6) Ap. 16:12-16
	II	Frogs
6) Ap. 9:13-21		6) Ap. 16:12-16
		Armageddon
(Euphrates)	(Gn. 15:18)	(Euphrates)
		4) Ap. 16:8 f.
		Burning heat
7) Ap. 11:14-19		
The third "Woe"		

This is a good example of the freedom with which the author uses the Old Testament; he does not trouble about consistency even in the parallel series of plagues. The plague of hail (first Trumpet) has been reserved for the last in the series of Bowls: it will destroy Babylon. The second and third Bowls, like the second and third Trumpets, make two parts of the plague of water turned into blood. The fifth Bowl has some of the details of the sixth Trumpet, but applies these details to the precise situation of the destruction of Rome. The Euphrates reappears, but in order to be dried up to form a passage for the kings of the East who come to destroy the city. The plague of frogs takes on an eschatological aspect, just like the plague of locusts in the vision of Trumpets. Here John says that the frogs are impure spirits: they have come forth from the mouths of the Dragon and of the two Beasts to deceive the kings of the earth and to assemble them for the final battle of the "Great Day" of God.[73]

Clearly, John is not hampered by the images and symbols he borrows, but freely adapts them; and he is not, of course, limited to Old Testament imagery, but also makes his own original contribution. When interpreting the images of Ap., we must bear two factors in mind.[74] First, imagination, especially oriental imagination, is not tied definitively to any one image and, on the other hand, an image may have more than one symbolical signification. For instance, in Ap. 12, the desert is a place of refuge, and in chapter 17 it is the abode of demons. Failure to take account of the varied symbolism of an image has led some to identify the white horseman of Ap. 6:2, who symbolizes victorious war, with him of Ap. 19:11 who symbolizes the Messiah. In the second place, there is the "historization" of images. By this we mean the tendency to take a symbol for the description of a concrete historical reality, the temptation to interpret the details of an image in terms of historical events. Thus, it would be wrong to regard the series of Seals, Trumpets, and Bowls as so many series of plagues that will come to pass successively at, or just before, the end of time. The sym-

---

[73]See L. Cerfaux and J. Cambier, *L'Apocalypse de saint Jean lue aux Chrétiens* (Paris: Cerf, 1955), pp. 144 f.

[74]See *ibid.*, pp. 216 f.

bols of Ap. are important, not for themselves, but for the truths they signify. Once they have yielded their symbolism, they must not be pressed into any system of interpretation.

3) *Purpose and Interpretation of Apocalypse*

THE PURPOSE   Like the Book of Daniel, the Apocalypse of John was written in a troubled time and for a special purpose; like Daniel, too, it carries a message that goes beyond the immediate crisis. Ap. is at once a declaration of Christian faith and hope and a manifesto against the official paganism of Rome. The author is a witness, and he speaks with the authority of the former prophets sent by God, echoing their words and images. His book is a commentary on the words of Jesus to his disciples: "In the world you have tribulation; but be of good cheer, I have overcome the world" (Jn. 16:33). Just as Dn. was aimed at rekindling the spiritual energy of the Jewish nation at a time when monotheism was menaced by pagan Hellenism (Dn. 7-12), so also Ap. was written to console and to strengthen Christians in the midst of persecution (Ap. 2:8-10, 12 f.; 6:9-11; 7:14; 13:11; 17:6; 20:4). In both cases, the intention is the same, and in both cases the method employed is the same. In the time of John, the persecutor was the Roman Empire and the most pressing danger to the faithful of the province of Asia was the cult of Rome and of the emperor. Emperor-worship demanded that sacrifice should be offered before an image of the Caesar, with the declaration: *Kyrios Kaisar*—"Caesar is Lord," that is, divine— sheer blasphemy in Christian eyes. For Christians, Jesus Christ was *Kyrios,* and they must "hold fast his name" (Ap. 2:13), reserve that title for him alone. The readers of Ap., contemporaries of John, to whom the book was addressed in the first place, were well able to understand its purpose and its veiled allusions to the contemporary situation and its polemic against the state religion.

A constant preoccupation of Ap. is the fate of the martyrs, readily understandable in the historical circumstances of the Book. The readers are being encouraged to face a violent persecution in which many of them may well find death. Thus, John, time and again, refers to the blessedness of the martyrs, and he becomes more and more explicit. In Ap. 6:9-11, the souls of those who had been slain for the witness they had borne—sacrificial victims—rest under the

altar of holocausts, but wearing the white robes of victory. Then
(Ap. 7:9-17) they are represented as celebrating, in heaven, an everlasting feast of Tabernacles (the most joyous of Jewish feasts). Satan
has no power over them: they are in heaven and he has been
cast out (Ap. 12:7-11). They are the close companions of the Lamb
(Ap. 14:1-5); a few verses further on their situation is stated in
explicit terms: "Blessed are the dead who die in the Lord—here and
now" (Ap. 14:13). Finally, they are those who reign with Christ
for a thousand years, beyond the power of Satan (Ap. 20:4-6).

What John had written for the churches of Asia remained as a
heritage for all suffering churches throughout the Empire; but he
seems to have been aware, too, that his work would have a wider
scope.

> There is some reason for believing that the writer of the Apoca-
> lypse, before his work was ended, realized that the book might find
> a larger field of service than the churches of Asia or even the
> churches of the Empire could offer. In the early chapters it is clear
> that St. John writes with a view to his message being read aloud in
> the local church assemblies (Ap. 1:3; 2:7, etc.). . . . But when he
> reaches the end a presentiment seems to enter his mind that the book
> will live: *I testify unto every man that heareth the words of the pro-*
> *phecy of this book. If any man shall add unto them, God shall add*
> *unto him the plagues which are written in this book; if any man shall*
> *take away . . . God shall take away his part of the tree of life* (Ap.
> 22:18 f.). . . . The words are based on two passages of Deuteronomy
> (4:2; 13:1) and they practically place the Apocalypse on a level with
> the Torah and anticipate for it a place among the Scriptures of the
> Church. St. John knew himself to be a prophet and his writing to
> be a prophecy; that he was commanded to consign his visions to a
> book was an assurance to him that their purpose would not be ful-
> filled in one generation or in two. He sees the book going down to
> posterity, and like the Deuteronomist, he endeavors to guard it against
> interpolation and excision. As he writes the last word upon the papyrus
> roll that lies upon his knee, the conviction dawns upon him that
> the *Revelation of Jesus Christ* was given for the warning and com-
> fort of the whole Church to the end of time.[75]

THE　　　　　　　　When the literary form of Ap. is taken into ac-
INTERPRETATION　　count, as it must be, a certain line of interpretation necessarily opens up—if violence is not to be done to the
work. For, as an apocalypse, the book was written in view of a

---

[75]Swete, *op. cit.*, pp. xcvii f.

crisis and it is concerned with concrete historical events. The author may well have been aware that his book would live and speak to ages yet to come, but he wrote primarily for the Christians of his own day, the communities of Asia Minor. This must be our starting point, and to ignore the historical milieu of Ap. is to invite inevitable misinterpretation.

Even granted this approach, however, there is much that we do not fully understand and there is scope for different interpretations of the writing. Here, perhaps more than anywhere else, we feel that an outline of opinions would not serve our purpose. Ap. is one of the most fascinating books of the New Testament, and although its literary form is strange to us and although parts of it remain obscure, the book itself can be made intelligible to the modern reader. We attempt, then, to break the seven seals and open up a writing that is indeed a closed book to one who may come upon it without some explanation of its nature, its purpose, and its meaning.[76]

1. A. *The Letters.* The letters to the seven churches (chaps. 1-3) have the same literary characteristics as the properly apocalyptic part of Ap. and are the work of the same author. Originally, they may have been independent of the rest, to be joined later to the apocalypse proper;[77] as such they form an integral part of the work as we know it. But the links between the letters and the rest are so close that the independent existence of the former seems unlikely.

The prologue (Ap. 1:1-3) introduces the Apocalypse as a letter of the prophet John, a letter destined to be read at the liturgical ceremonies; but the author is conscious that it is, in fact, a message from the supreme Pastor of the Church. The introduction (Ap. 1:4-8) addresses the Christian congregations to which John had ministered; it is notable for a trinitarian formula which, in Christian fashion, lingers over the Son: his Incarnation, death, and glory.

In a striking vision (Ap. 1:9-20), John is commissioned by the glorified Son of Man to write what is to be revealed to him and to send the message to seven churches of Asia. The Messiah appears

---

[76]I follow closely A. Feuillet, *L'Apocalypse, État de la question, op. cit.*; also, *Études Johanniques, op. cit.*, pp. 193-271. See Cerfaux-Cambier, *op. cit.*; Swete, *op. cit.* Division I above indicates the main lines of the interpretation given here.

[77]This is, for instance, the view of M.-E. Boismard. See p. 461.

as Judge (as in Dn. 7:13) and here the details of the vision have a symbolical value: he wears the long robe of priesthood, the golden cincture of royalty, the white hair of eternity. Eyes like a flame of fire represent his divine knowledge, and feet of bronze indicate stability. He holds in his right hand (that is, in his power) the seven lampstands representing the seven churches, and the stars, the angel guardians or protectors of the churches. The overall effect is one of terrifying majesty.

The vision of the Son of Man effectively brings out the oracular character of this first part of Ap., for it is closely parallel to the inaugural visions of the prophets (cf. Is. 6; Jer. 1; Ezek. 1). But where the latter proceeded to speak in the name of Yaweh ("thus says Yaweh"), John will make known the "revelation of Jesus Christ." And since, in the eyes of the inspired writer, the seven churches represent the universal Church, his message—the message of the Lord—has meaning for the Church until the end of time.

The seven churches are not listed haphazardly, but in order. They were linked by a circular road that, from Ephesus, went north to Smyrna and Pergamum and then swung southwards to take in the others. Each church receives a judgment which is based upon a full knowledge of its condition, both external (there are several topical references) and spiritual. The churches receive praise or blame (or both), usually with some qualifications, and in this there seems to be a definite plan and progression. Ephesus receives censure and commendation; then Smyrna, Thyatira, and Philadelphia (the even numbers) are praised—the latter without reservation, while Pergamum, Sardis, and Laodicea are censured—the latter very severely.[78] Their chief faults are a cooling in first fervor and a decline in charity, together with indulgence of or concessions to Nicolaitanism, a Gnostic heresy similar to that in question in the Johannine Epistles.

2. B. *The Prophetical Visions.* Ap. is certainly not concerned with the "seven ages of the world"—a theory popular in the Middle Ages; nor does it regard, in any detailed manner, the future of the Church. On the other hand, certain capital stages of human history are in view. All the while, John is concerned with the meaning of

---

[78]See M. Hubert, "L'architecture des lettres aux sept églises," *Revue Biblique,* 67 (1960), 349-53.

events rather than with the events themselves. Thus, he brings out the significance of the destruction of Jerusalem in 70 A.D. and then goes on to point to the inevitable issue of the persecution that had just begun.

A consideration of Dn. 7-12 can help us to understand Ap. Dn. was written in the Maccabaean age; hence, it is largely concerned with events of the past. Yet, the succession of empires is seen in relation to the purpose of the divine plan: the final establishment of the kingdom of God. That future event is not treated in detail; it is simply foretold that the persecution will end in failure and that God will have the last word. The perspective of Ap. is no different. "In both cases the presentation of historical realities, past, present, or near at hand is meant to be an example and a type of what will happen afterwards. God's plan is one and the author, convinced of that, can shorten his perspective and see the eschatological event just beyond the historical crisis of which he writes."[79]

1. *Part I. The Church and Israel (chaps 4-11)*. We are justified in dividing the central section of Ap. into two parts (Ap. 4—11; 12:1—21:8), for the first part may be regarded as a complete apocalypse. Swete remarks that, "had all our manuscripts broken off at Ap. 11:19 and no vestige of the last eleven chapters survived, it is conceivable that the loss might never have been suspected."[80] In Ap. 12:1, the author marks a fresh beginning for which the reader had been prepared in Ap. 10:11. We have, then, two complete apocalypses, each of which reaches to the end of time.[81] From chapter 12 onward, the author is concerned with the Church and pagan Rome, while in chapters 4-11 he was preoccupied with the Church's relation to the Chosen People. His work has about it something of the structure of the Old Testament prophetical books: first, oracles against Israel, and then oracles against the nations.[82]

---

[79]Feuillet, *L'Apocalypse, État de la question, op. cit.*, pp. 42 f.; English trans., pp. 51 f.

[80]*Op. cit.*, p. xl.

[81]It should be noted that this view is not necessarily in conflict with Boismard's theory of the *prehistory* of Ap. The two apocalypses which he identifies were eventually blended in the form known to us.

[82]See Feuillet, *L'Apocalypse, État de la question, op. cit.*, p. 48; English trans., p. 58.

The opening vision of the throne of God (chap. 4) is manifestly inspired by several prophetical texts (Is. 6:1-5; Ezek. 1:4-10, 25-27; Dn. 7:9 f.). Before the throne, the "twenty-four elders" represent the saints of Israel[83] and the "four living creatures" represent the created world. Then (chap. 5), "he who was seated on the throne" —a designation of God throughout Ap.—gave to the Lamb the sealed scroll which he held in his right hand (a transfer of power). The chapter ends with the first of the heavenly liturgies that recur so frequently in the Book; these are early Christian hymns or were modeled on such hymns. The scroll contained the divine decrees against an Israel that had not believed in Christ. As a sealed book it may well be the Old Testament: "To this day whenever Moses is read a veil lies over their minds" (2 Cor. 3:15).[84]

The breaking of the seals unleashes a series of plagues (Ap. 6:1— 8:1), a series which follows the pattern of events in the synoptic apocalypse (Mk. 13, parr.): war, strife among nations, famine, pestilence, persecution, cosmic phenomena (earthquakes, eclipses, etc.). The description of the first four, war and its attendant evils (Ap. 6:1-8), is inspired by the vision of the four chariots (Zech. 6:1-5). At the breaking of the fifth seal, the martyrs appear; here, the martyrs of the Old Law (Ap. 6:9-11) and the cosmic phenomena appear at the opening of the sixth seal. Before the last seal was broken, the servants of God were signed with the seal of the living God— one hundred and forty-four thousand of them (Ap. 7:1-8): the saved Remnant of Israel. The great multitude, from all nations, celebrating a feast of Tabernacles in heaven (Ap. 7:9-17) seem to be Christian martyrs, the "fellow servants and brethren" of the Jewish martyrs of Ap. 6:9-11. A solemn silence precedes the second series of plagues (Ap. 8:1).

The trumpets are presented in much the same way as the seals: the first four (Ap. 8:7-12) are described in a few verses, while the others are unfolded at greater length, interspersed with other visions. The plagues of Ap. 8:7-12 strike only *one-third* of the earth and of the heavenly bodies, and again in Ap. 9:15 only one-third of man-

---

[83]See Feuillet, *Études Johanniques, op. cit.,* pp. 193-227.
[84]Cerfaux-Cambier, *op. cit.,* pp. 55-57.

kind is striken by the sixth plague; there is no such qualification in the parallel plagues of Bowls which are aimed at the pagan world. We may seek the reason for this difference in the prophetic doctrine of the Remnant (compare the "third" of Ezek. 5:1-4; Zech. 13:8 f.). It follows that the plagues of Bowls are not a doublet of the plagues of Trumpets: the former are inflicted on the adorers of the Beast, while the latter are closely related to that judgment of God on an unbelieving Israel, the destruction of Jerusalem. Since the seals are the prelude and preparation of trumpets, they must be understood in the same context. The first two "Woes" (fifth and sixth Trumpets) are a highly-colored development of the plague of locusts (Ex. 10:12-15), already utilized in striking fashion by Joel (1:6–2:11)—a passage that immediately influenced John.

Chapter 10 opens with a vision of a mighty angel coming down from heaven wrapped in a cloud and with a rainbow over his head. He had a little scroll open in his hand and he set his right foot on the sea and his left foot on the land (vv. 1 f.). In Ap. 5:2, the invitation of a "strong angel" led to the opening of the sealed scroll: there is a parallel between angels and scrolls. The angels of chapter 10, with traits of the Son of Man of Daniel (Dn. 7:14), is more majestic than the other; of giant stature, he stands on sea and land because his message is for all mankind. This is in contrast to Ap. 5:1-12, where the title given to Christ (the Lion of the tribe of Judah, the Root of David) and the role of the twenty-four Elders (the saints of the Old Law) point to the Chosen People—without, however, overlooking the rest of humanity (Ap. 5:9) which receives the light from Israel. The sealed book is the Old Testament, especially the prophetic oracles, to which Christ has supplied the key. The little book (less extensive than the Old Testament, but open and universalist in scope) is the message of Jesus.

In Ap. 10:3-7, we find two antithetical scenes: one (vv. 3 f.) signifies that the universal judgment is still far off ("seal up what the seven thunders [the voice of God, cf. Ps. 29 (28):3-9] have said"), and the other (vv. 5-7), that the end is near (there shall be "no more delay"). Dn. 12:4-9, which has inspired the antithesis, also explains it. Daniel had been ordered to seal up the revelations he had received and the angel swore by the Creator that they will be accomplished after a certain delay, "a time, two times and a half a time." John also seals what he has heard, but here the angel swears by the Creator that there is no more delay: the old situation has been transformed.

This is followed by a new prophetic investiture (parallel to that of Ap. 1:9-20), patently based on the investiture of Ezekiel (Ap. 10:8-10; cf. Ezek. 3:1-3). Then (Ap. 10:11), John is told: "You must again prophesy about many peoples and nations and tongues and kings." In the context of these chapters, this means that he is called to a new mission: he must prophesy as he had not done up to now. The message of the sealed scroll bears directly on the Chosen People (cf. Ap. 7:4-8), and it is only from chapter 12 onward that there is question of "peoples and nations and tongues" (cf. Ap. 12:5; 13:7; 14:6, 8; 15:41; 17:15). It seems that the purpose of chapter 10 is to introduce the period of preaching to the Gentiles and to bring out the paradox of the Gospel: the end is near (we live in the last age), and yet the final episode may be long delayed.

Chapter 11 is by no means easy, but a study of it appears to confirm the interpretation of chapters 4-11 in terms of Israel and the Church. John received a measuring rod and was bidden to measure the temple and the altar and the worshipers—what is thus measured is under God's special protection. But he must "cast out the court which is outside" the temple (*tēn aulēn tēn exōthen ekbale exōthen*) for, "it is given over to the nations, and they will trample over the holy city for forty-two months" (Ap. 11:1 f.). Lk. 21:24 springs to mind at once: unbelieving Jerusalem "will be trodden down by the Gentiles, until the times of the Gentiles are fulfilled." Another text of Luke casts light on the enigmatic phrase, "cast out the court which is outside." In Lk. 13:25-28—the parable of The Closed Door —the unbelieving contemporaries of Jesus are represented as standing outside their Lord's door and knocking in vain for admittance (v. 25); and yet, a few verses later, they are "thrust out" (*ekballomenous exō*)(v. 28).[85] In both cases, we have the same para-

---

[85]The discrepancy in Luke is due to the fact that the passage is not an original parable of Jesus but one composed of various sayings of his. Cf. Wilfrid J. Harrington, *A Key to the Parables* (New York: Paulist Press, 1964), pp. 113-16. However, the resultant parable must be interpreted as it stands.

dox: those already outside are cast out. As Swete has noted,[86] the measured temple represents the Church and the outer court is the rejected synagogue; John refers to the final break between Church and Synagogue brought about by the catastrophe of 70 A.D. The true Temple of God, which Titus could not destroy, was constituted in the first place by the Jews faithful to Christ, the messianic Remnant (cf. the 144,000 of Ap. 7:4-8). The unbelieving Jews, until then rather like the outer court of the true temple, were now no longer part of it.[87]

However, the prospect is not one of unrelieved gloom: the court will be trampled for "forty-two months"; this is nothing else than the "time, two times and half a time" of Dn. 7:25. In Ap., the expression, or its equivalent, is a symbolic designation of the temporary time of persecution which separates Christians from the perfect establishment of the kingdom of God. The sufferings of the unconverted Jewish world will last just so long—"until the times of the Gentiles are fulfilled" (Lk. 21:24). Then, with Paul (Rm. 11:25 f.), we can look to the salvation of Israel.

The two witnesses (Ap. 11:3-13) are modeled on Elijah (power to bring about drought [v. 6]) and Moses (power to turn water into blood and to smite the earth with every plague [v. 6]). Their ministry lasts for 1,260 days, that is to say, the forty-two months of verse 2—the whole time of the Church. It appears that the witnesses are the incarnation of the testimony—from the Law and the Prophets—borne to Christ by the Church in the presence of the Jewish world. The puzzling verse 7: "When they have finished their testimony, the beast that ascends from the bottomless pit will make war upon them and conquer them and kill them," which abruptly introduces the Beast, is best understood of the final assault on the Church. For, indeed, the death and speedy resurrection of the witnesses will happen at the end of the forty-two months (they are to testify for 1,260 days [v. 3], and they are slain only "when they have finished their testimony" [v. 7]), and the victory of the Beast is ephemeral. One-tenth of the city (Jerusalem) was destroyed and

---

[86]See *op. cit.*, p. 133.
[87]See Feuillet, *L'Apocalypse, État de la question, op. cit.*, pp. 48 f.; English trans., pp. 58 f.; *Études Johanniques, op. cit.*, pp. 248-54.

seven thousand were killed (v. 13), but the rest "gave glory to God." This typically Jewish expression signifies the conversion of Israel at the end of the "times of the Gentiles."

In Rm. 11:25 f., the conversion of Israel, coming after that of the Gentiles, seems to mark the culminating point of the divine plan. The same is true here. Now is the end: the punishment of the wicked is implied in the third "Woe" (v. 14); then the seventh trumpet can sound to announce the end of the world and the definitive inauguration of the kingdom of God and of his Christ. Significantly, the canticle (Ap. 11:17 f.) is put in the mouths of the twenty-four elders, for its language is thoroughly Jewish. Finally, God's Temple was opened and the heavenly Ark of the Covenant was seen within it (Ap. 11:19).

It seems, then, that the historical background of Ap. 11 is the catastrophe of 70 A.D. which brought about the final separation of Church and Synagogue. This explains the artificial antedating of Ap.; for, in Ap. 17:10 f., the sixth of a list of seven emperors in whose reign the writing is set, is, reasonably, Vespasian. By using the customary apocalyptic procedure, John could thus place himself before the destruction of Jerusalem and from that vantage point bring out the theological significance of the event.

We may regard chapters 4-11 of Ap., with their series of seals and of trumpets, as no more than a development of the data of the synoptic apocalypse. It is an explanation based on the history of the events foretold in the Synoptics: the Jewish war and the destruction of Jerusalem which, when Ap. was written, were events of the past, events of great significance. "The destruction of Jerusalem and its sanctuary was not the end of the world, but it was the end of a world. It marked the definitive separation of synagogue and Church. Henceforth, the latter turned principally to the Gentiles."[88] We have seen[89] how Luke has distinguished three periods of salvation history: the time of Israel; the time of Christ; and the time of the Church. Ap. is not a gospel, and the author does not insist on the time of Christ, but he does discern the time of Israel

[88]Feuillet, *Études Johanniques, op. cit.*, p. 244.
[89]Pp. 191 f.

and the time of the Church, each period closing with a divine judgment.

Whatever may be said of our interpretation of Ap. 4-11, it is at least certain that chapter 11 marks a climax, while chapter 12 is a new departure. H. B. Swete (who does not refer these chapters to Israel and the Church) has made the point very clearly.

> With the seventh trumpet-blast the kingdom of God has come, and the general judgment is at hand. Thus, this section of the Apocalypse brings the course of history down to the verge of the Parousia. If the Book had ended here, it would have been within these limits complete. But the Seer pauses for a moment only to take up his role again with a fresh presentation of the future, in which the vision is to be carried to its issue. A new prophecy begins in chapter 12, the contents of the open *biblaridion* [little scroll] which the Seer had been directed to take from the hand of the Angel and consume. Impelled by a fresh gift of prophetic energy, he feels himself bound to prophesy again to a larger circle of hearers and with wider aims (Ap. 10:11); and this second message occupies the remainder of the Book.[90]

2. *Part II. The Church and Pagan Rome (Ap. 12:1—21:8).* The second part, although it offers its own particular problems, has met with a greater measure of agreement in its general interpretation. The historical background is undoubtedly the persecution of the Church by Rome, and the precise occasion of the persecution is the Church's refusal to countenance Caesar-worship; the two Beasts represent Rome and the religion of Rome. These pages attack the blasphemous pretensions of the emperors, which must end in disaster: Rome will go the way of Babylon.

Chapter 12 falls into three parts: (1) a diptych which introduces the two symbolical figures, the Woman and the Dragon (vv. 1-4a); (2) assault on Christ and the victory of Christ (vv. 4b-12); (3) persecution of the Christians (vv. 13-17).[91] The Woman symbolizes the people of God which brings forth the Messianic Age and the Messiah (cf. Mi. 4:9 f.; Is. 66:7). The Dragon is the "ancient serpent" of Gn. 3: once again the Woman and Satan are face-to-face. The Dragon seeks to destroy her Son, but the child was snatched out of his power to the throne of God—a reference to the ascension

---

[90]*Op. cit.,* p. 146.
[91]See Cerfaux-Cambier, *op. cit.,* p. 109.

and the triumph of Christ, which will bring about the fall of the Dragon. Meanwhile, the Woman (the people of God of the Old Testament which, having given Christ to the world, thereby became the Christian Church) found refuge in the desert where she is cared for by God for 1,260 days, that is, the equivalent of forty-two months or three and one-half years—the whole earthly duration of the Church. The fall of the Dragon is dramatized in Ap. 12:7-12; and although Michael has cast Satan out of heaven, it really is the victory of Christ (vv. 10 f.). The martyrs (who represent all Christians) share in the victory of Christ; death has set them free from the devil's power. Thus, in heaven there is great rejoicing; but, on earth, Satan can still, for a little while, give vent to his wrath.

The Dragon's attempt to destroy the Woman, implicit in Ap. 12:6, is described in Ap. 12:13-16. She is protected for "a time, two times and half a time" (cf. Ap. 12:6): the Church, as such, is under God's special care all the time of its historical duration. However, the faithful on earth are vulnerable: Satan, through his instruments, can make war on them; they will be persecuted and put to death. But the message of Ap. is precisely that those who are steadfast to the end share in the glorious victory of the Lamb.

Apropos of Ap. 12, we may ask if there is a basis in the text for a Mariological interpretation. At the outset, it is well to be clear that the Woman is certainly not, in the first place, Mary the mother of Christ, for the context and the Old Testament background leave no doubt that the Woman symbolizes, first and foremost, the people of God which gives birth to the Messiah and the messianic people. The only possibility is that the Woman may also, and in a secondary sense, symbolize Mary. Many eminent exegetes believe that she does.[92] However, I share the hesitation of M.-E. Boismard. He notes:

> It is not sufficient to say that, in the eyes of a Christian, the "Woman who brings forth the Messiah" must *necessarily* evoke Mary, the mother of Jesus. It remains to prove that the author of Apocalypse *intends* to attach a special importance to Mary as personal mother of Christ. More serious is the argument from Gn. 3:15. It is certain, in fact, that the Woman of Ap. 12 is described in terms of Eve: she is tried

---

[92]E.g., F.-M. Braun, *La Mère des Fidèles* (Paris, 1954²); Cerfaux-Cambier, *op. cit.*, pp. 109-12; Feuillet, *Études Johanniques, op. cit.*, pp. 272-310.

by Satan, the "ancient Serpent" (Ap. 12:9; cf. Gn. 3:1 ff.), she brings forth in anguish (Ap. 12:2; cf. Gn. 3:16), she is subject to the persecutions of Satan (Ap. 12:6, 14; cf. Gn. 3:15)—she and all her children (Ap. 12:17; cf. Gn. 3:15). The question is whether, *for the author of Apocalypse*, the Eve of Gn. 3:15 pointed to Mary or simply stood for the people of God called to take its revenge on the Serpent that had led it astray? In short, the Woman of Ap. 12 represents certainly, and primarily, the people of God which brings forth the Messiah and the messianic times. Has the author of Apocalypse intended that she should *also* represent Mary, the personal mother of the Messiah? It is possible, but the arguments in favor of this view do not quite carry conviction.[93]

The two Beasts of chapter 13, instruments of Satan, are Rome and the imperial religion in the service of Rome. The latter induces "the inhabitants of the earth" (a term that corresponds to the *kosmos* of the Fourth Gospel and Johannine Epistles: the unbelieving world) to worship the Beast and to bear its mark. The number of the Beast (Ap. 13:18) stands for his name which can be discovered by the process of gematria (that is, by addition of the numerical value of the letters of his name—in Hebrew and Greek, in place of numerals, the letters of the alphabet have a numerical value). In Hebrew, Nero Caesar (*nrwn qsr*) gives 666; the identification is probable, but not certain, especially in view of a variant reading, 616 instead of 666.

In deliberate and striking antithesis to the Beast and his followers, stand the Lamb and his companions, bearing on their foreheads the name of the Lamb and of his Father (Ap. 14:1-5). The 144,000 are not those of Ap. 7:4-8, the Remnant of Israel; they are instead the faithful remnant of the New Israel—the martyrs. The designation "virgins" must be understood in a metaphorical sense. The Old Testament prophets, especially Hosea, Jeremiah, and Ezekiel, frequently represented the Covenant of Sinai as a marriage of God with his people; therefore, all idolatry was regarded as adultery or fornication (and, in fact, Canaanite worship did involve ritual prostitution). In Ap., the 144,000 are contrasted with the followers of the Beast precisely because they have not adored the Beast but have remained faithful to the Lamb. They have remained virgins because they have not given themselves to the cult of the Beast

[93]IB, p. 738.

but have clung to God; in the context, there is no question of Christian ascetics.[94]

Satan, the two Beasts, and their followers, the "inhabitants of the earth," the Woman and her children, the Lamb and his companions —the *dramatis personnae* of the great eschatological struggle—have been introduced. Now comes the proclamation of the hour of Judgment (Ap. 14:6-13), followed by the symbolical harvest and vintage (Ap. 14:14-20). This last is based on Jl. 4:13, but the Old Testament text has been adapted and developed in the manner of John. In Joel, both images refer to the extermination of the pagan nations; here the Son of Man reaps the harvest of his elect (Ap. 14:14-16), and an angel gathers the vintage of the earth. "There is a delicate beauty in the assignment of the ingathering of the Vintage to an angel, while the Son of Man himself reaps the Wheat-harvest. The work of death is fittingly left in the hands of a minister of justice; the Savior of men appears *eis sōtērian* (['unto salvation']) (Heb. 9:28)."[95]

The seven plagues *which are the last* (Ap. 15:1)—and hence distinct from the plagues of Trumpets—are announced in chapter 15; the following chapter shows their execution. The Bowls (like the Trumpets) are based on the plagues of Egypt, but this time the chastisement is universal and definitive: all the worshipers of the Beast and the persecutors of Christians are stricken. Moreover, they are already gathered at Armageddon ("the mountain of Megiddo": ever since the defeat of Josiah at Megiddo [2 Kgs. 23:29 f.] it had remained a symbol of disaster) to await their destruction (Ap. 19:17-21).

Although in Ap. 16:19 ("the great city was split into three parts") the fall of Rome is indicated, the end of that city cannot be treated so casually. The whole of chapter 17 is given over to a description of Babylon—the goddess Rome—seated on the satanic Beast; the fall of Rome is solemnly proclaimed in Ap. 18:1-8. Then follows a satirical lament (Ap. 19:9-24) and a triumphal liturgy in heaven (Ap. 19:1-10).

---

[94]See M.-E. Boismard, "Notes sur l'Apocalypse," *Revue Biblique,* 59 (1952), 161-72.

[95]Swete, *op. cit.*, p. 190.

After the fall of Rome, the end comes swiftly. The Rider on the white horse leads out the armies of heaven (Ap. 19:11-16) against the two Beasts and their followers. Victory is complete: the two Beasts are cast into the "lake of fire"—the place of final punishment—and their followers are slain with the sword (Ap. 19:17-21). Now Satan alone is left.

The passage, Ap. 20:1-10, is perhaps the most difficult in the whole Book and it is necessary to linger over it. First and foremost we must determine the origin of the "millennium," the notion of a special messianic reign. We rightly look to Jewish speculation on the messianic reign. In the Old Testament (for example, Dn. 2:44; 7:27), this reign is something permanent, but later Jewish writers (100 B.C.-100 A.D.) looked for a temporary triumph of righteousness before the consummation of all things. To this golden age various periods were assigned: 100, 600, 1,000, 2,000, 7,000 years. Without doubt, John was familiar with these conceptions, but just as he freely adapts Old Testament imagery, so also he takes this idea too and bends it to his own purpose. Merely because the original Jewish idea envisaged a temporary messianic reign on earth, it does not necessarily follow that John is thinking along the same lines in Ap. The symbol must be seen, not in its original setting, but according to the significance that John attaches to it.

Many Christian writers of the early centuries (such as Papias, Justin, Irenaeus, Tertullian, and Hippolytus) had taken the millennium literally: Christ would reign for a thousand years in Jerusalem before the final judgment. St. Augustine at first accepted this view, but eventually came to oppose it; his explanation became the classic and accepted one in the Church. He saw in the captivity of Satan nothing else than the binding of the strong man by the Stronger than he, which the Lord had foretold (Mk. 3:27; Lk. 11:22); in the thousand years, the whole interval from the resurrection of Christ to the last conflict, that is, the whole duration of the Church; in the "first resurrection," baptism (cf. Rm. 6:1-10).

However, it seems more satisfactory to regard the resurrection of martyrs as symbolizing the renewal of the Church after the persecution of Rome: the "millennium," therefore, corresponds to the earthly phase of the kingdom of Christ, from the end of persecution (the fall of Rome) to the eschatological combat (Ap. 20:7-10). The key seems to be provided by Ezek. 37-39: in chapter 37 (the vision of the dry bones), the metaphorical resurrection of the people of God immediately precedes the attack on the Holy Land by Gog, king of Magog (chaps. 38-39; cf. Ap. 20:8).[96]

Perhaps, after all, we should try a different approach.[97] If we consider the whole passage Ap. 20:1-10 we find that two events are juxtaposed: on the one hand, there is the overthrow of Satan, in two phases; on the other hand, there is the reign of a thousand years. Chapter 7 of Daniel furnishes the background of the vision and explains the literary construction. The first condemnation of the Dragon coincides with the moment of judgment when dominion is given to the Son of man (Dn. 7:9-14); henceforth, the power is taken from the beast and belongs to the Son of Man and the saints. Thus, in Ap., while Christ and his faithful reign, the devil will remain imprisoned in the abyss, his "place." The binding of Satan for a thousand years also coincides with the punishment indicated in the parallel passage, Ap. 12:7-12: Satan, the "accuser of the brethren," is cast out of heaven by the victory of Christ; he can no longer touch the faithful who are in heaven with Christ.

The reign of the saints and the imprisonment of Satan last a thousand years. John has in mind the Jewish idea of a temporal messianic reign, but for him the thousand years is a symbol. In fact, his preoccupation with the martyrs comes once again to the fore, and this is the reason the passage Ap. 20:7-10 is a doublet of the eschatological battle of Ap. 19:17-21. These are still the same troops and the battle is that of Armageddon. The final assault of the Dragon was made through the intermediary of the Beasts and their followers and all are destroyed together. But, because of his concern with the martyrs—his desire to show yet again that Satan

---

[96]See M.-E. Boismard, (BJ), p. 81; Feuillet, *L'Apocalypse, État de la question, op. cit.,* p. 100; English trans., p. 121.

[97]See Cerfaux-Cambier, *op. cit.,* pp. 172-78; A. Wikenhauser, *Offenbarung des Johannes* (Regensburg: Pustet, 1949), pp. 127-31. Although aware that it raises difficulties of its own (for instance, how is one to explain Ap. 20:3: ". . . that he should deceive the nations no more"?), I still regard this solution as the most satisfactory and as best suiting the outlook of Ap.

has no power over them—he has to describe, separately, the fall of Satan.

Only the martyrs reign with Christ for a thousand years; only they had risen from the dead—it is the "first resurrection." The same point of interest recurs throughout the book: it must be shown that the martyrs are happy "here and now" (Ap. 14:13), that is, before the Parousia and the general resurrection. Here, the effect is achieved by reference to Dn. 7: a judgment anticipates the general judgment (thrones were placed and the judges took their seats); the martyrs are assured of definitive happiness ("over them the second death has no power"), thanks to a resurrection which anticipates the general resurrection. For a Semite like John, happiness, a true concrete happiness, must involve the whole person; hence, there must be a "resurrection" if the dead are to be eternally happy.

In reality, the thousand years begins when a Christian has shed his blood for Christ. The reign of a thousand years coincides with the feast of Tabernacles which the martyrs celebrate in heaven (Ap. 7:9-17); it is the reign of the companions of the Lamb (Ap. 14:1-5). It gives concrete expression to the solemn affirmation of Ap. 14:13: "Blessed are the dead who die in the Lord, here and now." The reign of a thousand years and the time of the Church ("a time, two times and half a time") are not consecutive but simultaneous.

But does our interpretation founder on Ap. 20:3? Largely on the basis of this verse, some would find in the passage an optimistic view of the relations between the temporal powers and the Church: after the first crisis, these will grow steadily better, at least until the last, definitive upheaval. This view would seem to conflict with the outlook of Ap.—the Beast carries out his campaign against the Church right up to the end—and verse 3 need not be interpreted so rigidly. For, if the Dragon is forbidden to deceive the nations, this can well mean that the satanic power, which is operative wherever Christ does not reign with his saints (for the martyrs represent the holiness of the Church), has no influence throughout the time of the Church, where the spiritual reign is accepted.

Briefly, in conclusion, we may say that John has made use of the Jewish tradition of a temporary messianic reign to symbolize the truth that the martyrs now reign with Christ. The thousand years, then, is a symbol—it has no chronological value. It must be interpreted as a symbol, and the reality which it typifies must be sought out. The reign of a thousand years signifies the reign of the martyrs with Christ who has won the final victory for them. Satan is bound for a thousand years: he cannot touch the martyrs, no more than he could touch those who have "conquered him by the blood of the Lamb" (Ap. 12:11). If he is represented as being set loose at the end of the thousand years, this is due to the literary construction of the passage; and he is loosed not to take action against the elect, but to hasten the doom of his followers, and his own doom, in the final cataclysm.

The conquest of all the powers hostile to God is followed by the general resurrection of the dead and the last judgment (Ap. 20:11-15); and the central part of Ap. ends with the vision of a new heaven and a new earth (Ap. 21:1-8) (the expression comes from Is. 65:17; cf. 66:22). The first heaven and the first earth have passed away (Ap. 21:1); this will be a new creation, but it will still be a heaven and an earth—a dwelling place for men.

3. *Part III. The Heavenly Jerusalem* (*Ap. 21:9—22:5*). The Book closes with a majestic vision of the New Jerusalem, the heavenly Church of the future, the veritable kingdom of God. Certain details in Ap. 21:24-27, which seem rather to refer to the historical stage of the Church, are explained by the fact that the author is echoing traditional Old Testament language. The heavenly city measured by God (therefore, immovable), and cubic (therefore, perfect), is also the Bride of the Lamb. We might expect the glowing description of the City (Ap. 21:16-21) to be followed by a particularly striking description of its Temple (the Temple was the glory of the earthly Jerusalem). Instead, a brilliant touch, we learn that there is no temple, nor any need for one: God himself dwells there, and the Lamb (Ap. 21:22). Consistently, the waters which in Ezek. 47 flow from the Temple, here flow from "the throne of God and of the Lamb" (Ap. 22:1). It is the river of the first paradise, and the tree of life is found again (Ap. 22:2). There, the elect shall look upon the face of God and of the Lamb and shall reign forever and ever.

Like the Fourth Gospel and 1 Jn., this Book also closes with an appendix or epilogue (Ap. 22:6-21), which gives the last words of the angel, the Seer, and the Lord. John ends his work with the prayer of the early Christians: *Marana tha* ("Our Lord, come!" [cf. 1 Cor. 16:22]), and a final blessing on the saints, the faithful of Christ. Swete comments finely:

> The saints, the men of consecrated lives, are, in the Apocalyptist's view, the men for whose advantage the whole course of human history is being carried to its end; and who are destined as a body to survive the wreck of cities and empires, and in the end to dominate a new world. But the grace of the Lord Jesus is the only source of their strength, and the guarantee of their triumph; and the last words of the Apocalypse are at once a reminder of this primary condition of success, and a prayer that it may be realized in the experience of the baptized, both in the cities of Asia and throughout the world.[98]

In the preceding pages, we have sought to outline the historical interpretation of Ap., its first and fundamental sense. It was written in concrete circumstances, in view of a particular crisis, but it is of abiding interest. Therefore, we can look again at the Book and read in it the message it has carried through the centuries and will carry to the end.

> Apocalypse is not a writing whose interest is lost, vanished like the circumstances that gave it birth: it is a Book for all time. Nothing really has passed away: Satan's struggle against the Church will last just as long as this world of ours; the persecution of Nero is the first, and the type, of all persecutions that the Church must suffer. All the actors of that great drama which was played out around the cradle of the Church walk the stage again throughout the centuries. So it is that, beyond the first and historical sense of Apocalypse, but *based on it*, we can discover another meaning, deeper and of universal scope. For, if the Beast of chapter 13 symbolizes the Roman Empire, the latter, in its turn, may be regarded as the type of all pagan powers and totalitarian regimes which stand against the Church. Similarly, the persecuted Christians of chapter 13 are, in the first place, those who suffered under Nero, but they are also, in a wider sense, all Christians of all time who are persecuted for their witness to Christ. The Apocalypse has an abiding value, it transcends time, it responds to Christian aspirations of succeeding ages. It is for this reason—as well as for its eschatological teaching—that it found its way into the canon of Scripture, beside the Gospels and the Epistles. And it is for the same reason

---

[98]*Op. cit.*, pp. 313 f.

that it has nourished the life of the Church and was abundantly used and commented on by the Fathers.[99]

4) Doctrine

THE CHURCH   The Church not only figures largely in Ap., but is indeed the center of interest in the Book. In the letters to the seven churches of Asia, John gives us a glimpse into the life of the first-century Church, and then he goes on to consider the relationship of the Church to Israel and to the pagan totalitarian state. It is the new people of God, redeemed by the blood of the Lamb, and it is the object of Satan's hate, the target of his war on God. For if the Church, protected by God, is safe from the assaults of the Dragon (Ap. 12:6, 14), the children of the Woman, on earth, can feel the brunt of his spite.

It is this awareness of the earthly dimensions of the Church, over against its other-worldly destiny, that saves Ap. from any hint of triumphalism. John's purpose is to support and encourage ordinary men and women who find themselves pitted against forces that seek relentlessly to crush them. They may be called upon to face death, but we may be sure that there was no glamour in their daily resistance to pressure on the part of an authority that may well have been rigid and unsympathetic rather than wantonly cruel. That is why they are called upon, again and again, to exercise *hypomonē* ("patient endurance") (Ap. 2:2, 3, 19; 3:10; 13:10; 14:12; cf. 1:9), the characteristic virtue of the persecuted, founded on faith in Christ. There can be no mistaking the harsh reality: "If any one is to be taken captive, to captivity he goes; if any one slays with the sword, with the sword must he be slain. Here is a call for the endurance and faith of the saints" (Ap. 13:10). These Christians were called upon to suffer patiently, to endure; who will say that the same message is not addressed to countless Christians of our time? Ap. holds out no prospect of peace and triumph for the Church (before the end); the two Beasts, instruments of Satan, will carry on their warfare to the last. And all the while, the letters to the seven churches, with their candid pilloring of shortcomings and abuses, show that John has no illusions about the human frailty of those who make up

---

[99]M.-E. Boismard, (BJ), p. 15.

the Church. His is that authentic vision of the Church so clearly stated in our day by the Fathers of Vatican II: "Christ completed the work of redemption in poverty and under persecution. In the same way, the Church is called to treat the same path. . . . With sinners clasped to her bosom, she is at once holy and in constant need of cleansing."[100]

At the same time, however, Christians form a priestly kingdom (Ap. 1:6), and already they share in the Kingship and Priesthood of Christ. And if the hour is not yet for the manifest glory and triumph of the Church, that too will come when the victory of Christ, already won, will reap its full harvest. Then will appear the Bride of the Lamb, clothed now "with fine linen, bright and pure" (Ap. 19:8), adorned for her Husband (Ap. 21:2), the Church, "holy and without blemish" (Eph. 5:27). She is the new Jerusalem, the dwelling place of "the Lord God the Almighty and the Lamb" (Ap. 21:22).

ESCHATOLOGY[101] The eschatological interest of Ap. is manifest; all the book is an apocalypse and hence this interest is to be expected— after all. On the other hand, the promises which close the seven letters (Ap. 2:7, 11, 17, 26 f.; 3:5, 12, 20 f.) look not to the Parousia but to heavenly blessedness after death. The same is true of Ap. 14:13: "Blessed are the dead who die in the Lord, henceforth," and of the care to portray the immediate happiness of the martyrs. However, elsewhere, Ap. consistently looks to the End.

God has promised men a new world in which he will "wipe away every tear from their eyes," a world from which all evil, even death itself, will have vanished. That will be the time of the new union of God with his people, now all purified and holy (Ap. 21:1-8). Before the inauguration of this perfect eschatological kingdom, the dead will rise and will be judged according to their works (Ap. 20:11-15). But, before these events, there will be a general offensive of the pagan nations on the Church (Ap. 19:17-21; 20:7-10); the enemies of God, including the two Beasts and Satan himself, will be definitively vanquished. It seems too that the final events will have

---

100*Dogmatic Constitution on the Church* (London: C.T.S.), Chap. 1, p. 8.
101See A. Feuillet, "Parousie," DBS, VI, cols. 1397-1403.

been preceded by the conversion of Israel (Ap. 11:14-18; cf. Rm. 11:25 f.).

Ap., then, emphatically assures us that history does move to a climax. More than that, the Lamb who was slain has won his victory; the fierce assaults of Satan are the desperate paroxysm of one mortally wounded. The final issue is not in doubt. For Christians, the problem is not the fact of ultimate victory, but the explanation of the delay of the Parousia. Christ has overcome the world—and yet, the world goes its way, the implacable enemy of the Church of Christ. How can this be and when will the End come? Ap. does face the problem and does, it seems, answer it.

The solution may be found in chapter 10, which we have considered at some length above.[102] We find ourselves very near the end: the coming of the Lion of Judah, the Root of David (Ap. 5:5), and the divine judgments (seals and trumpets) which have struck the unbelieving Jews have led humanity almost to the end of its course; the "mystery of God" (Ap. 10:7), his plan for the world, is about to be realized. The new people of God has taken the place of the old, and nothing remains but the sounding of the seventh trumpet-blast. In other words, the appearance of Christ on the stage of history has given a new impetus to the plan of salvation. All that is left now is the consummation of that plan by the resurrection of the dead and the judgment of nations (Ap. 11:15-19).

We seem to have reached the term of human history, and the author of Ap. does not seek to attenuate that feeling of the nearness of the end which earlier Christians had felt (cf. Ap. 1:3, 7; 3:11; 22:10, 12, 20). His prologue assures his readers—those who hear the words of the prophecy, the revelation of Jesus Christ—that "the time is near." In this phrase, two worlds are contrasted: this world of time and the heavenly world beyond; the world that, in Hebrew imagination, like the New Jerusalem (Ap. 21:10) and the Ark of the Covenant (Heb. 8:5; 9:12), already exists in heaven. With the coming of Christ, this other world has drawn near to us, time has lost its value; the end is near. These two worlds have drawn close together; the heavenly realities have penetrated the temporal order

---

[102]Pp. 472 f.

and have diminished the significance of time. Quantitatively, it remains the same, it may have a long course to run; and yet, it is short because it is no longer of much importance in comparison with the timeless realities that are now manifest.[103]

So it is that John, with Dn. 12:7-9 in view, can consciously change the perspective. There the angel swore that, before the things of the end would come to pass, there was yet to be "a time, two times and a half a time"; here (Ap. 10:6), he declares that "there should be no more delay." This brings out the difference between the two economies, the old and the new. Christians live in the age of fulfillment; now is "the last hour" (1 Jn. 2:18). Yet, the consummation is to come, and John is ordered to "seal up" the revelations of the seven thunders (Ap. 10:4). Similarly, he assimilates the decrees of the little scroll and receives a new prophetic investiture, a mission to all nations (Ap. 10:8-11); all the events of Ap. 13:1—20:15 must come to pass—the end is not yet.

> This paradox of an end near at hand and yet chronologically distant, which the author of Apocalypse has underscored more heavily than any of his predecessors, obliges us to see in the traditional theme of the nearness of the end something quite other than a question of date. Of course, in putting forward this view, John is not proposing a doctrine altogether new, but he has thrown a revealing light on the most obscure part of the New Testament message.[104]

It seems that Ap. 4-11 is a commentary on the synoptic apocalypse; and John has seen more clearly than the other New Testament writers that there is a real distinction between the end of Jerusalem and the end of the world. He understands that, when Jesus declares that the glorious coming of the Son of Man is near at hand, he is not indicating a date, but offering a truth of faith. Because Christ has come and by his resurrection—the first-fruits of those who rise—has introduced the new era of a new life, the Lord is henceforth near, even though his Parousia may be delayed. John—writing at the close of the first century—had no intention of reviving the naïve expectation of an imminent Parousia. His purpose was to convince his persecuted

---

103See Cerfaux-Cambier, *op. cit.*, pp. 13-16.
104A. Feuillet, DBS, VI, col. 1402.

brethren that their Christ, risen and glorious, was absolute Master of human history; that his victory was complete and that he would come to usher in the new world.

Bibliography

This bibliography is not meant to be exhaustive and has been restricted, as far as possible, to works in English. An asterisk (*) indicates that a work carries an *Imprimatur*.

GENERAL

*Ahern, B. M., *New Horizons: Studies in Biblical Theology*. Notre Dame, Ind.: Fides, 1963.

*Bauer, J. B., editor, *Bibeltheologisches Wörterbuch*. Graz: Verlag Styria, 1962². I, II.

*Benoit, P., *Exégèse et Théologie*. Paris: Cerf, 1961. I, II.

*————, and Boismard, M.-E., *Synopse des Quatre Évangiles en Français*. Paris: Cerf, 1965.

Black, M., *An Aramaic Approach to the Gospel and Acts*. Oxford University Press, 1954².

————, and Rowley, H. H., editors, *Peake's Commentary on the Bible*. London: Nelson, 1962².

*Bonsirven, J., *Theology of the New Testament*. Westminster, Md.: Newman Press, 1964.

*Brown, R. E., *New Testament Essays*. Milwaukee: Bruce, 1965.

*Castelot, J., *Meet the Bible*. Baltimore-Dublin: Helicon, 1960. III.

*Charlier, C., *The Christian Approach to the Bible*. Westminster, Md.: Newman Press, 1958.

Cullmann, O., *The Christology of the New Testament*. Philadelphia: Westminster Press, 1959.

————, *Christ and Time*. Philadelphia: Westminster Press, 1964.

Dodd, C. H., *According to the Scriptures*. The Sub-structure of New Testament Theology. London: Nisbet, 1952.

————, *New Testament Studies*. Manchester: The University Press, 1953.

————, *The Bible Today*. New York: Cambridge University Press, 1961.

Greek, Latin, English New Testament Students' Workbook. Collegeville, Minn.: Liturgical Press.

Hoskyns, E., and Davey, N., *The Riddle of the New Testament*. Naperville, Ill.: Allenson, 1957.

Jeremias, J., *The Central Message of the New Testament*. New York: Scribner's, 1965.

*Jones, A., *God's Living Word*. Glen Rock, N.J.: Paulist Press, 1965.

Kee, H. C., and Young, F. W., *Understanding the New Testament*. Englewood Cliffs, N.J.: Prentice-Hall, 1957.

La Sainte Bible. Trans. into French under the direction of l'École Biblique de Jérusalem. Paris: Cerf, 1957. (Revised edition in fascicle form.)

*Léon-Dufour, X., editor, *Vocabulaire de Théologie Biblique*. Paris: Cerf, 1961.

Manson, T. W., *The Teaching of Jesus*. New York: Cambridge University Press, 1935[2].

————, *Studies in the Gospels and Epistles*. Philadelphia: Westminster Press, 1962.

*McKenzie, J. L., *The Power and the Wisdom:* An Interpretation of the New Testament. Milwaukee: Bruce, 1965.

*————, *Dictionary of the Bible*. Milwaukee: Bruce, 1965.

McNeile, A. H., *An Introduction to the Study of the New Testament*. New York: Oxford University Press, 1953[2].

Neill, S., *The Interpretation of the New Testament 1861-1961*. New York: Oxford University Press, 1964.

New Testament Reading Guide. Collegeville, Minn.: Liturgical Press, 1960.

*Orchard, B., editor, *A Catholic Commentary on Holy Scripture*. London: Nelson, 1953.

*Quesnell, Q., *This Good News*. Milwaukee: Bruce, 1964.

Richardson, A., *An Introduction to the Theology of the New Testament*. New York: Harper & Row, 1959.

*Robert, A., and Feuillet, A., editors, *Introduction to the New Testament*. New York: Desclee, 1966.

*————, and Tricot, A., editors, *Guide to the Bible*. Trans. E. P. Arbez, and M. R. P. McGuire; New York: Desclee, 1960[2]. II.

Rowlingson, D. T., *Introduction to New Testament Study*. New York: Macmillan, 1956.

*Schnackenburg, R., *New Testament Theology Today*. New York: Herder & Herder, 1963.

*————, *The Moral Teaching of the New Testament*. New York: Herder & Herder, 1965.

*Spicq, C., *Agape in the New Testament*. St. Louis: B. Herder, 1963-1965. I, II.

*Stanley, D. M., *The Apostolic Church in the New Testament*. Westminster, Md.: Newman Press, 1965.

Taylor, V., *The Person of Christ in New Testament Teaching.* New York: St. Martin's Press, 1958.

*Wikenhauser, A., *New Testament Introduction.* New York: Herder & Herder, 1958.

CHAPTER ONE

*Bonsirven, J., *Palestinian Judaism in the Time of Jesus Christ.* New York: Holt, Rinehart, & Winston, 1964.

Burrows, M., *The Dead Sea Scrolls.* New York: Viking Press, 1955.

————, *More Light on the Dead Sea Scrolls.* New York: Viking Press, 1958.

*Copleston, F., *A History of Philosophy.* New York: Doubleday, 1962². I.

Cross, F. M., *The Ancient Library of Qumran.* Garden City, N.Y.: Doubleday, 1958.

Cullmann, O., *The Early Church.* Philadelphia: Westminster Press, 1965.

Doresse, J., *The Secret Books of the Egyptian Gnostics.* New York: Viking Press, 1959.

Filson, F. V., *A New Testament History.* Philadelphia: Westminster Press, 1964.

Grant, R. M., and Freedman, D. N., *The Secret Sayings of Jesus.* Garden City, N.Y.: Doubleday, 1960.

Jeremias, J., *Unknown Sayings of Jesus.* London: S.P.C.K., 1964.

*Lemaire, P., and Baldi, D., *Atlante Storico della Bibbia.* Rome: Marietti, 1955.

*Milik, J. T., *Ten Years of Discovery in the Wilderness of Judaea.* Naperville, Ill.: Allenson, 1959.

Pfeiffer, R. H., *History of New Testament Times.* London: A. & C. Black, 1963².

Ramsay, W. M., *St. Paul the Traveler and the Roman Citizen.* Grand Rapids, Mich.: Baker Book House, 1960.

*Ricciotti, G., *Paul the Apostle.* Milwaukee: Bruce, 1953.

*Sutcliffe, E. F., *The Monks of Qumran.* Westminster, Md.: Newman Press, 1960.

Van der Heyden, A. A. M., and Scullard, H. H., editors, *Atlas of the Classical World.* London: Nelson, 1960.

Vermès, G., *Discovery in the Judaean Desert.* New York: Desclee, 1956.

CHAPTER TWO

*Bea, A. Cardinal, *The Study of the Synoptic Gospels.* New York: Harper & Row, 1965.

*Butler, B. C., *The Originality of St. Matthew.* New York: Cambridge University Press, 1951.

Dodd, C. H., *History and the Gospel.* London: Nisbet, 1938.

————, *About the Gospels.* New York: Cambridge University Press, 1952.

————, *The Parables of the Kingdom.* New York: Scribner's, 1961.

*Harrington, W. J., *Explaining the Gospels*. Glen Rock, N. J.: Paulist Press, 1963.

*——————, *A Key to the Parables*. Glen Rock, N.J.: Paulist Press, 1964.

Jeremias, J., *Paroles de Jésus*. Paris: Cerf, 1963.

——————, *The Parables of Jesus*. New York: Scribner's, 1963.

*Léon-Dufour, X., *Les Évangiles et l'histoire de Jésus*. Paris: Éditions du Seuil, 1963.

Robinson, J. M., *A New Quest of the Historical Jesus*. Naperville, Ill.: Allenson, 1959.

Streeter, B. H., *The Four Gospels:* A Study of Origins. New York: St. Martin's Press, 1930[4].

Taylor, V., *The Formation of the Gospel Tradition*. New York: St. Martin's Press, 1933.

*Vaganay, L., *Le Problème Synoptique*. Paris: Desclée, 1954.

CHAPTER THREE

Cranfield, C. E. B., *The Gospel according to St. Mark*. New York: Cambridge University Press, 1959.

*Huby, J., and Benoit, P., *L'évangile selon Saint Marc*, (BJ). Paris: Cerf, 1961[3].

Johnson, S. E., *The Gospel according to St. Mark*. New York: Harper & Row, 1961.

*Jones, A., *The Gospel according to St. Mark*. New York: Sheed & Ward, 1963.

*Lagrange, M. J., *Évangile selon saint Marc*. Paris: Gabalda, 1947[8].

Lightfoot, R. H., *The Gospel Message of St. Mark*. New York: Oxford University Press, 1952.

Rawlinson, A. E., *The Gospel according to St. Mark*. London: Methuen, 1925.

*Schmid, J., *Das Evangelium nach Markus*. Regensburg: Pustet, 1954[3].

Swete, H. D., *The Gospel according to St. Mark*. London: Macmillan, 1927[3].

Taylor, V., *The Gospel according to St. Mark*. New York: St. Martin's Press, 1953.

CHAPTER FOUR

Allen, W. C., *The Gospel according to St. Matthew*, (ICC). Edinburgh: Clark, 1912[3].

*Benoit, P., *L'Évangile selon Saint Matthieu*, (BJ). Paris: Cerf, 1961[3].

Davies, W. D., *The Setting of the Sermon on the Mount*. New York: Cambridge University Press, 1964.

*Dupont, J., *Les Béatitudes*. Bruges: Abbaye de Saint-André, 1958[2].

Filson, F. V., *The Gospel according to St. Matthew*. New York: Harper & Row, 1960.

*Jones, A., *The Gospel according to St. Matthew*. New York: Sheed & Ward, 1965.

*Lagrange, M. J., *Évangile selon S. Matthieu*. Paris: Gabalda, 1941[5].

McNeile, A. H., *The Gospel according to St. Matthew*. London: Macmillan, 1915.

Plummer, A., *An Exegetical Commentary on the Gospel according to St. Matthew*. Grand Rapids, Mich.: Eerdmans, 1953.

*Schmid, J., *Das Evangelium nach Matthäus*. Regensburg: Pustet, 1956[3].

*Schnackenburg, R., *God's Rule and Kingdom*. New York: Herder & Herder, 1963.

Stendahl, K., *The School of St. Matthew*. Uppsala, 1954.

CHAPTER FIVE

Browning, W. R. E., *The Gospel according to St. Luke*. New York: Macmillan, 1960.

Conzelmann, H., *The Theology of St. Luke*. New York: Harper & Row, 1960.

Creed, J. M., *The Gospel according to St. Luke*. New York: St. Martin's Press.

*Lagrange, M. J., *Évangile selon Saint Luc*. Paris: Gabalda, 1941[5].

*Laurentin, R., *Structure et Théologie de Luc 1-2*. Paris: Gabalda, 1957.

Leaney, A. R. C., *A Commentary on the Gospel according to St. Luke*. New York: Harper & Row, 1958.

*Osty, E., *L'Évangile selon saint Luc*, (BJ). Paris: Cerf, 1961[3].

Plummer, A., *The Gospel according to St. Luke* (ICC). Edinburgh: Clark, 1922[5].

*Schmid, J., *Das Evangelium nach Lukas*. Regensburg: Pustet, 1960[4].

Tinsley, E. J., editor, *The Gospel according to Luke*. New York: Cambridge University Press, 1965.

CHAPTER SIX

Bruce, F. F., *The Acts of the Apostles*. Grand Rapids, Mich.: Eerdmans, 1960[2].

Cadbury, H. J., *The Making of Luke-Acts*. Naperville, Ill.: Allenson, 1958[2].

*Cerfaux, L., and Dupont, J., *Les Actes des Apôtres*, (BJ). Paris: Cerf, 1958[2].

Clark, A. C., *The Acts of the Apostles*. Oxford: The Clarendon Press, 1933.

Dodd, C. H., *The Apostolic Preaching and Its Developments*. London: Hodder & Stoughton, 1963[3].

*Dupont, J., *The Sources of Acts*. New York: Herder & Herder, 1964.

Foakes-Jackson, F. J., *The Acts of the Apostles*. New York: Harper & Row, 1931.

——————, and Lake, K., *The Beginnings of Christianity. I. Acts of the Apostles*. London: Macmillan, 1933. IV, V.

Knox, W. L., *The Acts of Apostles*. New York: Cambridge University Press, 1948.

*Wikenhauser, A., *Die Apostelgeschichte*. Regensburg: Pustet, 1965[3].

CHAPTER SEVEN

Abbott, T. K., *The Epistles to the Ephesians and to the Colossians*. Naperville, Ill.: Allenson, 1956.

*Amiot, F., *The Key Concepts of St. Paul*. New York: Herder & Herder, 1962.

Barrett, C. K., *The Epistle to the Romans*. New York: Harper & Row, 1957.

*Benoit, P., *Les Épîtres de Saint Paul aux Philippiens, à Philémon, aux Colossiens, aux Ephésiens*, (BJ). Paris: Cerf, 1959³.

*Boylan, P., *St. Paul's Epistle to the Romans*. Dublin: Gill, 1934.

Bruce, F. F., *The Epistle to the Romans*. London: Tyndale Press, 1963.

*Callan, C., *The Epistles of St. Paul*. New York: Wagner, 1922-1931. I, II.

*Cerfaux, L., *Christ in the Theology of St. Paul*. New York: Herder & Herder, 1959.

*————, *The Church in the Theology of St. Paul*. New York: Herder & Herder, 1959.

Dodd, C. H., *The Epistle of St. Paul to the Romans*. London: Collins, 1959².

*Dornier, P., *Les Épîtres de Saint Paul à Timothée et à Tite*, (BJ). Paris: Cerf, 1958².

*Dubarle, A. M., *The Biblical Doctrine of Original Sin*. New York: Herder & Herder, 1965.

*Grossouw, W., *In Christ: A Sketch of the Theology of St. Paul*. Westminster, Md.: Newman Press, 1959.

Lightfoot, J. B., *St. Paul's Epistle to the Galatians*. London: Macmillan, 1880⁶.

*————, *St. Paul's Epistle to the Philippians*. London: Macmillan, 1896¹².

*————, *St. Paul's Epistles to the Colossians and to Philemon*. London: Macmillan, 1904.

Lock, W., *The Pastoral Epistles*. Naperville, Ill.: Allenson, 1959.

*Lyonnet, S., *Les Épîtres de Saint Paul aux Galates, aux Romains*, (BJ). Paris: Cerf, 1959².

Moffatt, J., *The Epistle to the Hebrews*. Naperville, Ill.: Allenson, 1963.

Moule, C. F. D., *The Epistles of Paul the Apostle to the Colossians and to Philemon*. New York: Cambridge University Press, 1957.

*Murphy-O'Connor, J., *Paul on Preaching*. New York: Sheed & Ward, 1964.

*Osty, E., *Les Épîtres de Saint Paul aux Corinthiens*, (BJ). Paris: Cerf, 1959³.

Plummer, A., *A Commentary on St. Paul's First Epistle to the Thessalonians*. London: Scott, 1918.

*————, *A Commentary on St. Paul's Second Epistle to the Thessalonians*. London: Scott, 1918.

*————, *A Commentary on St. Paul's Epistle to the Philippians*. London: Scott, 1919.

*————, *The Second Epistle of St. Paul to the Corinthians* (ICC). Edinburgh: Clark, 1925.

Ramsay, W. M., *An Historical Commentary on St. Paul's Epistle to the Galatians.* London: Hodder & Stoughton, 1899.

*Rigaux, B., *Saint Paul: Les Épîtres aux Thessaloniciens.* Paris: Gabalda, 1965.

*——————, *Saint Paul et ses Lettres:* État de la question. Paris-Bruges: Desclée de Brouwer, 1962.

Robertson, A., and Plummer, A., *The First Epistle of St. Paul to the Corinthians* (ICC). Edinburgh: Clark, 1929[2].

Sanday, W., and Headlam, A. C., *The Epistle to the Romans,* (ICC). Edinburgh: Clark, 1905[5].

Scott, E. F., *The Pastoral Epistles.* New York: Harper & Row.

*Schnackenburg, R., *Baptism in the Thought of St. Paul: A Study in Pauline Theology.* New York: Herder & Herder, 1964.

*——————, *The Church in the New Testament.* New York: Herder & Herder, 1965.

Simpson, E. K., and Bruce, F. F., *Commentary on the Epistles to the Ephesians and the Colossians.* Grand Rapids, Mich.: Eerdmans, 1957.

*Spicq, C., *L'Épître aux Hébreux.* Paris: Gabalda, 1952-1953. I, II.

*——————, *L'Épître aux Hébreux,* (BJ). Paris: Cerf, 1950.

*Vanhoye, A., *La Structure Littéraire de l'Épître aux Hébreux.* Paris-Bruges: Desclée de Brouwer, 1963.

Westcott, B. F., *The Epistle to the Hebrews.* Grand Rapids, Mich.: Eerdmans, 1950.

CHAPTER EIGHT

Beare, F. W., *The First Epistle of Peter.* Oxford: Blackwell, 1947.

Bigg, C., *The Epistles of St. Peter and St. Jude.* Naperville, Ill.: Allenson, 1956.

*Leconte, R., *Les Épîtres Catholiques de saint Jacques, saint Jude et saint Pierre,* (BJ). Paris: Cerf, 1961[2].

Mayor, J. B., *The Epistle of St. James.* London: Macmillan, 1897[2].

Moffatt, J., *The Catholic Epistles.* London: Hodder & Stoughton, 1928.

Reicke, B., *The Epistles of James, Peter, and Jude.* New York: Doubleday, 1964.

Ropes, J. H., *The Epistle of St. James.* Naperville, Ill.: Allenson, 1961.

*Schelkle, K. H., *Die Petrusbriefe, Der Judasbrief.* Frieburg-Basel-Wien: Herder, 1961.

Selwyn, E. G., *The First Epistle of St. Peter.* London: Macmillan, 1946.

CHAPTER NINE

Barrett, C. K., *The Gospel according to St. John.* New York: Seabury Press (S.P.C.K.), 1955.

Bernard, J. H., and McNeile, A. H., *The Gospel according to John* (ICC). Edinburgh: Clark, 1942. I, II.

*Boismard, M.-E., *L'Apocalypse,* (BJ). Paris: Cerf, 1959[3].

Brooke, A. E., *The Johannine Epistles.* Naperville, Ill.: Allenson, 1957.

*Cerfaux, L., and Cambier, J., *L'Apocalypse de Saint Jean lue aux Chrétiens*. Paris: Cerf, 1955.

Charles, R. H., *The Revelation of St. John* (ICC). · Edinburgh: Clark, 1920. I, II.

Cullmann, O., *Early Christian Worship*. Naperville, Ill.: Allenson, 1956.

Dodd, C. H., *The Johannine Epistles*. New York: Harper & Row, 1946.

————, *The Interpretation of the Fourth Gospel*. New York: Cambridge University Press, 1965.

————, *Historical Truth in the Fourth Gospel*. New York: Cambridge University Press, 1963.

Farrer, A., *The Revelation of St. John the Divine*. New York: Oxford University Press, 1964.

*Feuillet, A., *Johannine Studies*. New York: Alba House, 1964.

*————, *The Apocalypse*. New York: Alba House, 1965.

*Grossouw, W., *Revelation and Redemption*. London: Chapman, 1958.

Hoskyns, E. C., and Davey, F. N., *The Fourth Gospel*. Naperville, Ill.: Allenson, 1956².

Hunter, A. M., editor, *The Gospel according to John*. New York: Cambridge University Press, 1965.

*Lagrange, M. J., *Évangile selon Saint Jean*. Paris: Gabalda, 1925.

Lightfoot, R. H., *St. John's Gospel: A Commentary*. New York: Oxford University Press, 1956.

*Mollat, D., and Braun, F. M., *L'Évangile et les Épîtres de Saint Jean*, (BJ). Paris: Cerf, 1960².

Ramsay, W. M., *The Letters to the Seven Churches of Asia*. Grand Rapids, Mich.: Baker Book House, 1963.

Richardson, A., *The Gospel according to St. John*. Naperville, Ill.: Allenson, 1959.

Rowley, H. H., *The Relevance of Apocalyptic*. New York: Association Press, 1964³.

*Schnackenburg, R., *Die Jonannesbriefe*. Freiburg: Herder, 1953.

Swete, H. B., *The Apocalypse of St. John*. London: Macmillan, 1922³.

Wescott, B. F., *The Gospel according to St. John*. London: Clarke, 1958².

*Wikenhauser, A., *Das Evangelium nach Johannes*. Regensburg: Pustet, 1957².

Index of Biblical References

General Index

(CARPATHIANS)
ODROG –
ERESZTUR
CULTURE
EARLY BRONZE AGE
TRIPOLYE B
CULTURE
(BLACK
MACEDONIA
THES-
SALY
Troy
City VI
OLD
(Halys River
MIDDLE
HELLADIC
II
Tarsus
Mersin
CYCLADES
Cnossus
CAPHTOR
CRETE
ALASHIYA
CYPRUS
AN
SEA)